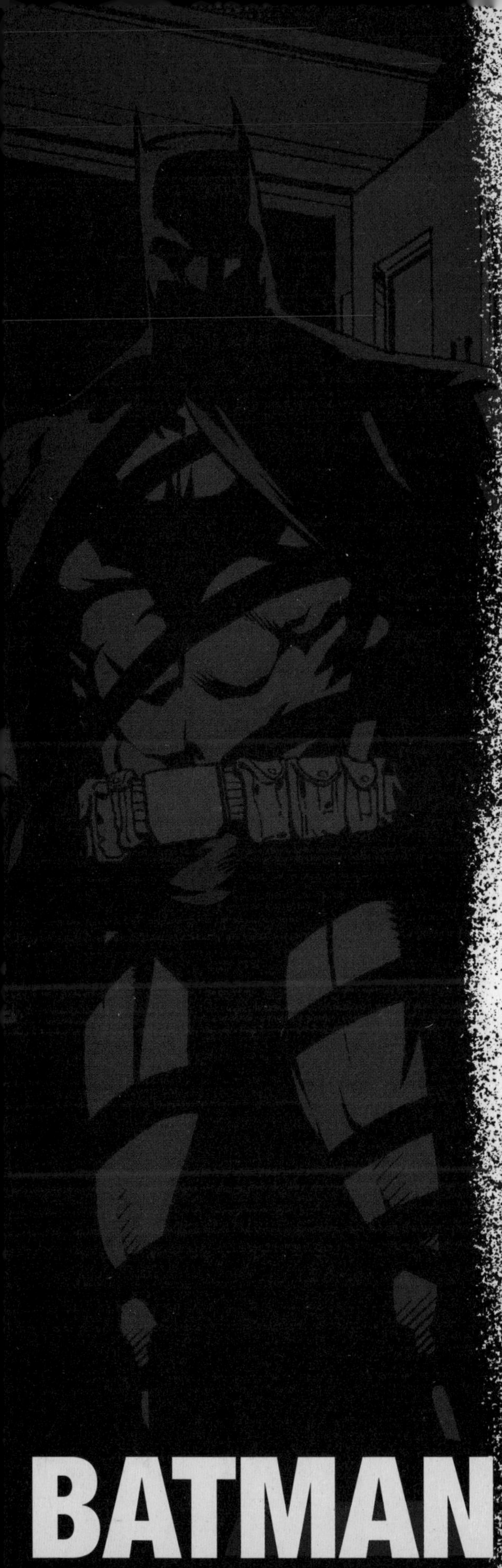

BATMAN WAR DRUMS

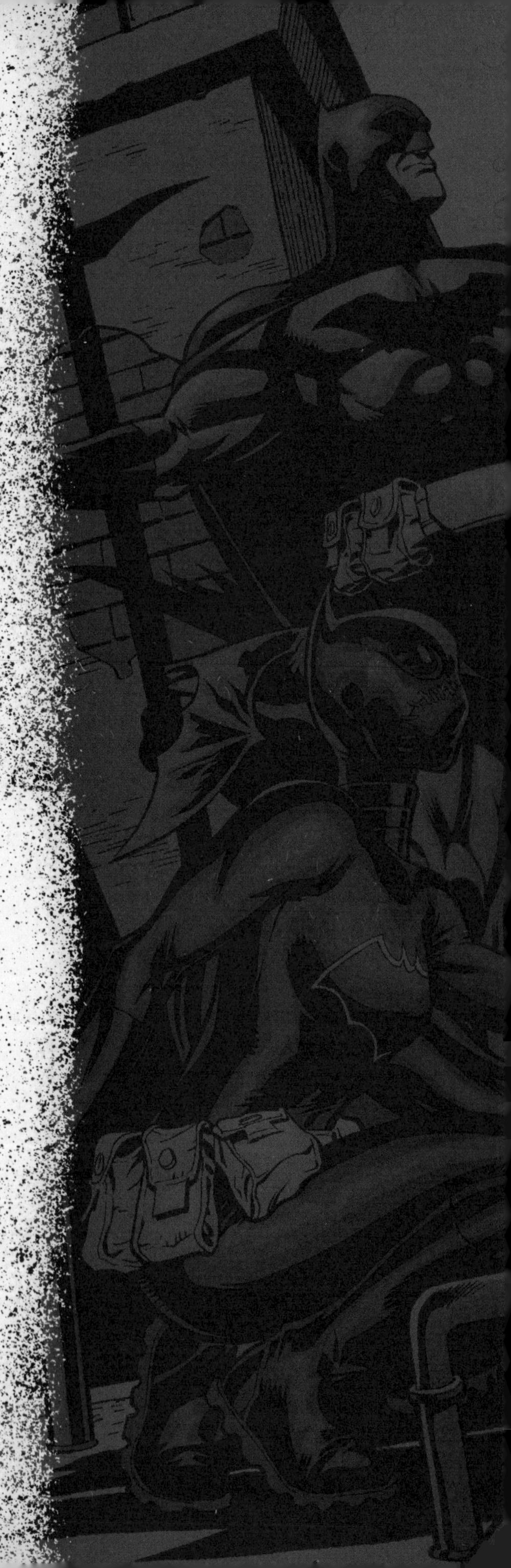

Dan DiDio
VP-EXECUTIVE EDITOR

Bob Schreck
Michael Wright
Matt Idelson
EDITORS-ORIGINAL SERIES

Nachie Castro
ASSISTANT EDITOR-ORIGINAL SERIES

Robert Greenberger
SENIOR EDITOR-COLLECTED EDITION

Robbin Brosterman
SENIOR ART DIRECTOR

Amie Brockway-Metcalf
ART DIRECTOR

Paul Levitz
PRESIDENT & PUBLISHER

Georg Brewer
VP-DESIGN & RETAIL PRODUCT DEVELOPMENT

Richard Bruning
SENIOR VP-CREATIVE DIRECTOR

Patrick Caldon
SENIOR VP-FINANCE & OPERATIONS

Chris Caramalis
VP-FINANCE

Terri Cunningham
VP-MANAGING EDITOR

Alison Gill
VP-MANUFACTURING

Rich Johnson
VP-BOOK TRADE SALES

Hank Kanalz
VP-GENERAL MANAGER, WILDSTORM

Lillian Laserson
SENIOR VP & GENERAL COUNSEL

Jim Lee
EDITORIAL DIRECTOR-WILDSTORM

David McKillips
VP-ADVERTISING & CUSTOM PUBLISHING

John Nee
VP-BUSINESS DEVELOPMENT

Gregory Noveck
SENIOR VP-CREATIVE AFFAIRS

Cheryl Rubin
SENIOR VP-BRAND MANAGEMENT

Bob Wayne
VP-SALES & MARKETING

BATMAN WAR DRUMS

DC Comics, 1700 Broadway, New York, NY 10019 -- a Warner Bros. Entertainment Company
Printed in Canada. Second Printing.
ISBN: 1-4012-0341-8
Cover illustration by James Jean

ANDERSEN GABRYCH
BILL WILLINGHAM
WRITERS

PETE WOODS
DAMION SCOTT
BRAD WALKER
PENCILLERS

CAM SMITH
DAMION SCOTT
TROY NIXEY
ROBERT CAMPANELLA
INKERS

CLEM ROBINS
PHIL BALSMAN
LETTERERS

JASON WRIGHT
GUY MAJOR
COLORISTS

TIM SALE
DAMION SCOTT
ORIGINAL COVERS

BATMAN CREATED BY
BOB KANE

BATMAN
WAR DRUMS

Despite being thought of as a loner, Batman has allowed several others to join his crusade to protect the streets of his beloved Gotham City. They have all been drawn to him and his fight but that relationship has never been an easy one, for any of them.

First, there was Dick Grayson, whose parents died through violence, similar to Bruce Wayne's loss. He had a child's sense of wonder coupled with grief and, in time, he trained and became the first Robin.

Later, Commissioner Gordon's niece Barbara followed as the first Batgirl. She was motivated more by hero worship and a sense of duty and was grudgingly welcomed to the fight. Even after she was crippled by the Joker, Barbara continued to prove invaluable. She now uses bits and bytes in lieu of batarangs and fists as Oracle.

Helena Bertinelli channeled her anger, an anger born of watching her underworld family slaughtered. As the Huntress, she sought to mete out a rough form of justice, and her methods and morals were ultimately rejected by the Batman. Undaunted, she has continued her fight on her own, sometimes with the aid of Oracle. Similarly, the costumed Orpheus has been allowed to operate in Gotham, after proving to Batman his sincere aims to clean up the section of Gotham known as "The Hill."

There have been other Robins, the second being Jason Todd, who never grew to accept the rules of right and wrong. His death at the hands of the Joker caused Batman to question risking a youth in what he continued to believe was a personal crusade. However, without Jason or Dick as a moral barometer, Batman grew even more obsessed with his mission. That's when Tim Drake arrived, having deduced Batman's identity and arguing that Batman needs a Robin. Tim has trained hard and has come to love the life of a costumed crimefighter, especially since he knows he can always walk away.

Recently, Tim's father discovered the secret and angrily confronted Wayne. The result of the argument was Tim's early retirement as Robin. He also withdrew from working on weekends with the Teen Titans.

Stephanie, daughter of the recently deceased minor criminal the Cluemaster, has longed to do good under the guise of The Spoiler. She has never measured up to any of the Robins or even the Huntress and after a time, Batman essentially "fired" her from his extended family. She has continued to do battle, briefly receiving help from

Black Canary but again, Stephanie never quite excelled.

Batman's family of operatives was also expanded to include young Cassandra Cain, trained by the assassin David Cain. Never taught to speak, she instead read body movement, ultimately rejecting her teachings when she realized she was expected to kill for David. Barbara took her in and gave her her blessing to continue the Batgirl legacy.

In recent times, this family has been tested again and again. When Bruce Wayne was framed by David Cain for killing his ex-girlfriend Vesper Fairchild, he went into hiding. Dick, now known as Nightwing, assembled the others to investigate who was truly behind the woman's death. Batman returned, apologizing to the others for ignoring them and then helped take down Cain, who admitted he had been hired by President Lex Luthor. Cain's real motivation, however, was to disgrace Wayne so he could win his daughter back. When Luthor ordered the crime, Cain saw a chance to ruin not only Wayne but Batman as well.

Shortly thereafter, Batman was targeted by a mysterious figure known as Hush. Through an elaborate series of attacks, carried out by the likes of Killer Croc and Poison Ivy, Hush whittled away at Batman's self-confidence. The injured Bruce asked Alfred to bring him to childhood friend Dr. Thomas Elliott for treatment, unaware that Elliott and the Riddler were behind the scheme to ruin Wayne. Elliott blamed the son for the sins of the father – Dr. Thomas Wayne saved the life of Elliott's mother after Elliott himself tried to kill his parents.

Batman was rescued, in part by the efforts of his other friends, former police commissioner Gordon and Harvey Dent, known to the world as Two-Face. Elliott performed the miracle that eluded others, surgically repairing Dent's half-scarred face, and Dent was repaying the favor by returning to an honest life. It was Dent who finally shot Elliott, bringing an end to the latest cycle of misery.

Tragically, Batman was again reminded of his failure with Jason when Clayface II imitated the teen, seemingly returned from the dead. After defeating him, Batman was shocked to learn Jason's body was missing from the grave. Once more he was flooded with guilt.

As this story opens, only a little time has passed since the Hush case ended.

BATMAN Dedicated to ridding the world of crime since the callous murder of his parents, billionaire Bruce Wayne dons the cape and cowl of the Dark Knight to battle evil from the shadows of Gotham City.

ALFRED Alfred Pennyworth followed his family's calling as butler to the Wayne family and raised young Bruce after Thomas and Mary were killed by a gunman. Over time, he has become Bruce's invaluable friend, tending not just to Wayne Manor and its occupant, but providing covert services when Bruce dons the cape and cowl. Batman and Bruce Wayne have no fiercer protector and confidant.

BATGIRL Cassandra Cain was trained from birth by her father, assassin David Cain. She never learned to speak, but mastered reading other people, perfecting one fighting form after another. She would have been Cain's masterwork had she not rejected killing and fled his care. In Gotham City she found a true calling, following the footsteps of Batman, and is now learning how to be a crimefighter. Under Barbara Gordon's watchful eye, she is also learning what it means to be a young woman.

SPOILER Stephanie Brown hasn't had it easy. Her father was career loser Arthur Brown, a.k.a. the Cluemaster. Frequently in jail, he was unable to help raise Stephanie. Rejecting her father's life, she donned a costume to right wrongs as Spoiler. Along the way, she met Robin, falling in love with Tim Drake. Tim helped train her and was even there when she gave birth to a child, whom she gave up for adoption. Batman, in order to protect her, has recently withdrawn his support of her fledgling career.

LESLIE THOMPKINS Right after his parents were murdered before his eyes, a grief-stricken Bruce Wayne was comforted by Dr. Leslie Thompkins. Her soothing words gave him the strength to quietly mourn his parents. She has since set up a clinic in Crime Alley, safe in the knowledge that she is protected by Bruce. Over time, she has come to abhor violence of any sort, philosophically clashing with her surrogate son time and again. She has also recently entered into a not-quite-platonic relationship with Alfred Pennyworth, the two brought together over their joint concern for Bruce's well-being.

ONYX Onyx was schooled in the Sanctuary, a monastery outside Star City. Pursued by an unknown agent who wanted to kill her, Onyx was admitted to the all-male Sanctuary by the Master, who trained her in martial arts and gave her a new identity. Upon the Master's death, Onyx sought out Green Arrow, another student of the Sanctuary, to protect the monastery from a takeover by one of the Master's more ambitious protégés, a man named Lars. Onyx stayed at the Sanctuary, guarding the key to the Master's mysterious Book of Ages. She has yet to discover the identity of the man, or woman, who pursued her to the doors of the Sanctuary.

ORPHEUS While other kids were shooting hoops or roaming Gotham City's mean streets and getting into trouble, teenager Gavin King turned his attention toward martial arts and dance. After finishing his schooling, Gavin joined a professional dance troupe and traveled the world, where he witnessed more of the same poverty and inequality that divided the races and inevitably led to violence. Determined to do something about these injustices, Gavin joined a shadowy secret organization, which provided him with the training and equipment. As Orpheus, Gavin took the fight back to Gotham, where he joined Batman in revealing a cabal of corrupt cops fomenting bloodshed between gangs and gun dealers in order to keep their own kind of enforced order. Batman maintains a watchful eye over Orpheus.

TARANTULA Former FBI trainee Catalina Flores admired Jonathan Law, the Tarantula from the first era of costumed heroes, going so far as to adopt a costumed persona to help battle Blüdhaven's rampant government corruption. An encounter with Nightwing on one of her first outings earned his disapproval of her more aggressive approach to crime fighting. When she killed Delmore Redhorn, the city's chief of police, Nightwing saw to it that she was arrested for the crime. Her brother, though, is a Blüdhaven assistant district attorney and secretly procured her freedom.

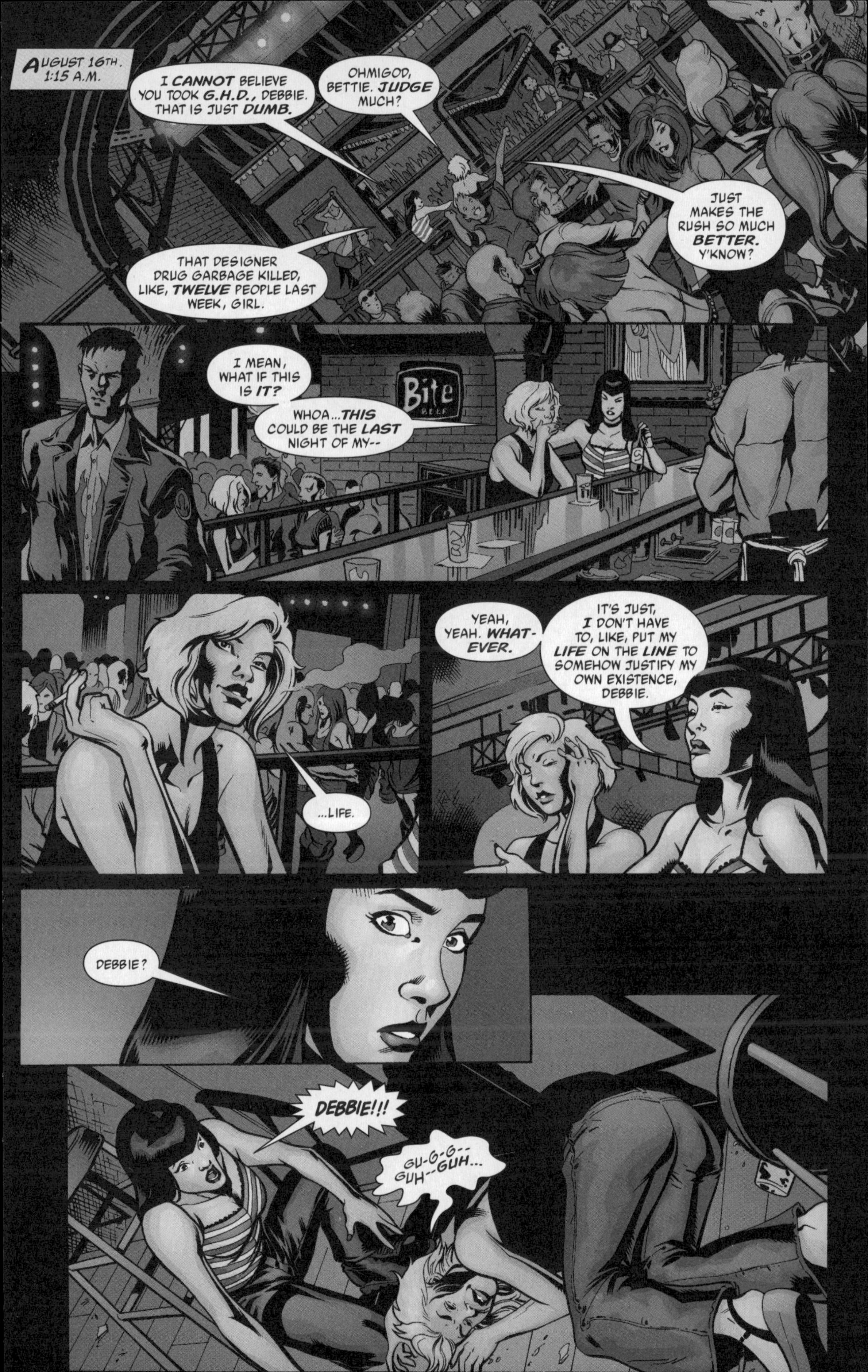

AUGUST 16TH. 1:15 A.M.
I CANNOT BELIEVE YOU TOOK G.H.D., DEBBIE. THAT IS JUST DUMB.
OHMIGOD, BETTIE. JUDGE MUCH?
JUST MAKES THE RUSH SO MUCH BETTER. Y'KNOW?
THAT DESIGNER DRUG GARBAGE KILLED, LIKE, TWELVE PEOPLE LAST WEEK, GIRL.
Bite
I MEAN, WHAT IF THIS IS IT?
WHOA...THIS COULD BE THE LAST NIGHT OF MY--
...LIFE.
YEAH, YEAH. WHAT-EVER.
IT'S JUST, I DON'T HAVE TO, LIKE, PUT MY LIFE ON THE LINE TO SOMEHOW JUSTIFY MY OWN EXISTENCE, DEBBIE.
DEBBIE?
DEBBIE!!!
GU-G-G-- GUH--GUH...

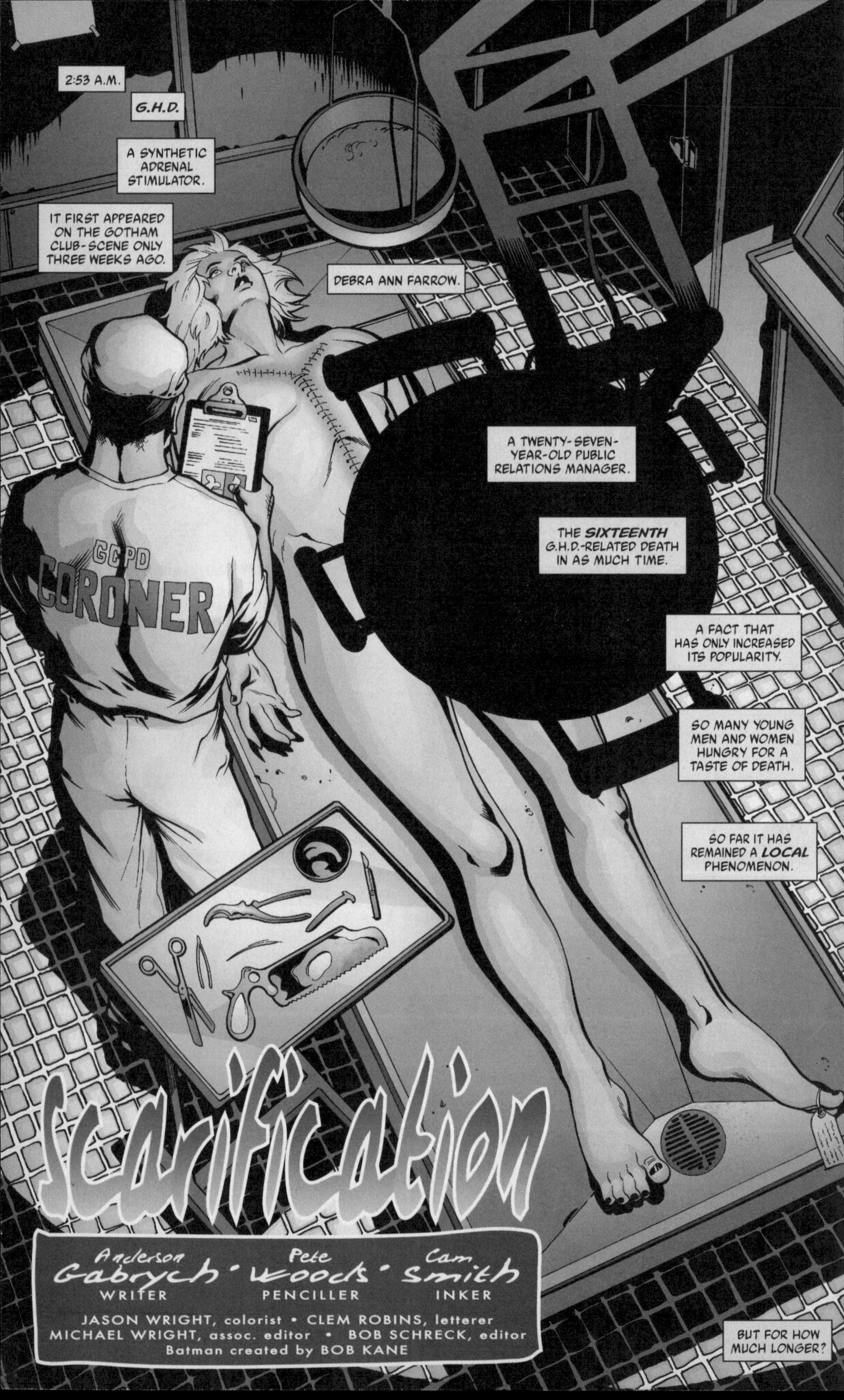
2:53 A.M.
G.H.D.
A SYNTHETIC ADRENAL STIMULATOR.
IT FIRST APPEARED ON THE GOTHAM CLUB-SCENE ONLY THREE WEEKS AGO.
DEBRA ANN FARROW.
GCPD
CORONER
A TWENTY-SEVEN-YEAR-OLD PUBLIC RELATIONS MANAGER.
THE SIXTEENTH G.H.D.-RELATED DEATH IN AS MUCH TIME.
A FACT THAT HAS ONLY INCREASED ITS POPULARITY.
SO MANY YOUNG MEN AND WOMEN HUNGRY FOR A TASTE OF DEATH.
SO FAR IT HAS REMAINED A LOCAL PHENOMENON.
Scarification
Anderson Gabrych WRITER
Pete Woods PENCILLER
Cam Smith INKER
JASON WRIGHT, colorist • CLEM ROBINS, letterer
MICHAEL WRIGHT, assoc. editor • BOB SCHRECK, editor
Batman created by BOB KANE
BUT FOR HOW MUCH LONGER?

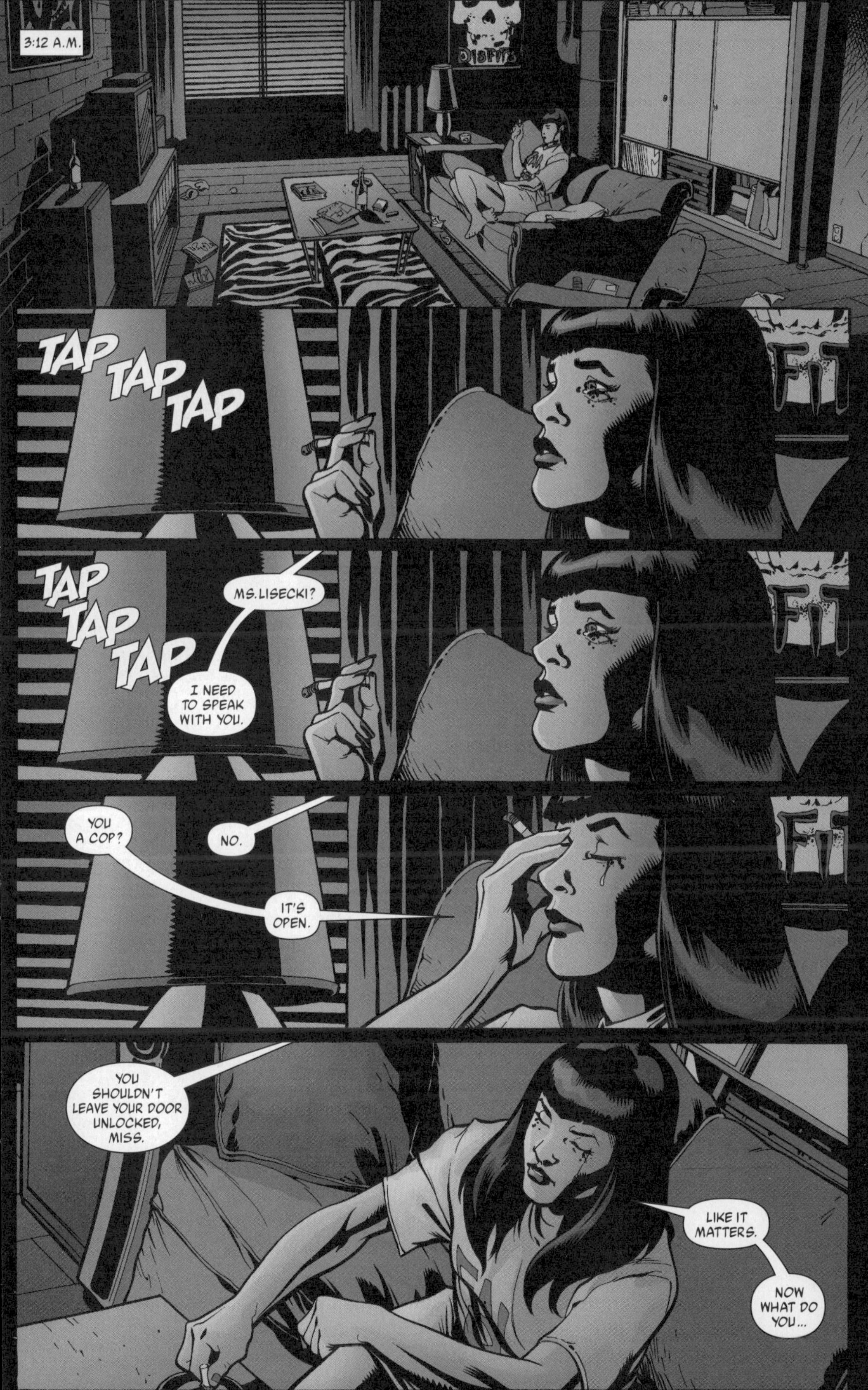
3:12 A.M.
DISFITS
TAP TAP TAP
TAP TAP TAP
MS. LISECKI?
I NEED TO SPEAK WITH YOU.
YOU A COP?
NO.
IT'S OPEN.
YOU SHOULDN'T LEAVE YOUR DOOR UNLOCKED, MISS.
LIKE IT MATTERS.
NOW WHAT DO YOU...

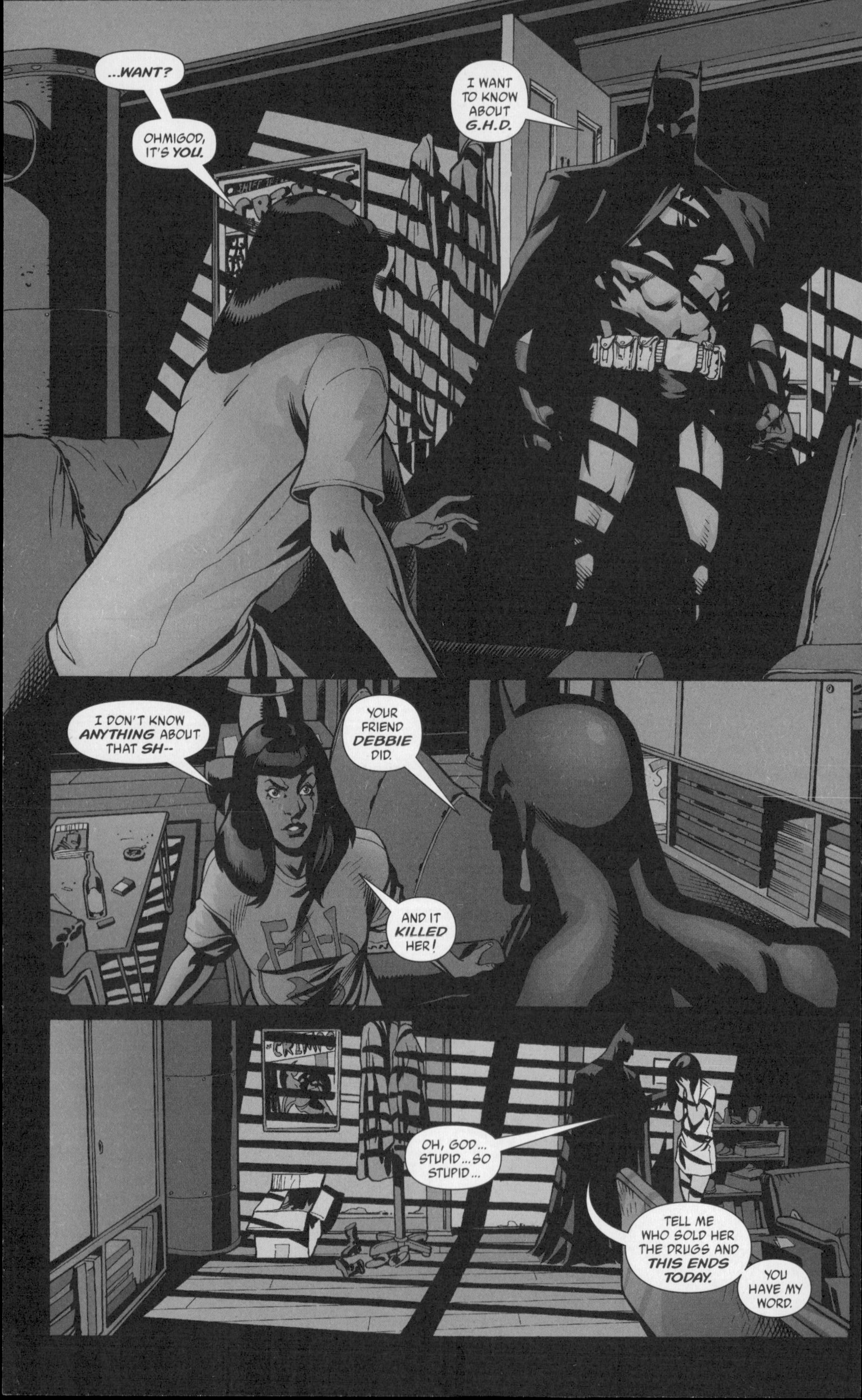
...WANT?
OHMIGOD, IT'S YOU.
I WANT TO KNOW ABOUT G.H.D.
I DON'T KNOW ANYTHING ABOUT THAT SH--
YOUR FRIEND DEBBIE DID.
AND IT KILLED HER!
OH, GOD... STUPID...SO STUPID...
TELL ME WHO SOLD HER THE DRUGS AND THIS ENDS TODAY.
YOU HAVE MY WORD.

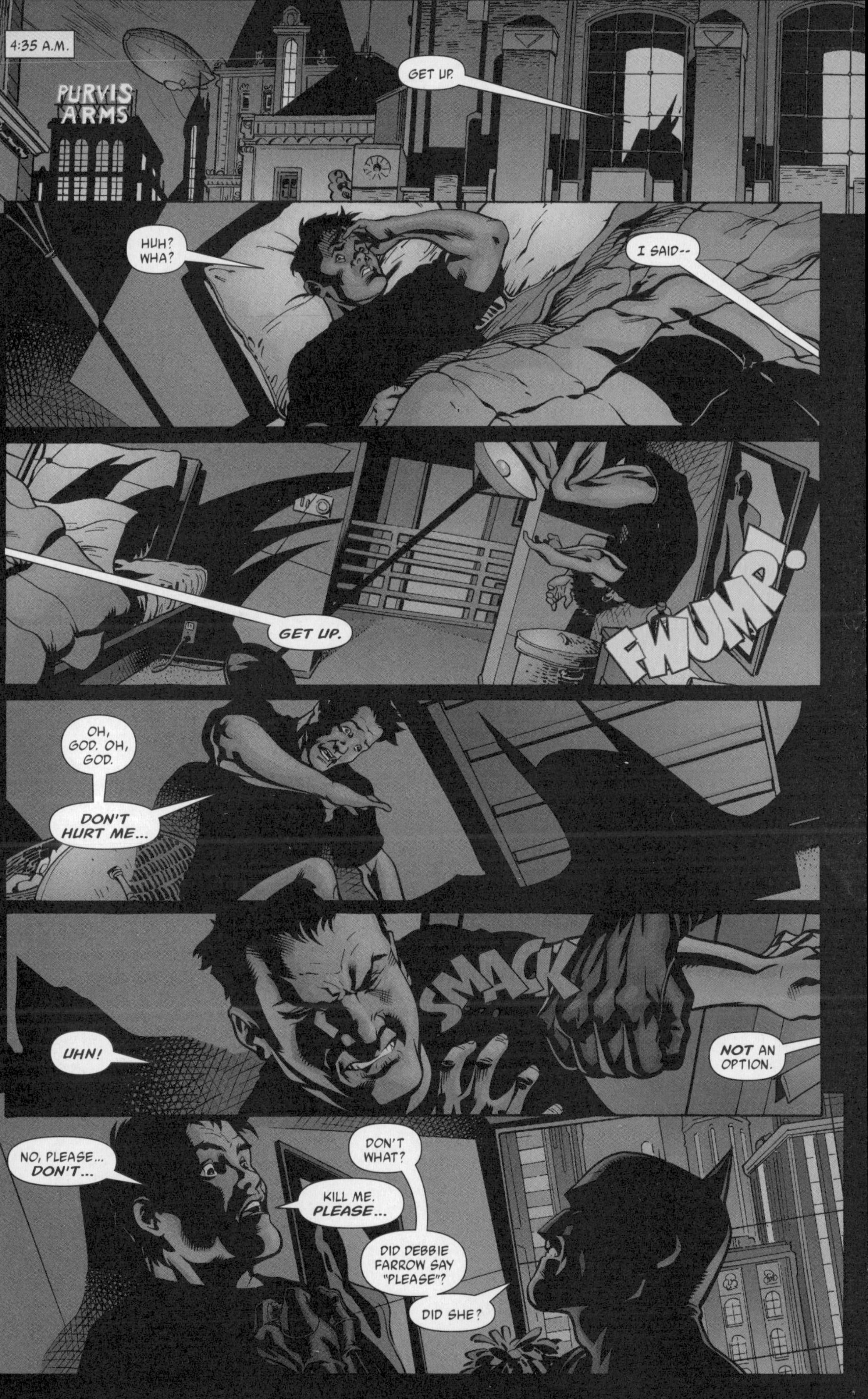
4:35 A.M.
PURVIS ARMS
GET UP.
HUH? WHA?
I SAID--
GET UP.
FWUMP!
OH, GOD. OH, GOD.
DON'T HURT ME...
SMACK
UHN!
NOT AN OPTION.
NO, PLEASE... DON'T...
DON'T WHAT?
KILL ME. PLEASE...
DID DEBBIE FARROW SAY "PLEASE"?
DID SHE?

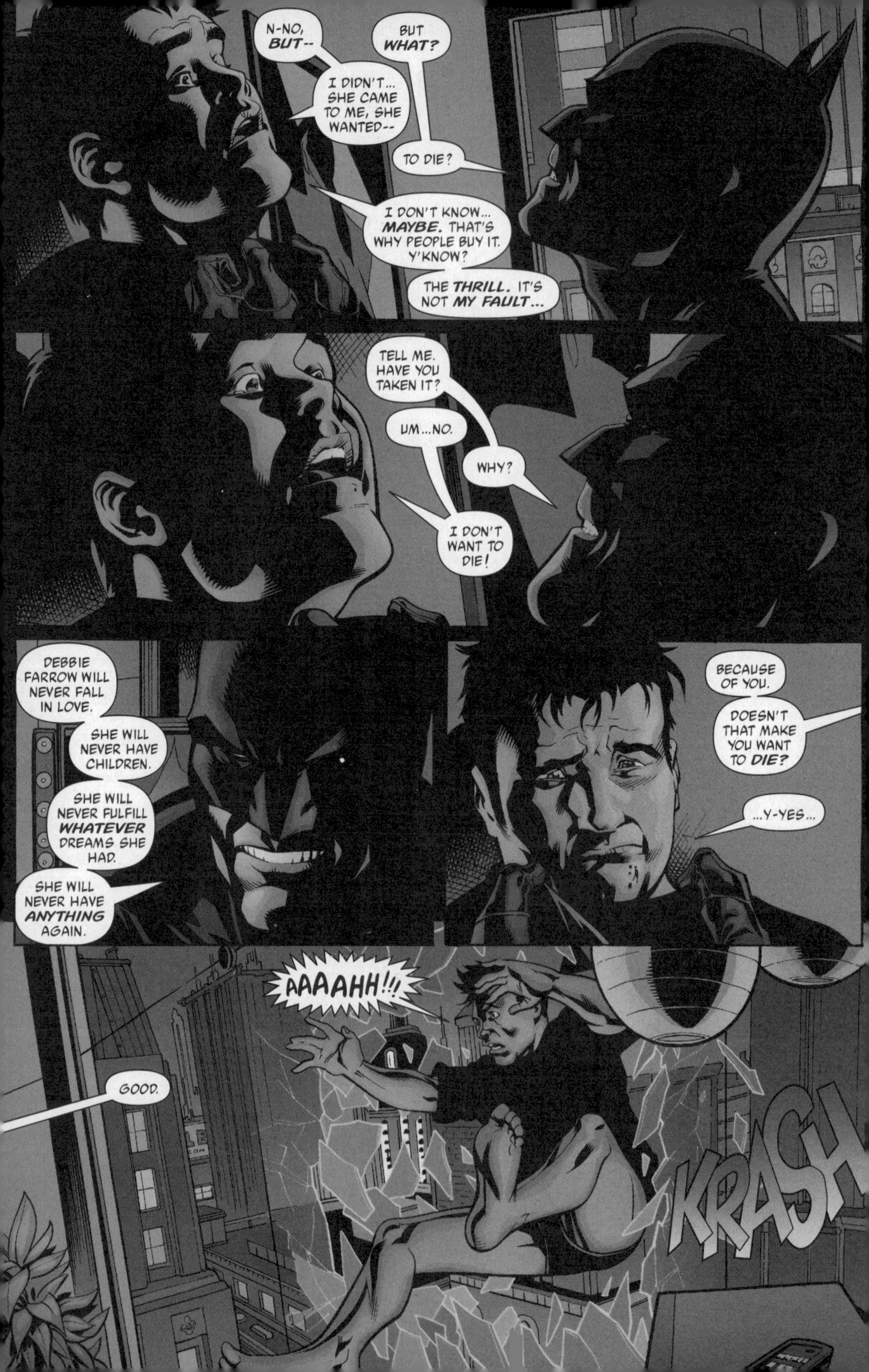
N-NO, BUT--
BUT WHAT?
I DIDN'T... SHE CAME TO ME, SHE WANTED--
TO DIE?
I DON'T KNOW... MAYBE. THAT'S WHY PEOPLE BUY IT. Y'KNOW?
THE THRILL. IT'S NOT MY FAULT...
TELL ME. HAVE YOU TAKEN IT?
UM...NO.
WHY?
I DON'T WANT TO DIE!
DEBBIE FARROW WILL NEVER FALL IN LOVE.
SHE WILL NEVER HAVE CHILDREN.
SHE WILL NEVER FULFILL WHATEVER DREAMS SHE HAD.
SHE WILL NEVER HAVE ANYTHING AGAIN.
BECAUSE OF YOU.
DOESN'T THAT MAKE YOU WANT TO DIE?
...Y-YES...
AAAAHH!!!
GOOD.
KRASH

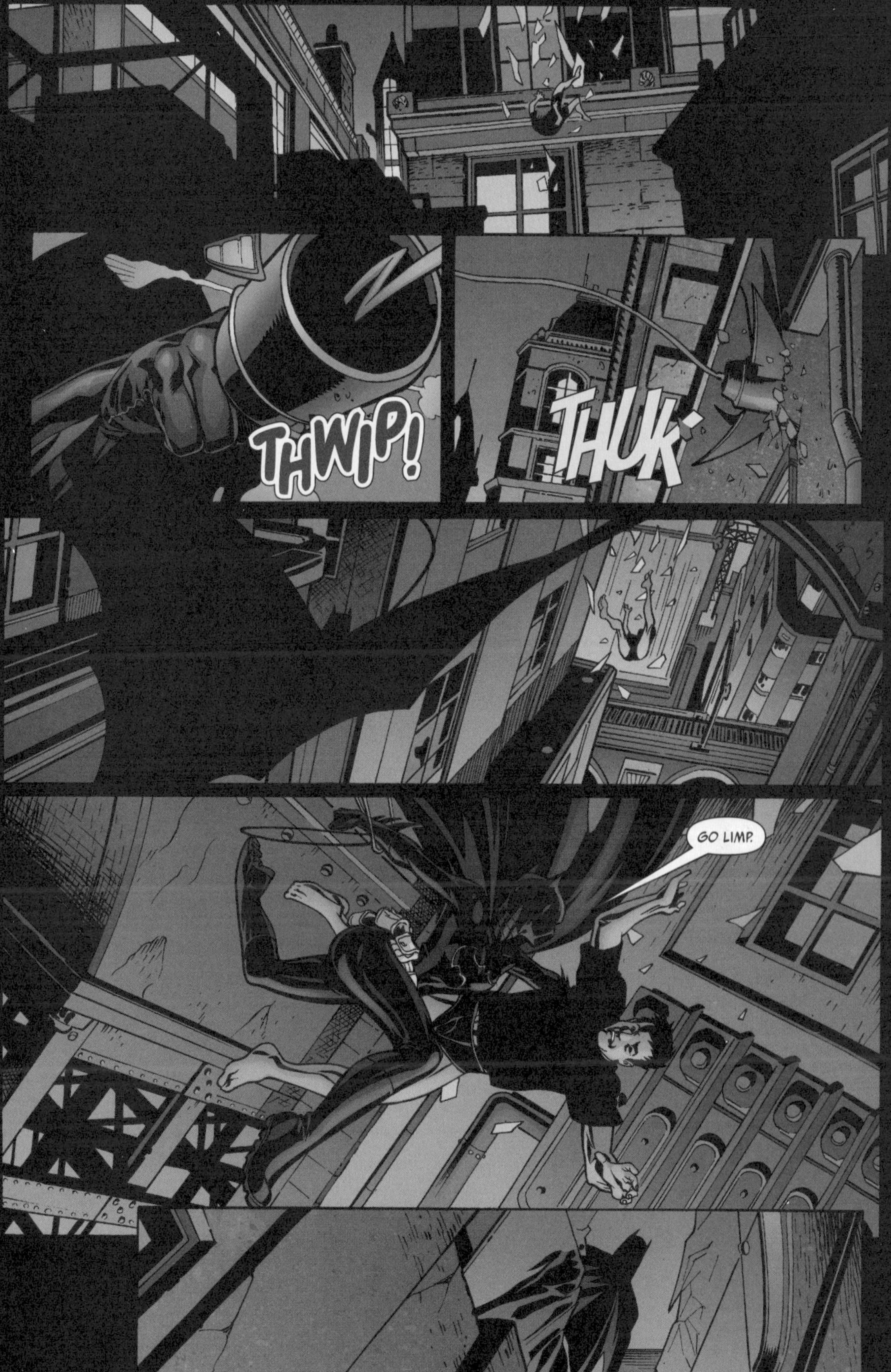
THWIP!
THUK
GO LIMP.

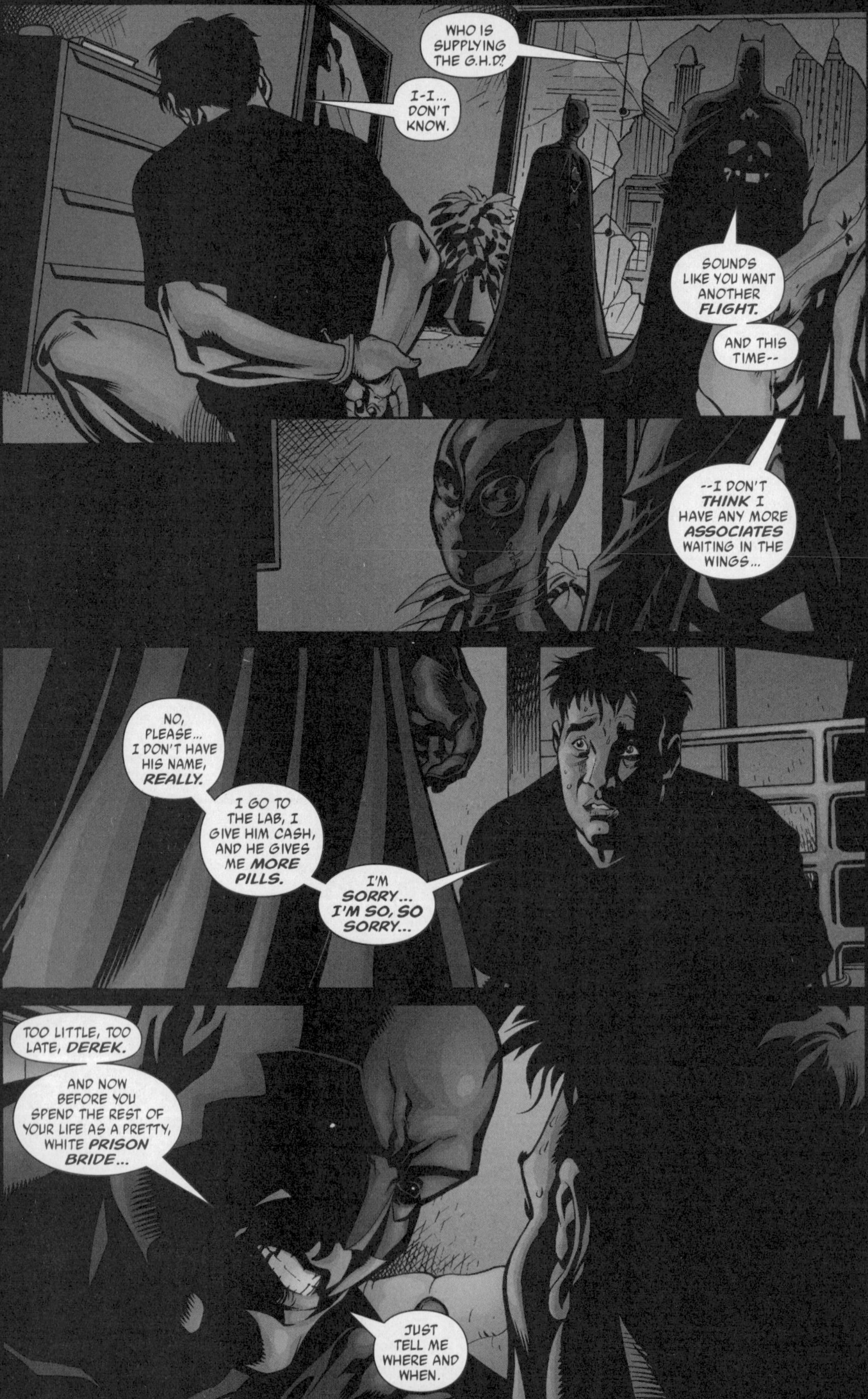
WHO IS SUPPLYING THE G.H.D.?
I-I... DON'T KNOW.
SOUNDS LIKE YOU WANT ANOTHER **FLIGHT.**
AND THIS TIME--
--I DON'T **THINK** I HAVE ANY MORE **ASSOCIATES** WAITING IN THE WINGS...
NO, PLEASE... I DON'T HAVE HIS NAME, **REALLY.**
I GO TO THE LAB, I GIVE HIM CASH, AND HE GIVES ME **MORE PILLS.**
I'M **SORRY... I'M SO, SO SORRY...**
TOO LITTLE, TOO LATE, **DEREK.**
AND NOW BEFORE YOU SPEND THE REST OF YOUR LIFE AS A PRETTY, WHITE **PRISON BRIDE...**
JUST TELL ME WHERE AND WHEN.

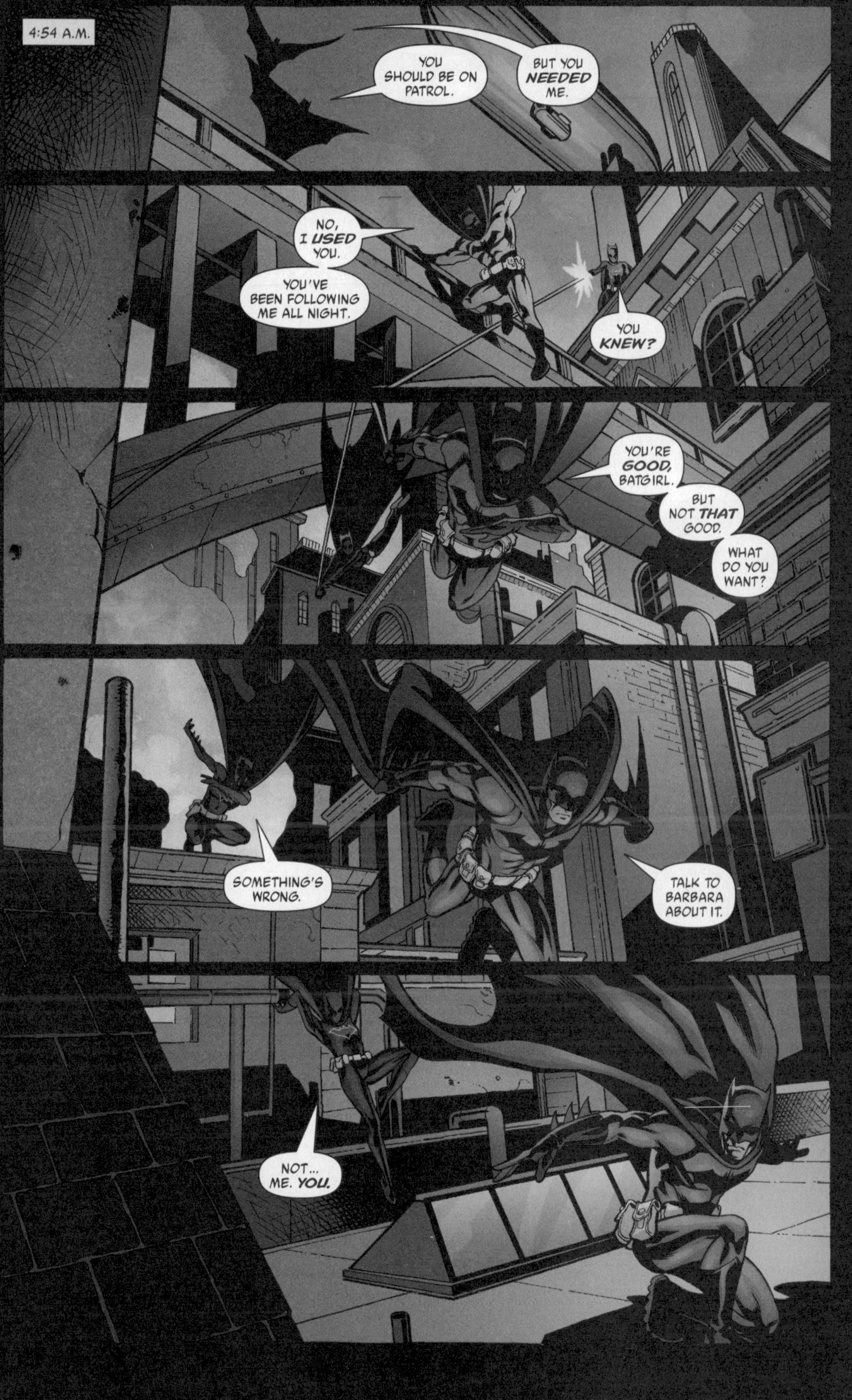
4:54 A.M.
YOU SHOULD BE ON PATROL.
BUT YOU NEEDED ME.
NO, I USED YOU.
YOU'VE BEEN FOLLOWING ME ALL NIGHT.
YOU KNEW?
YOU'RE GOOD, BATGIRL.
BUT NOT THAT GOOD.
WHAT DO YOU WANT?
SOMETHING'S WRONG.
TALK TO BARBARA ABOUT IT.
NOT... ME. YOU.

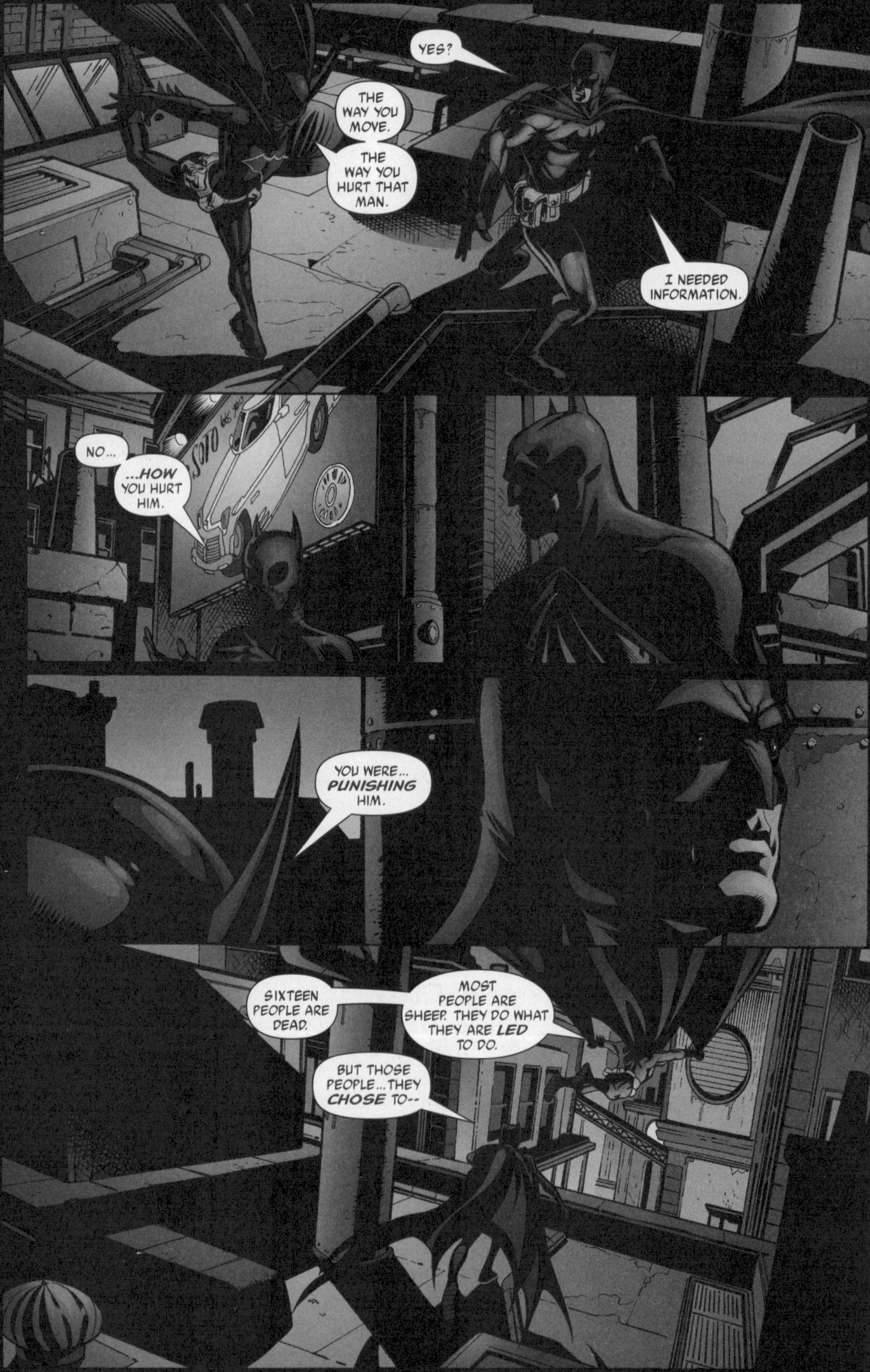
YES?
THE WAY YOU MOVE.
THE WAY YOU HURT THAT MAN.
I NEEDED INFORMATION.
NO...
...*HOW* YOU HURT HIM.
YOU WERE... *PUNISHING* HIM.
SIXTEEN PEOPLE ARE DEAD.
MOST PEOPLE ARE SHEEP. THEY DO WHAT THEY ARE *LED* TO DO.
BUT THOSE PEOPLE... THEY *CHOSE* TO--

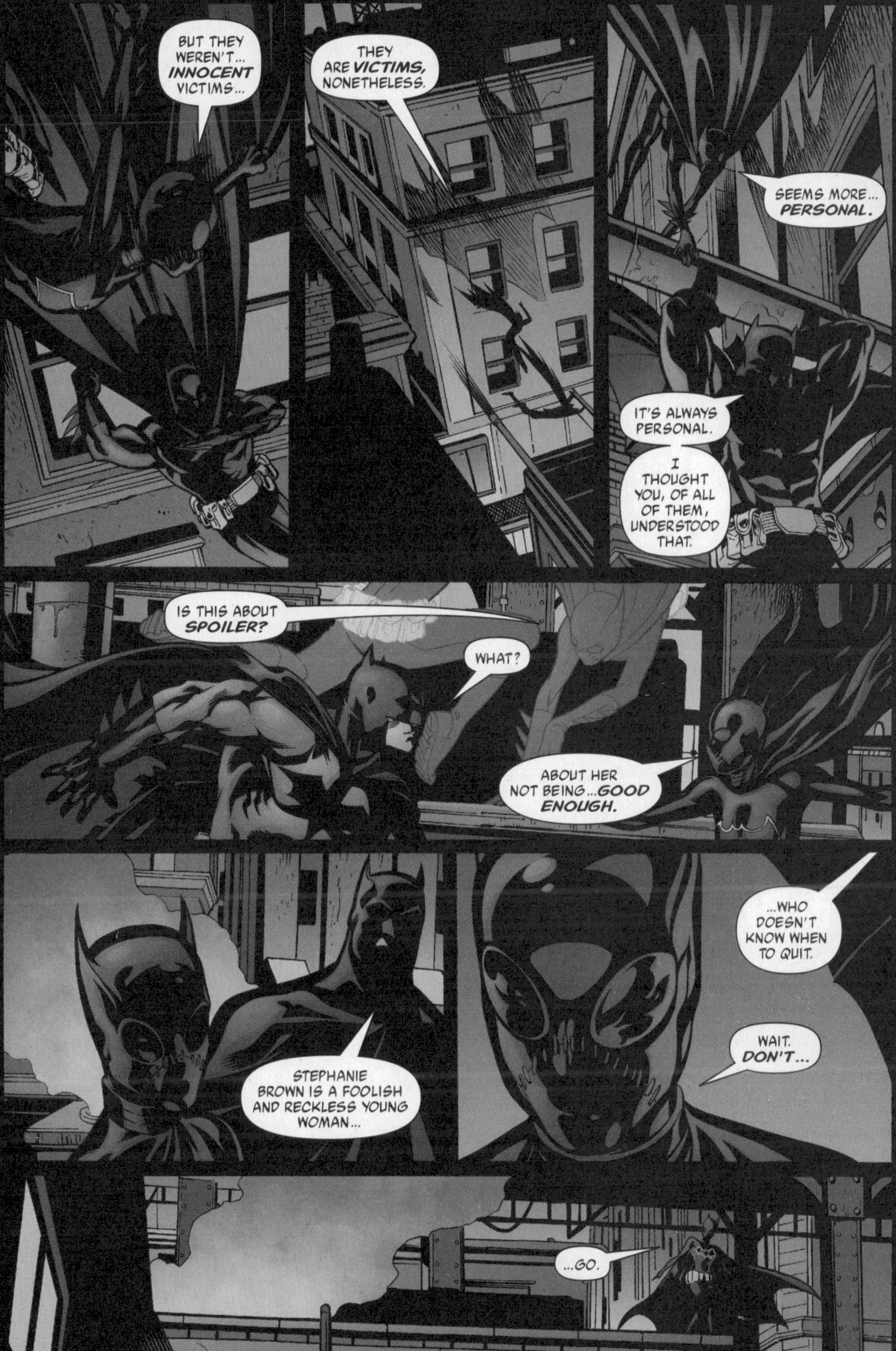

BUT THEY WEREN'T... INNOCENT VICTIMS...
THEY ARE VICTIMS, NONETHELESS.
SEEMS MORE... PERSONAL.
IT'S ALWAYS PERSONAL.
I THOUGHT YOU, OF ALL OF THEM, UNDERSTOOD THAT.
IS THIS ABOUT SPOILER?
WHAT?
ABOUT HER NOT BEING...GOOD ENOUGH.
STEPHANIE BROWN IS A FOOLISH AND RECKLESS YOUNG WOMAN...
...WHO DOESN'T KNOW WHEN TO QUIT.
WAIT. DON'T...
...GO.

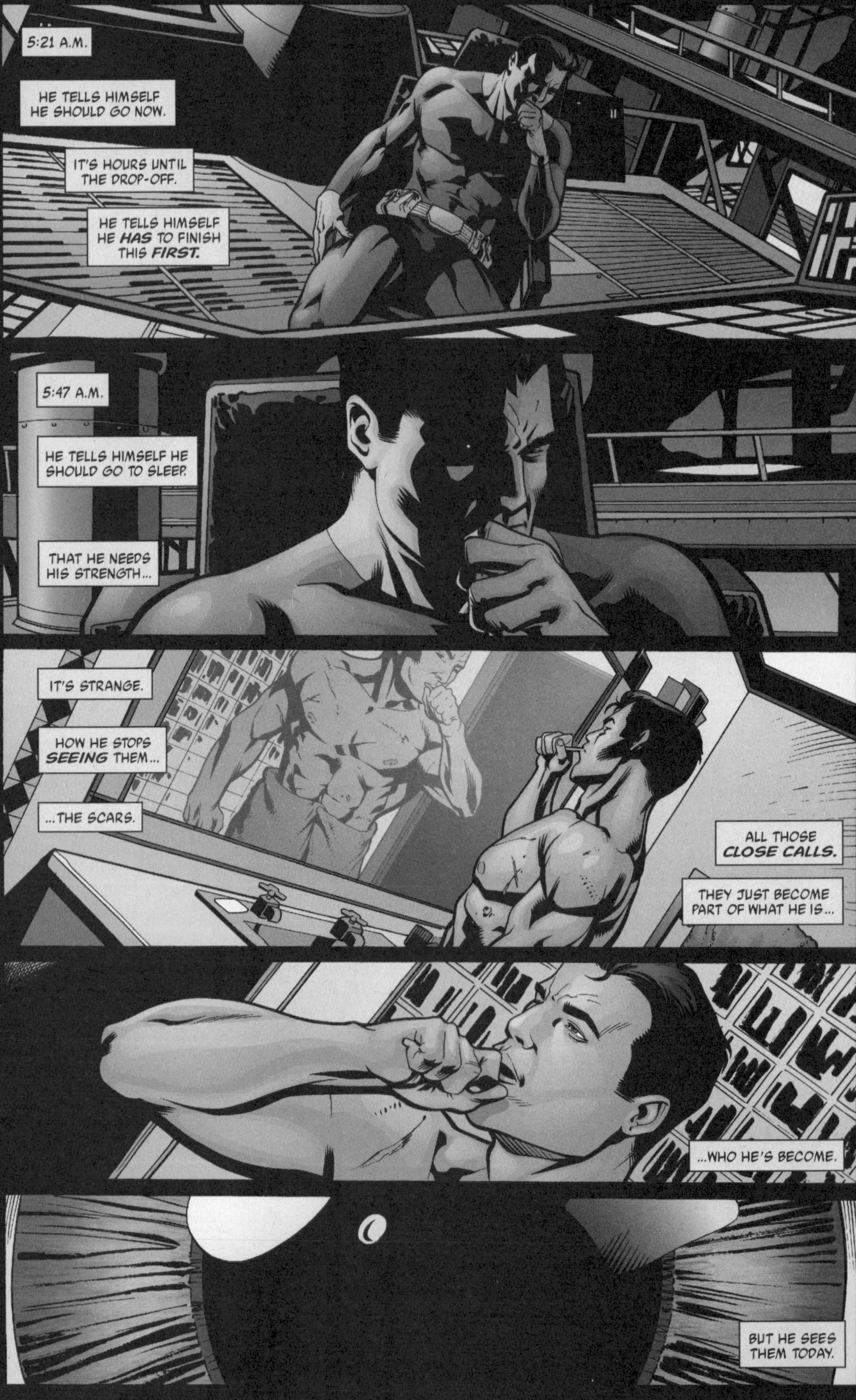
5:21 A.M.
HE TELLS HIMSELF HE SHOULD GO NOW.
IT'S HOURS UNTIL THE DROP-OFF.
HE TELLS HIMSELF HE HAS TO FINISH THIS FIRST.
5:47 A.M.
HE TELLS HIMSELF HE SHOULD GO TO SLEEP.
THAT HE NEEDS HIS STRENGTH...
IT'S STRANGE.
HOW HE STOPS SEEING THEM...
...THE SCARS.
ALL THOSE CLOSE CALLS.
THEY JUST BECOME PART OF WHAT HE IS...
...WHO HE'S BECOME.
BUT HE SEES THEM TODAY.

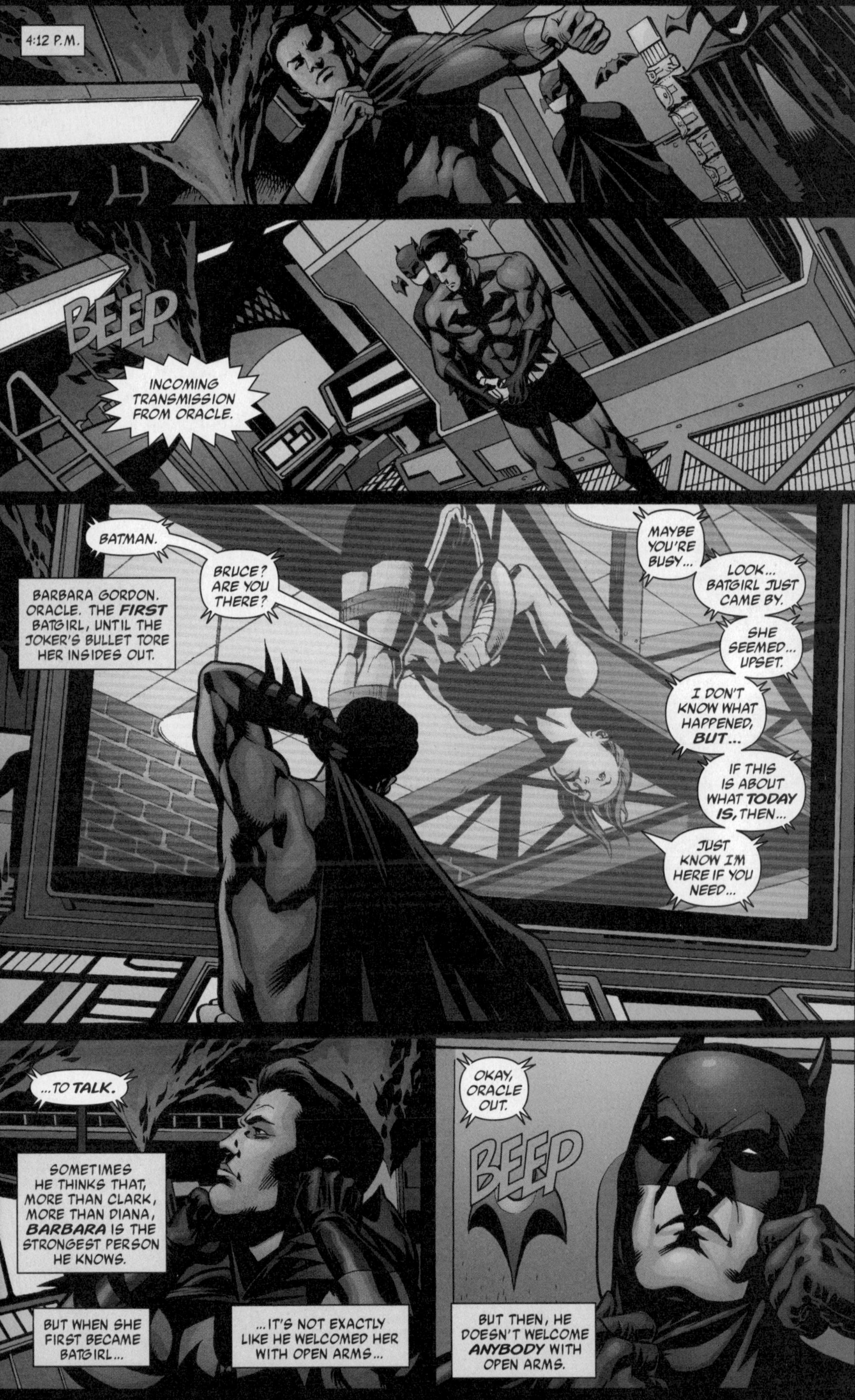
4:12 P.M.
BEEP
INCOMING TRANSMISSION FROM ORACLE.
BATMAN.
BRUCE? ARE YOU THERE?
BARBARA GORDON. ORACLE. THE FIRST BATGIRL, UNTIL THE JOKER'S BULLET TORE HER INSIDES OUT.
MAYBE YOU'RE BUSY...
LOOK... BATGIRL JUST CAME BY.
SHE SEEMED... UPSET.
I DON'T KNOW WHAT HAPPENED, BUT...
IF THIS IS ABOUT WHAT TODAY IS, THEN...
JUST KNOW I'M HERE IF YOU NEED...
...TO TALK.
SOMETIMES HE THINKS THAT, MORE THAN CLARK, MORE THAN DIANA, BARBARA IS THE STRONGEST PERSON HE KNOWS.
BUT WHEN SHE FIRST BECAME BATGIRL...
...IT'S NOT EXACTLY LIKE HE WELCOMED HER WITH OPEN ARMS...
OKAY, ORACLE OUT.
BEEP
BUT THEN, HE DOESN'T WELCOME ANYBODY WITH OPEN ARMS.

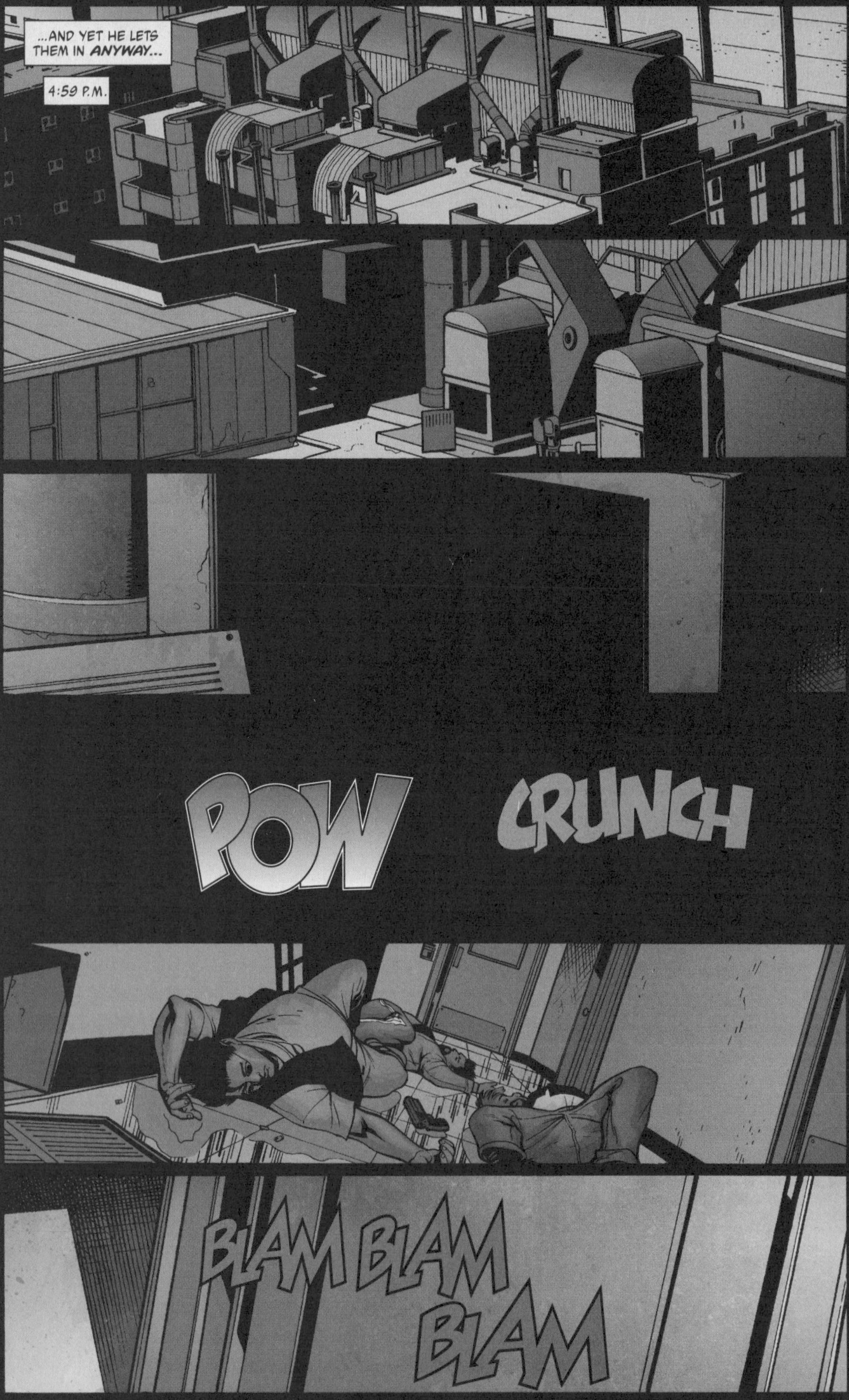
...AND YET HE LETS THEM IN *ANYWAY*...
4:59 P.M.
POW
CRUNCH
BLAM BLAM BLAM

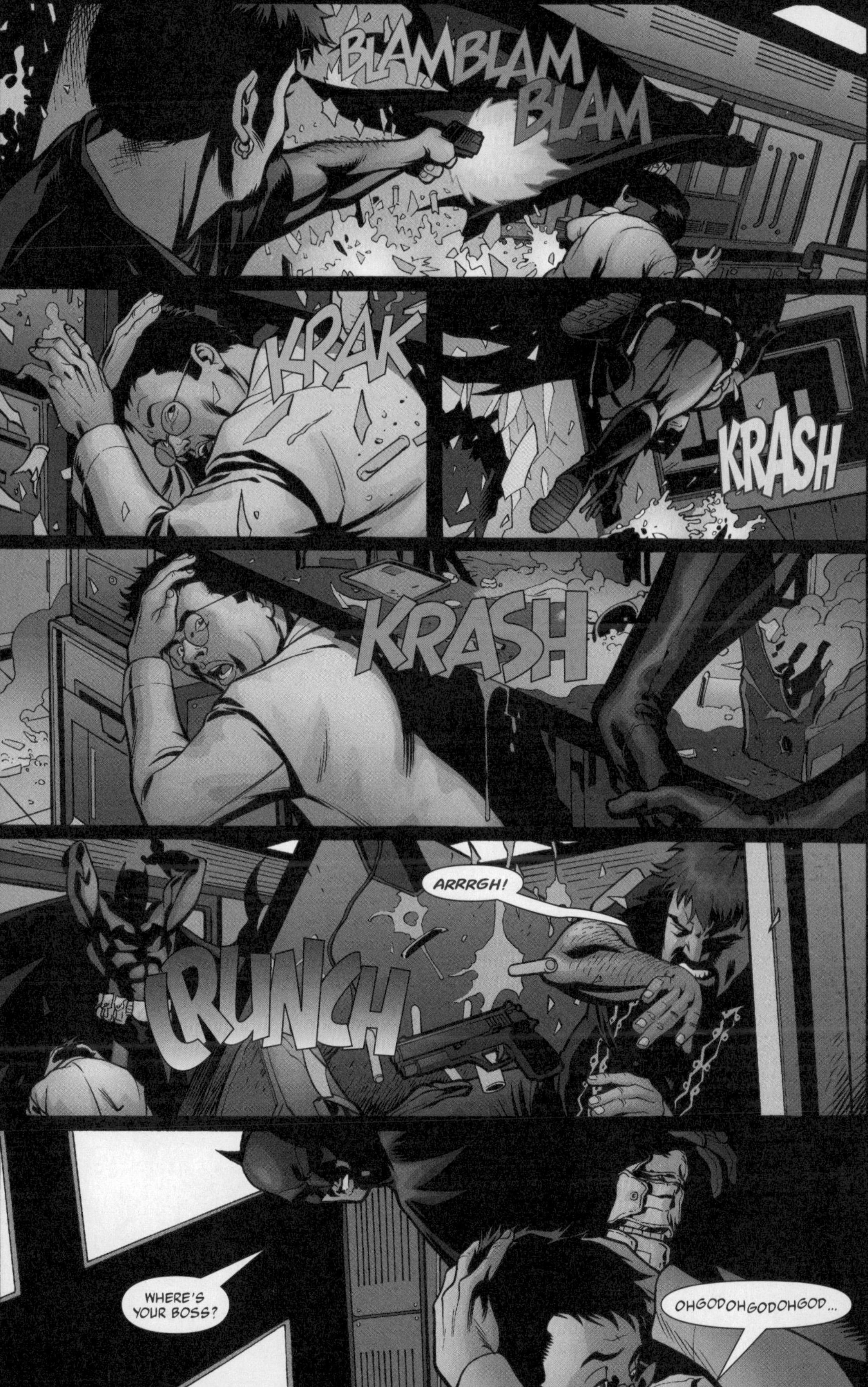
BLAMBLAM
BLAM
KRAK
KRASH
KRASH
ARRRGH!
CRUNCH
WHERE'S YOUR BOSS?
OHGODOHGODOHGOD...

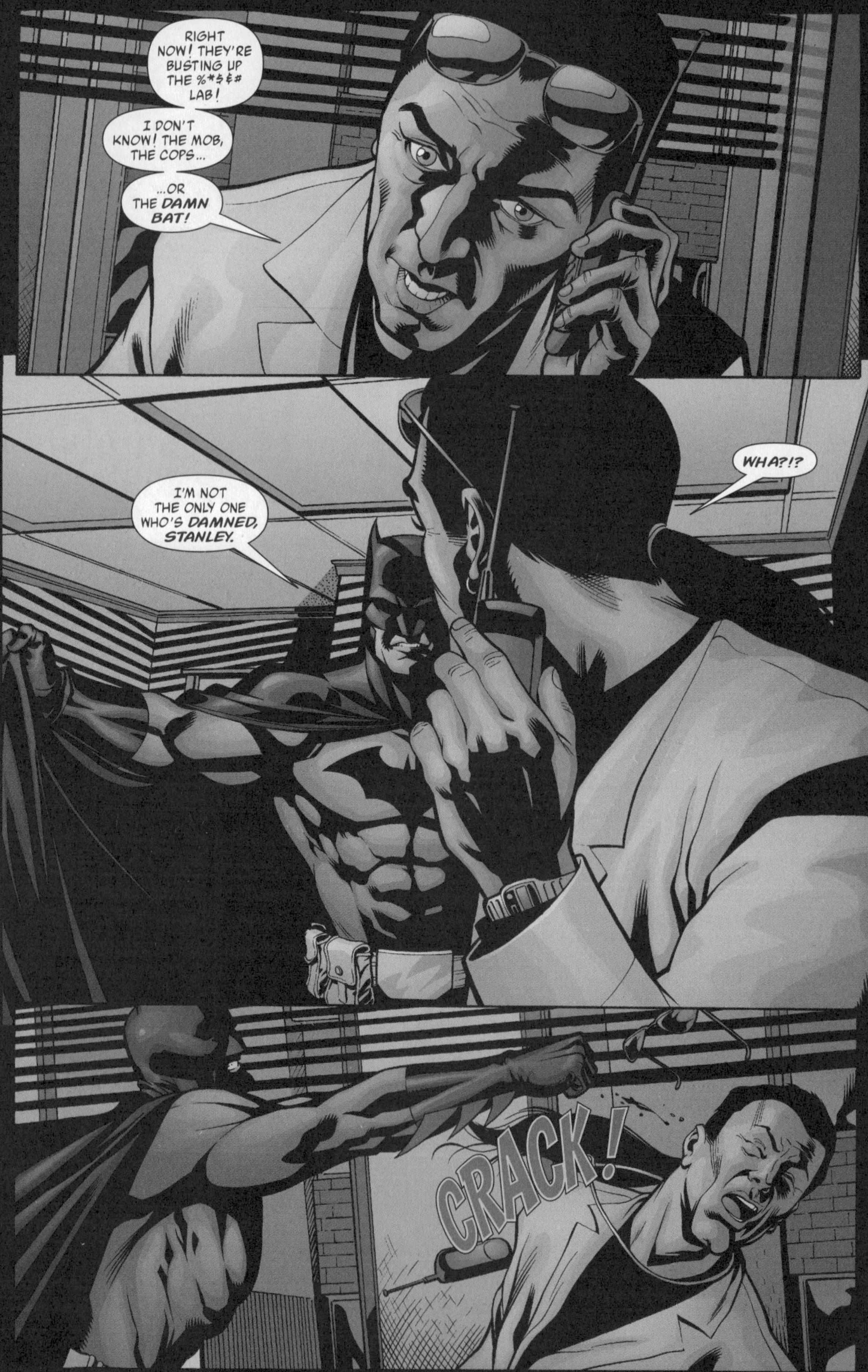

RIGHT NOW! THEY'RE BUSTING UP THE %*$&# LAB!
I DON'T KNOW! THE MOB, THE COPS...
...OR THE DAMN BAT!
WHA?!?
I'M NOT THE ONLY ONE WHO'S DAMNED, STANLEY.
CRACK!

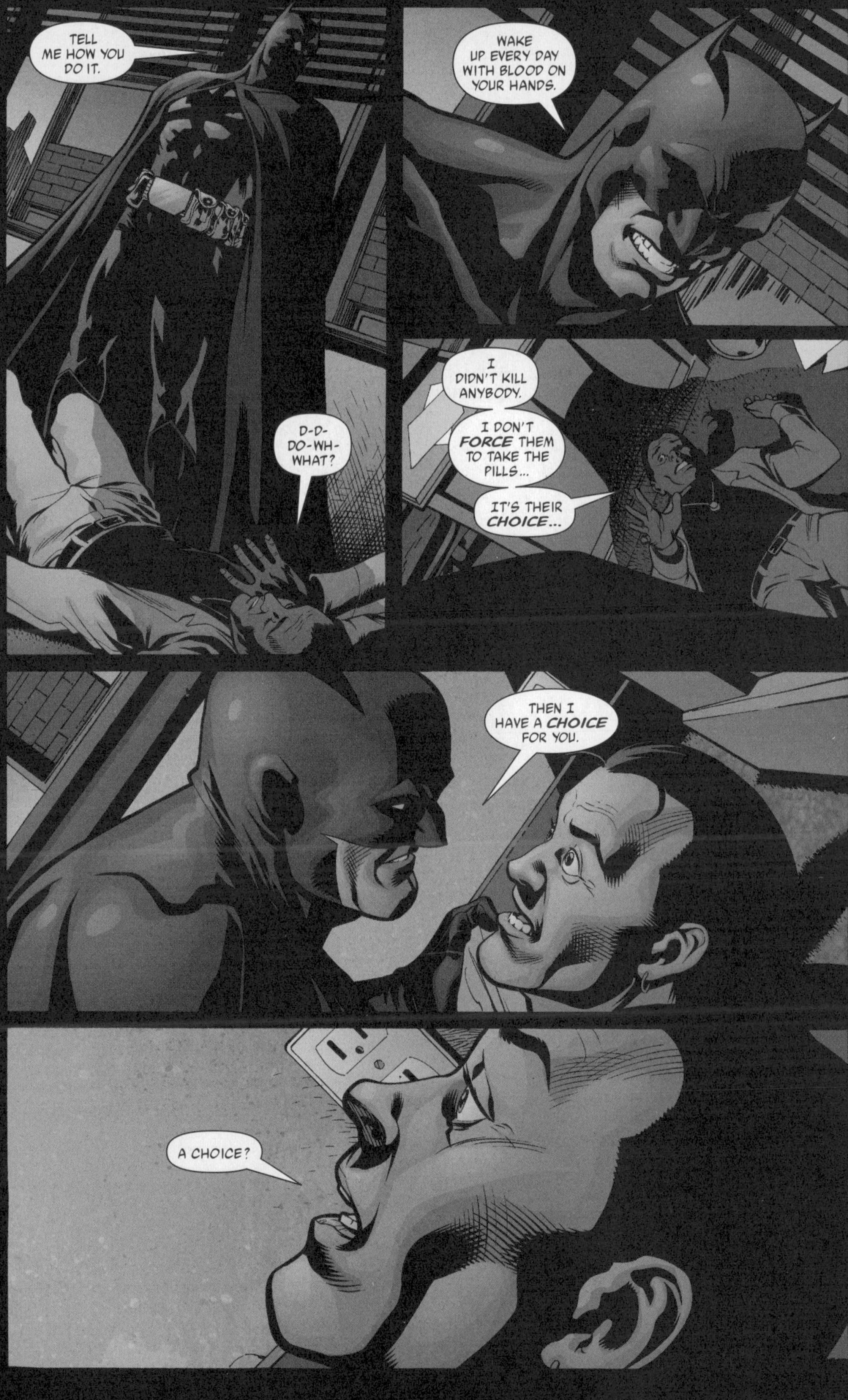
TELL ME HOW YOU DO IT.
WAKE UP EVERY DAY WITH BLOOD ON YOUR HANDS.
D-D-DO-WH-WHAT?
I DIDN'T KILL ANYBODY.
I DON'T FORCE THEM TO TAKE THE PILLS...
IT'S THEIR CHOICE...
THEN I HAVE A CHOICE FOR YOU.
A CHOICE?

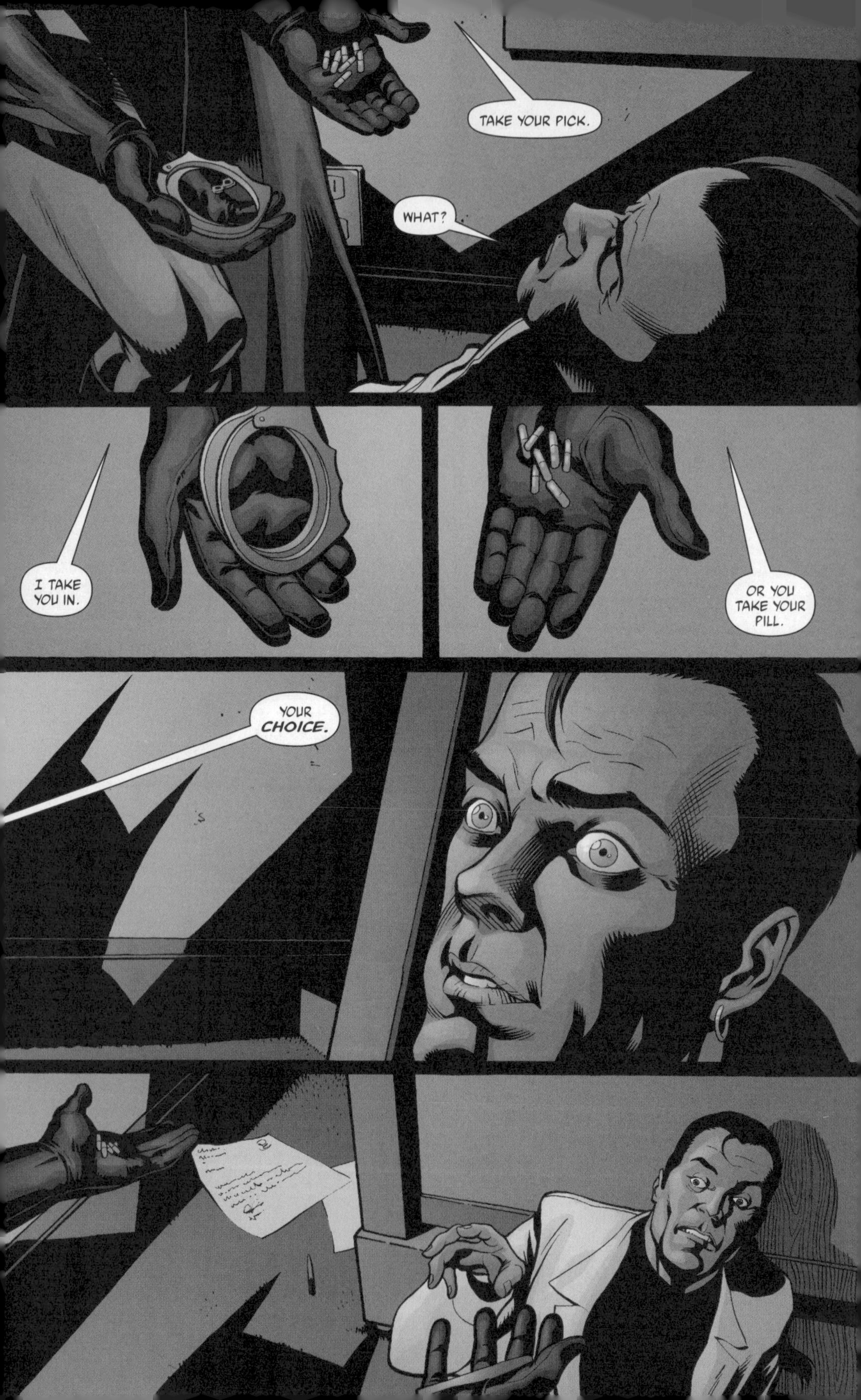
TAKE YOUR PICK.
WHAT?
I TAKE YOU IN.
OR YOU TAKE YOUR PILL.
YOUR *CHOICE.*

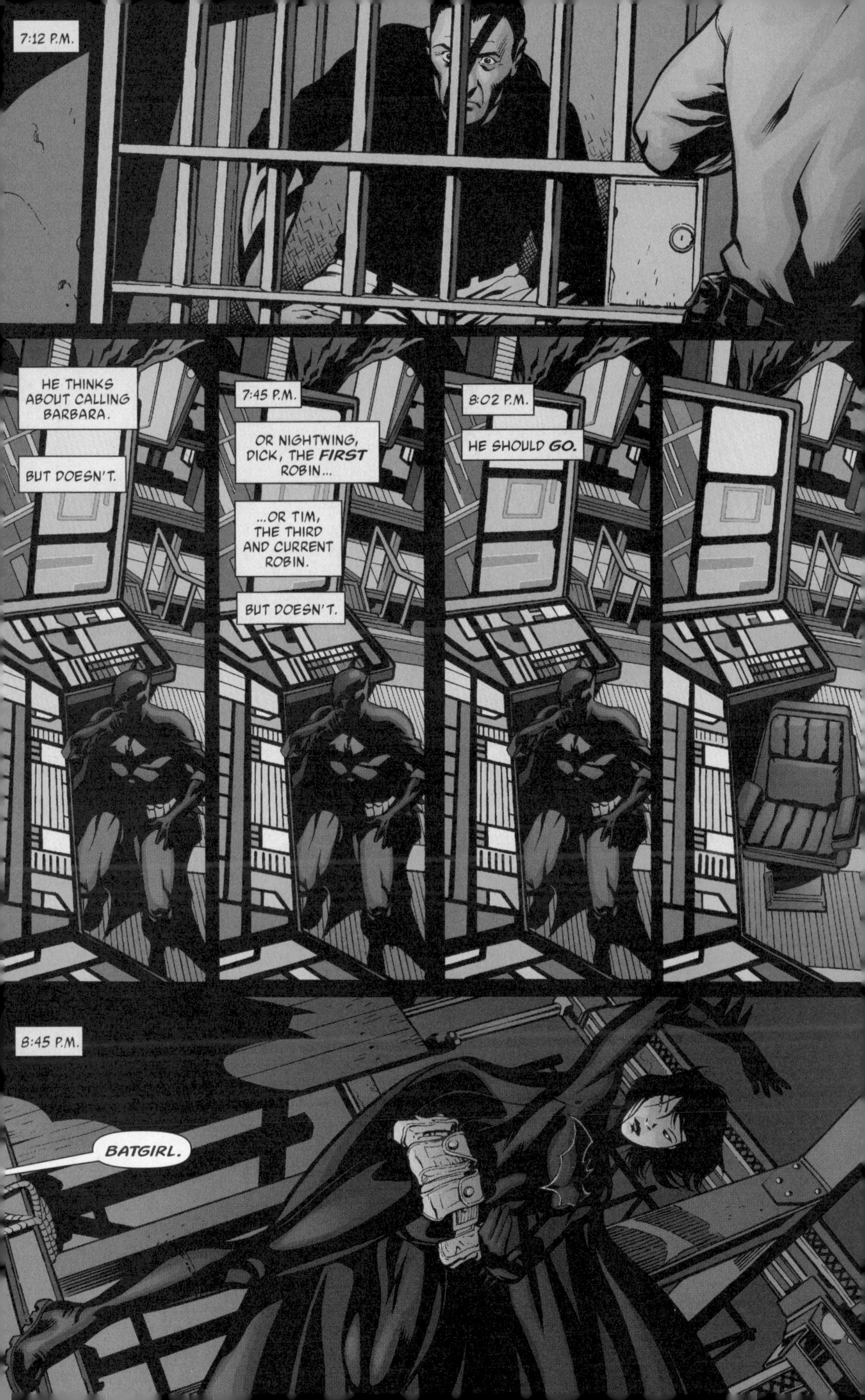
7:12 P.M.
HE THINKS ABOUT CALLING BARBARA.
BUT DOESN'T.
7:45 P.M.
OR NIGHTWING, DICK, THE FIRST ROBIN...
...OR TIM, THE THIRD AND CURRENT ROBIN.
BUT DOESN'T.
8:02 P.M.
HE SHOULD GO.
8:45 P.M.
BATGIRL.

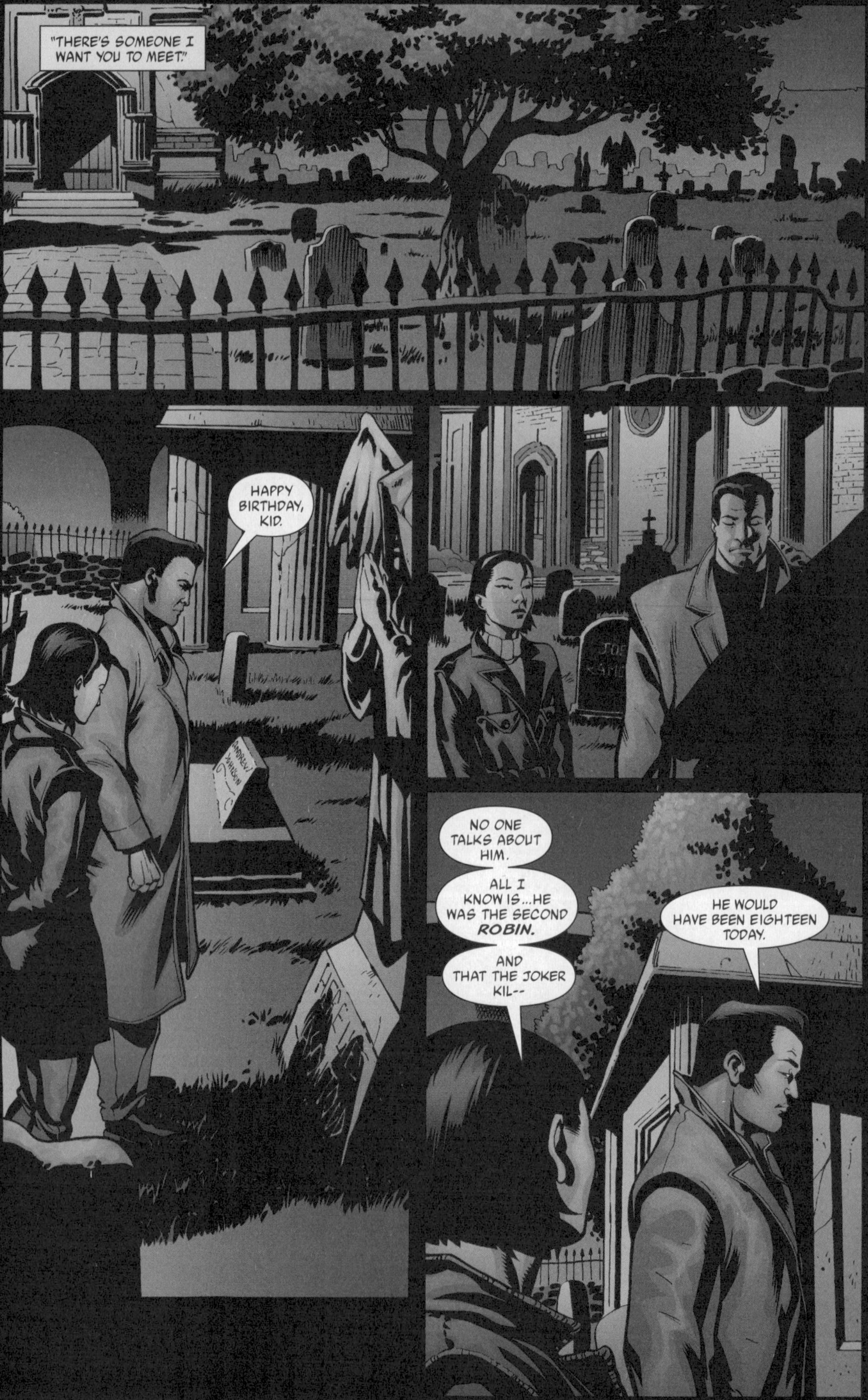
"THERE'S SOMEONE I WANT YOU TO MEET."
HAPPY BIRTHDAY, KID.
NO ONE TALKS ABOUT HIM.
ALL I KNOW IS...HE WAS THE SECOND ROBIN.
AND THAT THE JOKER KIL--
HE WOULD HAVE BEEN EIGHTEEN TODAY.

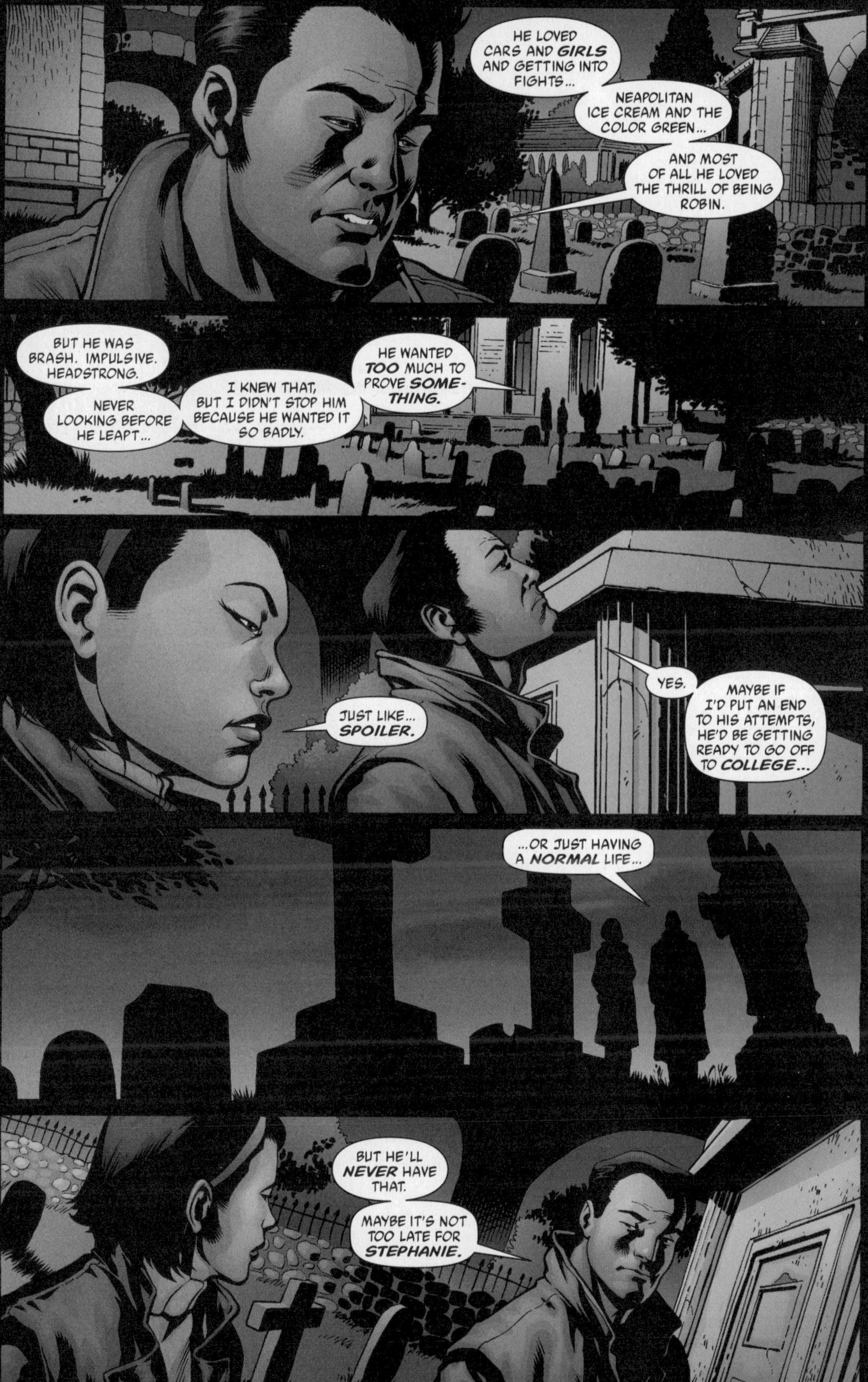
HE LOVED CARS AND GIRLS AND GETTING INTO FIGHTS...
NEAPOLITAN ICE CREAM AND THE COLOR GREEN...
AND MOST OF ALL HE LOVED THE THRILL OF BEING ROBIN.
BUT HE WAS BRASH. IMPULSIVE. HEADSTRONG.
NEVER LOOKING BEFORE HE LEAPT...
I KNEW THAT, BUT I DIDN'T STOP HIM BECAUSE HE WANTED IT SO BADLY.
HE WANTED TOO MUCH TO PROVE SOME-THING.
JUST LIKE... SPOILER.
YES.
MAYBE IF I'D PUT AN END TO HIS ATTEMPTS, HE'D BE GETTING READY TO GO OFF TO COLLEGE...
...OR JUST HAVING A NORMAL LIFE...
BUT HE'LL NEVER HAVE THAT.
MAYBE IT'S NOT TOO LATE FOR STEPHANIE.

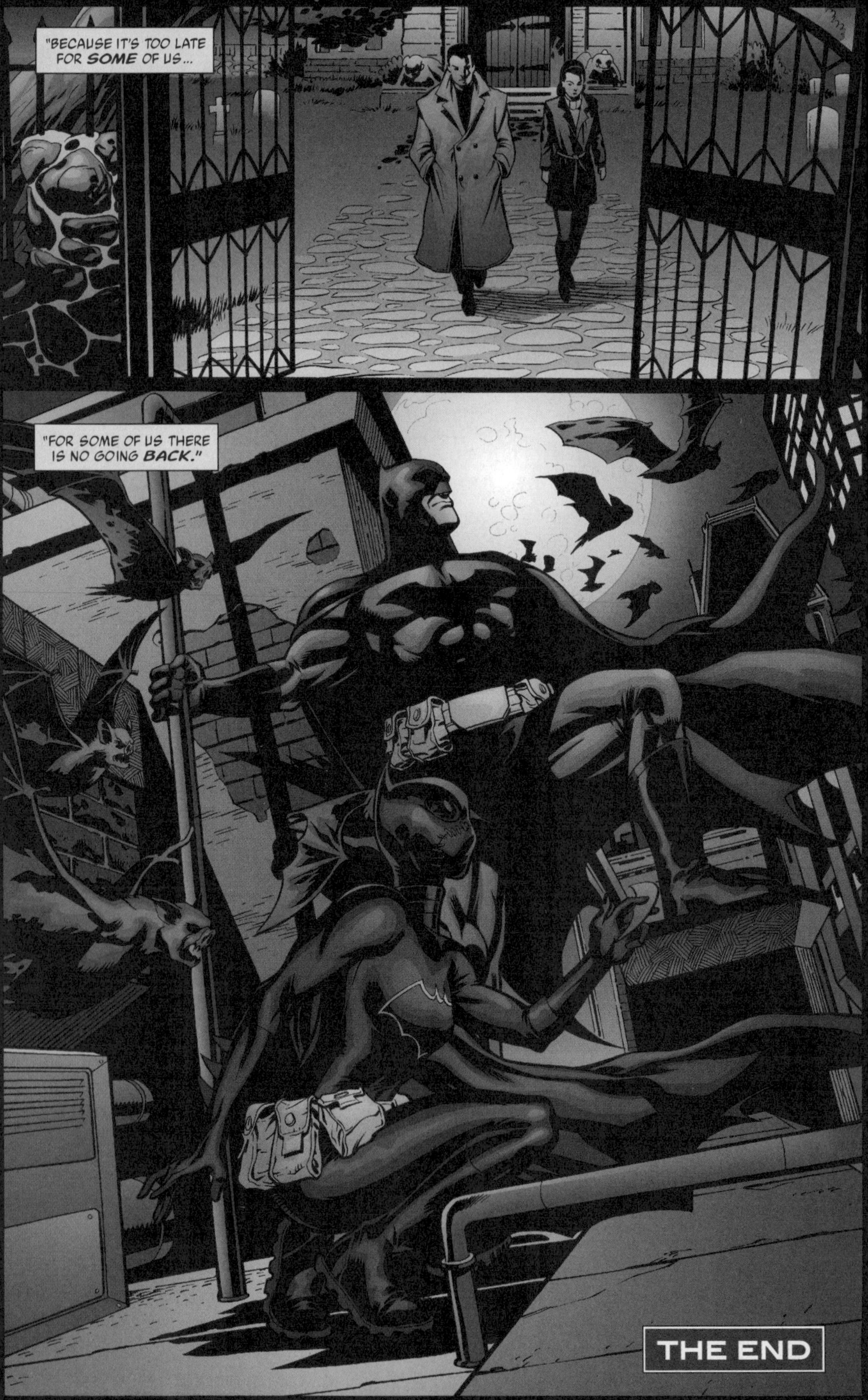
"BECAUSE IT'S TOO LATE FOR SOME OF US...
"FOR SOME OF US THERE IS NO GOING BACK."
THE END

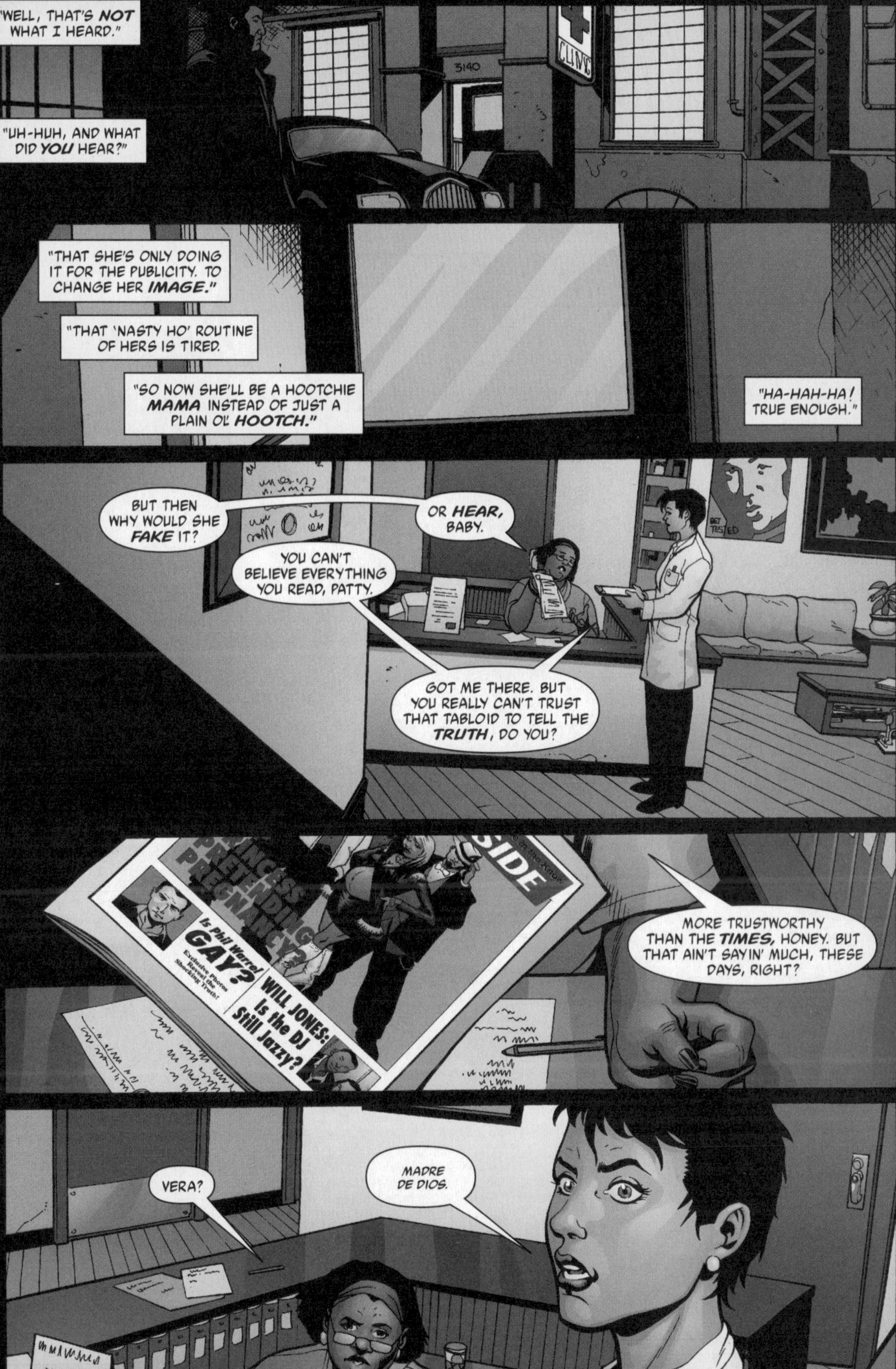
"WELL, THAT'S NOT WHAT I HEARD."
"UH-HUH, AND WHAT DID YOU HEAR?"
3140
CLINIC
"THAT SHE'S ONLY DOING IT FOR THE PUBLICITY. TO CHANGE HER IMAGE."
"THAT 'NASTY HO' ROUTINE OF HERS IS TIRED.
"SO NOW SHE'LL BE A HOOTCHIE MAMA INSTEAD OF JUST A PLAIN OL' HOOTCH."
"HA-HAH-HA! TRUE ENOUGH."
BUT THEN WHY WOULD SHE FAKE IT?
OR HEAR, BABY.
YOU CAN'T BELIEVE EVERYTHING YOU READ, PATTY.
GOT ME THERE. BUT YOU REALLY CAN'T TRUST THAT TABLOID TO TELL THE TRUTH, DO YOU?
GET TESTED
SIDE
PREGNANCY?
Is Phil Warrel GAY?
Exclusive Photos Reveal the Shocking Truth!
WILL JONES: Is the DJ Still Jazzy?
MORE TRUSTWORTHY THAN THE TIMES, HONEY. BUT THAT AIN'T SAYIN' MUCH, THESE DAYS, RIGHT?
VERA?
MADRE DE DIOS.

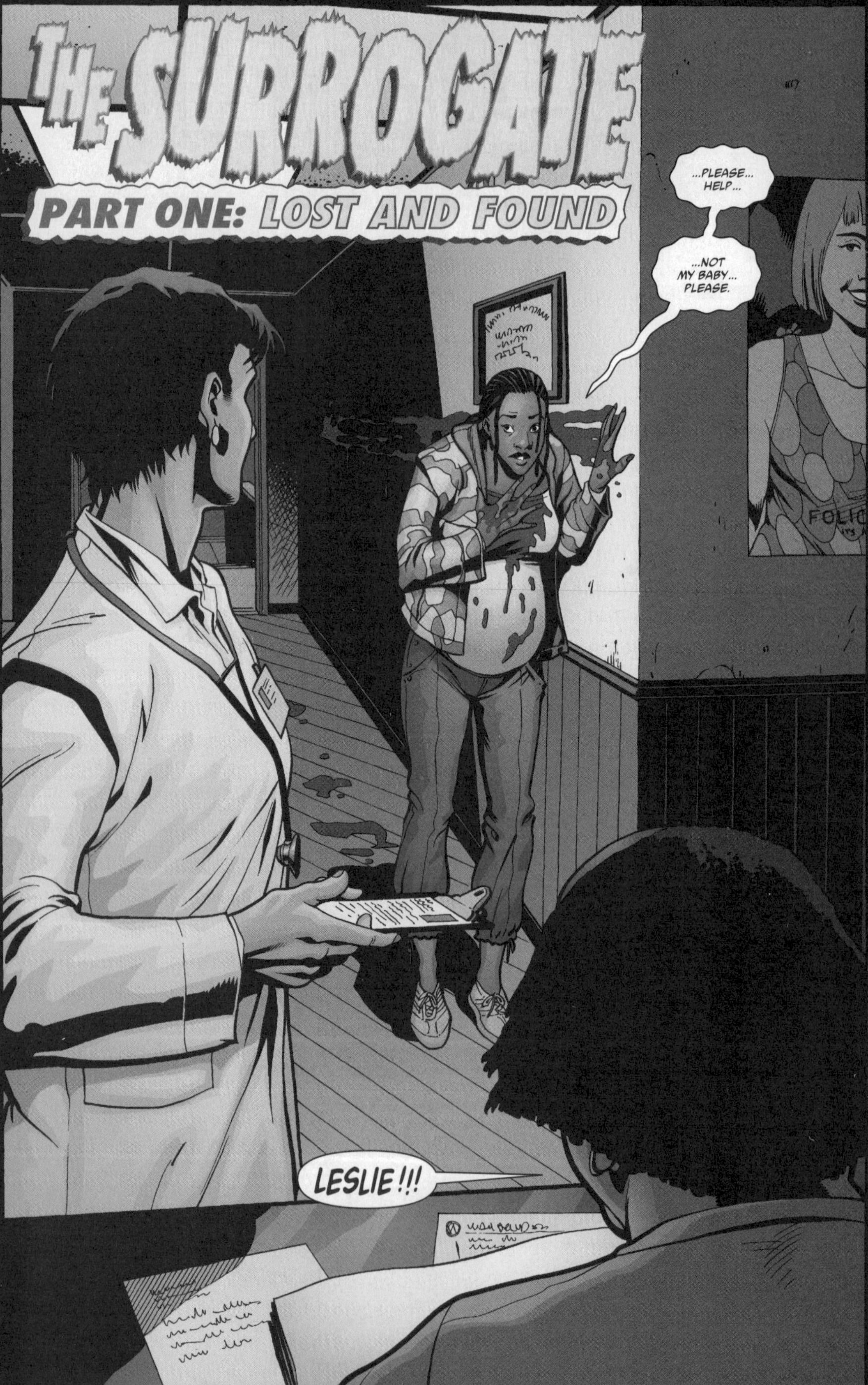
THE SURROGATE
PART ONE: LOST AND FOUND
...PLEASE... HELP...
...NOT MY BABY... PLEASE.
LESLIE!!!

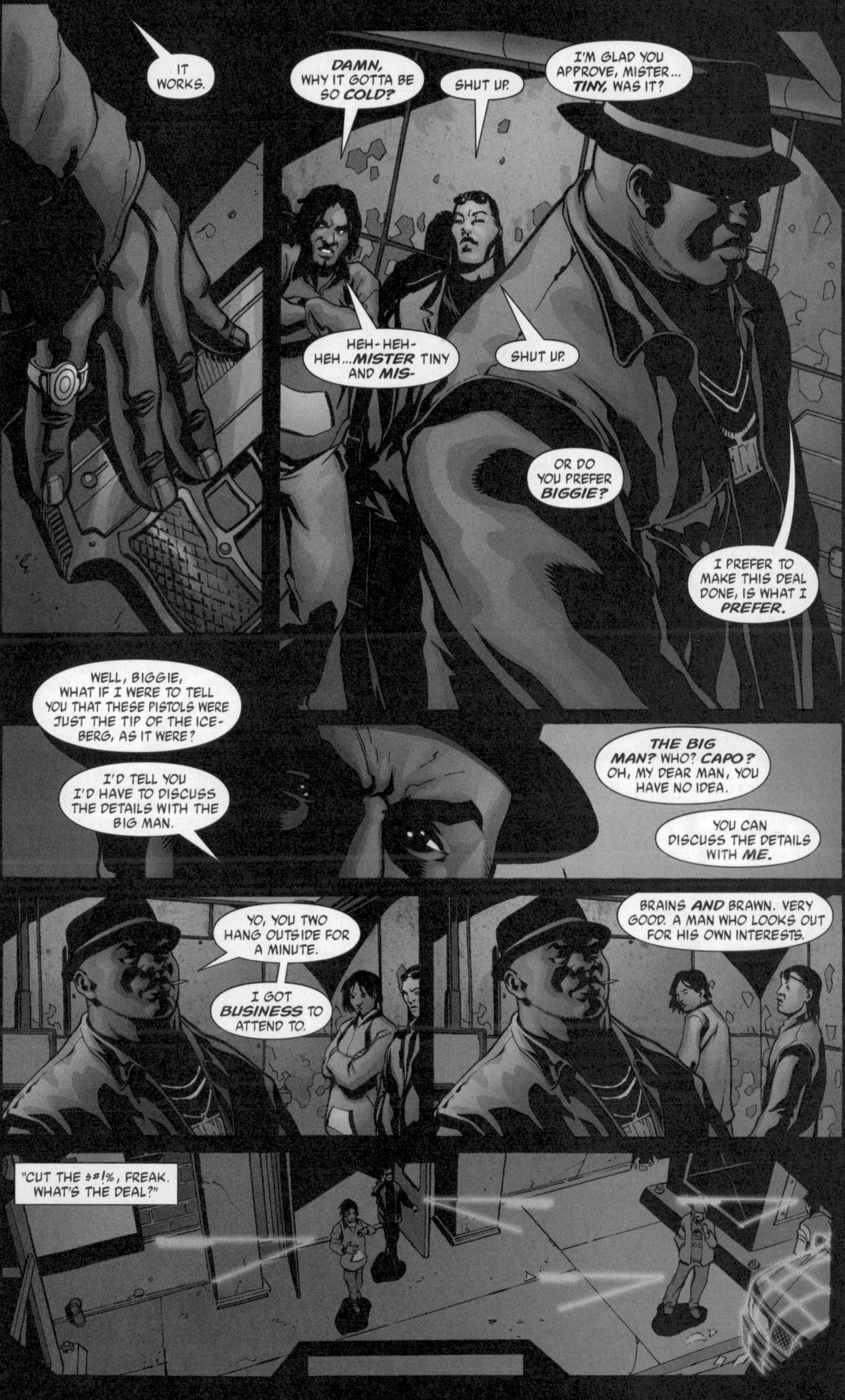
IT WORKS.
DAMN, WHY IT GOTTA BE SO COLD?
SHUT UP.
I'M GLAD YOU APPROVE, MISTER... TINY, WAS IT?
HEH-HEH-HEH...MISTER TINY AND MIS-
SHUT UP.
OR DO YOU PREFER BIGGIE?
I PREFER TO MAKE THIS DEAL DONE, IS WHAT I PREFER.
WELL, BIGGIE, WHAT IF I WERE TO TELL YOU THAT THESE PISTOLS WERE JUST THE TIP OF THE ICE-BERG, AS IT WERE?
I'D TELL YOU I'D HAVE TO DISCUSS THE DETAILS WITH THE BIG MAN.
THE BIG MAN? WHO? CAPO? OH, MY DEAR MAN, YOU HAVE NO IDEA.
YOU CAN DISCUSS THE DETAILS WITH ME.
YO, YOU TWO HANG OUTSIDE FOR A MINUTE.
I GOT BUSINESS TO ATTEND TO.
BRAINS AND BRAWN. VERY GOOD. A MAN WHO LOOKS OUT FOR HIS OWN INTERESTS.
"CUT THE $#!%, FREAK. WHAT'S THE DEAL?"

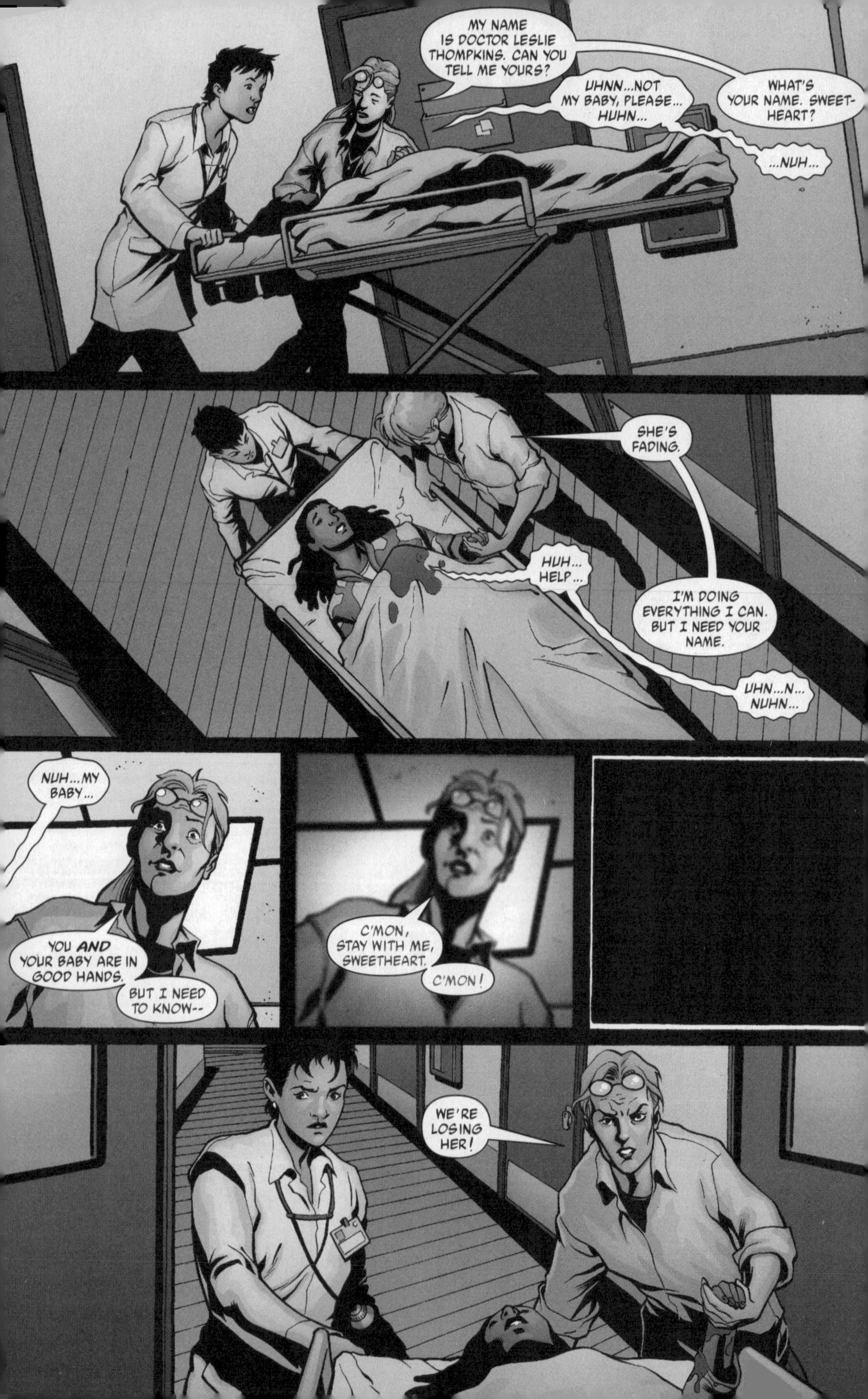
MY NAME IS DOCTOR LESLIE THOMPKINS. CAN YOU TELL ME YOURS?
UHNN...NOT MY BABY, PLEASE... HUHN...
WHAT'S YOUR NAME. SWEET-HEART?
...NUH...
SHE'S FADING.
HUH... HELP...
I'M DOING EVERYTHING I CAN. BUT I NEED YOUR NAME.
UHN...N... NUHN...
NUH...MY BABY...
YOU AND YOUR BABY ARE IN GOOD HANDS.
BUT I NEED TO KNOW--
C'MON, STAY WITH ME, SWEETHEART.
C'MON!
WE'RE LOSING HER!

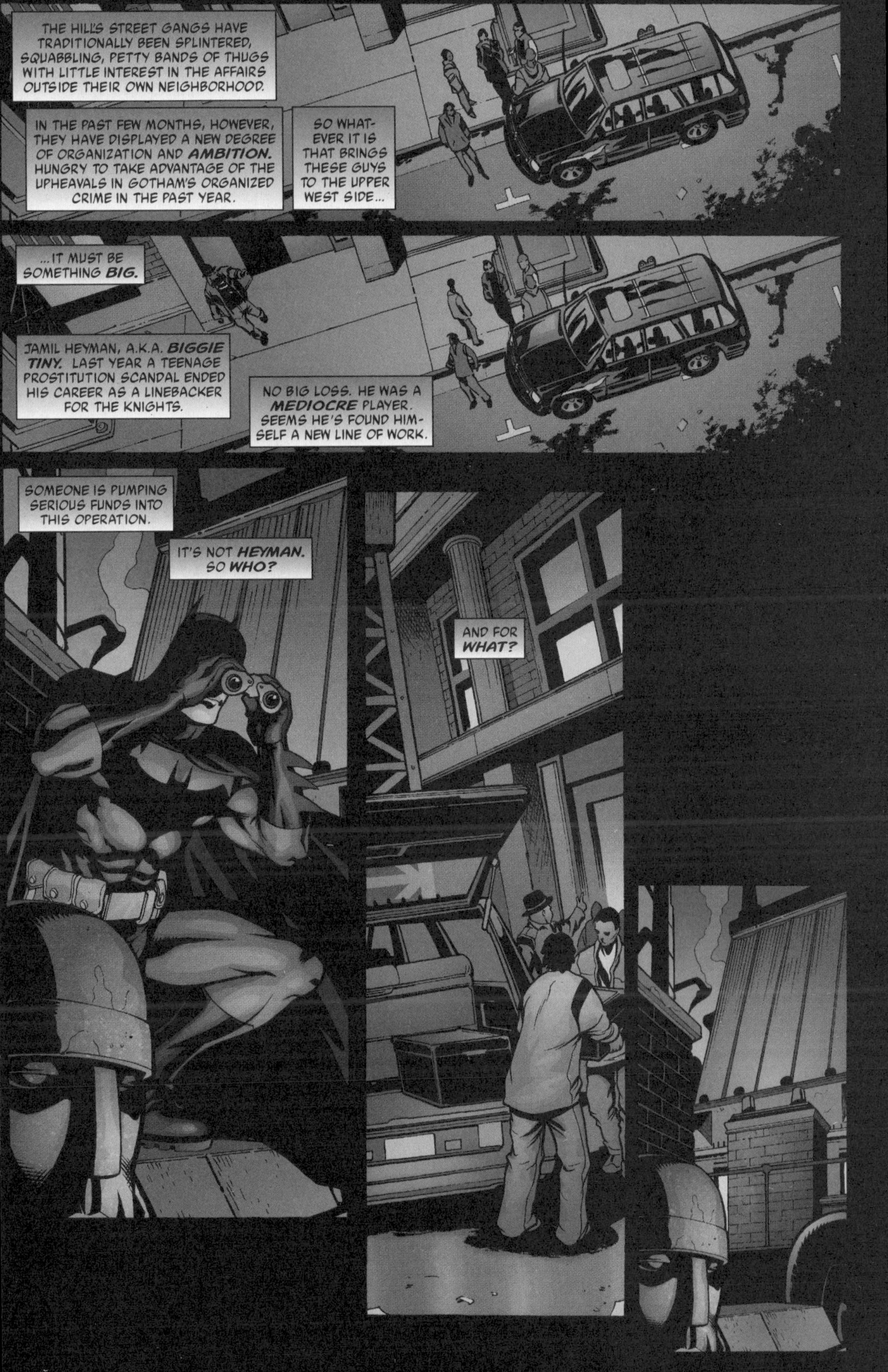
THE HILL'S STREET GANGS HAVE TRADITIONALLY BEEN SPLINTERED, SQUABBLING, PETTY BANDS OF THUGS WITH LITTLE INTEREST IN THE AFFAIRS OUTSIDE THEIR OWN NEIGHBORHOOD.
IN THE PAST FEW MONTHS, HOWEVER, THEY HAVE DISPLAYED A NEW DEGREE OF ORGANIZATION AND AMBITION. HUNGRY TO TAKE ADVANTAGE OF THE UPHEAVALS IN GOTHAM'S ORGANIZED CRIME IN THE PAST YEAR.
SO WHATEVER IT IS THAT BRINGS THESE GUYS TO THE UPPER WEST SIDE...
...IT MUST BE SOMETHING BIG.
JAMIL HEYMAN, A.K.A. BIGGIE TINY. LAST YEAR A TEENAGE PROSTITUTION SCANDAL ENDED HIS CAREER AS A LINEBACKER FOR THE KNIGHTS.
NO BIG LOSS. HE WAS A MEDIOCRE PLAYER. SEEMS HE'S FOUND HIMSELF A NEW LINE OF WORK.
SOMEONE IS PUMPING SERIOUS FUNDS INTO THIS OPERATION.
IT'S NOT HEYMAN. SO WHO?
AND FOR WHAT?

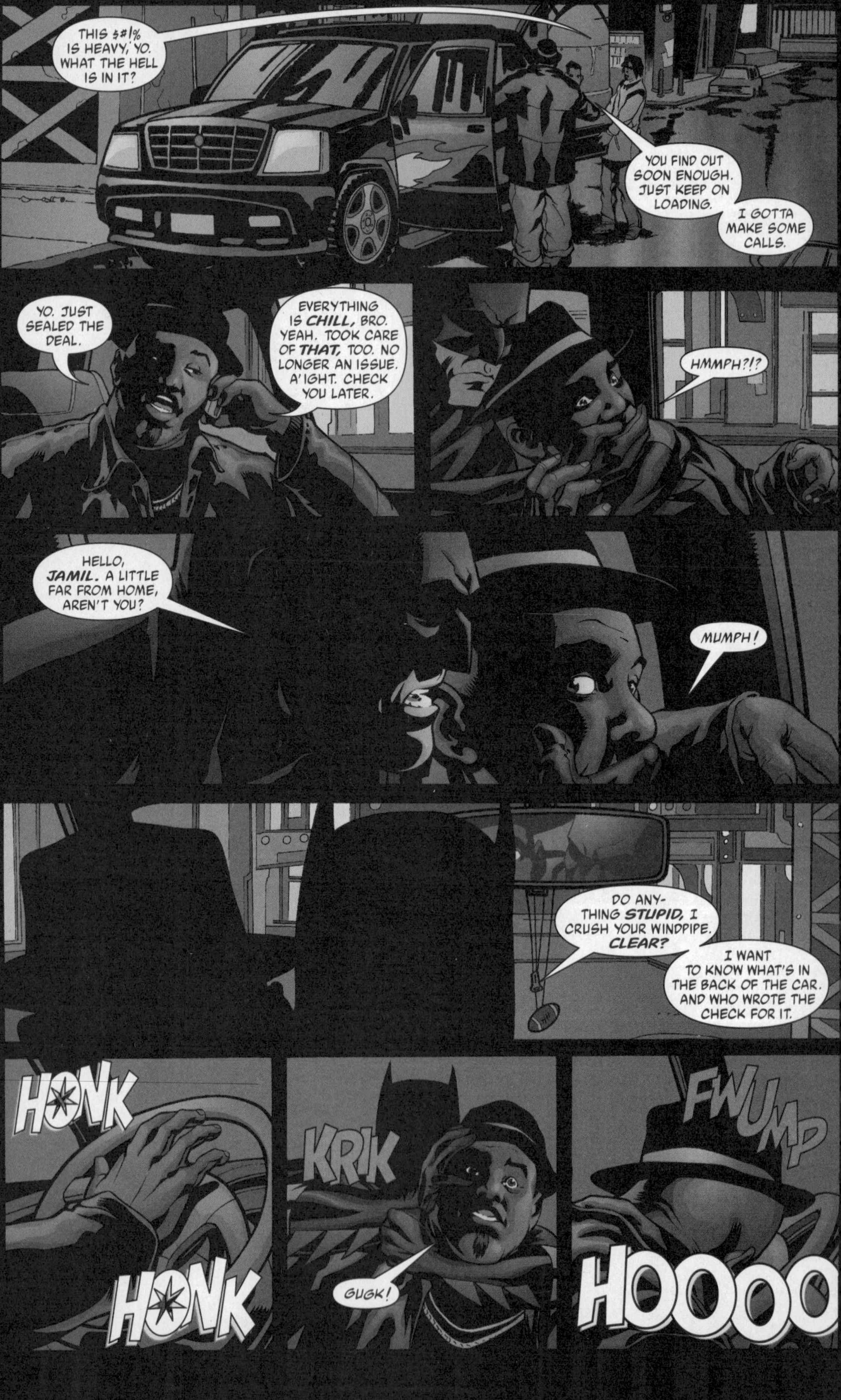
THIS $#!% IS HEAVY, YO. WHAT THE HELL IS IN IT?
YOU FIND OUT SOON ENOUGH. JUST KEEP ON LOADING.
I GOTTA MAKE SOME CALLS.
YO. JUST SEALED THE DEAL.
EVERYTHING IS CHILL, BRO. YEAH. TOOK CARE OF THAT, TOO. NO LONGER AN ISSUE. A'IGHT. CHECK YOU LATER.
HMMPH?!?
HELLO, JAMIL. A LITTLE FAR FROM HOME, AREN'T YOU?
MUMPH!
DO ANY-THING STUPID, I CRUSH YOUR WINDPIPE. CLEAR?
I WANT TO KNOW WHAT'S IN THE BACK OF THE CAR. AND WHO WROTE THE CHECK FOR IT.
HONK
HONK
KRIK
GUGK!
FWUMP
HOOOO

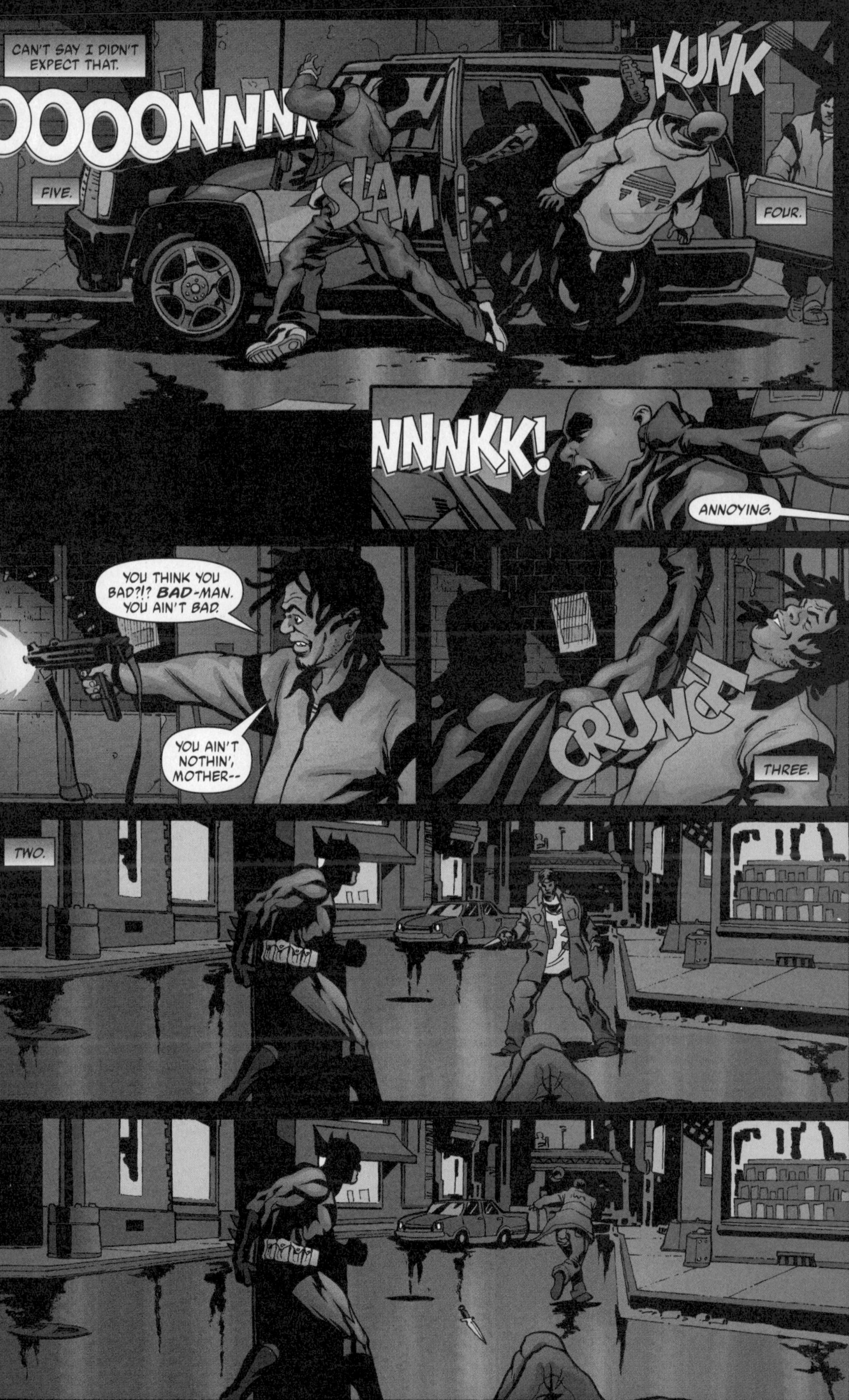
CAN'T SAY I DIDN'T EXPECT THAT.
OOOONNNN
KUNK
SLAM
FIVE.
FOUR.
NNNKK!
ANNOYING.
YOU THINK YOU BAD?!? BAD-MAN. YOU AIN'T BAD.
YOU AIN'T NOTHIN', MOTHER--
CRUNCH
THREE.
TWO.

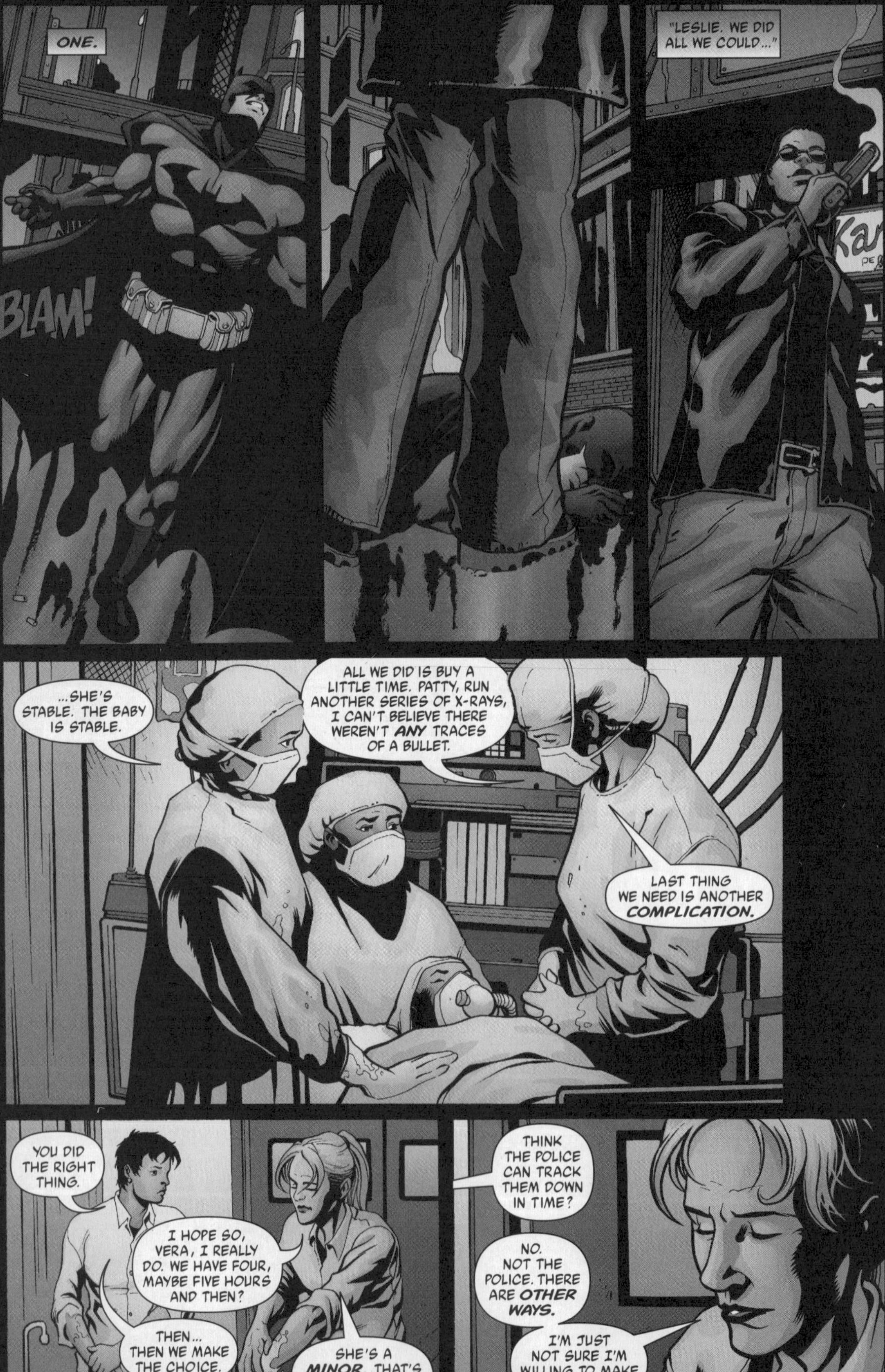
ONE.
BLAM!
"LESLIE. WE DID ALL WE COULD..."
...SHE'S STABLE. THE BABY IS STABLE.
ALL WE DID IS BUY A LITTLE TIME. PATTY, RUN ANOTHER SERIES OF X-RAYS, I CAN'T BELIEVE THERE WEREN'T ANY TRACES OF A BULLET.
LAST THING WE NEED IS ANOTHER COMPLICATION.
YOU DID THE RIGHT THING.
I HOPE SO, VERA, I REALLY DO. WE HAVE FOUR, MAYBE FIVE HOURS AND THEN?
THEN... THEN WE MAKE THE CHOICE.
SHE'S A MINOR. THAT'S FOR HER FAMILY TO DECIDE.
THINK THE POLICE CAN TRACK THEM DOWN IN TIME?
NO. NOT THE POLICE. THERE ARE OTHER WAYS.
I'M JUST NOT SURE I'M WILLING TO MAKE THAT CALL.

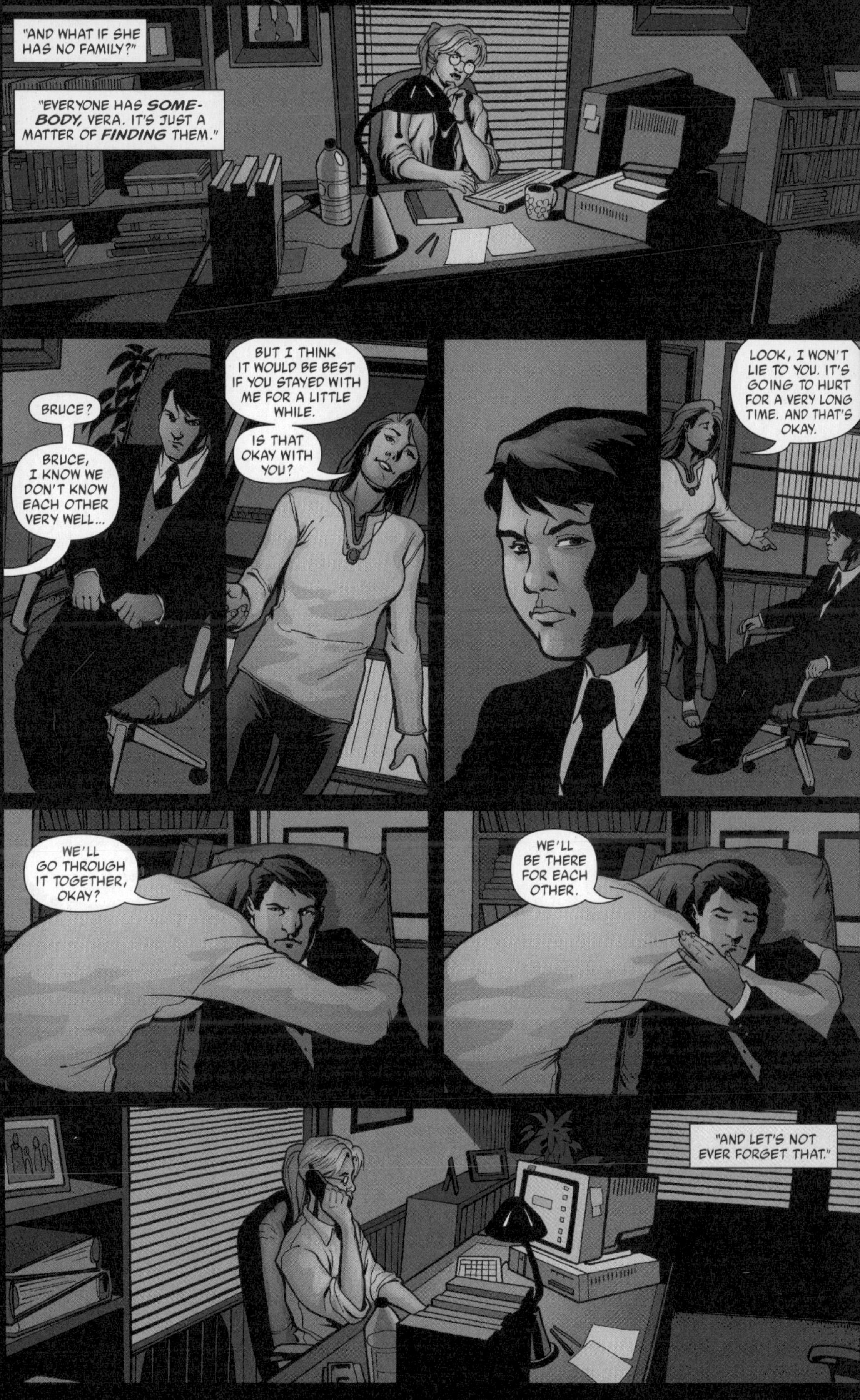
"AND WHAT IF SHE HAS NO FAMILY?"
"EVERYONE HAS SOME-BODY, VERA. IT'S JUST A MATTER OF FINDING THEM."
BRUCE?
BRUCE, I KNOW WE DON'T KNOW EACH OTHER VERY WELL...
BUT I THINK IT WOULD BE BEST IF YOU STAYED WITH ME FOR A LITTLE WHILE.
IS THAT OKAY WITH YOU?
LOOK, I WON'T LIE TO YOU. IT'S GOING TO HURT FOR A VERY LONG TIME. AND THAT'S OKAY.
WE'LL GO THROUGH IT TOGETHER, OKAY?
WE'LL BE THERE FOR EACH OTHER.
"AND LET'S NOT EVER FORGET THAT."

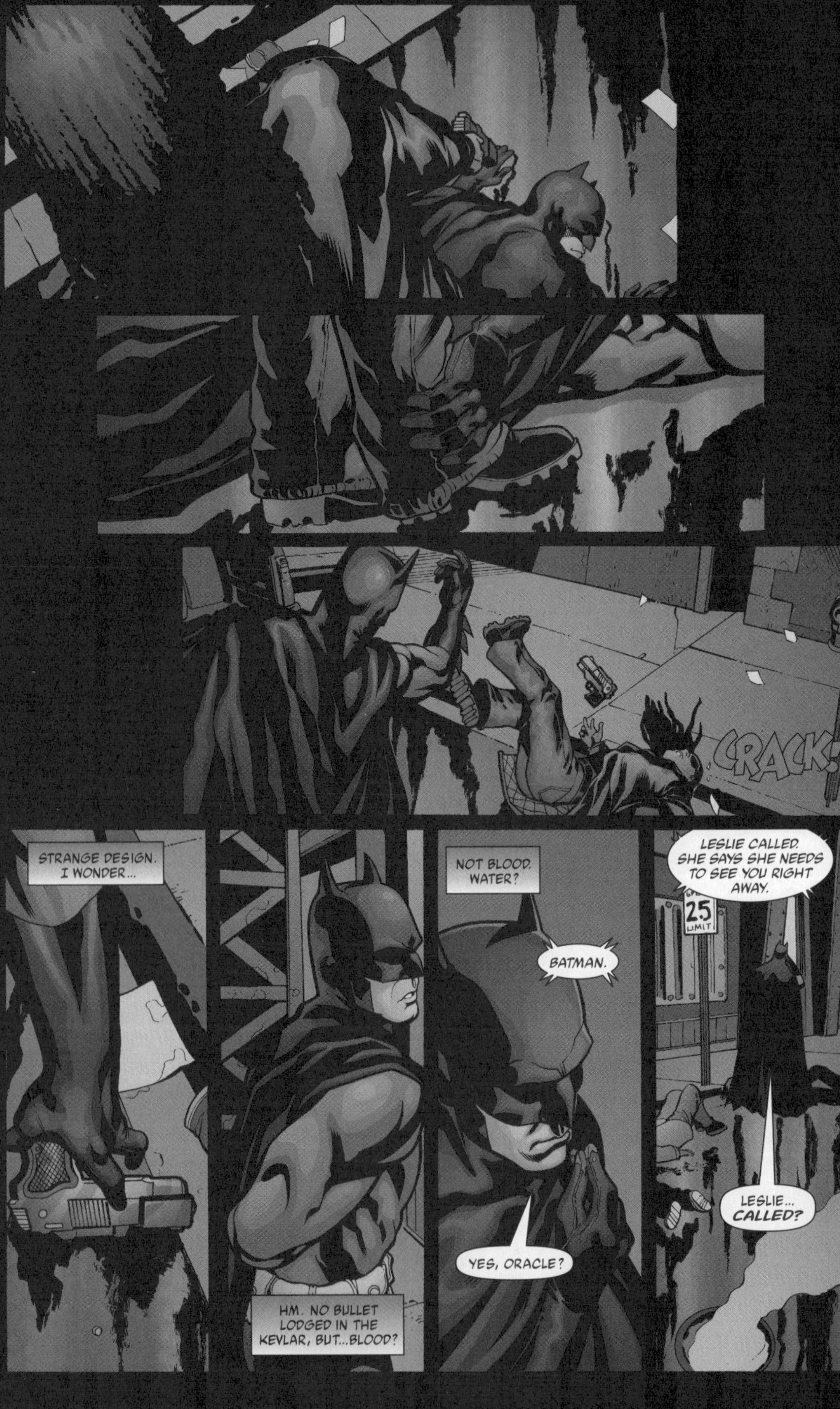
CRACK!
STRANGE DESIGN. I WONDER...
HM. NO BULLET LODGED IN THE KEVLAR, BUT...BLOOD?
NOT BLOOD. WATER?
BATMAN.
YES, ORACLE?
LESLIE CALLED. SHE SAYS SHE NEEDS TO SEE YOU RIGHT AWAY.
25 LIMIT
LESLIE... CALLED?

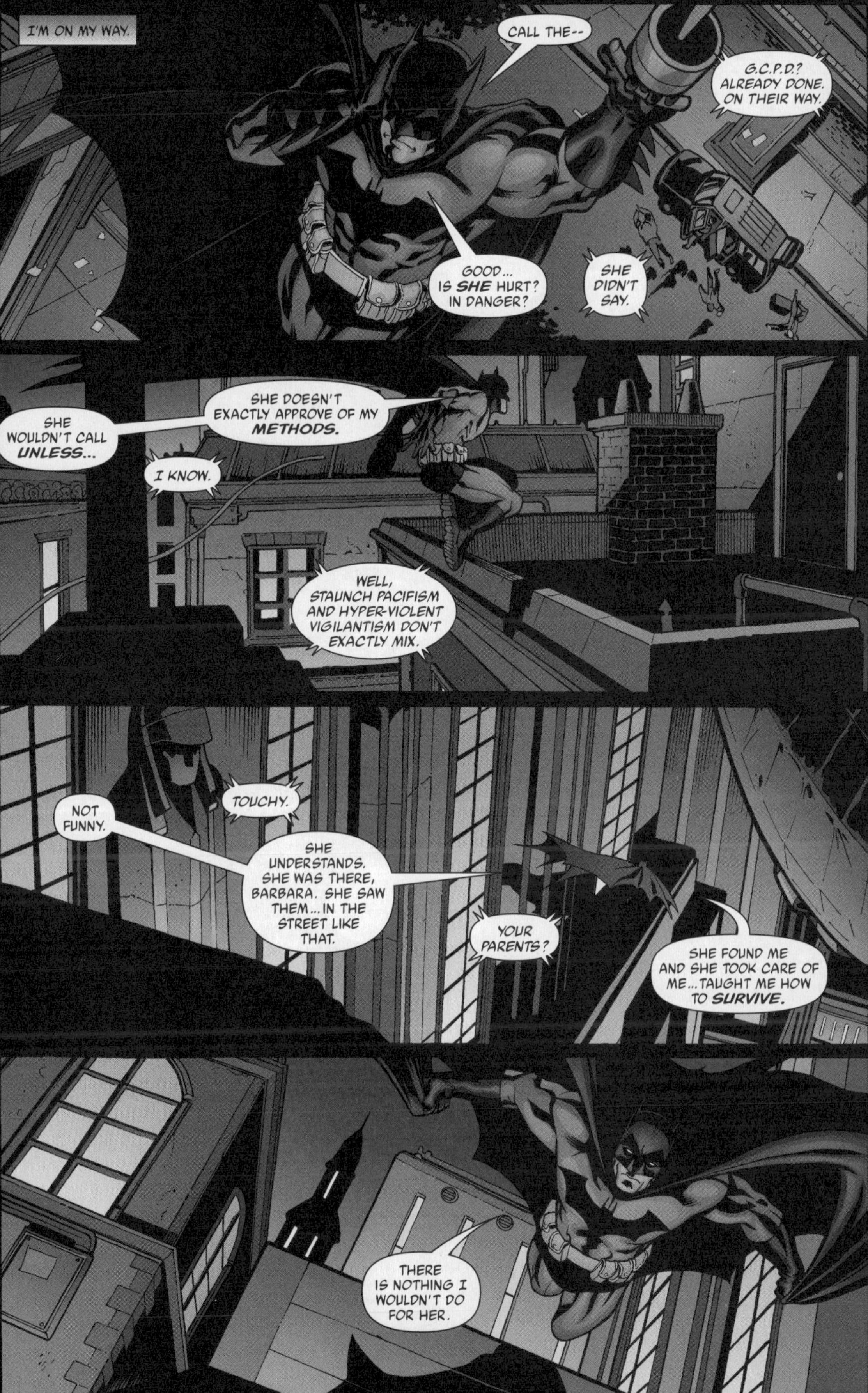
I'M ON MY WAY.
CALL THE--
G.C.P.D.? ALREADY DONE. ON THEIR WAY.
GOOD... IS SHE HURT? IN DANGER?
SHE DIDN'T SAY.
SHE WOULDN'T CALL UNLESS...
SHE DOESN'T EXACTLY APPROVE OF MY METHODS.
I KNOW.
WELL, STAUNCH PACIFISM AND HYPER-VIOLENT VIGILANTISM DON'T EXACTLY MIX.
NOT FUNNY.
TOUCHY.
SHE UNDERSTANDS. SHE WAS THERE, BARBARA. SHE SAW THEM... IN THE STREET LIKE THAT.
YOUR PARENTS?
SHE FOUND ME AND SHE TOOK CARE OF ME... TAUGHT ME HOW TO SURVIVE.
THERE IS NOTHING I WOULDN'T DO FOR HER.

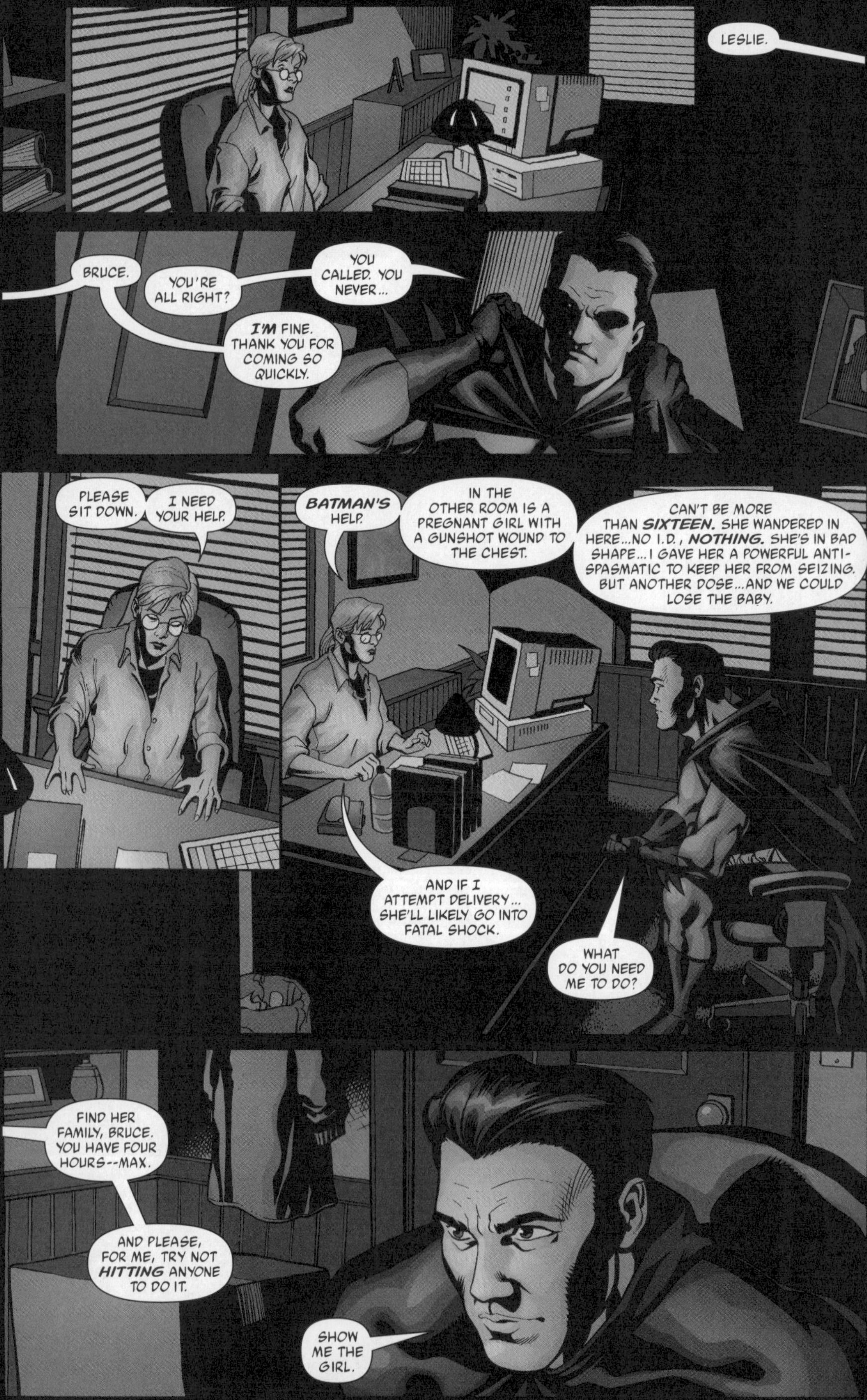

LESLIE.
BRUCE.
YOU'RE ALL RIGHT?
YOU CALLED. YOU NEVER...
I'M FINE. THANK YOU FOR COMING SO QUICKLY.
PLEASE SIT DOWN.
I NEED YOUR HELP.
BATMAN'S HELP.
IN THE OTHER ROOM IS A PREGNANT GIRL WITH A GUNSHOT WOUND TO THE CHEST.
CAN'T BE MORE THAN SIXTEEN. SHE WANDERED IN HERE...NO I.D., NOTHING. SHE'S IN BAD SHAPE...I GAVE HER A POWERFUL ANTI-SPASMATIC TO KEEP HER FROM SEIZING. BUT ANOTHER DOSE...AND WE COULD LOSE THE BABY.
AND IF I ATTEMPT DELIVERY... SHE'LL LIKELY GO INTO FATAL SHOCK.
WHAT DO YOU NEED ME TO DO?
FIND HER FAMILY, BRUCE. YOU HAVE FOUR HOURS--MAX.
AND PLEASE, FOR ME, TRY NOT HITTING ANYONE TO DO IT.
SHOW ME THE GIRL.

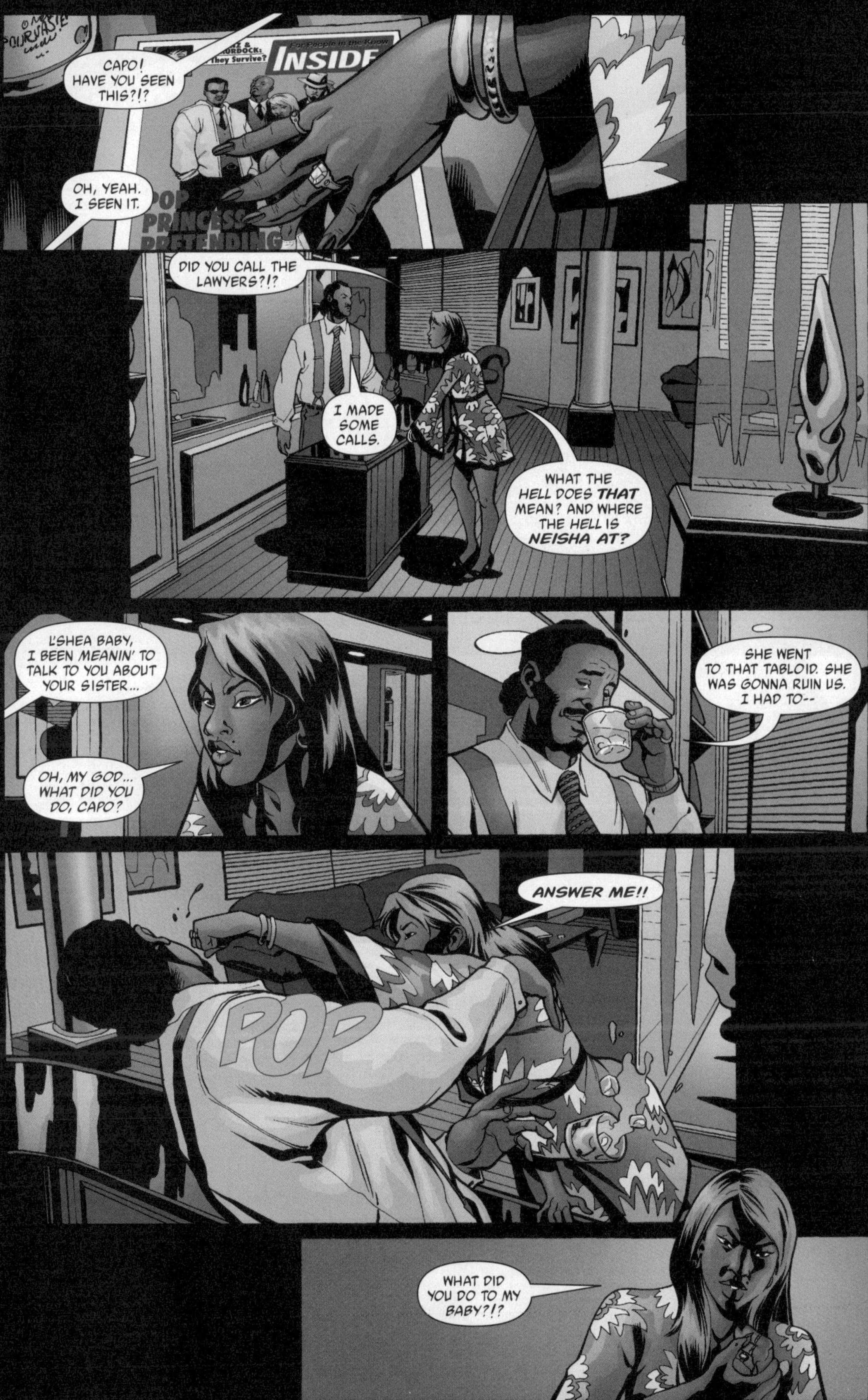
CAPO! HAVE YOU SEEN THIS?!?
INSIDE
For People in the Know
OH, YEAH. I SEEN IT.
POP PRINCESS
DID YOU CALL THE LAWYERS?!?
I MADE SOME CALLS.
WHAT THE HELL DOES THAT MEAN? AND WHERE THE HELL IS NEISHA AT?
L'SHEA BABY, I BEEN MEANIN' TO TALK TO YOU ABOUT YOUR SISTER...
OH, MY GOD... WHAT DID YOU DO, CAPO?
SHE WENT TO THAT TABLOID. SHE WAS GONNA RUIN US. I HAD TO--
ANSWER ME!!
POP
WHAT DID YOU DO TO MY BABY?!?

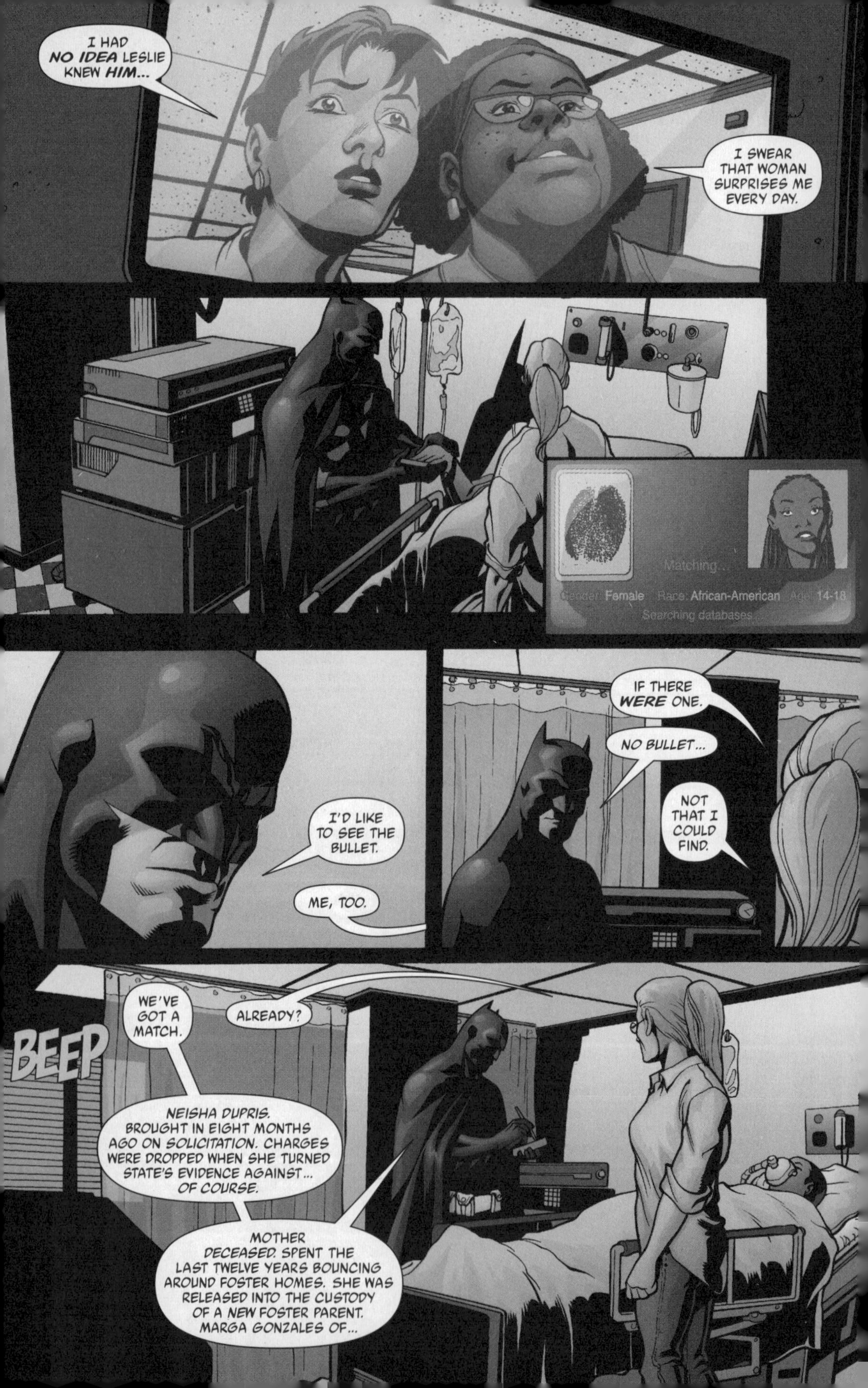
I HAD *NO IDEA* LESLIE KNEW *HIM*...
I SWEAR THAT WOMAN SURPRISES ME EVERY DAY.
Matching...
Gender: Female Race: African-American Age: 14-18
Searching databases...
I'D LIKE TO SEE THE BULLET.
ME, TOO.
IF THERE *WERE* ONE.
NO BULLET...
NOT THAT I COULD FIND.
BEEP
WE'VE GOT A MATCH.
ALREADY?
NEISHA DUPRIS. BROUGHT IN EIGHT MONTHS AGO ON *SOLICITATION*. CHARGES WERE DROPPED WHEN SHE TURNED STATE'S EVIDENCE AGAINST... OF COURSE.
MOTHER DECEASED. SPENT THE LAST TWELVE YEARS BOUNCING AROUND FOSTER HOMES. SHE WAS RELEASED INTO THE CUSTODY OF A *NEW* FOSTER PARENT. MARGA GONZALES OF...

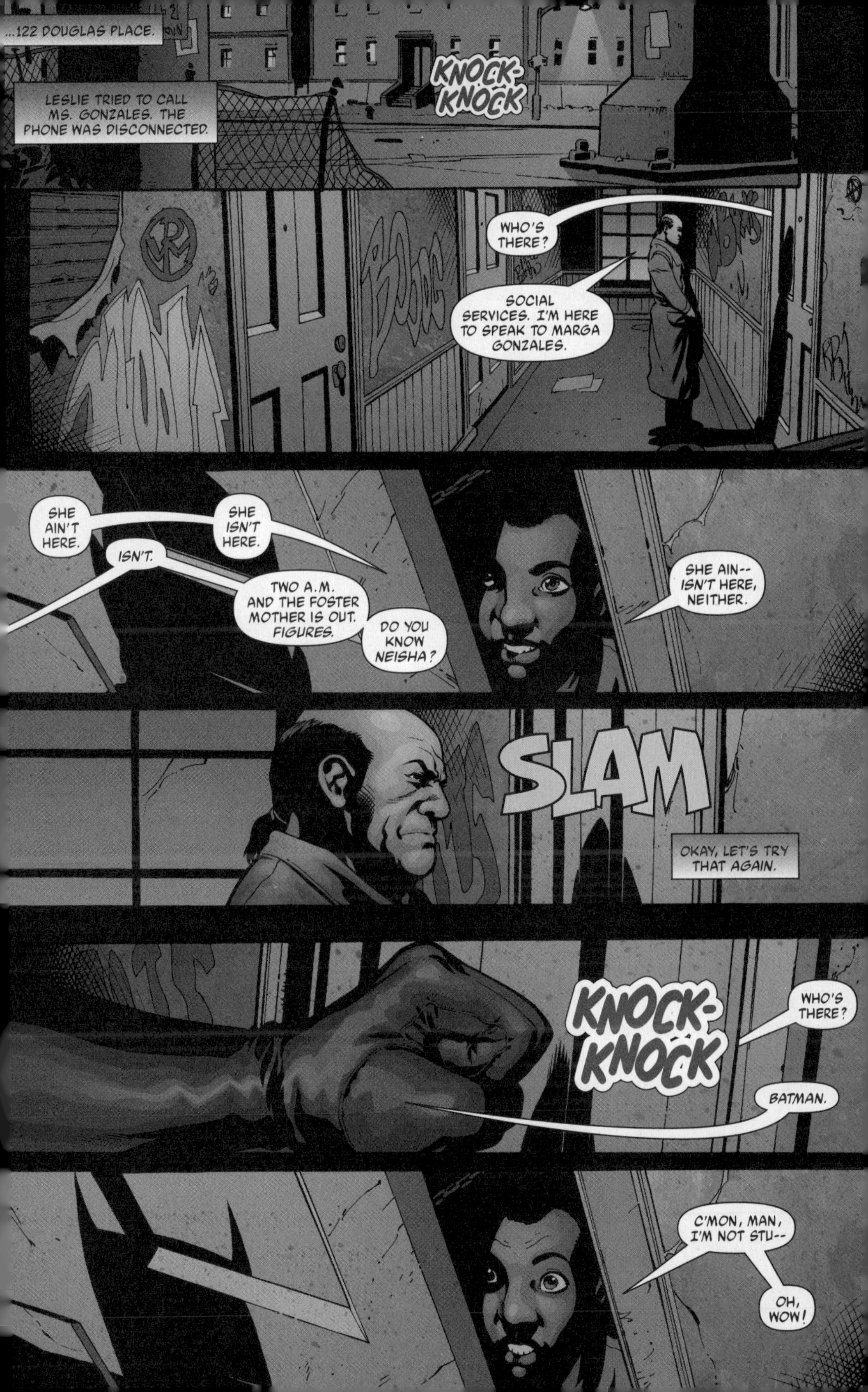
...122 DOUGLAS PLACE.
LESLIE TRIED TO CALL MS. GONZALES. THE PHONE WAS DISCONNECTED.
KNOCK-KNOCK
WHO'S THERE?
SOCIAL SERVICES. I'M HERE TO SPEAK TO MARGA GONZALES.
SHE AIN'T HERE.
SHE ISN'T HERE.
ISN'T.
TWO A.M. AND THE FOSTER MOTHER IS OUT. FIGURES.
DO YOU KNOW NEISHA?
SHE AIN-- ISN'T HERE, NEITHER.
SLAM
OKAY, LET'S TRY THAT AGAIN.
KNOCK-KNOCK
WHO'S THERE?
BATMAN.
C'MON, MAN, I'M NOT STU--
OH, WOW!

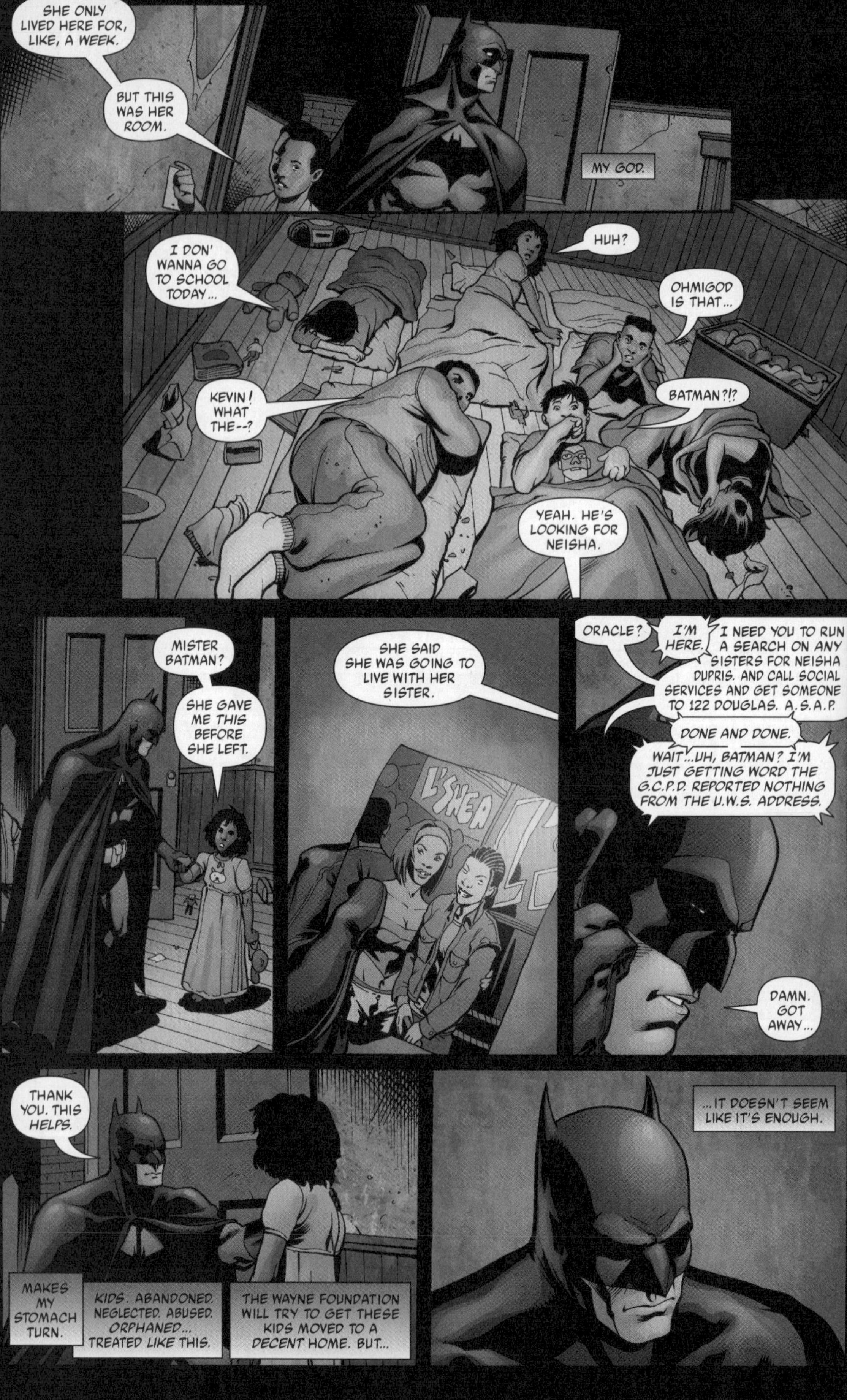

SHE ONLY LIVED HERE FOR, LIKE, A WEEK.
BUT THIS WAS HER ROOM.
MY GOD.
I DON' WANNA GO TO SCHOOL TODAY...
HUH?
OHMIGOD IS THAT...
KEVIN! WHAT THE--?
BATMAN?!?
YEAH. HE'S LOOKING FOR NEISHA.
MISTER BATMAN?
SHE GAVE ME THIS BEFORE SHE LEFT.
SHE SAID SHE WAS GOING TO LIVE WITH HER SISTER.
L'SHEA
ORACLE?
I'M HERE.
I NEED YOU TO RUN A SEARCH ON ANY SISTERS FOR NEISHA DUPRIS. AND CALL SOCIAL SERVICES AND GET SOMEONE TO 122 DOUGLAS. A.S.A.P.
DONE AND DONE.
WAIT...UH, BATMAN? I'M JUST GETTING WORD THE G.C.P.D. REPORTED NOTHING FROM THE U.W.S. ADDRESS.
DAMN. GOT AWAY...
THANK YOU. THIS HELPS.
MAKES MY STOMACH TURN.
KIDS. ABANDONED. NEGLECTED. ABUSED. ORPHANED... TREATED LIKE THIS.
THE WAYNE FOUNDATION WILL TRY TO GET THESE KIDS MOVED TO A DECENT HOME. BUT...
...IT DOESN'T SEEM LIKE IT'S ENOUGH.

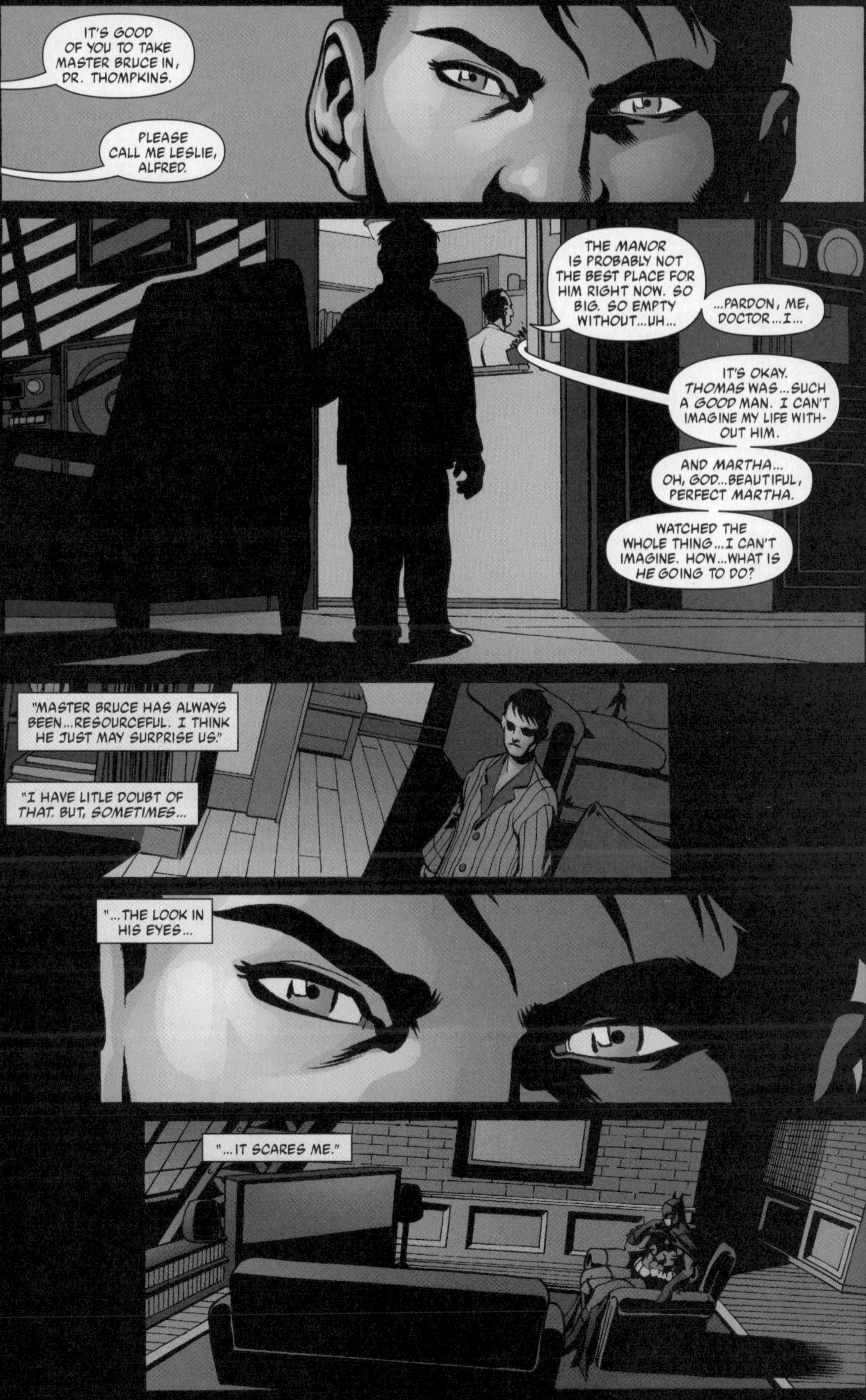
IT'S GOOD OF YOU TO TAKE MASTER BRUCE IN, DR. THOMPKINS.
PLEASE CALL ME LESLIE, ALFRED.
THE MANOR IS PROBABLY NOT THE BEST PLACE FOR HIM RIGHT NOW. SO BIG. SO EMPTY WITHOUT...UH...
...PARDON, ME, DOCTOR...I...
IT'S OKAY. THOMAS WAS...SUCH A GOOD MAN. I CAN'T IMAGINE MY LIFE WITH-OUT HIM.
AND MARTHA... OH, GOD...BEAUTIFUL, PERFECT MARTHA.
WATCHED THE WHOLE THING...I CAN'T IMAGINE. HOW...WHAT IS HE GOING TO DO?
"MASTER BRUCE HAS ALWAYS BEEN...RESOURCEFUL. I THINK HE JUST MAY SURPRISE US."
"I HAVE LITLE DOUBT OF THAT. BUT, SOMETIMES...
"...THE LOOK IN HIS EYES...
"...IT SCARES ME."

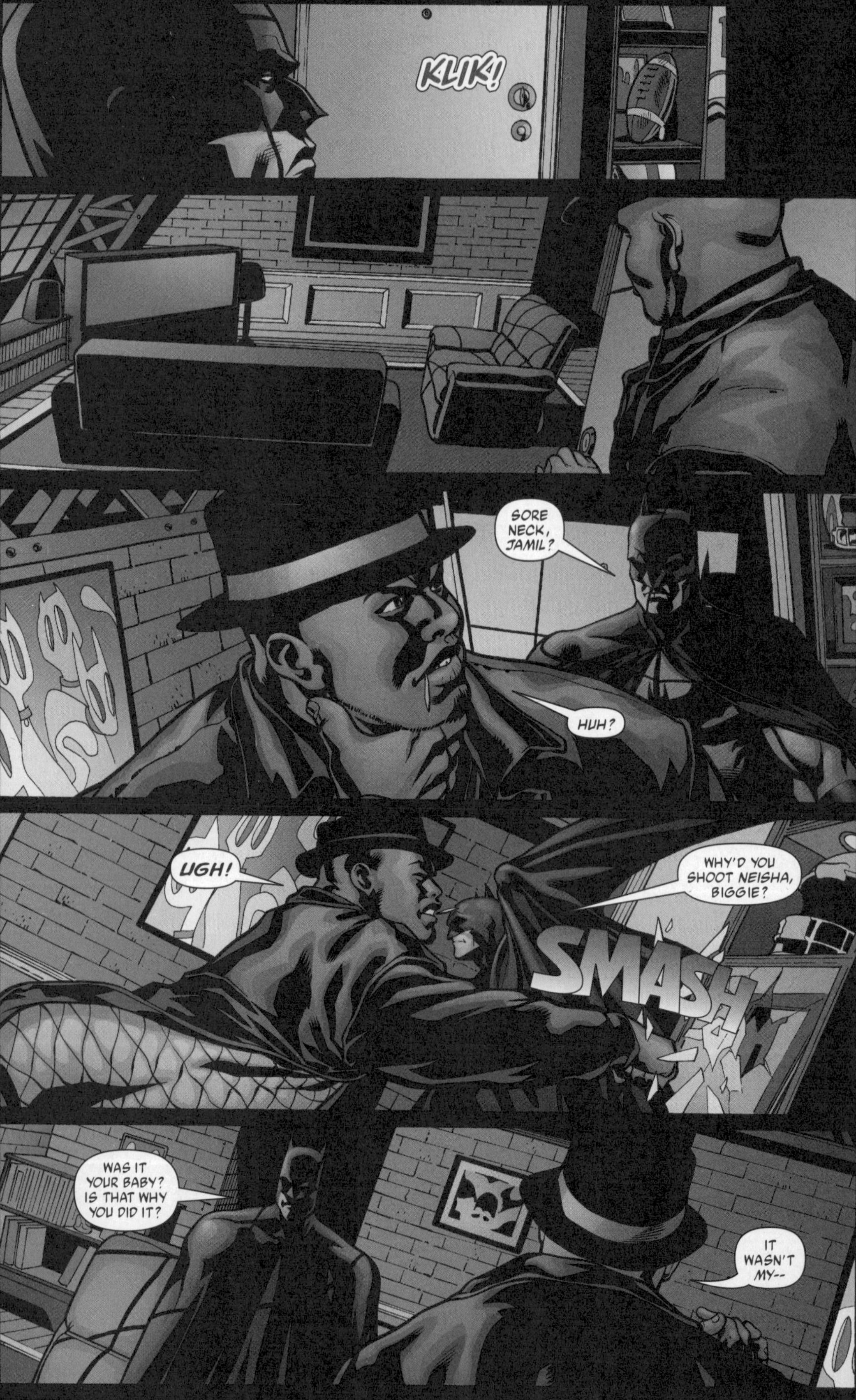
KLIK!
SORE NECK, JAMIL?
HUH?
UGH!
WHY'D YOU SHOOT NEISHA, BIGGIE?
SMASH
WAS IT YOUR BABY? IS THAT WHY YOU DID IT?
IT WASN'T MY--

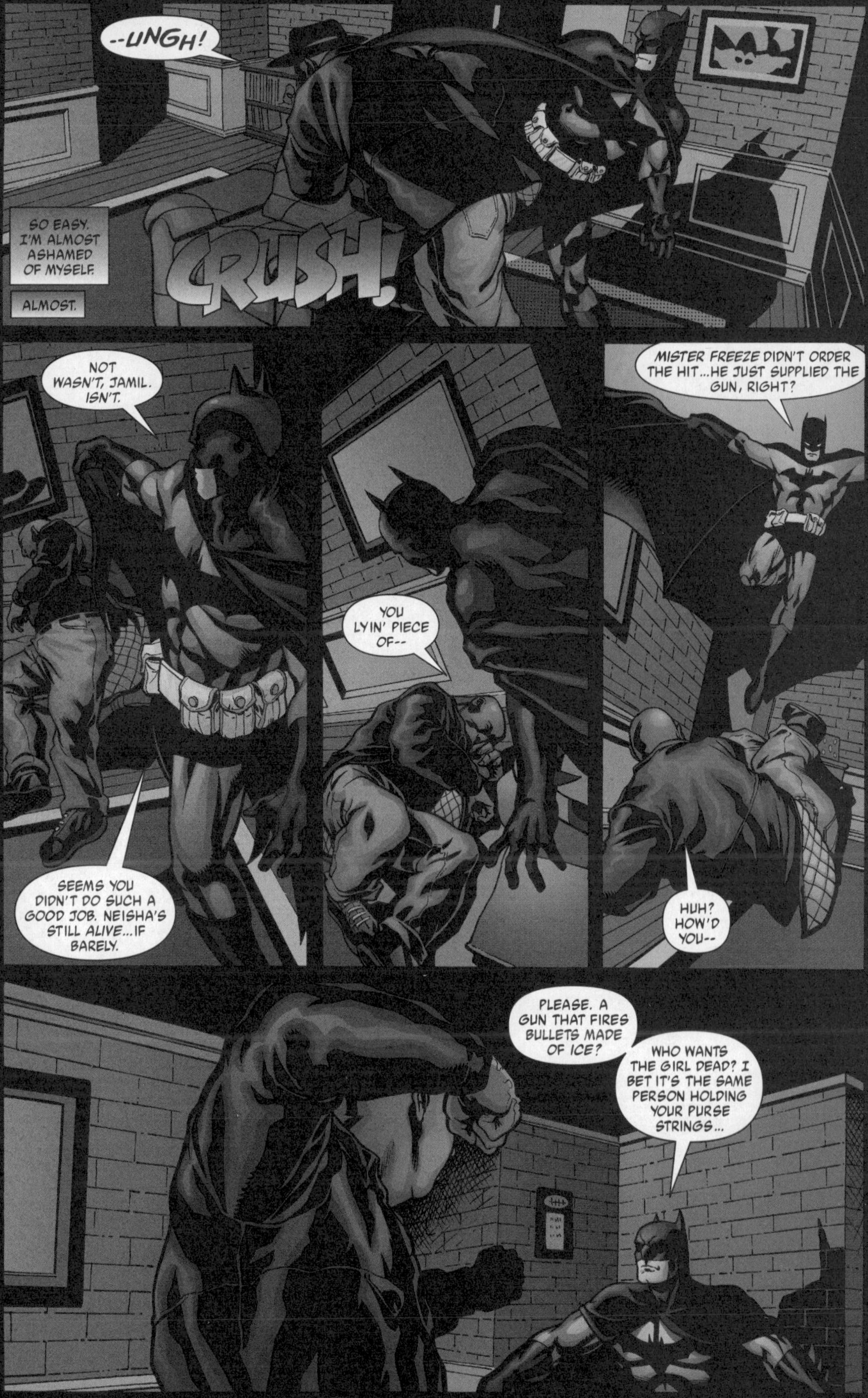
--UNGH!
SO EASY. I'M ALMOST ASHAMED OF MYSELF.
ALMOST.
CRUSH!
NOT WASN'T, JAMIL. ISN'T.
SEEMS YOU DIDN'T DO SUCH A GOOD JOB. NEISHA'S STILL ALIVE...IF BARELY.
YOU LYIN' PIECE OF--
MISTER FREEZE DIDN'T ORDER THE HIT...HE JUST SUPPLIED THE GUN, RIGHT?
HUH? HOW'D YOU--
PLEASE. A GUN THAT FIRES BULLETS MADE OF ICE?
WHO WANTS THE GIRL DEAD? I BET IT'S THE SAME PERSON HOLDING YOUR PURSE STRINGS...

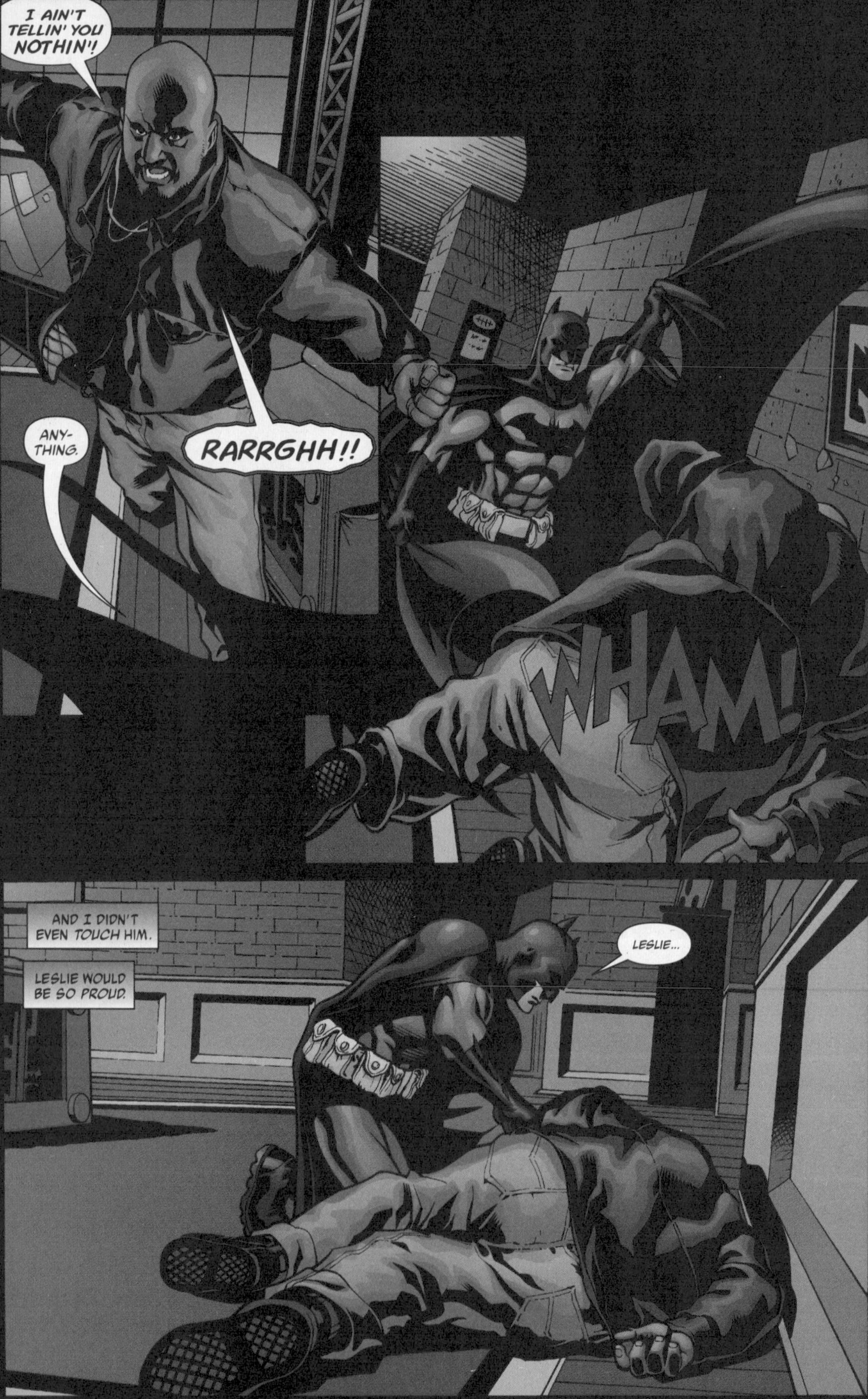
I AIN'T TELLIN' YOU NOTHIN'!
RARRGHH!!
ANY-THING.
WHAM!
AND I DIDN'T EVEN TOUCH HIM.
LESLIE WOULD BE SO PROUD.
LESLIE...

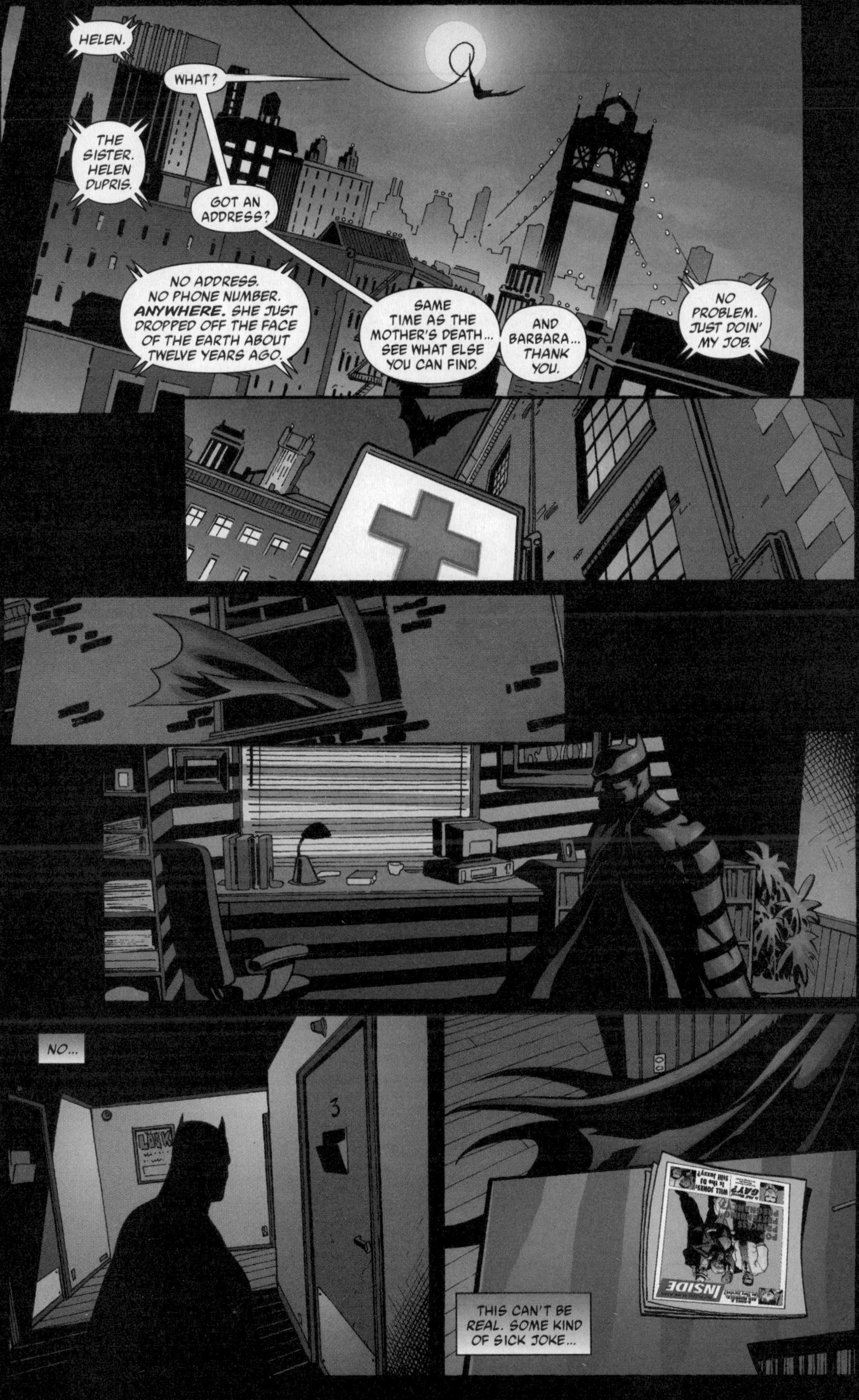
HELEN.
WHAT?
THE SISTER. HELEN DUPRIS.
GOT AN ADDRESS?
NO ADDRESS. NO PHONE NUMBER. ANYWHERE. SHE JUST DROPPED OFF THE FACE OF THE EARTH ABOUT TWELVE YEARS AGO.
SAME TIME AS THE MOTHER'S DEATH... SEE WHAT ELSE YOU CAN FIND.
AND BARBARA... THANK YOU.
NO PROBLEM. JUST DOIN' MY JOB.
NO...
THIS CAN'T BE REAL. SOME KIND OF SICK JOKE...
INSIDE

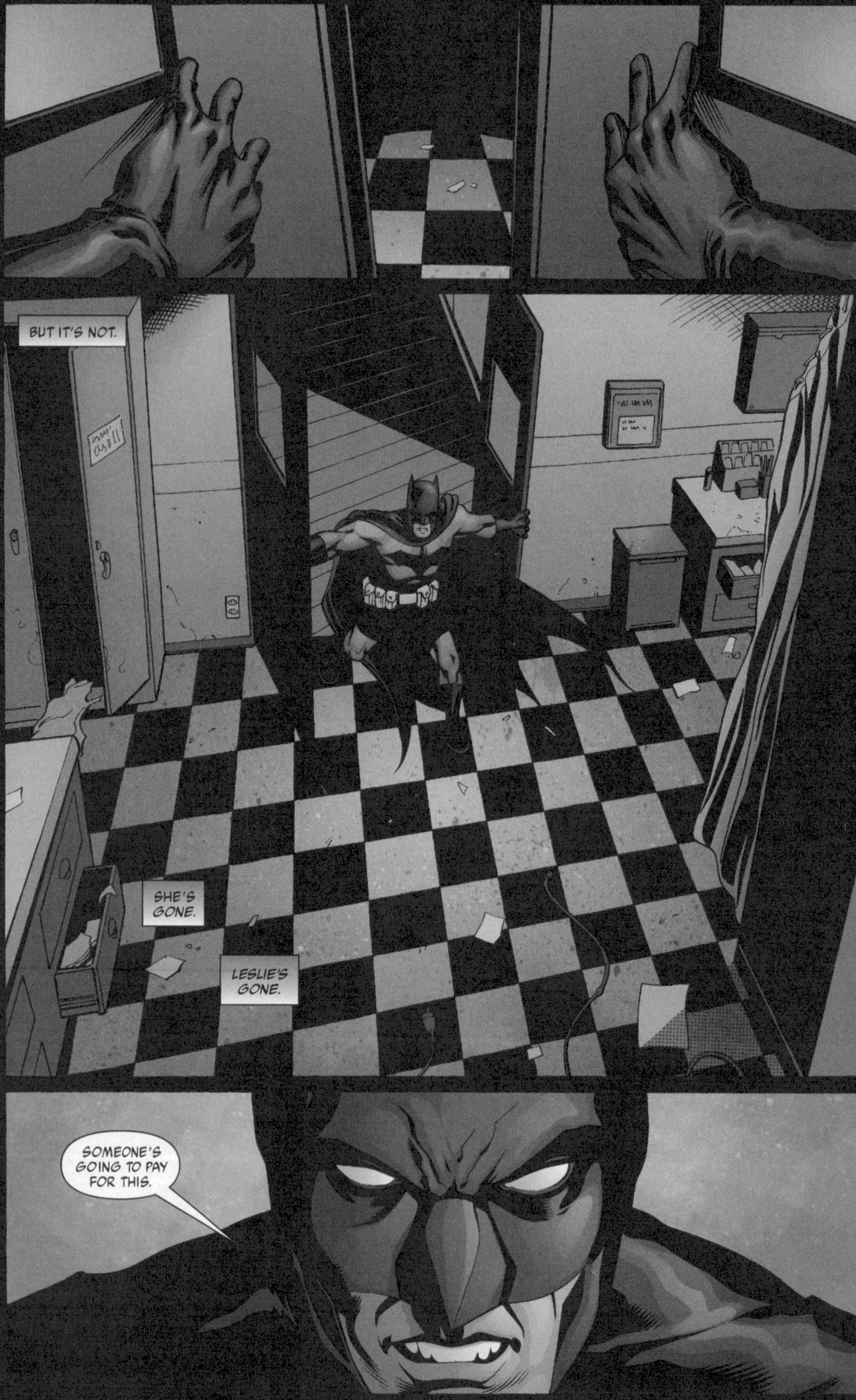
BUT IT'S NOT.
SHE'S GONE.
LESLIE'S GONE.
SOMEONE'S GOING TO PAY FOR THIS.

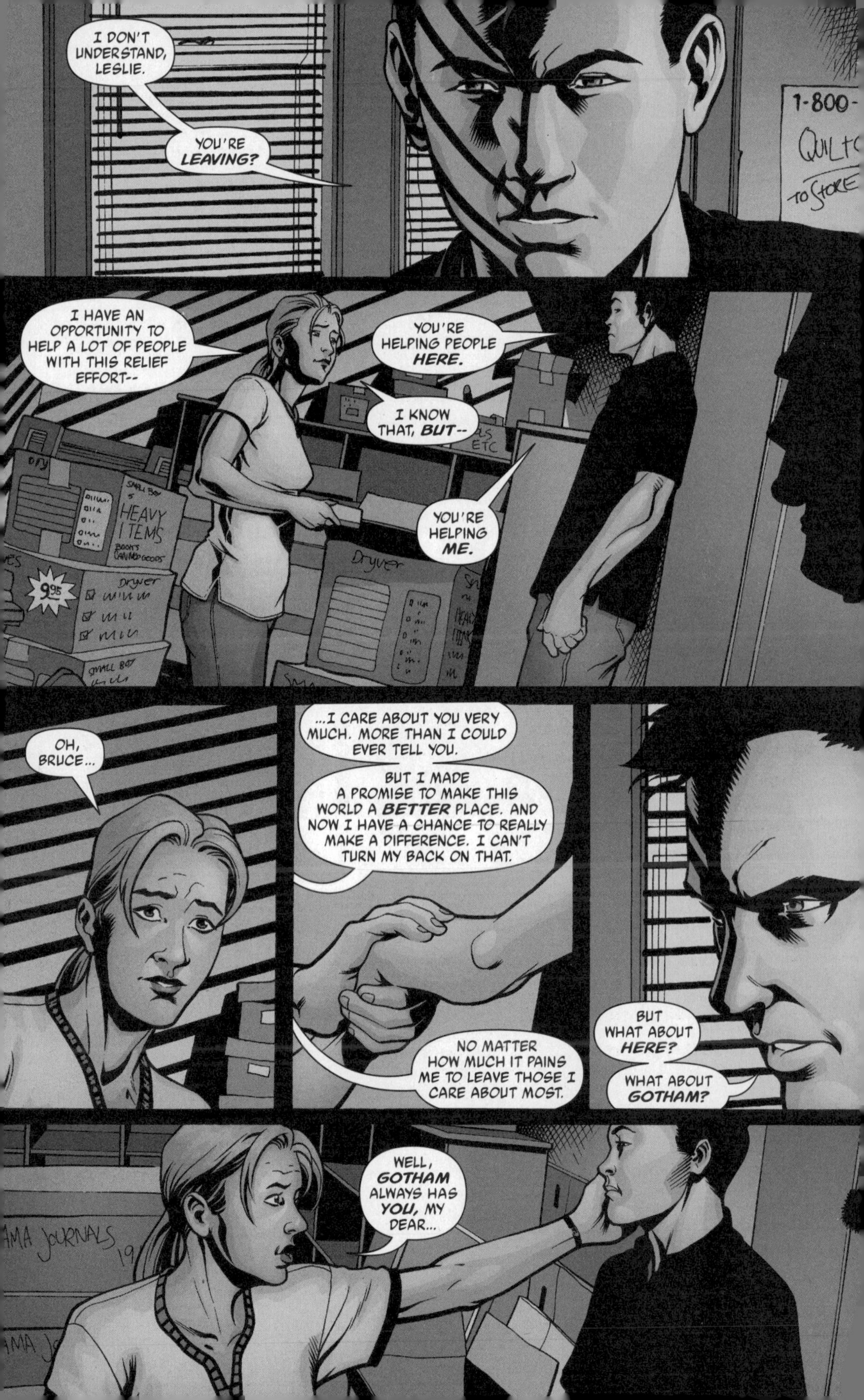
I DON'T UNDERSTAND, LESLIE.
YOU'RE LEAVING?
1-800-
QUILTS
TO STORE
I HAVE AN OPPORTUNITY TO HELP A LOT OF PEOPLE WITH THIS RELIEF EFFORT--
YOU'RE HELPING PEOPLE HERE.
I KNOW THAT, BUT--
YOU'RE HELPING ME.
HEAVY ITEMS
9.95
OH, BRUCE...
...I CARE ABOUT YOU VERY MUCH. MORE THAN I COULD EVER TELL YOU.
BUT I MADE A PROMISE TO MAKE THIS WORLD A BETTER PLACE. AND NOW I HAVE A CHANCE TO REALLY MAKE A DIFFERENCE. I CAN'T TURN MY BACK ON THAT.
NO MATTER HOW MUCH IT PAINS ME TO LEAVE THOSE I CARE ABOUT MOST.
BUT WHAT ABOUT HERE?
WHAT ABOUT GOTHAM?
WELL, GOTHAM ALWAYS HAS YOU, MY DEAR...

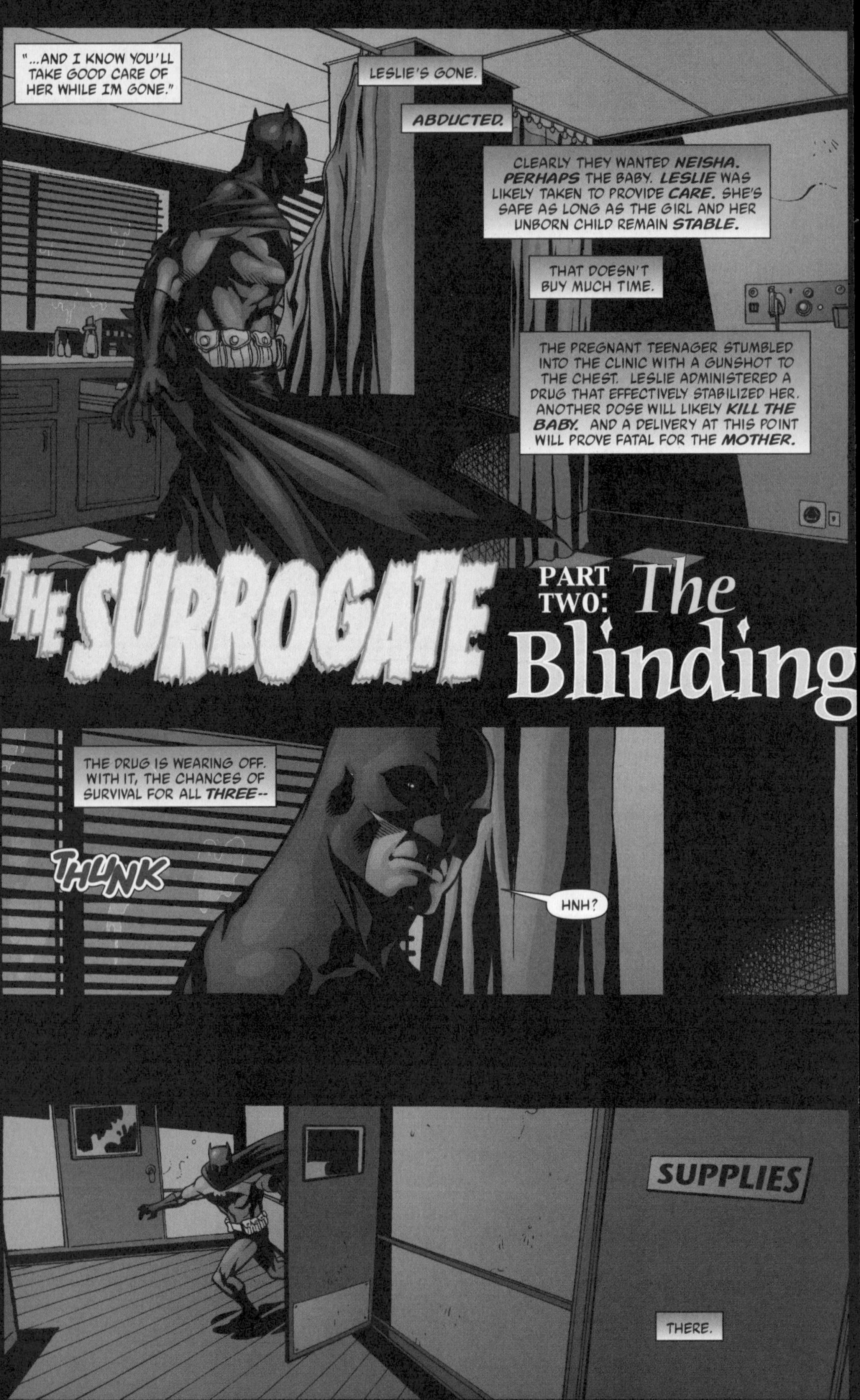

"...AND I KNOW YOU'LL TAKE GOOD CARE OF HER WHILE IM GONE."
LESLIE'S GONE.
ABDUCTED.
CLEARLY THEY WANTED NEISHA. PERHAPS THE BABY. LESLIE WAS LIKELY TAKEN TO PROVIDE CARE. SHE'S SAFE AS LONG AS THE GIRL AND HER UNBORN CHILD REMAIN STABLE.
THAT DOESN'T BUY MUCH TIME.
THE PREGNANT TEENAGER STUMBLED INTO THE CLINIC WITH A GUNSHOT TO THE CHEST. LESLIE ADMINISTERED A DRUG THAT EFFECTIVELY STABILIZED HER. ANOTHER DOSE WILL LIKELY KILL THE BABY. AND A DELIVERY AT THIS POINT WILL PROVE FATAL FOR THE MOTHER.
THE SURROGATE
PART TWO: The Blinding
THE DRUG IS WEARING OFF. WITH IT, THE CHANCES OF SURVIVAL FOR ALL THREE--
THUNK
HNH?
SUPPLIES
THERE.

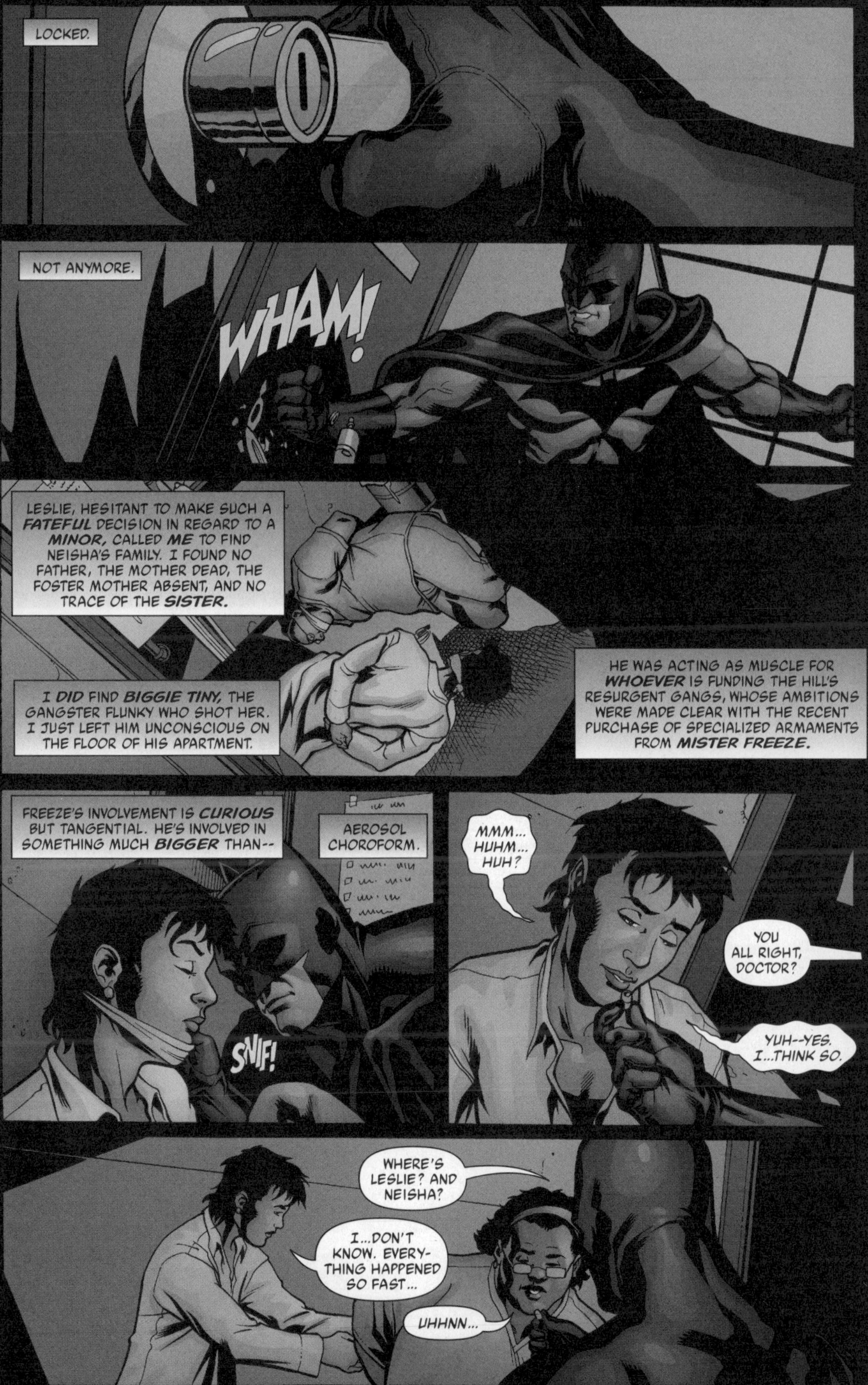
LOCKED.
NOT ANYMORE.
WHAM!
LESLIE, HESITANT TO MAKE SUCH A FATEFUL DECISION IN REGARD TO A MINOR, CALLED ME TO FIND NEISHA'S FAMILY. I FOUND NO FATHER, THE MOTHER DEAD, THE FOSTER MOTHER ABSENT, AND NO TRACE OF THE SISTER.
I DID FIND BIGGIE TINY, THE GANGSTER FLUNKY WHO SHOT HER. I JUST LEFT HIM UNCONSCIOUS ON THE FLOOR OF HIS APARTMENT.
HE WAS ACTING AS MUSCLE FOR WHOEVER IS FUNDING THE HILL'S RESURGENT GANGS, WHOSE AMBITIONS WERE MADE CLEAR WITH THE RECENT PURCHASE OF SPECIALIZED ARMAMENTS FROM MISTER FREEZE.
FREEZE'S INVOLVEMENT IS CURIOUS BUT TANGENTIAL. HE'S INVOLVED IN SOMETHING MUCH BIGGER THAN--
AEROSOL CHOROFORM.
SNIF!
MMM... HUHM... HUH?
YOU ALL RIGHT, DOCTOR?
YUH--YES. I...THINK SO.
WHERE'S LESLIE? AND NEISHA?
I...DON'T KNOW. EVERYTHING HAPPENED SO FAST...
UHHNN...

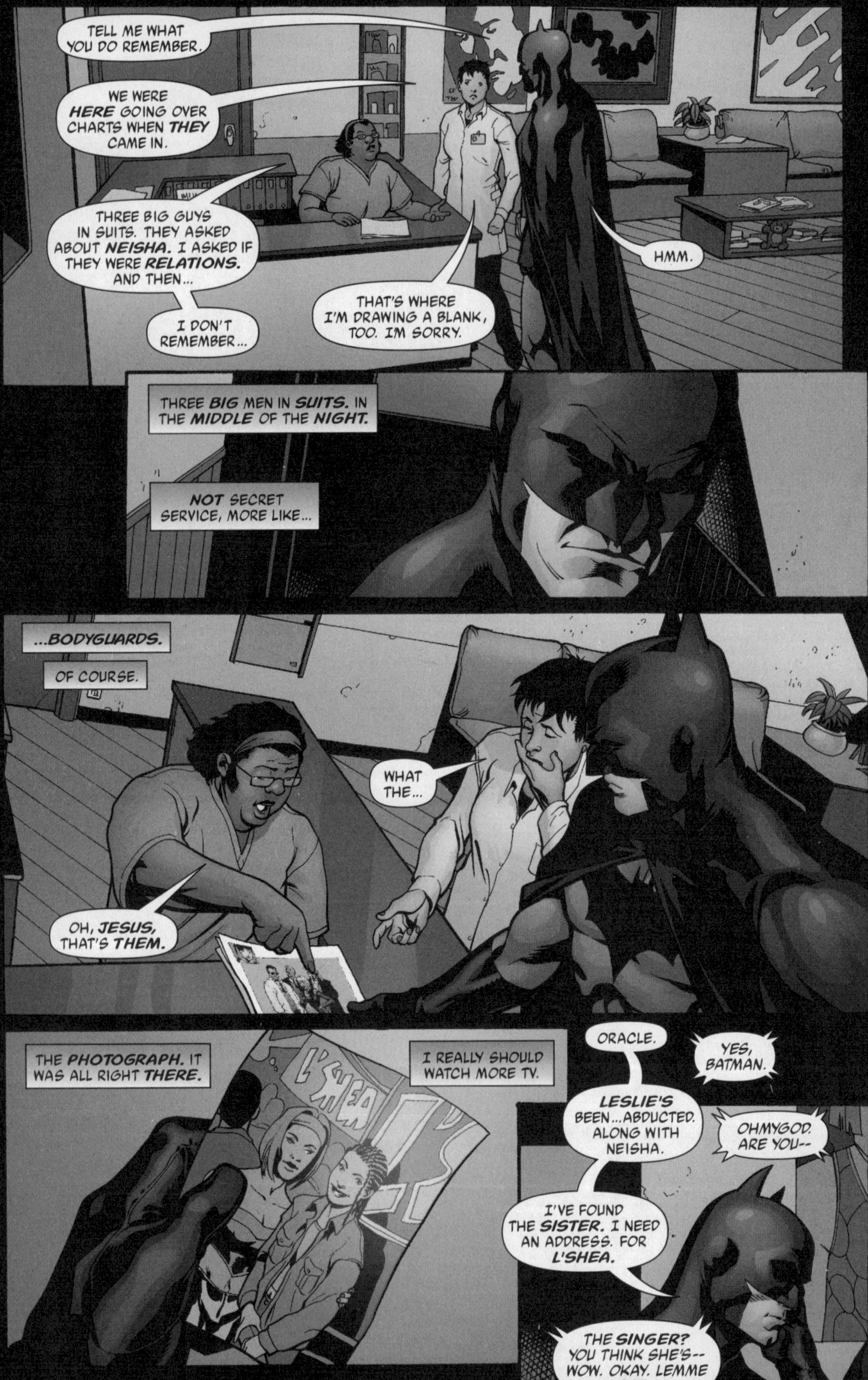

TELL ME WHAT YOU DO REMEMBER.
WE WERE HERE GOING OVER CHARTS WHEN THEY CAME IN.
THREE BIG GUYS IN SUITS. THEY ASKED ABOUT NEISHA. I ASKED IF THEY WERE RELATIONS. AND THEN...
I DON'T REMEMBER...
THAT'S WHERE I'M DRAWING A BLANK, TOO. I'M SORRY.
HMM.
THREE BIG MEN IN SUITS. IN THE MIDDLE OF THE NIGHT.
NOT SECRET SERVICE, MORE LIKE...
...BODYGUARDS.
OF COURSE.
WHAT THE...
OH, JESUS, THAT'S THEM.
THE PHOTOGRAPH. IT WAS ALL RIGHT THERE.
I REALLY SHOULD WATCH MORE TV.
L'SHEA
ORACLE.
YES, BATMAN.
LESLIE'S BEEN...ABDUCTED. ALONG WITH NEISHA.
OHMYGOD. ARE YOU--
I'VE FOUND THE SISTER. I NEED AN ADDRESS. FOR L'SHEA.
THE SINGER? YOU THINK SHE'S-- WOW. OKAY. LEMME SEE...

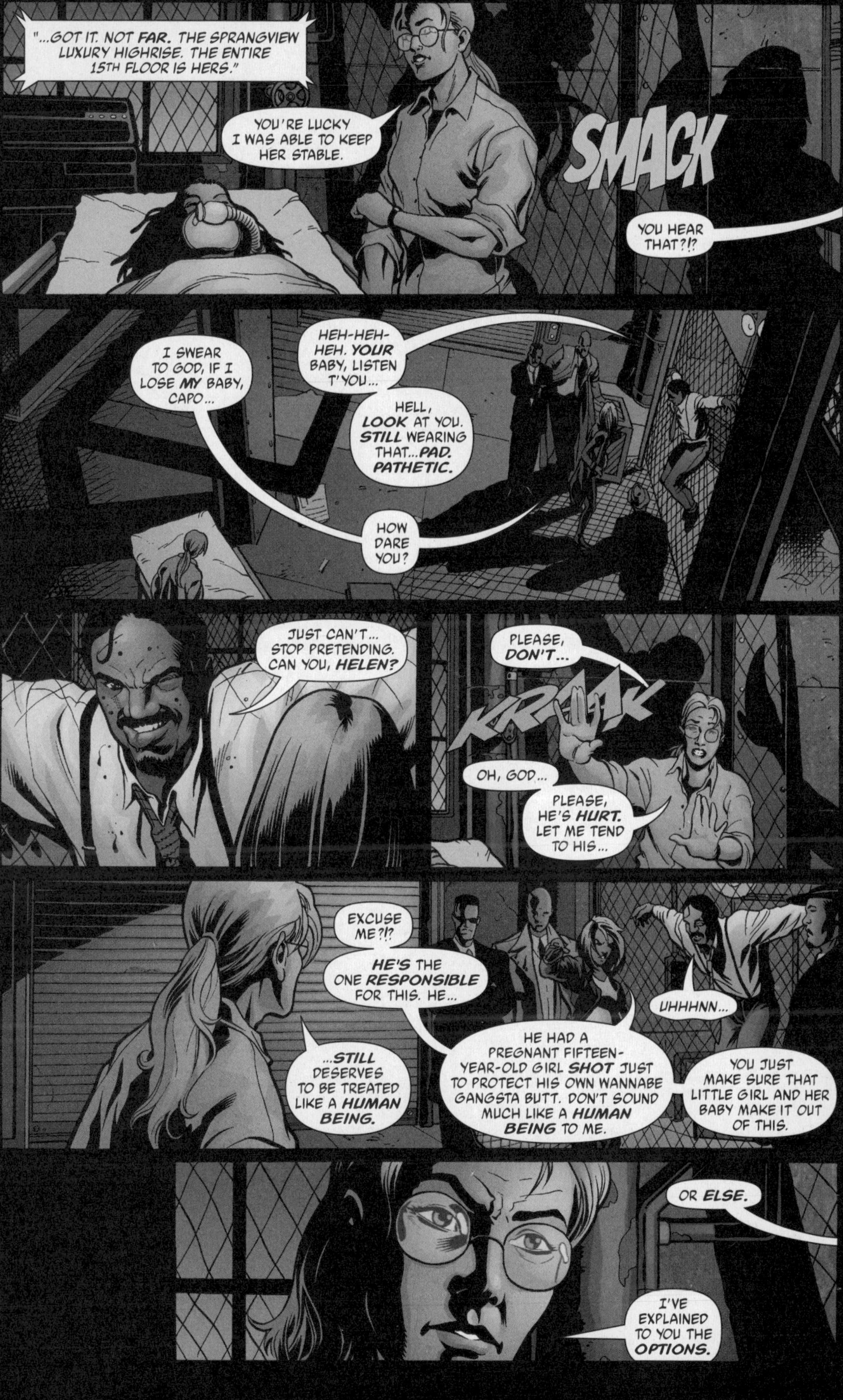
"...GOT IT. NOT FAR. THE SPRANGVIEW LUXURY HIGHRISE. THE ENTIRE 15TH FLOOR IS HERS."
YOU'RE LUCKY I WAS ABLE TO KEEP HER STABLE.
SMACK
YOU HEAR THAT?!?
I SWEAR TO GOD, IF I LOSE MY BABY, CAPO...
HEH-HEH-HEH. YOUR BABY, LISTEN T'YOU...
HELL, LOOK AT YOU. STILL WEARING THAT...PAD. PATHETIC.
HOW DARE YOU?
JUST CAN'T... STOP PRETENDING. CAN YOU, HELEN?
PLEASE, DON'T...
KRAAK
OH, GOD...
PLEASE, HE'S HURT. LET ME TEND TO HIS...
EXCUSE ME?!?
HE'S THE ONE RESPONSIBLE FOR THIS. HE...
...STILL DESERVES TO BE TREATED LIKE A HUMAN BEING.
HE HAD A PREGNANT FIFTEEN-YEAR-OLD GIRL SHOT JUST TO PROTECT HIS OWN WANNABE GANGSTA BUTT. DON'T SOUND MUCH LIKE A HUMAN BEING TO ME.
UHHHNN...
YOU JUST MAKE SURE THAT LITTLE GIRL AND HER BABY MAKE IT OUT OF THIS.
OR ELSE.
I'VE EXPLAINED TO YOU THE OPTIONS.

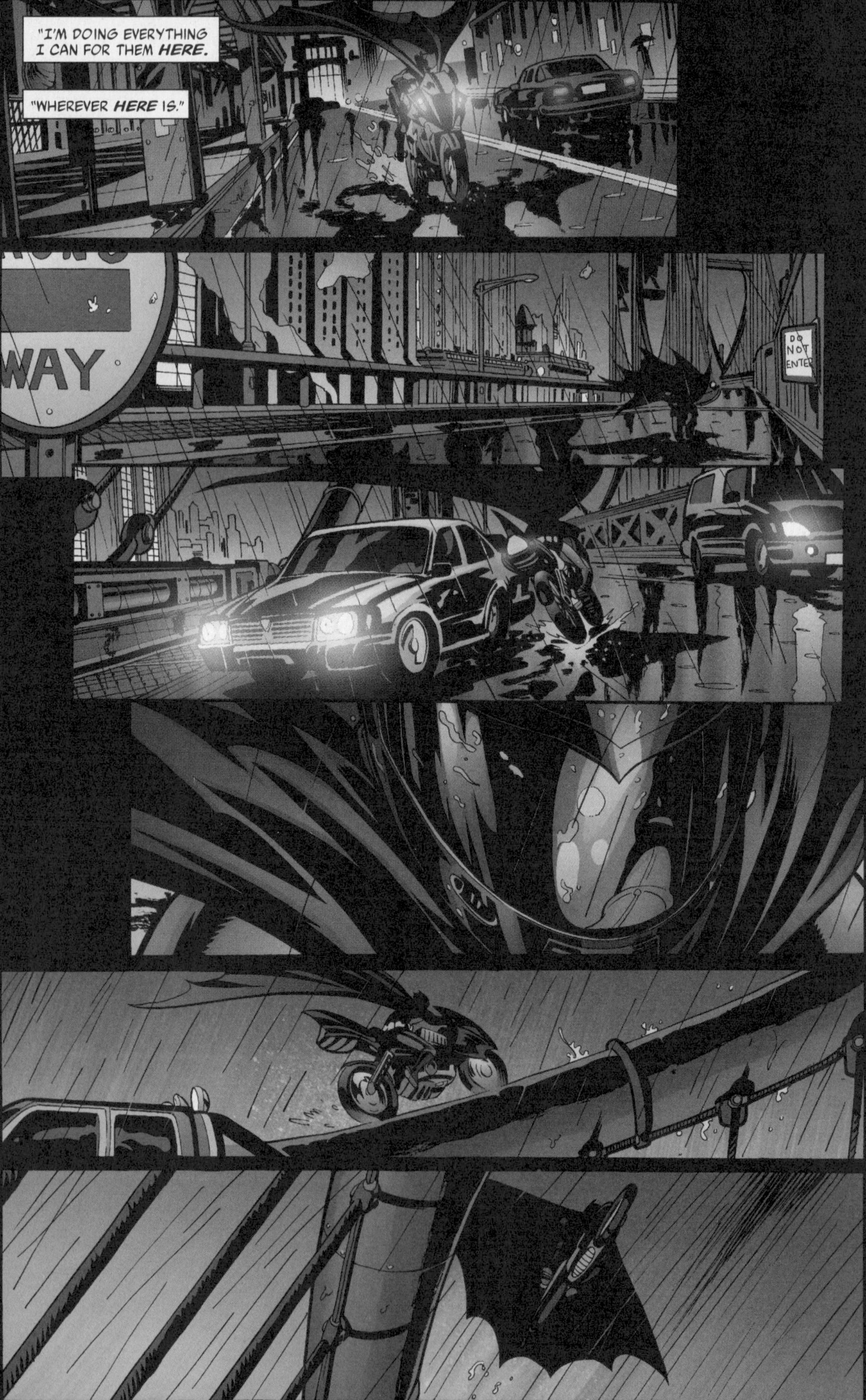
"I'M DOING EVERYTHING I CAN FOR THEM HERE.
"WHEREVER HERE IS."
WAY
DO NOT ENTER

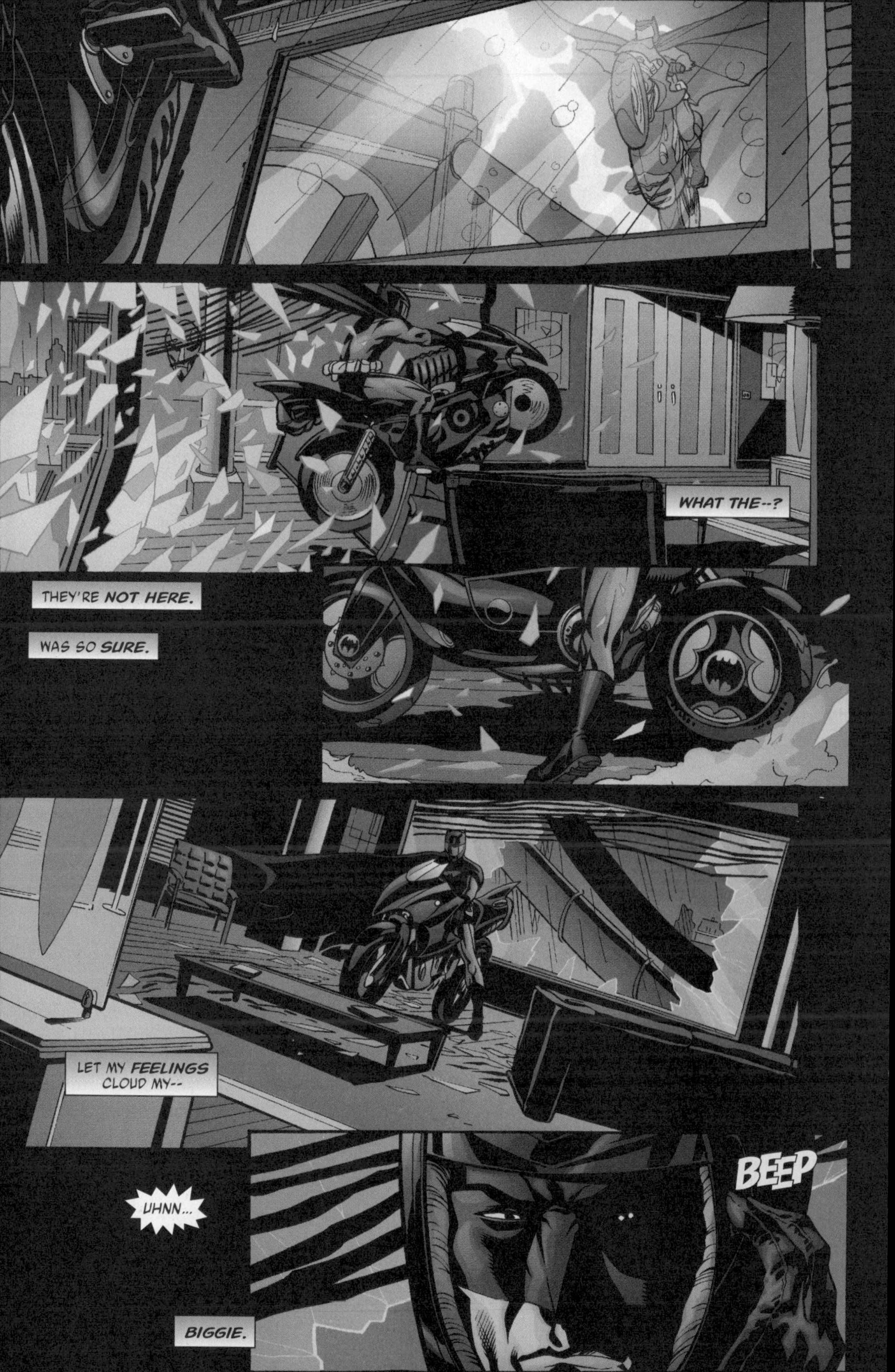
WHAT THE--?
THEY'RE NOT HERE.
WAS SO SURE.
LET MY FEELINGS CLOUD MY--
BEEP
UHNN...
BIGGIE.

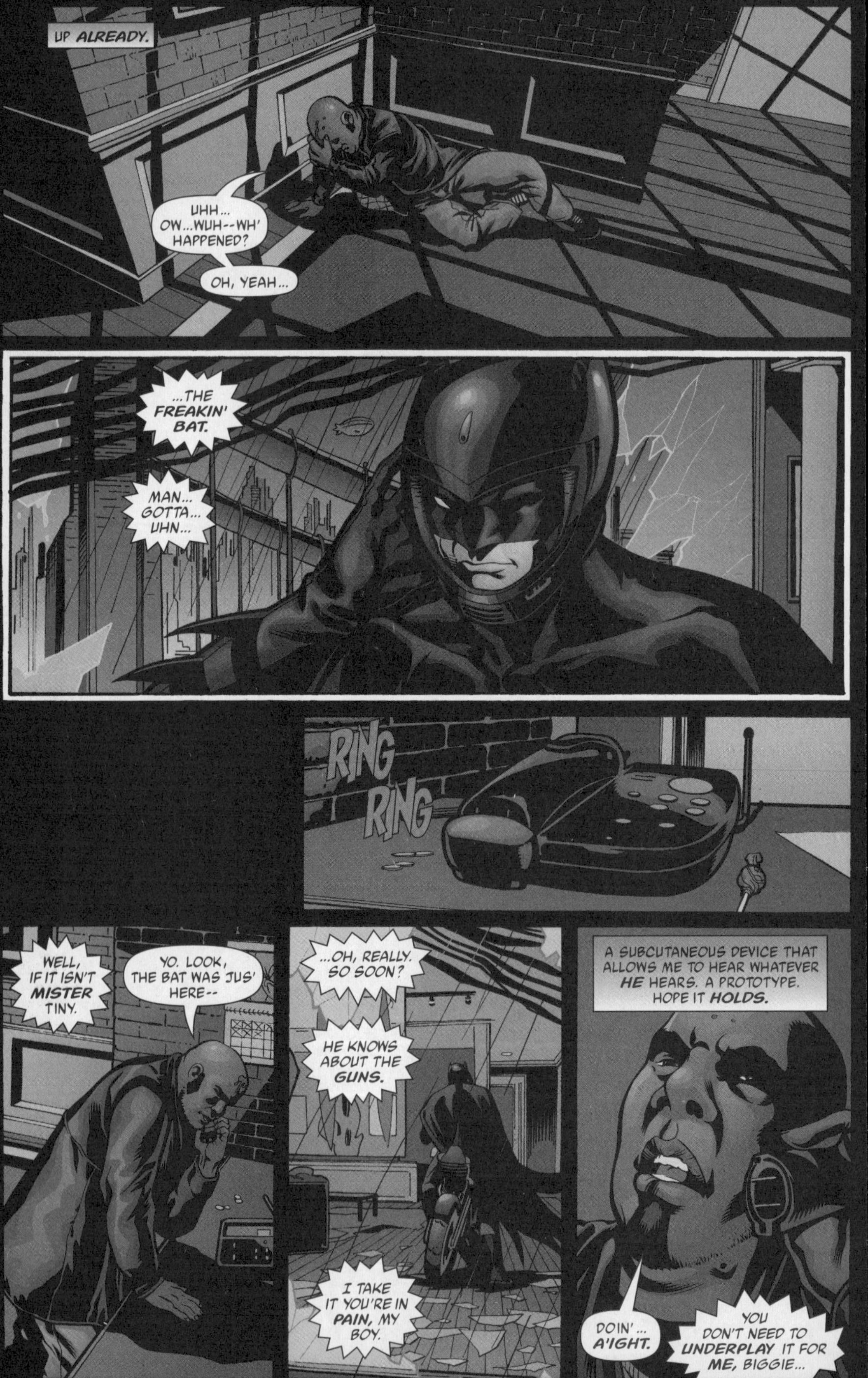
UP ALREADY.
UHH... OW...WUH--WH' HAPPENED?
OH, YEAH...
...THE FREAKIN' BAT.
MAN... GOTTA... UHN...
RING RING
WELL, IF IT ISN'T MISTER TINY.
YO. LOOK, THE BAT WAS JUS' HERE--
...OH, REALLY. SO SOON?
HE KNOWS ABOUT THE GUNS.
I TAKE IT YOU'RE IN PAIN, MY BOY.
A SUBCUTANEOUS DEVICE THAT ALLOWS ME TO HEAR WHATEVER HE HEARS. A PROTOTYPE. HOPE IT HOLDS.
DOIN'... A'IGHT.
YOU DON'T NEED TO UNDERPLAY IT FOR ME, BIGGIE...

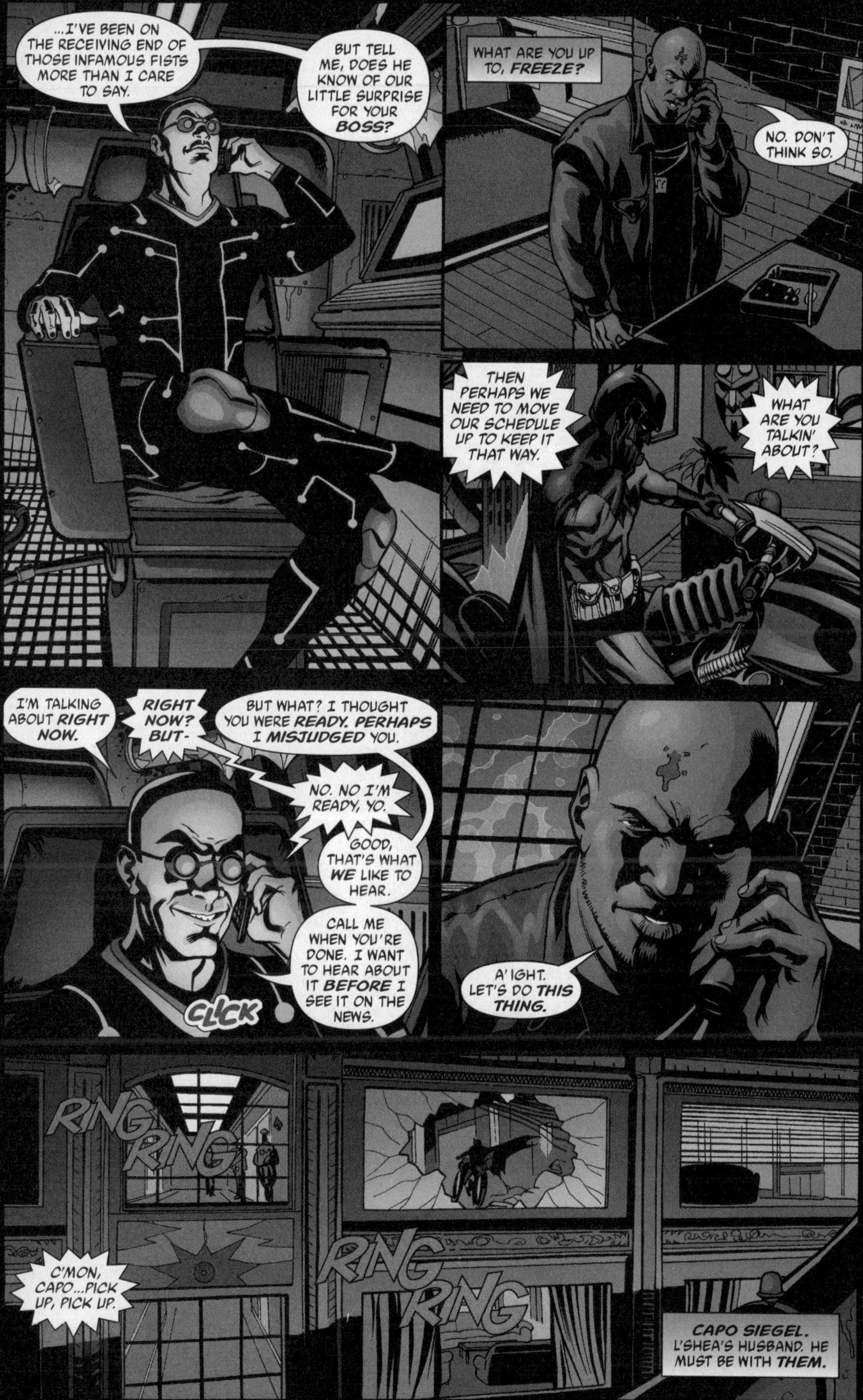
...I'VE BEEN ON THE RECEIVING END OF THOSE INFAMOUS FISTS MORE THAN I CARE TO SAY.
BUT TELL ME, DOES HE KNOW OF OUR LITTLE SURPRISE FOR YOUR BOSS?
WHAT ARE YOU UP TO, FREEZE?
NO. DON'T THINK SO.
THEN PERHAPS WE NEED TO MOVE OUR SCHEDULE UP TO KEEP IT THAT WAY.
WHAT ARE YOU TALKIN' ABOUT?
I'M TALKING ABOUT RIGHT NOW.
RIGHT NOW? BUT-
BUT WHAT? I THOUGHT YOU WERE READY. PERHAPS I MISJUDGED YOU.
NO. NO I'M READY, YO.
GOOD, THAT'S WHAT WE LIKE TO HEAR.
CALL ME WHEN YOU'RE DONE. I WANT TO HEAR ABOUT IT BEFORE I SEE IT ON THE NEWS.
CLICK
A'IGHT. LET'S DO THIS THING.
RING RING
C'MON, CAPO...PICK UP, PICK UP.
RING RING
CAPO SIEGEL. L'SHEA'S HUSBAND. HE MUST BE WITH THEM.

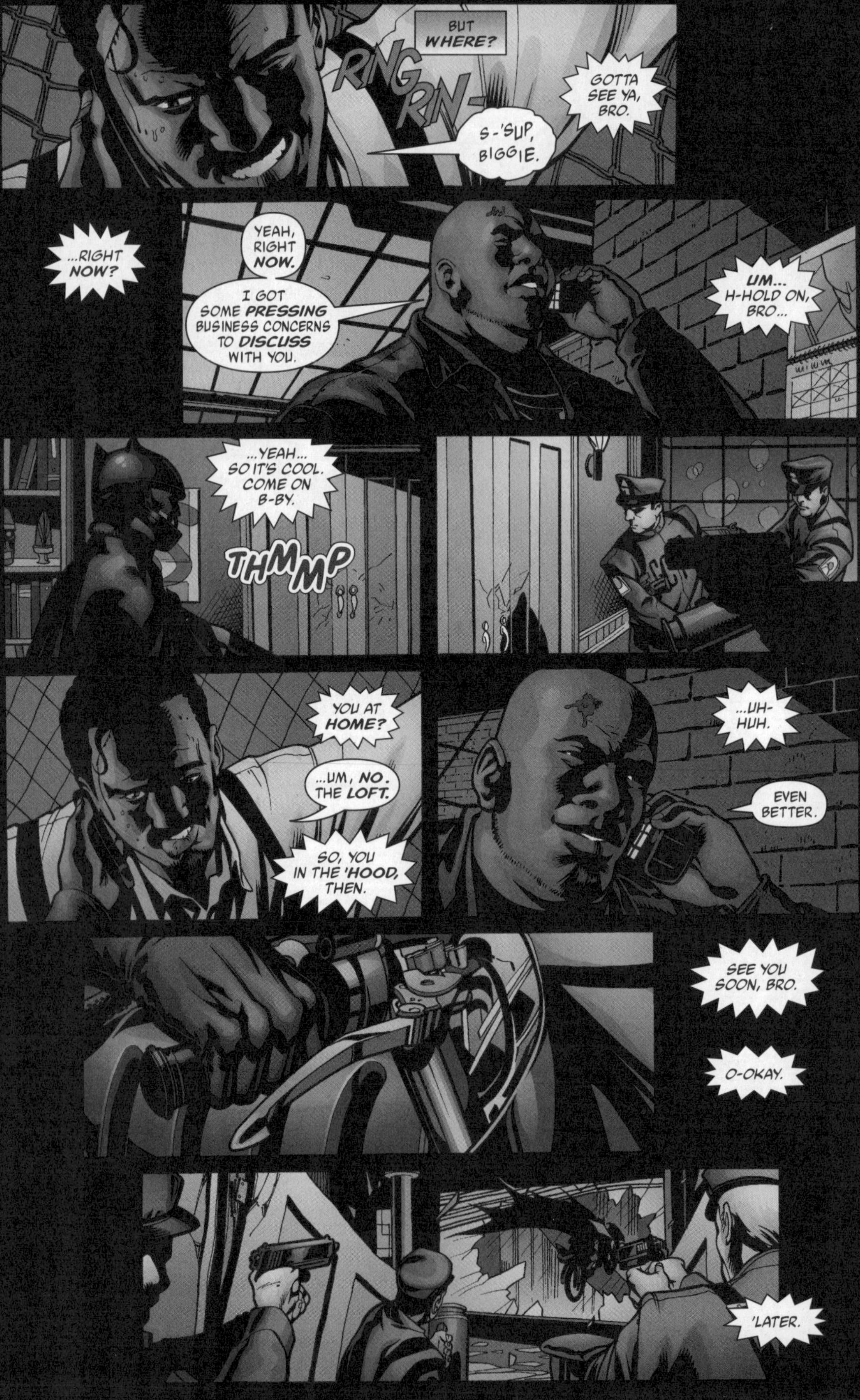

BUT WHERE?
RING RIN-
S-'SUP, BIGGIE.
GOTTA SEE YA, BRO.
...RIGHT NOW?
YEAH, RIGHT NOW.
I GOT SOME PRESSING BUSINESS CONCERNS TO DISCUSS WITH YOU.
UM... H-HOLD ON, BRO...
...YEAH... SO IT'S COOL. COME ON B-BY.
THMMP
YOU AT HOME?
...UM, NO. THE LOFT.
SO, YOU IN THE 'HOOD, THEN.
...UH-HUH.
EVEN BETTER.
SEE YOU SOON, BRO.
O-OKAY.
'LATER.

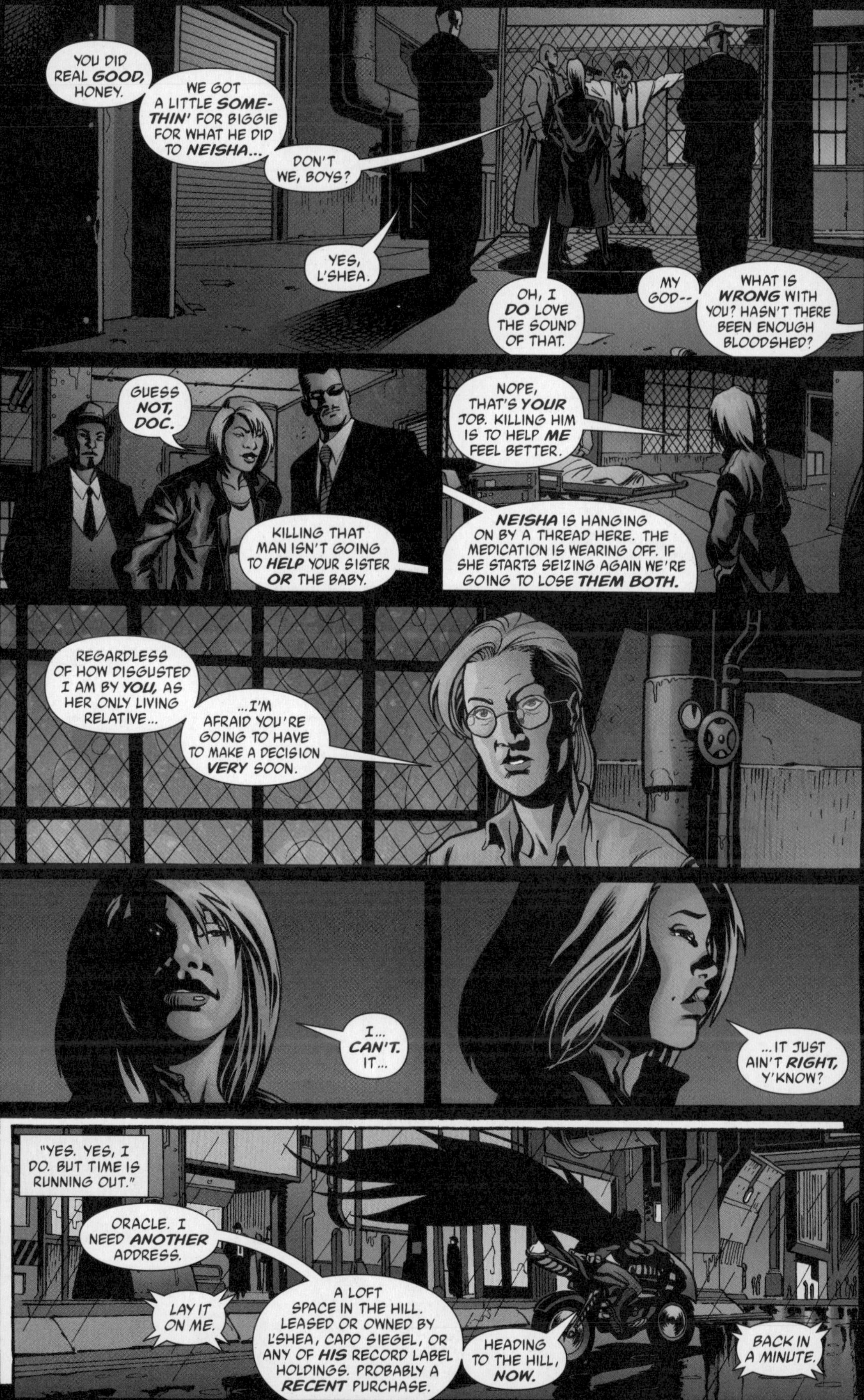
YOU DID REAL **GOOD,** HONEY.
WE GOT A LITTLE **SOME-THIN'** FOR BIGGIE FOR WHAT HE DID TO **NEISHA...**
DON'T WE, BOYS?
YES, L'SHEA.
OH, I **DO** LOVE THE SOUND OF THAT.
MY GOD--
WHAT IS **WRONG** WITH YOU? HASN'T THERE BEEN ENOUGH BLOODSHED?
GUESS **NOT, DOC.**
KILLING THAT MAN ISN'T GOING TO **HELP** YOUR SISTER **OR** THE BABY.
NOPE, THAT'S **YOUR** JOB. KILLING HIM IS TO HELP **ME** FEEL BETTER.
NEISHA IS HANGING ON BY A THREAD HERE. THE MEDICATION IS WEARING OFF. IF SHE STARTS SEIZING AGAIN WE'RE GOING TO LOSE **THEM BOTH.**
REGARDLESS OF HOW DISGUSTED I AM BY **YOU,** AS HER ONLY LIVING RELATIVE...
...I'M AFRAID YOU'RE GOING TO HAVE TO MAKE A DECISION **VERY** SOON.
I... **CAN'T.** IT...
...IT JUST AIN'T **RIGHT,** Y'KNOW?
"YES. YES, I DO. BUT TIME IS RUNNING OUT."
ORACLE. I NEED **ANOTHER** ADDRESS.
LAY IT ON ME.
A LOFT SPACE IN THE HILL. LEASED OR OWNED BY L'SHEA, CAPO SIEGEL, OR ANY OF **HIS** RECORD LABEL HOLDINGS. PROBABLY A **RECENT** PURCHASE.
HEADING TO THE HILL, **NOW.**
BACK IN A MINUTE.

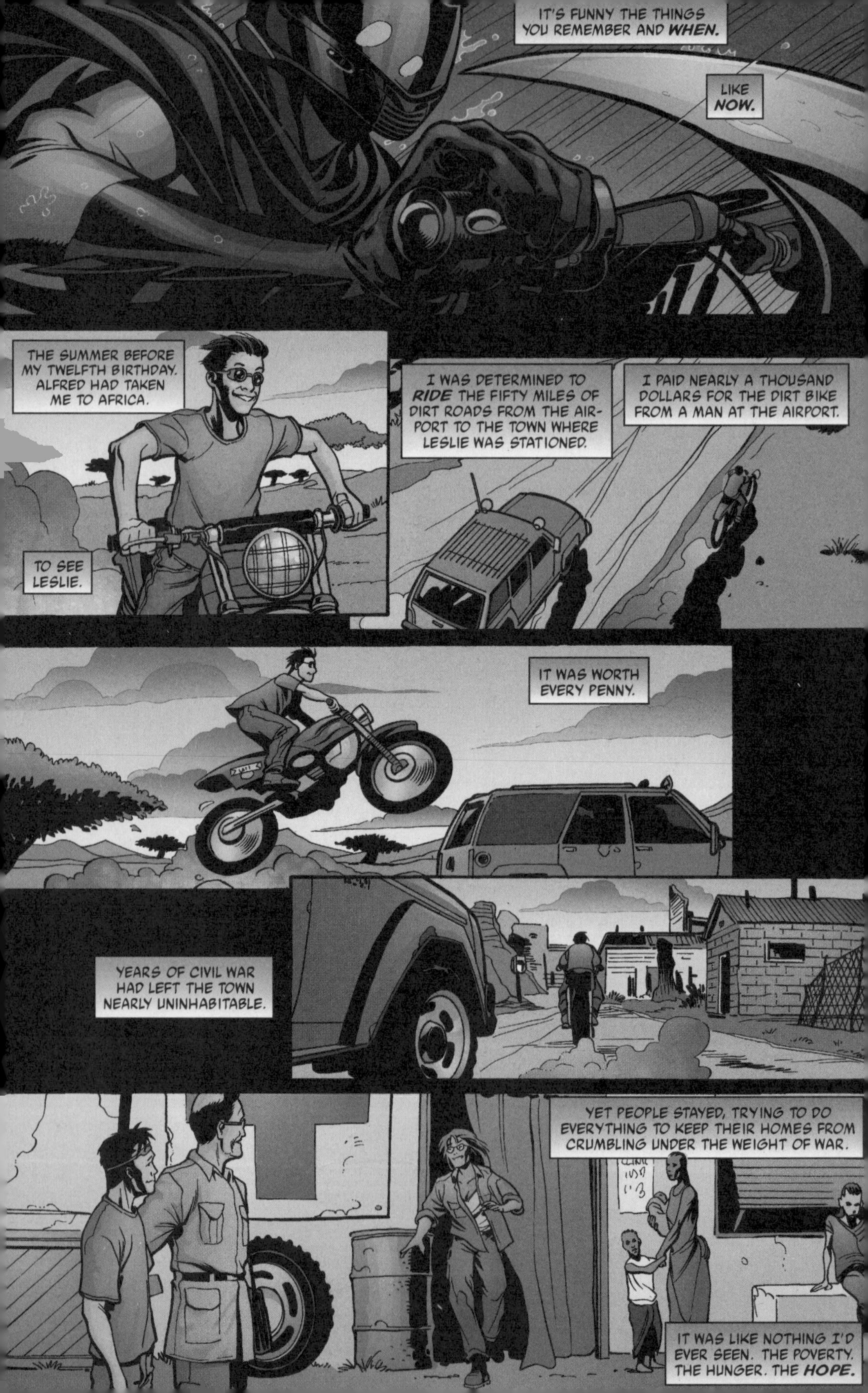

IT'S FUNNY THE THINGS YOU REMEMBER AND WHEN.
LIKE NOW.
THE SUMMER BEFORE MY TWELFTH BIRTHDAY. ALFRED HAD TAKEN ME TO AFRICA.
TO SEE LESLIE.
I WAS DETERMINED TO RIDE THE FIFTY MILES OF DIRT ROADS FROM THE AIRPORT TO THE TOWN WHERE LESLIE WAS STATIONED.
I PAID NEARLY A THOUSAND DOLLARS FOR THE DIRT BIKE FROM A MAN AT THE AIRPORT.
IT WAS WORTH EVERY PENNY.
YEARS OF CIVIL WAR HAD LEFT THE TOWN NEARLY UNINHABITABLE.
YET PEOPLE STAYED, TRYING TO DO EVERYTHING TO KEEP THEIR HOMES FROM CRUMBLING UNDER THE WEIGHT OF WAR.
IT WAS LIKE NOTHING I'D EVER SEEN. THE POVERTY. THE HUNGER. THE HOPE.

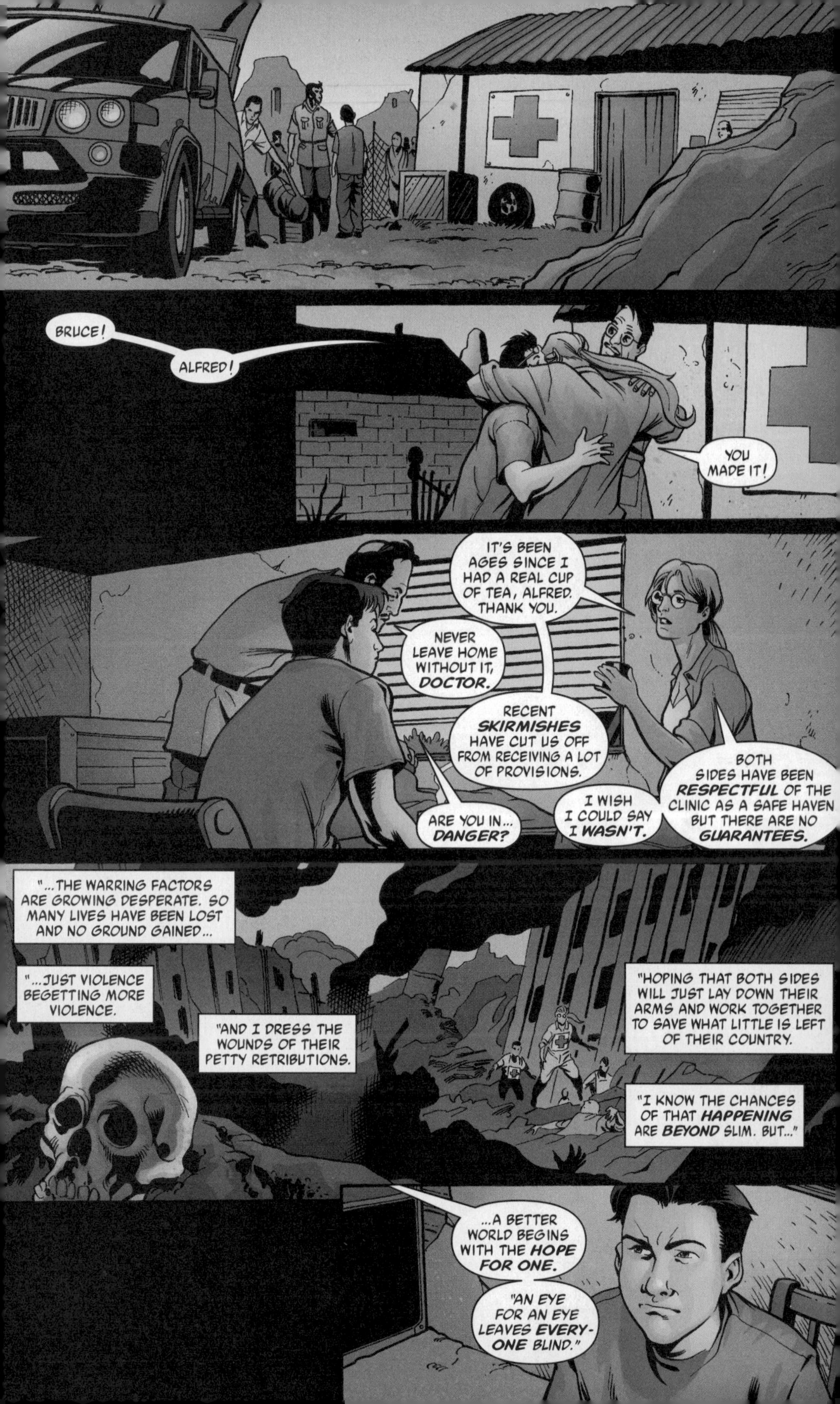
BRUCE!
ALFRED!
YOU MADE IT!
IT'S BEEN AGES SINCE I HAD A REAL CUP OF TEA, ALFRED. THANK YOU.
NEVER LEAVE HOME WITHOUT IT, DOCTOR.
RECENT SKIRMISHES HAVE CUT US OFF FROM RECEIVING A LOT OF PROVISIONS.
ARE YOU IN... DANGER?
I WISH I COULD SAY I WASN'T.
BOTH SIDES HAVE BEEN RESPECTFUL OF THE CLINIC AS A SAFE HAVEN BUT THERE ARE NO GUARANTEES.
"...THE WARRING FACTORS ARE GROWING DESPERATE. SO MANY LIVES HAVE BEEN LOST AND NO GROUND GAINED...
"...JUST VIOLENCE BEGETTING MORE VIOLENCE.
"AND I DRESS THE WOUNDS OF THEIR PETTY RETRIBUTIONS.
"HOPING THAT BOTH SIDES WILL JUST LAY DOWN THEIR ARMS AND WORK TOGETHER TO SAVE WHAT LITTLE IS LEFT OF THEIR COUNTRY.
"I KNOW THE CHANCES OF THAT HAPPENING ARE BEYOND SLIM. BUT..."
...A BETTER WORLD BEGINS WITH THE HOPE FOR ONE.
"AN EYE FOR AN EYE LEAVES EVERY-ONE BLIND."

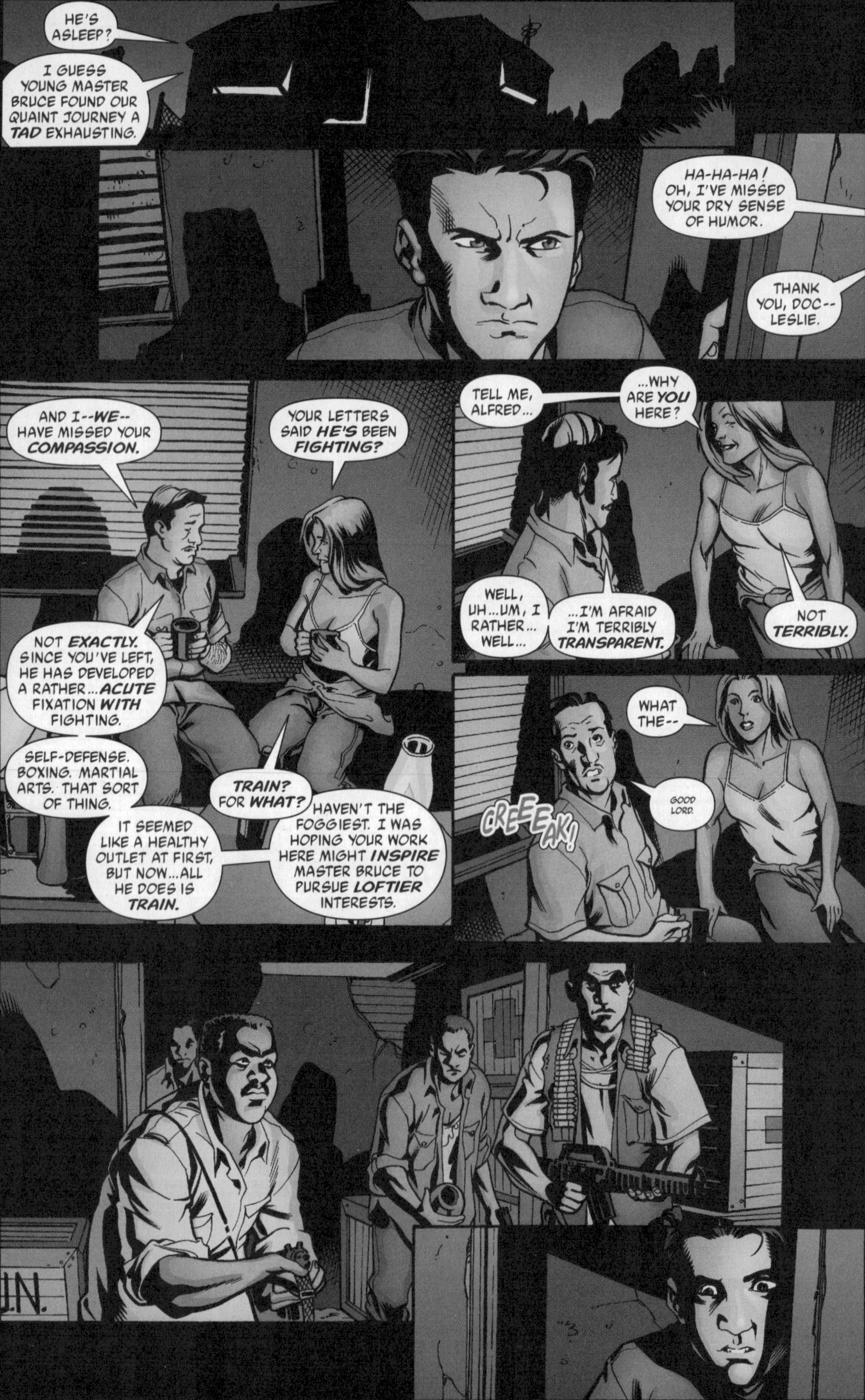
HE'S ASLEEP?
I GUESS YOUNG MASTER BRUCE FOUND OUR QUAINT JOURNEY A TAD EXHAUSTING.
HA-HA-HA! OH, I'VE MISSED YOUR DRY SENSE OF HUMOR.
THANK YOU, DOC--LESLIE.
AND I--WE--HAVE MISSED YOUR COMPASSION.
YOUR LETTERS SAID HE'S BEEN FIGHTING?
NOT EXACTLY. SINCE YOU'VE LEFT, HE HAS DEVELOPED A RATHER...ACUTE FIXATION WITH FIGHTING.
SELF-DEFENSE. BOXING. MARTIAL ARTS. THAT SORT OF THING.
IT SEEMED LIKE A HEALTHY OUTLET AT FIRST, BUT NOW...ALL HE DOES IS TRAIN.
TRAIN? FOR WHAT?
HAVEN'T THE FOGGIEST. I WAS HOPING YOUR WORK HERE MIGHT INSPIRE MASTER BRUCE TO PURSUE LOFTIER INTERESTS.
TELL ME, ALFRED...
...WHY ARE YOU HERE?
WELL, UH...UM, I RATHER... WELL...
...I'M AFRAID I'M TERRIBLY TRANSPARENT.
NOT TERRIBLY.
WHAT THE--
CREEEEAK!
GOOD LORD.
U.N.

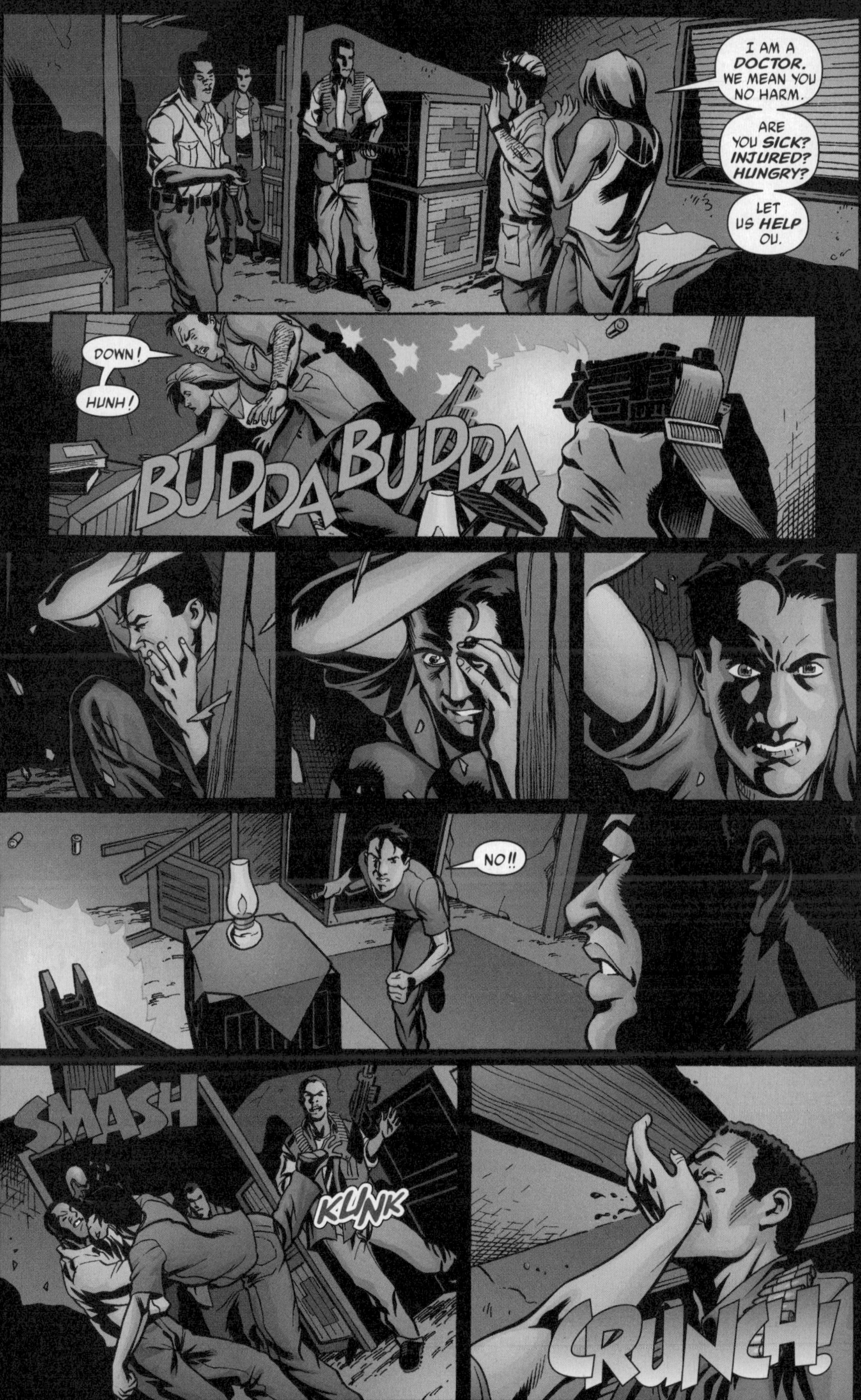

I AM A DOCTOR. WE MEAN YOU NO HARM.
ARE YOU SICK? INJURED? HUNGRY?
LET US HELP OU.
DOWN!
HUNH!
BUDDA BUDDA
NO!!
SMASH
KLUNK
CRUNCH!

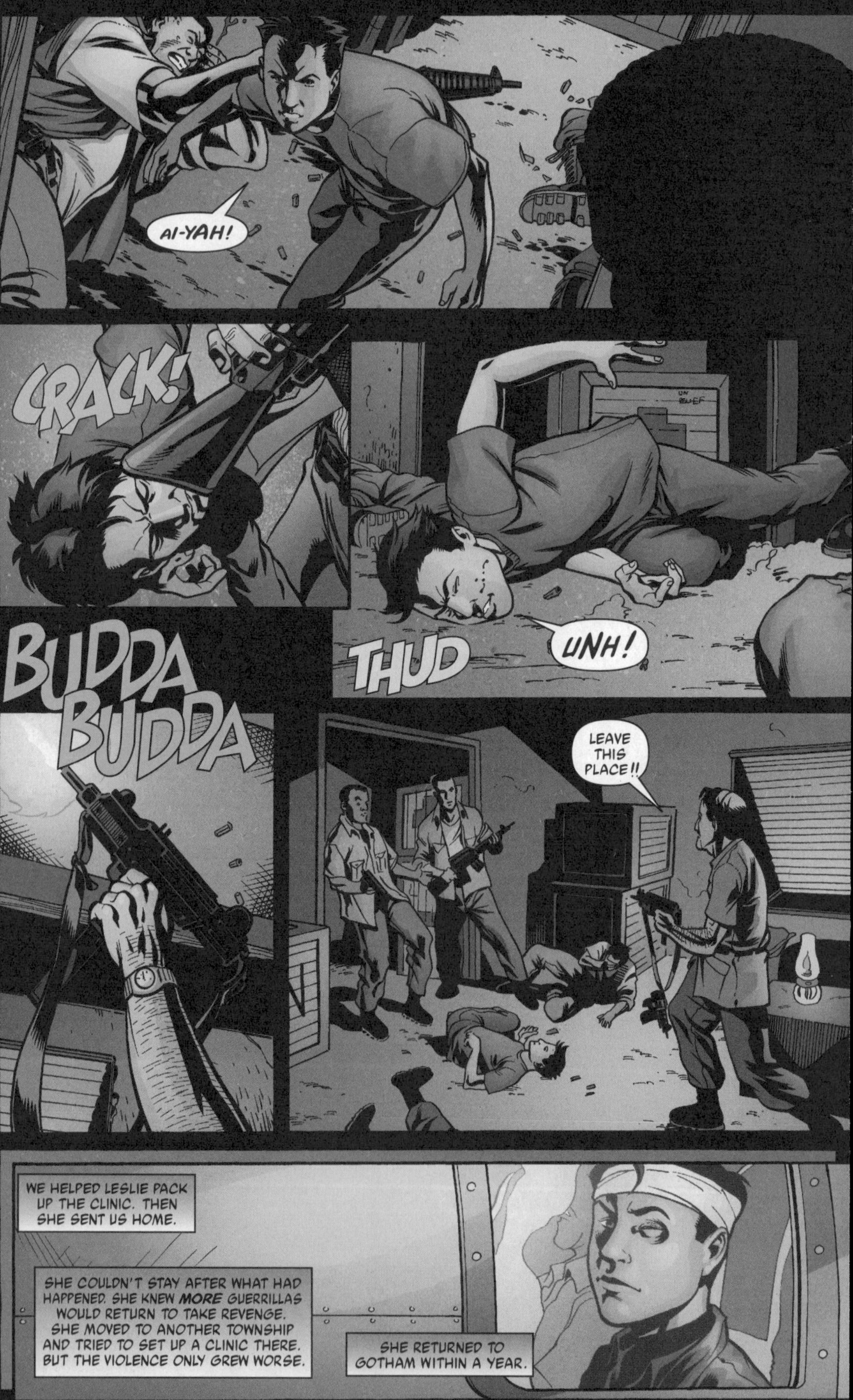
AI-YAH!
CRACK!
THUD
UNH!
BUDDA
BUDDA
LEAVE THIS PLACE!!
WE HELPED LESLIE PACK UP THE CLINIC. THEN SHE SENT US HOME.
SHE COULDN'T STAY AFTER WHAT HAD HAPPENED. SHE KNEW MORE GUERRILLAS WOULD RETURN TO TAKE REVENGE. SHE MOVED TO ANOTHER TOWNSHIP AND TRIED TO SET UP A CLINIC THERE. BUT THE VIOLENCE ONLY GREW WORSE.
SHE RETURNED TO GOTHAM WITHIN A YEAR.

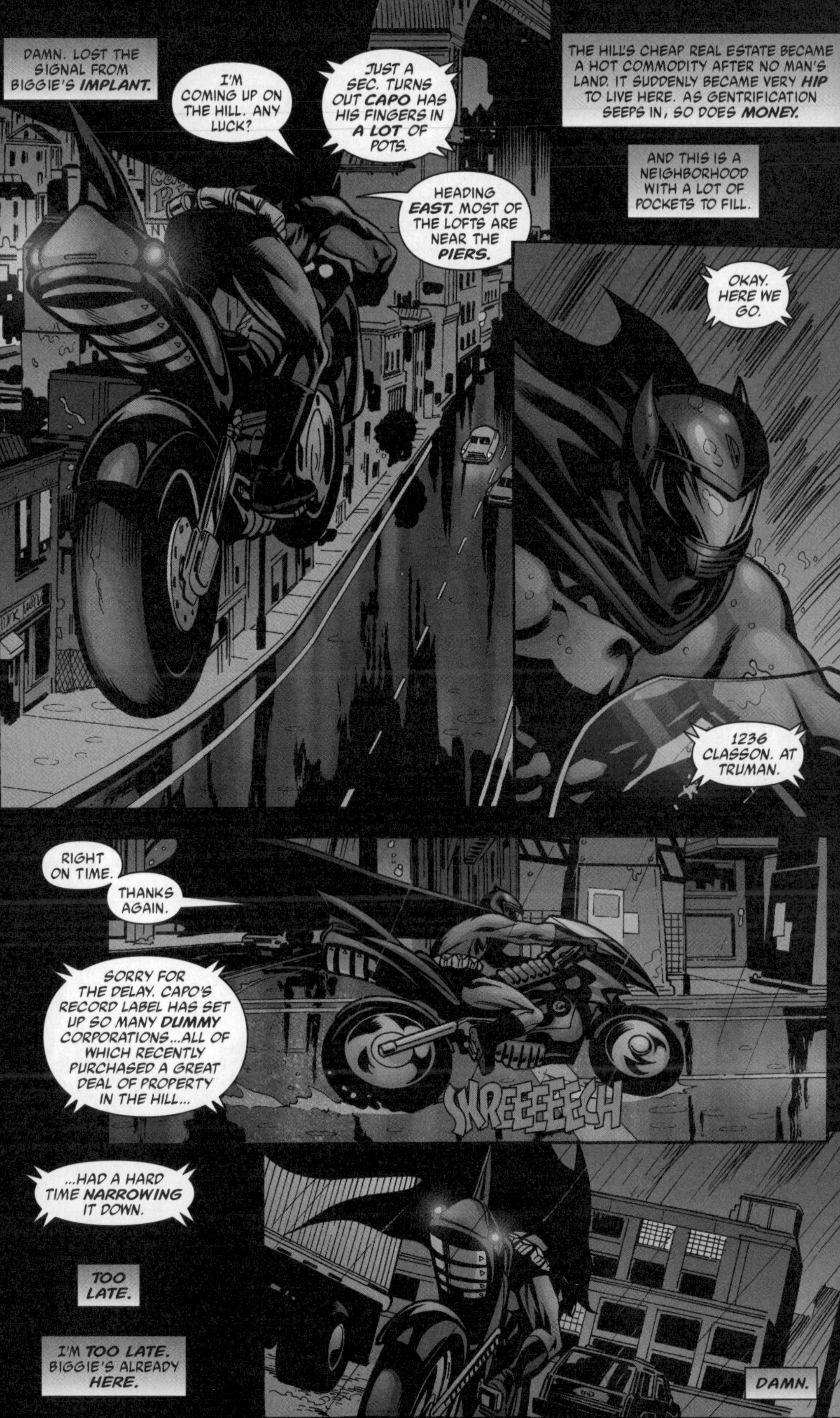
DAMN. LOST THE SIGNAL FROM BIGGIE'S IMPLANT.
I'M COMING UP ON THE HILL. ANY LUCK?
JUST A SEC. TURNS OUT CAPO HAS HIS FINGERS IN A LOT OF POTS.
HEADING EAST. MOST OF THE LOFTS ARE NEAR THE PIERS.
THE HILL'S CHEAP REAL ESTATE BECAME A HOT COMMODITY AFTER NO MAN'S LAND. IT SUDDENLY BECAME VERY HIP TO LIVE HERE. AS GENTRIFICATION SEEPS IN, SO DOES MONEY.
AND THIS IS A NEIGHBORHOOD WITH A LOT OF POCKETS TO FILL.
OKAY. HERE WE GO.
1236 CLASSON. AT TRUMAN.
RIGHT ON TIME.
THANKS AGAIN.
SORRY FOR THE DELAY. CAPO'S RECORD LABEL HAS SET UP SO MANY DUMMY CORPORATIONS...ALL OF WHICH RECENTLY PURCHASED A GREAT DEAL OF PROPERTY IN THE HILL...
SKREEEEECH
...HAD A HARD TIME NARROWING IT DOWN.
TOO LATE.
I'M TOO LATE. BIGGIE'S ALREADY HERE.
DAMN.

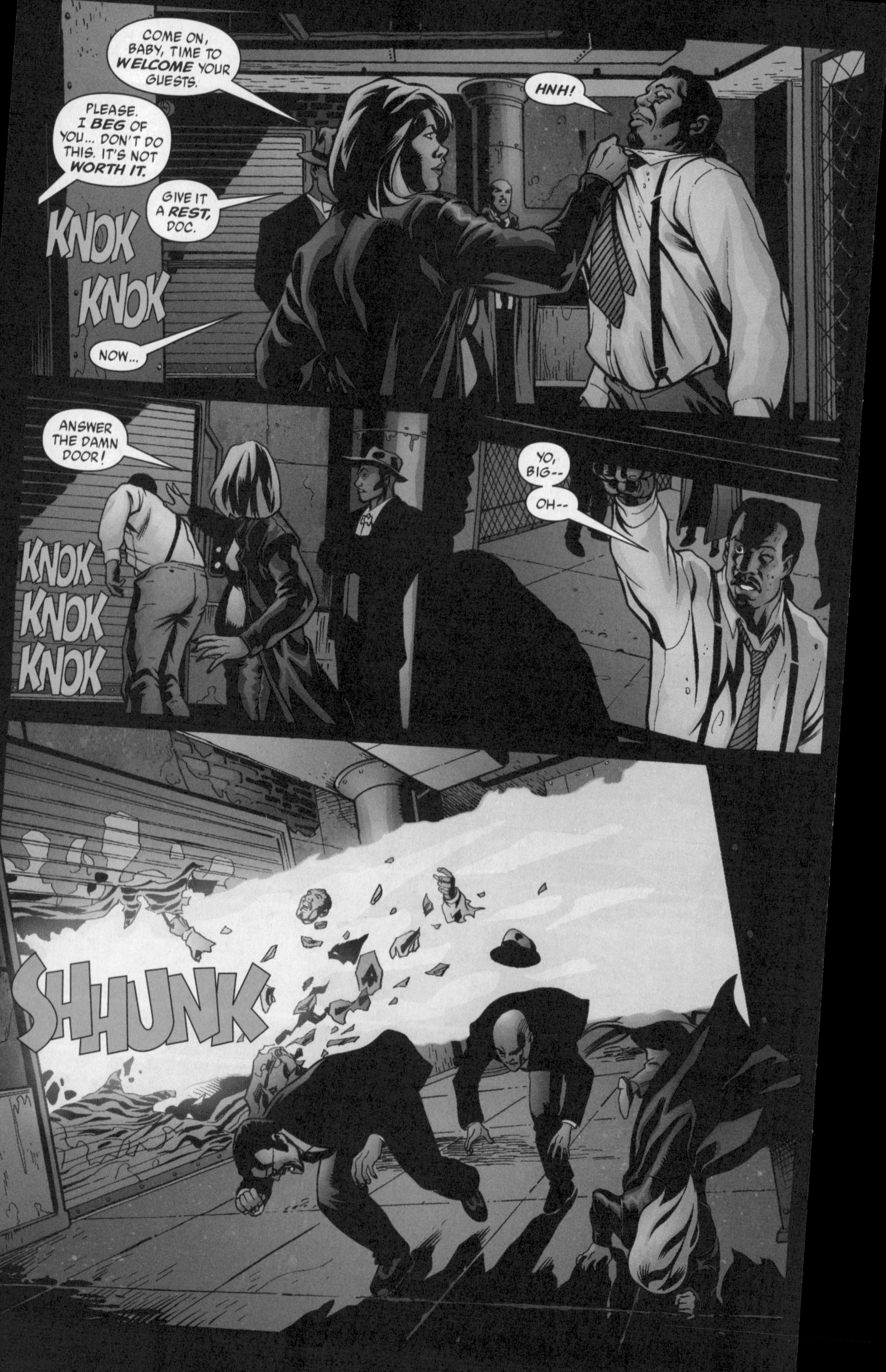
COME ON, BABY, TIME TO WELCOME YOUR GUESTS.
HNH!
PLEASE. I BEG OF YOU... DON'T DO THIS. IT'S NOT WORTH IT.
GIVE IT A REST, DOC.
KNOK KNOK
NOW...
ANSWER THE DAMN DOOR!
KNOK KNOK KNOK
YO, BIG--
OH--
SHHUNK

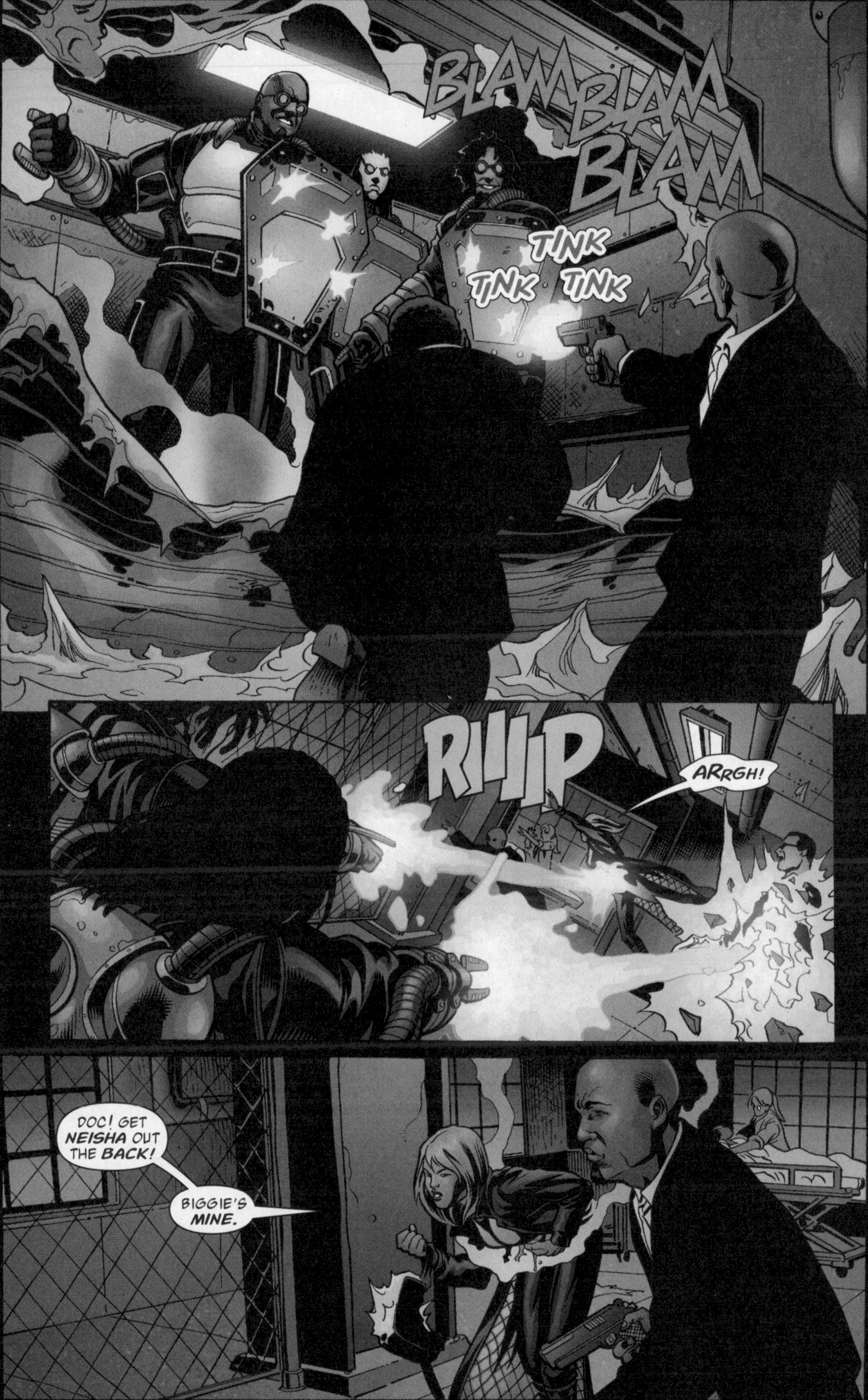
BLAM BLAM
BLAM
TINK
TINK TINK
RIIIP
ARRGH!
DOC! GET NEISHA OUT THE BACK!
BIGGIE'S MINE.

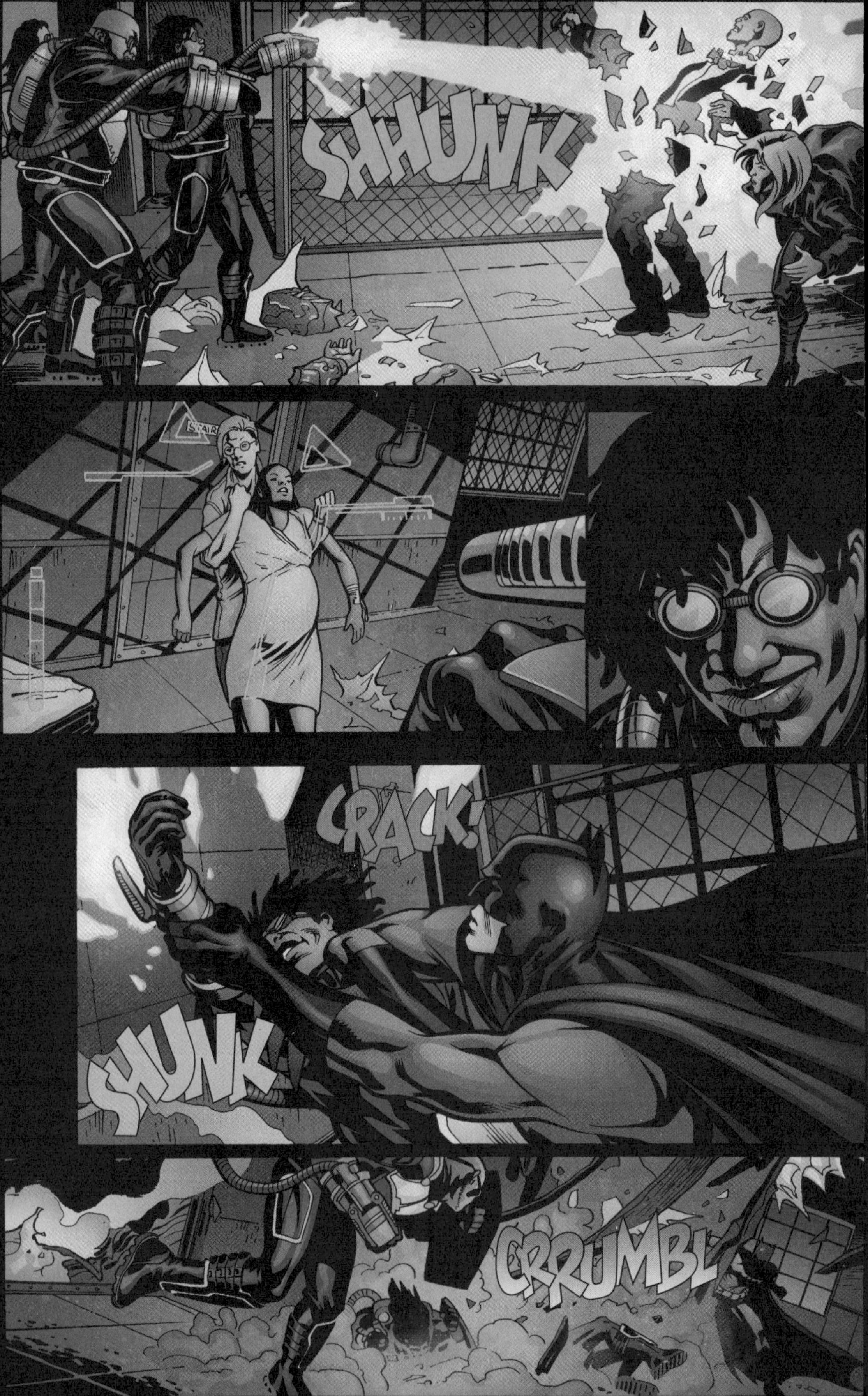
SHHUNK
STAIR
CRACK!
SHUNK
CRRUMBL

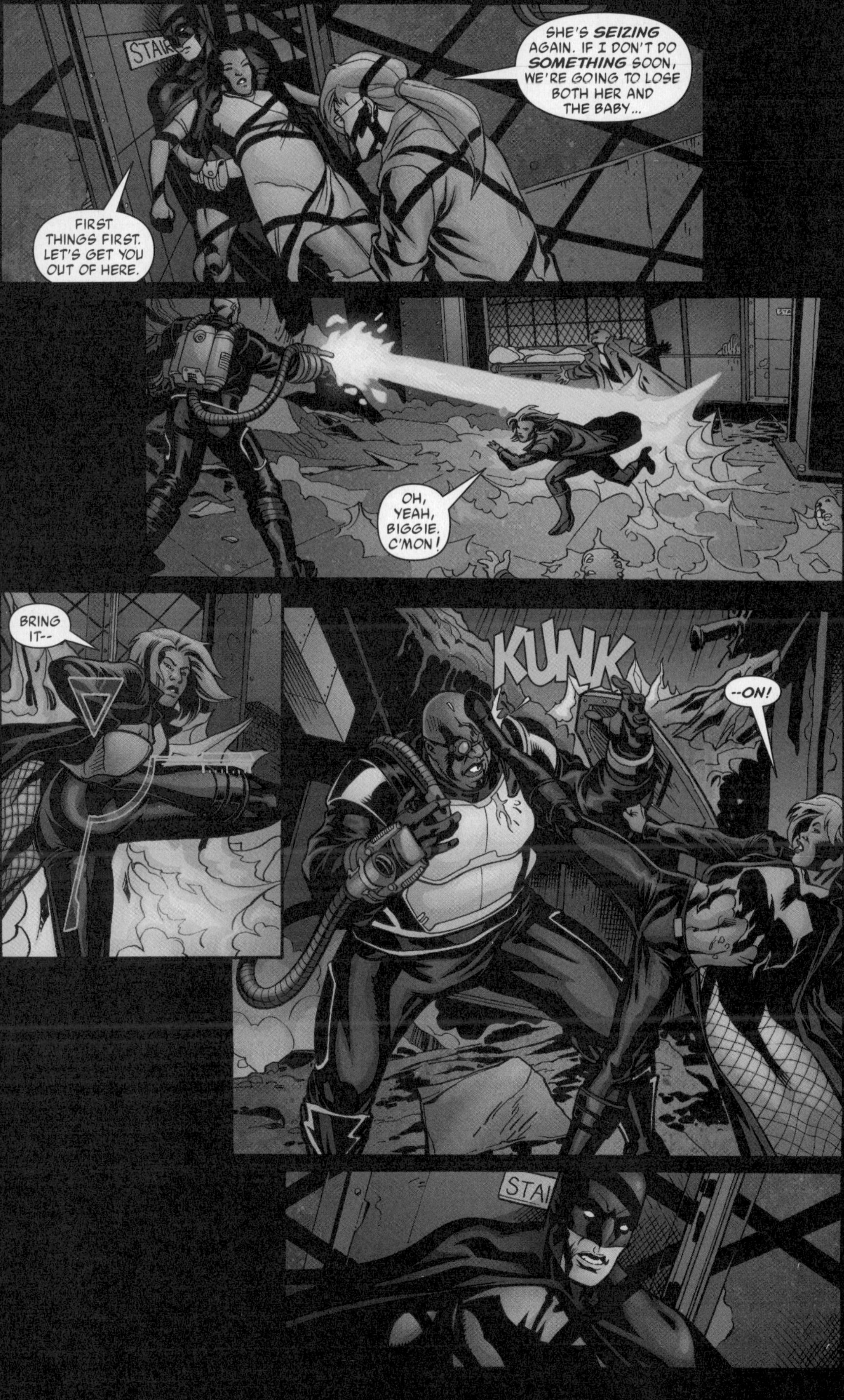
SHE'S **SEIZING** AGAIN. IF I DON'T DO **SOMETHING** SOON, WE'RE GOING TO LOSE BOTH HER AND THE BABY...
FIRST THINGS FIRST. LET'S GET YOU OUT OF HERE.
OH, YEAH, BIGGIE. C'MON!
BRING IT--
KUNK
--ON!

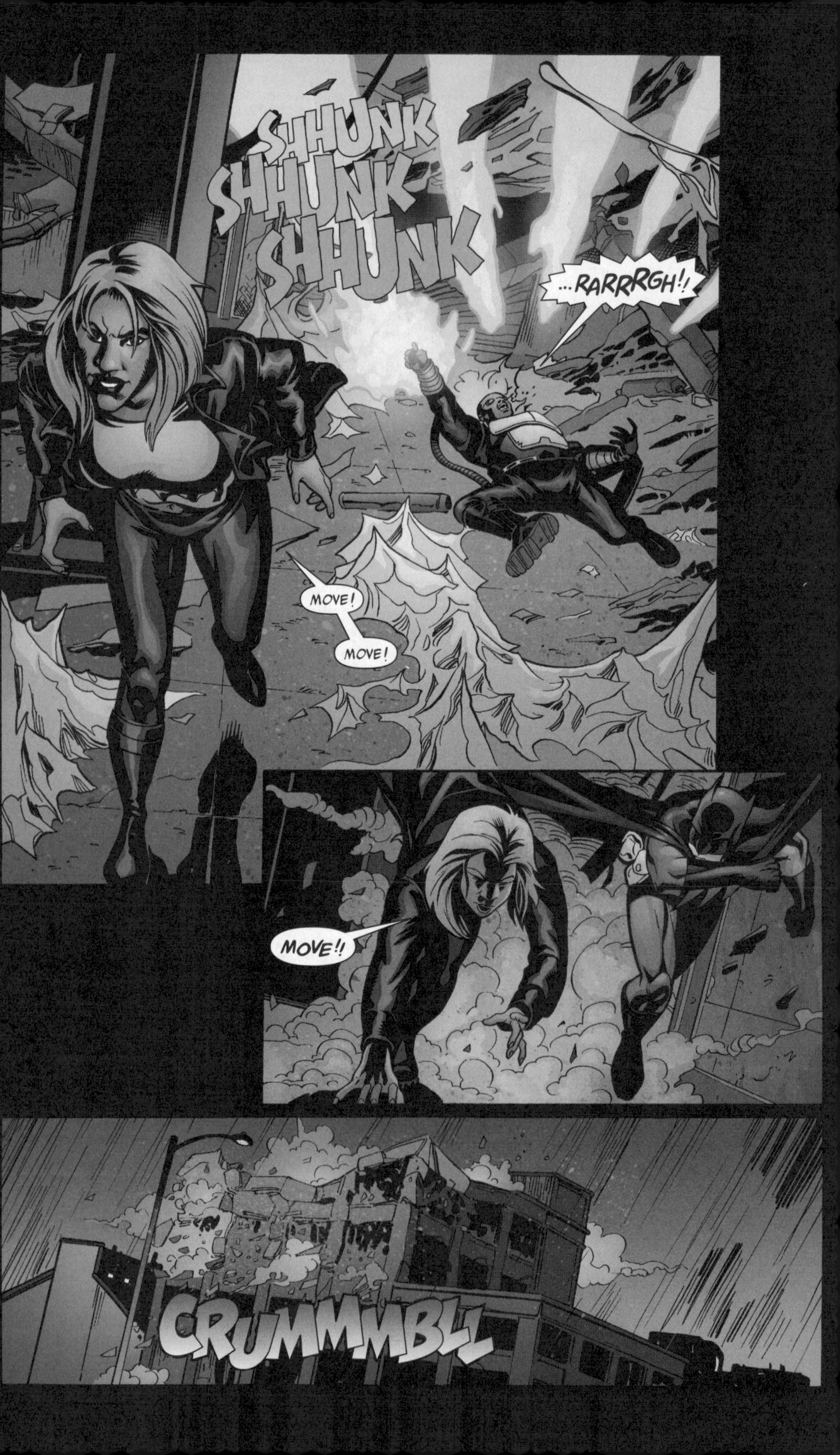
SHHUNK SHHUNK SHHUNK
...RARRRGH!!
MOVE!
MOVE!
MOVE!!
CRUMMMBLL

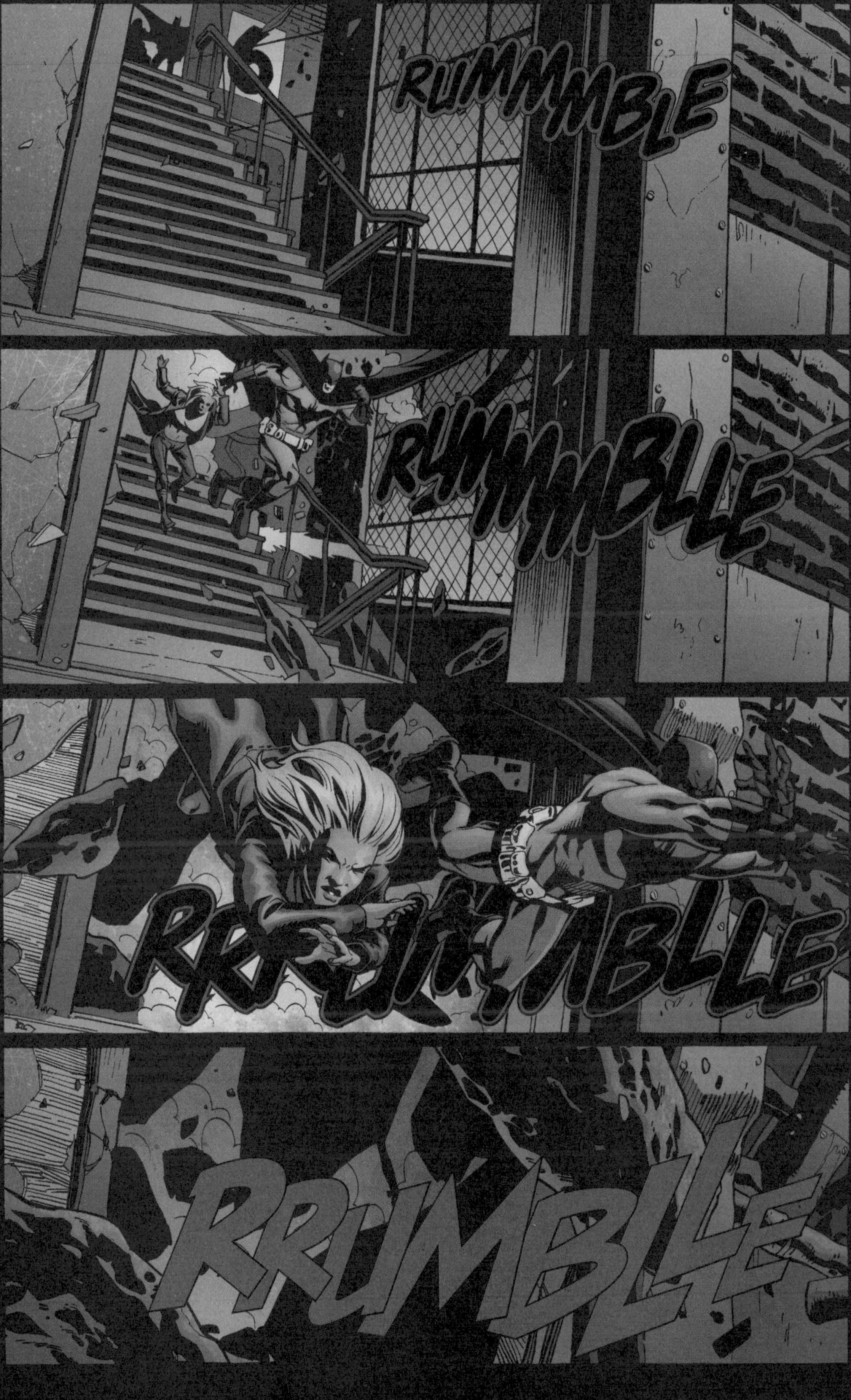
RUMMMMBLE
RUMMMMBLLE
RRRUMMMBLLE
RRUMBLLE

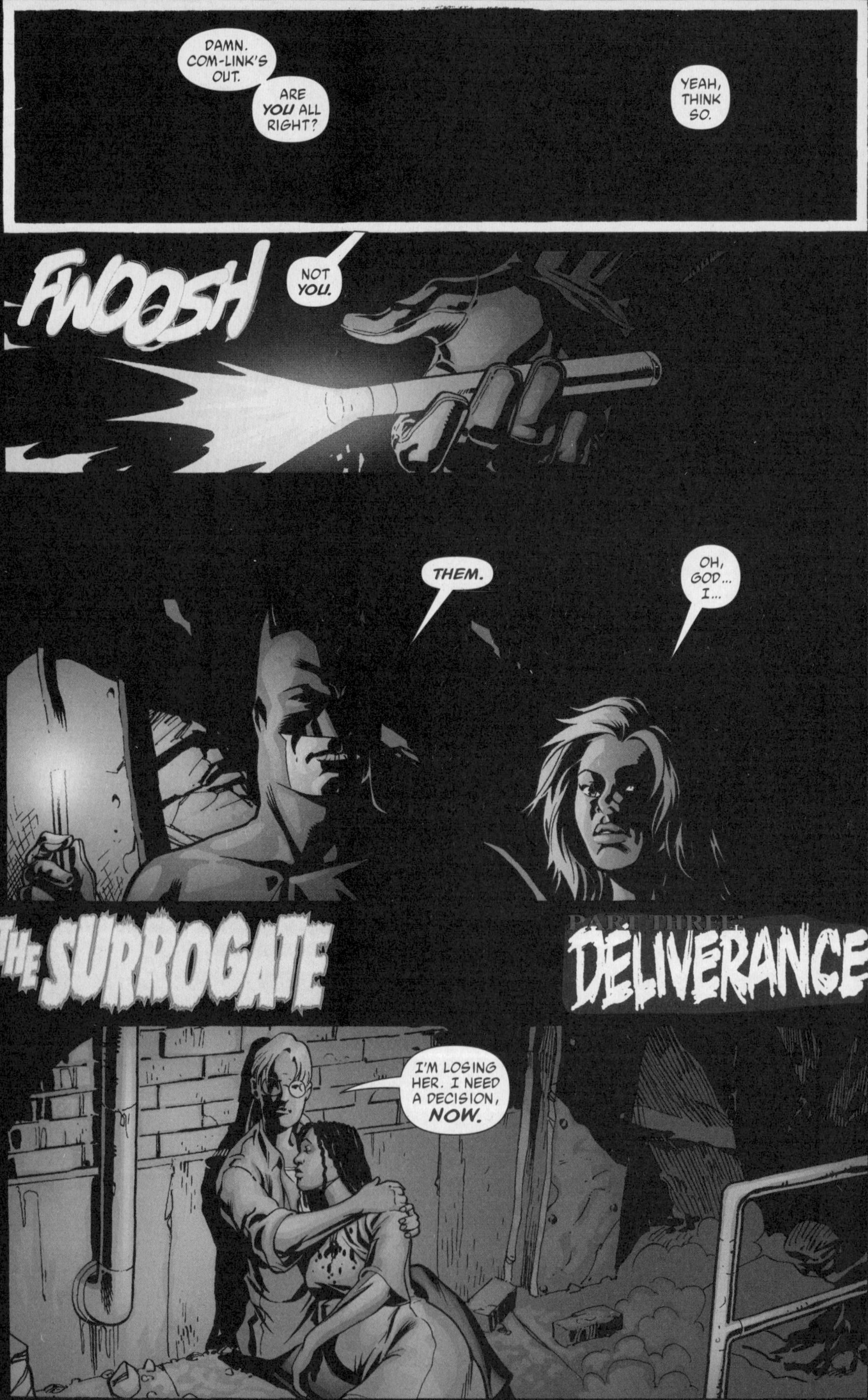
DAMN. COM-LINK'S OUT.
ARE YOU ALL RIGHT?
YEAH, THINK SO.
FWOOSH
NOT YOU.
THEM.
OH, GOD... I...
THE SURROGATE
PART THREE: DELIVERANCE
I'M LOSING HER. I NEED A DECISION, NOW.

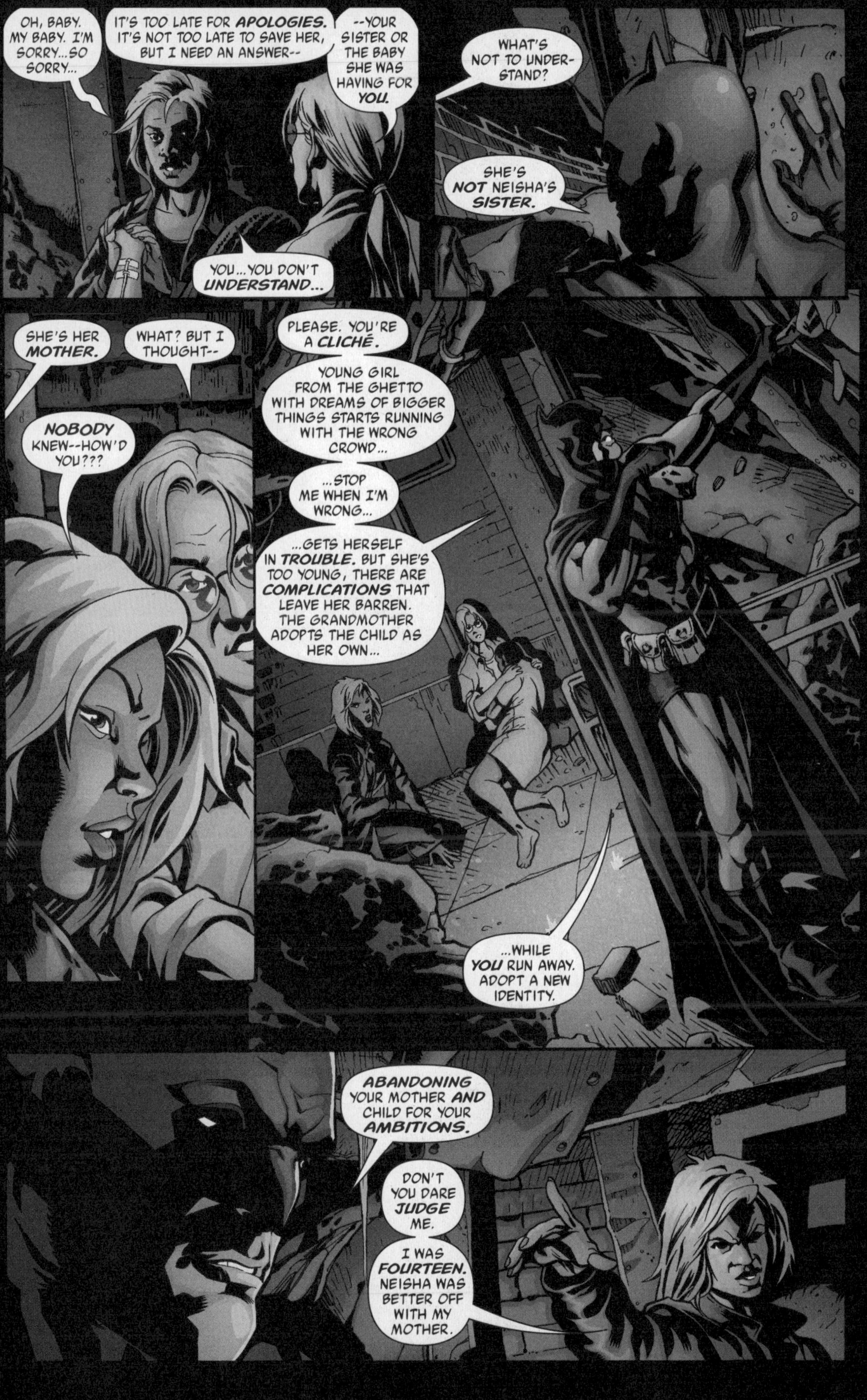

OH, BABY. MY BABY. I'M SORRY...SO SORRY...
IT'S TOO LATE FOR APOLOGIES. IT'S NOT TOO LATE TO SAVE HER, BUT I NEED AN ANSWER--
--YOUR SISTER OR THE BABY SHE WAS HAVING FOR YOU.
YOU...YOU DON'T UNDERSTAND...
WHAT'S NOT TO UNDERSTAND?
SHE'S NOT NEISHA'S SISTER.
SHE'S HER MOTHER.
WHAT? BUT I THOUGHT--
NOBODY KNEW--HOW'D YOU???
PLEASE. YOU'RE A CLICHÉ.
YOUNG GIRL FROM THE GHETTO WITH DREAMS OF BIGGER THINGS STARTS RUNNING WITH THE WRONG CROWD...
...STOP ME WHEN I'M WRONG...
...GETS HERSELF IN TROUBLE. BUT SHE'S TOO YOUNG, THERE ARE COMPLICATIONS THAT LEAVE HER BARREN. THE GRANDMOTHER ADOPTS THE CHILD AS HER OWN...
...WHILE YOU RUN AWAY. ADOPT A NEW IDENTITY.
ABANDONING YOUR MOTHER AND CHILD FOR YOUR AMBITIONS.
DON'T YOU DARE JUDGE ME.
I WAS FOURTEEN. NEISHA WAS BETTER OFF WITH MY MOTHER.

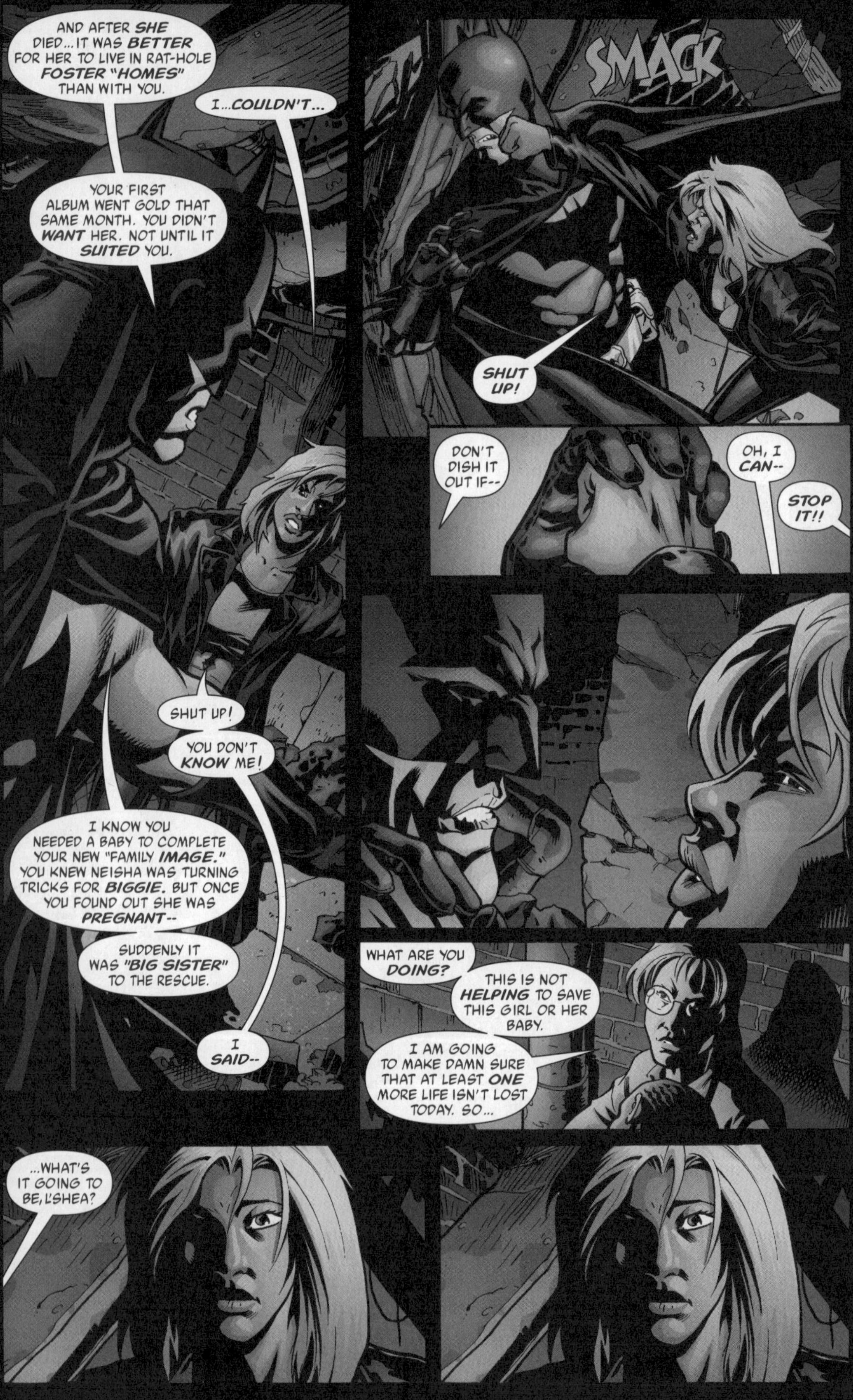
AND AFTER SHE DIED... IT WAS BETTER FOR HER TO LIVE IN RAT-HOLE FOSTER "HOMES" THAN WITH YOU.
I...COULDN'T...
YOUR FIRST ALBUM WENT GOLD THAT SAME MONTH. YOU DIDN'T WANT HER. NOT UNTIL IT SUITED YOU.
SHUT UP!
YOU DON'T KNOW ME!
I KNOW YOU NEEDED A BABY TO COMPLETE YOUR NEW "FAMILY IMAGE." YOU KNEW NEISHA WAS TURNING TRICKS FOR BIGGIE. BUT ONCE YOU FOUND OUT SHE WAS PREGNANT--
SUDDENLY IT WAS "BIG SISTER" TO THE RESCUE.
I SAID--
SMACK
SHUT UP!
DON'T DISH IT OUT IF--
OH, I CAN--
STOP IT!!
WHAT ARE YOU DOING?
THIS IS NOT HELPING TO SAVE THIS GIRL OR HER BABY.
I AM GOING TO MAKE DAMN SURE THAT AT LEAST ONE MORE LIFE ISN'T LOST TODAY. SO...
...WHAT'S IT GOING TO BE, L'SHEA?

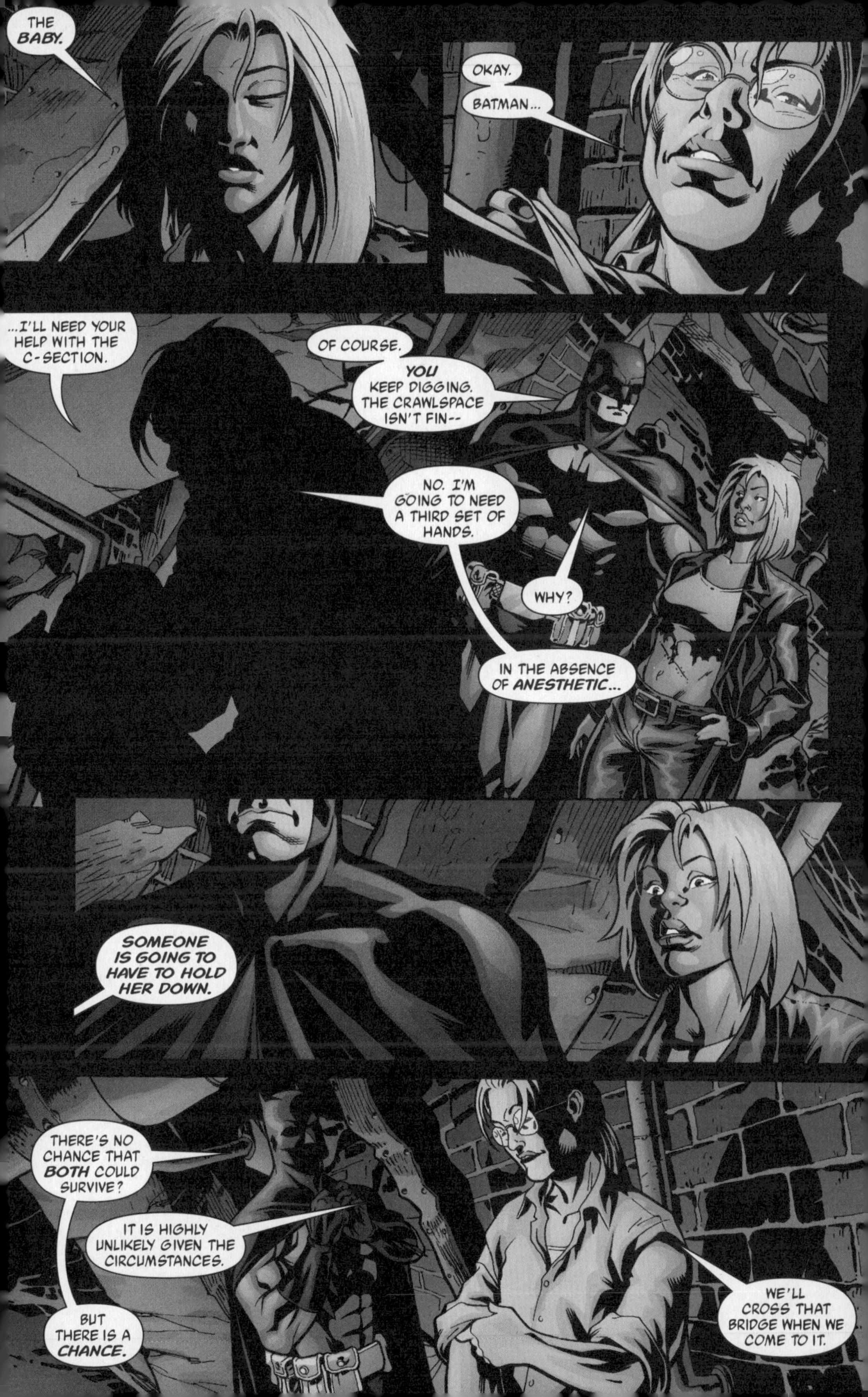
THE BABY.
OKAY.
BATMAN...
...I'LL NEED YOUR HELP WITH THE C-SECTION.
OF COURSE.
YOU KEEP DIGGING. THE CRAWLSPACE ISN'T FIN--
NO. I'M GOING TO NEED A THIRD SET OF HANDS.
WHY?
IN THE ABSENCE OF ANESTHETIC...
SOMEONE IS GOING TO HAVE TO HOLD HER DOWN.
THERE'S NO CHANCE THAT BOTH COULD SURVIVE?
IT IS HIGHLY UNLIKELY GIVEN THE CIRCUMSTANCES.
BUT THERE IS A CHANCE.
WE'LL CROSS THAT BRIDGE WHEN WE COME TO IT.

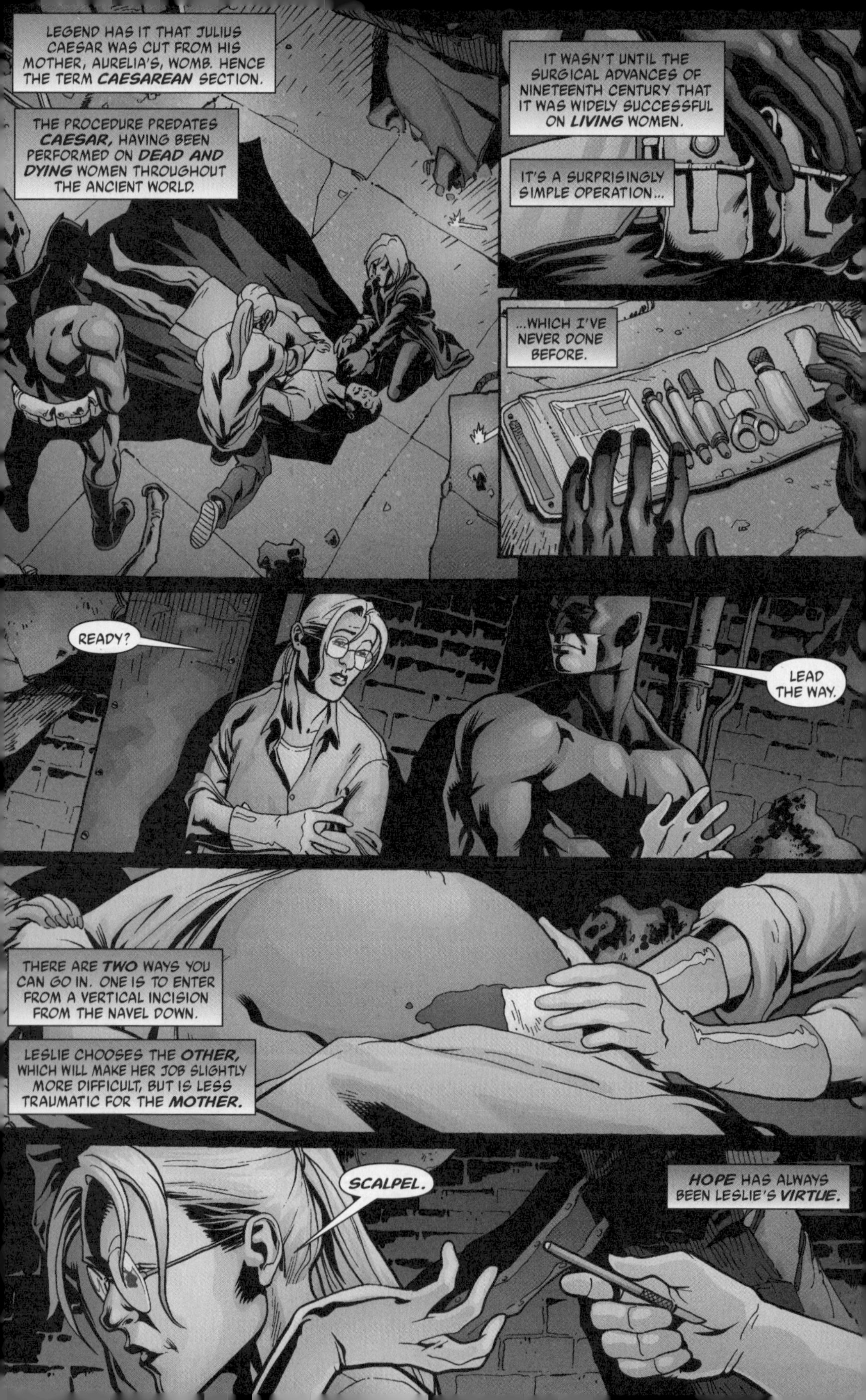
LEGEND HAS IT THAT JULIUS CAESAR WAS CUT FROM HIS MOTHER, AURELIA'S, WOMB. HENCE THE TERM CAESAREAN SECTION.
THE PROCEDURE PREDATES CAESAR, HAVING BEEN PERFORMED ON DEAD AND DYING WOMEN THROUGHOUT THE ANCIENT WORLD.
IT WASN'T UNTIL THE SURGICAL ADVANCES OF NINETEENTH CENTURY THAT IT WAS WIDELY SUCCESSFUL ON LIVING WOMEN.
IT'S A SURPRISINGLY SIMPLE OPERATION...
...WHICH I'VE NEVER DONE BEFORE.
READY?
LEAD THE WAY.
THERE ARE TWO WAYS YOU CAN GO IN. ONE IS TO ENTER FROM A VERTICAL INCISION FROM THE NAVEL DOWN.
LESLIE CHOOSES THE OTHER, WHICH WILL MAKE HER JOB SLIGHTLY MORE DIFFICULT, BUT IS LESS TRAUMATIC FOR THE MOTHER.
SCALPEL.
HOPE HAS ALWAYS BEEN LESLIE'S VIRTUE.

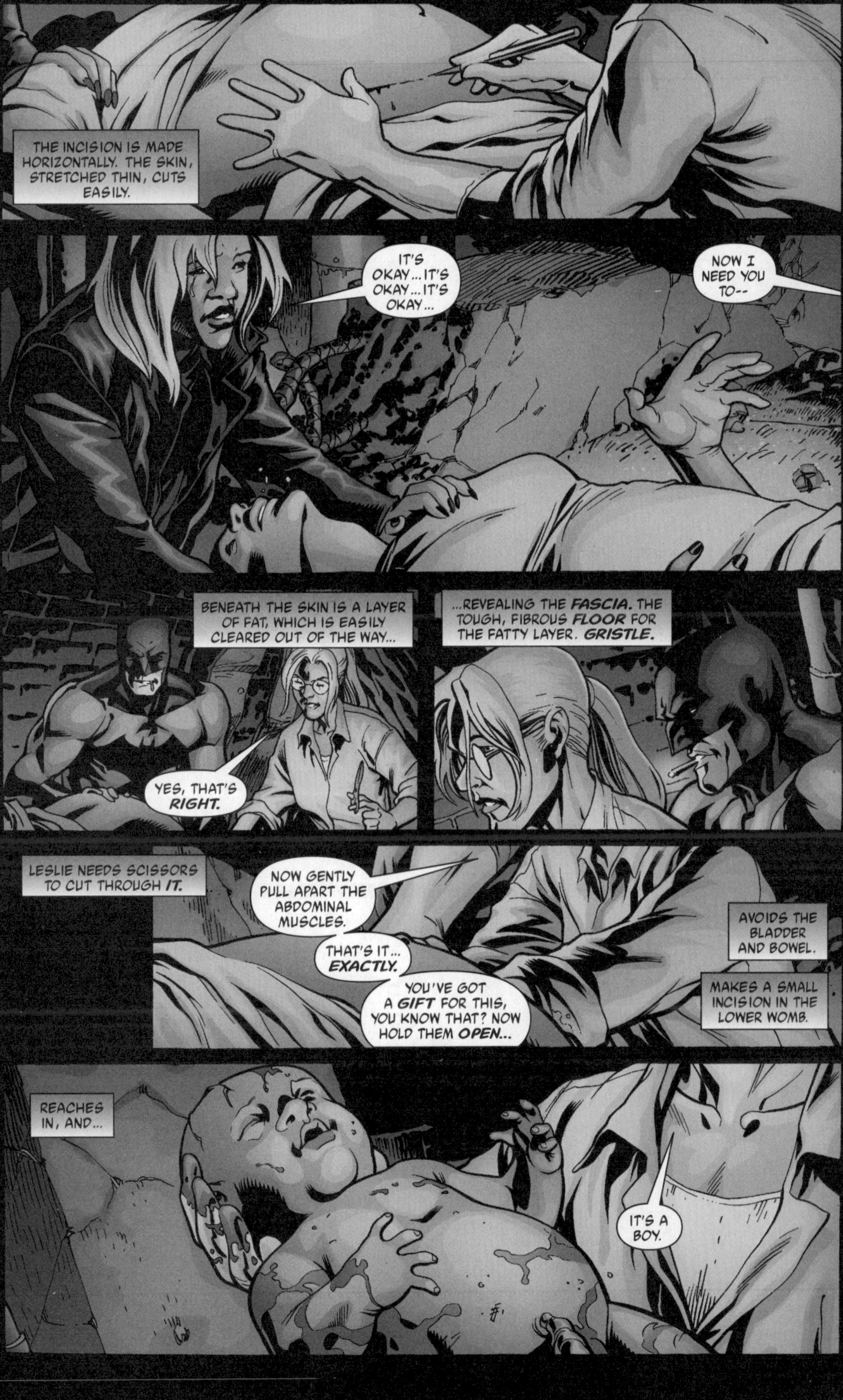
THE INCISION IS MADE HORIZONTALLY. THE SKIN, STRETCHED THIN, CUTS EASILY.
IT'S OKAY... IT'S OKAY... IT'S OKAY...
NOW I NEED YOU TO--
BENEATH THE SKIN IS A LAYER OF FAT, WHICH IS EASILY CLEARED OUT OF THE WAY...
YES, THAT'S RIGHT.
...REVEALING THE FASCIA. THE TOUGH, FIBROUS FLOOR FOR THE FATTY LAYER. GRISTLE.
LESLIE NEEDS SCISSORS TO CUT THROUGH IT.
NOW GENTLY PULL APART THE ABDOMINAL MUSCLES.
THAT'S IT... EXACTLY.
YOU'VE GOT A GIFT FOR THIS, YOU KNOW THAT? NOW HOLD THEM OPEN...
AVOIDS THE BLADDER AND BOWEL.
MAKES A SMALL INCISION IN THE LOWER WOMB.
REACHES IN, AND...
IT'S A BOY.

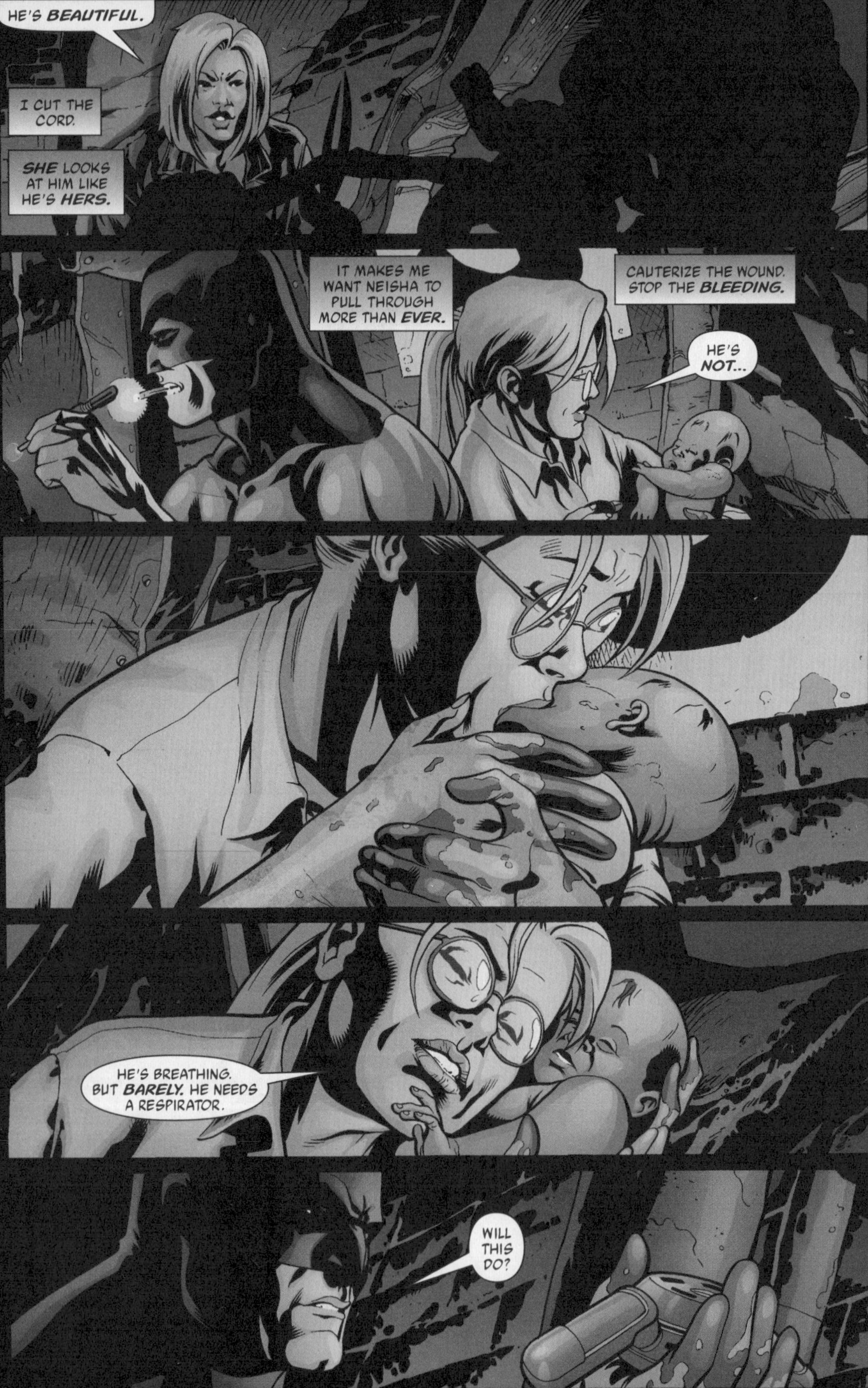
HE'S BEAUTIFUL.
I CUT THE CORD.
SHE LOOKS AT HIM LIKE HE'S HERS.
IT MAKES ME WANT NEISHA TO PULL THROUGH MORE THAN EVER.
CAUTERIZE THE WOUND. STOP THE BLEEDING.
HE'S NOT...
HE'S BREATHING. BUT BARELY. HE NEEDS A RESPIRATOR.
WILL THIS DO?

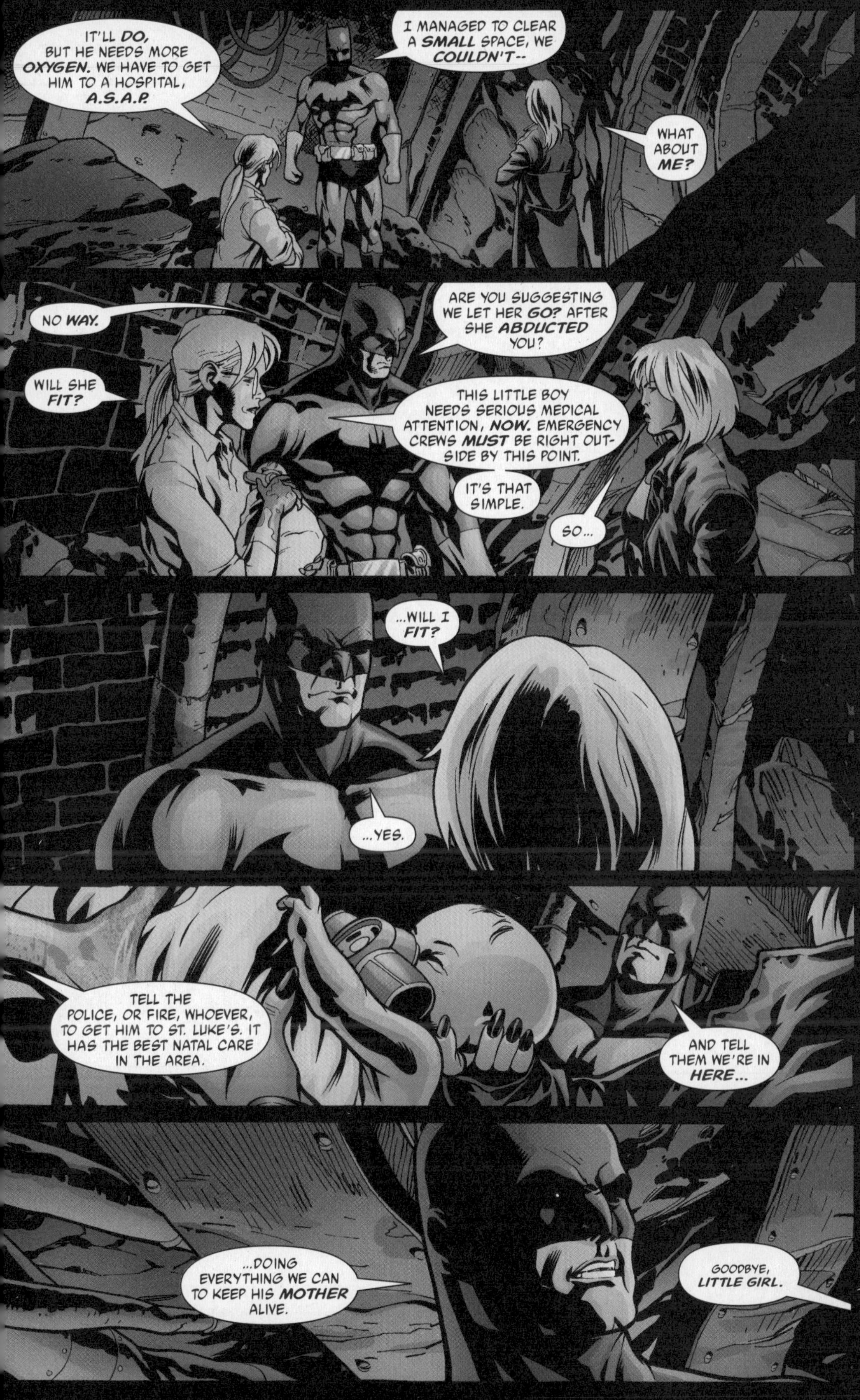
IT'LL DO, BUT HE NEEDS MORE OXYGEN. WE HAVE TO GET HIM TO A HOSPITAL, A.S.A.P.
I MANAGED TO CLEAR A SMALL SPACE, WE COULDN'T--
WHAT ABOUT ME?
NO WAY.
ARE YOU SUGGESTING WE LET HER GO? AFTER SHE ABDUCTED YOU?
WILL SHE FIT?
THIS LITTLE BOY NEEDS SERIOUS MEDICAL ATTENTION, NOW. EMERGENCY CREWS MUST BE RIGHT OUTSIDE BY THIS POINT.
IT'S THAT SIMPLE.
SO...
...WILL I FIT?
...YES.
TELL THE POLICE, OR FIRE, WHOEVER, TO GET HIM TO ST. LUKE'S. IT HAS THE BEST NATAL CARE IN THE AREA.
AND TELL THEM WE'RE IN HERE...
...DOING EVERYTHING WE CAN TO KEEP HIS MOTHER ALIVE.
GOODBYE, LITTLE GIRL.

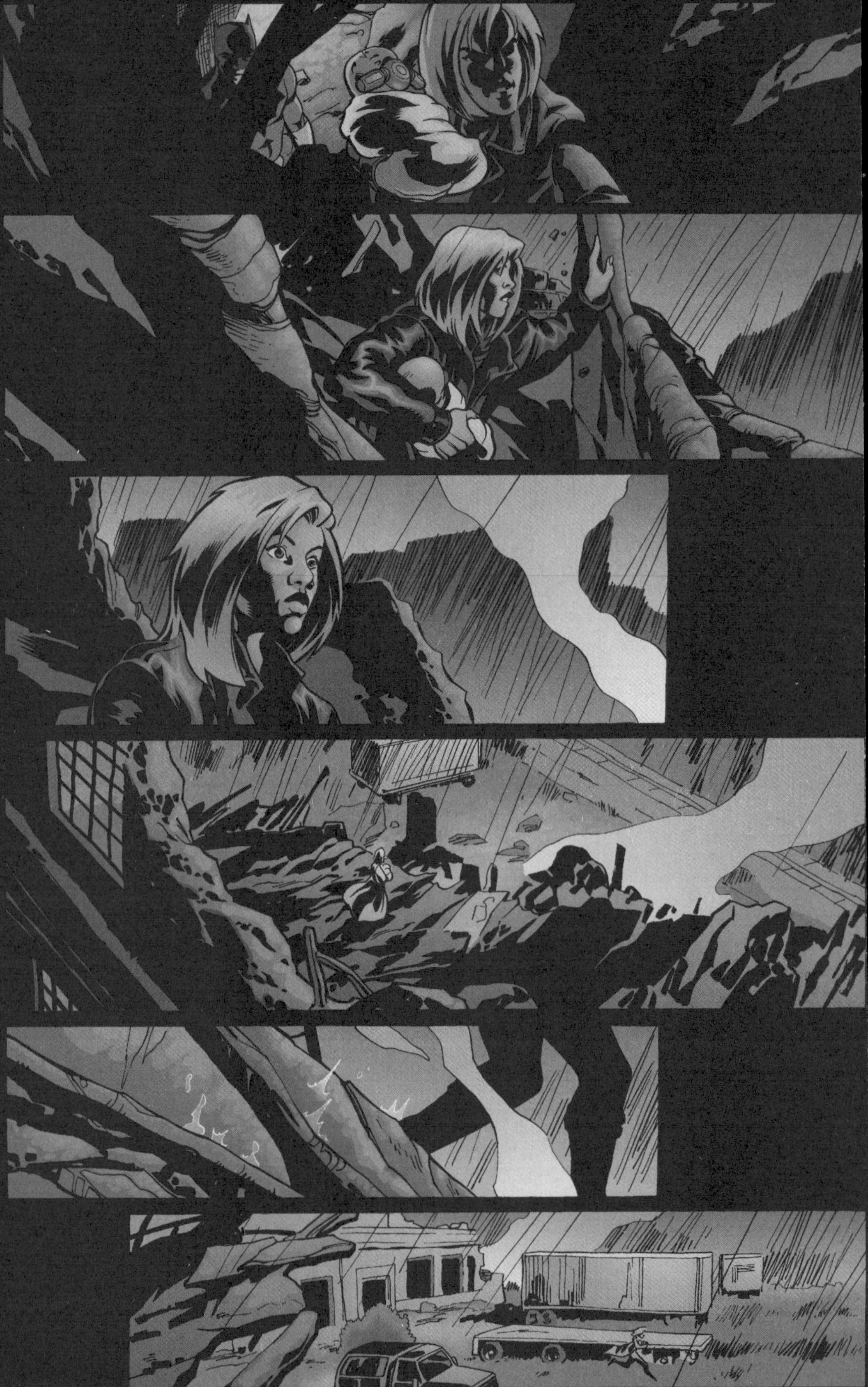

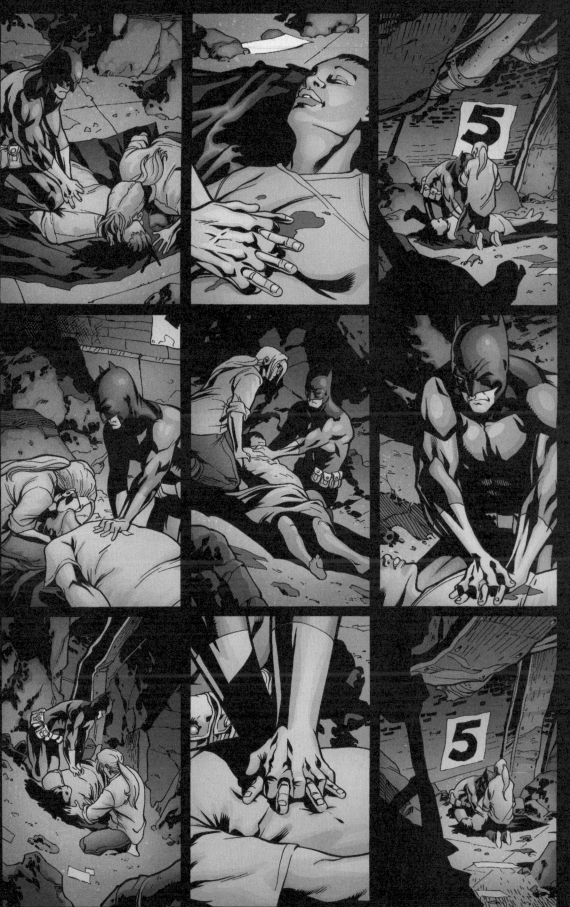

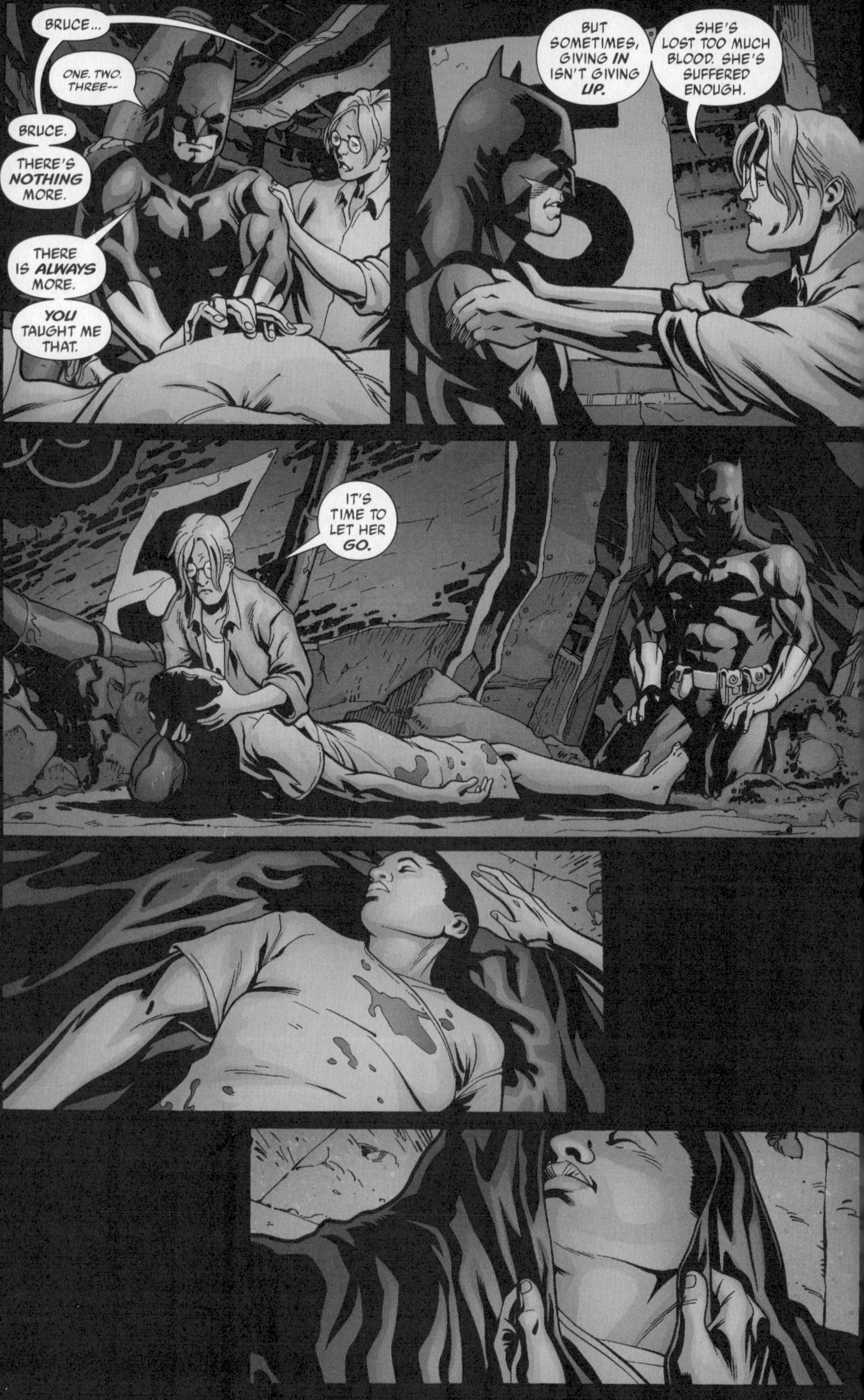
BRUCE...
ONE. TWO. THREE--
BRUCE.
THERE'S NOTHING MORE.
THERE IS ALWAYS MORE.
YOU TAUGHT ME THAT.
SHE'S LOST TOO MUCH BLOOD. SHE'S SUFFERED ENOUGH.
BUT SOMETIMES, GIVING IN ISN'T GIVING UP.
IT'S TIME TO LET HER GO.

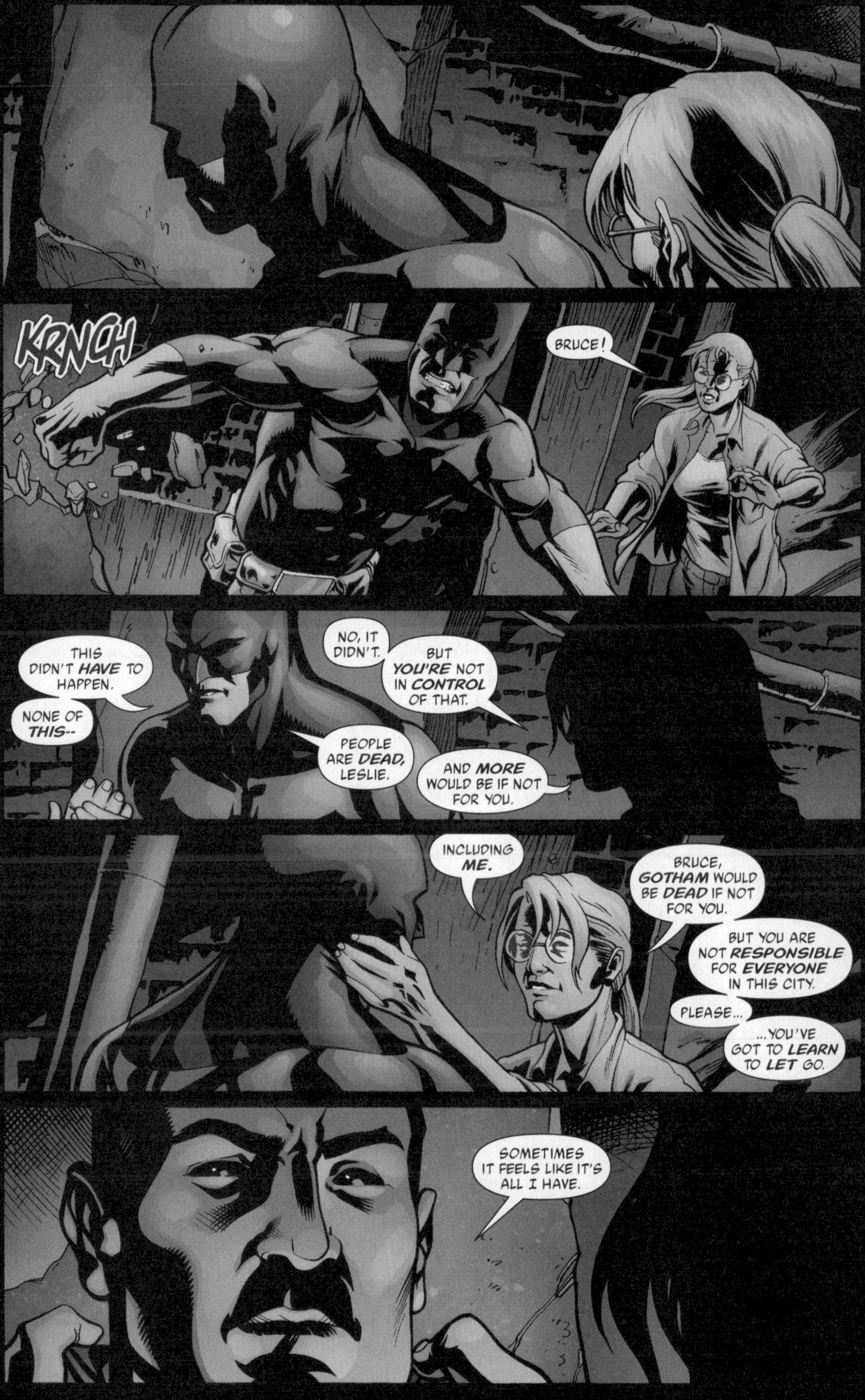
KRNCH
BRUCE!
THIS DIDN'T HAVE TO HAPPEN.
NONE OF THIS--
NO, IT DIDN'T.
BUT YOU'RE NOT IN CONTROL OF THAT.
PEOPLE ARE DEAD, LESLIE.
AND MORE WOULD BE IF NOT FOR YOU.
INCLUDING ME.
BRUCE, GOTHAM WOULD BE DEAD IF NOT FOR YOU.
BUT YOU ARE NOT RESPONSIBLE FOR EVERYONE IN THIS CITY.
PLEASE...
...YOU'VE GOT TO LEARN TO LET GO.
SOMETIMES IT FEELS LIKE IT'S ALL I HAVE.

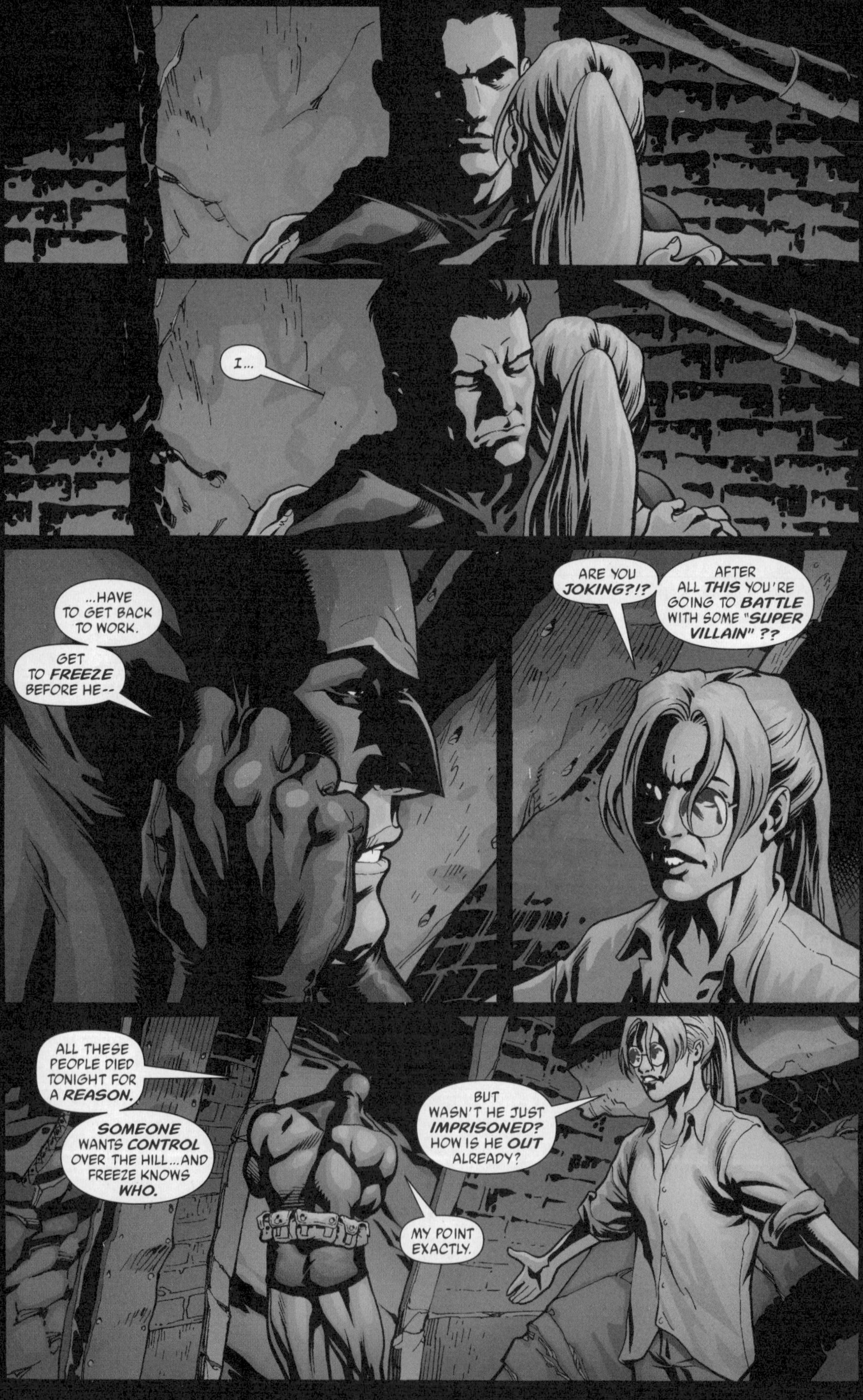
I...
...HAVE TO GET BACK TO WORK.
GET TO FREEZE BEFORE HE--
ARE YOU JOKING?!?
AFTER ALL THIS YOU'RE GOING TO BATTLE WITH SOME "SUPER VILLAIN"??
ALL THESE PEOPLE DIED TONIGHT FOR A REASON.
SOMEONE WANTS CONTROL OVER THE HILL...AND FREEZE KNOWS WHO.
BUT WASN'T HE JUST IMPRISONED? HOW IS HE OUT ALREADY?
MY POINT EXACTLY.

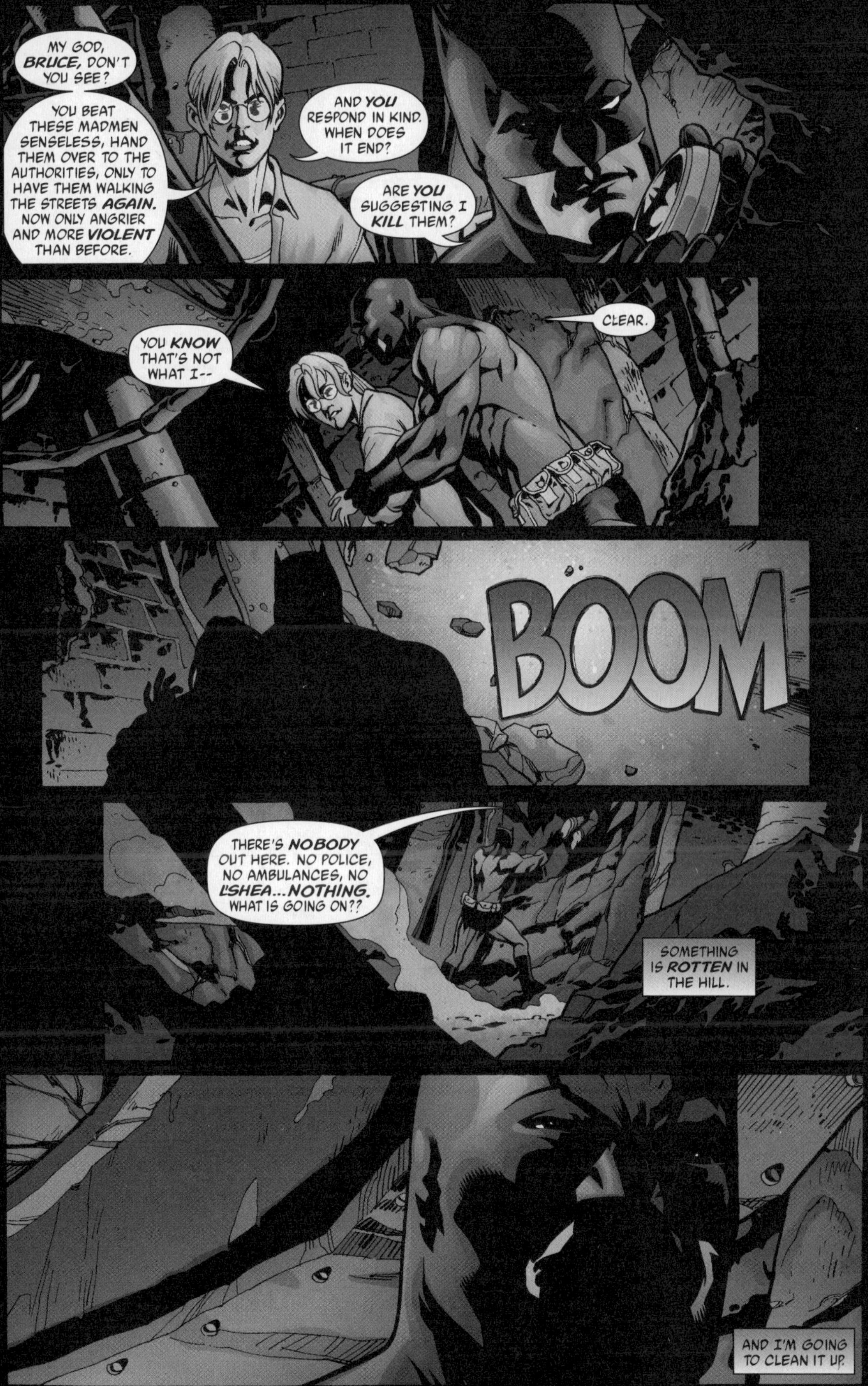
MY GOD, BRUCE, DON'T YOU SEE?
YOU BEAT THESE MADMEN SENSELESS, HAND THEM OVER TO THE AUTHORITIES, ONLY TO HAVE THEM WALKING THE STREETS AGAIN. NOW ONLY ANGRIER AND MORE VIOLENT THAN BEFORE.
AND YOU RESPOND IN KIND. WHEN DOES IT END?
ARE YOU SUGGESTING I KILL THEM?
YOU KNOW THAT'S NOT WHAT I--
CLEAR.
BOOM
THERE'S NOBODY OUT HERE. NO POLICE, NO AMBULANCES, NO L'SHEA...NOTHING. WHAT IS GOING ON??
SOMETHING IS ROTTEN IN THE HILL.
AND I'M GOING TO CLEAN IT UP.

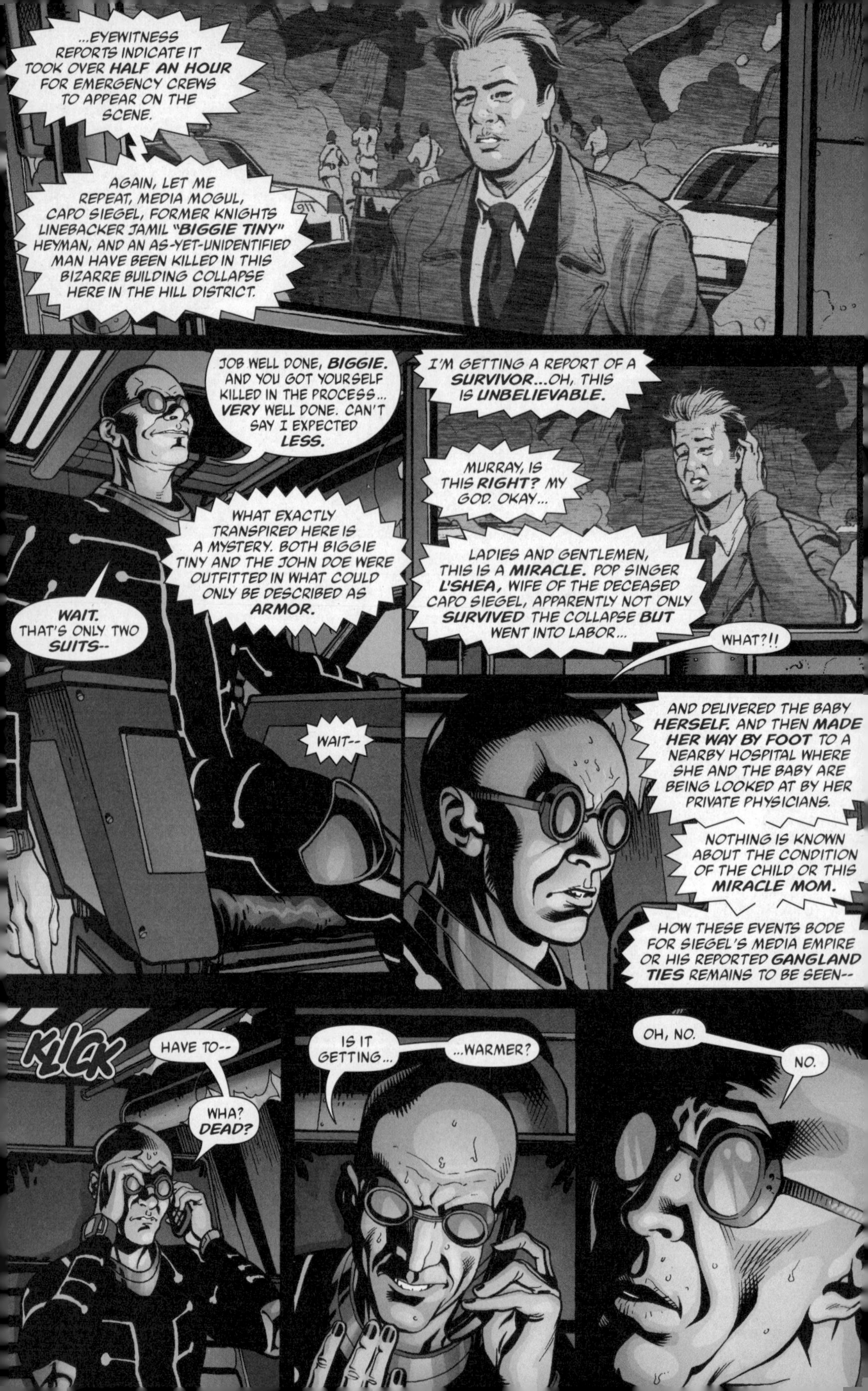
...EYEWITNESS REPORTS INDICATE IT TOOK OVER HALF AN HOUR FOR EMERGENCY CREWS TO APPEAR ON THE SCENE.
AGAIN, LET ME REPEAT, MEDIA MOGUL, CAPO SIEGEL, FORMER KNIGHTS LINEBACKER JAMIL "BIGGIE TINY" HEYMAN, AND AN AS-YET-UNIDENTIFIED MAN HAVE BEEN KILLED IN THIS BIZARRE BUILDING COLLAPSE HERE IN THE HILL DISTRICT.
JOB WELL DONE, BIGGIE. AND YOU GOT YOURSELF KILLED IN THE PROCESS... VERY WELL DONE. CAN'T SAY I EXPECTED LESS.
WHAT EXACTLY TRANSPIRED HERE IS A MYSTERY. BOTH BIGGIE TINY AND THE JOHN DOE WERE OUTFITTED IN WHAT COULD ONLY BE DESCRIBED AS ARMOR.
WAIT. THAT'S ONLY TWO SUITS--
I'M GETTING A REPORT OF A SURVIVOR...OH, THIS IS UNBELIEVABLE.
MURRAY, IS THIS RIGHT? MY GOD. OKAY...
LADIES AND GENTLEMEN, THIS IS A MIRACLE. POP SINGER L'SHEA, WIFE OF THE DECEASED CAPO SIEGEL, APPARENTLY NOT ONLY SURVIVED THE COLLAPSE BUT WENT INTO LABOR...
WHAT?!!
WAIT--
AND DELIVERED THE BABY HERSELF. AND THEN MADE HER WAY BY FOOT TO A NEARBY HOSPITAL WHERE SHE AND THE BABY ARE BEING LOOKED AT BY HER PRIVATE PHYSICIANS.
NOTHING IS KNOWN ABOUT THE CONDITION OF THE CHILD OR THIS MIRACLE MOM.
HOW THESE EVENTS BODE FOR SIEGEL'S MEDIA EMPIRE OR HIS REPORTED GANGLAND TIES REMAINS TO BE SEEN--
KLICK
HAVE TO--
WHA? DEAD?
IS IT GETTING...
...WARMER?
OH, NO.
NO.

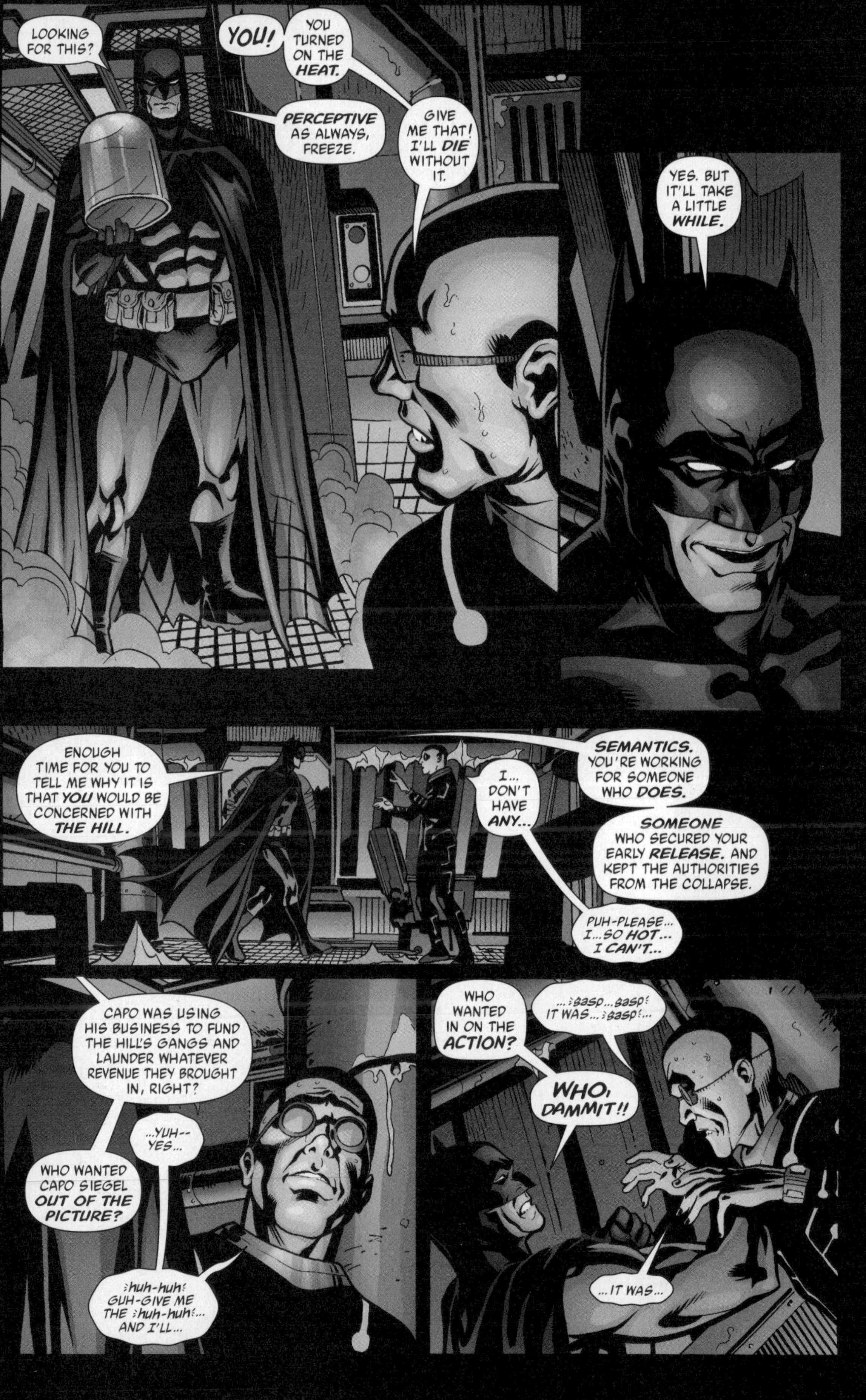
LOOKING FOR THIS?
YOU!
YOU TURNED ON THE HEAT.
PERCEPTIVE AS ALWAYS, FREEZE.
GIVE ME THAT! I'LL DIE WITHOUT IT.
YES. BUT IT'LL TAKE A LITTLE WHILE.
ENOUGH TIME FOR YOU TO TELL ME WHY IT IS THAT YOU WOULD BE CONCERNED WITH THE HILL.
I... DON'T HAVE ANY...
SEMANTICS. YOU'RE WORKING FOR SOMEONE WHO DOES.
SOMEONE WHO SECURED YOUR EARLY RELEASE. AND KEPT THE AUTHORITIES FROM THE COLLAPSE.
PUH-PLEASE... I...SO HOT... I CAN'T...
CAPO WAS USING HIS BUSINESS TO FUND THE HILL'S GANGS AND LAUNDER WHATEVER REVENUE THEY BROUGHT IN, RIGHT?
...YUH--YES...
WHO WANTED CAPO SIEGEL OUT OF THE PICTURE?
huh-huh GUH-GIVE ME THE huh-huh... AND I'LL...
WHO WANTED IN ON THE ACTION?
...gasp...gasp IT WAS...gasp...
WHO, DAMMIT!!
...IT WAS...

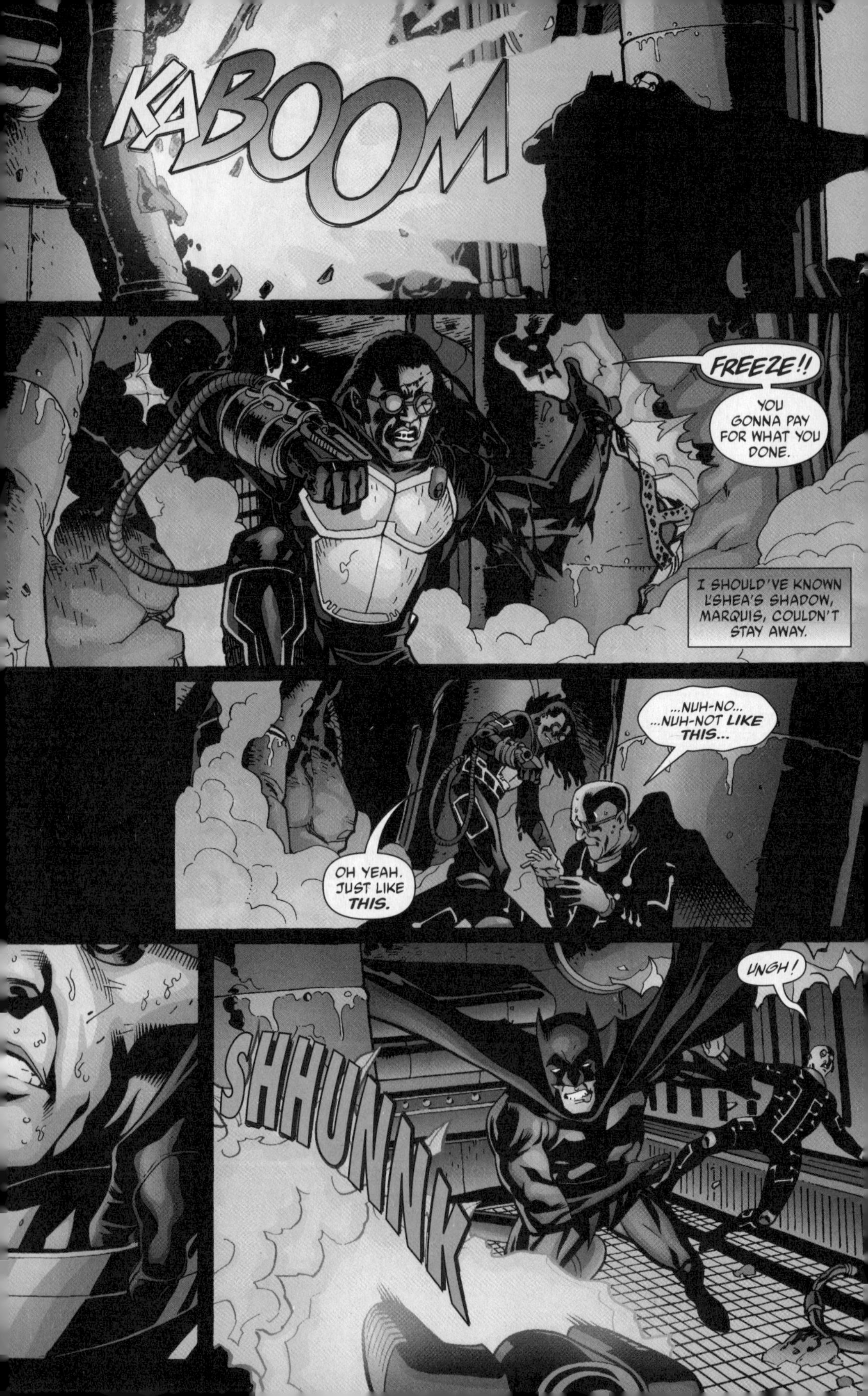
KABOOM
FREEZE!!
YOU GONNA PAY FOR WHAT YOU DONE.
I SHOULD'VE KNOWN L'SHEA'S SHADOW, MARQUIS, COULDN'T STAY AWAY.
...NUH-NO... ...NUH-NOT LIKE THIS...
OH YEAH. JUST LIKE THIS.
SHHUNNNK
UNGH!

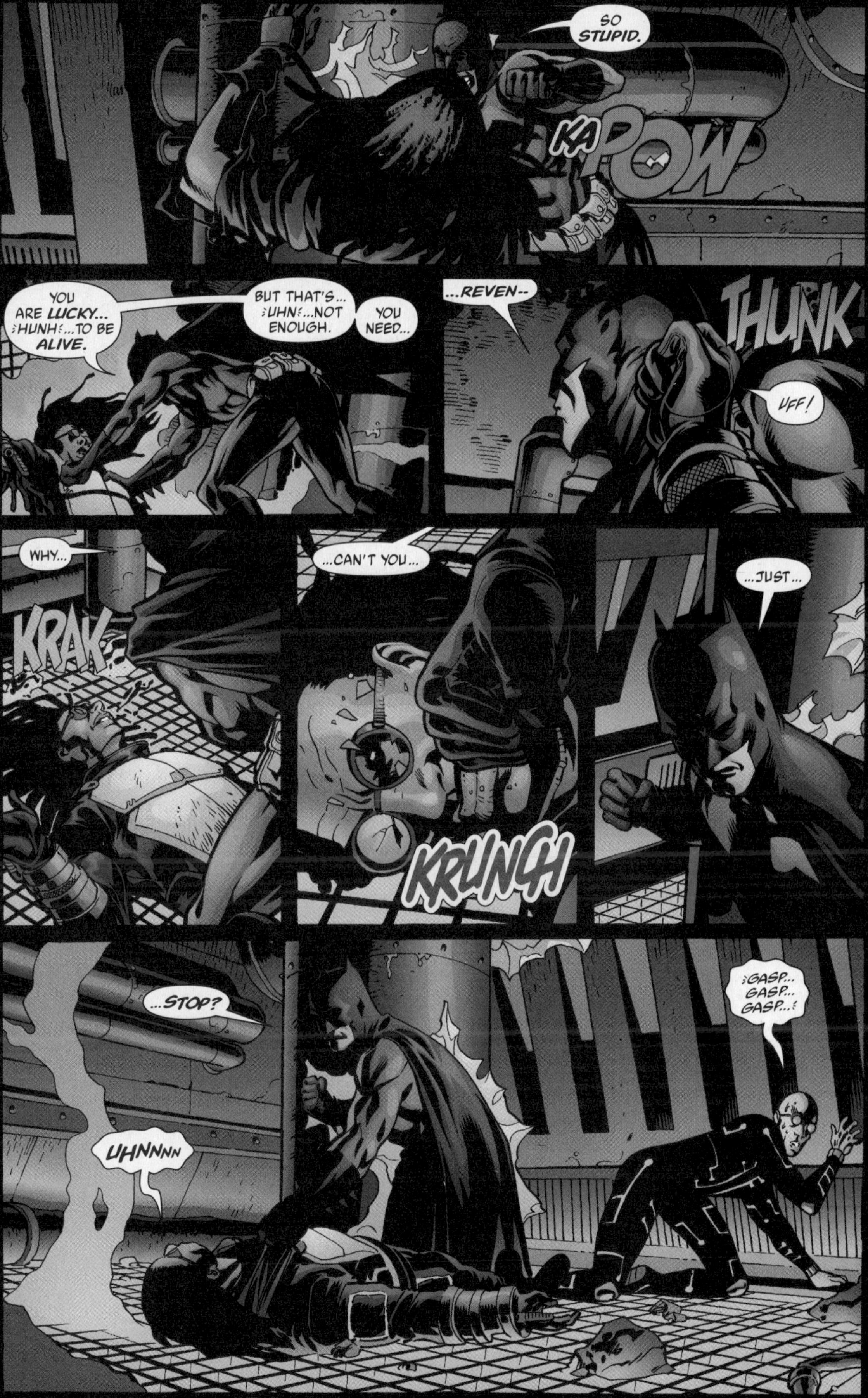
SO STUPID.
KA POW
YOU ARE LUCKY... HUNH ...TO BE ALIVE.
BUT THAT'S... UHN ...NOT ENOUGH.
YOU NEED...
...REVEN--
THUNK
UFF!
WHY...
KRAK
...CAN'T YOU...
KRUNCH
...JUST...
...STOP?
UHNNNN
GASP... GASP... GASP...

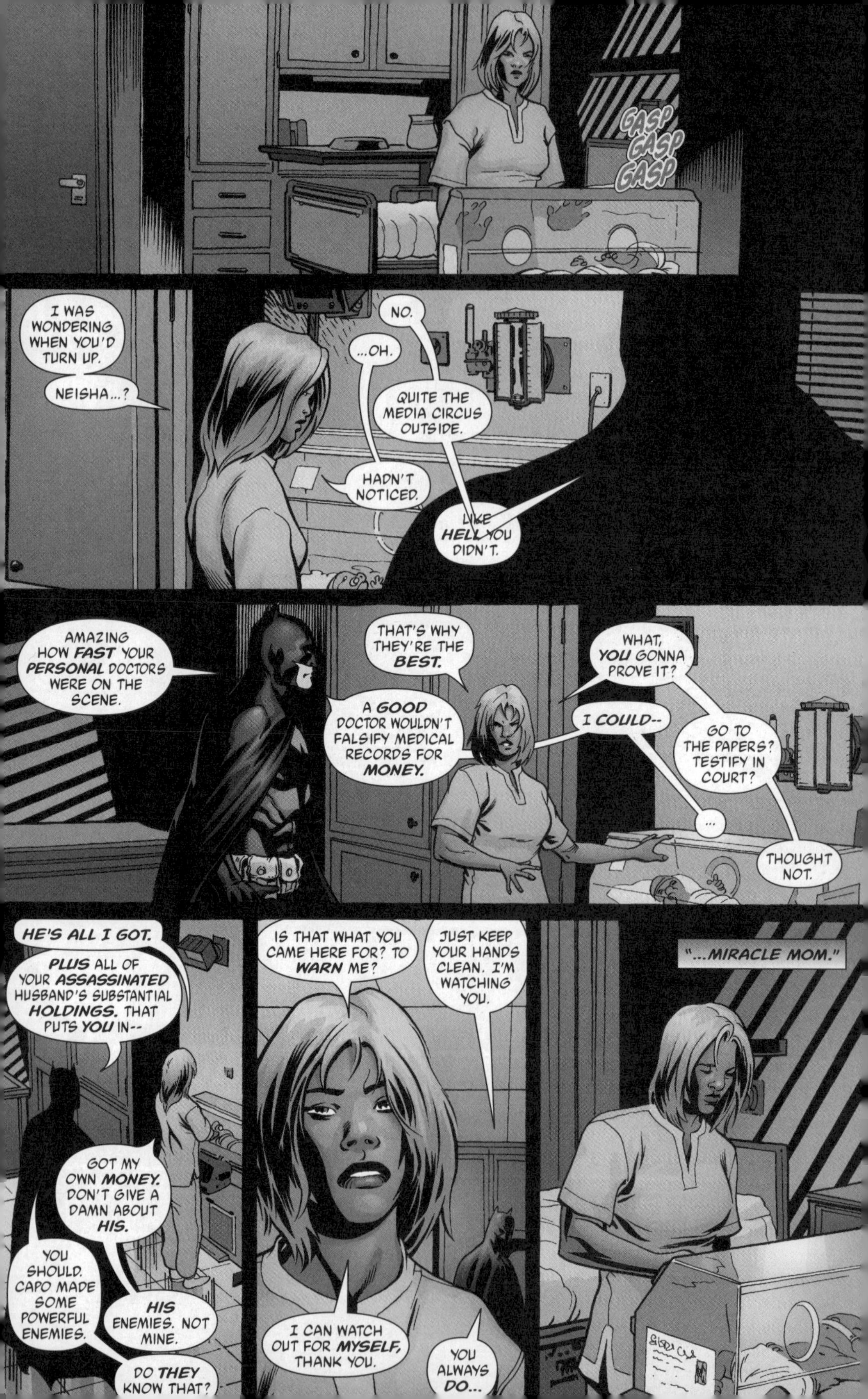
GASP GASP GASP
I WAS WONDERING WHEN YOU'D TURN UP.
NEISHA...?
NO.
...OH.
QUITE THE MEDIA CIRCUS OUTSIDE.
HADN'T NOTICED.
LIKE HELL YOU DIDN'T.
AMAZING HOW FAST YOUR PERSONAL DOCTORS WERE ON THE SCENE.
THAT'S WHY THEY'RE THE BEST.
A GOOD DOCTOR WOULDN'T FALSIFY MEDICAL RECORDS FOR MONEY.
WHAT, YOU GONNA PROVE IT?
I COULD--
GO TO THE PAPERS? TESTIFY IN COURT?
...
THOUGHT NOT.
HE'S ALL I GOT.
PLUS ALL OF YOUR ASSASSINATED HUSBAND'S SUBSTANTIAL HOLDINGS. THAT PUTS YOU IN--
GOT MY OWN MONEY. DON'T GIVE A DAMN ABOUT HIS.
YOU SHOULD. CAPO MADE SOME POWERFUL ENEMIES.
HIS ENEMIES. NOT MINE.
DO THEY KNOW THAT?
IS THAT WHAT YOU CAME HERE FOR? TO WARN ME?
JUST KEEP YOUR HANDS CLEAN. I'M WATCHING YOU.
I CAN WATCH OUT FOR MYSELF, THANK YOU.
YOU ALWAYS DO...
"...MIRACLE MOM."

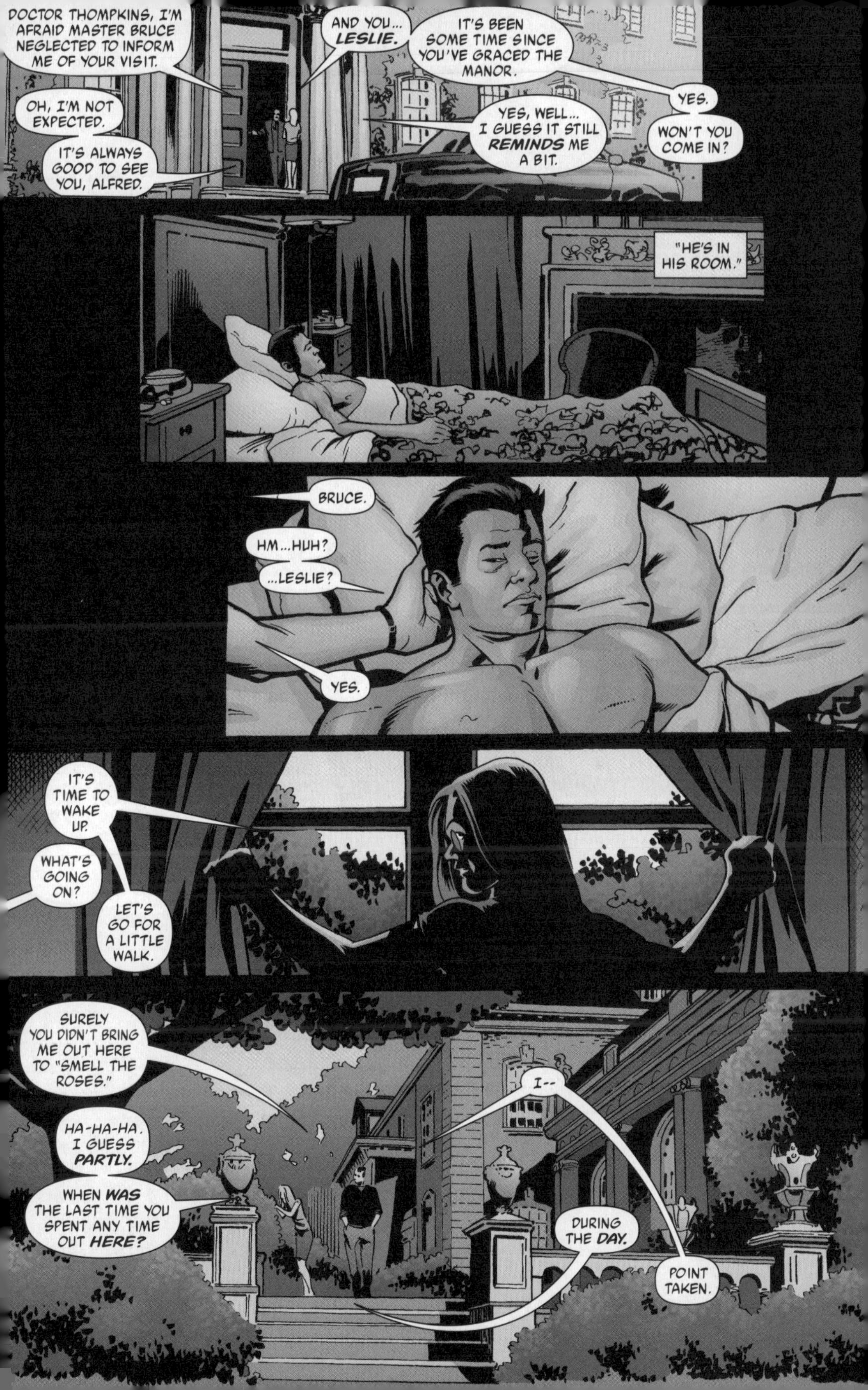
DOCTOR THOMPKINS, I'M AFRAID MASTER BRUCE NEGLECTED TO INFORM ME OF YOUR VISIT.
OH, I'M NOT EXPECTED.
IT'S ALWAYS GOOD TO SEE YOU, ALFRED.
AND YOU... LESLIE.
IT'S BEEN SOME TIME SINCE YOU'VE GRACED THE MANOR.
YES, WELL... I GUESS IT STILL REMINDS ME A BIT.
YES.
WON'T YOU COME IN?
"HE'S IN HIS ROOM."
BRUCE.
HM...HUH?
...LESLIE?
YES.
IT'S TIME TO WAKE UP.
WHAT'S GOING ON?
LET'S GO FOR A LITTLE WALK.
SURELY YOU DIDN'T BRING ME OUT HERE TO "SMELL THE ROSES."
HA-HA-HA. I GUESS PARTLY.
WHEN WAS THE LAST TIME YOU SPENT ANY TIME OUT HERE?
I--
DURING THE DAY.
POINT TAKEN.

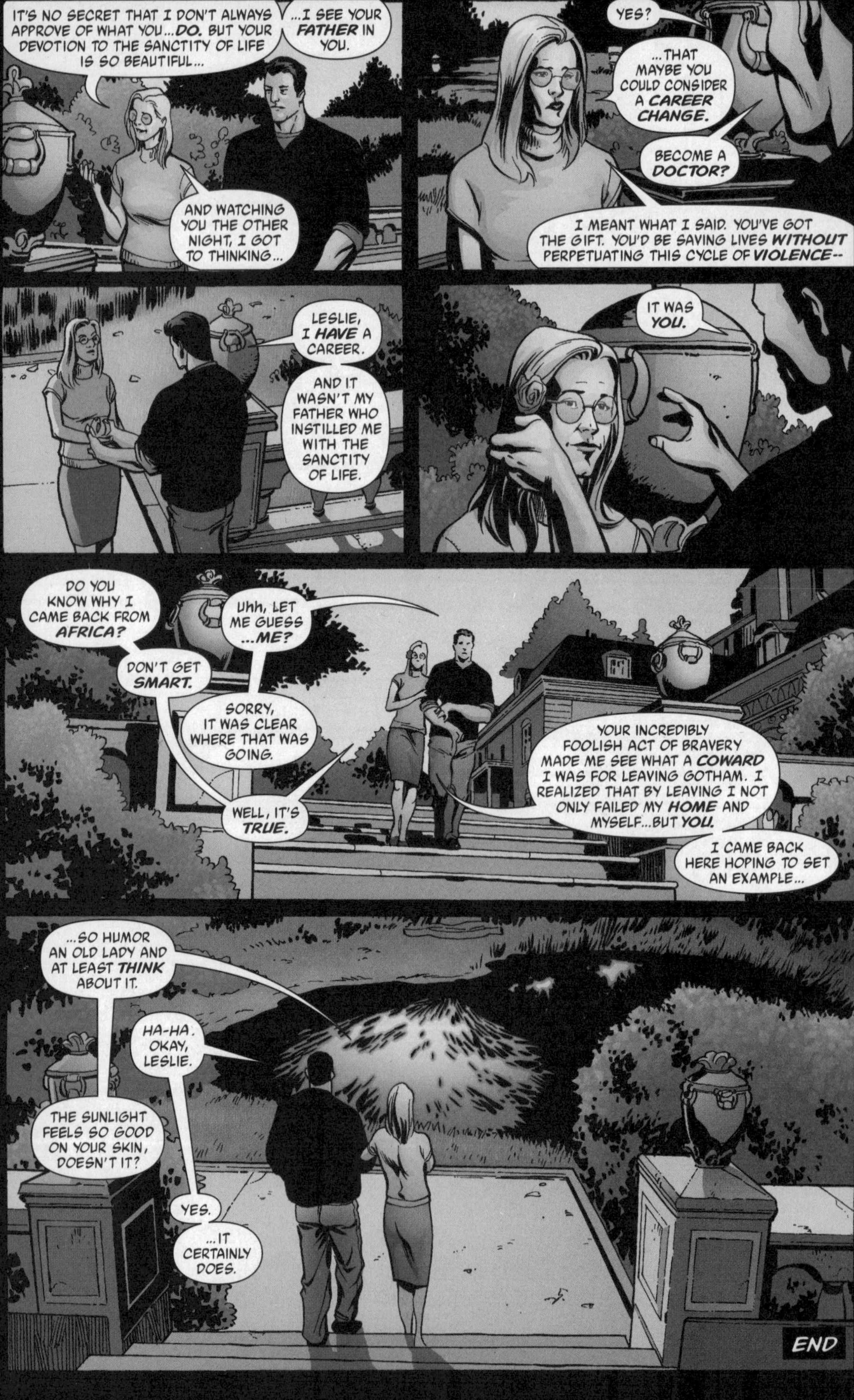
IT'S NO SECRET THAT I DON'T ALWAYS APPROVE OF WHAT YOU...DO. BUT YOUR DEVOTION TO THE SANCTITY OF LIFE IS SO BEAUTIFUL...
...I SEE YOUR FATHER IN YOU.
AND WATCHING YOU THE OTHER NIGHT, I GOT TO THINKING...
YES?
...THAT MAYBE YOU COULD CONSIDER A CAREER CHANGE.
BECOME A DOCTOR?
I MEANT WHAT I SAID. YOU'VE GOT THE GIFT. YOU'D BE SAVING LIVES WITHOUT PERPETUATING THIS CYCLE OF VIOLENCE--
LESLIE, I HAVE A CAREER.
AND IT WASN'T MY FATHER WHO INSTILLED ME WITH THE SANCTITY OF LIFE.
IT WAS YOU.
DO YOU KNOW WHY I CAME BACK FROM AFRICA?
UHH, LET ME GUESS ...ME?
DON'T GET SMART.
SORRY, IT WAS CLEAR WHERE THAT WAS GOING.
WELL, IT'S TRUE.
YOUR INCREDIBLY FOOLISH ACT OF BRAVERY MADE ME SEE WHAT A COWARD I WAS FOR LEAVING GOTHAM. I REALIZED THAT BY LEAVING I NOT ONLY FAILED MY HOME AND MYSELF...BUT YOU.
I CAME BACK HERE HOPING TO SET AN EXAMPLE...
...SO HUMOR AN OLD LADY AND AT LEAST THINK ABOUT IT.
HA-HA. OKAY, LESLIE.
THE SUNLIGHT FEELS SO GOOD ON YOUR SKIN, DOESN'T IT?
YES.
...IT CERTAINLY DOES.
END

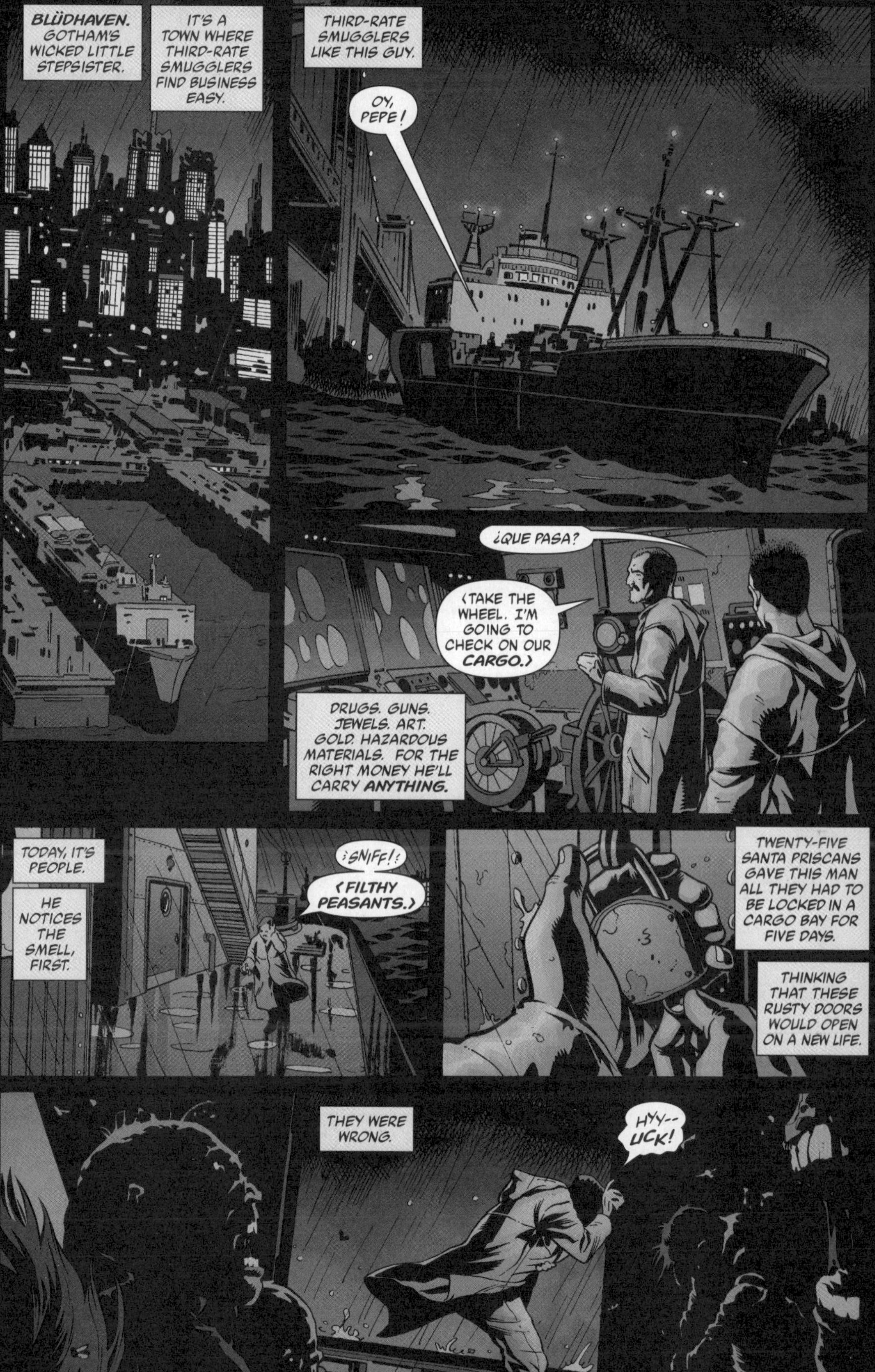
BLÜDHAVEN. GOTHAM'S WICKED LITTLE STEPSISTER.
IT'S A TOWN WHERE THIRD-RATE SMUGGLERS FIND BUSINESS EASY.
THIRD-RATE SMUGGLERS LIKE THIS GUY.
OY, PEPE!
¿QUE PASA?
‹TAKE THE WHEEL. I'M GOING TO CHECK ON OUR CARGO.›
DRUGS. GUNS. JEWELS. ART. GOLD. HAZARDOUS MATERIALS. FOR THE RIGHT MONEY HE'LL CARRY ANYTHING.
TODAY, IT'S PEOPLE.
HE NOTICES THE SMELL, FIRST.
SNIFF!
‹FILTHY PEASANTS.›
TWENTY-FIVE SANTA PRISCANS GAVE THIS MAN ALL THEY HAD TO BE LOCKED IN A CARGO BAY FOR FIVE DAYS.
THINKING THAT THESE RUSTY DOORS WOULD OPEN ON A NEW LIFE.
THEY WERE WRONG.
HYY-- UCK!

MONSTERS OF ROT

part one: CLEANSING FIRES

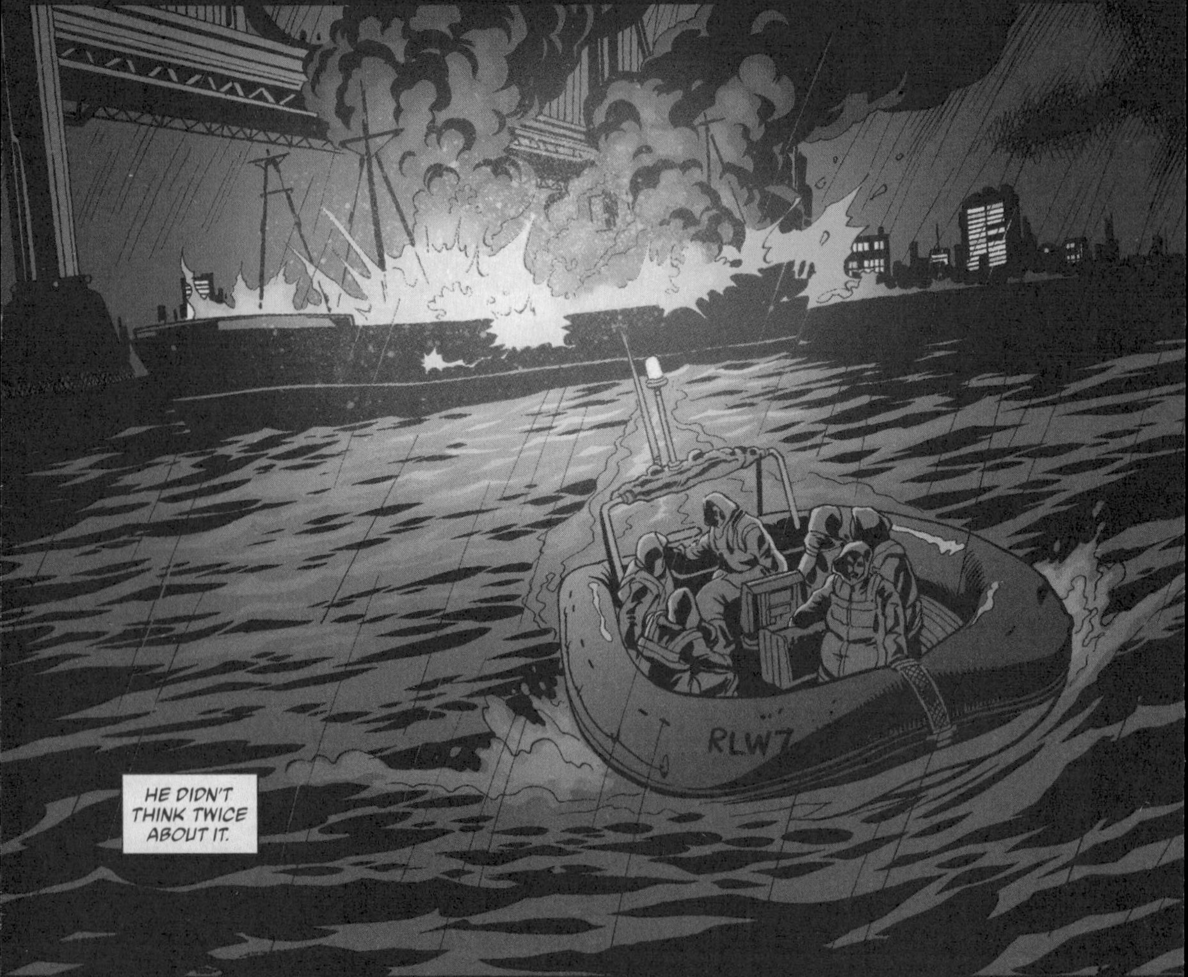
HE DIDN'T THINK TWICE ABOUT IT.
RLW7

written by **ANDERSEN GABRYCH**
pencilled by **PETE WOODS**
inked by **CAM SMITH / NATHAN MASSENGILL**

colorist **JASON WRIGHT**
letterer **CLEM ROBINS**
associate editor **MICHAEL WRIGHT**
editor **BOB SCHRECK**
Batman created by **BOB KANE**

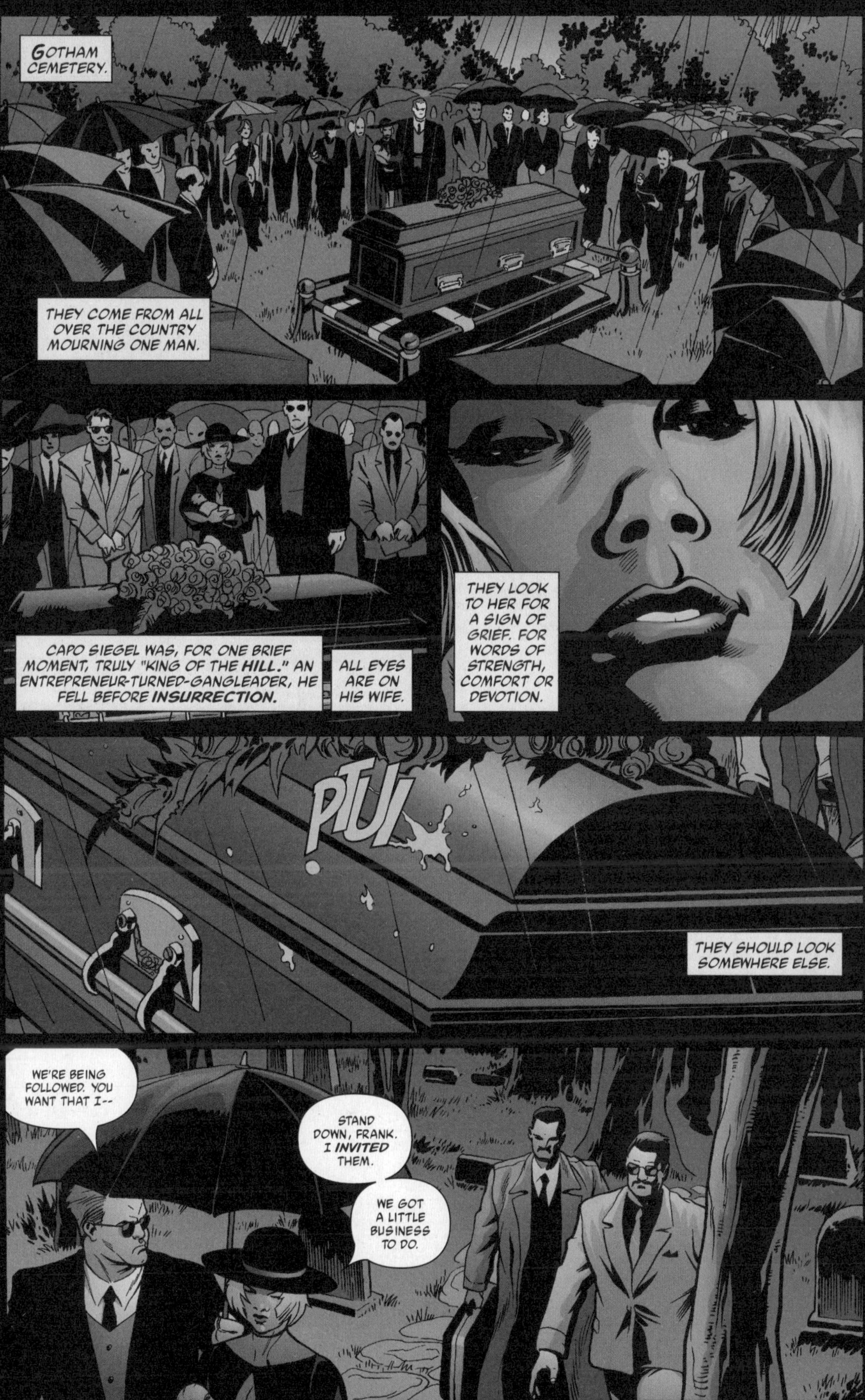
GOTHAM CEMETERY.
THEY COME FROM ALL OVER THE COUNTRY MOURNING ONE MAN.
CAPO SIEGEL WAS, FOR ONE BRIEF MOMENT, TRULY "KING OF THE HILL." AN ENTREPRENEUR-TURNED-GANGLEADER, HE FELL BEFORE INSURRECTION.
ALL EYES ARE ON HIS WIFE.
THEY LOOK TO HER FOR A SIGN OF GRIEF. FOR WORDS OF STRENGTH, COMFORT OR DEVOTION.
PTUI
THEY SHOULD LOOK SOMEWHERE ELSE.
WE'RE BEING FOLLOWED. YOU WANT THAT I--
STAND DOWN, FRANK. I INVITED THEM.
WE GOT A LITTLE BUSINESS TO DO.

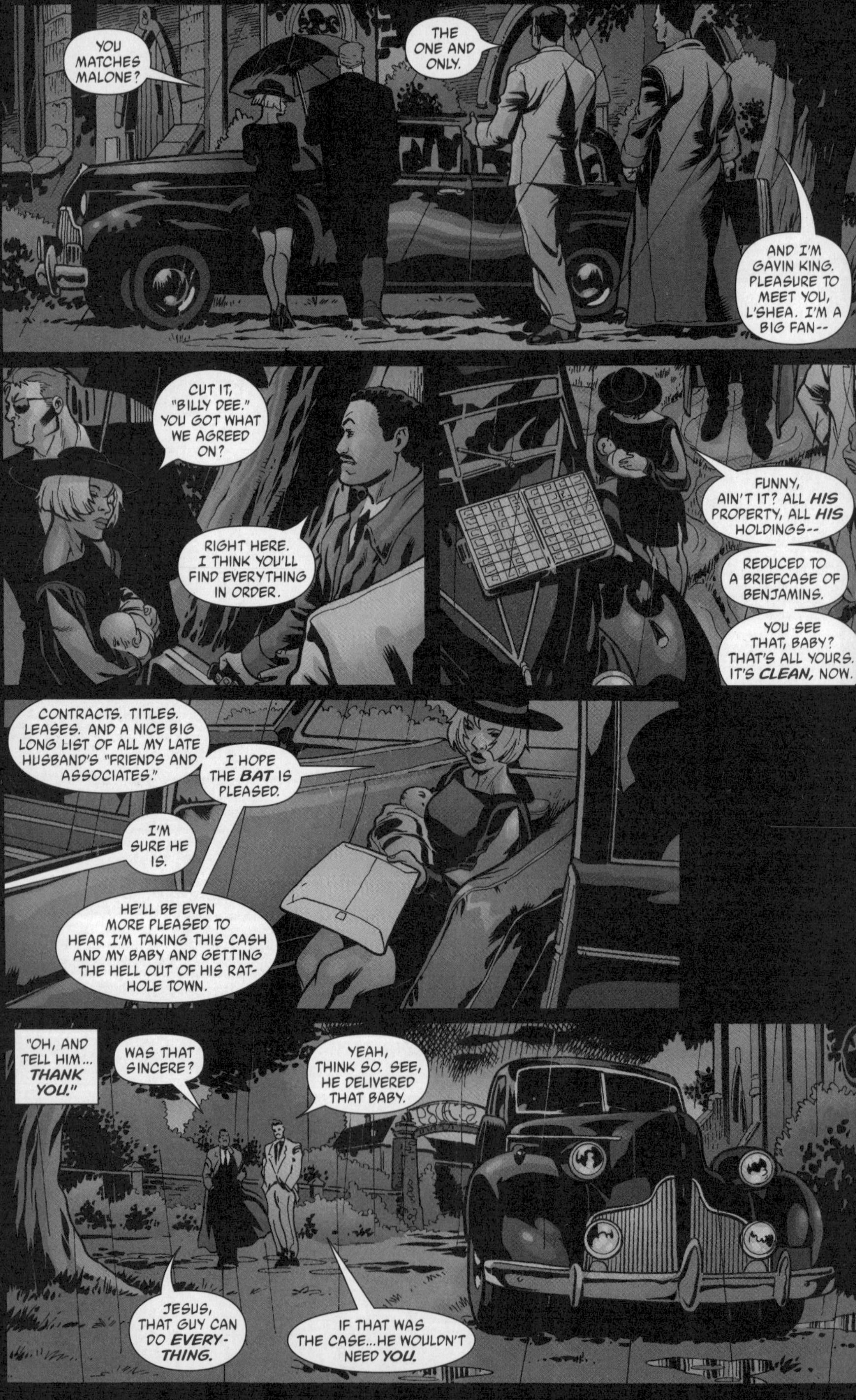
YOU MATCHES MALONE?
THE ONE AND ONLY.
AND I'M GAVIN KING. PLEASURE TO MEET YOU, L'SHEA. I'M A BIG FAN--
CUT IT, "BILLY DEE." YOU GOT WHAT WE AGREED ON?
RIGHT HERE. I THINK YOU'LL FIND EVERYTHING IN ORDER.
FUNNY, AIN'T IT? ALL **HIS** PROPERTY, ALL **HIS** HOLDINGS--
REDUCED TO A BRIEFCASE OF BENJAMINS.
YOU SEE THAT, BABY? THAT'S ALL YOURS. IT'S ***CLEAN,*** NOW.
CONTRACTS. TITLES. LEASES. AND A NICE BIG LONG LIST OF ALL MY LATE HUSBAND'S "FRIENDS AND ASSOCIATES."
I HOPE THE ***BAT*** IS PLEASED.
I'M SURE HE IS.
HE'LL BE EVEN MORE PLEASED TO HEAR I'M TAKING THIS CASH AND MY BABY AND GETTING THE HELL OUT OF HIS RAT-HOLE TOWN.
"OH, AND TELL HIM... ***THANK YOU.***"
WAS THAT SINCERE?
YEAH, THINK SO. SEE, HE DELIVERED THAT BABY.
JESUS, THAT GUY CAN DO ***EVERY-THING.***
IF THAT WAS THE CASE...HE WOULDN'T NEED ***YOU.***

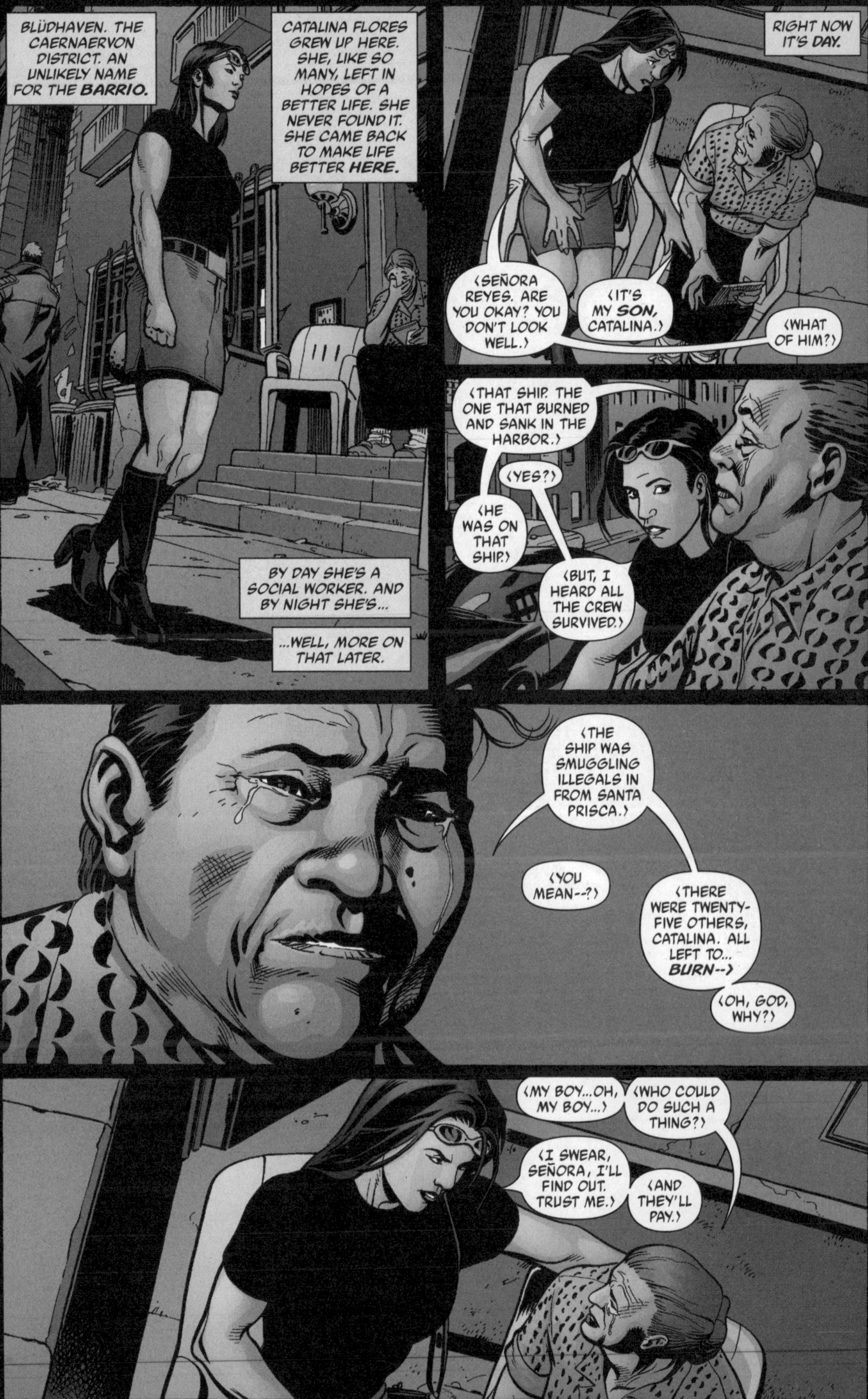
BLÜDHAVEN. THE CAERNAERVON DISTRICT. AN UNLIKELY NAME FOR THE **BARRIO.**
CATALINA FLORES GREW UP HERE. SHE, LIKE SO MANY, LEFT IN HOPES OF A BETTER LIFE. SHE NEVER FOUND IT. SHE CAME BACK TO MAKE LIFE BETTER **HERE.**
BY DAY SHE'S A SOCIAL WORKER. AND BY NIGHT SHE'S...
...WELL, MORE ON THAT LATER.
RIGHT NOW IT'S *DAY.*
‹SEÑORA REYES. ARE YOU OKAY? YOU DON'T LOOK WELL.›
‹IT'S MY **SON,** CATALINA.›
‹WHAT OF HIM?›
‹THAT SHIP. THE ONE THAT BURNED AND SANK IN THE HARBOR.›
‹YES?›
‹HE WAS ON THAT SHIP.›
‹BUT, I HEARD ALL THE CREW SURVIVED.›
‹THE SHIP WAS SMUGGLING ILLEGALS IN FROM SANTA PRISCA.›
‹YOU MEAN--?›
‹THERE WERE TWENTY-FIVE OTHERS, CATALINA. ALL LEFT TO... ***BURN--***›
‹OH, GOD, WHY?›
‹MY BOY...OH, MY BOY...›
‹WHO COULD DO SUCH A THING?›
‹I SWEAR, SEÑORA, I'LL FIND OUT. TRUST ME.›
‹AND THEY'LL PAY.›

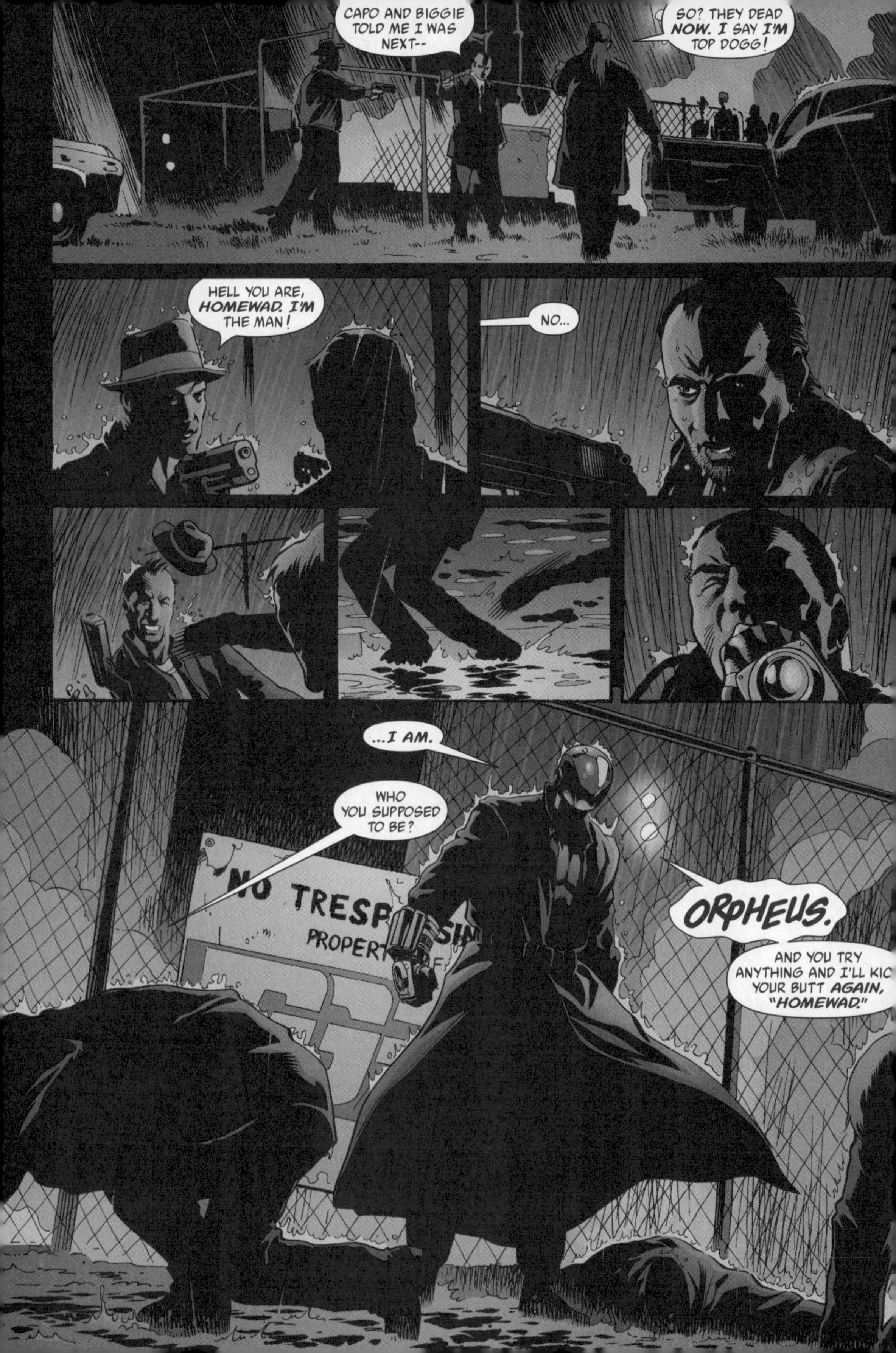
CAPO AND BIGGIE TOLD ME I WAS NEXT--
SO? THEY DEAD NOW. I SAY I'M TOP DOGG!
HELL YOU ARE, HOMEWAD. I'M THE MAN!
NO...
...I AM.
WHO YOU SUPPOSED TO BE?
NO TRESP
PROPERT
ORPHEUS.
AND YOU TRY ANYTHING AND I'LL KIC YOUR BUTT AGAIN, "HOMEWAD."

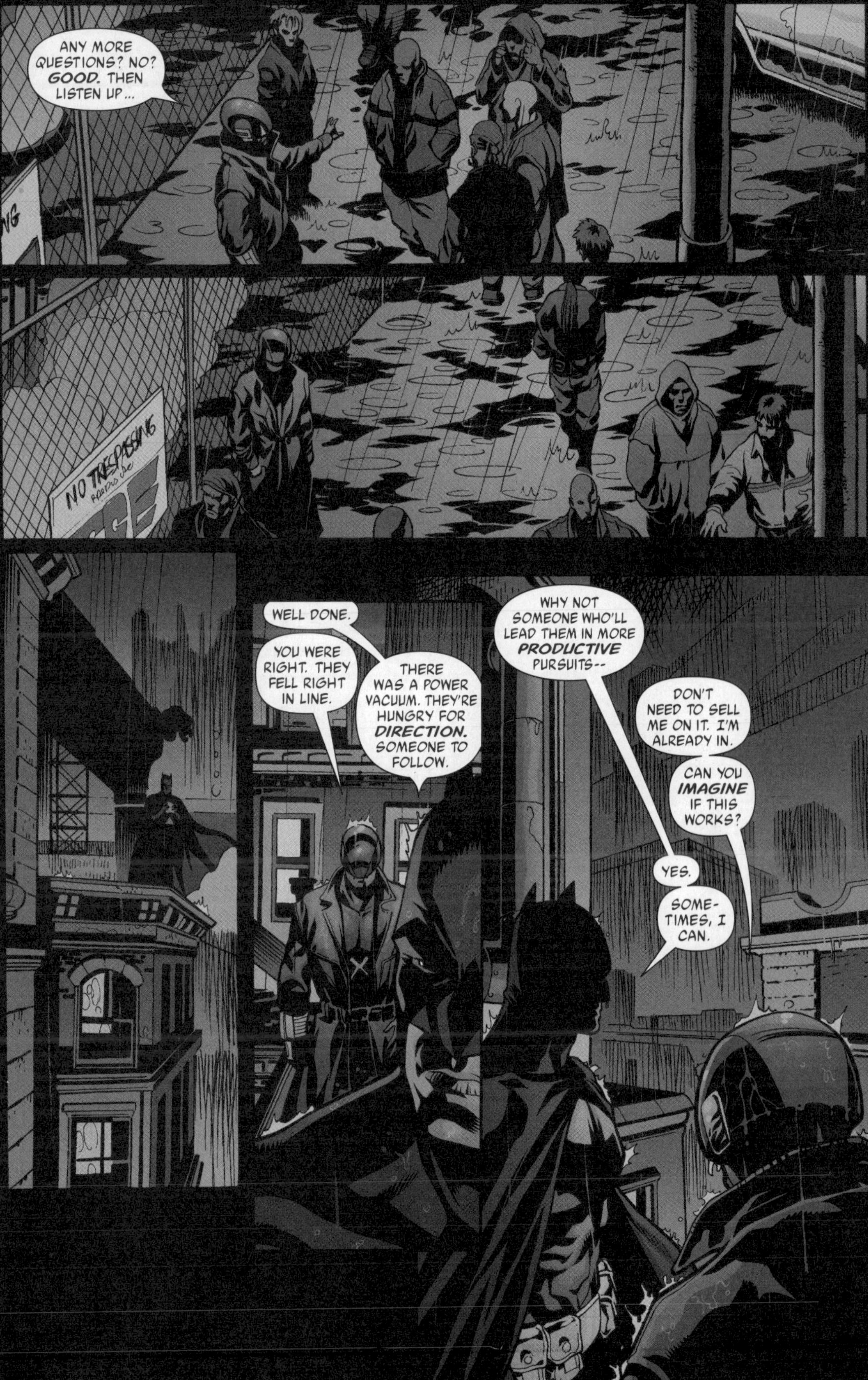
ANY MORE QUESTIONS? NO? **GOOD.** THEN LISTEN UP...
NO TRESPASSING
WELL DONE.
YOU WERE RIGHT. THEY FELL RIGHT IN LINE.
THERE WAS A POWER VACUUM. THEY'RE HUNGRY FOR ***DIRECTION.*** SOMEONE TO FOLLOW.
WHY NOT SOMEONE WHO'LL LEAD THEM IN MORE ***PRODUCTIVE*** PURSUITS--
DON'T NEED TO SELL ME ON IT. I'M ALREADY IN.
CAN YOU ***IMAGINE*** IF THIS WORKS?
YES.
SOME-TIMES, I CAN.

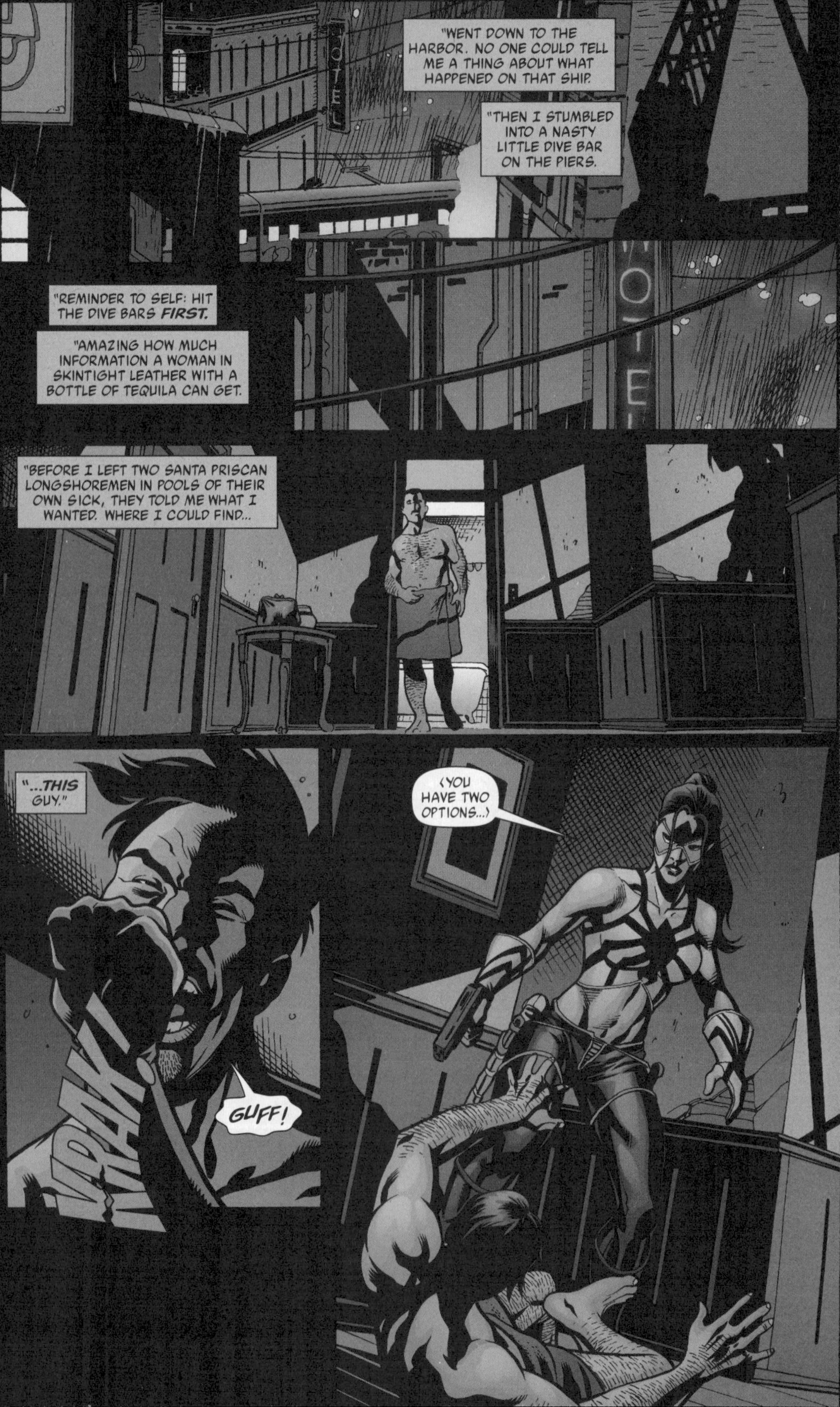
"WENT DOWN TO THE HARBOR. NO ONE COULD TELL ME A THING ABOUT WHAT HAPPENED ON THAT SHIP.
"THEN I STUMBLED INTO A NASTY LITTLE DIVE BAR ON THE PIERS.
MOTEL
"REMINDER TO SELF: HIT THE DIVE BARS *FIRST.*
"AMAZING HOW MUCH INFORMATION A WOMAN IN SKINTIGHT LEATHER WITH A BOTTLE OF TEQUILA CAN GET.
"BEFORE I LEFT TWO SANTA PRISCAN LONGSHOREMEN IN POOLS OF THEIR OWN SICK, THEY TOLD ME WHAT I WANTED. WHERE I COULD FIND...
"...*THIS* GUY."
WHAK
GUFF!
‹YOU HAVE TWO OPTIONS...›

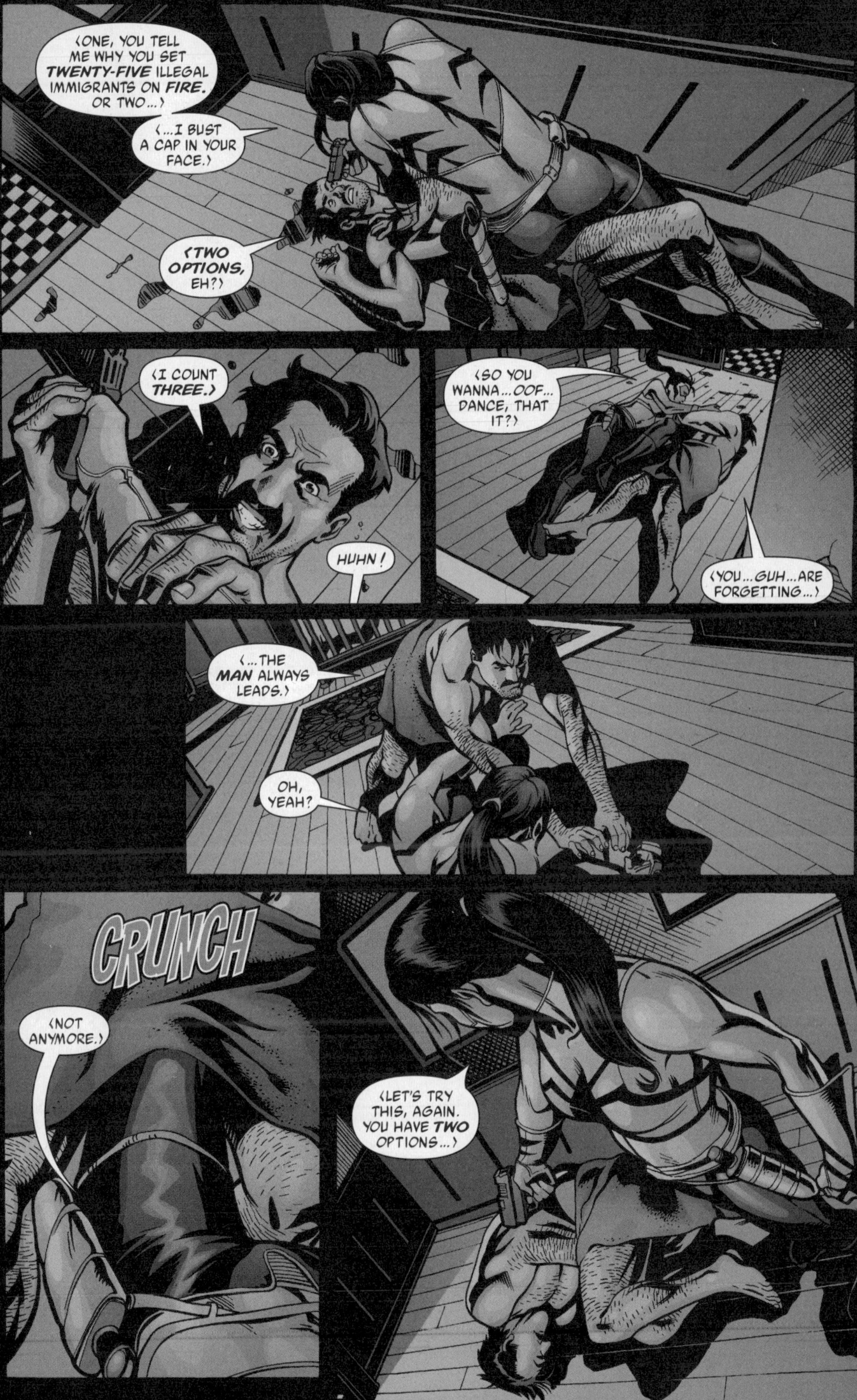
‹ONE, YOU TELL ME WHY YOU SET **TWENTY-FIVE** ILLEGAL IMMIGRANTS ON **FIRE.** OR TWO...›
‹...I BUST A CAP IN YOUR FACE.›
‹**TWO OPTIONS,** EH?›
‹I COUNT **THREE.**›
HUHN!
‹SO YOU WANNA...OOF... DANCE, THAT IT?›
‹YOU...GUH...ARE FORGETTING...›
‹...THE **MAN** ALWAYS LEADS.›
OH, YEAH?
CRUNCH
‹NOT ANYMORE.›
‹LET'S TRY THIS, AGAIN. YOU HAVE **TWO** OPTIONS...›

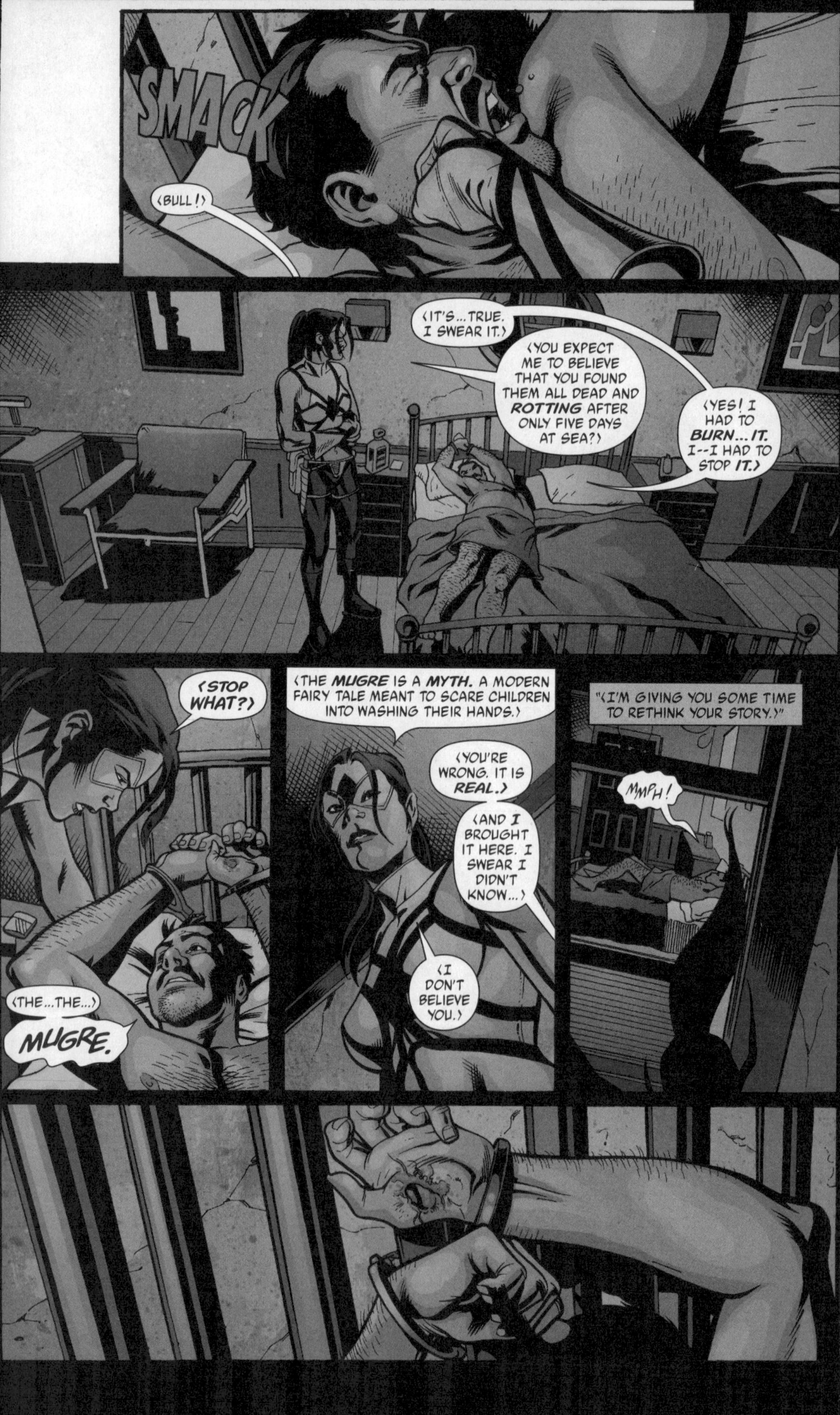
SMACK
‹BULL!›
‹IT'S...TRUE. I SWEAR IT.›
‹YOU EXPECT ME TO BELIEVE THAT YOU FOUND THEM ALL DEAD AND ROTTING AFTER ONLY FIVE DAYS AT SEA?›
‹YES! I HAD TO BURN...IT. I--I HAD TO STOP IT.›
‹STOP WHAT?›
‹THE...THE...›
MUGRE.
‹THE MUGRE IS A MYTH. A MODERN FAIRY TALE MEANT TO SCARE CHILDREN INTO WASHING THEIR HANDS.›
‹YOU'RE WRONG. IT IS REAL.›
‹AND I BROUGHT IT HERE. I SWEAR I DIDN'T KNOW...›
‹I DON'T BELIEVE YOU.›
"‹I'M GIVING YOU SOME TIME TO RETHINK YOUR STORY.›"
MMPH!

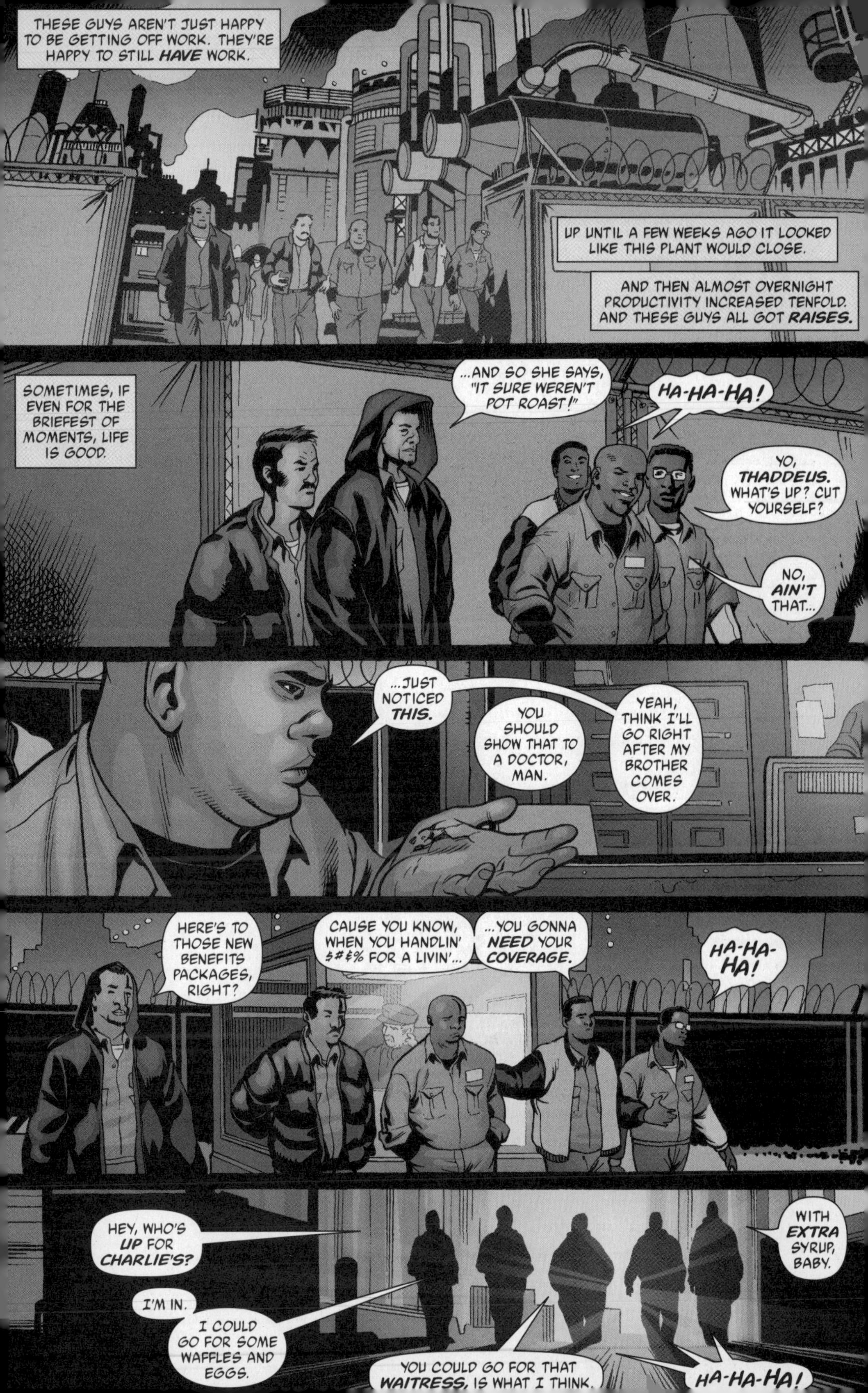

THESE GUYS AREN'T JUST HAPPY TO BE GETTING OFF WORK. THEY'RE HAPPY TO STILL **HAVE** WORK.
UP UNTIL A FEW WEEKS AGO IT LOOKED LIKE THIS PLANT WOULD CLOSE.
AND THEN ALMOST OVERNIGHT PRODUCTIVITY INCREASED TENFOLD. AND THESE GUYS ALL GOT **RAISES.**
SOMETIMES, IF EVEN FOR THE BRIEFEST OF MOMENTS, LIFE IS GOOD.
...AND SO SHE SAYS, "IT SURE WEREN'T POT ROAST!"
HA-HA-HA!
YO, **THADDEUS.** WHAT'S UP? CUT YOURSELF?
NO, **AIN'T** THAT...
...JUST NOTICED **THIS.**
YOU SHOULD SHOW THAT TO A DOCTOR, MAN.
YEAH, THINK I'LL GO RIGHT AFTER MY BROTHER COMES OVER.
HERE'S TO THOSE NEW BENEFITS PACKAGES, RIGHT?
CAUSE YOU KNOW, WHEN YOU HANDLIN' $#&% FOR A LIVIN'...
...YOU GONNA **NEED** YOUR **COVERAGE.**
HA-HA-HA!
HEY, WHO'S **UP** FOR **CHARLIE'S?**
WITH **EXTRA** SYRUP, BABY.
I'M IN.
I COULD GO FOR SOME WAFFLES AND EGGS.
YOU COULD GO FOR THAT **WAITRESS**, IS WHAT I THINK.
HA-HA-HA!

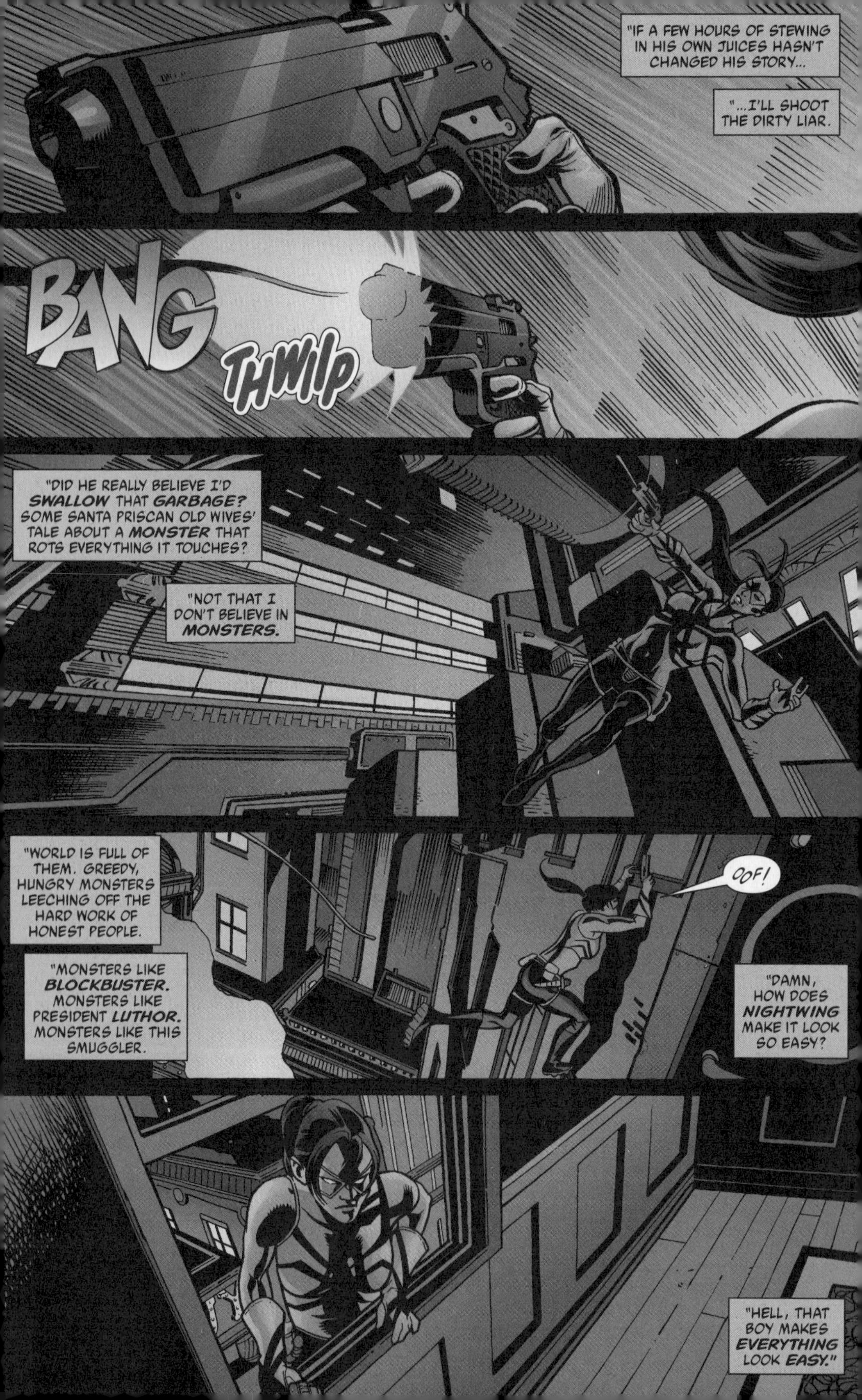
"IF A FEW HOURS OF STEWING IN HIS OWN JUICES HASN'T CHANGED HIS STORY...
"...I'LL SHOOT THE DIRTY LIAR.
BANG
THWIP
"DID HE REALLY BELIEVE I'D SWALLOW THAT GARBAGE? SOME SANTA PRISCAN OLD WIVES' TALE ABOUT A MONSTER THAT ROTS EVERYTHING IT TOUCHES?
"NOT THAT I DON'T BELIEVE IN MONSTERS.
"WORLD IS FULL OF THEM. GREEDY, HUNGRY MONSTERS LEECHING OFF THE HARD WORK OF HONEST PEOPLE.
OOF!
"MONSTERS LIKE BLOCKBUSTER. MONSTERS LIKE PRESIDENT LUTHOR. MONSTERS LIKE THIS SMUGGLER.
"DAMN, HOW DOES NIGHTWING MAKE IT LOOK SO EASY?
"HELL, THAT BOY MAKES EVERYTHING LOOK EASY."

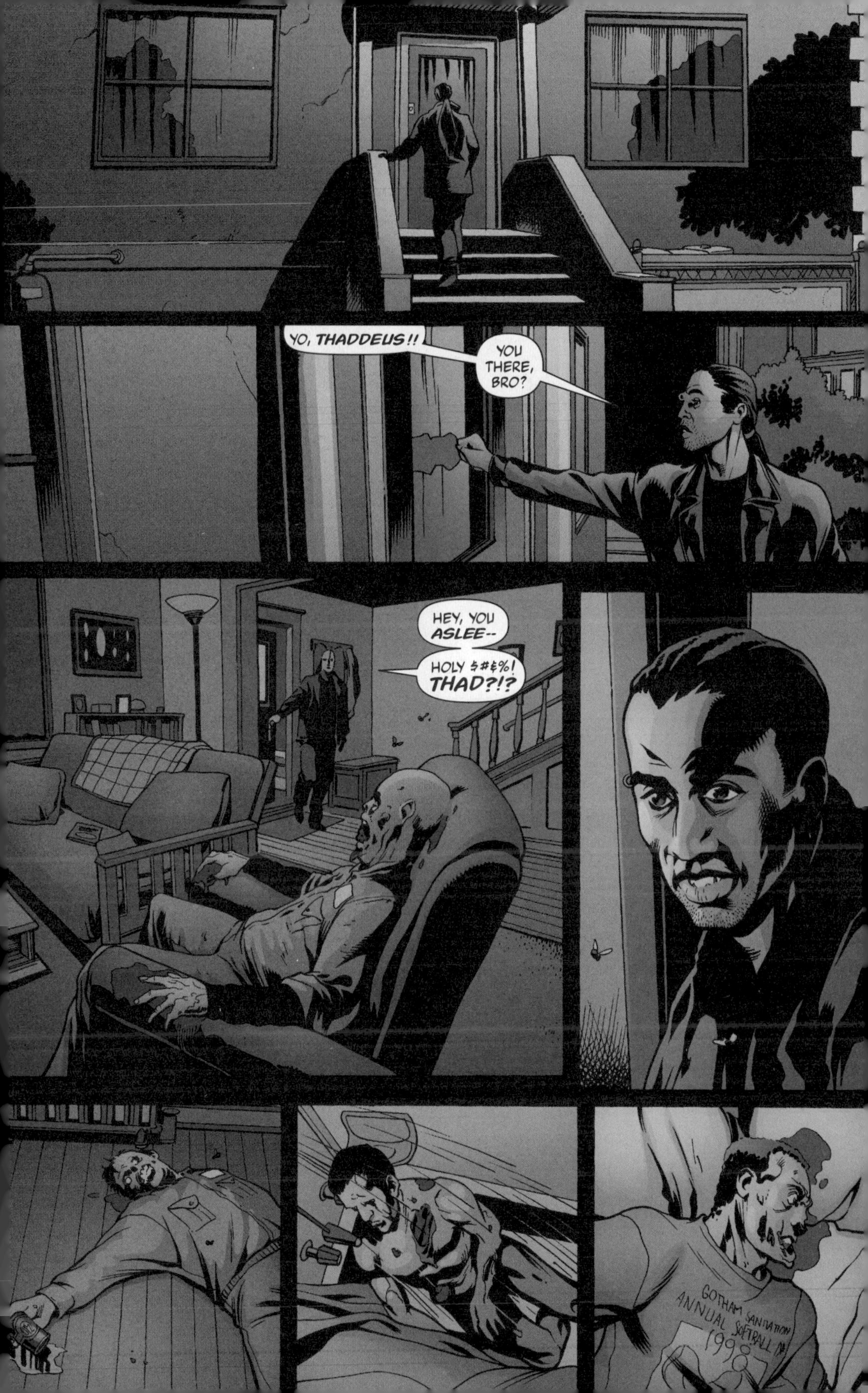
YO, THADDEUS!!
YOU THERE, BRO?
HEY, YOU ASLEE--
HOLY $#&%! THAD?!?
GOTHAM SANITATION ANNUAL SOFTBALL
1998

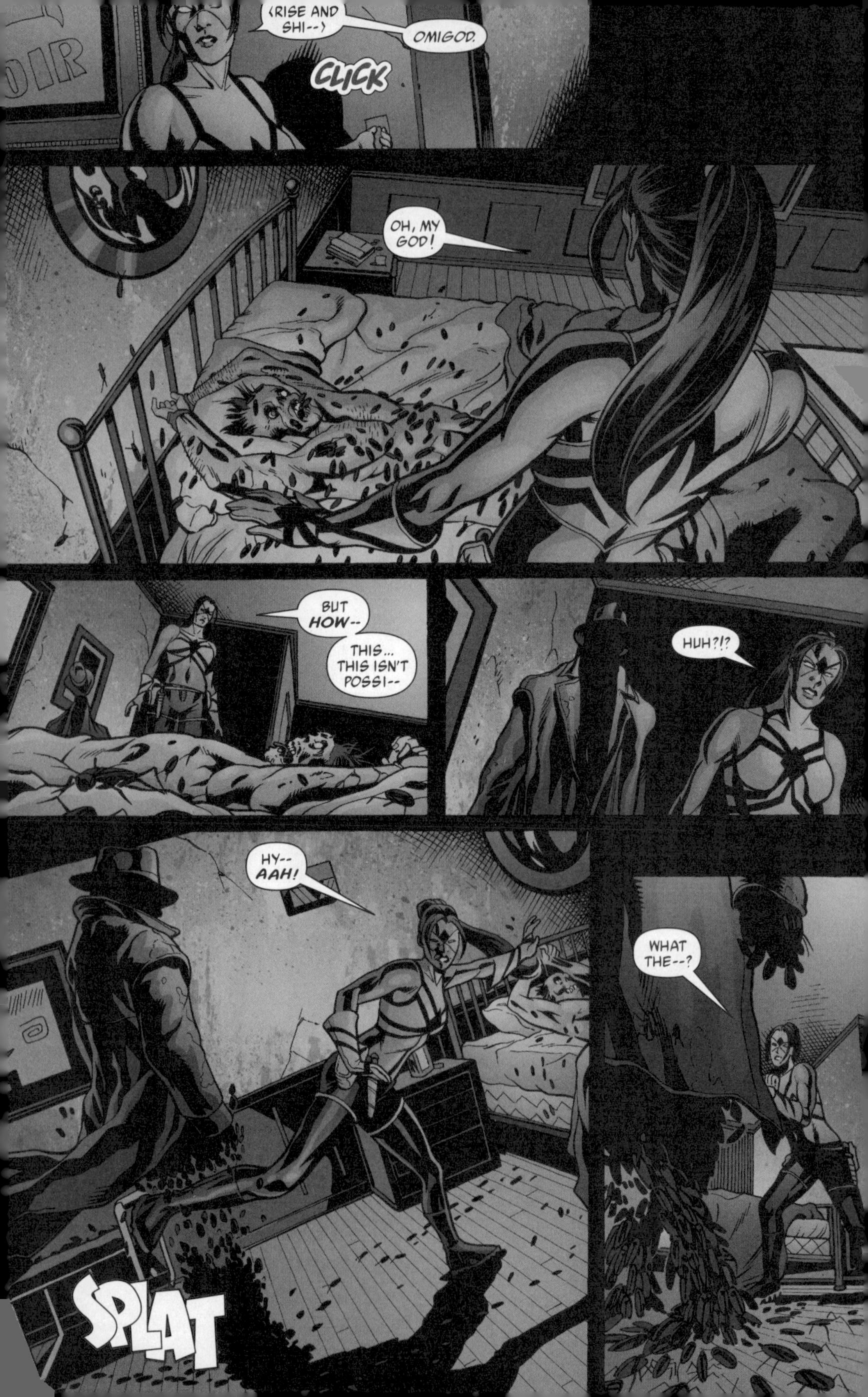
‹RISE AND SHI--›
OMIGOD.
CLICK
OH, MY GOD!
BUT HOW--
THIS... THIS ISN'T POSSI--
HUH?!?
HY-- AAH!
SPLAT
WHAT THE--?

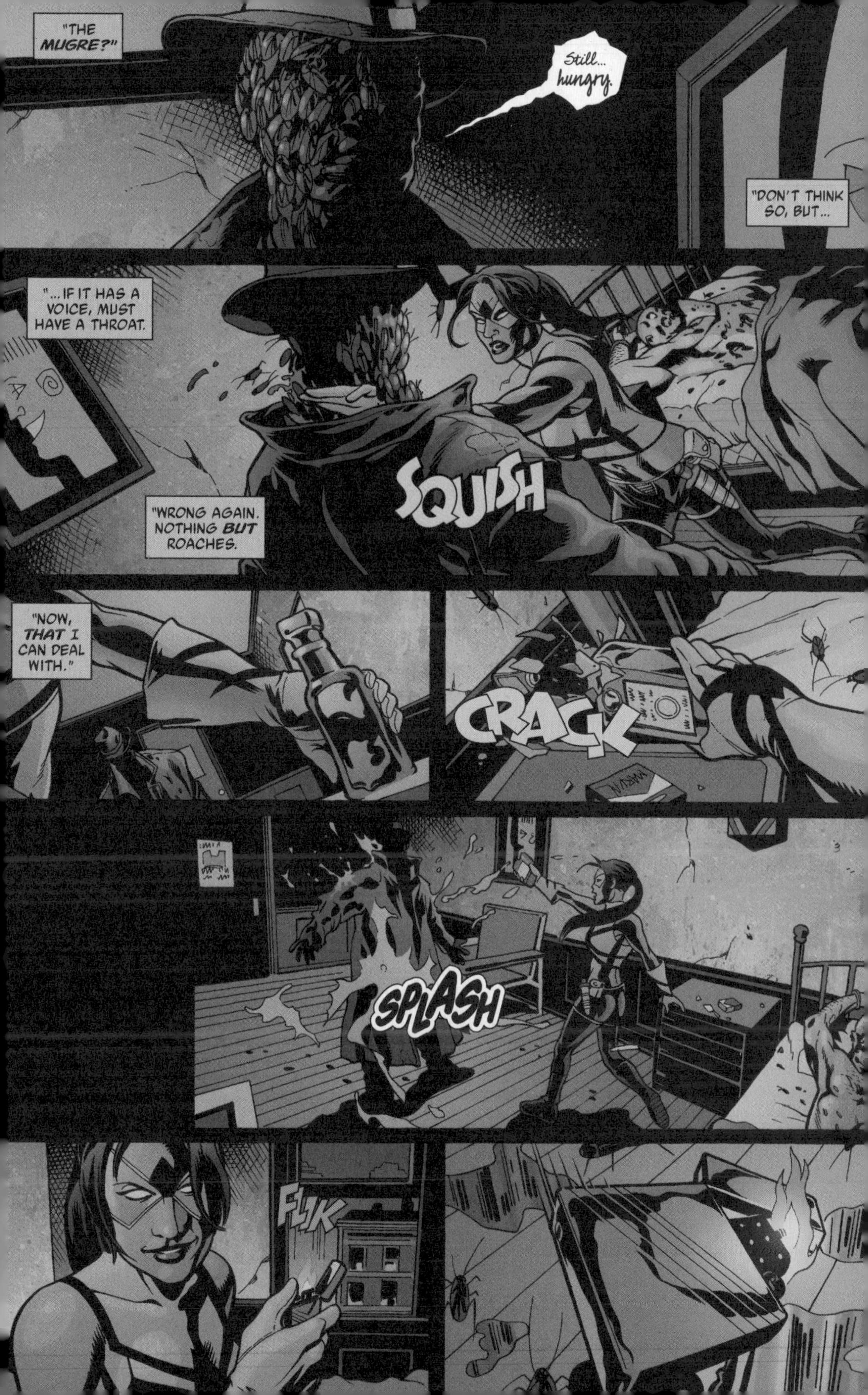
"THE MUGRE?"
Still... hungry.
"DON'T THINK SO, BUT...
"...IF IT HAS A VOICE, MUST HAVE A THROAT.
SQUISH
"WRONG AGAIN. NOTHING BUT ROACHES.
"NOW, THAT I CAN DEAL WITH."
CRACK
SPLASH
FLIK

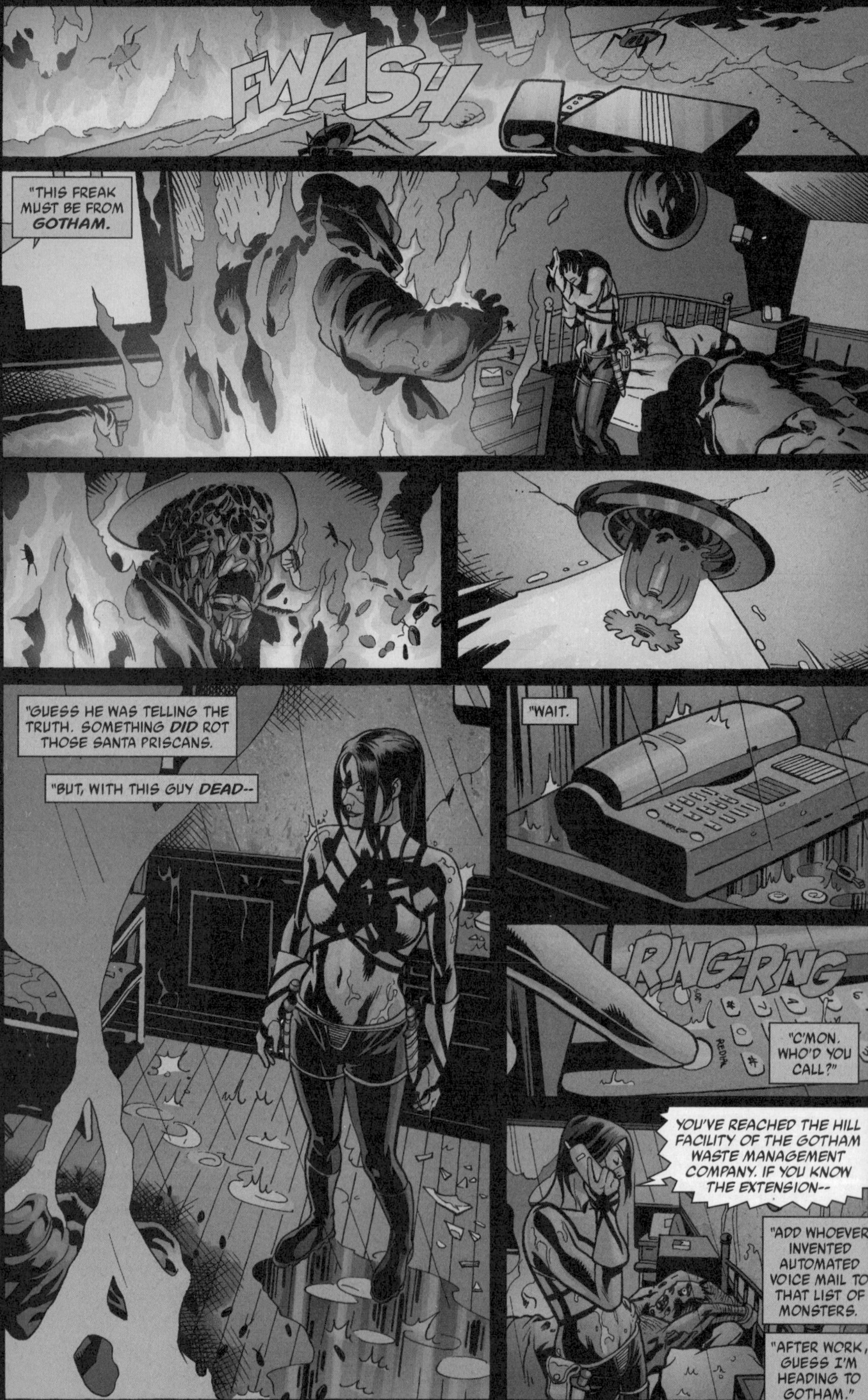
FWASH
"THIS FREAK MUST BE FROM GOTHAM.
"GUESS HE WAS TELLING THE TRUTH. SOMETHING DID ROT THOSE SANTA PRISCANS.
"BUT, WITH THIS GUY DEAD--
"WAIT.
RNG RNG
REDIAL
"C'MON. WHO'D YOU CALL?"
YOU'VE REACHED THE HILL FACILITY OF THE GOTHAM WASTE MANAGEMENT COMPANY. IF YOU KNOW THE EXTENSION--
"ADD WHOEVER INVENTED AUTOMATED VOICE MAIL TO THAT LIST OF MONSTERS.
"AFTER WORK, GUESS I'M HEADING TO GOTHAM."

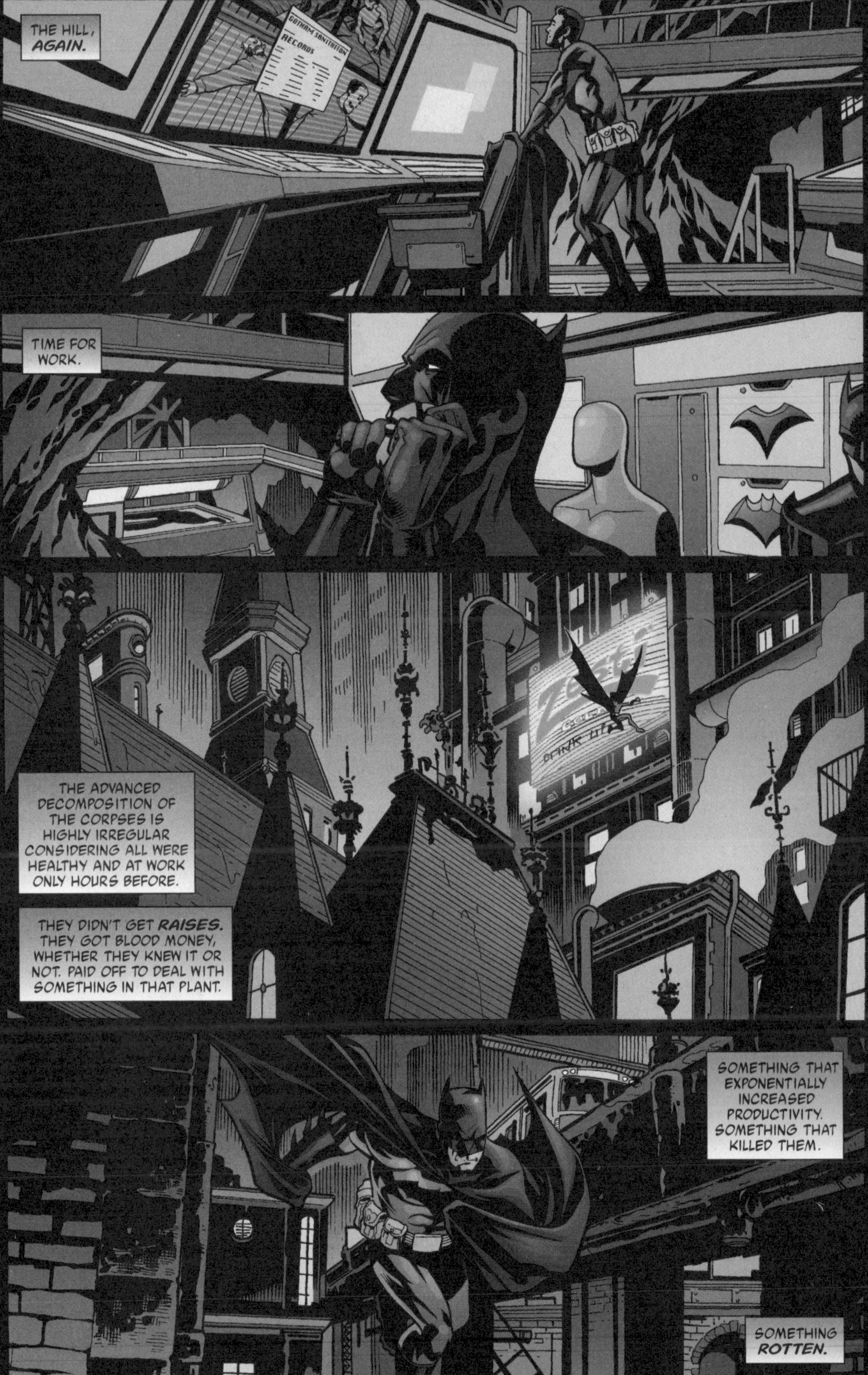
THE HILL, *AGAIN.*
GOTHAM SANITATION
RECORDS
TIME FOR WORK.
THE ADVANCED DECOMPOSITION OF THE CORPSES IS HIGHLY IRREGULAR CONSIDERING ALL WERE HEALTHY AND AT WORK ONLY HOURS BEFORE.
THEY DIDN'T GET *RAISES.* THEY GOT BLOOD MONEY, WHETHER THEY KNEW IT OR NOT. PAID OFF TO DEAL WITH SOMETHING IN THAT PLANT.
SOMETHING THAT EXPONENTIALLY INCREASED PRODUCTIVITY. SOMETHING THAT KILLED THEM.
SOMETHING *ROTTEN.*

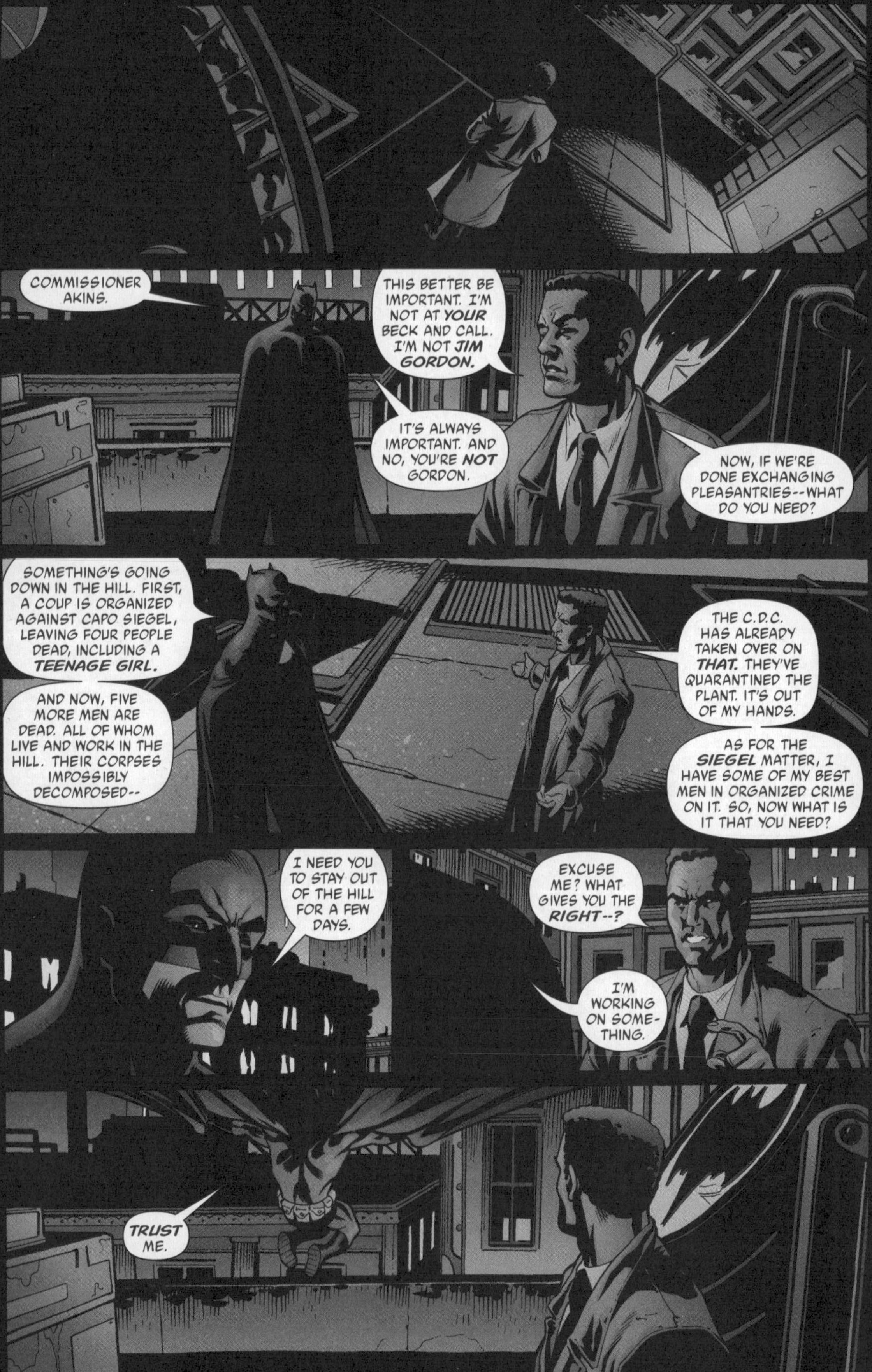
COMMISSIONER AKINS.
THIS BETTER BE IMPORTANT. I'M NOT AT YOUR BECK AND CALL. I'M NOT JIM GORDON.
IT'S ALWAYS IMPORTANT. AND NO, YOU'RE NOT GORDON.
NOW, IF WE'RE DONE EXCHANGING PLEASANTRIES--WHAT DO YOU NEED?
SOMETHING'S GOING DOWN IN THE HILL. FIRST, A COUP IS ORGANIZED AGAINST CAPO SIEGEL, LEAVING FOUR PEOPLE DEAD, INCLUDING A TEENAGE GIRL.
AND NOW, FIVE MORE MEN ARE DEAD. ALL OF WHOM LIVE AND WORK IN THE HILL. THEIR CORPSES IMPOSSIBLY DECOMPOSED--
THE C.D.C. HAS ALREADY TAKEN OVER ON THAT. THEY'VE QUARANTINED THE PLANT. IT'S OUT OF MY HANDS.
AS FOR THE SIEGEL MATTER, I HAVE SOME OF MY BEST MEN IN ORGANIZED CRIME ON IT. SO, NOW WHAT IS IT THAT YOU NEED?
I NEED YOU TO STAY OUT OF THE HILL FOR A FEW DAYS.
EXCUSE ME? WHAT GIVES YOU THE RIGHT--?
I'M WORKING ON SOME-THING.
TRUST ME.

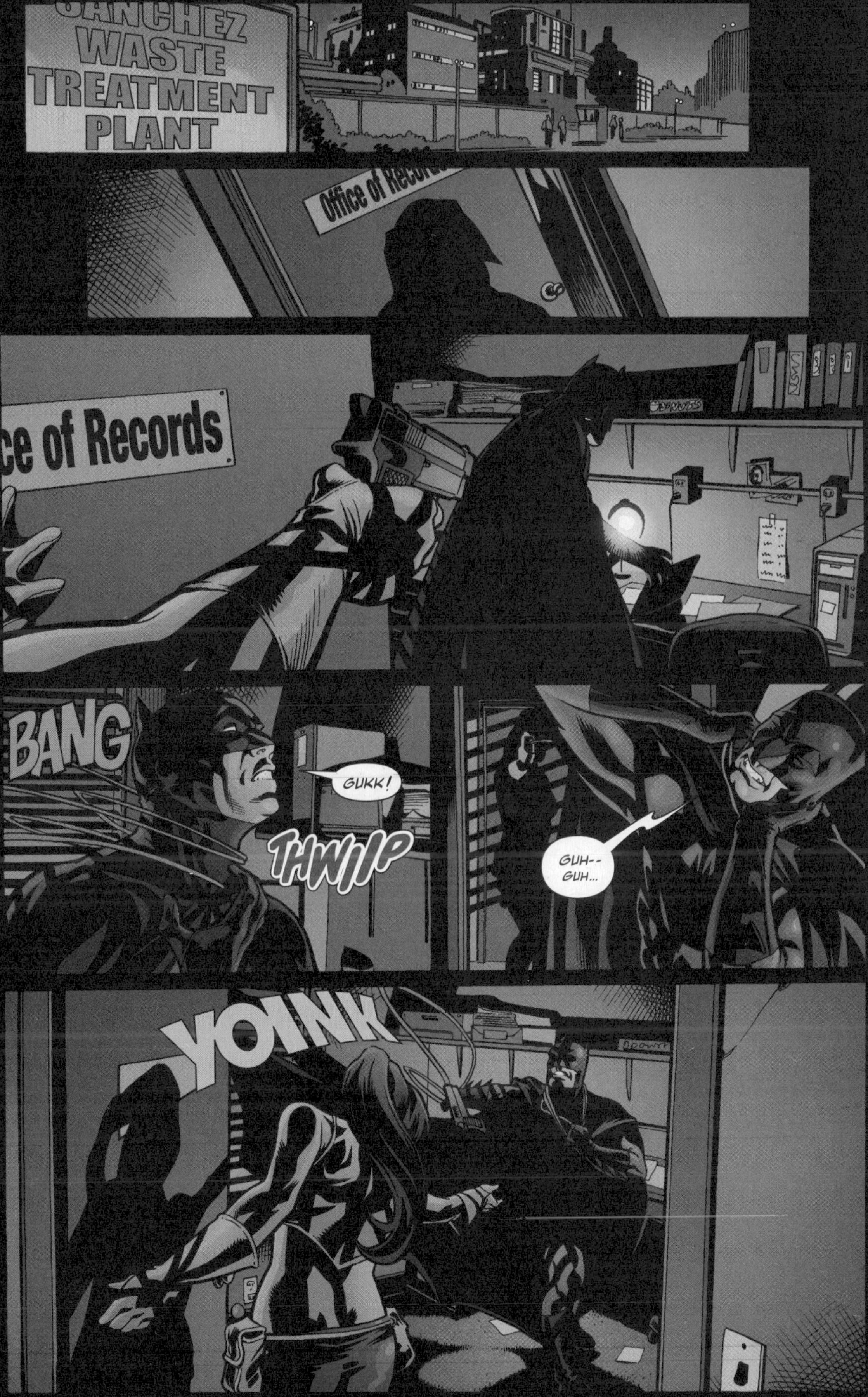
SANCHEZ WASTE TREATMENT PLANT
Office of Records
Office of Records
BANG
GUKK!
THWIIP
GUH-- GUH...
YOINK

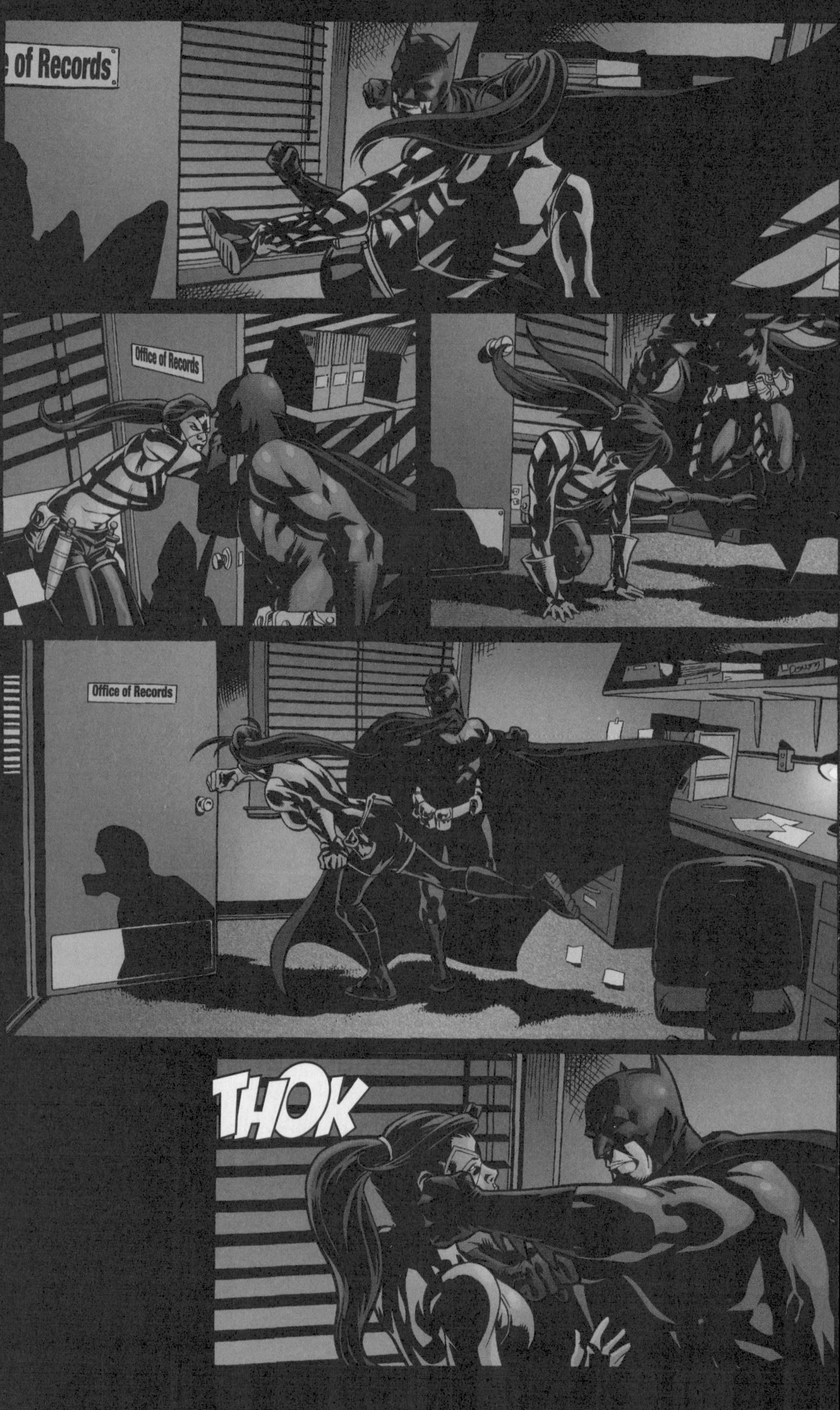

of Records
Office of Records
Office of Records
THOK

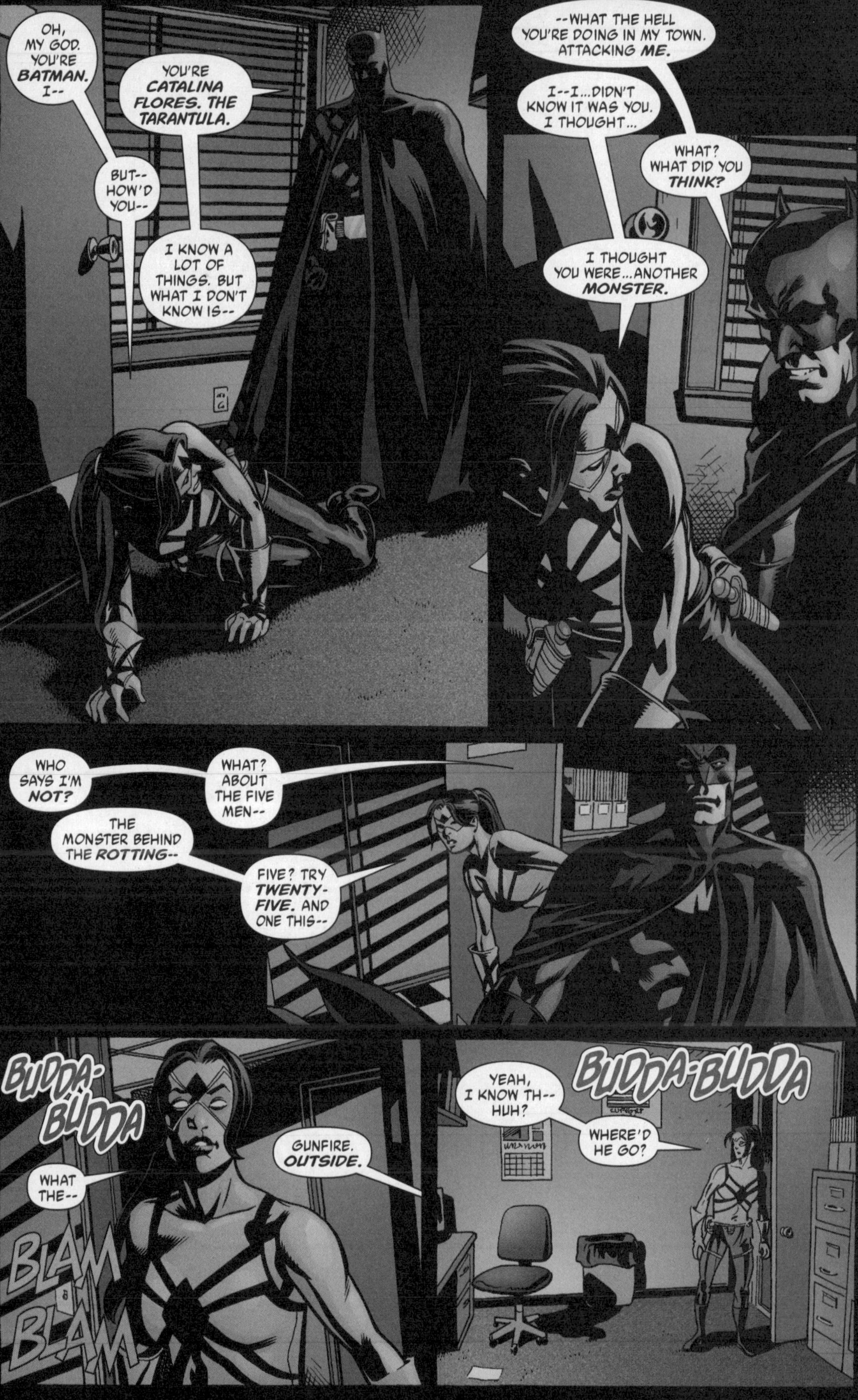
OH, MY GOD. YOU'RE BATMAN. I--
YOU'RE CATALINA FLORES. THE TARANTULA.
BUT-- HOW'D YOU--
I KNOW A LOT OF THINGS. BUT WHAT I DON'T KNOW IS--
--WHAT THE HELL YOU'RE DOING IN MY TOWN. ATTACKING ME.
I--I...DIDN'T KNOW IT WAS YOU. I THOUGHT...
WHAT? WHAT DID YOU THINK?
I THOUGHT YOU WERE...ANOTHER MONSTER.
WHO SAYS I'M NOT?
WHAT? ABOUT THE FIVE MEN--
THE MONSTER BEHIND THE ROTTING--
FIVE? TRY TWENTY-FIVE. AND ONE THIS--
BUDDA-BUDDA
WHAT THE--
BLAM BLAM
GUNFIRE. OUTSIDE.
BUDDA-BUDDA
YEAH, I KNOW TH-- HUH?
WHERE'D HE GO?

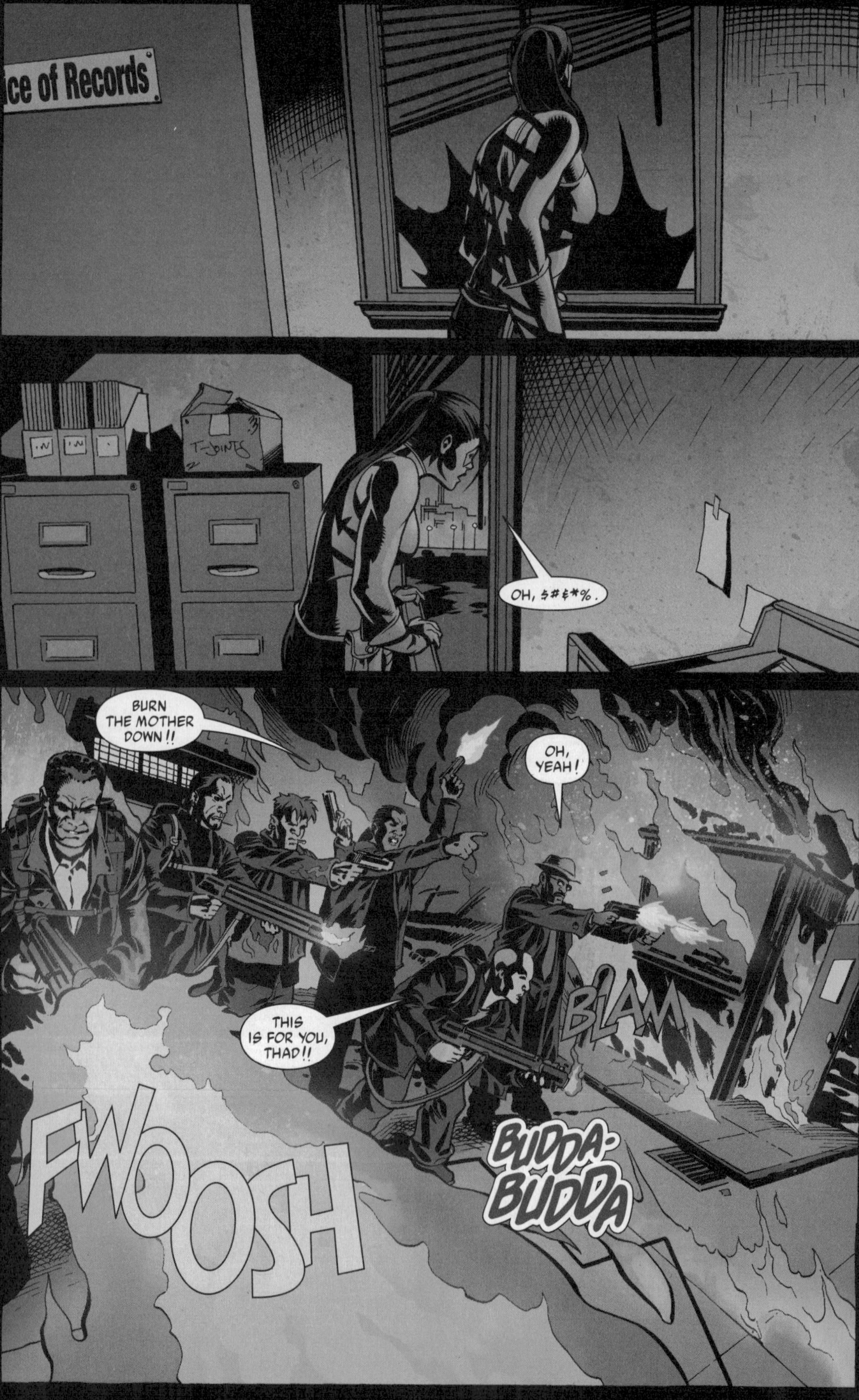
ice of Records
OH, $#&*%.
BURN THE MOTHER DOWN!!
OH, YEAH!
THIS IS FOR YOU, THAD!!
BLAM
FWOOSH
BUDDA-BUDDA

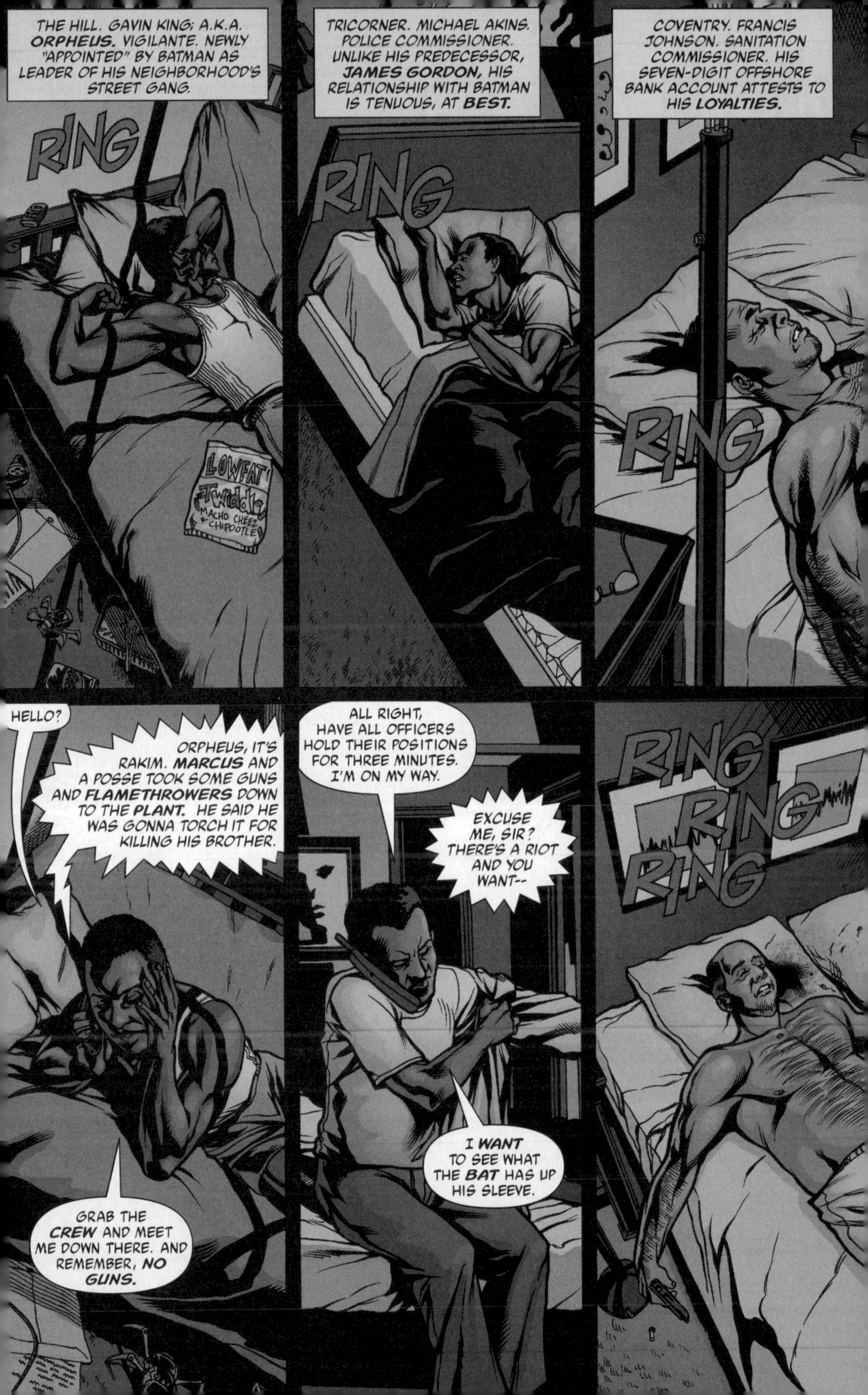
THE HILL. GAVIN KING; A.K.A. ORPHEUS. VIGILANTE. NEWLY "APPOINTED" BY BATMAN AS LEADER OF HIS NEIGHBORHOOD'S STREET GANG.
RING
LOWFAT TWIDDLIS MACHO CHEEZ & CHIPOOTLE
TRICORNER. MICHAEL AKINS. POLICE COMMISSIONER. UNLIKE HIS PREDECESSOR, JAMES GORDON, HIS RELATIONSHIP WITH BATMAN IS TENUOUS, AT BEST.
RING
COVENTRY. FRANCIS JOHNSON. SANITATION COMMISSIONER. HIS SEVEN-DIGIT OFFSHORE BANK ACCOUNT ATTESTS TO HIS LOYALTIES.
RING
HELLO?
ORPHEUS, IT'S RAKIM. MARCUS AND A POSSE TOOK SOME GUNS AND FLAMETHROWERS DOWN TO THE PLANT. HE SAID HE WAS GONNA TORCH IT FOR KILLING HIS BROTHER.
GRAB THE CREW AND MEET ME DOWN THERE. AND REMEMBER, NO GUNS.
ALL RIGHT, HAVE ALL OFFICERS HOLD THEIR POSITIONS FOR THREE MINUTES. I'M ON MY WAY.
EXCUSE ME, SIR? THERE'S A RIOT AND YOU WANT--
I WANT TO SEE WHAT THE BAT HAS UP HIS SLEEVE.
RING RING RING

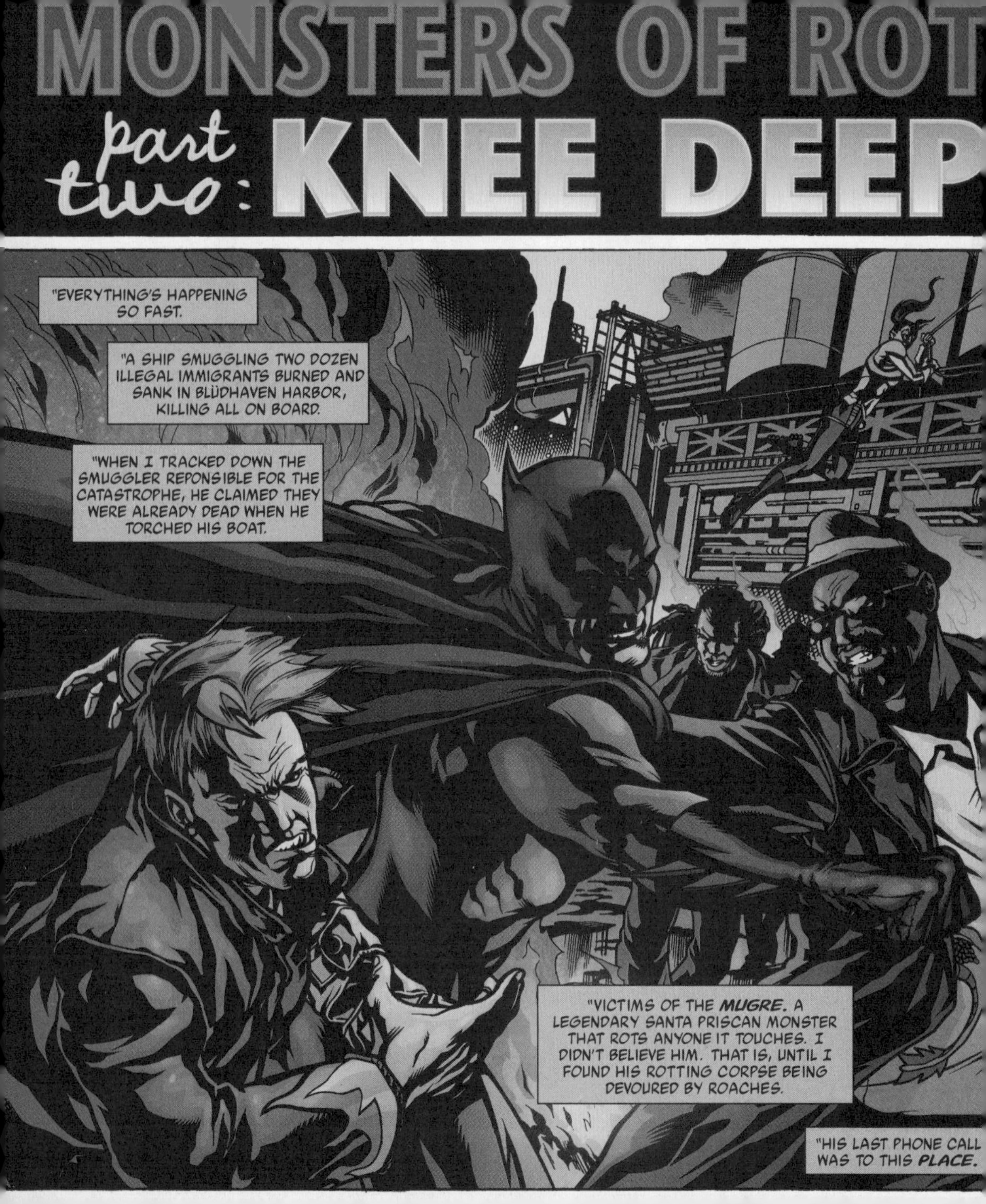
MONSTERS OF ROT
part two: KNEE DEEP
"EVERYTHING'S HAPPENING SO FAST.
"A SHIP SMUGGLING TWO DOZEN ILLEGAL IMMIGRANTS BURNED AND SANK IN BLÜDHAVEN HARBOR, KILLING ALL ON BOARD.
"WHEN I TRACKED DOWN THE SMUGGLER REPONSIBLE FOR THE CATASTROPHE, HE CLAIMED THEY WERE ALREADY DEAD WHEN HE TORCHED HIS BOAT.
"VICTIMS OF THE MUGRE. A LEGENDARY SANTA PRISCAN MONSTER THAT ROTS ANYONE IT TOUCHES. I DIDN'T BELIEVE HIM. THAT IS, UNTIL I FOUND HIS ROTTING CORPSE BEING DEVOURED BY ROACHES.
"HIS LAST PHONE CALL WAS TO THIS PLACE.

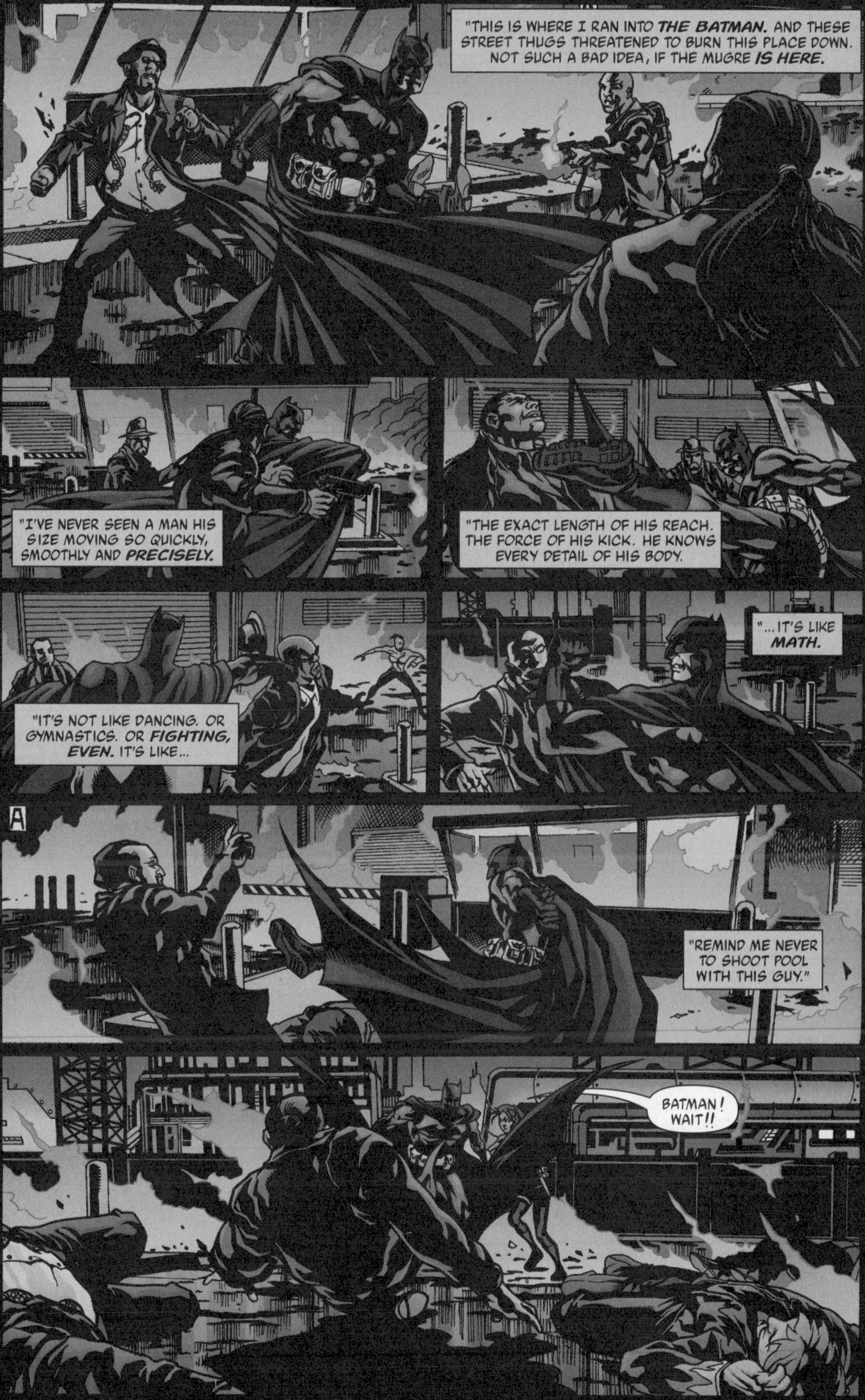
"THIS IS WHERE I RAN INTO THE BATMAN. AND THESE STREET THUGS THREATENED TO BURN THIS PLACE DOWN. NOT SUCH A BAD IDEA, IF THE MUGRE IS HERE.
"I'VE NEVER SEEN A MAN HIS SIZE MOVING SO QUICKLY, SMOOTHLY AND PRECISELY.
"THE EXACT LENGTH OF HIS REACH. THE FORCE OF HIS KICK. HE KNOWS EVERY DETAIL OF HIS BODY.
"IT'S NOT LIKE DANCING. OR GYMNASTICS. OR FIGHTING, EVEN. IT'S LIKE...
"...IT'S LIKE MATH.
"REMIND ME NEVER TO SHOOT POOL WITH THIS GUY."
BATMAN! WAIT!!

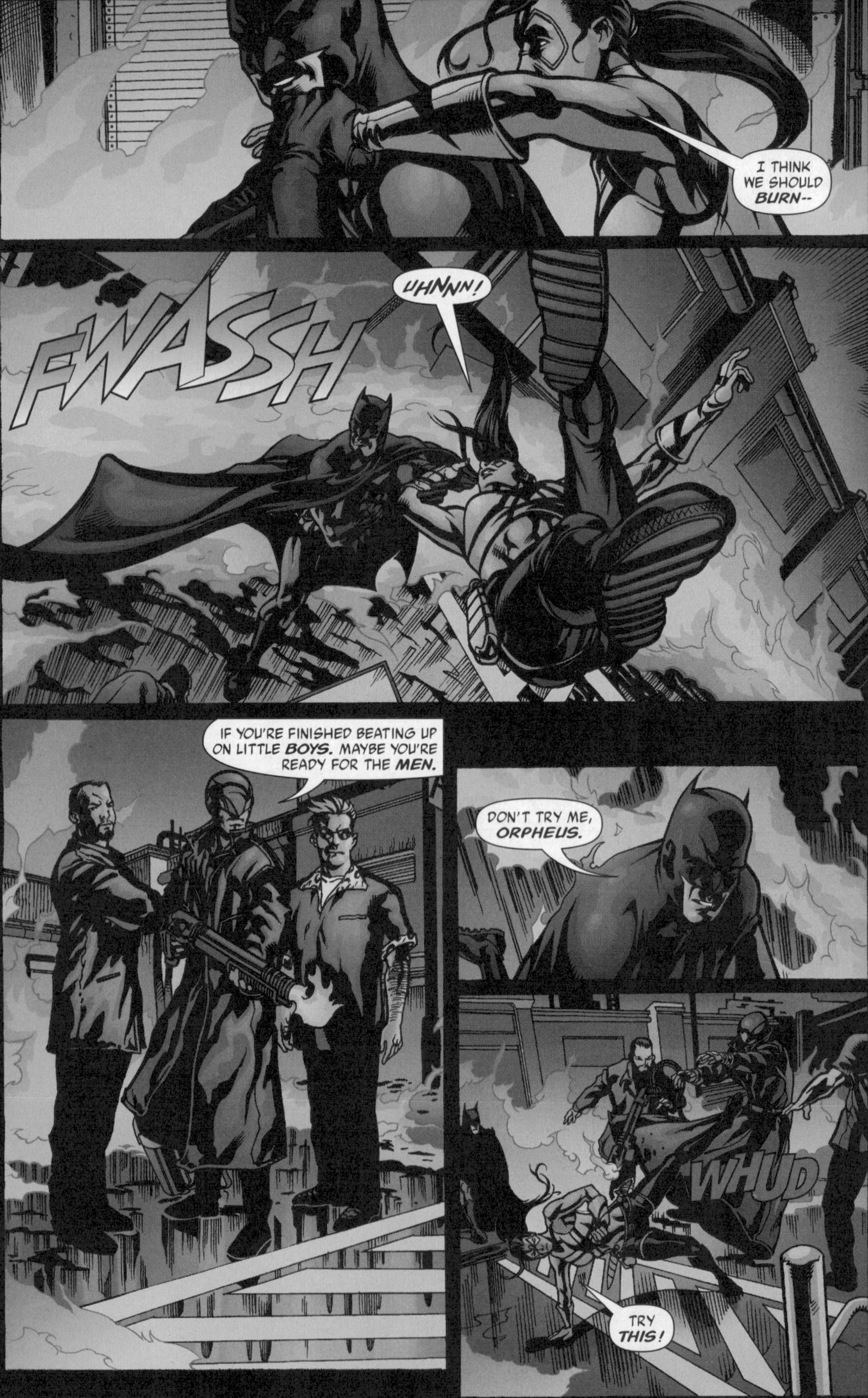

I THINK WE SHOULD BURN--
FWASSH
UHNNN!
IF YOU'RE FINISHED BEATING UP ON LITTLE BOYS. MAYBE YOU'RE READY FOR THE MEN.
DON'T TRY ME, ORPHEUS.
WHUD
TRY THIS!

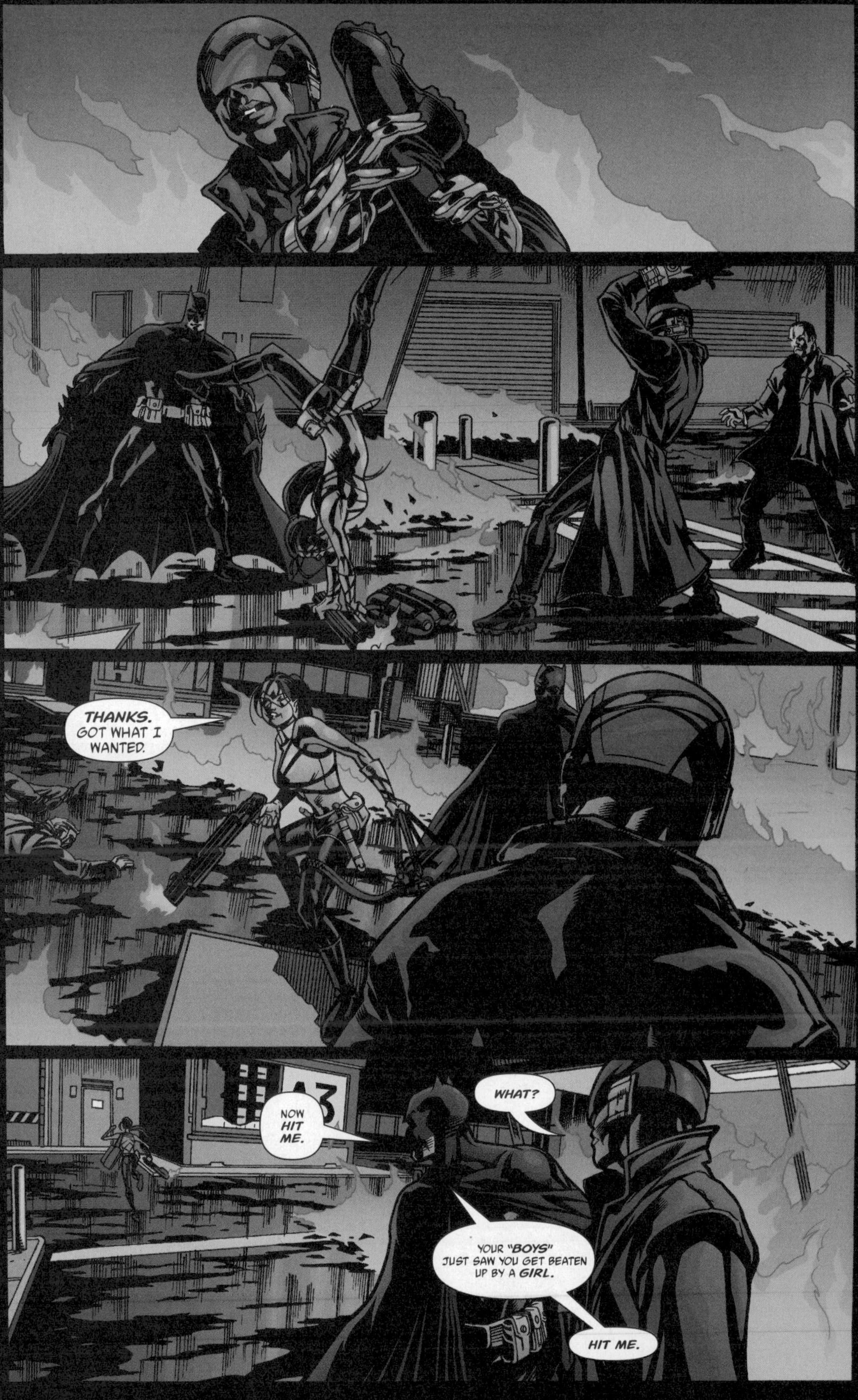
THANKS. GOT WHAT I WANTED.
NOW HIT ME.
WHAT?
YOUR "BOYS" JUST SAW YOU GET BEATEN UP BY A GIRL.
HIT ME.
A3

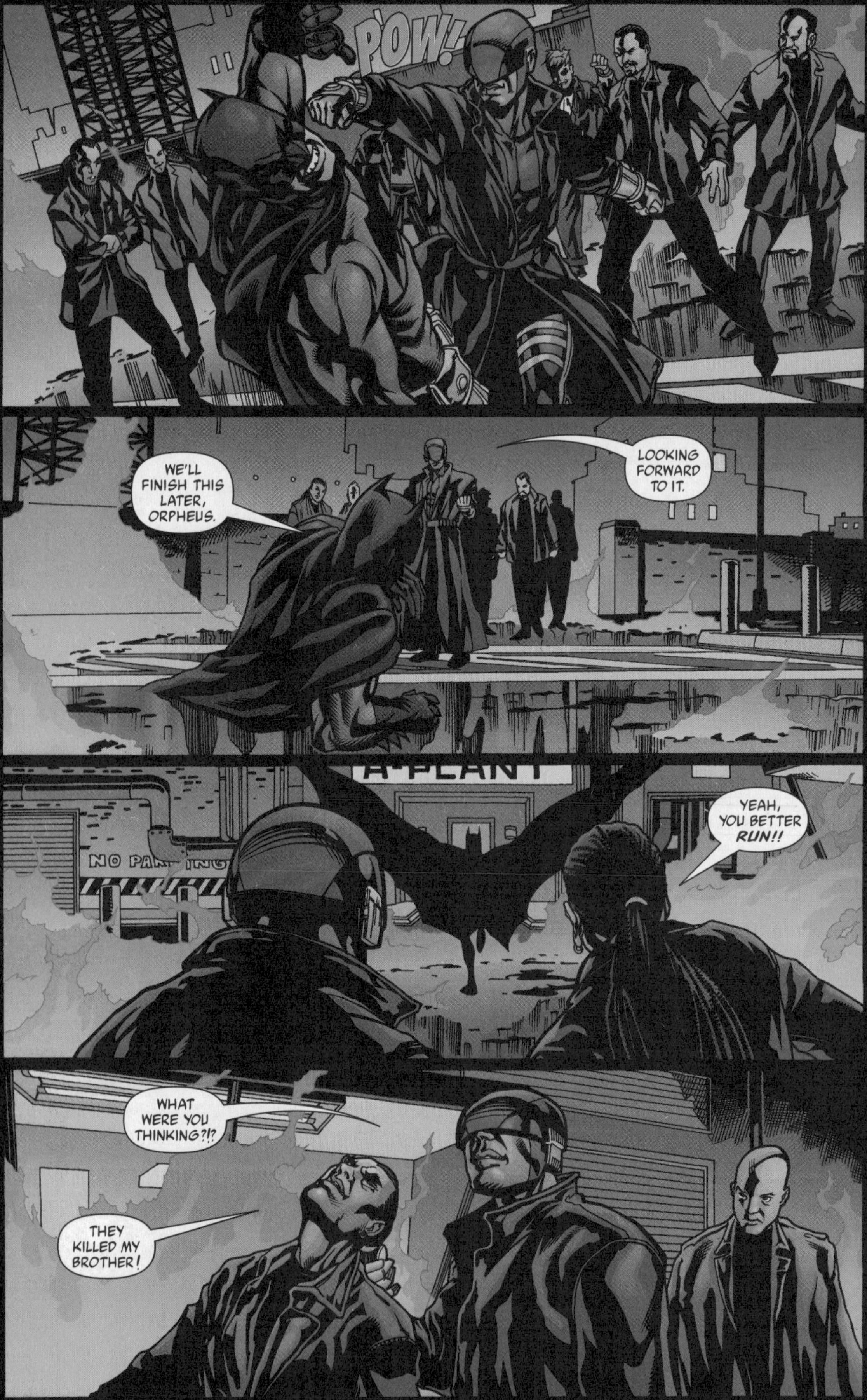
POW!!
WE'LL FINISH THIS LATER, ORPHEUS.
LOOKING FORWARD TO IT.
A-PLANT
NO PARKING
YEAH, YOU BETTER RUN!!
WHAT WERE YOU THINKING?!?
THEY KILLED MY BROTHER!

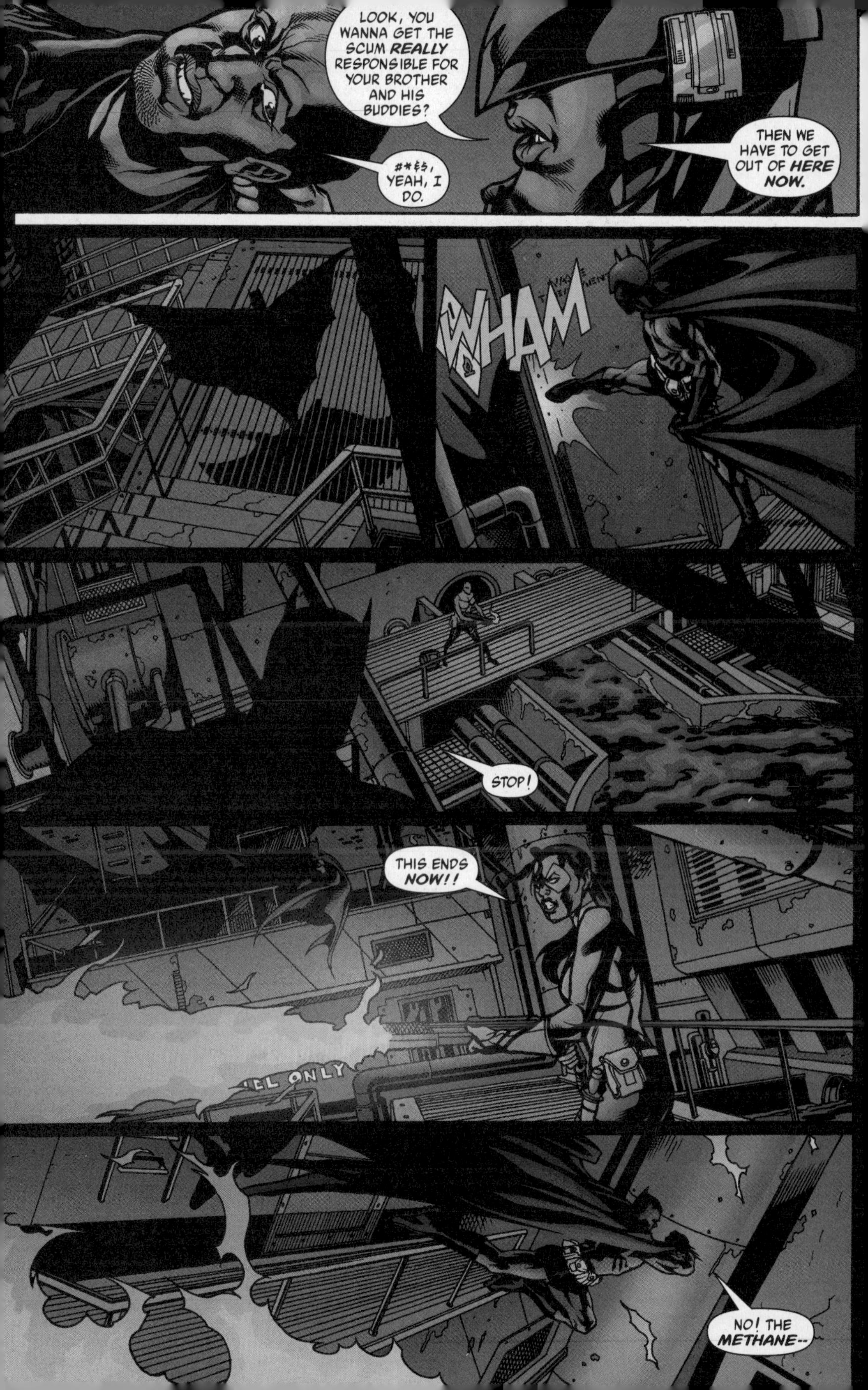
LOOK, YOU WANNA GET THE SCUM REALLY RESPONSIBLE FOR YOUR BROTHER AND HIS BUDDIES?
#*$%, YEAH, I DO.
THEN WE HAVE TO GET OUT OF HERE NOW.
WHAM
STOP!
THIS ENDS NOW!!
EL ONLY
NO! THE METHANE--

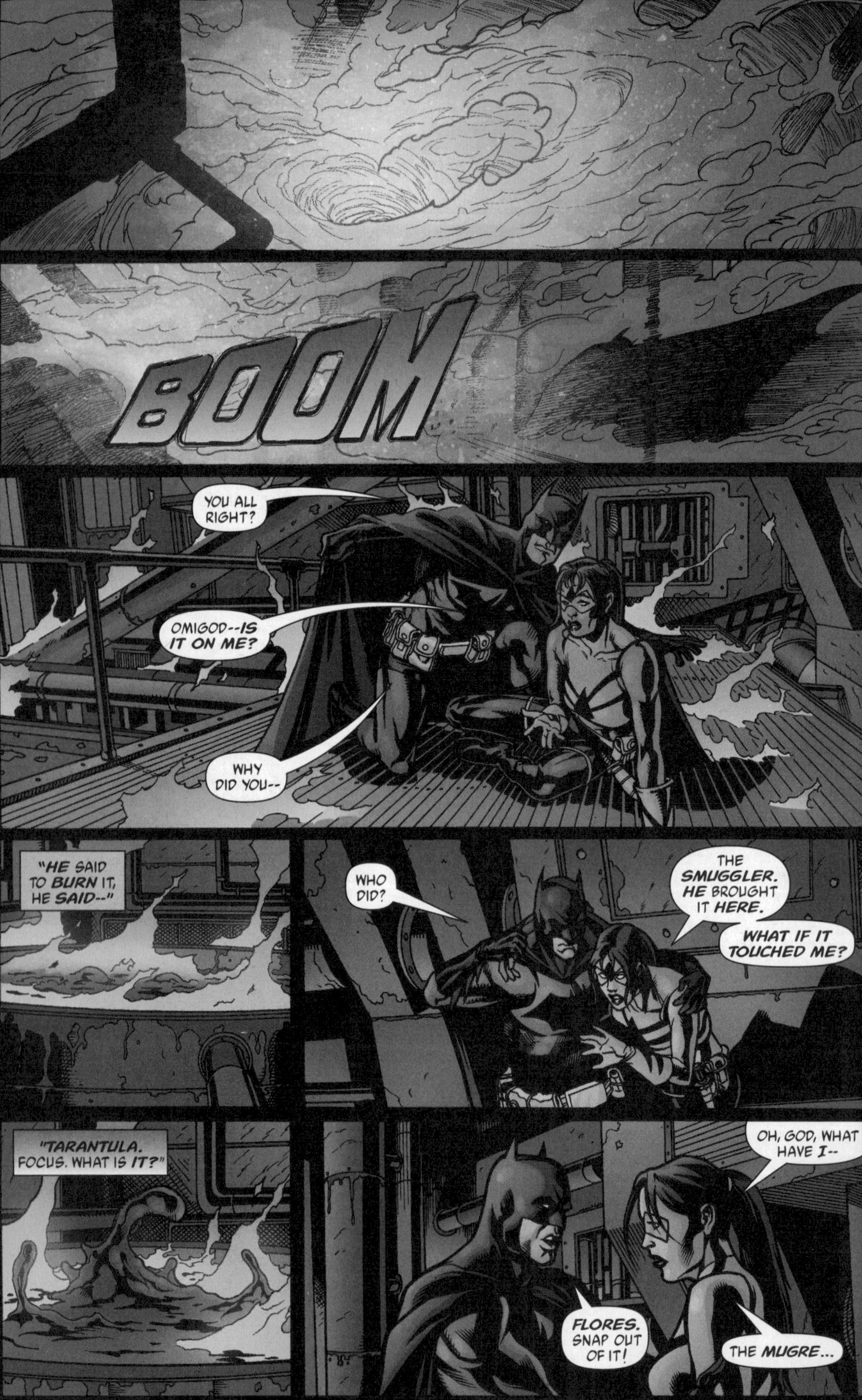
BOOM
YOU ALL RIGHT?
OMIGOD--IS IT ON ME?
WHY DID YOU--
"HE SAID TO BURN IT, HE SAID--"
WHO DID?
THE SMUGGLER. HE BROUGHT IT HERE.
WHAT IF IT TOUCHED ME?
"TARANTULA. FOCUS. WHAT IS IT?"
OH, GOD, WHAT HAVE I--
FLORES. SNAP OUT OF IT!
THE MUGRE...

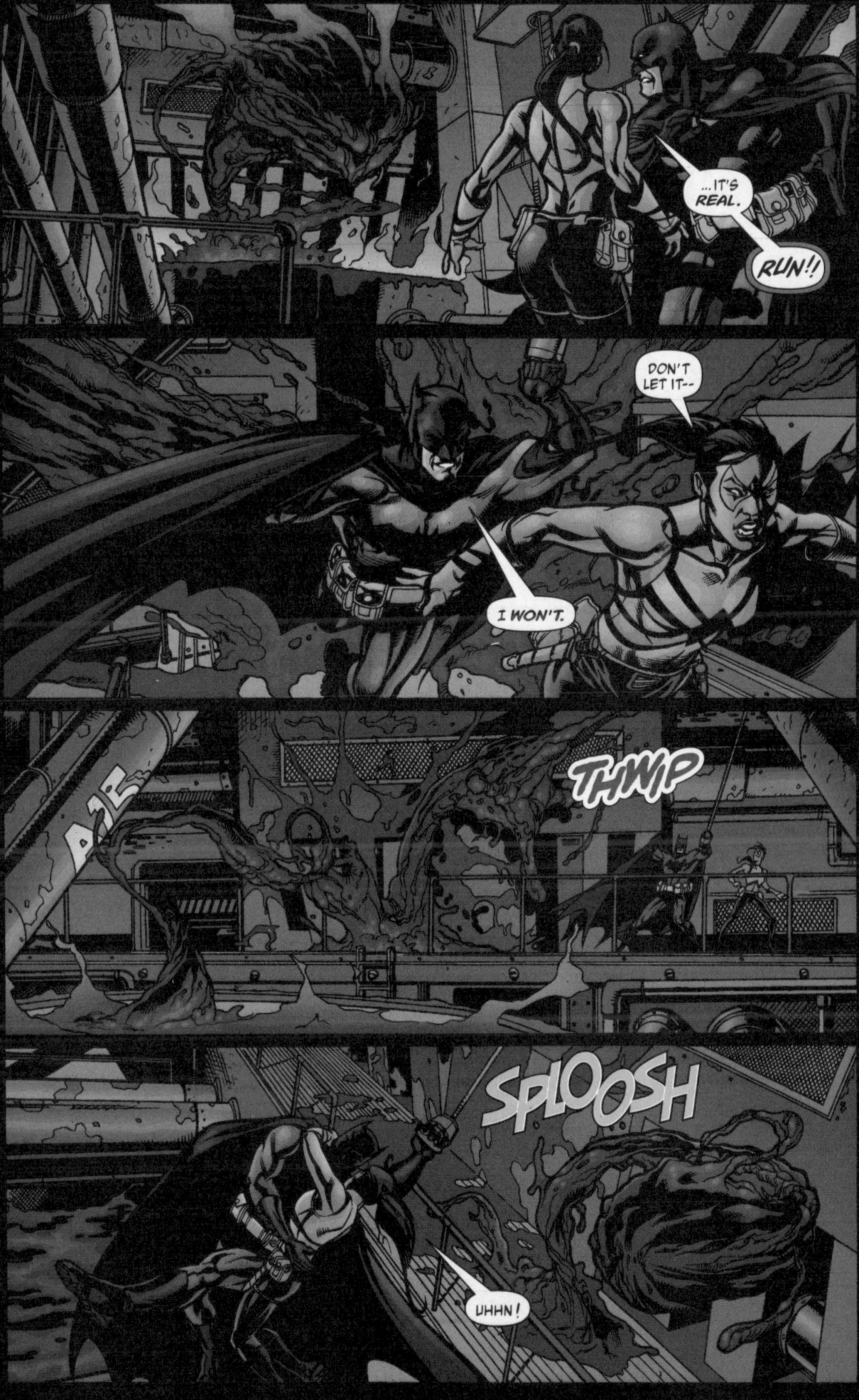
...IT'S REAL.
RUN!!
DON'T LET IT--
I WON'T.
THWIP
SPLOOSH
UHHN!

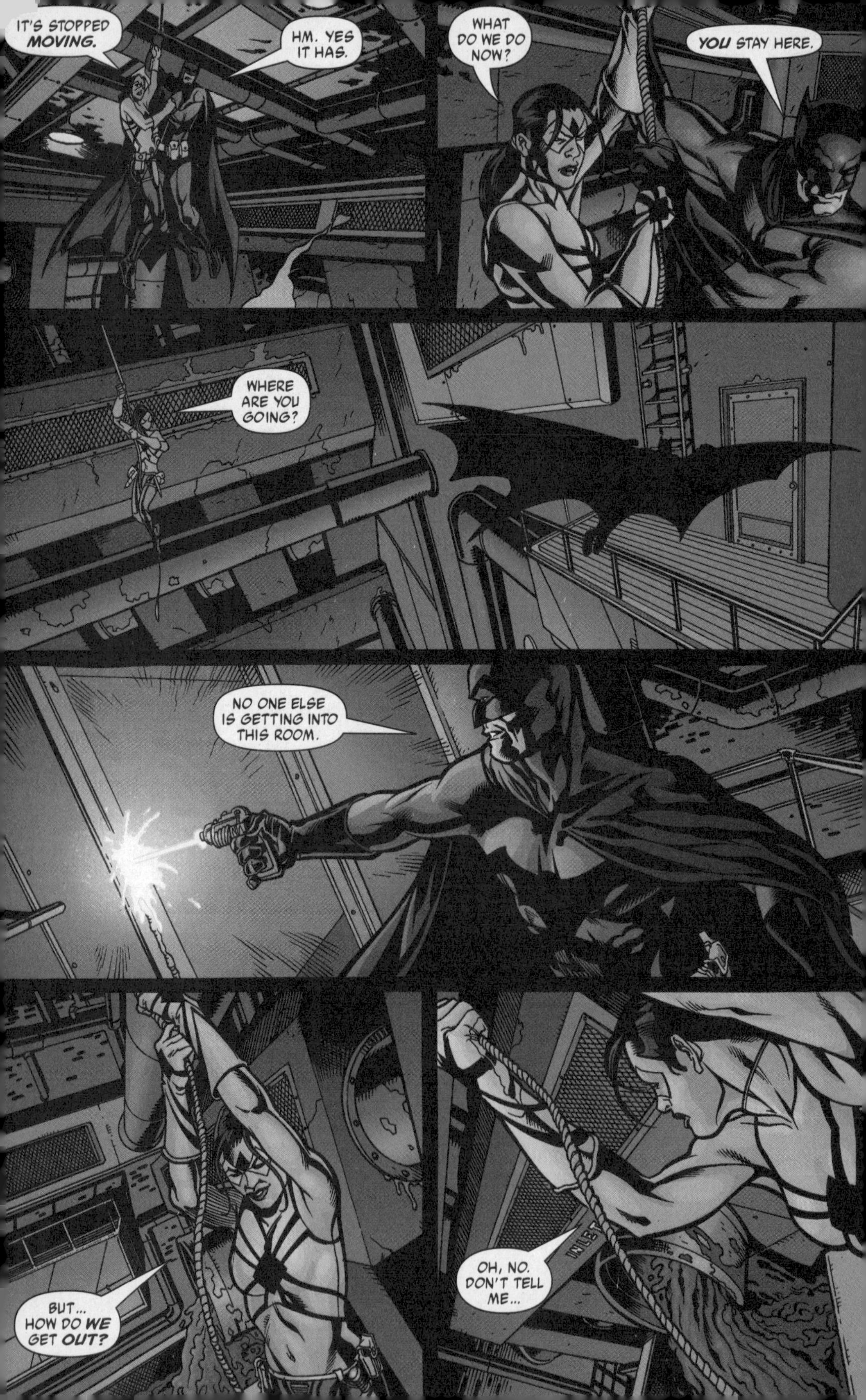
IT'S STOPPED **MOVING.**
HM. YES IT HAS.
WHAT DO WE DO NOW?
YOU STAY HERE.
WHERE ARE YOU GOING?
NO ONE ELSE IS GETTING INTO THIS ROOM.
BUT... HOW DO **WE** GET **OUT?**
OH, NO. DON'T TELL ME...
INLET

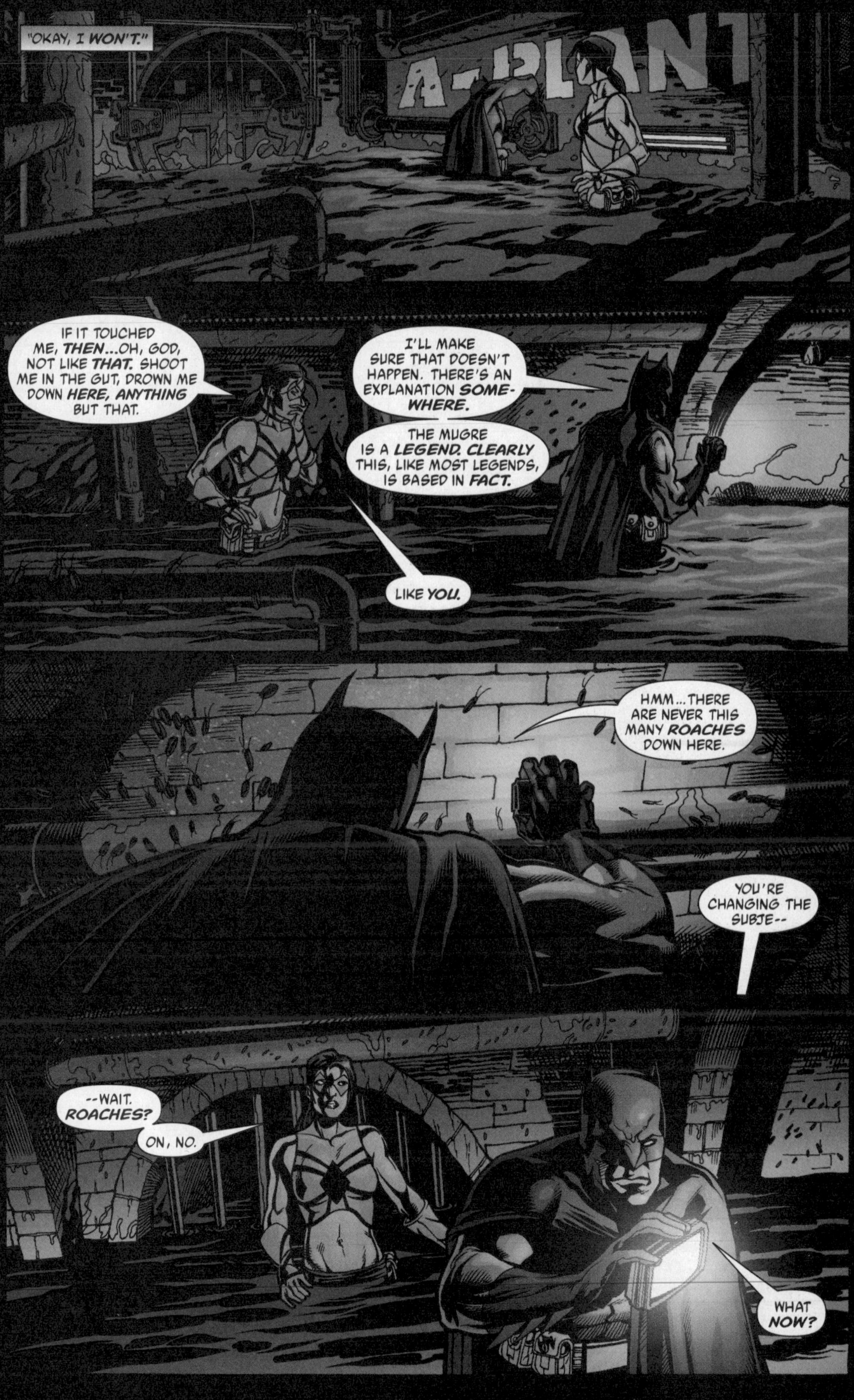
"OKAY, I WON'T."
A-PLANT
IF IT TOUCHED ME, THEN...OH, GOD, NOT LIKE THAT. SHOOT ME IN THE GUT, DROWN ME DOWN HERE, ANYTHING BUT THAT.
I'LL MAKE SURE THAT DOESN'T HAPPEN. THERE'S AN EXPLANATION SOME-WHERE.
THE MUGRE IS A LEGEND. CLEARLY THIS, LIKE MOST LEGENDS, IS BASED IN FACT.
LIKE YOU.
HMM...THERE ARE NEVER THIS MANY ROACHES DOWN HERE.
YOU'RE CHANGING THE SUBJE--
--WAIT. ROACHES?
ON, NO.
WHAT NOW?

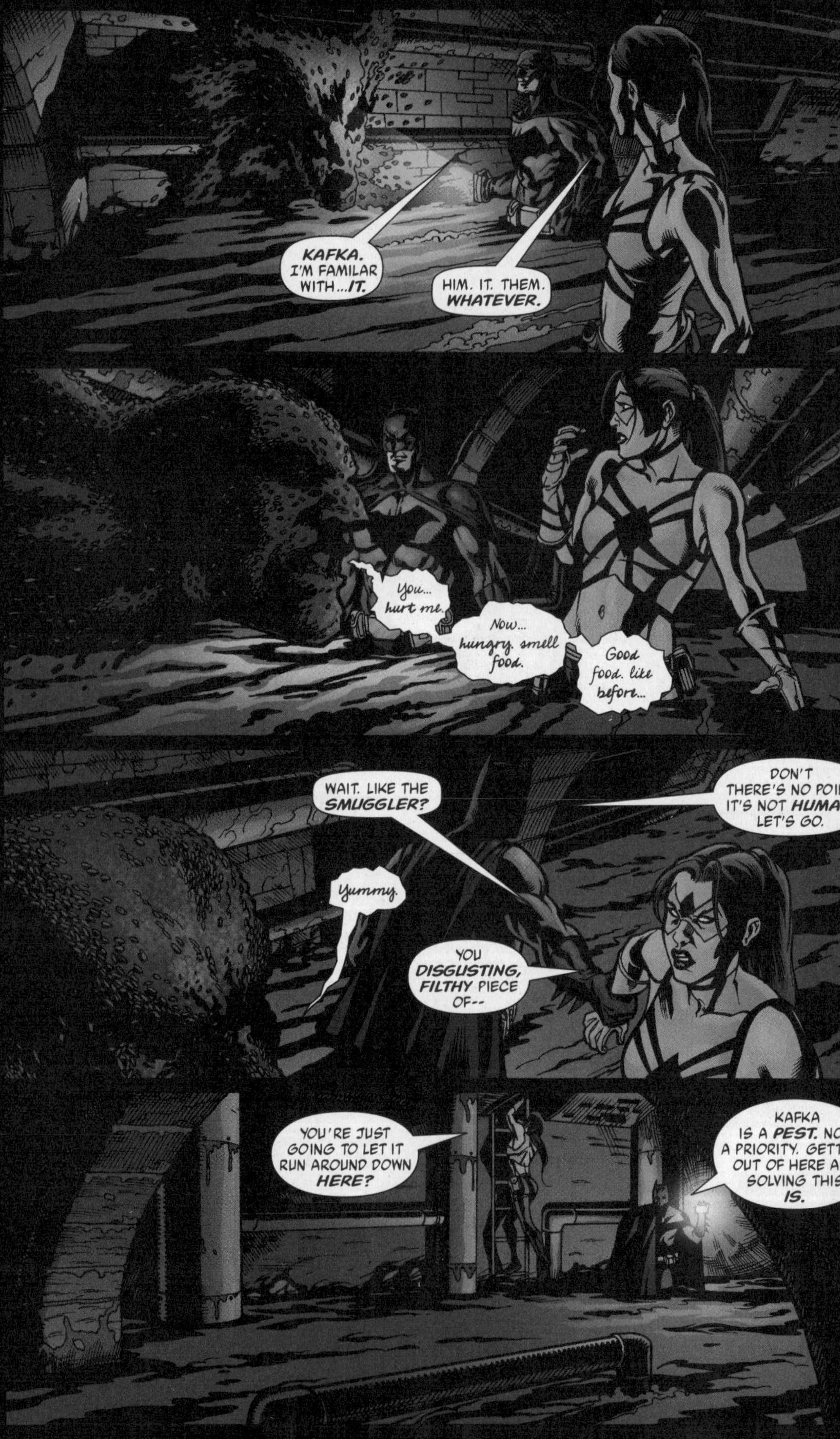
KAFKA. I'M FAMILAR WITH ...IT.
HIM. IT. THEM. WHATEVER.
You... hurt me.
Now... hungry. smell food.
Good food. like before...
WAIT. LIKE THE SMUGGLER?
DON'T THERE'S NO POINT, IT'S NOT HUMAN. LET'S GO.
Yummy.
YOU DISGUSTING, FILTHY PIECE OF--
YOU'RE JUST GOING TO LET IT RUN AROUND DOWN HERE?
KAFKA IS A PEST. NOT A PRIORITY. GETTING OUT OF HERE AND SOLVING THIS IS.

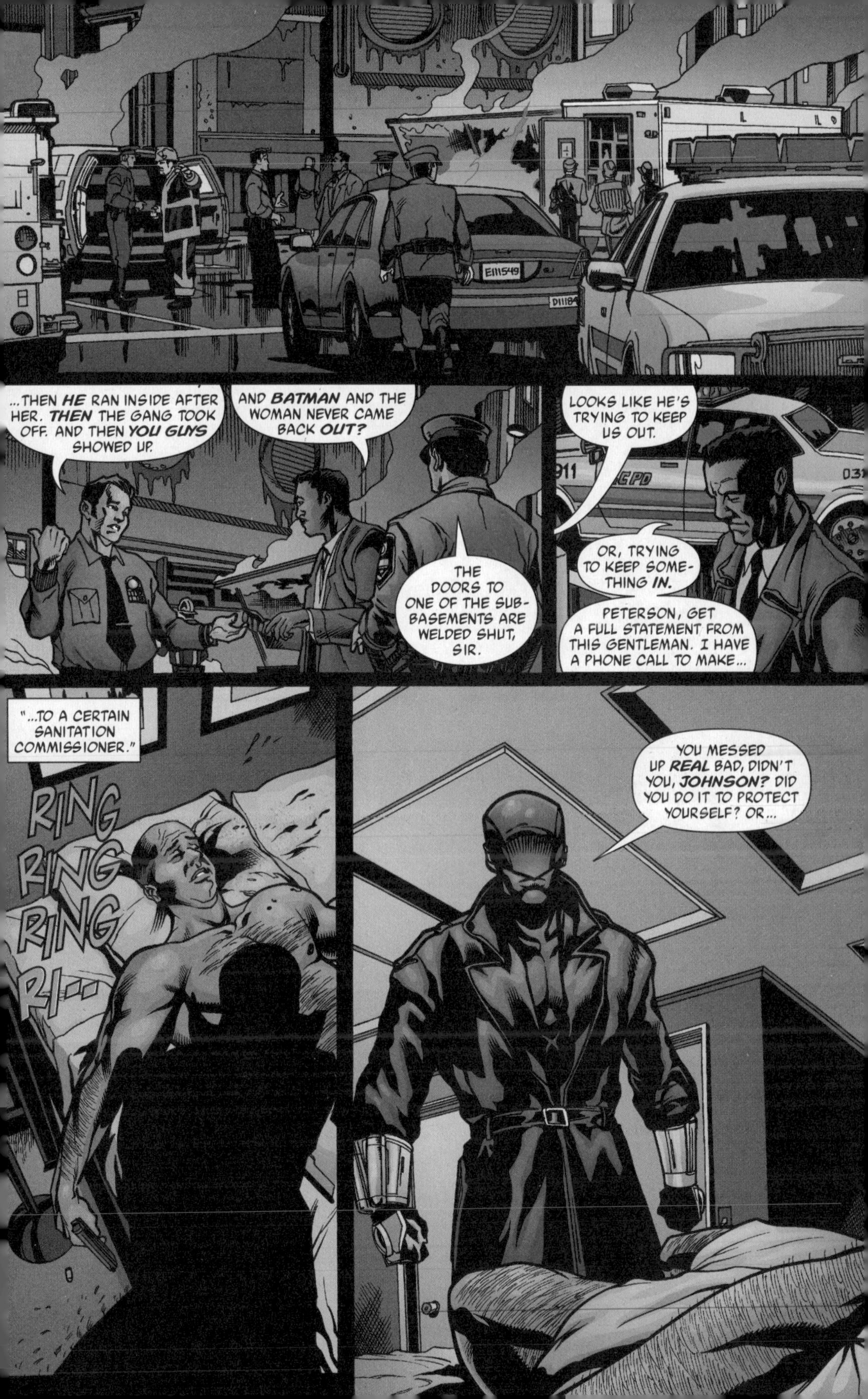
...THEN HE RAN INSIDE AFTER HER. THEN THE GANG TOOK OFF. AND THEN YOU GUYS SHOWED UP.
AND BATMAN AND THE WOMAN NEVER CAME BACK OUT?
THE DOORS TO ONE OF THE SUB-BASEMENTS ARE WELDED SHUT, SIR.
LOOKS LIKE HE'S TRYING TO KEEP US OUT.
OR, TRYING TO KEEP SOME-THING IN.
PETERSON, GET A FULL STATEMENT FROM THIS GENTLEMAN. I HAVE A PHONE CALL TO MAKE...
"...TO A CERTAIN SANITATION COMMISSIONER."
RING RING RING RI--
YOU MESSED UP REAL BAD, DIDN'T YOU, JOHNSON? DID YOU DO IT TO PROTECT YOURSELF? OR...

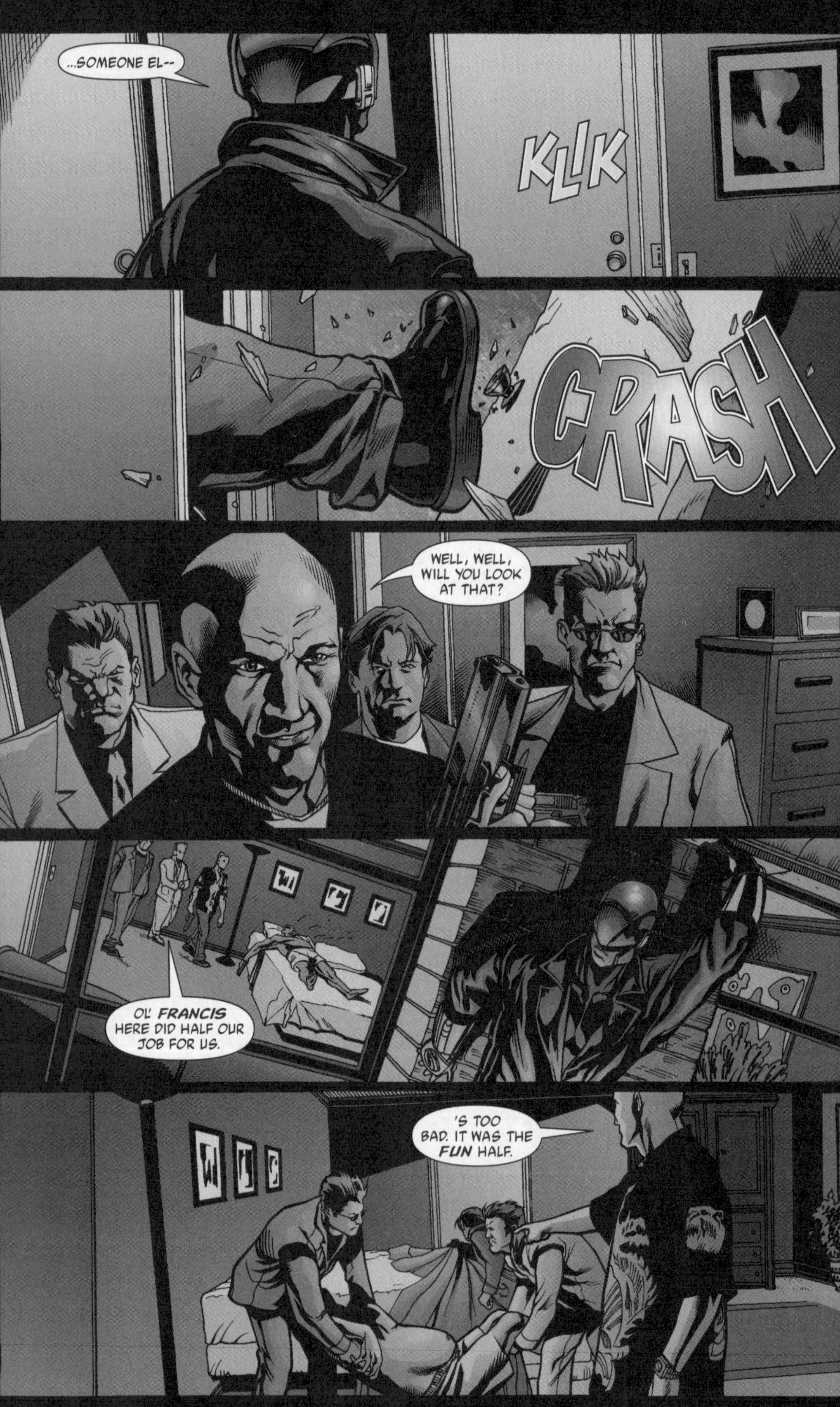
...SOMEONE EL--
KLIK
CRASH
WELL, WELL, WILL YOU LOOK AT THAT?
OL' FRANCIS HERE DID HALF OUR JOB FOR US.
'S TOO BAD. IT WAS THE FUN HALF.

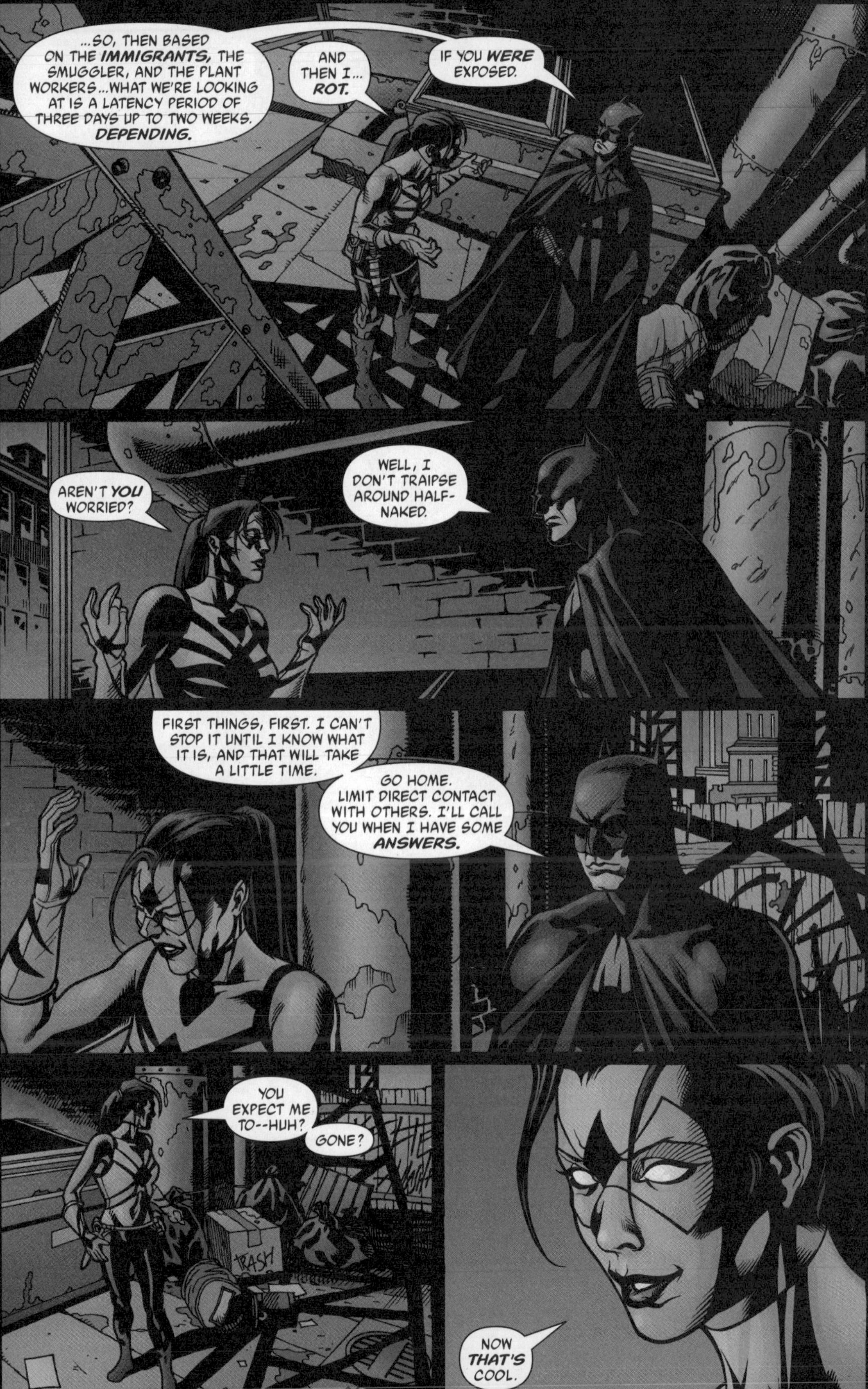
...SO, THEN BASED ON THE IMMIGRANTS, THE SMUGGLER, AND THE PLANT WORKERS...WHAT WE'RE LOOKING AT IS A LATENCY PERIOD OF THREE DAYS UP TO TWO WEEKS. DEPENDING.
AND THEN I... ROT.
IF YOU WERE EXPOSED.
AREN'T YOU WORRIED?
WELL, I DON'T TRAIPSE AROUND HALF-NAKED.
FIRST THINGS, FIRST. I CAN'T STOP IT UNTIL I KNOW WHAT IT IS, AND THAT WILL TAKE A LITTLE TIME.
GO HOME. LIMIT DIRECT CONTACT WITH OTHERS. I'LL CALL YOU WHEN I HAVE SOME ANSWERS.
YOU EXPECT ME TO--HUH?
GONE?
TRASH
NOW THAT'S COOL.

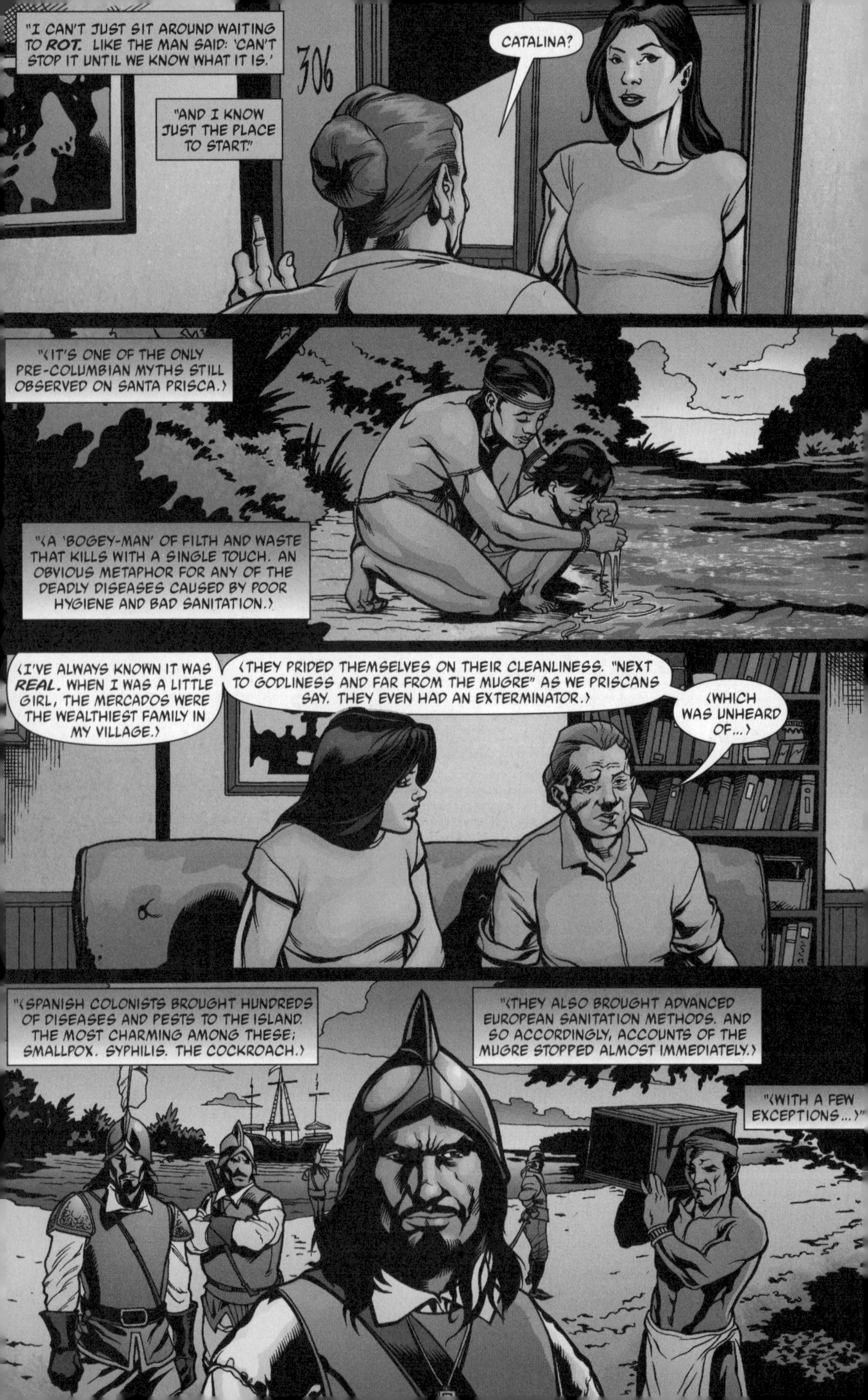
"I CAN'T JUST SIT AROUND WAITING TO ROT. LIKE THE MAN SAID: 'CAN'T STOP IT UNTIL WE KNOW WHAT IT IS.'
306
CATALINA?
"AND I KNOW JUST THE PLACE TO START."
"‹IT'S ONE OF THE ONLY PRE-COLUMBIAN MYTHS STILL OBSERVED ON SANTA PRISCA.›
"‹A 'BOGEY-MAN' OF FILTH AND WASTE THAT KILLS WITH A SINGLE TOUCH. AN OBVIOUS METAPHOR FOR ANY OF THE DEADLY DISEASES CAUSED BY POOR HYGIENE AND BAD SANITATION.›
‹I'VE ALWAYS KNOWN IT WAS REAL. WHEN I WAS A LITTLE GIRL, THE MERCADOS WERE THE WEALTHIEST FAMILY IN MY VILLAGE.›
‹THEY PRIDED THEMSELVES ON THEIR CLEANLINESS. "NEXT TO GODLINESS AND FAR FROM THE MUGRE" AS WE PRISCANS SAY. THEY EVEN HAD AN EXTERMINATOR.›
‹WHICH WAS UNHEARD OF...›
"‹SPANISH COLONISTS BROUGHT HUNDREDS OF DISEASES AND PESTS TO THE ISLAND. THE MOST CHARMING AMONG THESE; SMALLPOX. SYPHILIS. THE COCKROACH.›
"‹THEY ALSO BROUGHT ADVANCED EUROPEAN SANITATION METHODS. AND SO ACCORDINGLY, ACCOUNTS OF THE MUGRE STOPPED ALMOST IMMEDIATELY.›
"‹WITH A FEW EXCEPTIONS...›"

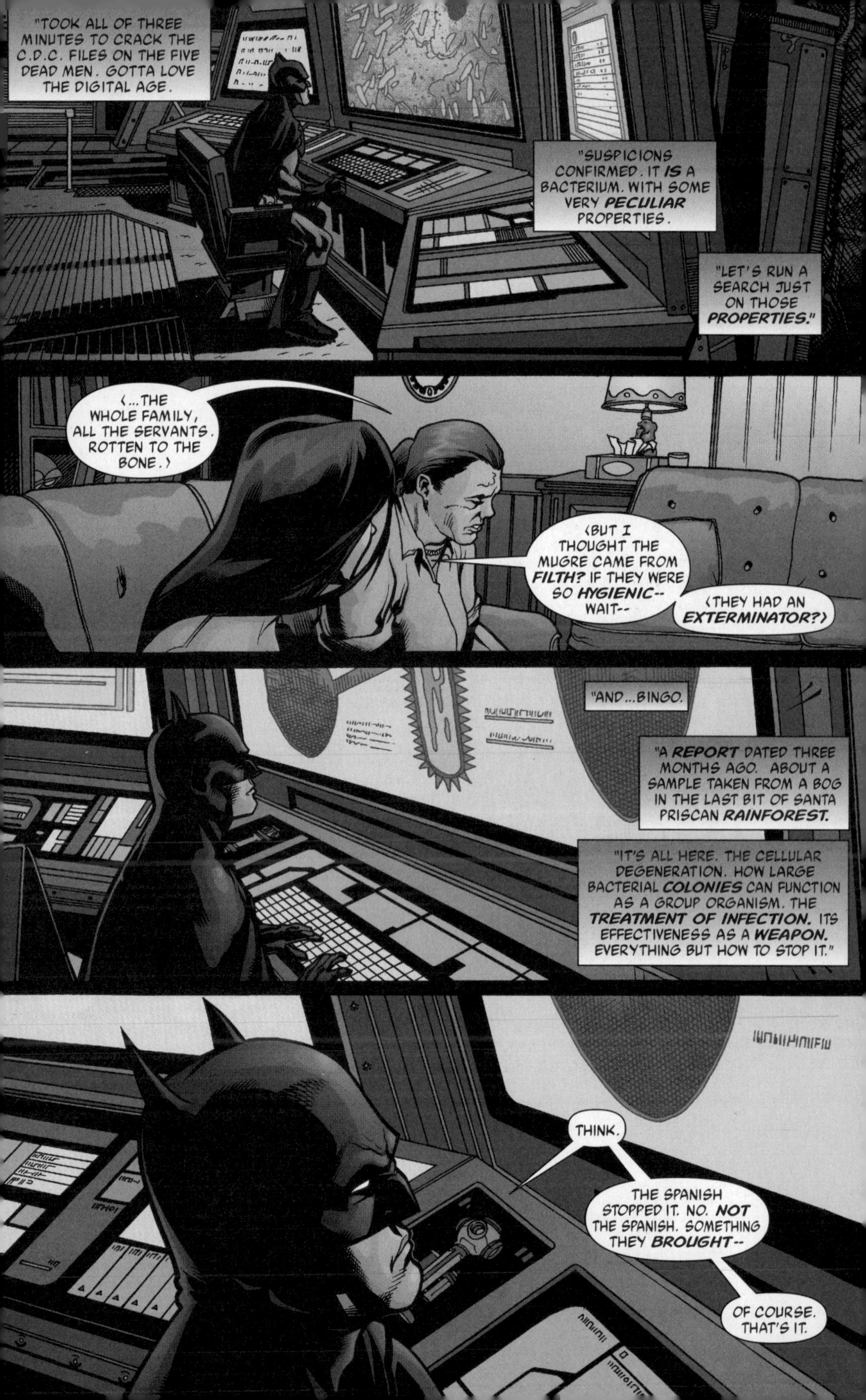
"TOOK ALL OF THREE MINUTES TO CRACK THE C.D.C. FILES ON THE FIVE DEAD MEN. GOTTA LOVE THE DIGITAL AGE.
"SUSPICIONS CONFIRMED. IT IS A BACTERIUM. WITH SOME VERY PECULIAR PROPERTIES.
"LET'S RUN A SEARCH JUST ON THOSE PROPERTIES."
‹...THE WHOLE FAMILY, ALL THE SERVANTS. ROTTEN TO THE BONE.›
‹BUT I THOUGHT THE MUGRE CAME FROM FILTH? IF THEY WERE SO HYGIENIC-- WAIT--
‹THEY HAD AN EXTERMINATOR?›
"AND...BINGO.
"A REPORT DATED THREE MONTHS AGO. ABOUT A SAMPLE TAKEN FROM A BOG IN THE LAST BIT OF SANTA PRISCAN RAINFOREST.
"IT'S ALL HERE. THE CELLULAR DEGENERATION. HOW LARGE BACTERIAL COLONIES CAN FUNCTION AS A GROUP ORGANISM. THE TREATMENT OF INFECTION. ITS EFFECTIVENESS AS A WEAPON. EVERYTHING BUT HOW TO STOP IT."
THINK.
THE SPANISH STOPPED IT. NO. NOT THE SPANISH. SOMETHING THEY BROUGHT--
OF COURSE. THAT'S IT.

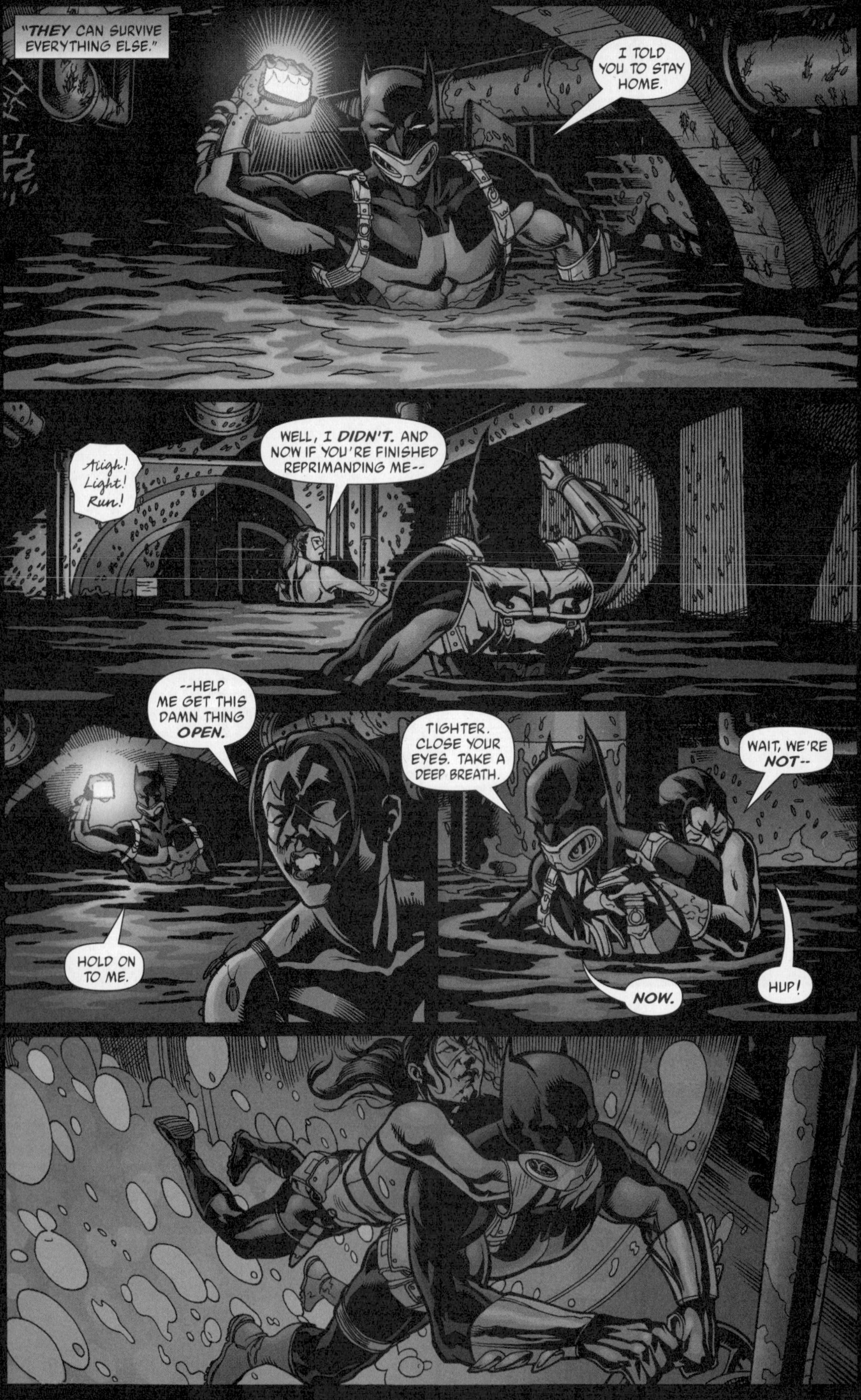
"THEY CAN SURVIVE EVERYTHING ELSE."
I TOLD YOU TO STAY HOME.
Aiigh! Light! Run!
WELL, I DIDN'T. AND NOW IF YOU'RE FINISHED REPRIMANDING ME--
--HELP ME GET THIS DAMN THING OPEN.
HOLD ON TO ME.
TIGHTER. CLOSE YOUR EYES. TAKE A DEEP BREATH.
WAIT, WE'RE NOT--
NOW.
HUP!

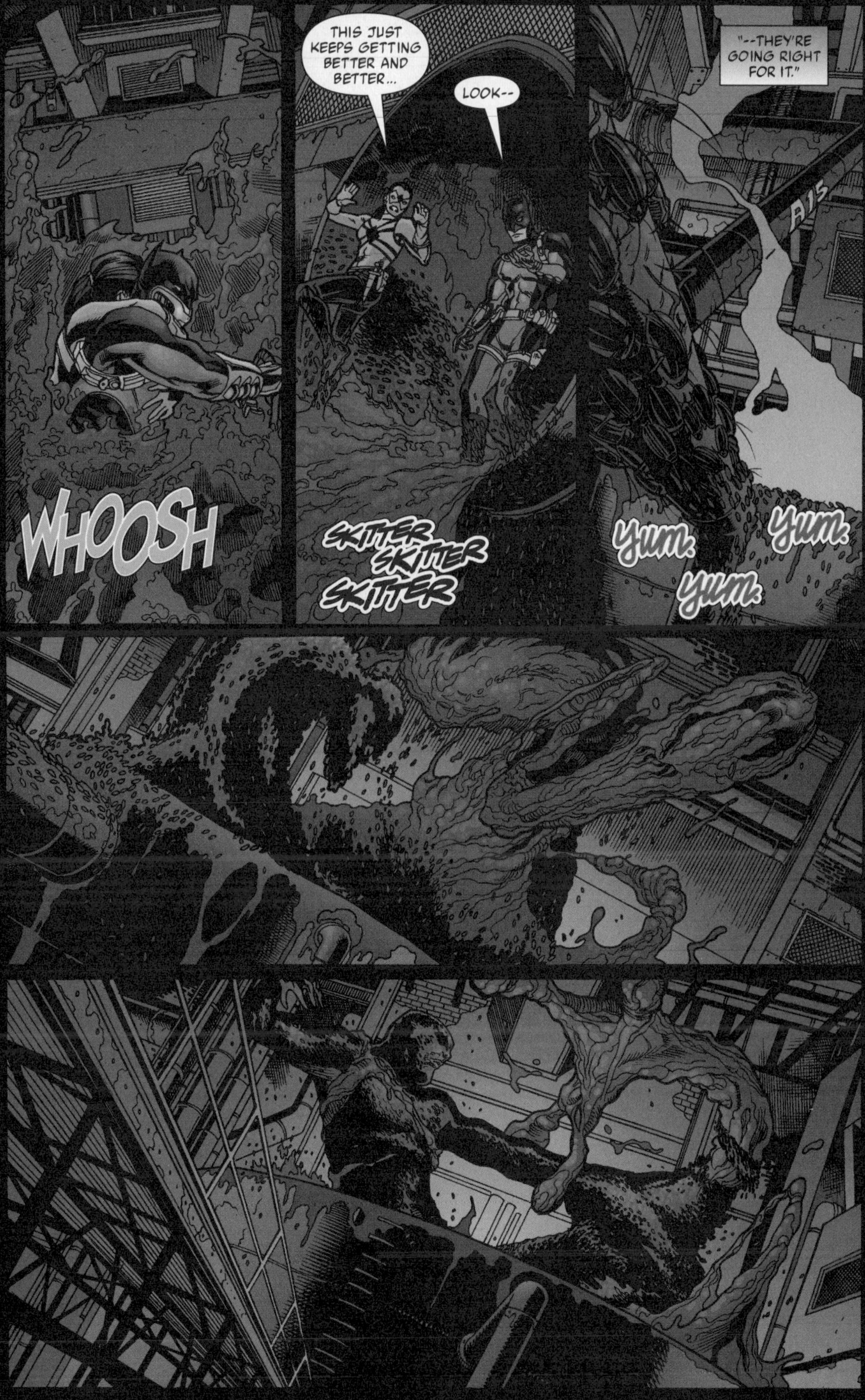
WHOOSH
THIS JUST KEEPS GETTING BETTER AND BETTER...
LOOK--
SKITTER SKITTER SKITTER
"--THEY'RE GOING RIGHT FOR IT."
A15
YUM. YUM. YUM.

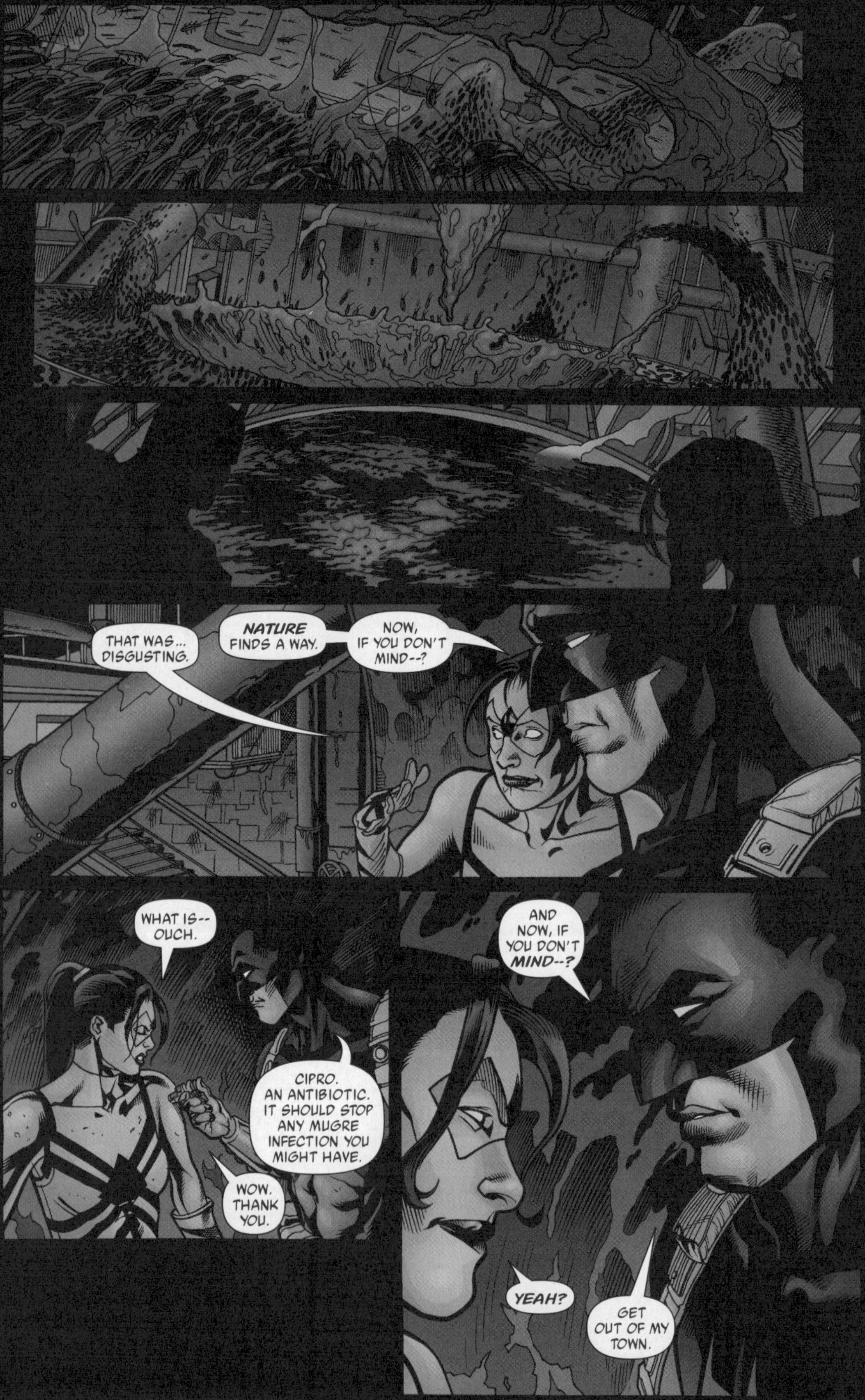
THAT WAS... DISGUSTING.
NATURE FINDS A WAY.
NOW, IF YOU DON'T MIND--?
WHAT IS-- OUCH.
CIPRO. AN ANTIBIOTIC. IT SHOULD STOP ANY MUGRE INFECTION YOU MIGHT HAVE.
WOW. THANK YOU.
AND NOW, IF YOU DON'T MIND--?
YEAH?
GET OUT OF MY TOWN.

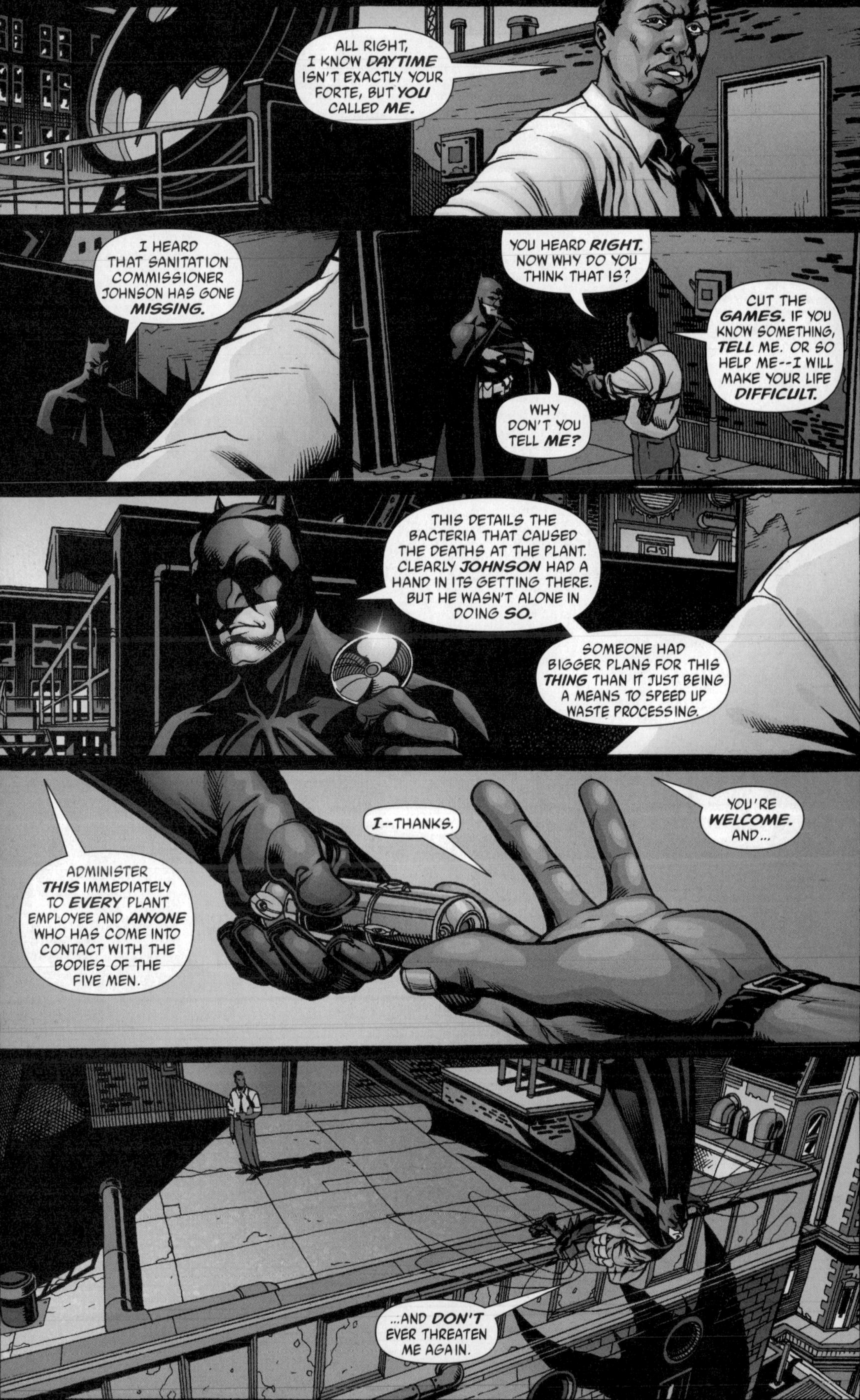
ALL RIGHT, I KNOW DAYTIME ISN'T EXACTLY YOUR FORTE, BUT YOU CALLED ME.
I HEARD THAT SANITATION COMMISSIONER JOHNSON HAS GONE MISSING.
YOU HEARD RIGHT. NOW WHY DO YOU THINK THAT IS?
WHY DON'T YOU TELL ME?
CUT THE GAMES. IF YOU KNOW SOMETHING, TELL ME. OR SO HELP ME--I WILL MAKE YOUR LIFE DIFFICULT.
THIS DETAILS THE BACTERIA THAT CAUSED THE DEATHS AT THE PLANT. CLEARLY JOHNSON HAD A HAND IN ITS GETTING THERE. BUT HE WASN'T ALONE IN DOING SO.
SOMEONE HAD BIGGER PLANS FOR THIS THING THAN IT JUST BEING A MEANS TO SPEED UP WASTE PROCESSING.
ADMINISTER THIS IMMEDIATELY TO EVERY PLANT EMPLOYEE AND ANYONE WHO HAS COME INTO CONTACT WITH THE BODIES OF THE FIVE MEN.
I--THANKS.
YOU'RE WELCOME. AND...
...AND DON'T EVER THREATEN ME AGAIN.

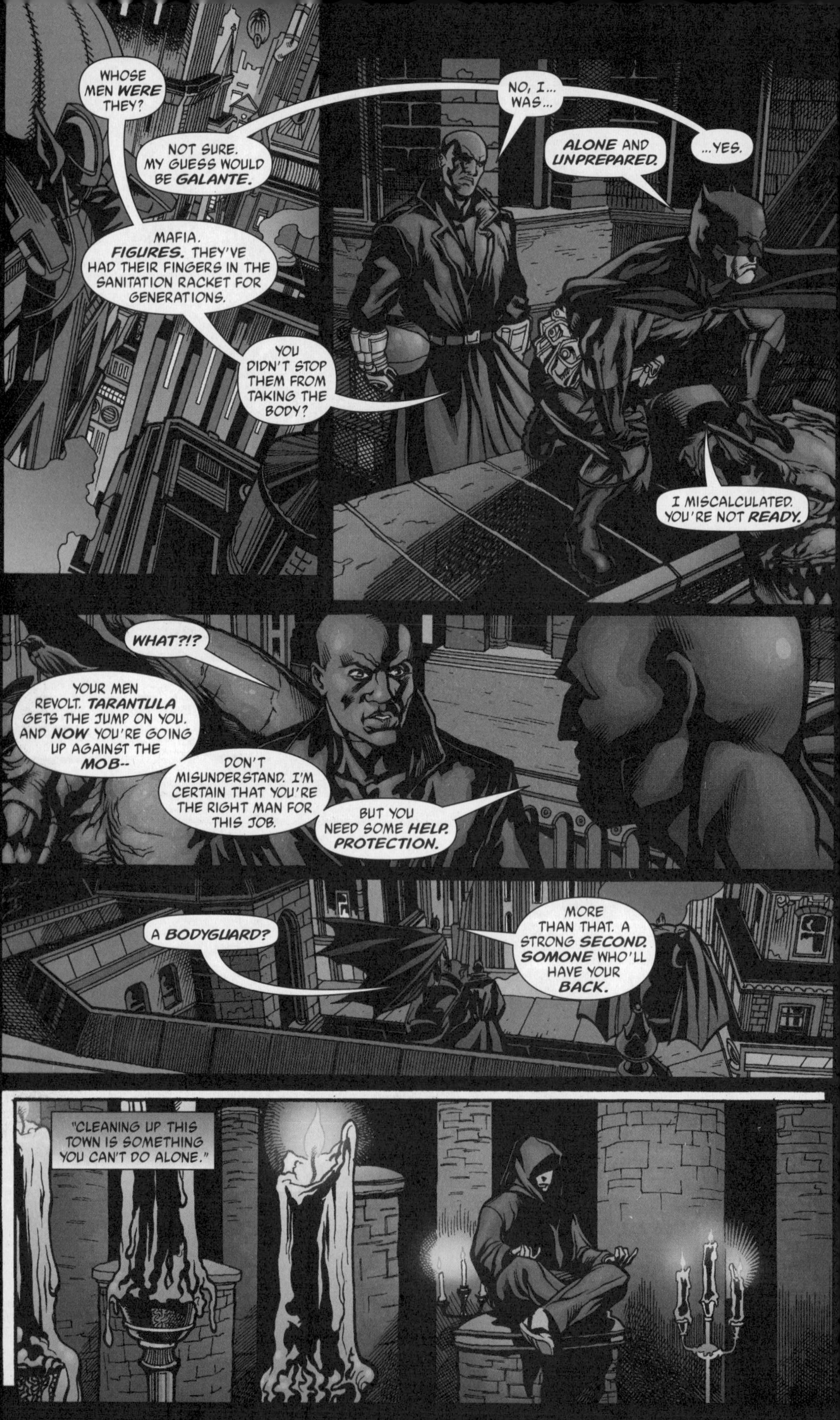

WHOSE MEN WERE THEY?
NOT SURE. MY GUESS WOULD BE GALANTE.
MAFIA. FIGURES. THEY'VE HAD THEIR FINGERS IN THE SANITATION RACKET FOR GENERATIONS.
YOU DIDN'T STOP THEM FROM TAKING THE BODY?
NO, I... WAS...
ALONE AND UNPREPARED.
...YES.
I MISCALCULATED. YOU'RE NOT READY.
WHAT?!?
YOUR MEN REVOLT. TARANTULA GETS THE JUMP ON YOU. AND NOW YOU'RE GOING UP AGAINST THE MOB--
DON'T MISUNDERSTAND. I'M CERTAIN THAT YOU'RE THE RIGHT MAN FOR THIS JOB.
BUT YOU NEED SOME HELP. PROTECTION.
A BODYGUARD?
MORE THAN THAT. A STRONG SECOND. SOMONE WHO'LL HAVE YOUR BACK.
"CLEANING UP THIS TOWN IS SOMETHING YOU CAN'T DO ALONE."

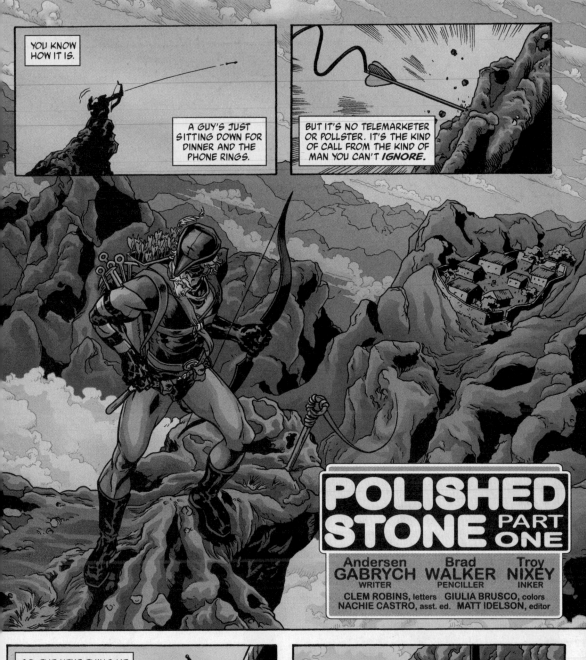

YOU KNOW HOW IT IS.

A GUY'S JUST SITTING DOWN FOR DINNER AND THE PHONE RINGS.

BUT IT'S NO TELEMARKETER OR POLLSTER. IT'S THE KIND OF CALL FROM THE KIND OF MAN YOU CAN'T *IGNORE.*

POLISHED STONE PART ONE

Andersen **GABRYCH** WRITER

Brad **WALKER** PENCILLER

Troy **NIXEY** INKER

CLEM ROBINS, letters GIULIA BRUSCO, colors
NACHIE CASTRO, asst. ed. MATT IDELSON, editor

SO, THE NEXT THING HE KNOWS, HE'S HALFWAY AROUND THE WORLD CLIMBING MOUNTAINS.

THOUGH *GREEN ARROW'S* MADE THIS TRIP BEFORE...

...IT NEVER GETS ANY *EASIER.*

DAMN *BAT* AND HIS FRIGGIN' *IDEAS.*

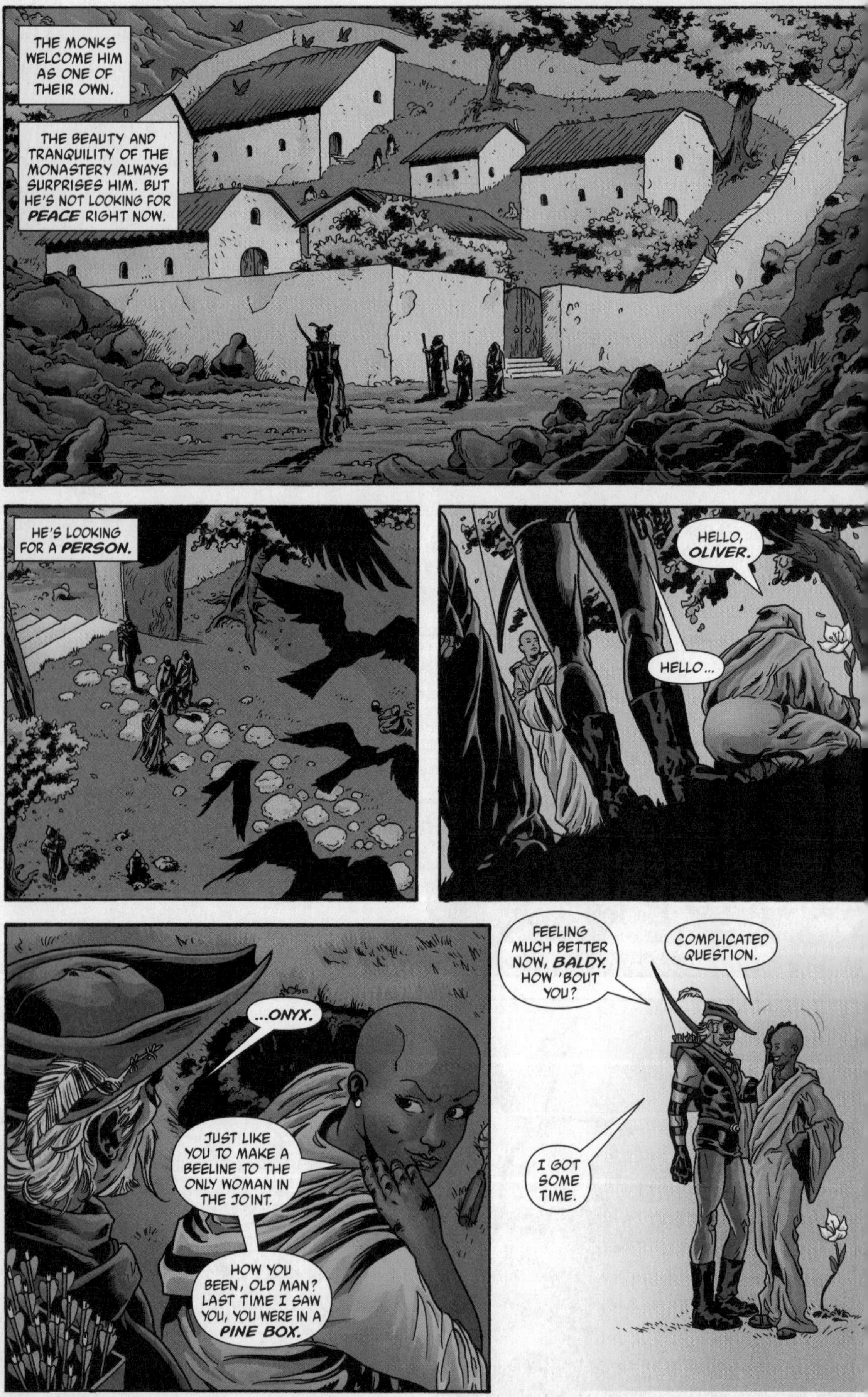
THE MONKS WELCOME HIM AS ONE OF THEIR OWN.
THE BEAUTY AND TRANQUILITY OF THE MONASTERY ALWAYS SURPRISES HIM. BUT HE'S NOT LOOKING FOR **PEACE** RIGHT NOW.
HE'S LOOKING FOR A **PERSON.**
HELLO, **OLIVER.**
HELLO...
...ONYX.
JUST LIKE YOU TO MAKE A BEELINE TO THE ONLY WOMAN IN THE JOINT.
HOW YOU BEEN, OLD MAN? LAST TIME I SAW YOU, YOU WERE IN A **PINE BOX.**
FEELING MUCH BETTER NOW, **BALDY.** HOW 'BOUT YOU?
COMPLICATED QUESTION.
I GOT SOME TIME.

...THEN I CAME BACK *HERE*. NEEDED TO CLEAR MY HEAD ABOUT SOME OF THE *THINGS* I'VE DONE...

LEAGUE OF ASSASSINS KINDA THINGS?

YOU GOT IT.

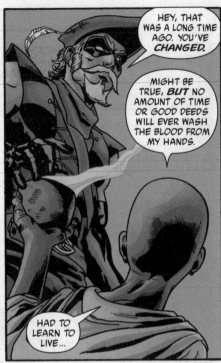

HEY, THAT WAS A LONG TIME AGO. YOU'VE *CHANGED*.

MIGHT BE TRUE, *BUT* NO AMOUNT OF TIME OR GOOD DEEDS WILL EVER WASH THE BLOOD FROM MY HANDS.

HAD TO LEARN TO LIVE...

...WITH DIRTY HANDS. Y'KNOW?

I HEAR *THAT*.

I FIGURED AFTER ALL THIS GARDENING, BASKET-WEAVING, AND SOUL-SEARCHING THAT YOU'D BE...

...BORED OUT OF YOUR SKULL.

HA HA! DAMN STRAIGHT I AM.

WHY? YOU GOT SOME *GOOD DEED* FOR ME TO DO?

WELL, IT'S NOT FOR *ME*...

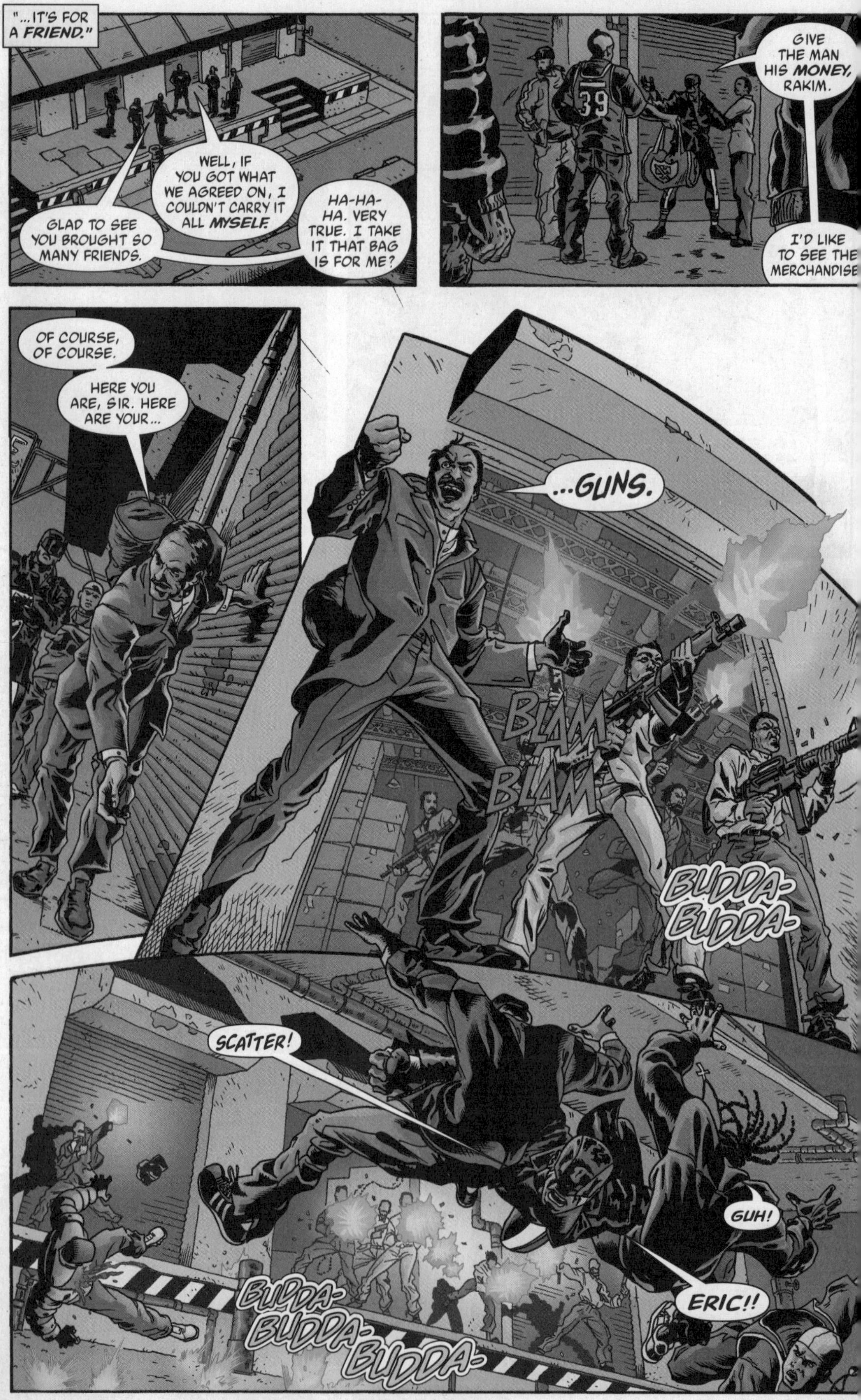
"...IT'S FOR A FRIEND."
WELL, IF YOU GOT WHAT WE AGREED ON, I COULDN'T CARRY IT ALL MYSELF.
GLAD TO SEE YOU BROUGHT SO MANY FRIENDS.
HA-HA-HA. VERY TRUE. I TAKE IT THAT BAG IS FOR ME?
GIVE THE MAN HIS MONEY, RAKIM.
I'D LIKE TO SEE THE MERCHANDISE
OF COURSE, OF COURSE.
HERE YOU ARE, SIR. HERE ARE YOUR...
...GUNS.
BLAM
BLAM
BUDDA-BUDDA-
SCATTER!
GUH!
ERIC!!
BUDDA-BUDDA-BUDDA-

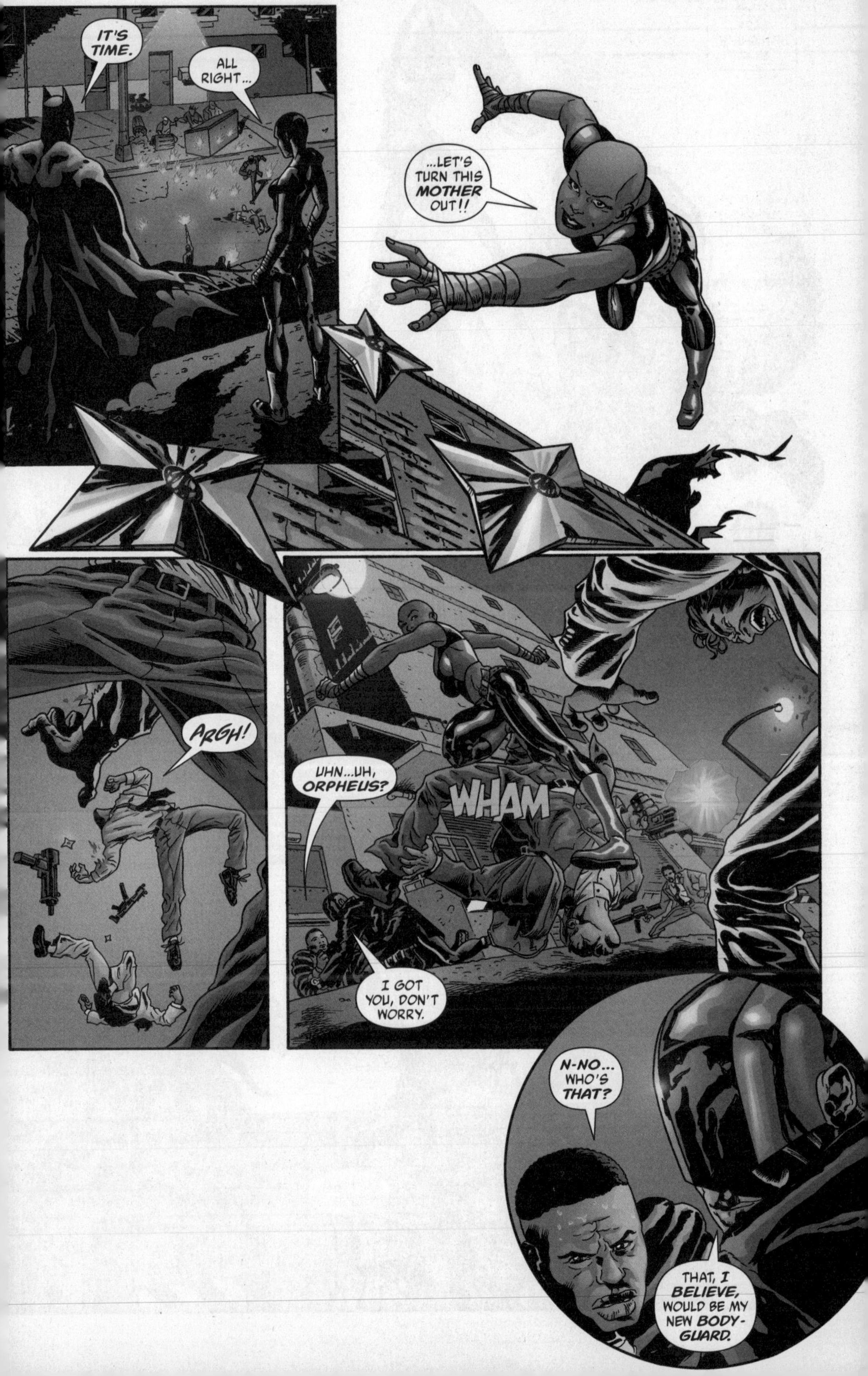

IT'S TIME.
ALL RIGHT...
...LET'S TURN THIS MOTHER OUT!!
ARGH!
UHN...UH, ORPHEUS?
WHAM
I GOT YOU, DON'T WORRY.
N-NO... WHO'S THAT?
THAT, I BELIEVE, WOULD BE MY NEW BODY-GUARD.

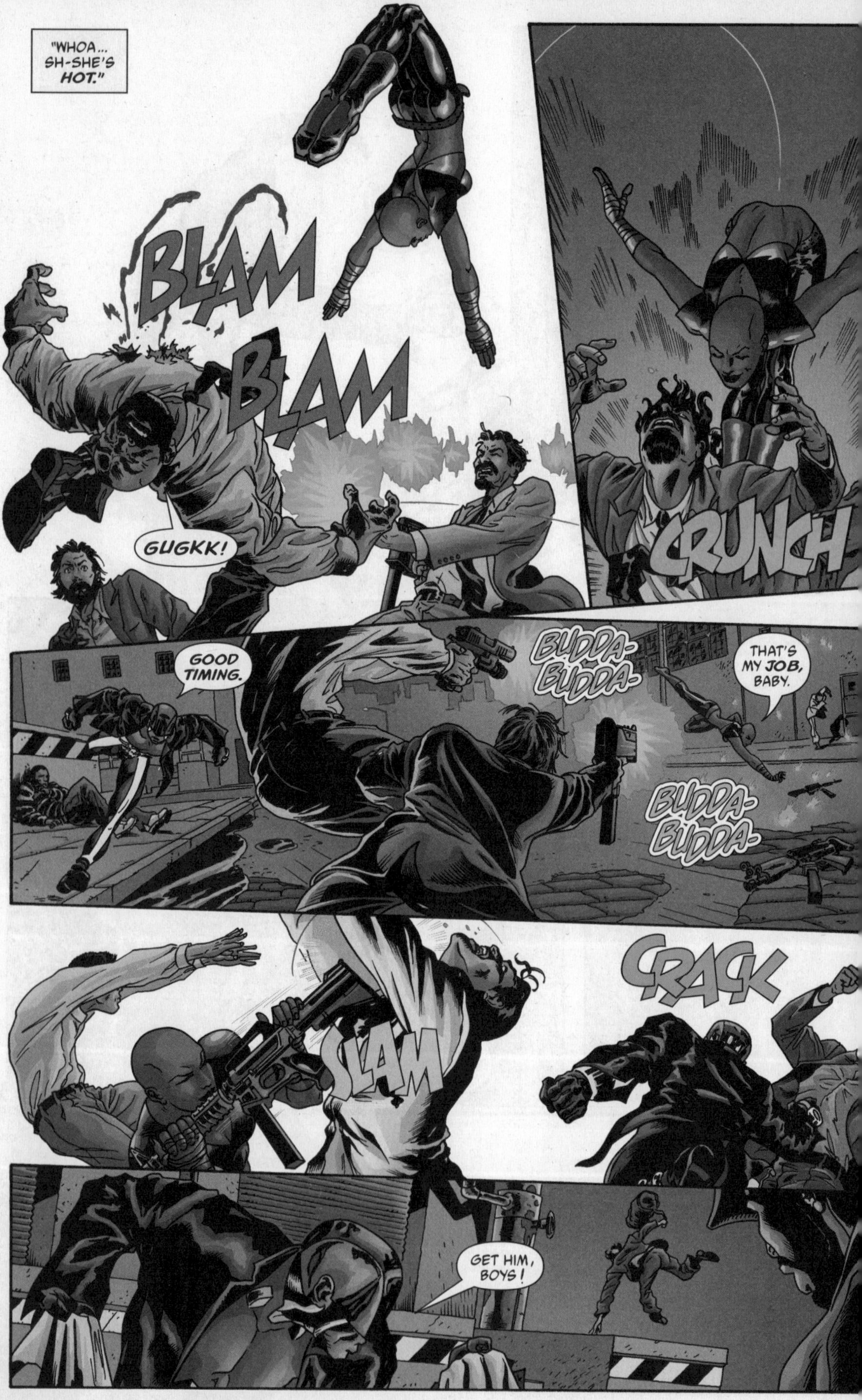

"WHOA... SH-SHE'S HOT."
BLAM
BLAM
GUGKK!
CRUNCH
GOOD TIMING.
BUDDA-BUDDA-
THAT'S MY JOB, BABY.
BUDDA-BUDDA-
SLAM
CRACK
GET HIM, BOYS!

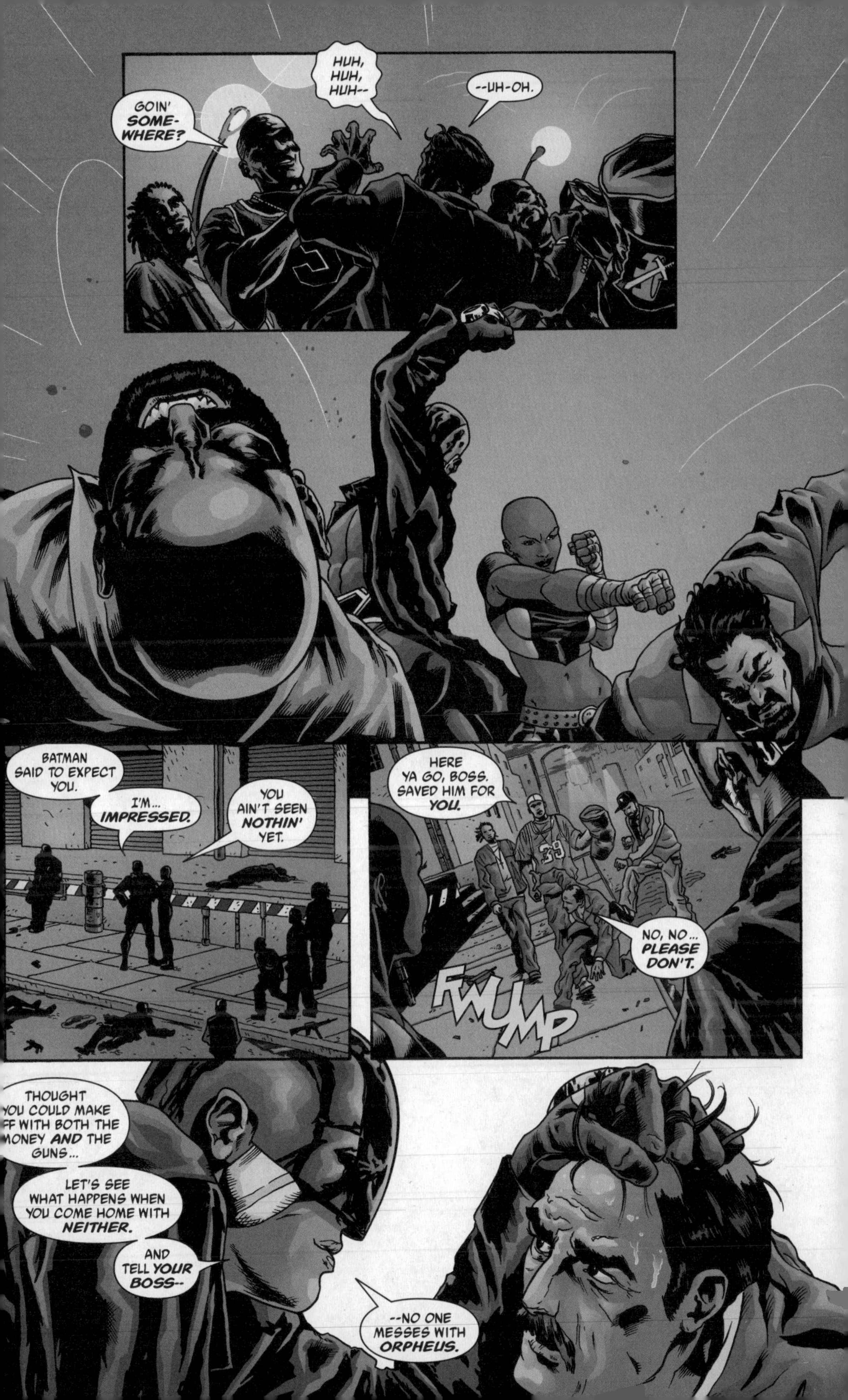
GOIN' SOME-WHERE?
HUH, HUH, HUH--
--UH-OH.
BATMAN SAID TO EXPECT YOU.
I'M... IMPRESSED.
YOU AIN'T SEEN NOTHIN' YET.
HERE YA GO, BOSS. SAVED HIM FOR YOU.
NO, NO... PLEASE DON'T.
FWUMP
THOUGHT YOU COULD MAKE FF WITH BOTH THE MONEY AND THE GUNS...
LET'S SEE WHAT HAPPENS WHEN YOU COME HOME WITH NEITHER.
AND TELL YOUR BOSS--
--NO ONE MESSES WITH ORPHEUS.

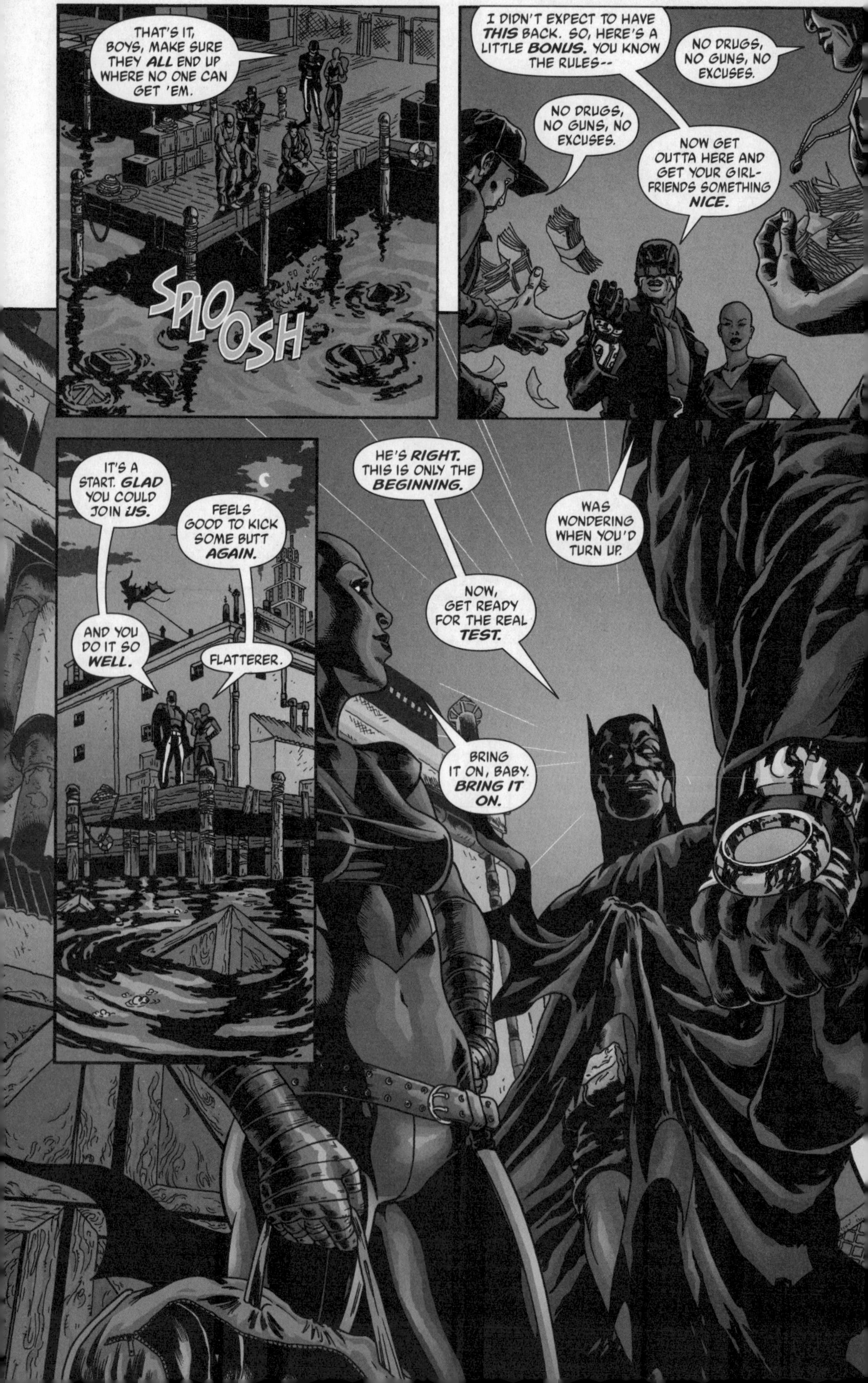
THAT'S IT, BOYS, MAKE SURE THEY ALL END UP WHERE NO ONE CAN GET 'EM.
SPLOOSH
I DIDN'T EXPECT TO HAVE THIS BACK. SO, HERE'S A LITTLE BONUS. YOU KNOW THE RULES--
NO DRUGS, NO GUNS, NO EXCUSES.
NO DRUGS, NO GUNS, NO EXCUSES.
NOW GET OUTTA HERE AND GET YOUR GIRLFRIENDS SOMETHING NICE.
IT'S A START. GLAD YOU COULD JOIN US.
FEELS GOOD TO KICK SOME BUTT AGAIN.
AND YOU DO IT SO WELL.
FLATTERER.
HE'S RIGHT. THIS IS ONLY THE BEGINNING.
NOW, GET READY FOR THE REAL TEST.
WAS WONDERING WHEN YOU'D TURN UP.
BRING IT ON, BABY. BRING IT ON.

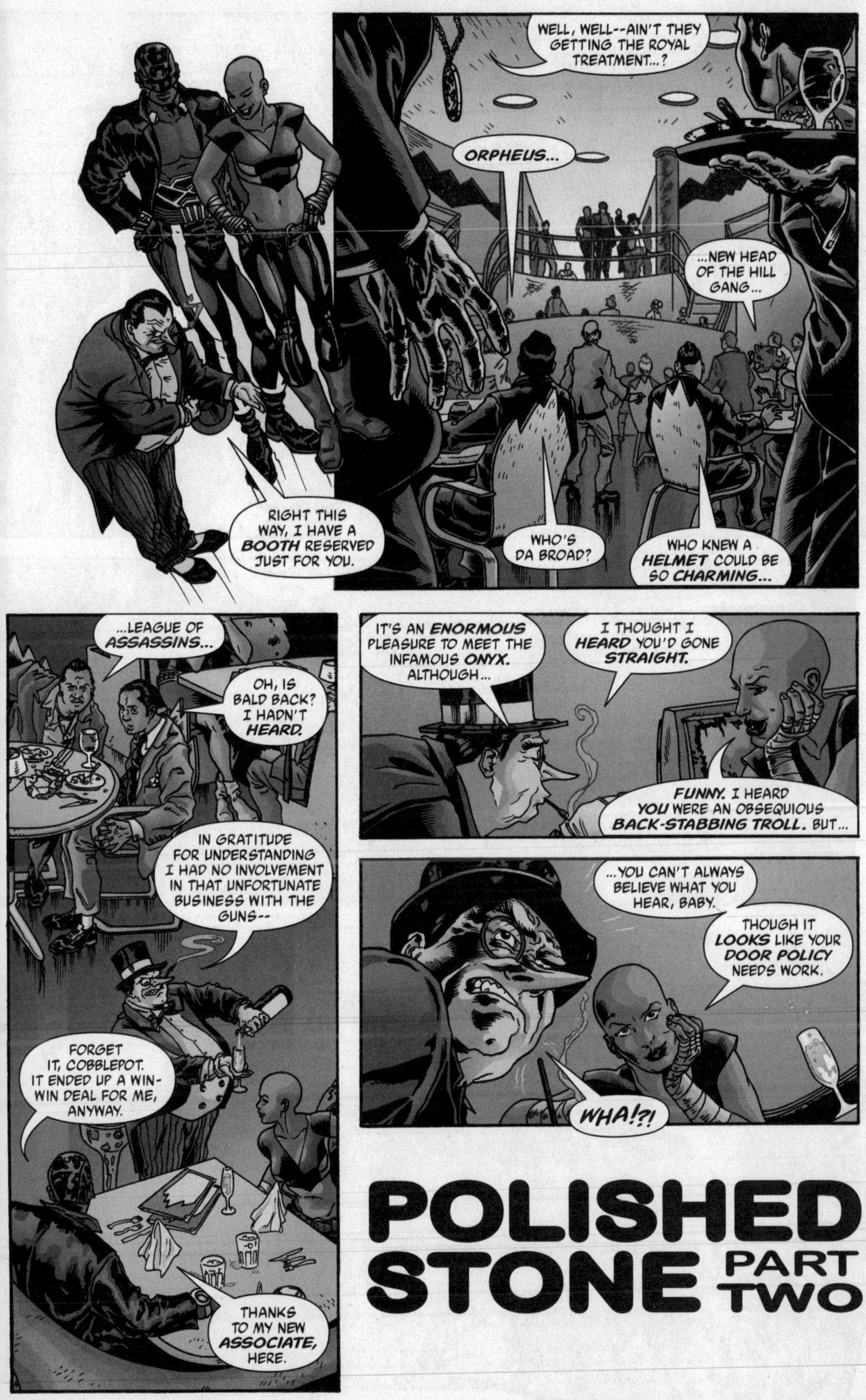
RIGHT THIS WAY, I HAVE A BOOTH RESERVED JUST FOR YOU.
WELL, WELL--AIN'T THEY GETTING THE ROYAL TREATMENT...?
ORPHEUS...
...NEW HEAD OF THE HILL GANG...
WHO'S DA BROAD?
WHO KNEW A HELMET COULD BE SO CHARMING...
...LEAGUE OF ASSASSINS...
OH, IS BALD BACK? I HADN'T HEARD.
IN GRATITUDE FOR UNDERSTANDING I HAD NO INVOLVEMENT IN THAT UNFORTUNATE BUSINESS WITH THE GUNS--
FORGET IT, COBBLEPOT. IT ENDED UP A WIN-WIN DEAL FOR ME, ANYWAY.
THANKS TO MY NEW ASSOCIATE, HERE.
IT'S AN ENORMOUS PLEASURE TO MEET THE INFAMOUS ONYX. ALTHOUGH...
I THOUGHT I HEARD YOU'D GONE STRAIGHT.
FUNNY. I HEARD YOU WERE AN OBSEQUIOUS BACK-STABBING TROLL. BUT...
...YOU CAN'T ALWAYS BELIEVE WHAT YOU HEAR, BABY.
THOUGH IT LOOKS LIKE YOUR DOOR POLICY NEEDS WORK.
WHA!?!

POLISHED STONE PART TWO

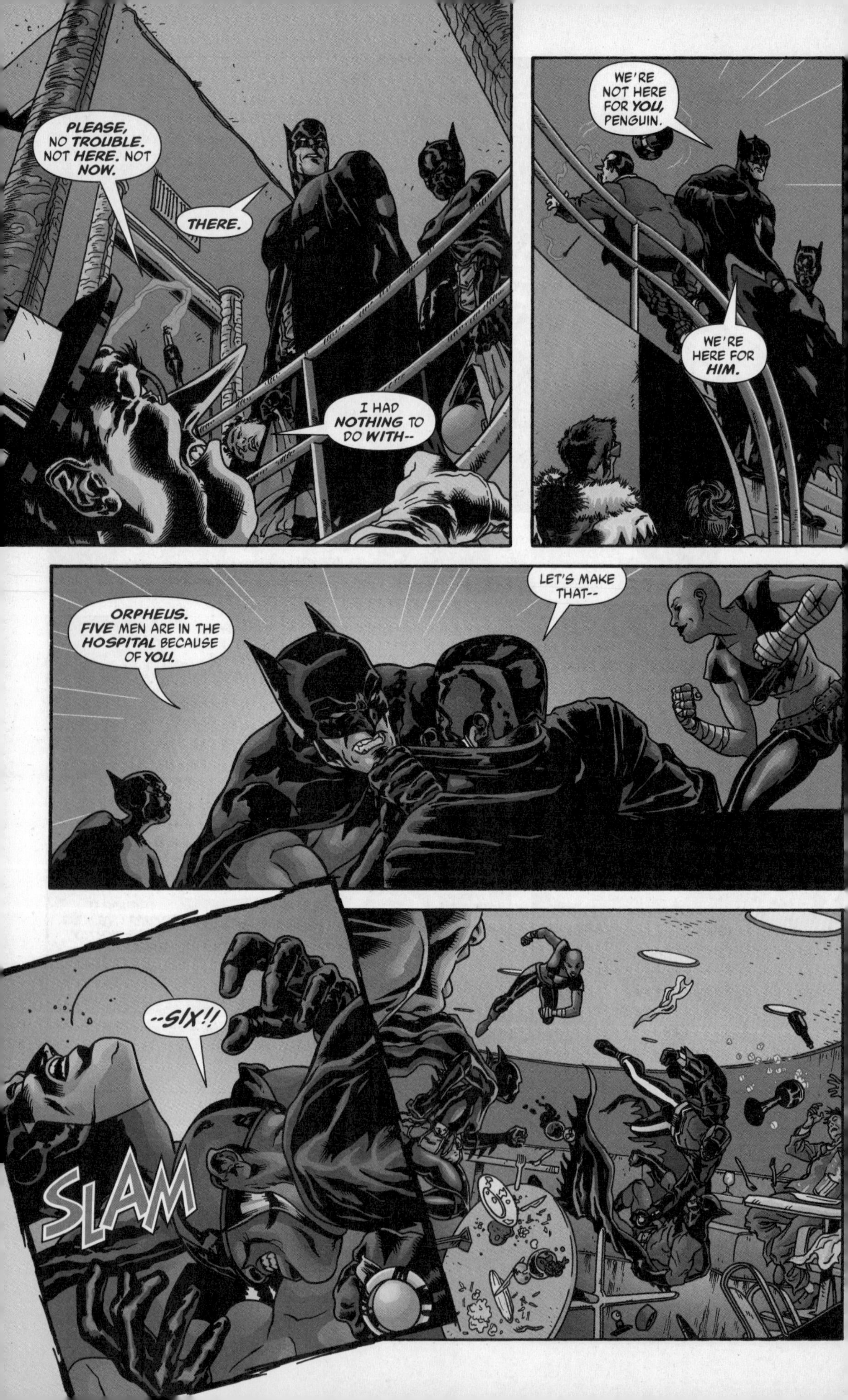
PLEASE, NO TROUBLE. NOT HERE. NOT NOW.
THERE.
I HAD NOTHING TO DO WITH--
WE'RE NOT HERE FOR YOU, PENGUIN.
WE'RE HERE FOR HIM.
ORPHEUS. FIVE MEN ARE IN THE HOSPITAL BECAUSE OF YOU.
LET'S MAKE THAT--
--SIX!!
SLAM

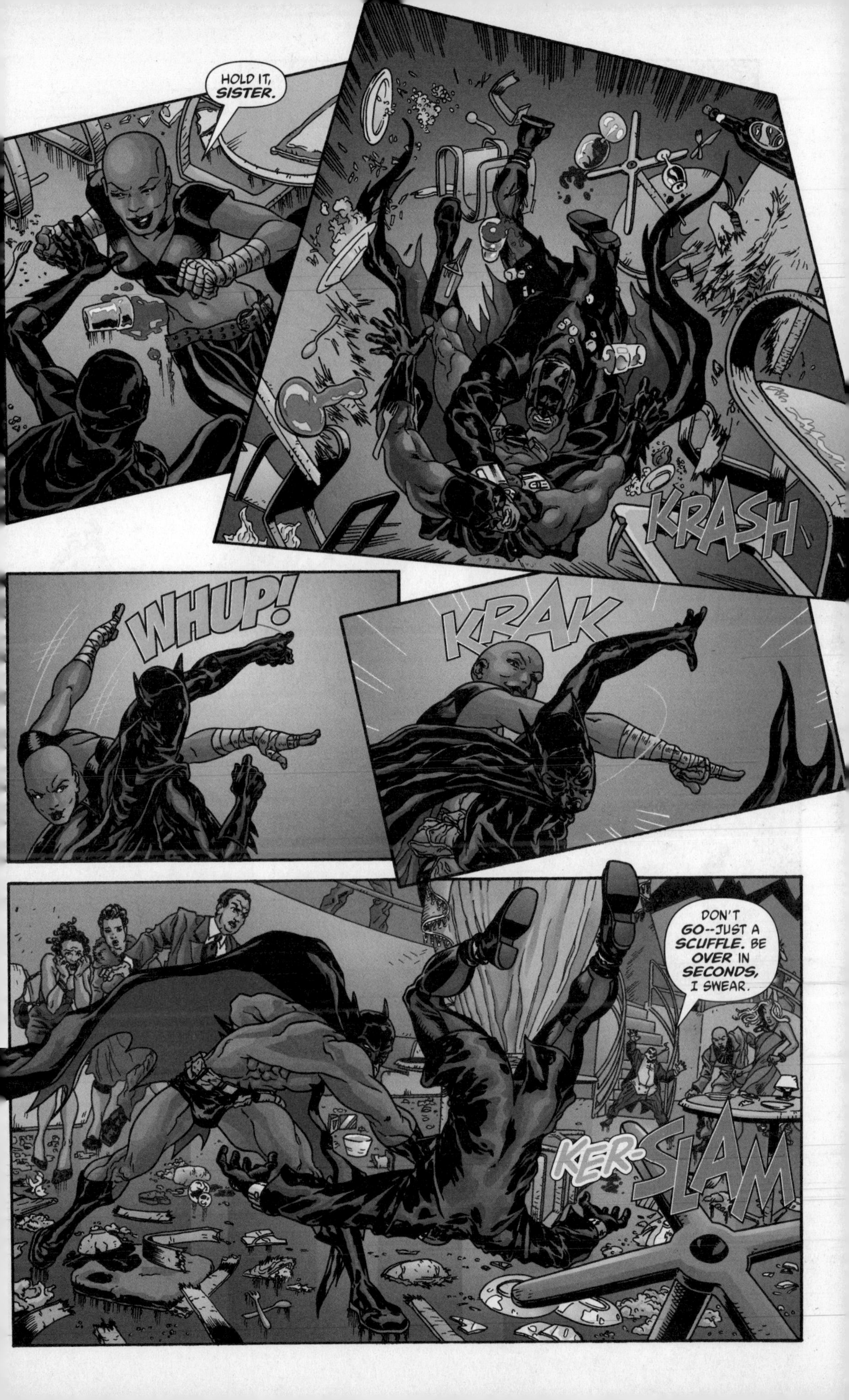
HOLD IT, SISTER.
KRASH
WHUP!
KRAK
DON'T GO--JUST A SCUFFLE. BE OVER IN SECONDS, I SWEAR.
KER-SLAM

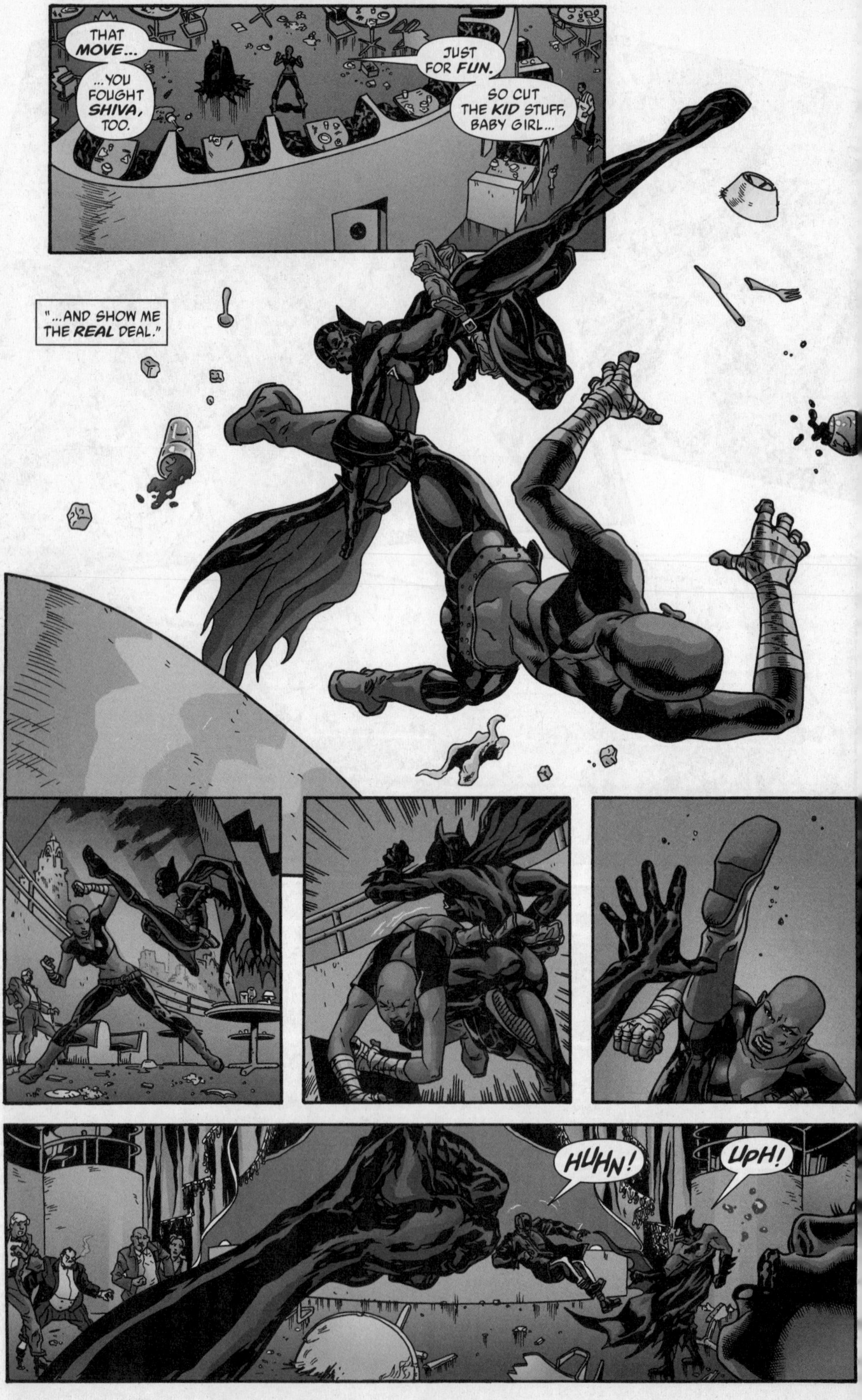

THAT MOVE...
...YOU FOUGHT SHIVA, TOO.
JUST FOR FUN.
SO CUT THE KID STUFF, BABY GIRL...
"...AND SHOW ME THE REAL DEAL."
HUHN!
UPH!

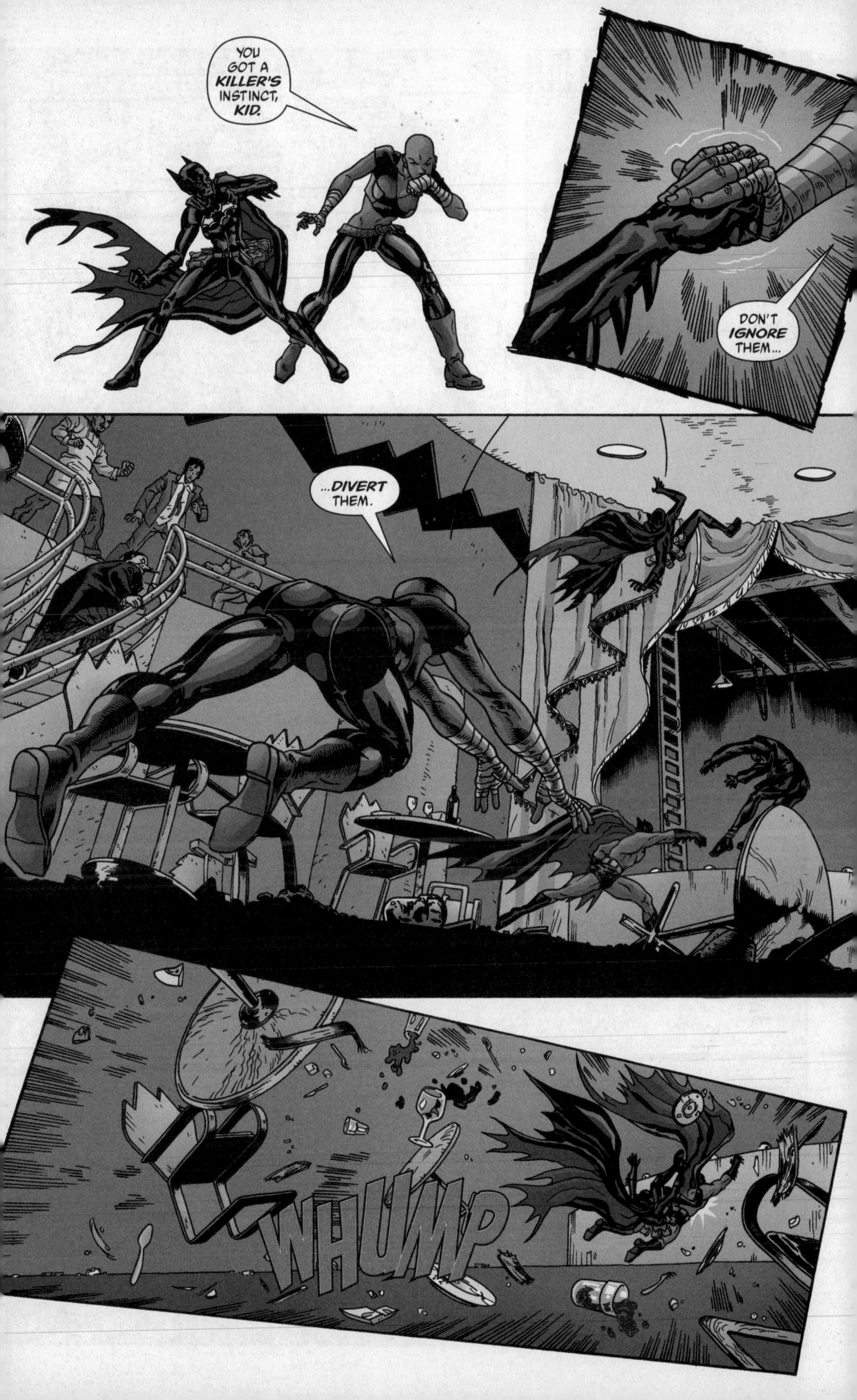

YOU GOT A KILLER'S INSTINCT, KID.
DON'T IGNORE THEM...
...DIVERT THEM.
WHUMP

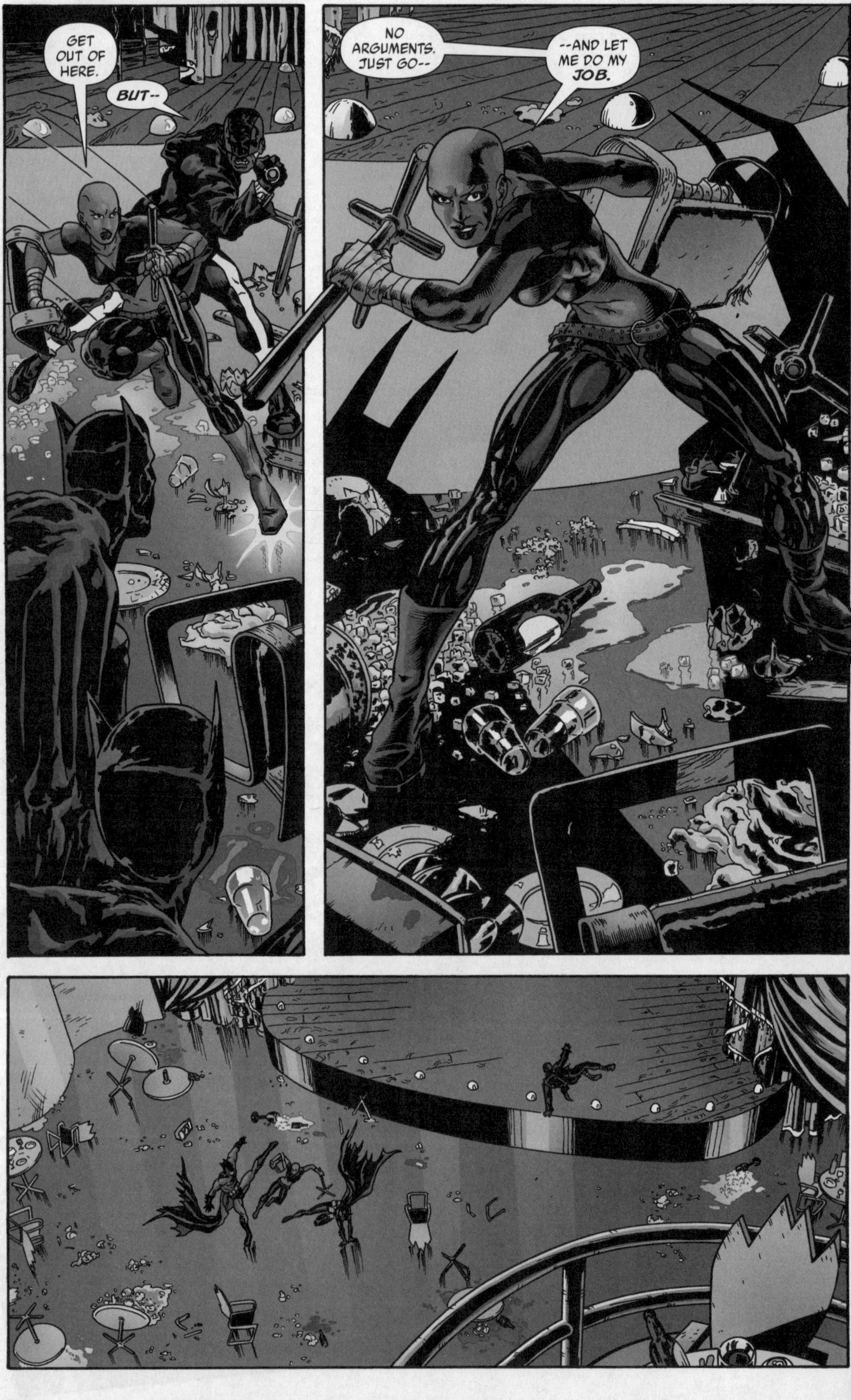
GET OUT OF HERE.
BUT--
NO ARGUMENTS. JUST GO--
--AND LET ME DO MY JOB.

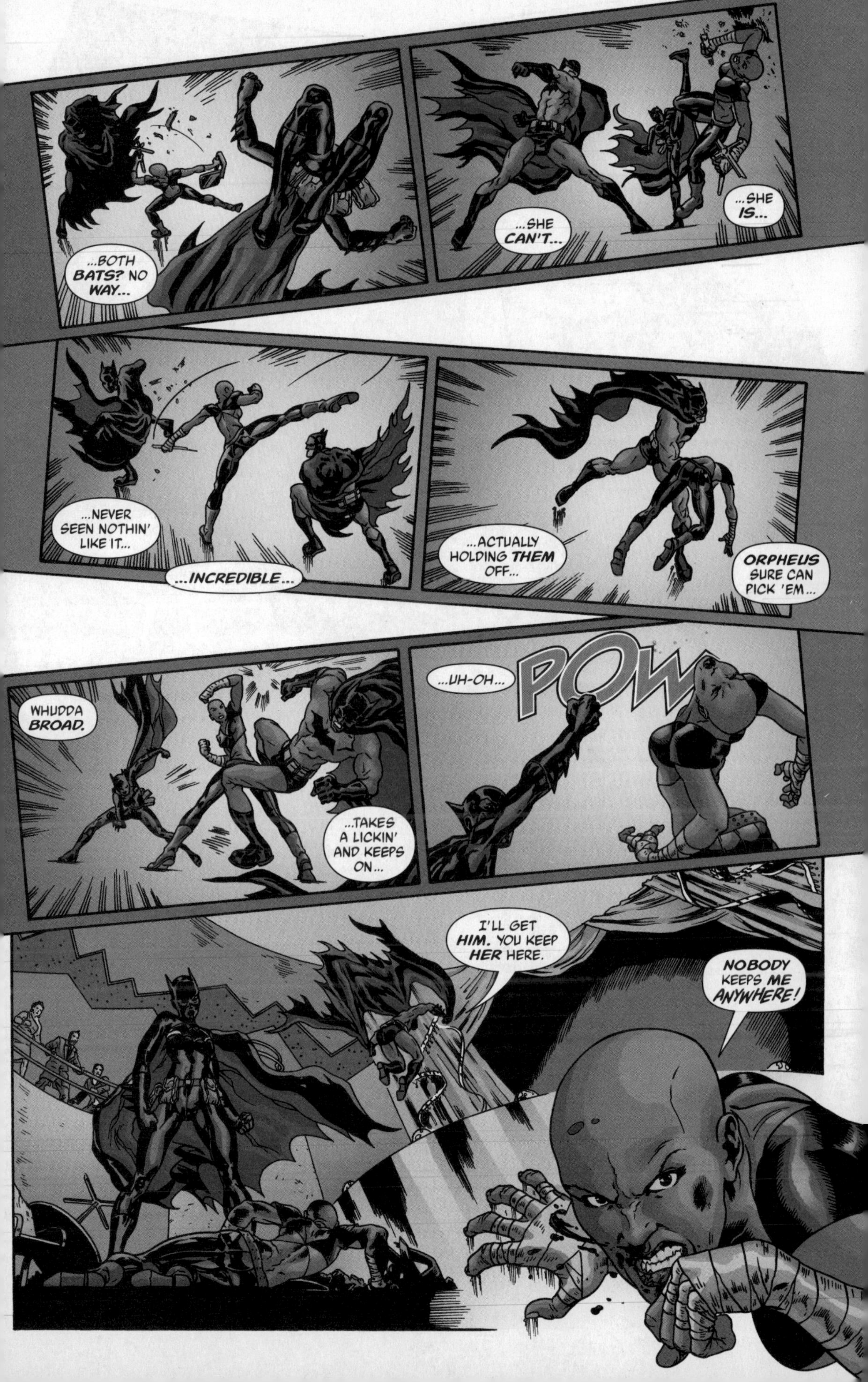
...BOTH BATS? NO WAY...
...SHE CAN'T...
...SHE IS...
...NEVER SEEN NOTHIN' LIKE IT...
...INCREDIBLE...
...ACTUALLY HOLDING THEM OFF...
ORPHEUS SURE CAN PICK 'EM...
WHUDDA BROAD.
...TAKES A LICKIN' AND KEEPS ON...
...UH-OH...
POW
I'LL GET HIM. YOU KEEP HER HERE.
NOBODY KEEPS ME ANYWHERE!

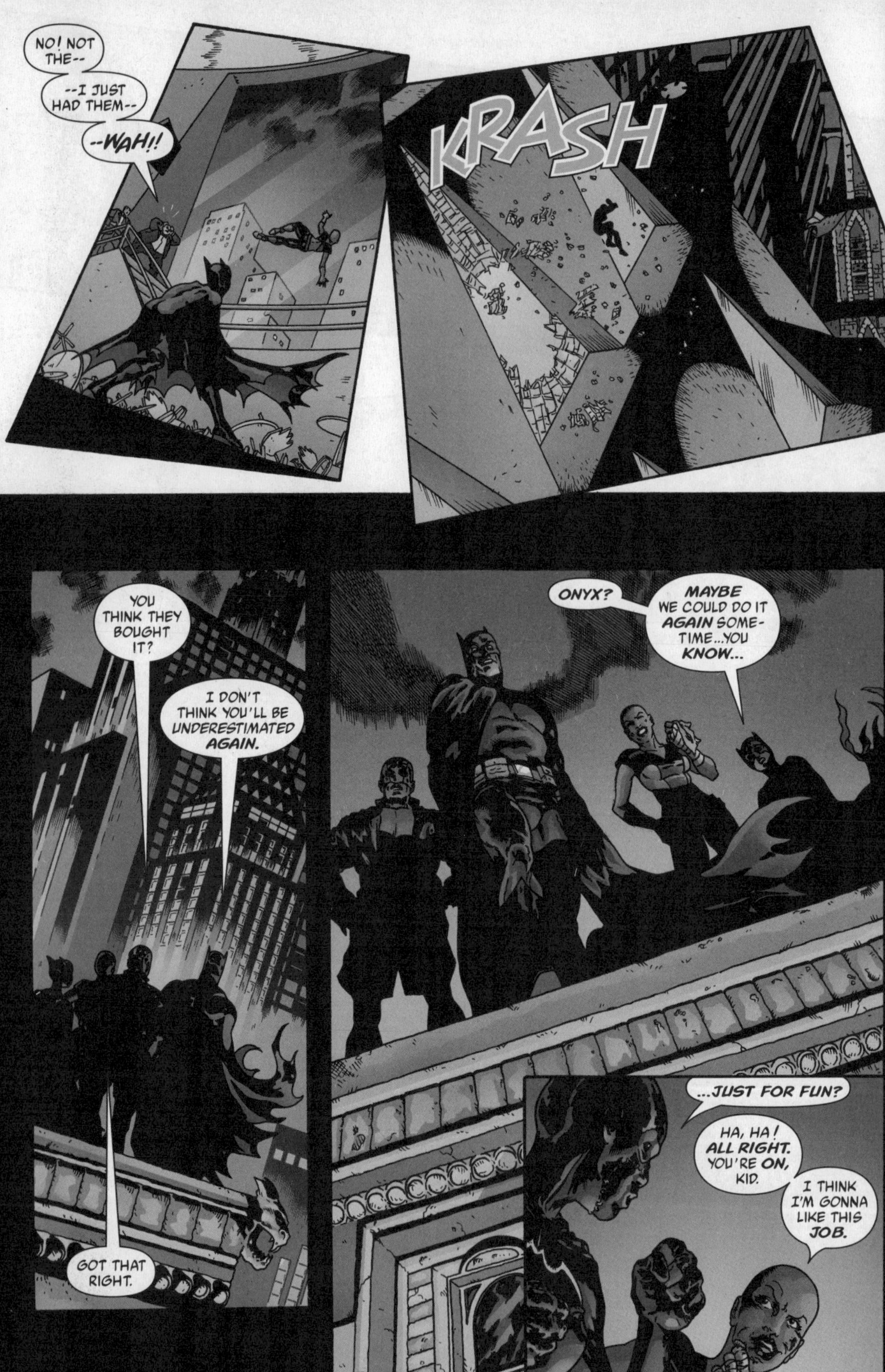
NO! NOT THE--
--I JUST HAD THEM--
--WAH!!
KRASH
YOU THINK THEY BOUGHT IT?
I DON'T THINK YOU'LL BE UNDERESTIMATED AGAIN.
GOT THAT RIGHT.
ONYX?
MAYBE WE COULD DO IT AGAIN SOME-TIME...YOU KNOW...
...JUST FOR FUN?
HA, HA! ALL RIGHT. YOU'RE ON, KID.
I THINK I'M GONNA LIKE THIS JOB.
the end

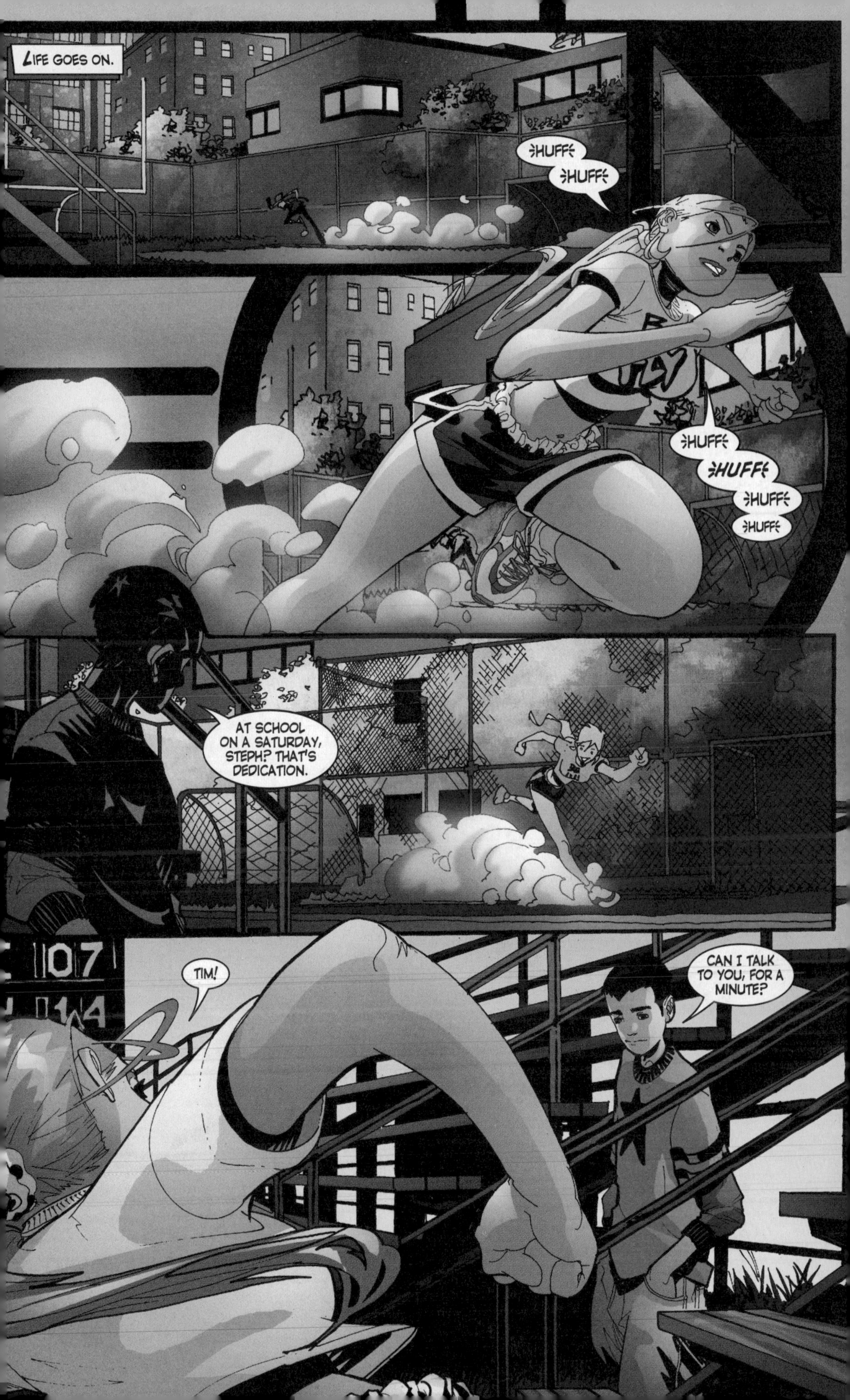
LIFE GOES ON.
HUFF HUFF
HUFF HUFF HUFF HUFF
AT SCHOOL ON A SATURDAY, STEPH? THAT'S DEDICATION.
TIM!
CAN I TALK TO YOU, FOR A MINUTE?

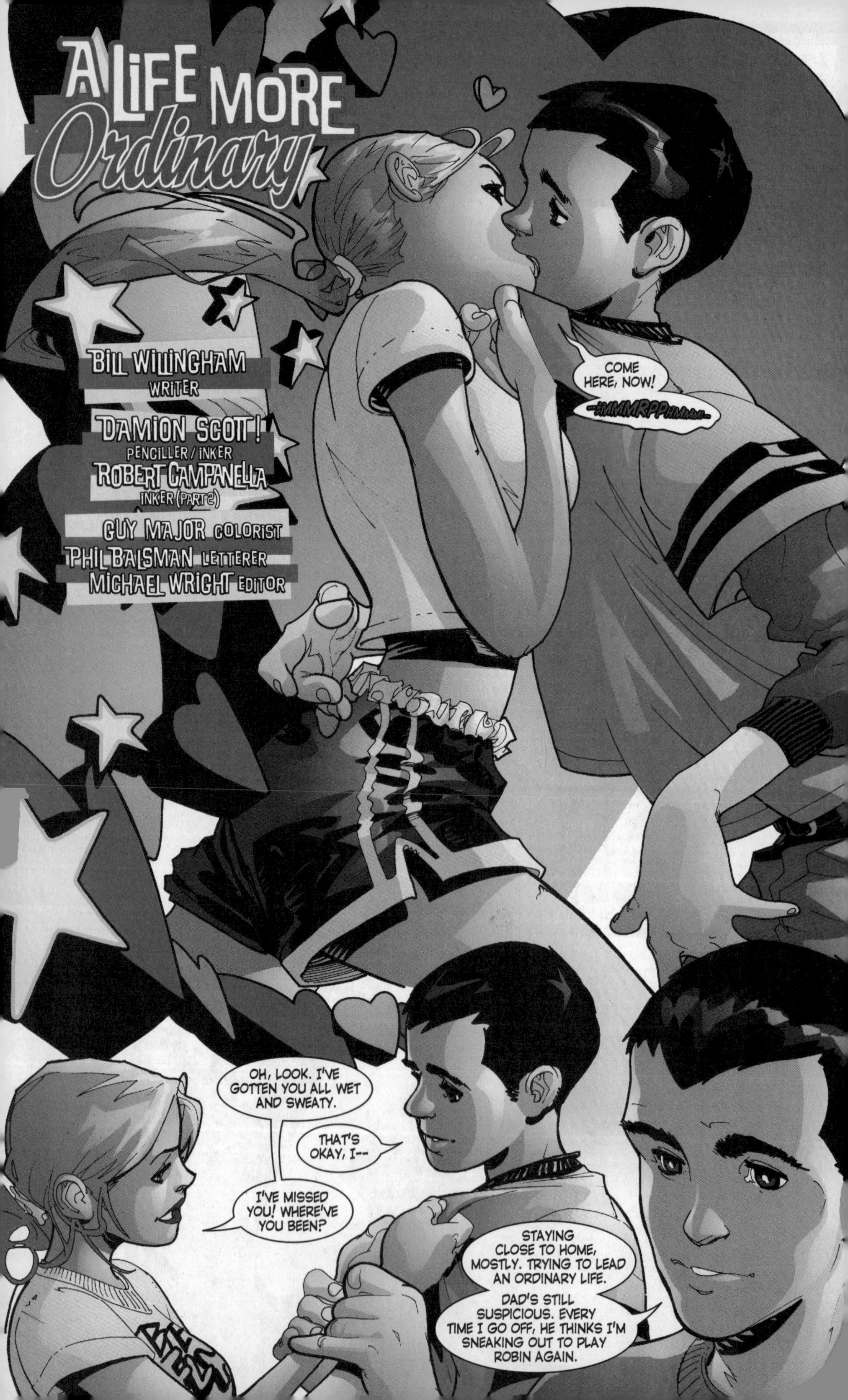
A LIFE MORE Ordinary
BILL WILLINGHAM WRITER
DAMION SCOTT! PENCILLER / INKER
ROBERT CAMPANELLA INKER (PART 2)
GUY MAJOR COLORIST
PHIL BALSMAN LETTERER
MICHAEL WRIGHT EDITOR
COME HERE, NOW!
--MMMMRPPHMMMM--
OH, LOOK. I'VE GOTTEN YOU ALL WET AND SWEATY.
THAT'S OKAY, I--
I'VE MISSED YOU! WHERE'VE YOU BEEN?
STAYING CLOSE TO HOME, MOSTLY. TRYING TO LEAD AN ORDINARY LIFE.
DAD'S STILL SUSPICIOUS. EVERY TIME I GO OFF, HE THINKS I'M SNEAKING OUT TO PLAY ROBIN AGAIN.

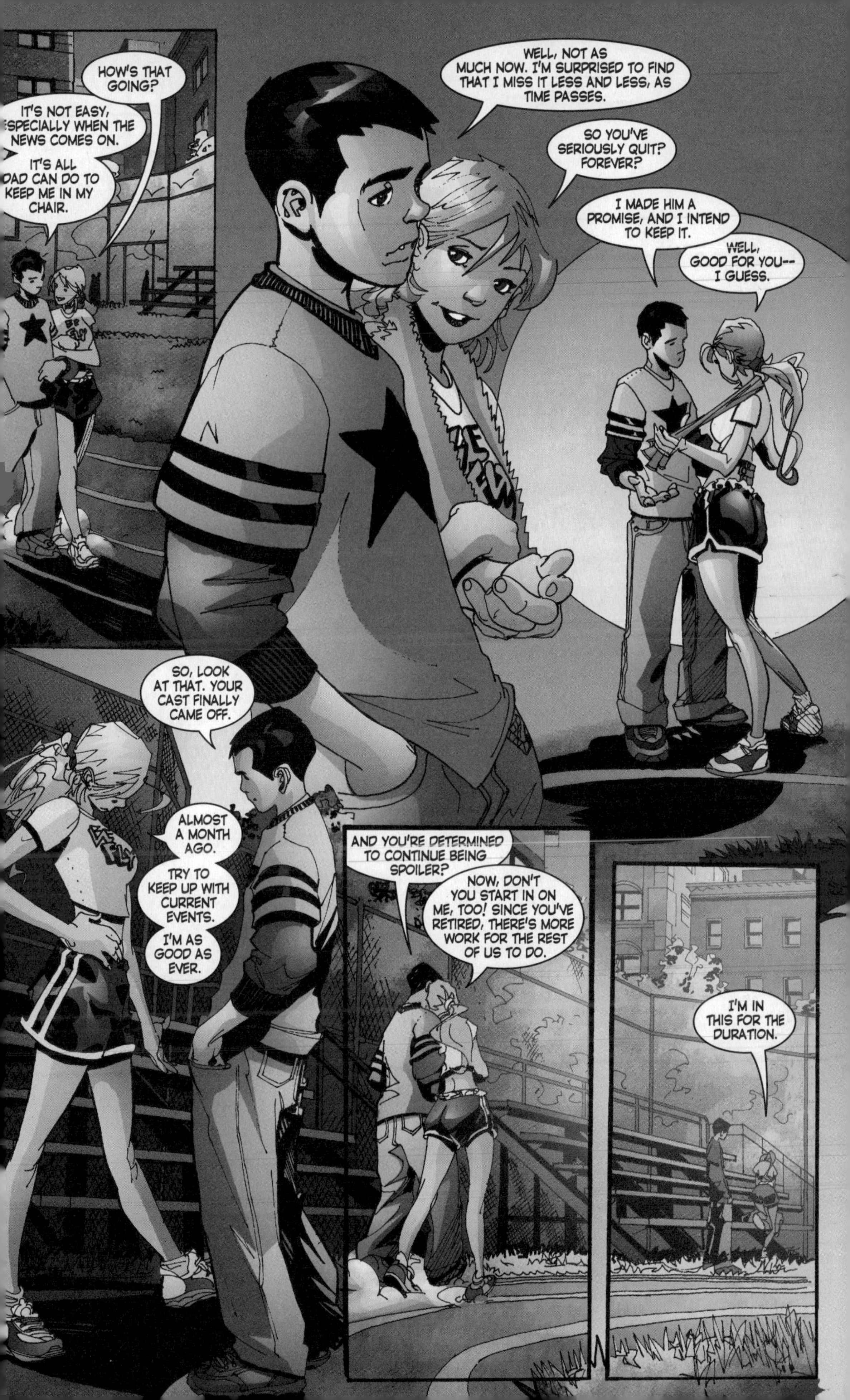
HOW'S THAT GOING?
IT'S NOT EASY, ESPECIALLY WHEN THE NEWS COMES ON.
IT'S ALL DAD CAN DO TO KEEP ME IN MY CHAIR.
WELL, NOT AS MUCH NOW. I'M SURPRISED TO FIND THAT I MISS IT LESS AND LESS, AS TIME PASSES.
SO YOU'VE SERIOUSLY QUIT? FOREVER?
I MADE HIM A PROMISE, AND I INTEND TO KEEP IT.
WELL, GOOD FOR YOU-- I GUESS.
SO, LOOK AT THAT. YOUR CAST FINALLY CAME OFF.
ALMOST A MONTH AGO.
TRY TO KEEP UP WITH CURRENT EVENTS.
I'M AS GOOD AS EVER.
AND YOU'RE DETERMINED TO CONTINUE BEING SPOILER?
NOW, DON'T YOU START IN ON ME, TOO! SINCE YOU'VE RETIRED, THERE'S MORE WORK FOR THE REST OF US TO DO.
I'M IN THIS FOR THE DURATION.

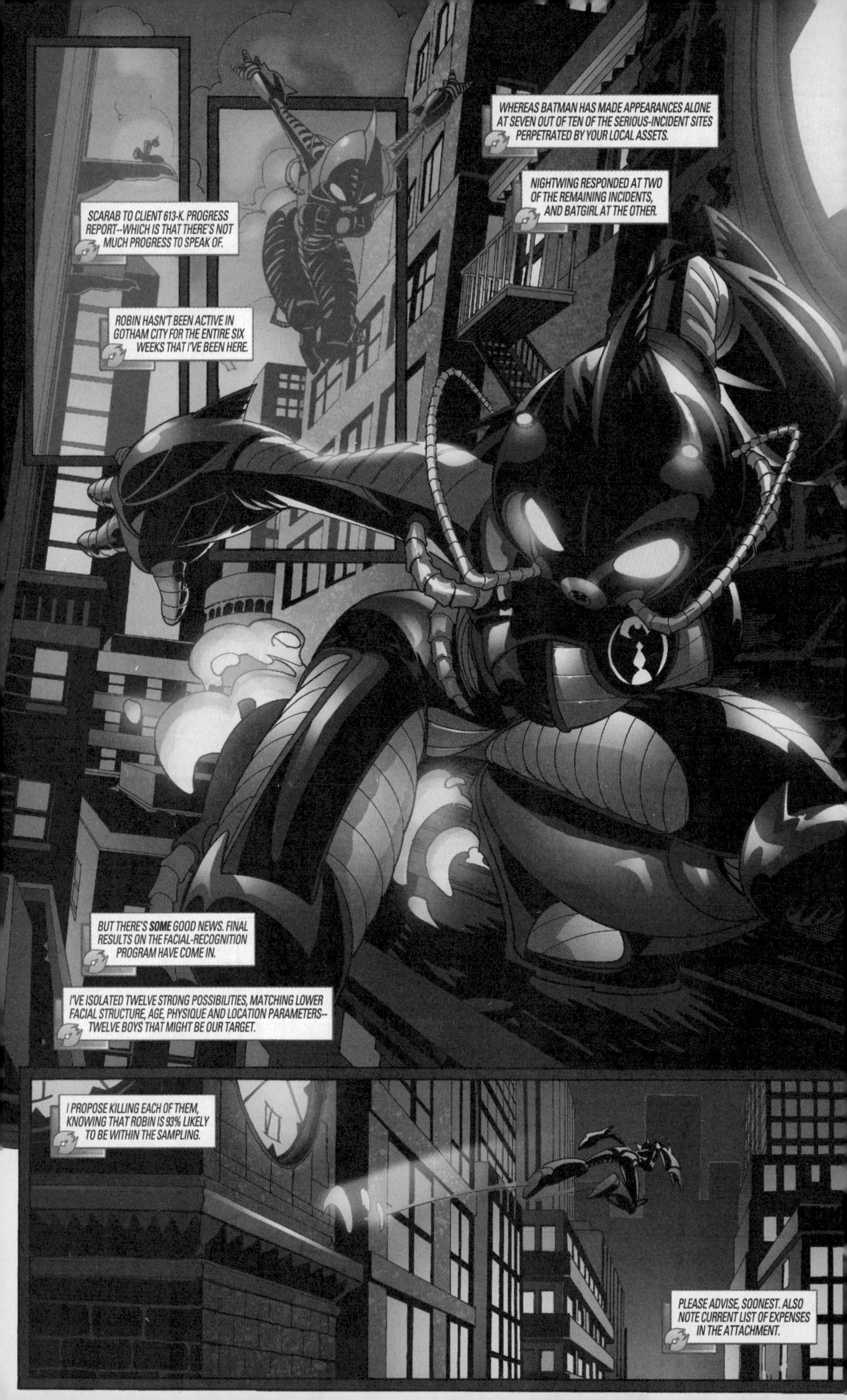
SCARAB TO CLIENT 613-K. PROGRESS REPORT--WHICH IS THAT THERE'S NOT MUCH PROGRESS TO SPEAK OF.
ROBIN HASN'T BEEN ACTIVE IN GOTHAM CITY FOR THE ENTIRE SIX WEEKS THAT I'VE BEEN HERE.
WHEREAS BATMAN HAS MADE APPEARANCES ALONE AT SEVEN OUT OF TEN OF THE SERIOUS-INCIDENT SITES PERPETRATED BY YOUR LOCAL ASSETS.
NIGHTWING RESPONDED AT TWO OF THE REMAINING INCIDENTS, AND BATGIRL AT THE OTHER.
BUT THERE'S **SOME** GOOD NEWS. FINAL RESULTS ON THE FACIAL-RECOGNITION PROGRAM HAVE COME IN.
I'VE ISOLATED TWELVE STRONG POSSIBILITIES, MATCHING LOWER FACIAL STRUCTURE, AGE, PHYSIQUE AND LOCATION PARAMETERS-- TWELVE BOYS THAT MIGHT BE OUR TARGET.
I PROPOSE KILLING EACH OF THEM, KNOWING THAT ROBIN IS 93% LIKELY TO BE WITHIN THE SAMPLING.
PLEASE ADVISE, SOONEST. ALSO NOTE CURRENT LIST OF EXPENSES IN THE ATTACHMENT.

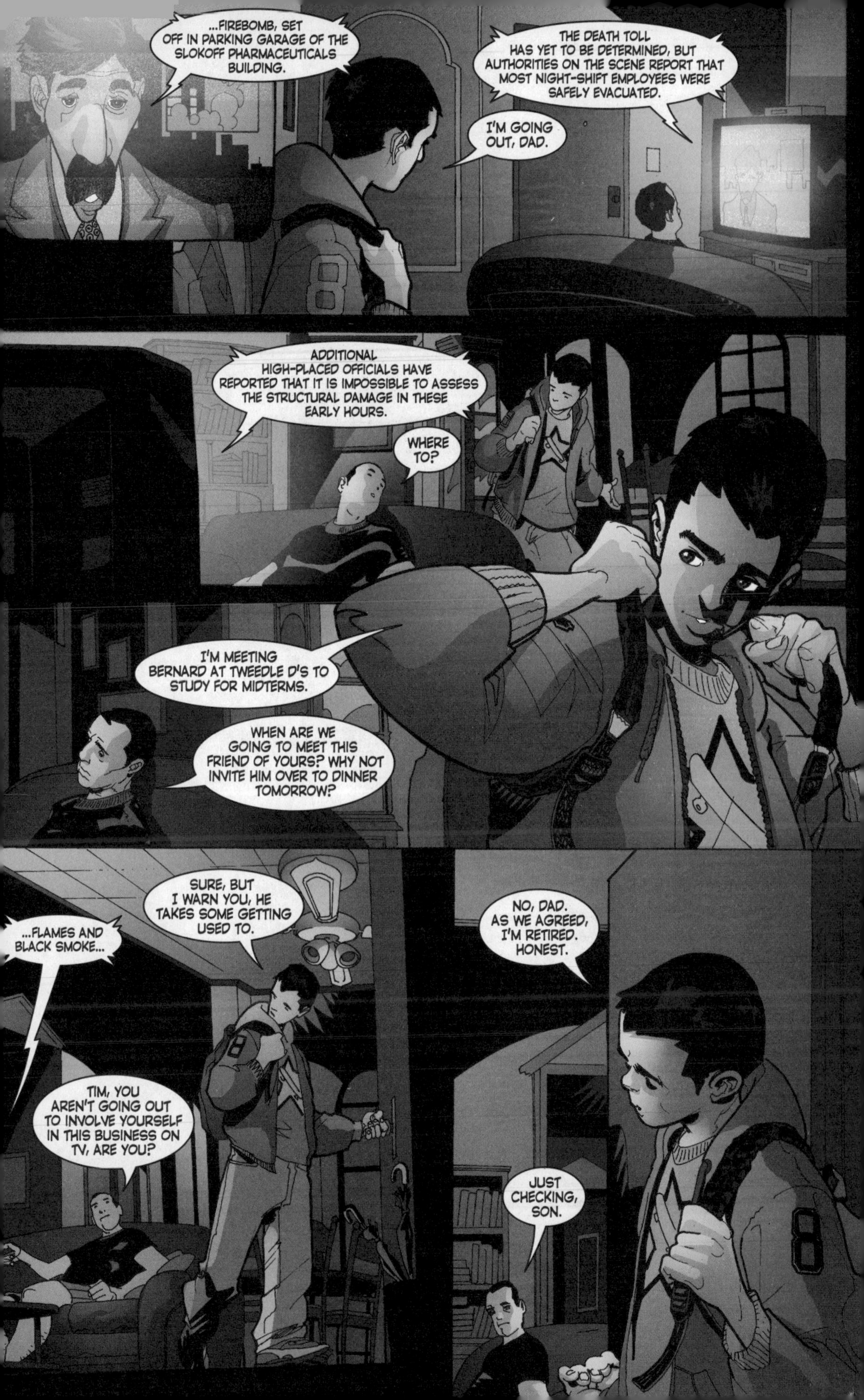
...FIREBOMB, SET OFF IN PARKING GARAGE OF THE SLOKOFF PHARMACEUTICALS BUILDING.
THE DEATH TOLL HAS YET TO BE DETERMINED, BUT AUTHORITIES ON THE SCENE REPORT THAT MOST NIGHT-SHIFT EMPLOYEES WERE SAFELY EVACUATED.
I'M GOING OUT, DAD.
ADDITIONAL HIGH-PLACED OFFICIALS HAVE REPORTED THAT IT IS IMPOSSIBLE TO ASSESS THE STRUCTURAL DAMAGE IN THESE EARLY HOURS.
WHERE TO?
I'M MEETING BERNARD AT TWEEDLE D'S TO STUDY FOR MIDTERMS.
WHEN ARE WE GOING TO MEET THIS FRIEND OF YOURS? WHY NOT INVITE HIM OVER TO DINNER TOMORROW?
SURE, BUT I WARN YOU, HE TAKES SOME GETTING USED TO.
...FLAMES AND BLACK SMOKE...
TIM, YOU AREN'T GOING OUT TO INVOLVE YOURSELF IN THIS BUSINESS ON TV, ARE YOU?
NO, DAD. AS WE AGREED, I'M RETIRED. HONEST.
JUST CHECKING, SON.

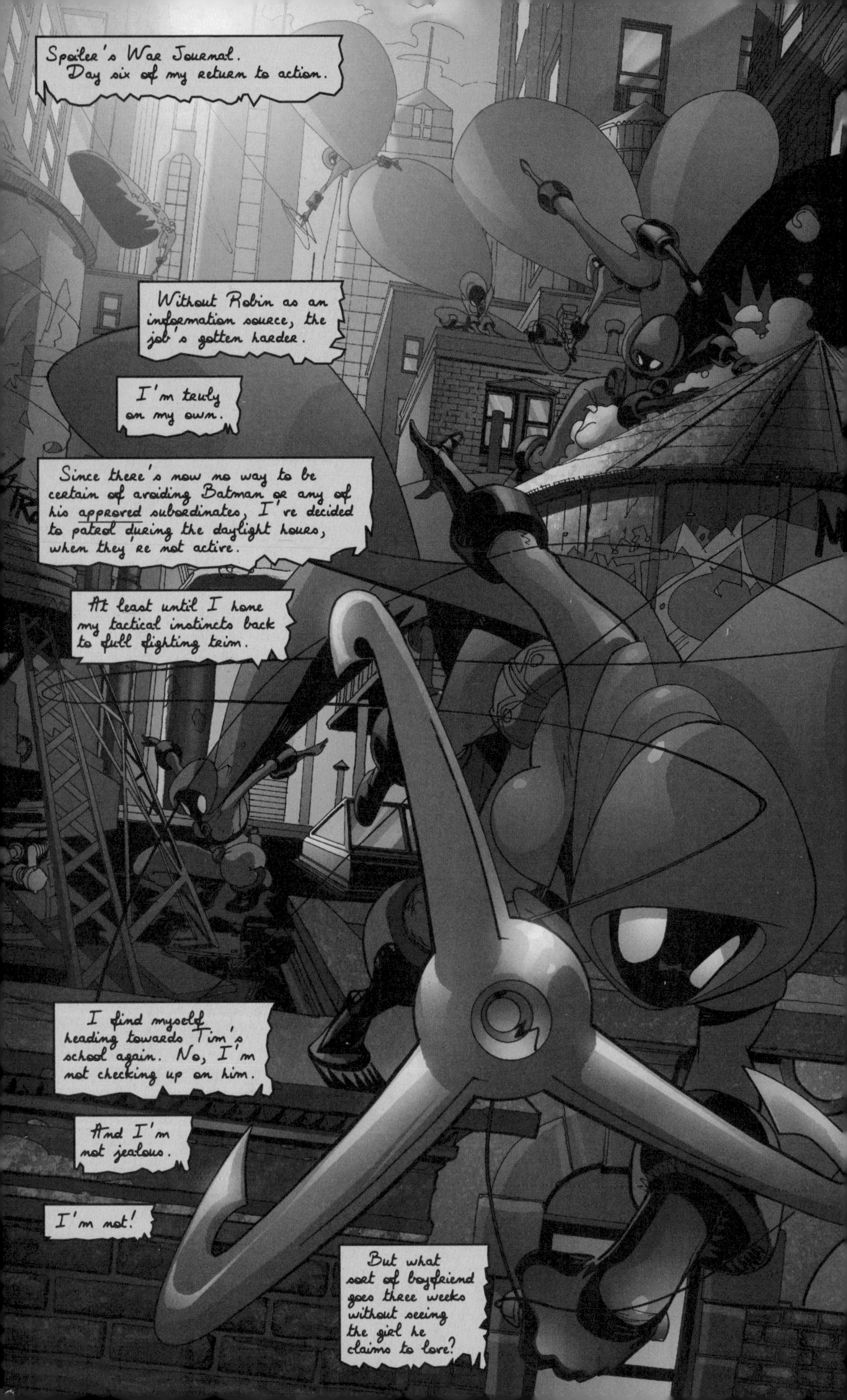

Spoiler's War Journal. Day six of my return to action.
Without Robin as an information source, the job's gotten harder.
I'm truly on my own.
Since there's now no way to be certain of avoiding Batman or any of his approved subordinates, I've decided to patrol during the daylight hours, when they're not active.
At least until I hone my tactical instincts back to full fighting trim.
I find myself heading towards Tim's school again. No, I'm not checking up on him.
And I'm not jealous.
I'm not!
But what sort of boyfriend goes three weeks without seeing the girl he claims to love?

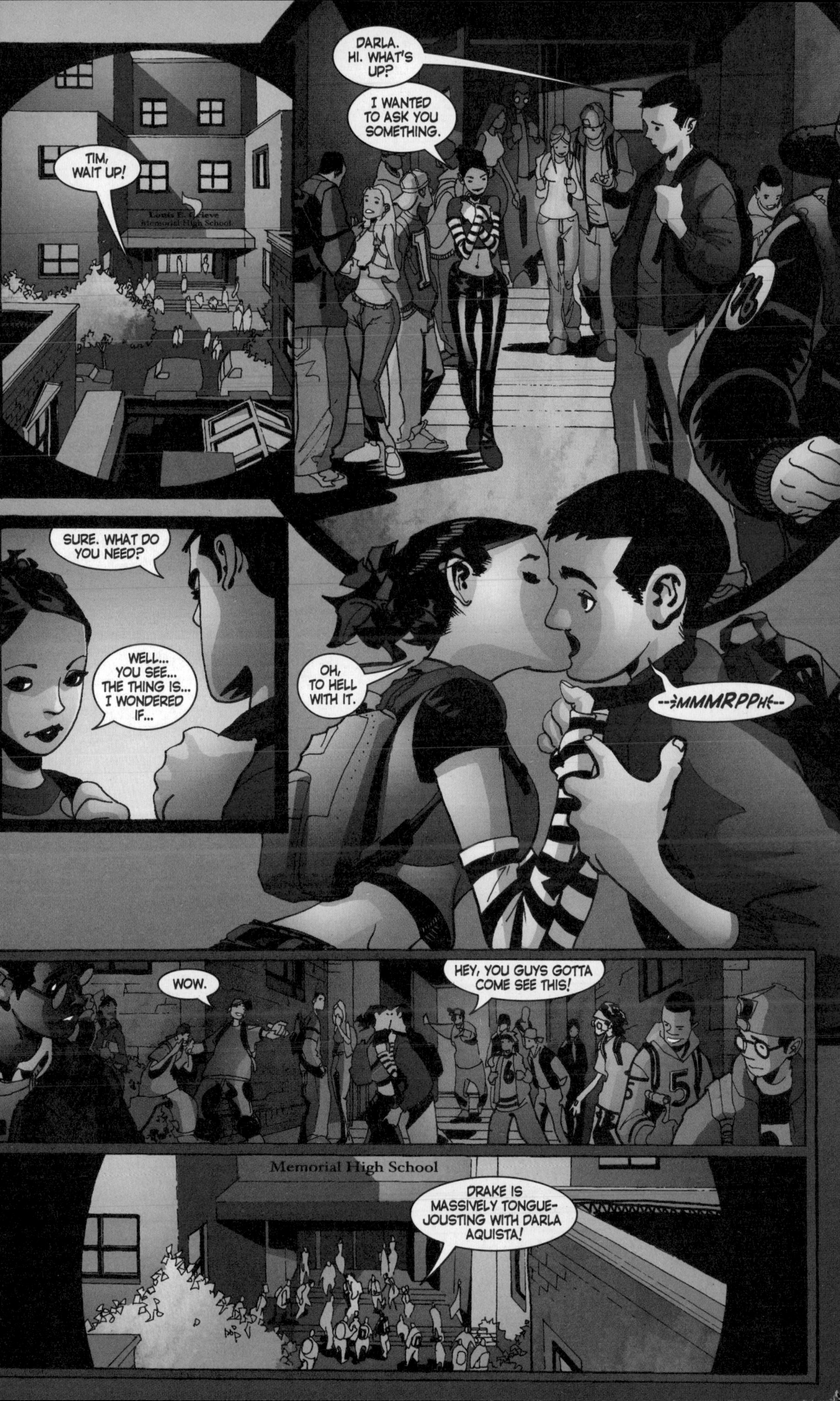

TIM, WAIT UP!
Louis E. Grieve Memorial High School
DARLA. HI. WHAT'S UP?
I WANTED TO ASK YOU SOMETHING.
SURE. WHAT DO YOU NEED?
WELL... YOU SEE... THE THING IS... I WONDERED IF...
OH, TO HELL WITH IT.
--MMMRPPH--
WOW.
HEY, YOU GUYS GOTTA COME SEE THIS!
Memorial High School
DRAKE IS MASSIVELY TONGUE-JOUSTING WITH DARLA AQUISTA!

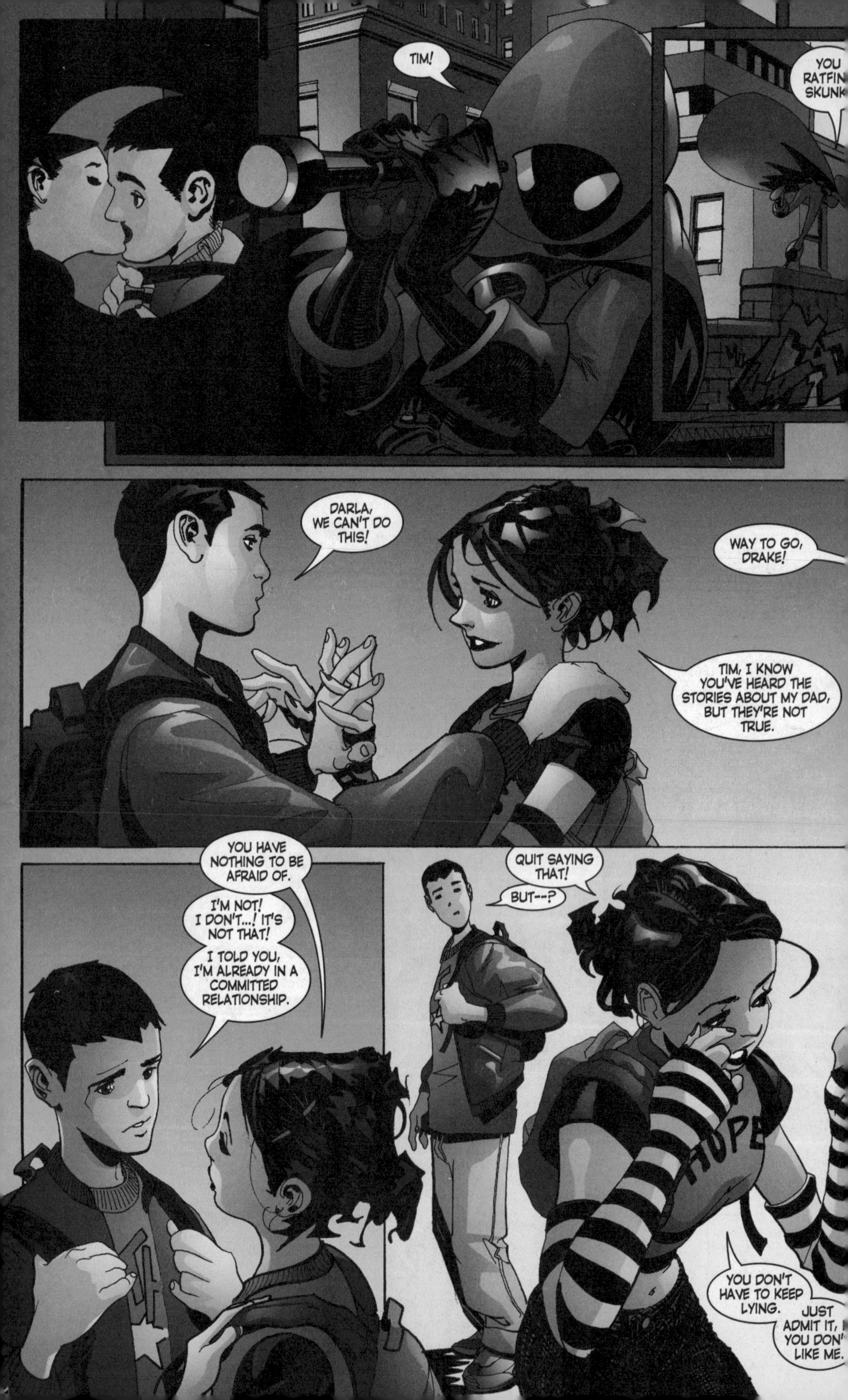
TIM!
YOU RATFIN SKUNK
DARLA, WE CAN'T DO THIS!
WAY TO GO, DRAKE!
TIM, I KNOW YOU'VE HEARD THE STORIES ABOUT MY DAD, BUT THEY'RE NOT TRUE.
YOU HAVE NOTHING TO BE AFRAID OF.
I'M NOT! I DON'T...! IT'S NOT THAT!
I TOLD YOU, I'M ALREADY IN A COMMITTED RELATIONSHIP.
QUIT SAYING THAT!
BUT--?
YOU DON'T HAVE TO KEEP LYING.
JUST ADMIT IT, YOU DON LIKE ME.
HOPE

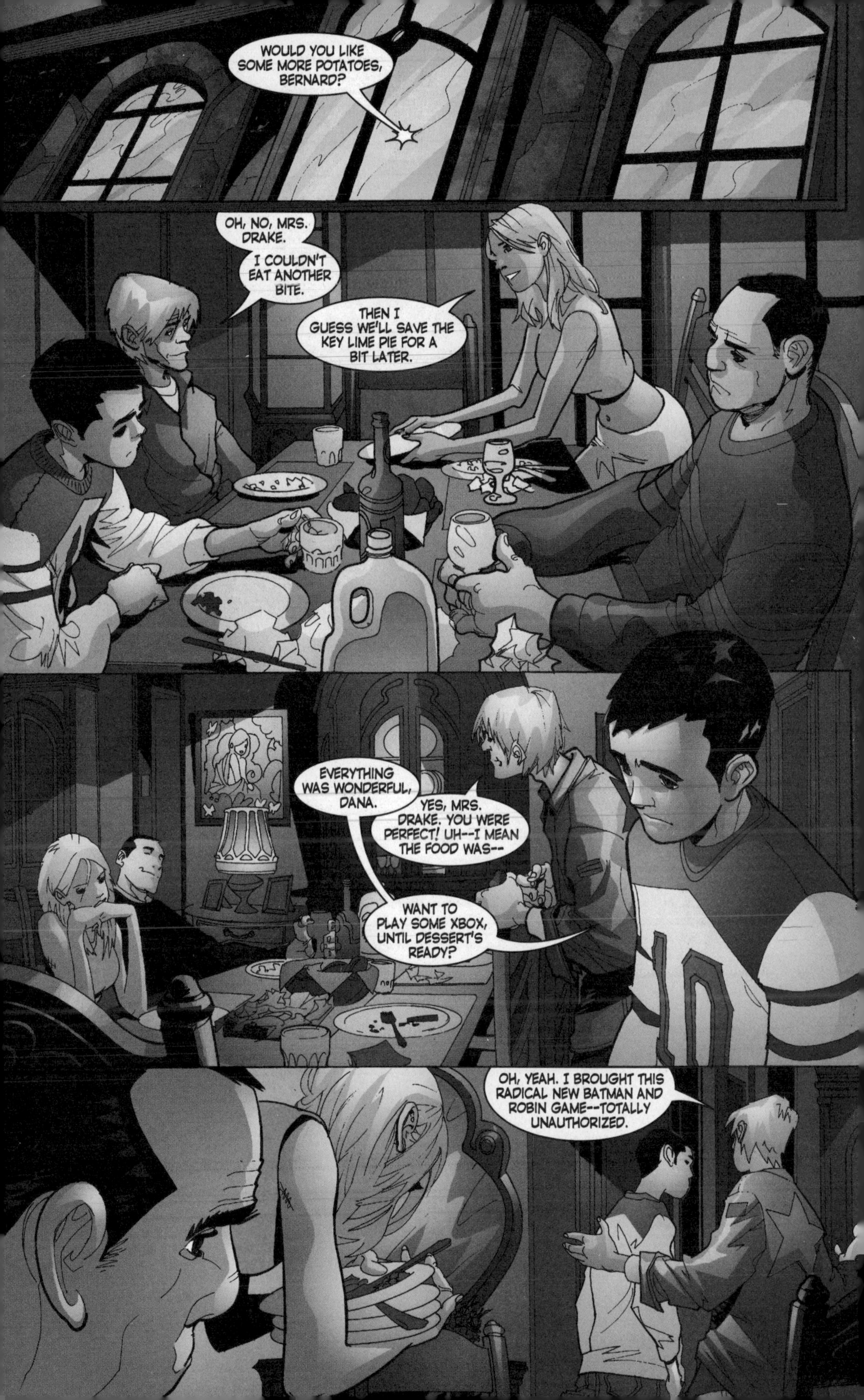
WOULD YOU LIKE SOME MORE POTATOES, BERNARD?
OH, NO, MRS. DRAKE.
I COULDN'T EAT ANOTHER BITE.
THEN I GUESS WE'LL SAVE THE KEY LIME PIE FOR A BIT LATER.
EVERYTHING WAS WONDERFUL, DANA.
YES, MRS. DRAKE. YOU WERE PERFECT! UH--I MEAN THE FOOD WAS--
WANT TO PLAY SOME XBOX, UNTIL DESSERT'S READY?
OH, YEAH. I BROUGHT THIS RADICAL NEW BATMAN AND ROBIN GAME--TOTALLY UNAUTHORIZED.

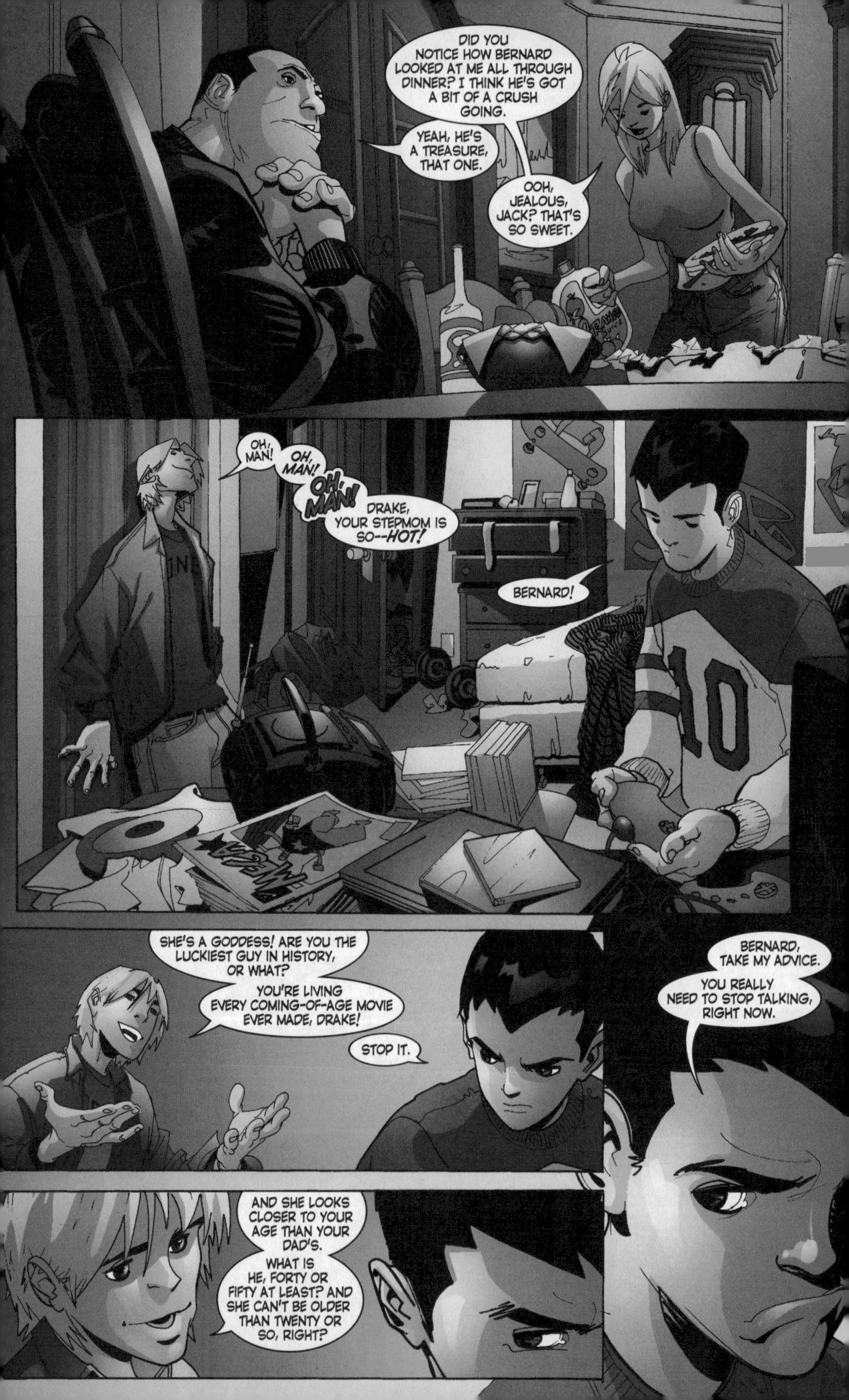
DID YOU NOTICE HOW BERNARD LOOKED AT ME ALL THROUGH DINNER? I THINK HE'S GOT A BIT OF A CRUSH GOING.
YEAH, HE'S A TREASURE, THAT ONE.
OOH, JEALOUS, JACK? THAT'S SO SWEET.
ORANGE JUICE
OH, MAN!
OH, MAN!
OH, MAN!
DRAKE, YOUR STEPMOM IS SO--HOT!
BERNARD!
10
MEGA
SHE'S A GODDESS! ARE YOU THE LUCKIEST GUY IN HISTORY, OR WHAT?
YOU'RE LIVING EVERY COMING-OF-AGE MOVIE EVER MADE, DRAKE!
STOP IT.
BERNARD, TAKE MY ADVICE.
YOU REALLY NEED TO STOP TALKING, RIGHT NOW.
AND SHE LOOKS CLOSER TO YOUR AGE THAN YOUR DAD'S.
WHAT IS HE, FORTY OR FIFTY AT LEAST? AND SHE CAN'T BE OLDER THAN TWENTY OR SO, RIGHT?

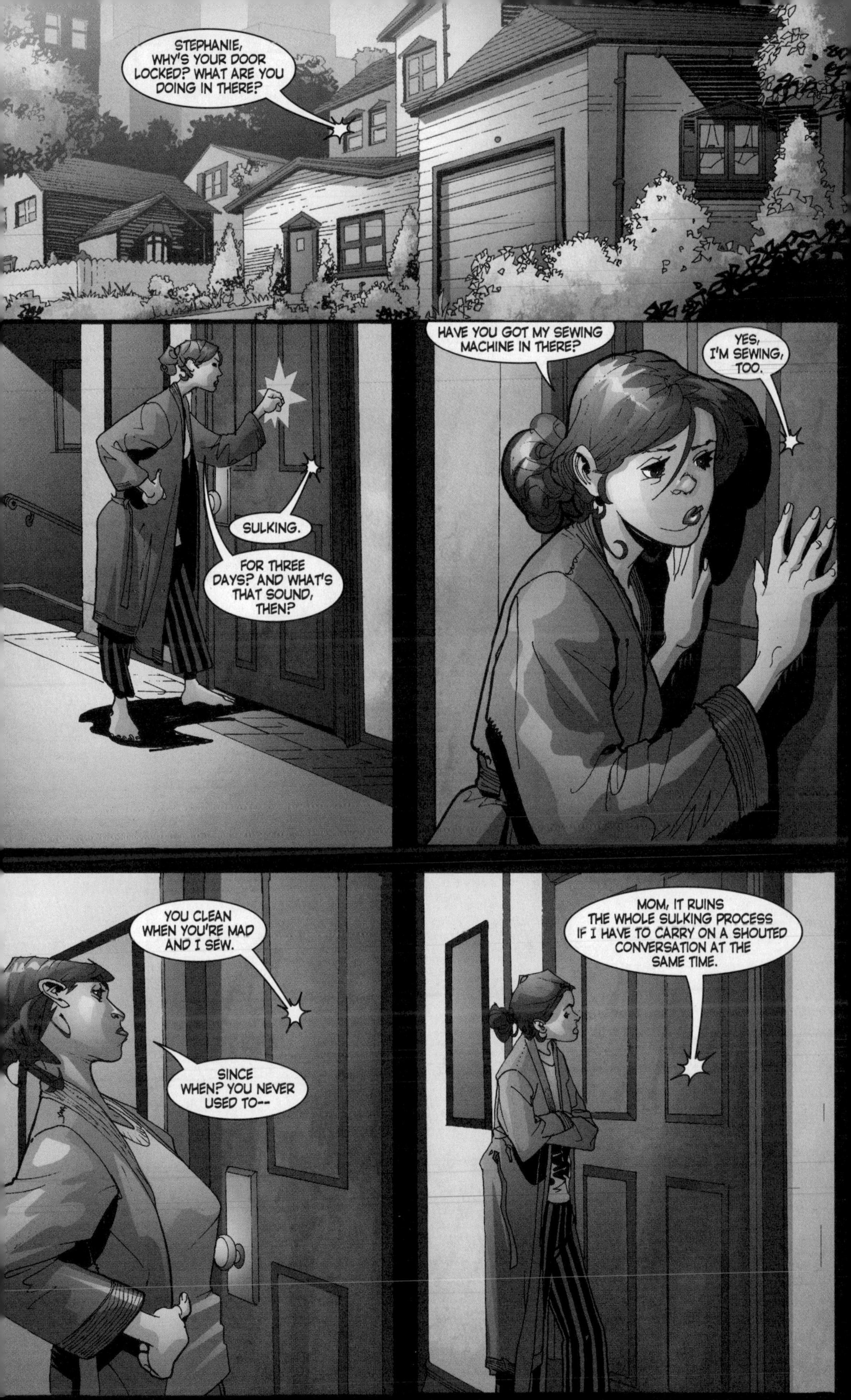
STEPHANIE, WHY'S YOUR DOOR LOCKED? WHAT ARE YOU DOING IN THERE?
SULKING.
FOR THREE DAYS? AND WHAT'S THAT SOUND, THEN?
HAVE YOU GOT MY SEWING MACHINE IN THERE?
YES, I'M SEWING, TOO.
YOU CLEAN WHEN YOU'RE MAD AND I SEW.
SINCE WHEN? YOU NEVER USED TO--
MOM, IT RUINS THE WHOLE SULKING PROCESS IF I HAVE TO CARRY ON A SHOUTED CONVERSATION AT THE SAME TIME.

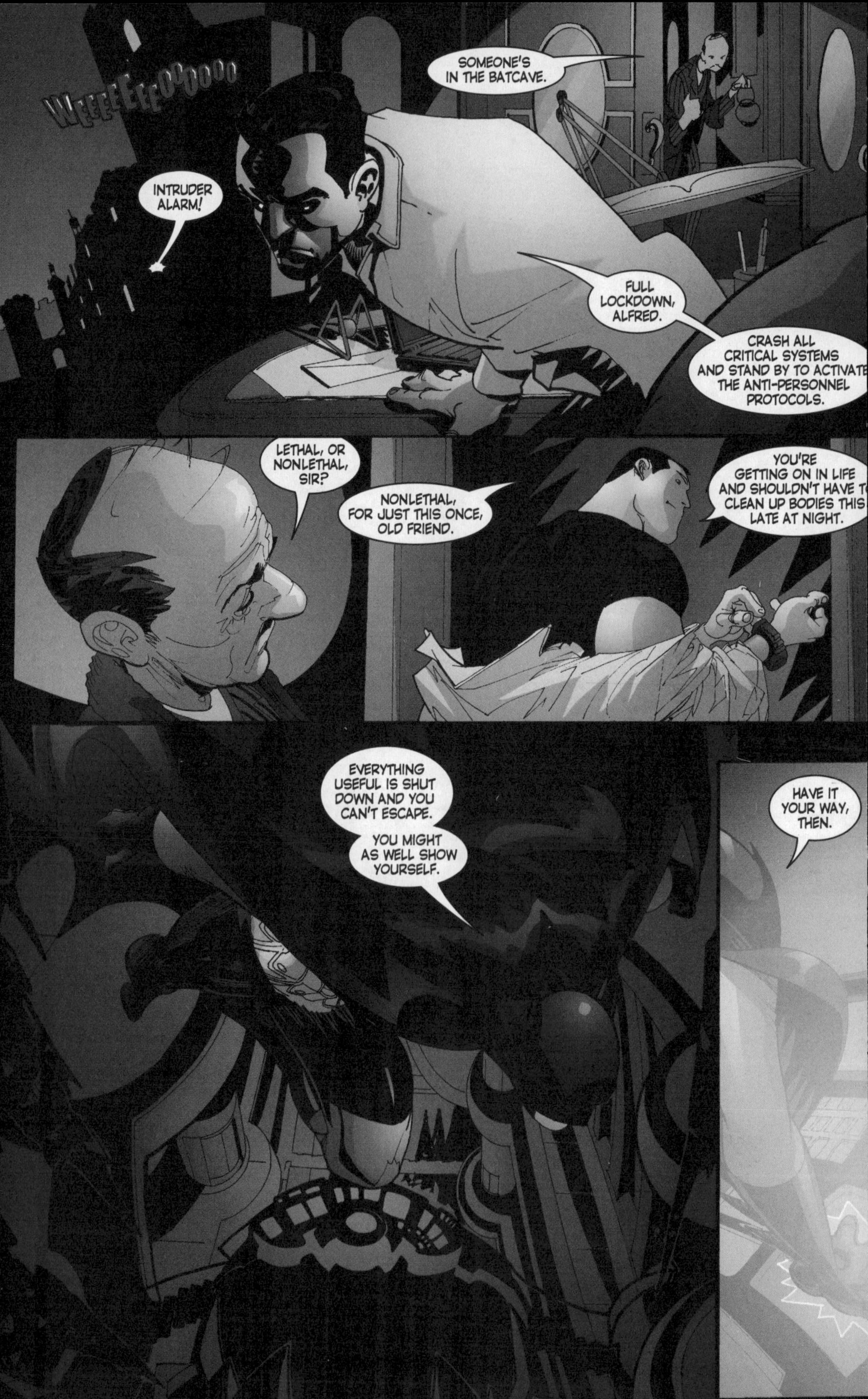
WEEEEEEEOOOOOO
SOMEONE'S IN THE BATCAVE.
INTRUDER ALARM!
FULL LOCKDOWN, ALFRED.
CRASH ALL CRITICAL SYSTEMS AND STAND BY TO ACTIVATE THE ANTI-PERSONNEL PROTOCOLS.
LETHAL, OR NONLETHAL, SIR?
NONLETHAL, FOR JUST THIS ONCE, OLD FRIEND.
YOU'RE GETTING ON IN LIFE AND SHOULDN'T HAVE TO CLEAN UP BODIES THIS LATE AT NIGHT.
EVERYTHING USEFUL IS SHUT DOWN AND YOU CAN'T ESCAPE.
YOU MIGHT AS WELL SHOW YOURSELF.
HAVE IT YOUR WAY, THEN.

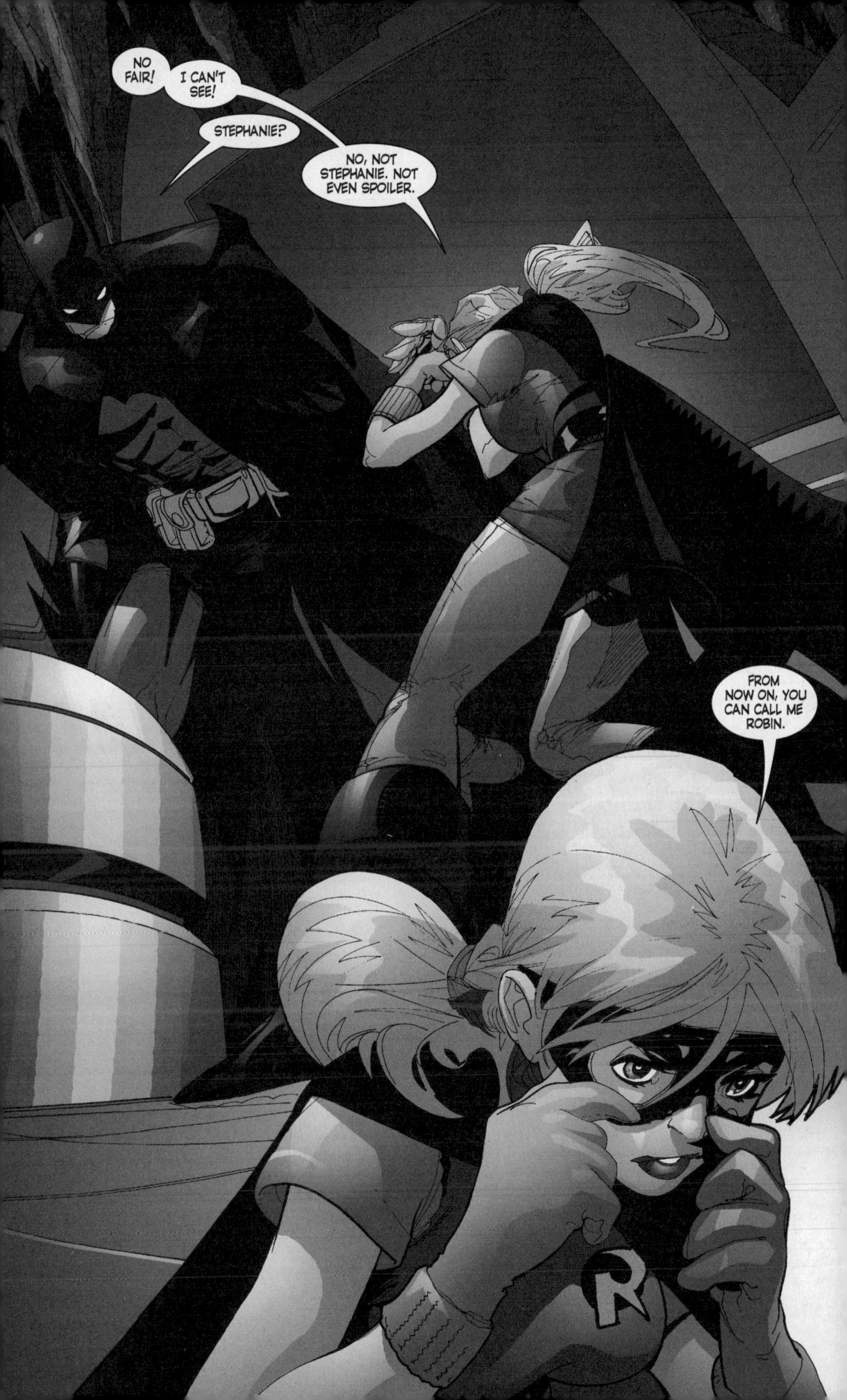
NO FAIR!
I CAN'T SEE!
STEPHANIE?
NO, NOT STEPHANIE. NOT EVEN SPOILER.
FROM NOW ON, YOU CAN CALL ME ROBIN.

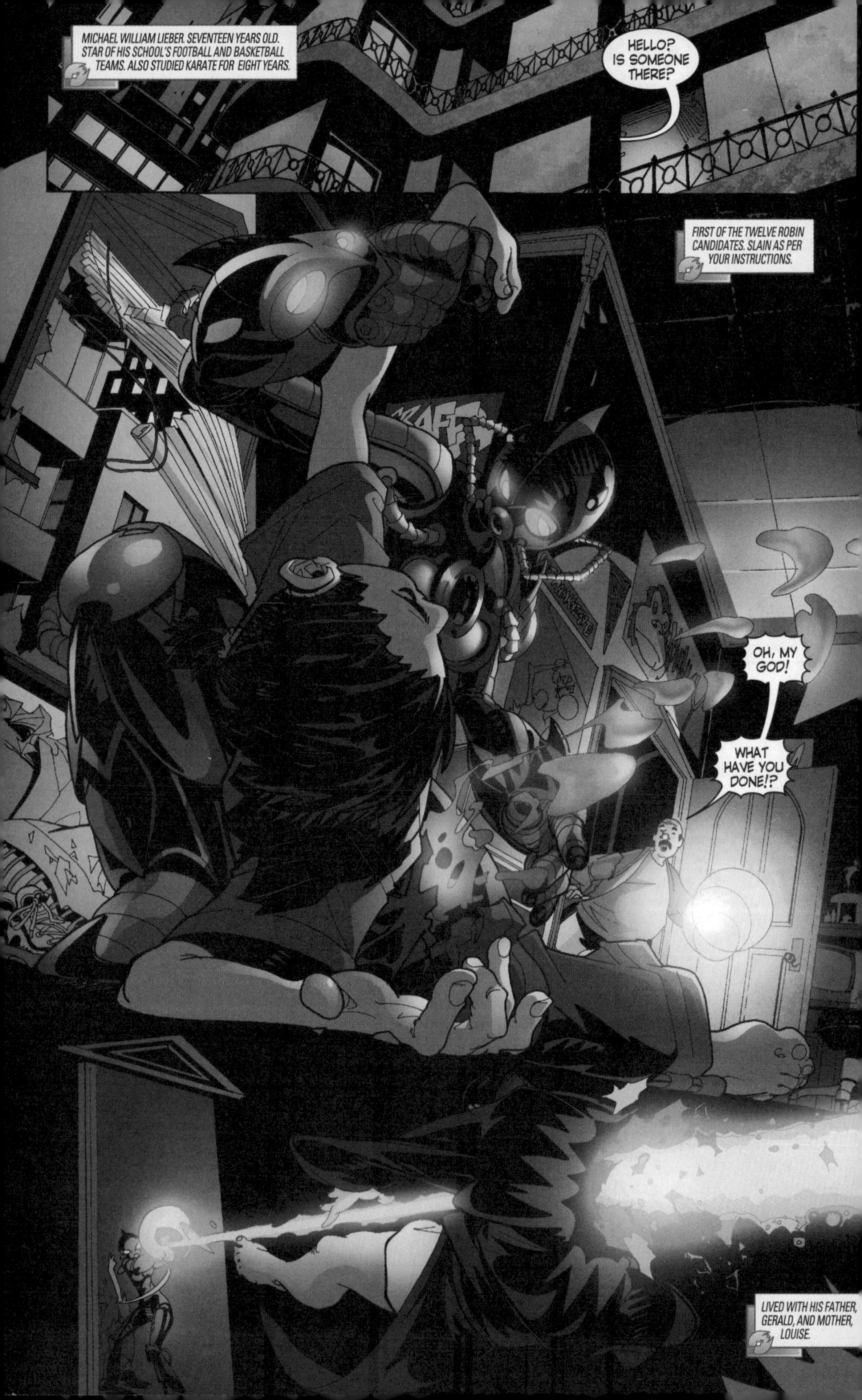
MICHAEL WILLIAM LIEBER. SEVENTEEN YEARS OLD. STAR OF HIS SCHOOL'S FOOTBALL AND BASKETBALL TEAMS. ALSO STUDIED KARATE FOR EIGHT YEARS.
HELLO? IS SOMEONE THERE?
FIRST OF THE TWELVE ROBIN CANDIDATES. SLAIN AS PER YOUR INSTRUCTIONS.
OH, MY GOD!
WHAT HAVE YOU DONE!?
LIVED WITH HIS FATHER, GERALD, AND MOTHER, LOUISE.

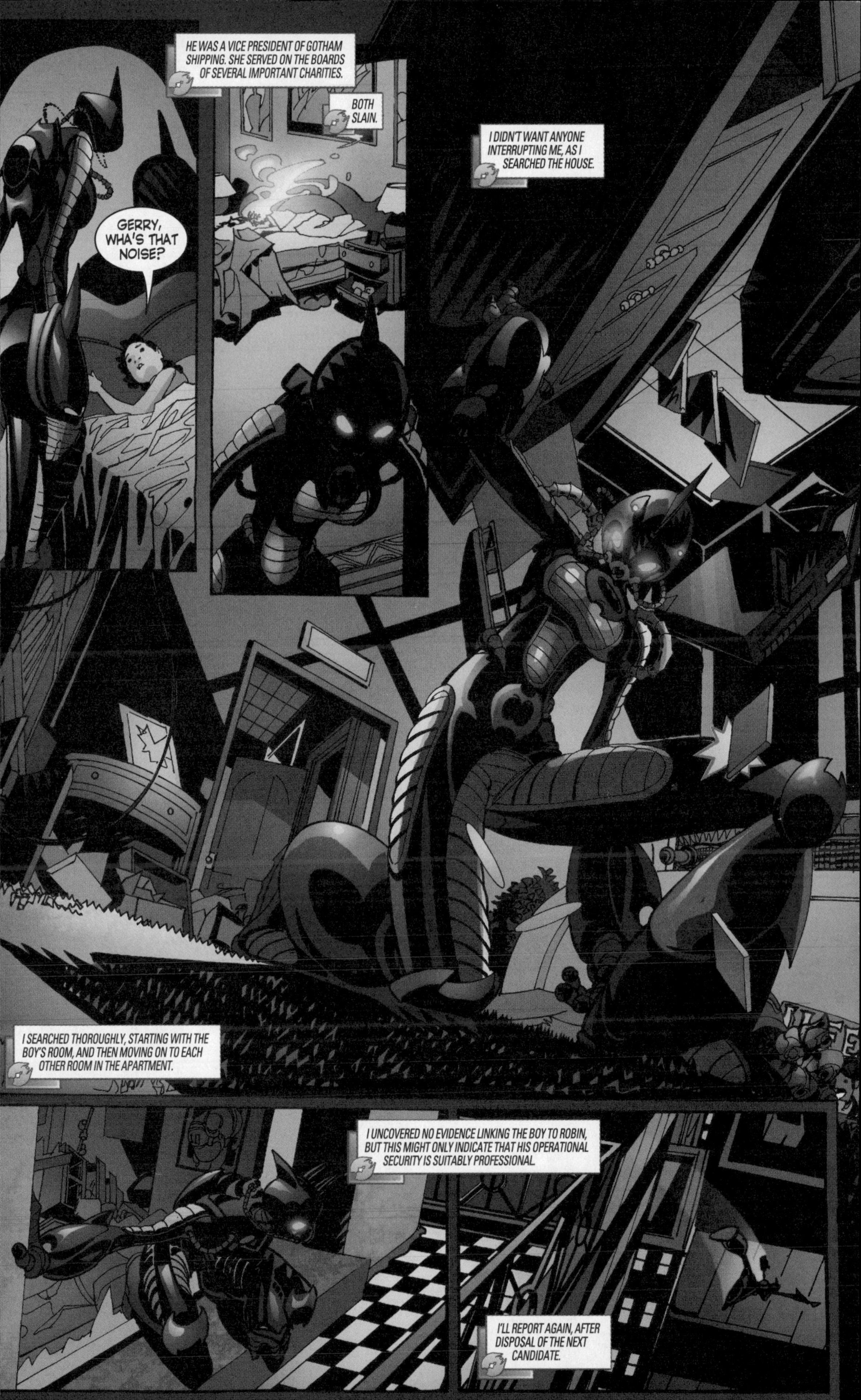
HE WAS A VICE PRESIDENT OF GOTHAM SHIPPING. SHE SERVED ON THE BOARDS OF SEVERAL IMPORTANT CHARITIES.
GERRY, WHA'S THAT NOISE?
BOTH SLAIN.
I DIDN'T WANT ANYONE INTERRUPTING ME, AS I SEARCHED THE HOUSE.
I SEARCHED THOROUGHLY, STARTING WITH THE BOY'S ROOM, AND THEN MOVING ON TO EACH OTHER ROOM IN THE APARTMENT.
I UNCOVERED NO EVIDENCE LINKING THE BOY TO ROBIN, BUT THIS MIGHT ONLY INDICATE THAT HIS OPERATIONAL SECURITY IS SUITABLY PROFESSIONAL.
I'LL REPORT AGAIN, AFTER DISPOSAL OF THE NEXT CANDIDATE.

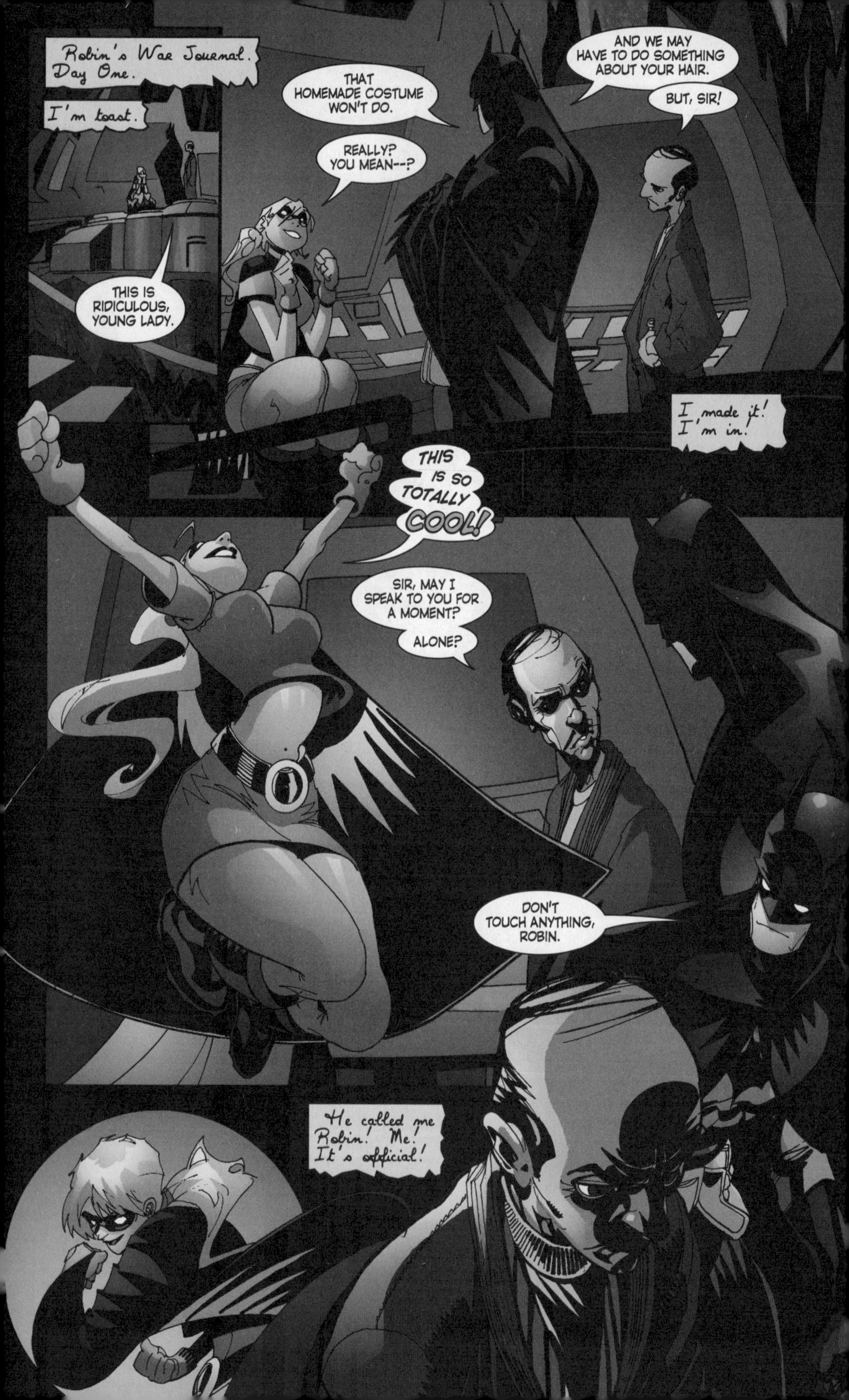
Robin's War Journal. Day One.
I'm toast.
THIS IS RIDICULOUS, YOUNG LADY.
THAT HOMEMADE COSTUME WON'T DO.
REALLY? YOU MEAN--?
AND WE MAY HAVE TO DO SOMETHING ABOUT YOUR HAIR.
BUT, SIR!
I made it! I'm in!
THIS IS SO TOTALLY COOL!
SIR, MAY I SPEAK TO YOU FOR A MOMENT?
ALONE?
DON'T TOUCH ANYTHING, ROBIN.
He called me Robin! Me! It's official!

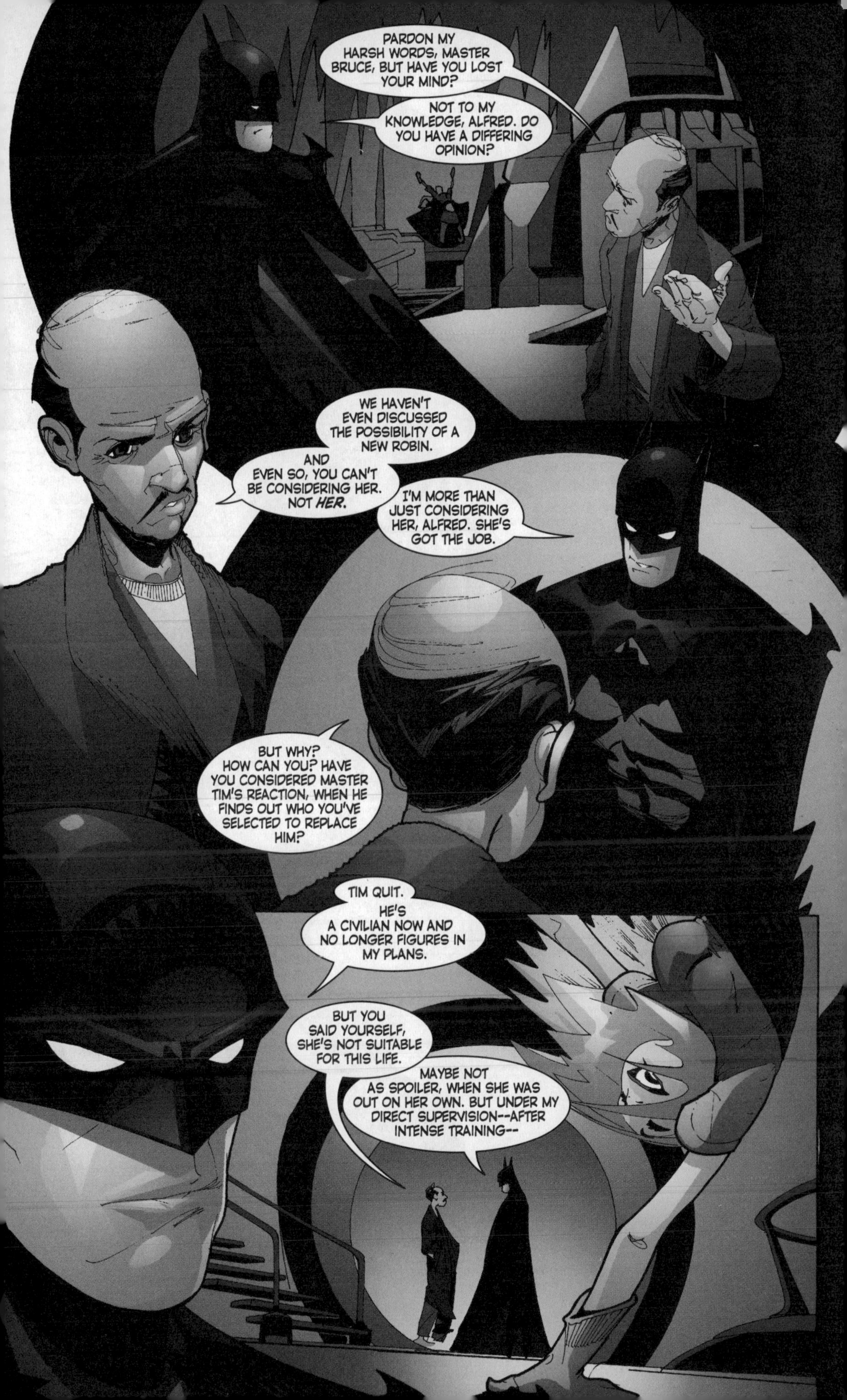
PARDON MY HARSH WORDS, MASTER BRUCE, BUT HAVE YOU LOST YOUR MIND?
NOT TO MY KNOWLEDGE, ALFRED. DO YOU HAVE A DIFFERING OPINION?
WE HAVEN'T EVEN DISCUSSED THE POSSIBILITY OF A NEW ROBIN.
AND EVEN SO, YOU CAN'T BE CONSIDERING HER. NOT *HER*.
I'M MORE THAN JUST CONSIDERING HER, ALFRED. SHE'S GOT THE JOB.
BUT WHY? HOW CAN YOU? HAVE YOU CONSIDERED MASTER TIM'S REACTION, WHEN HE FINDS OUT WHO YOU'VE SELECTED TO REPLACE HIM?
TIM QUIT.
HE'S A CIVILIAN NOW AND NO LONGER FIGURES IN MY PLANS.
BUT YOU SAID YOURSELF, SHE'S NOT SUITABLE FOR THIS LIFE.
MAYBE NOT AS SPOILER, WHEN SHE WAS OUT ON HER OWN. BUT UNDER MY DIRECT SUPERVISION--AFTER INTENSE TRAINING--

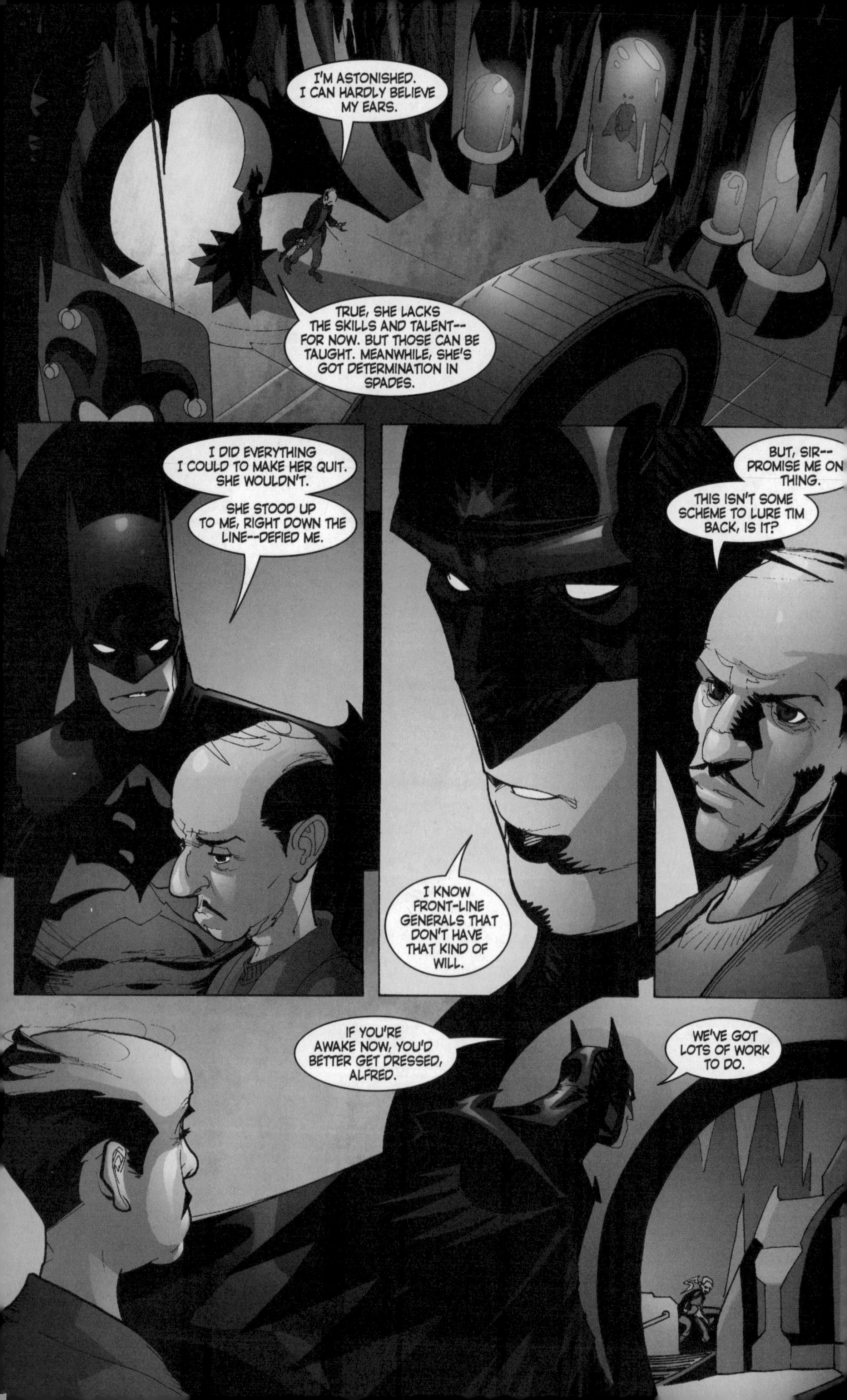
I'M ASTONISHED. I CAN HARDLY BELIEVE MY EARS.
TRUE, SHE LACKS THE SKILLS AND TALENT-- FOR NOW. BUT THOSE CAN BE TAUGHT. MEANWHILE, SHE'S GOT DETERMINATION IN SPADES.
I DID EVERYTHING I COULD TO MAKE HER QUIT. SHE WOULDN'T.
SHE STOOD UP TO ME, RIGHT DOWN THE LINE--DEFIED ME.
I KNOW FRONT-LINE GENERALS THAT DON'T HAVE THAT KIND OF WILL.
BUT, SIR-- PROMISE ME ON THING.
THIS ISN'T SOME SCHEME TO LURE TIM BACK, IS IT?
IF YOU'RE AWAKE NOW, YOU'D BETTER GET DRESSED, ALFRED.
WE'VE GOT LOTS OF WORK TO DO.

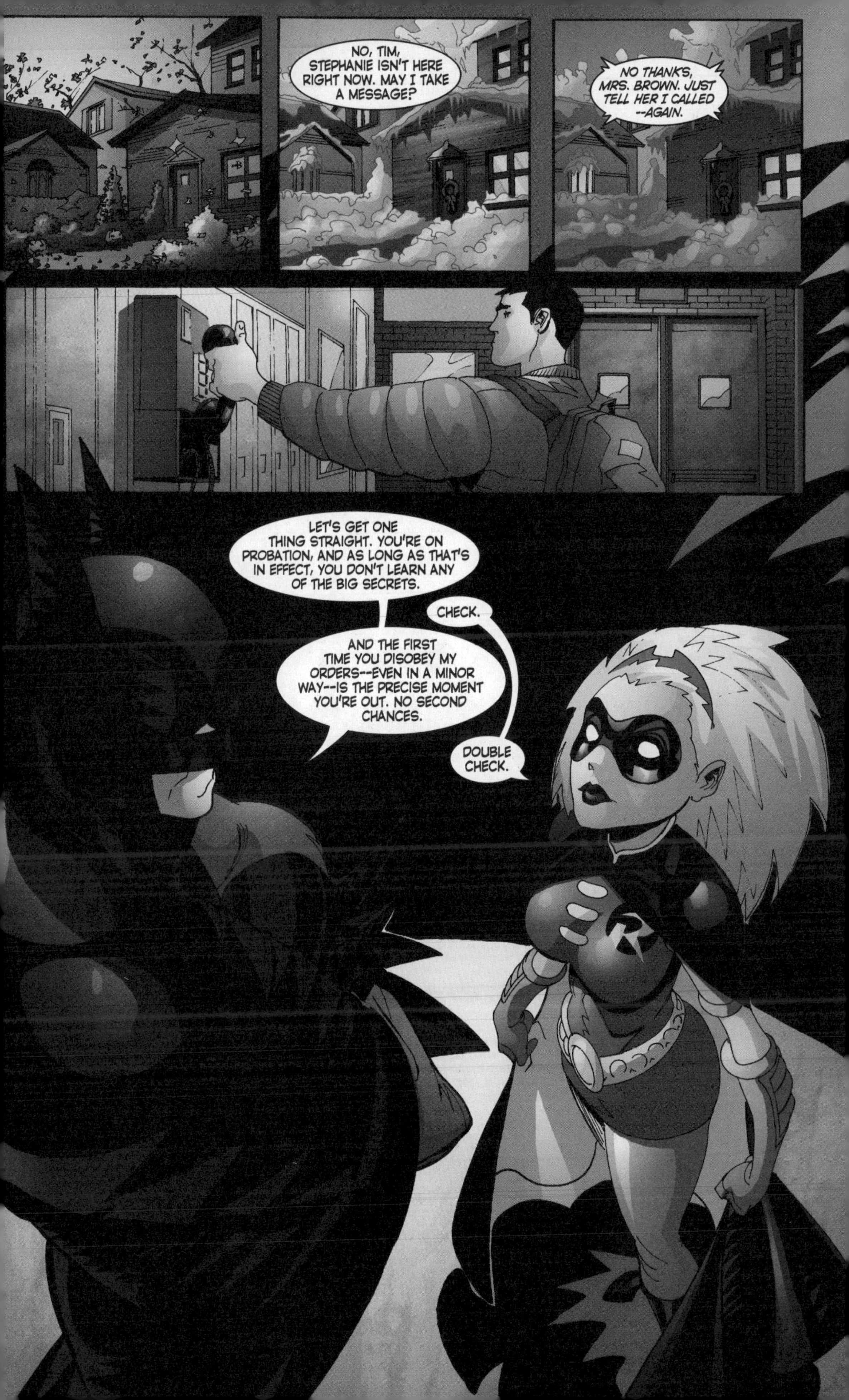
NO, TIM, STEPHANIE ISN'T HERE RIGHT NOW. MAY I TAKE A MESSAGE?
NO THANKS, MRS. BROWN. JUST TELL HER I CALLED --AGAIN.
LET'S GET ONE THING STRAIGHT. YOU'RE ON PROBATION, AND AS LONG AS THAT'S IN EFFECT, YOU DON'T LEARN ANY OF THE BIG SECRETS.
CHECK.
AND THE FIRST TIME YOU DISOBEY MY ORDERS--EVEN IN A MINOR WAY--IS THE PRECISE MOMENT YOU'RE OUT. NO SECOND CHANCES.
DOUBLE CHECK.

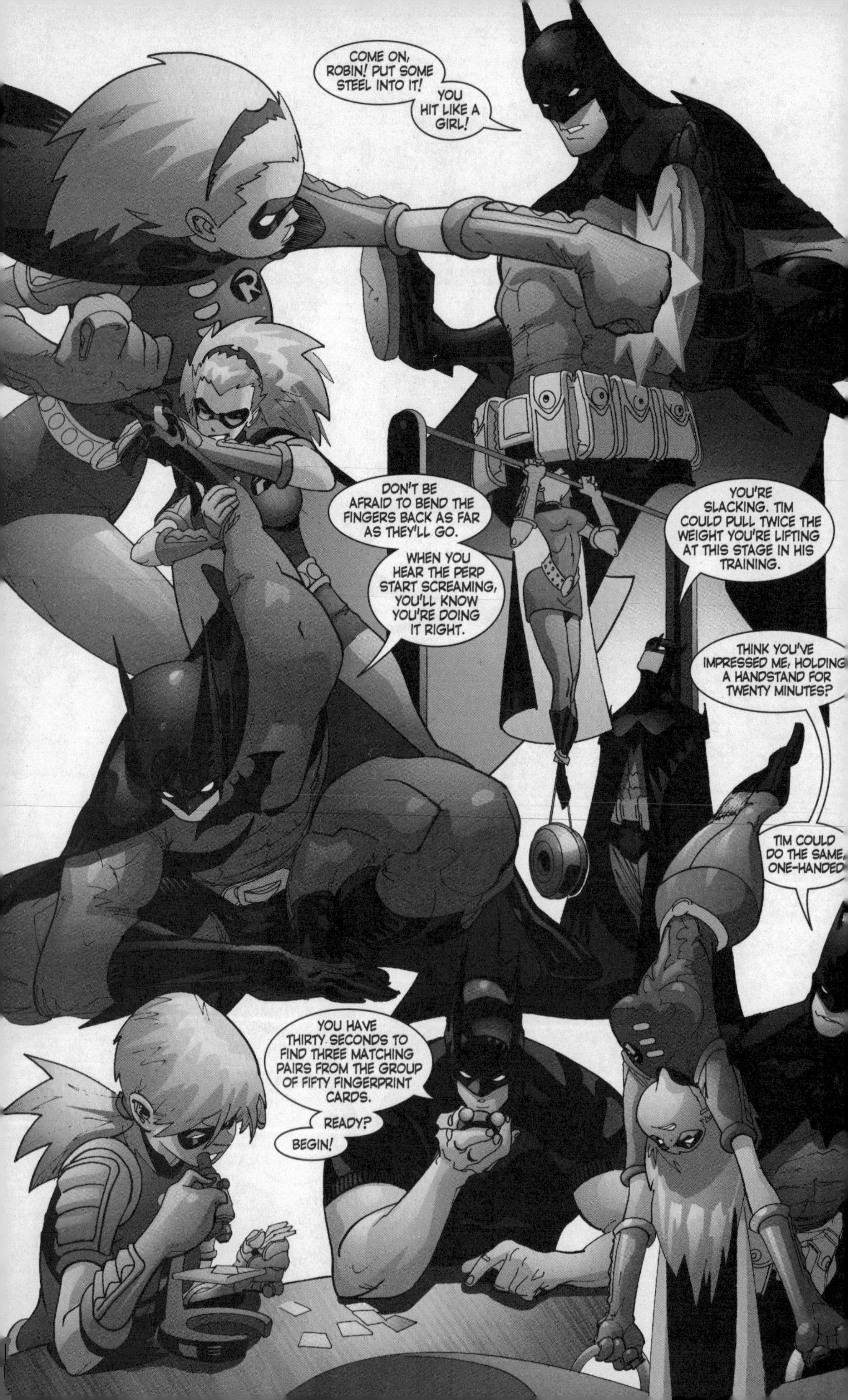
COME ON, ROBIN! PUT SOME STEEL INTO IT!
YOU HIT LIKE A GIRL!
DON'T BE AFRAID TO BEND THE FINGERS BACK AS FAR AS THEY'LL GO.
WHEN YOU HEAR THE PERP START SCREAMING, YOU'LL KNOW YOU'RE DOING IT RIGHT.
YOU'RE SLACKING. TIM COULD PULL TWICE THE WEIGHT YOU'RE LIFTING AT THIS STAGE IN HIS TRAINING.
THINK YOU'VE IMPRESSED ME, HOLDING A HANDSTAND FOR TWENTY MINUTES?
TIM COULD DO THE SAME, ONE-HANDED
YOU HAVE THIRTY SECONDS TO FIND THREE MATCHING PAIRS FROM THE GROUP OF FIFTY FINGERPRINT CARDS.
READY?
BEGIN!

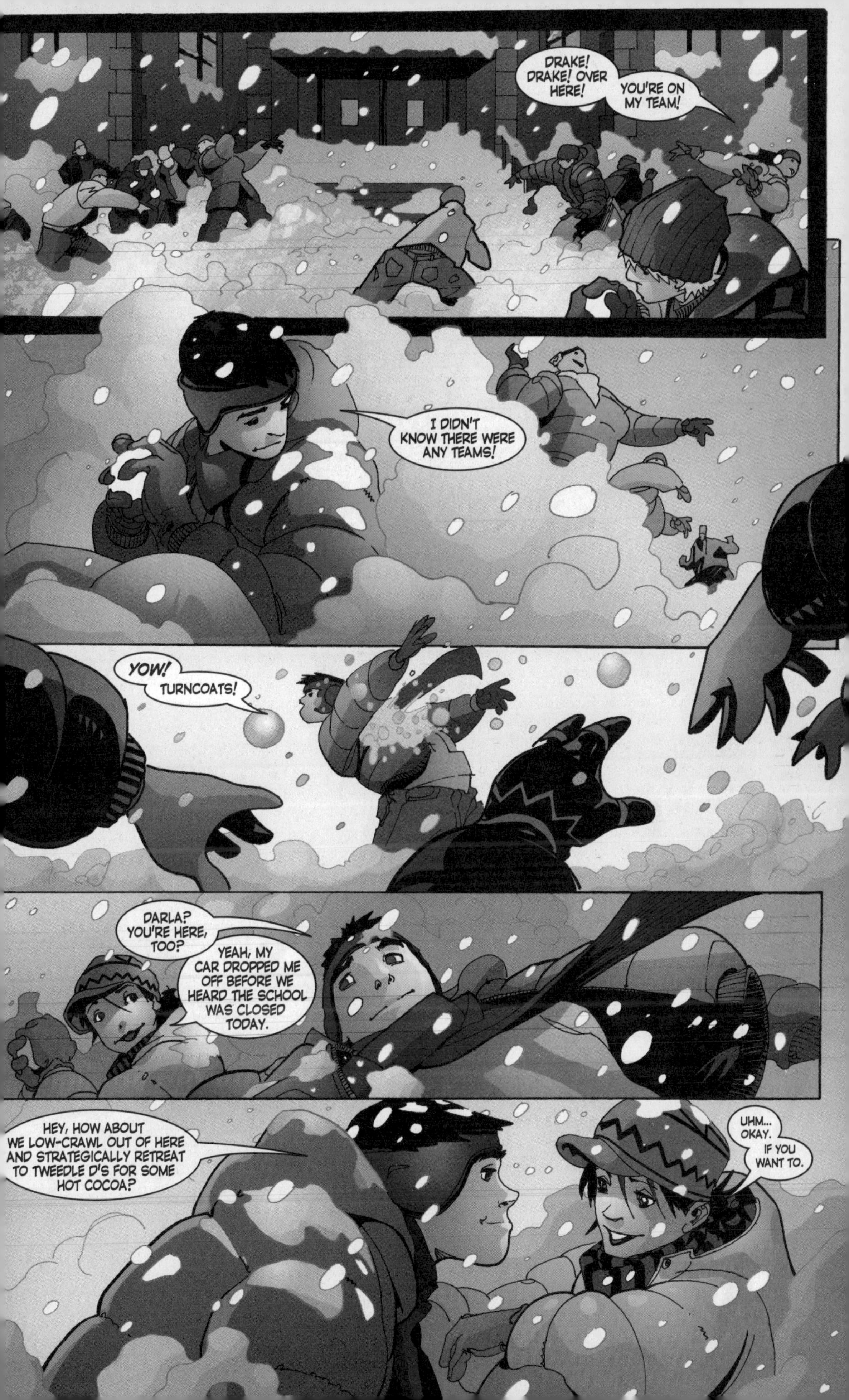

DRAKE! DRAKE! OVER HERE!
YOU'RE ON MY TEAM!
I DIDN'T KNOW THERE WERE ANY TEAMS!
YOW!
TURNCOATS!
DARLA? YOU'RE HERE, TOO?
YEAH, MY CAR DROPPED ME OFF BEFORE WE HEARD THE SCHOOL WAS CLOSED TODAY.
HEY, HOW ABOUT WE LOW-CRAWL OUT OF HERE AND STRATEGICALLY RETREAT TO TWEEDLE D'S FOR SOME HOT COCOA?
UHM... OKAY.
IF YOU WANT TO.

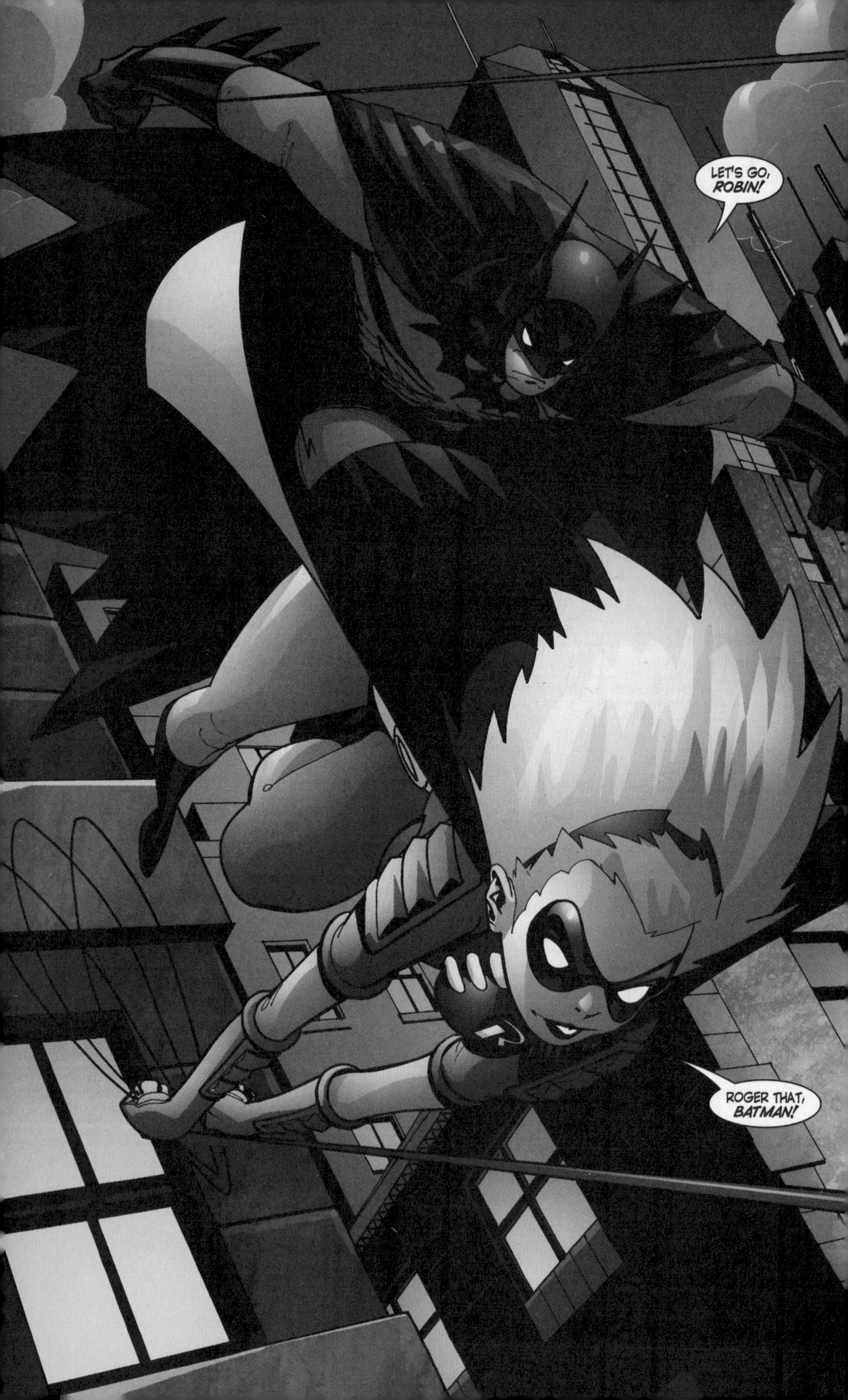
LET'S GO, ROBIN!
ROGER THAT, BATMAN!

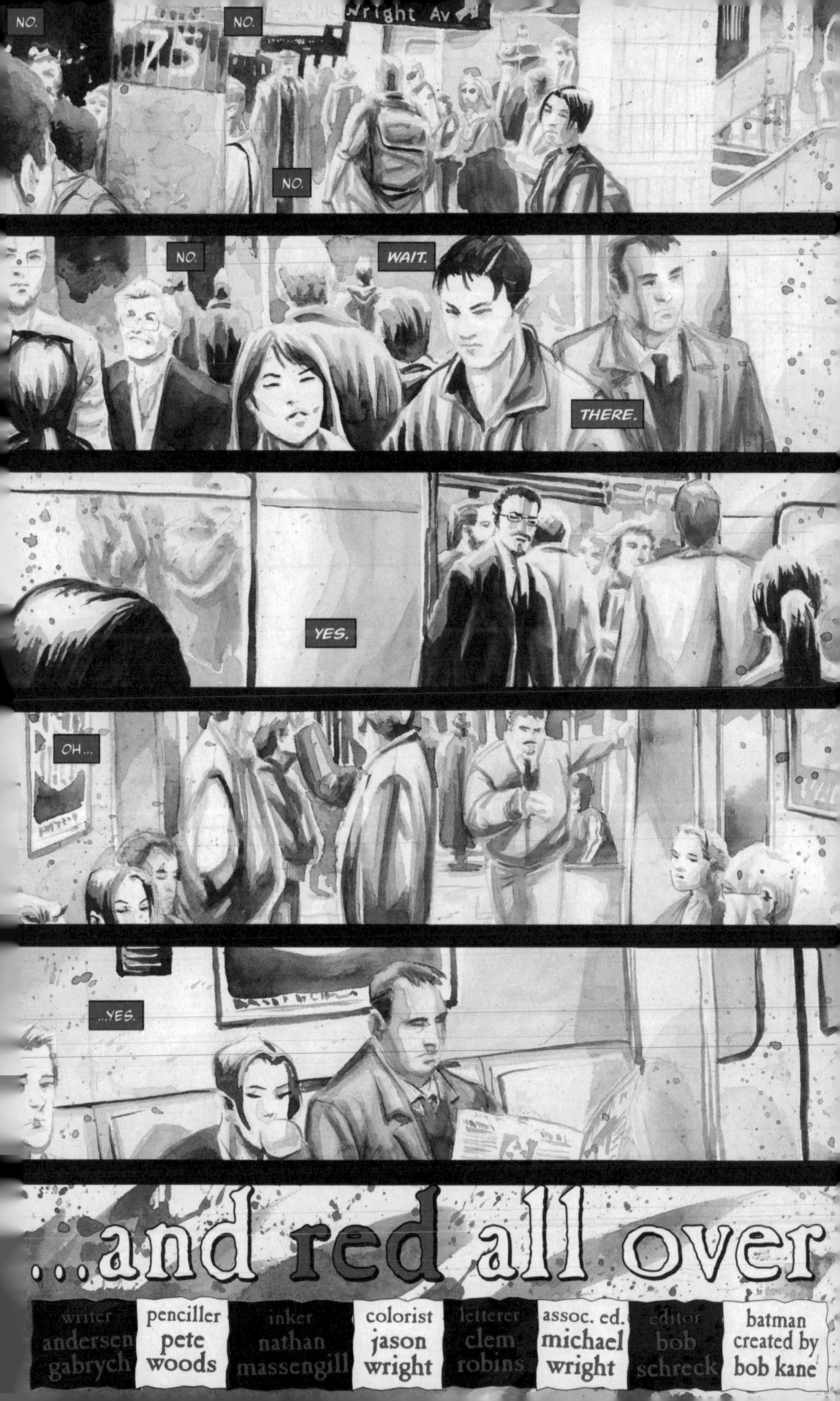
Wright Av
NO.
NO.
NO.
NO.
WAIT.
THERE.
YES.
OH...
...YES.
...and red all over
writer andersen gabrych
penciller pete woods
inker nathan massengill
colorist jason wright
letterer clem robins
assoc. ed. michael wright
editor bob schreck
batman created by bob kane

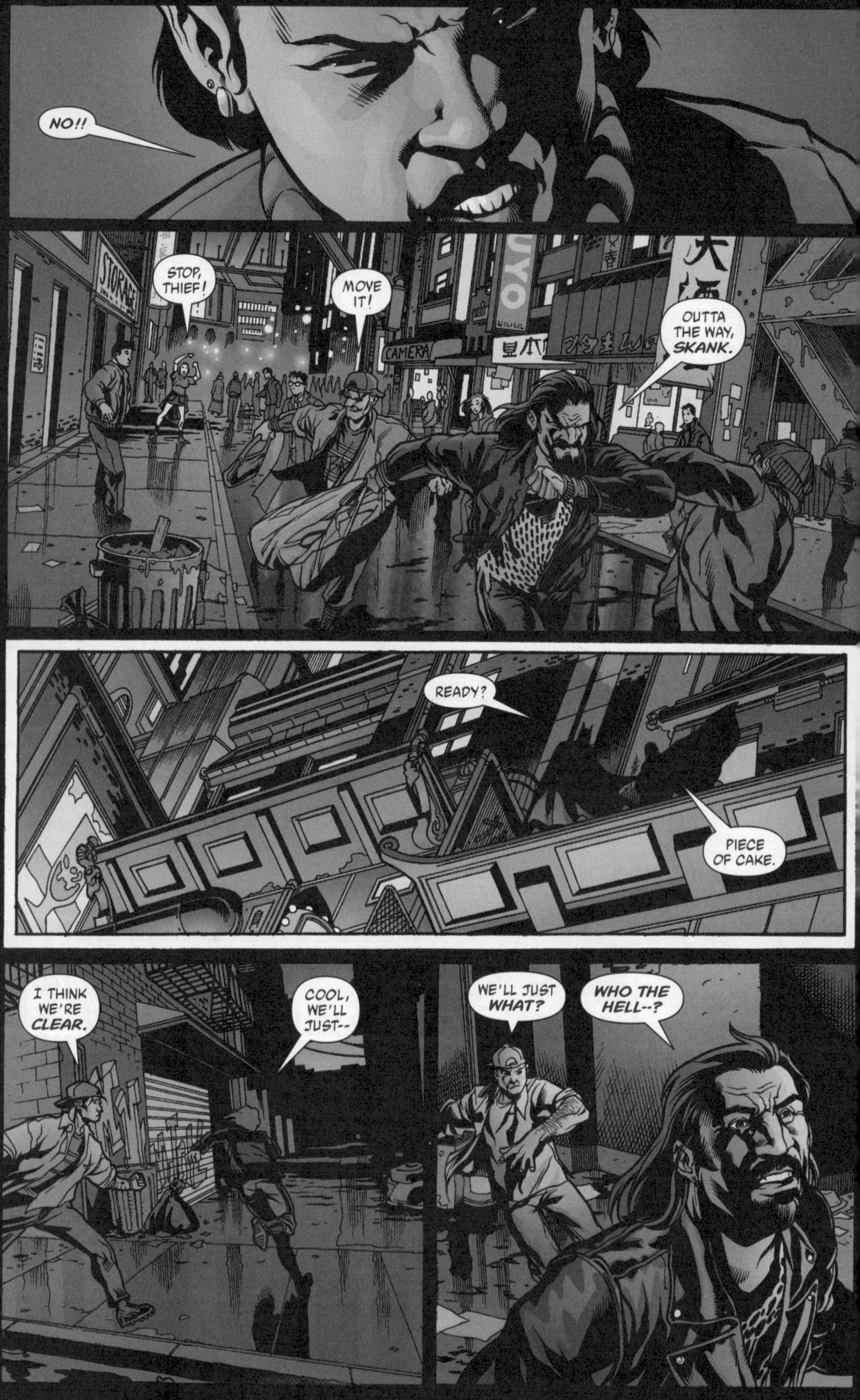
NO!!
STOP, THIEF!
MOVE IT!
OUTTA THE WAY, SKANK.
STORAGE
CAMERA
READY?
PIECE OF CAKE.
I THINK WE'RE CLEAR.
COOL, WE'LL JUST--
WE'LL JUST WHAT?
WHO THE HELL--?

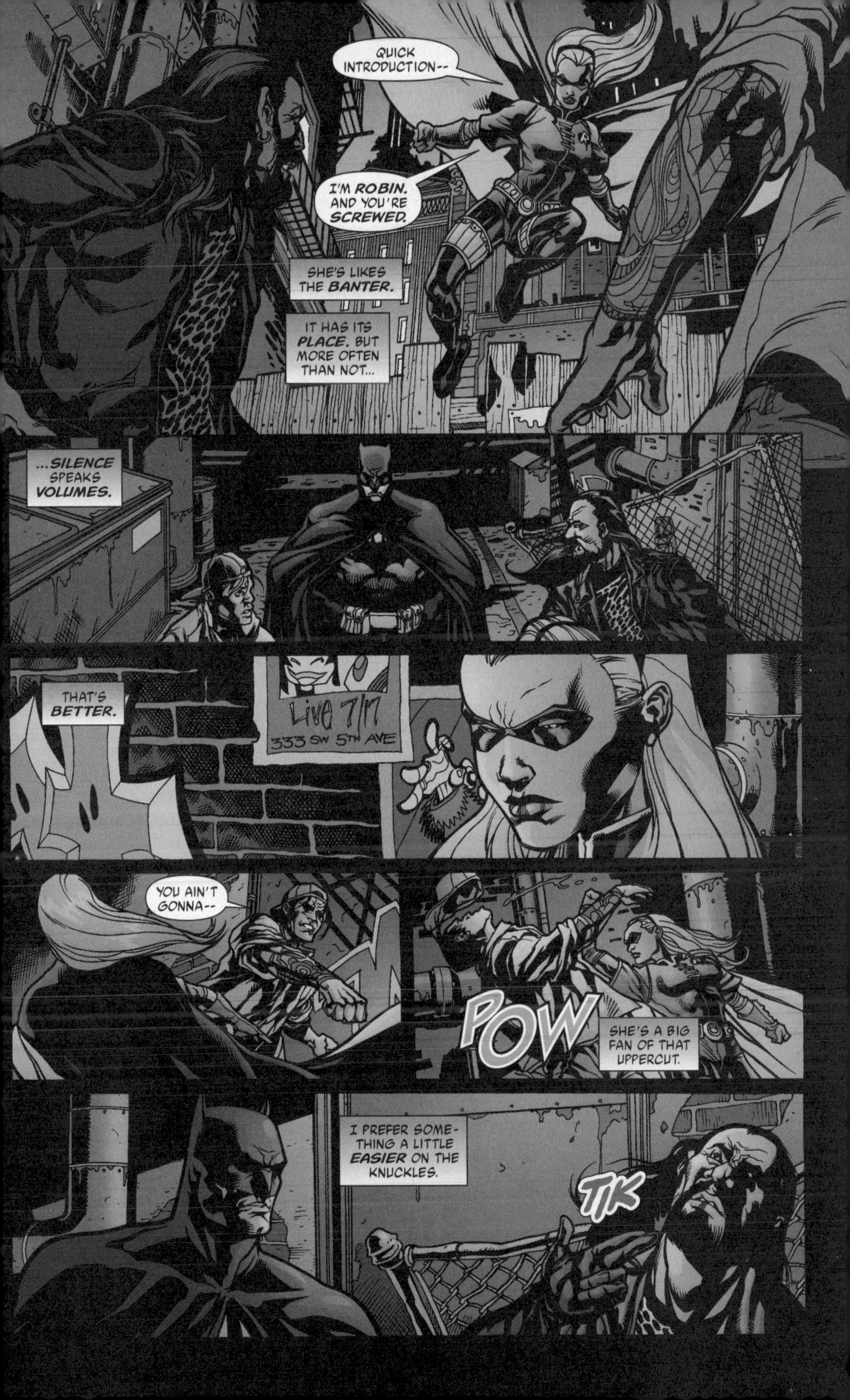
QUICK INTRODUCTION--
I'M ROBIN. AND YOU'RE SCREWED.
SHE'S LIKES THE BANTER.
IT HAS ITS PLACE. BUT MORE OFTEN THAN NOT...
...SILENCE SPEAKS VOLUMES.
THAT'S BETTER.
Live 7/17
333 SW 5TH AVE
YOU AIN'T GONNA--
POW
SHE'S A BIG FAN OF THAT UPPERCUT.
I PREFER SOME-THING A LITTLE EASIER ON THE KNUCKLES.
TIK

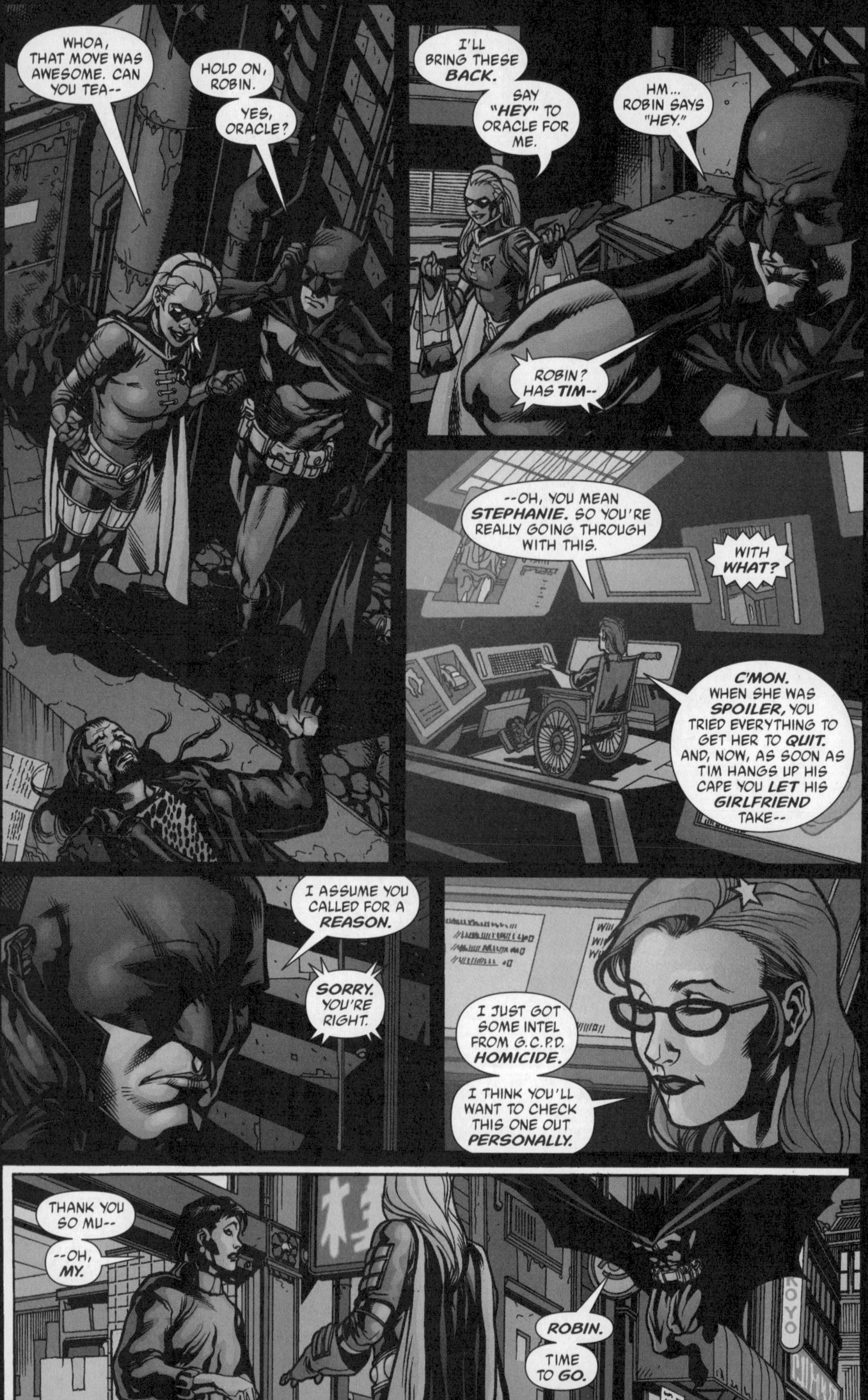
WHOA, THAT MOVE WAS AWESOME. CAN YOU TEA--
HOLD ON, ROBIN.
YES, ORACLE?
I'LL BRING THESE BACK.
SAY "HEY" TO ORACLE FOR ME.
HM... ROBIN SAYS "HEY."
ROBIN? HAS TIM--
--OH, YOU MEAN STEPHANIE. SO YOU'RE REALLY GOING THROUGH WITH THIS.
WITH WHAT?
C'MON. WHEN SHE WAS SPOILER, YOU TRIED EVERYTHING TO GET HER TO QUIT. AND, NOW, AS SOON AS TIM HANGS UP HIS CAPE YOU LET HIS GIRLFRIEND TAKE--
I ASSUME YOU CALLED FOR A REASON.
SORRY. YOU'RE RIGHT.
I JUST GOT SOME INTEL FROM G.C.P.D. HOMICIDE.
I THINK YOU'LL WANT TO CHECK THIS ONE OUT PERSONALLY.
THANK YOU SO MU--
--OH, MY.
ROBIN.
TIME TO GO.

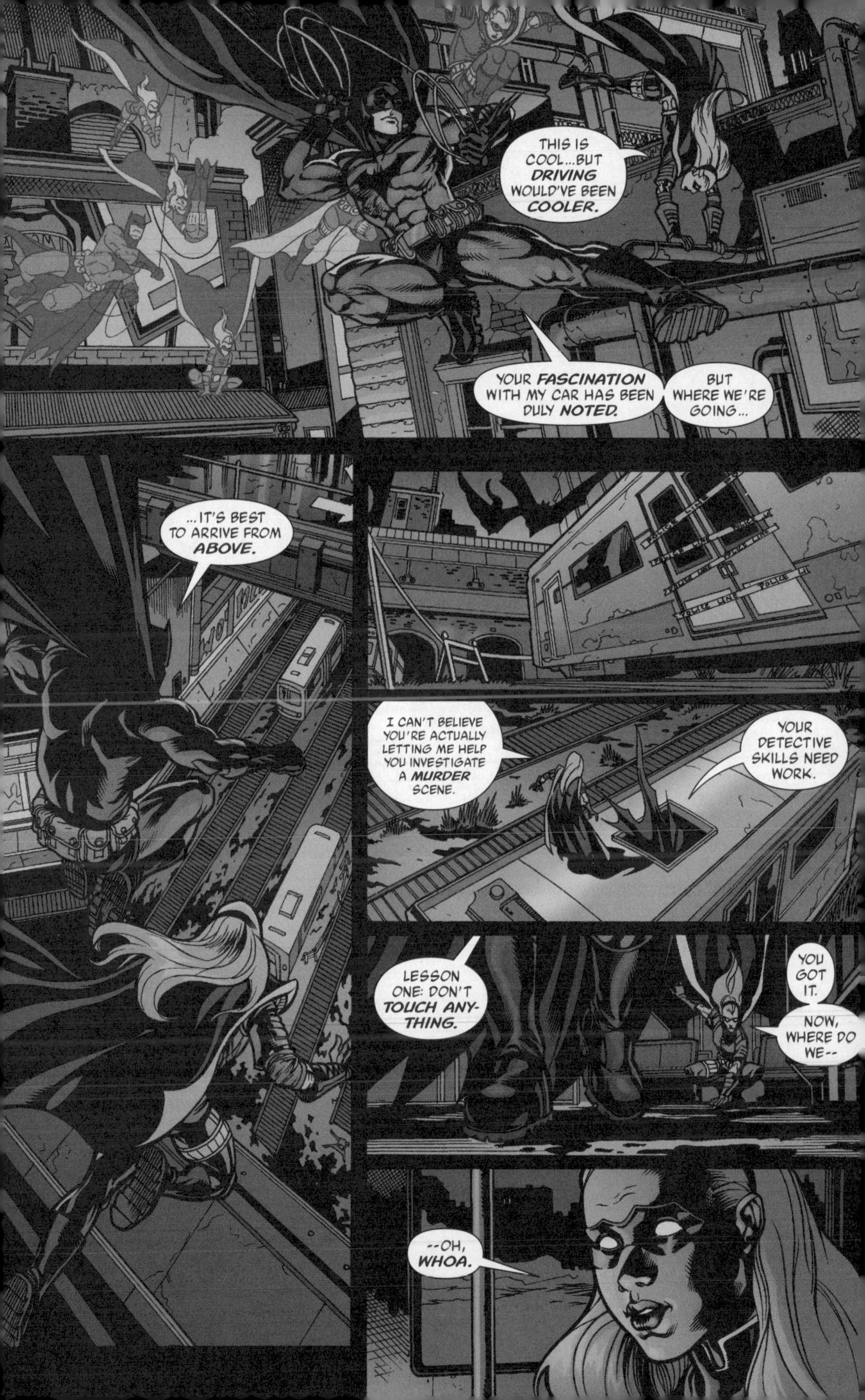
THIS IS COOL...BUT DRIVING WOULD'VE BEEN COOLER.
YOUR FASCINATION WITH MY CAR HAS BEEN DULY NOTED.
BUT WHERE WE'RE GOING...
...IT'S BEST TO ARRIVE FROM ABOVE.
I CAN'T BELIEVE YOU'RE ACTUALLY LETTING ME HELP YOU INVESTIGATE A MURDER SCENE.
YOUR DETECTIVE SKILLS NEED WORK.
LESSON ONE: DON'T TOUCH ANYTHING.
YOU GOT IT.
NOW, WHERE DO WE--
--OH, WHOA.

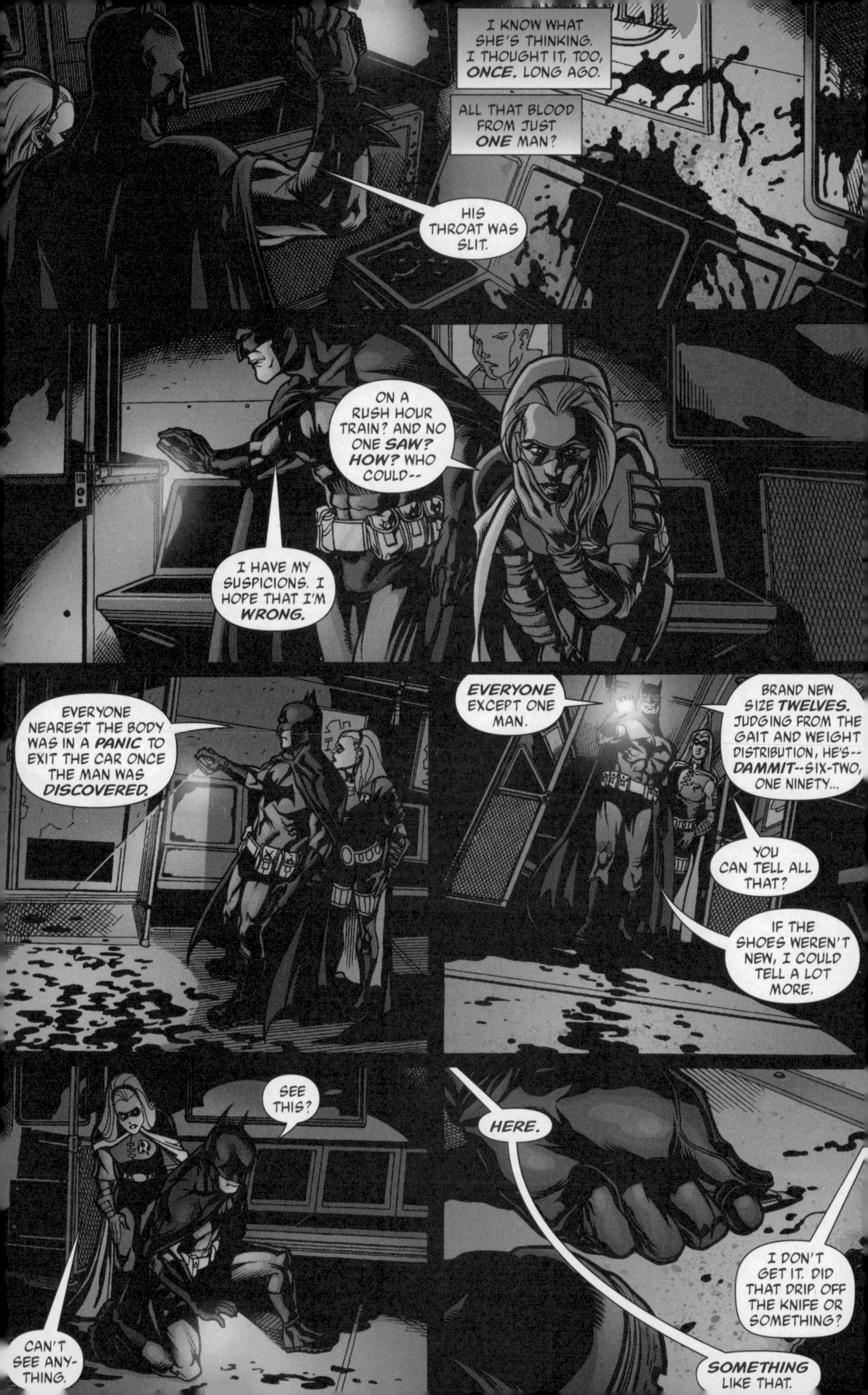
I KNOW WHAT SHE'S THINKING. I THOUGHT IT, TOO, ONCE. LONG AGO.
ALL THAT BLOOD FROM JUST ONE MAN?
HIS THROAT WAS SLIT.
ON A RUSH HOUR TRAIN? AND NO ONE SAW? HOW? WHO COULD--
I HAVE MY SUSPICIONS. I HOPE THAT I'M WRONG.
EVERYONE NEAREST THE BODY WAS IN A PANIC TO EXIT THE CAR ONCE THE MAN WAS DISCOVERED.
EVERYONE EXCEPT ONE MAN.
BRAND NEW SIZE TWELVES. JUDGING FROM THE GAIT AND WEIGHT DISTRIBUTION, HE'S--DAMMIT--SIX-TWO, ONE NINETY...
YOU CAN TELL ALL THAT?
IF THE SHOES WEREN'T NEW, I COULD TELL A LOT MORE.
SEE THIS?
CAN'T SEE ANY-THING.
HERE.
I DON'T GET IT. DID THAT DRIP OFF THE KNIFE OR SOMETHING?
SOMETHING LIKE THAT.

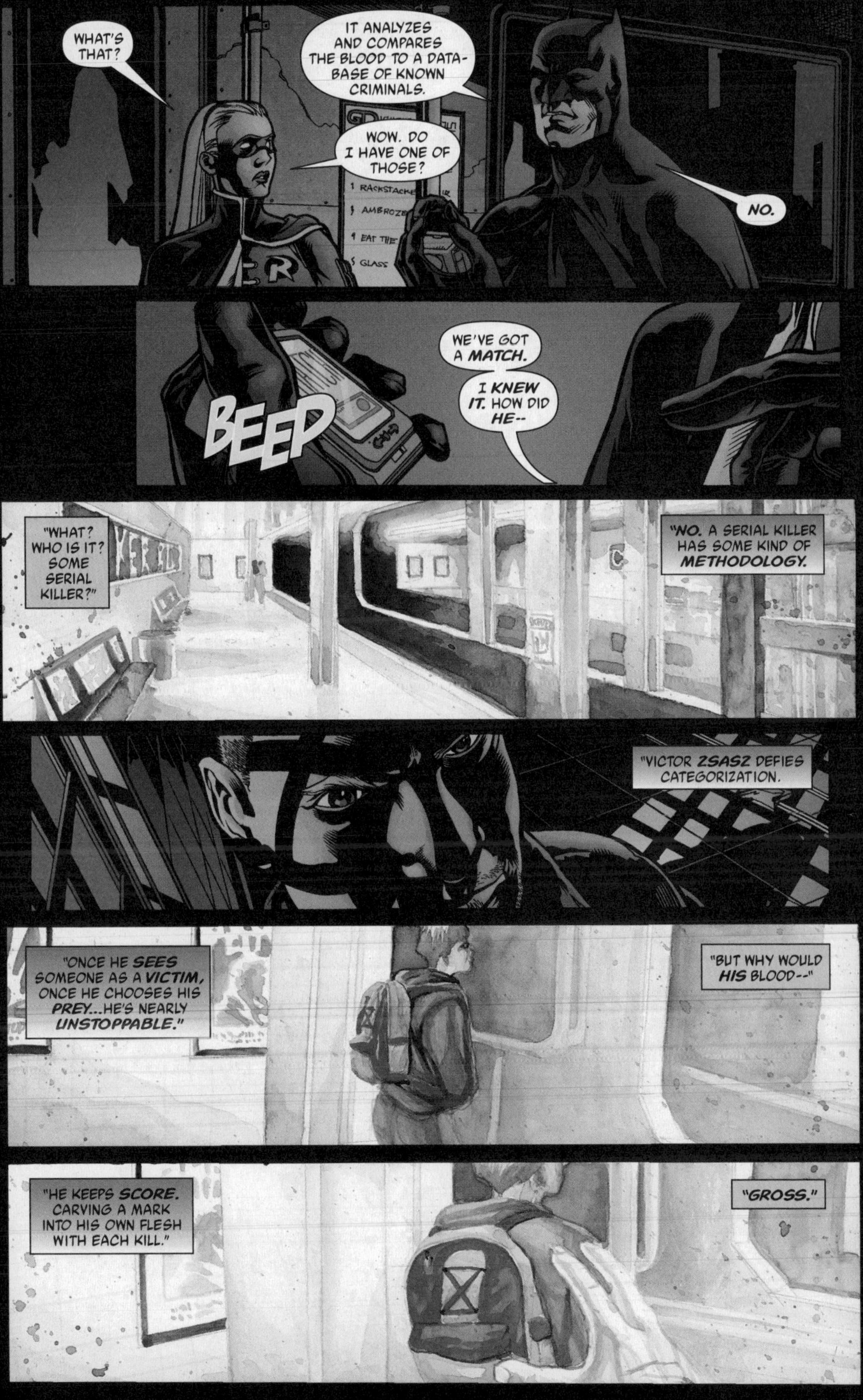
WHAT'S THAT?
IT ANALYZES AND COMPARES THE BLOOD TO A DATA-BASE OF KNOWN CRIMINALS.
WOW. DO I HAVE ONE OF THOSE?
NO.
BEEP
WE'VE GOT A MATCH.
I KNEW IT. HOW DID HE--
"WHAT? WHO IS IT? SOME SERIAL KILLER?"
"NO. A SERIAL KILLER HAS SOME KIND OF METHODOLOGY.
"VICTOR ZSASZ DEFIES CATEGORIZATION.
"ONCE HE SEES SOMEONE AS A VICTIM, ONCE HE CHOOSES HIS PREY...HE'S NEARLY UNSTOPPABLE."
"BUT WHY WOULD HIS BLOOD--"
"HE KEEPS SCORE. CARVING A MARK INTO HIS OWN FLESH WITH EACH KILL."
"GROSS."

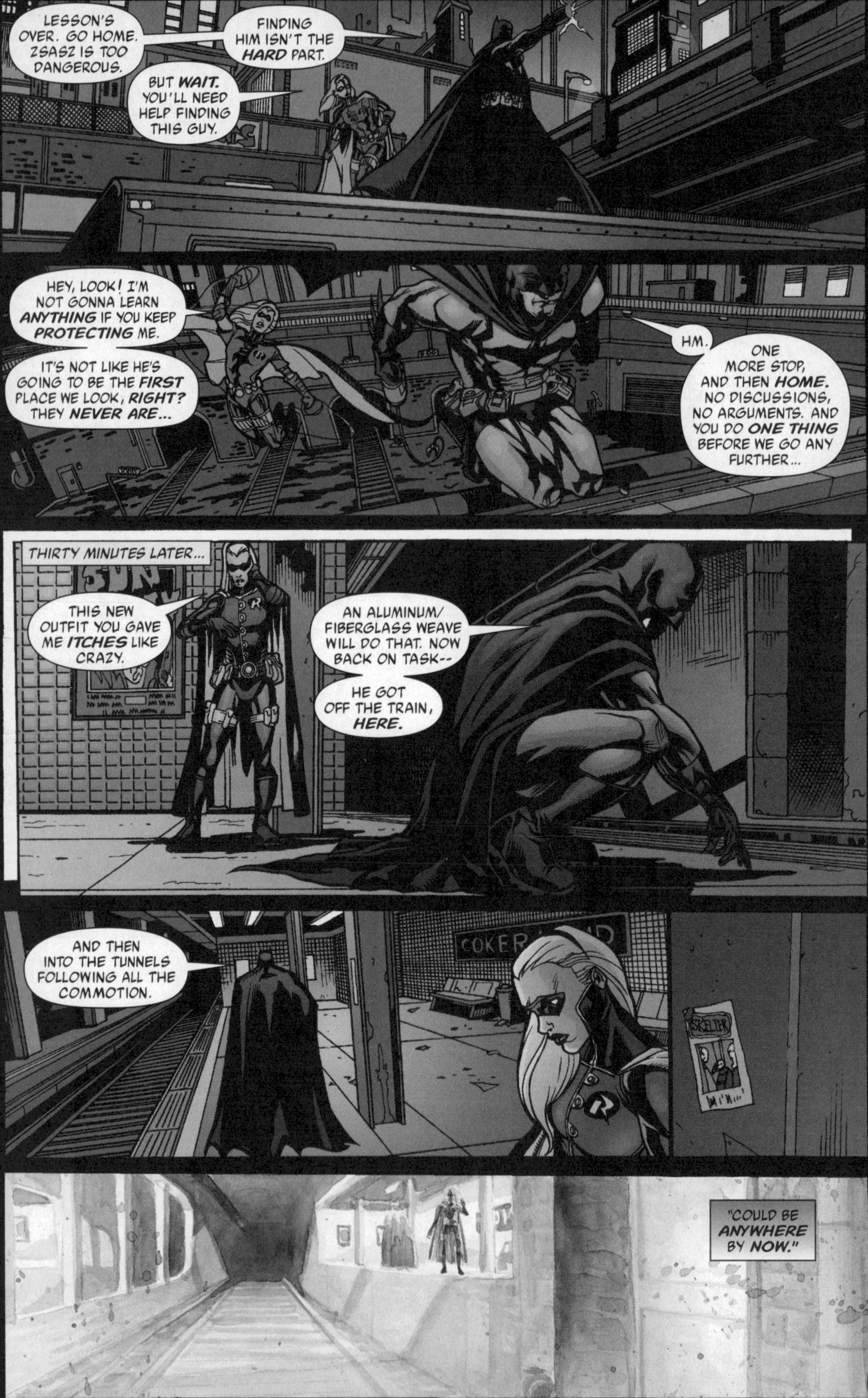

LESSON'S OVER. GO HOME. ZSASZ IS TOO DANGEROUS.
FINDING HIM ISN'T THE **HARD** PART.
BUT **WAIT.** YOU'LL NEED HELP FINDING THIS GUY.
HEY, LOOK! I'M NOT GONNA LEARN **ANYTHING** IF YOU KEEP **PROTECTING** ME.
IT'S NOT LIKE HE'S GOING TO BE THE **FIRST** PLACE WE LOOK, **RIGHT?** THEY **NEVER ARE...**
HM.
ONE MORE STOP, AND THEN **HOME.** NO DISCUSSIONS, NO ARGUMENTS. AND YOU DO **ONE THING** BEFORE WE GO ANY FURTHER...
THIRTY MINUTES LATER...
THIS NEW OUTFIT YOU GAVE ME **ITCHES** LIKE CRAZY.
AN ALUMINUM/ FIBERGLASS WEAVE WILL DO THAT. NOW BACK ON TASK--
HE GOT OFF THE TRAIN, **HERE.**
AND THEN INTO THE TUNNELS FOLLOWING ALL THE COMMOTION.
"COULD BE **ANYWHERE** BY **NOW.**"

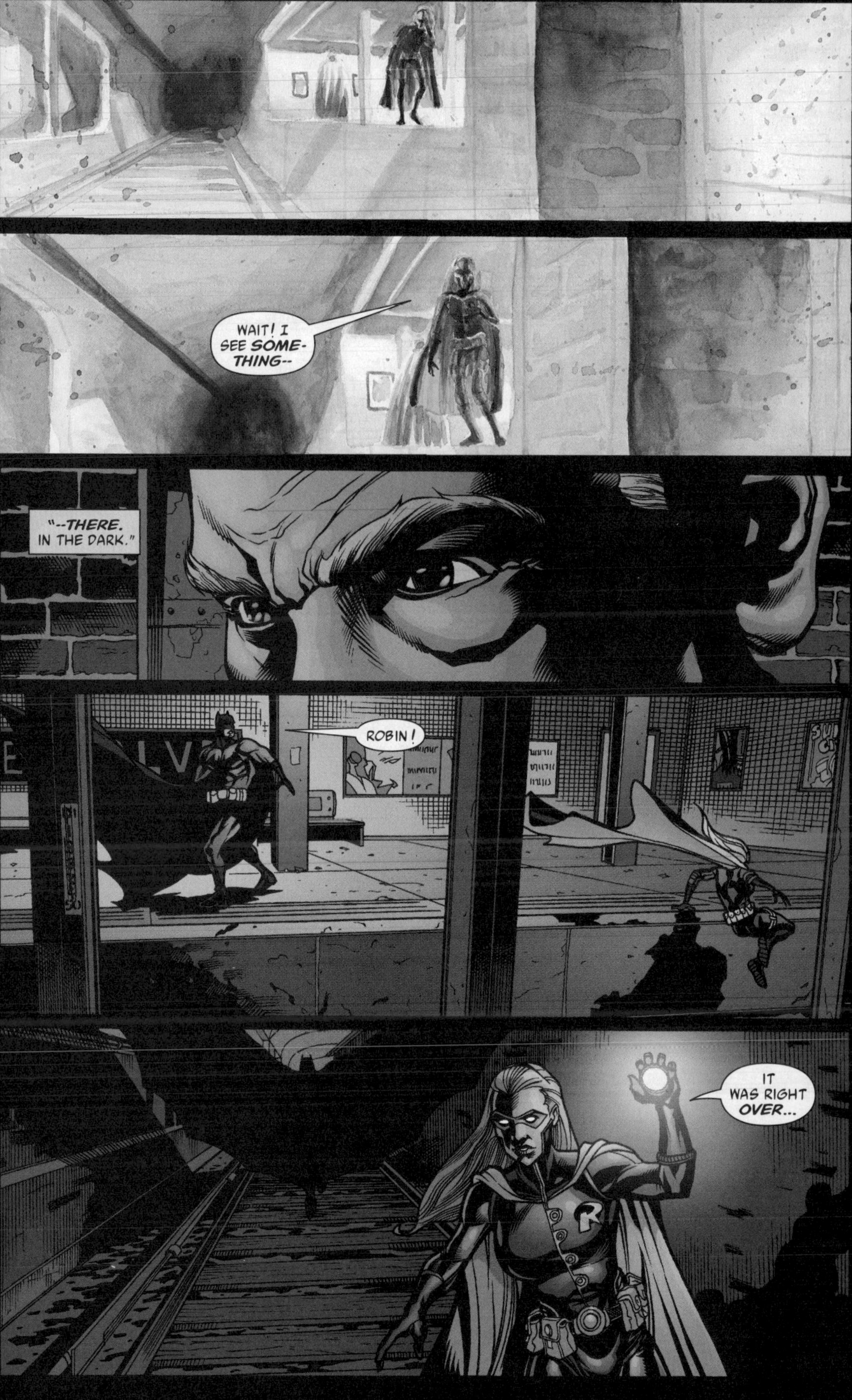
WAIT! I SEE SOME-THING--
"--THERE. IN THE DARK."
ROBIN!
IT WAS RIGHT OVER...

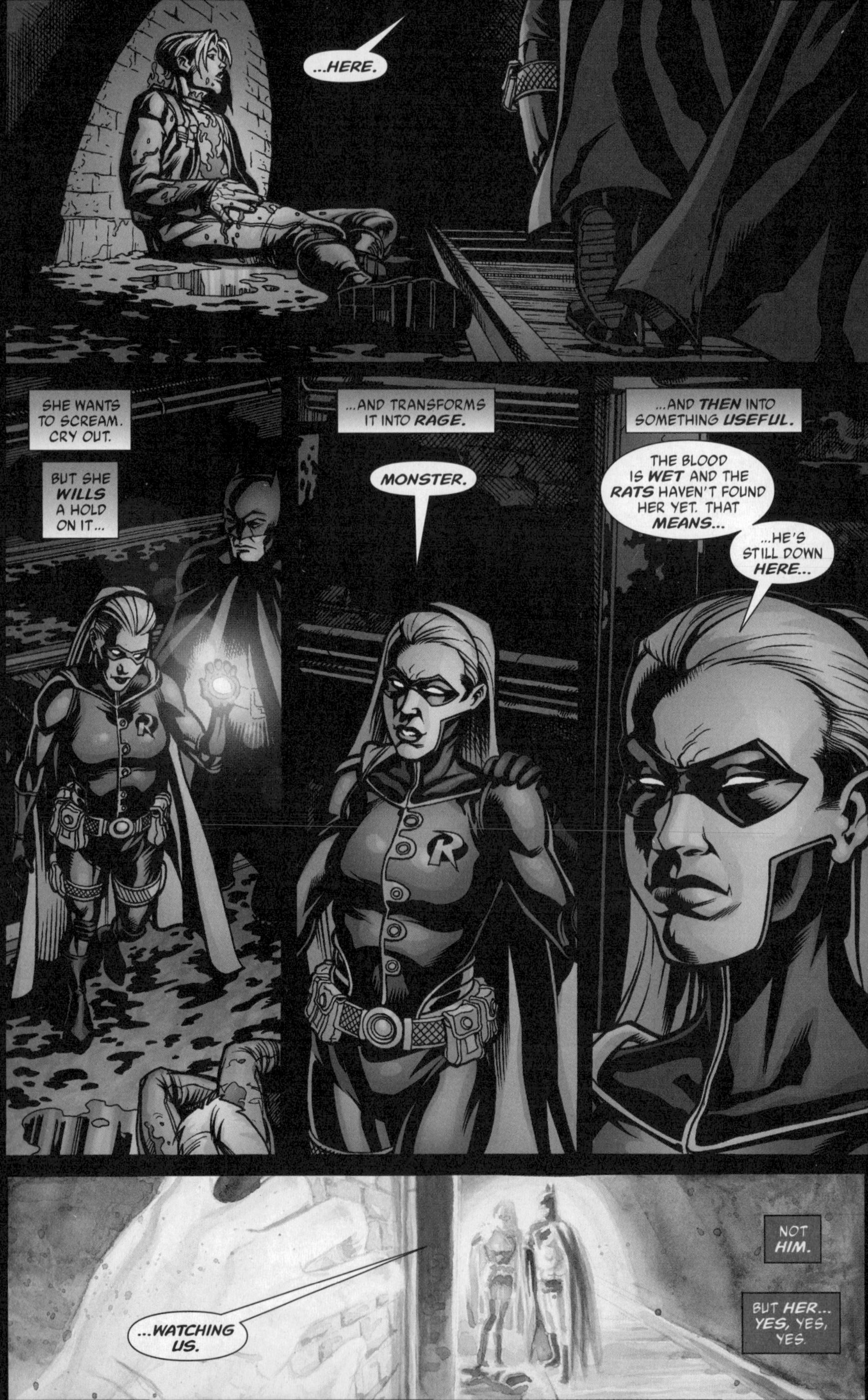
...HERE.
SHE WANTS TO SCREAM. CRY OUT.
BUT SHE WILLS A HOLD ON IT...
...AND TRANSFORMS IT INTO RAGE.
MONSTER.
...AND THEN INTO SOMETHING USEFUL.
THE BLOOD IS WET AND THE RATS HAVEN'T FOUND HER YET. THAT MEANS...
...HE'S STILL DOWN HERE...
...WATCHING US.
NOT HIM.
BUT HER... YES, YES, YES.

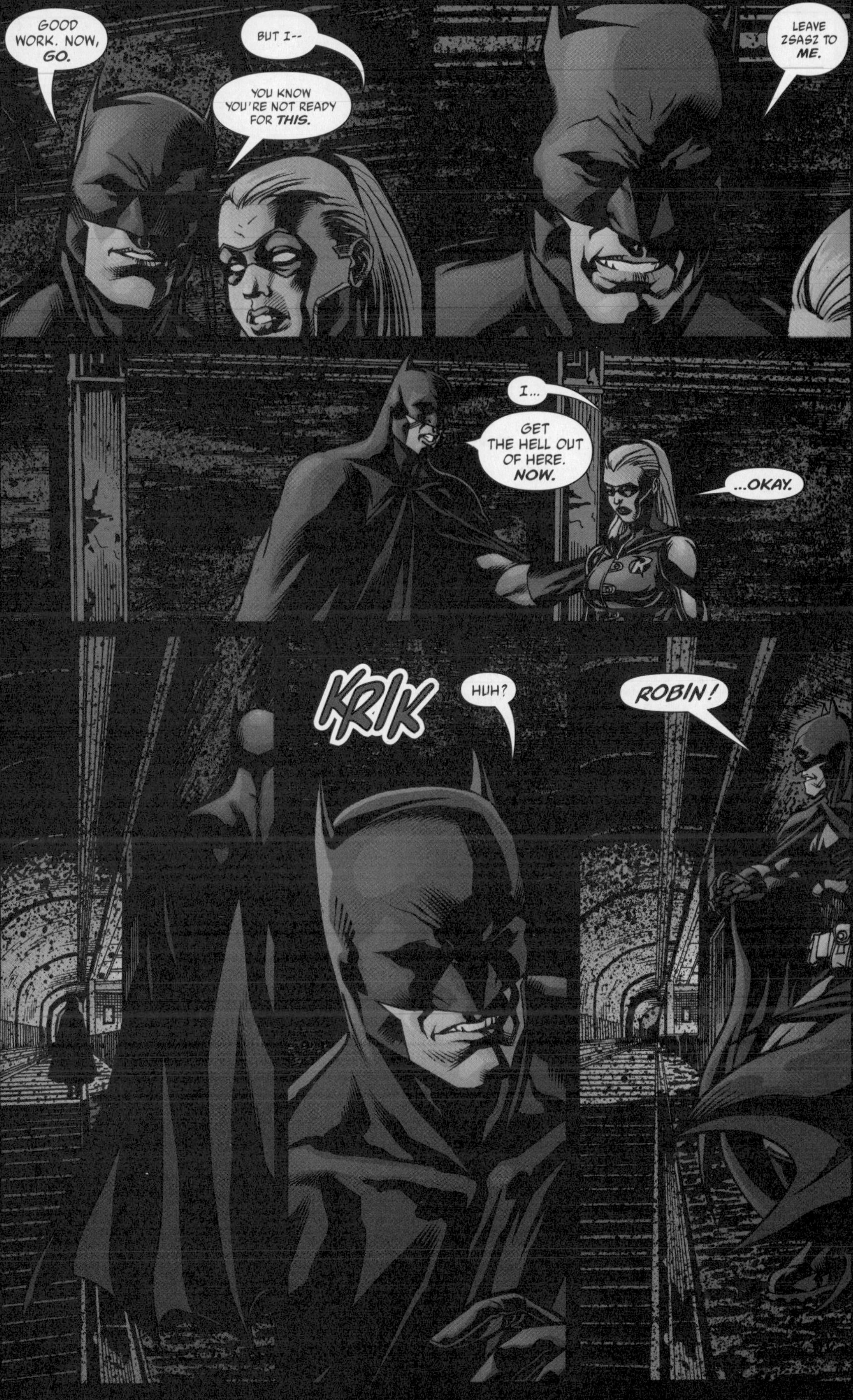
GOOD WORK. NOW, GO.
BUT I--
YOU KNOW YOU'RE NOT READY FOR THIS.
LEAVE ZSASZ TO ME.
I...
GET THE HELL OUT OF HERE. NOW.
...OKAY.
KRIK
HUH?
ROBIN!

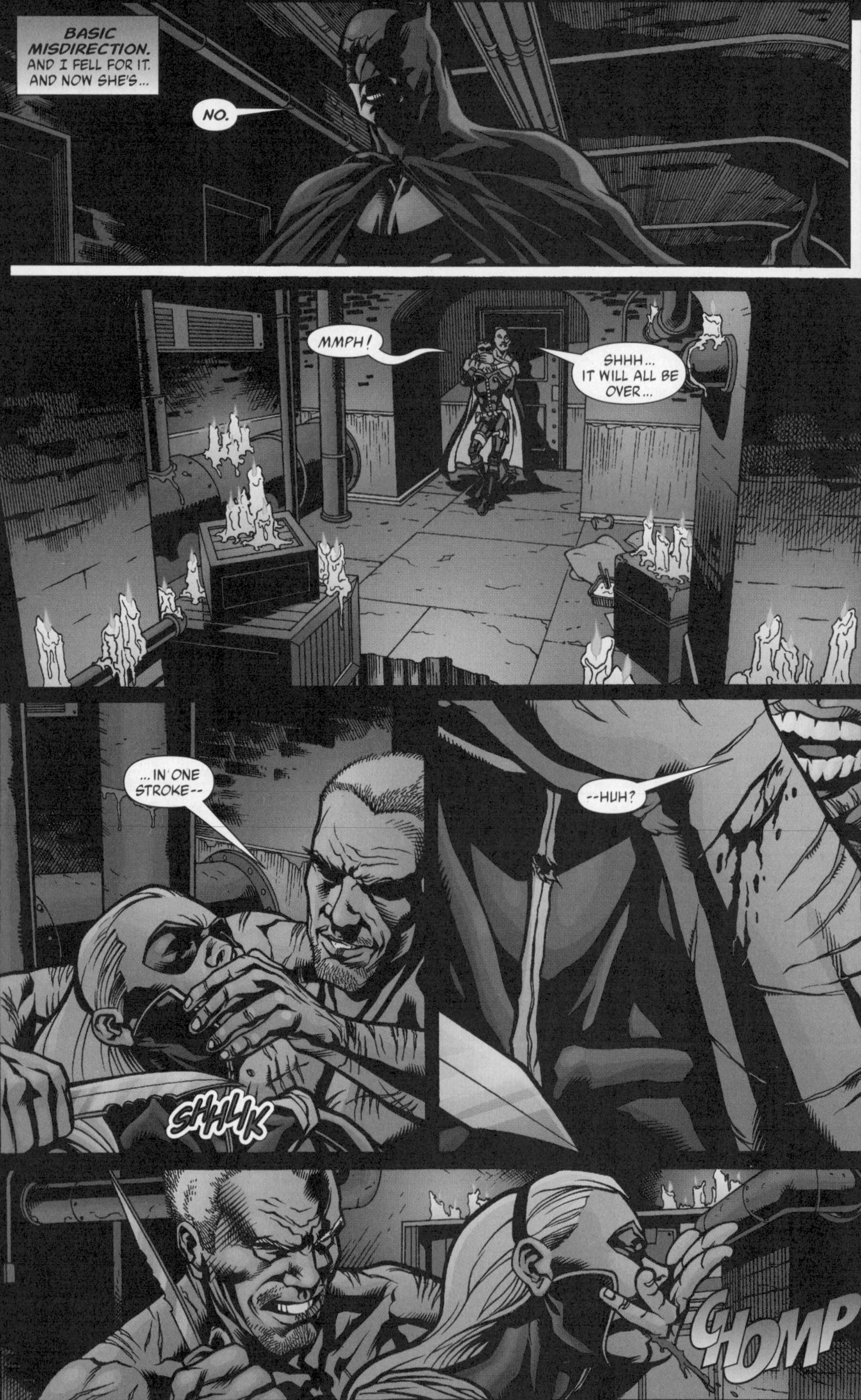
BASIC MISDIRECTION. AND I FELL FOR IT. AND NOW SHE'S...
NO.
MMPH!
SHHH... IT WILL ALL BE OVER...
...IN ONE STROKE--
SHHLIK
--HUH?
CHOMP

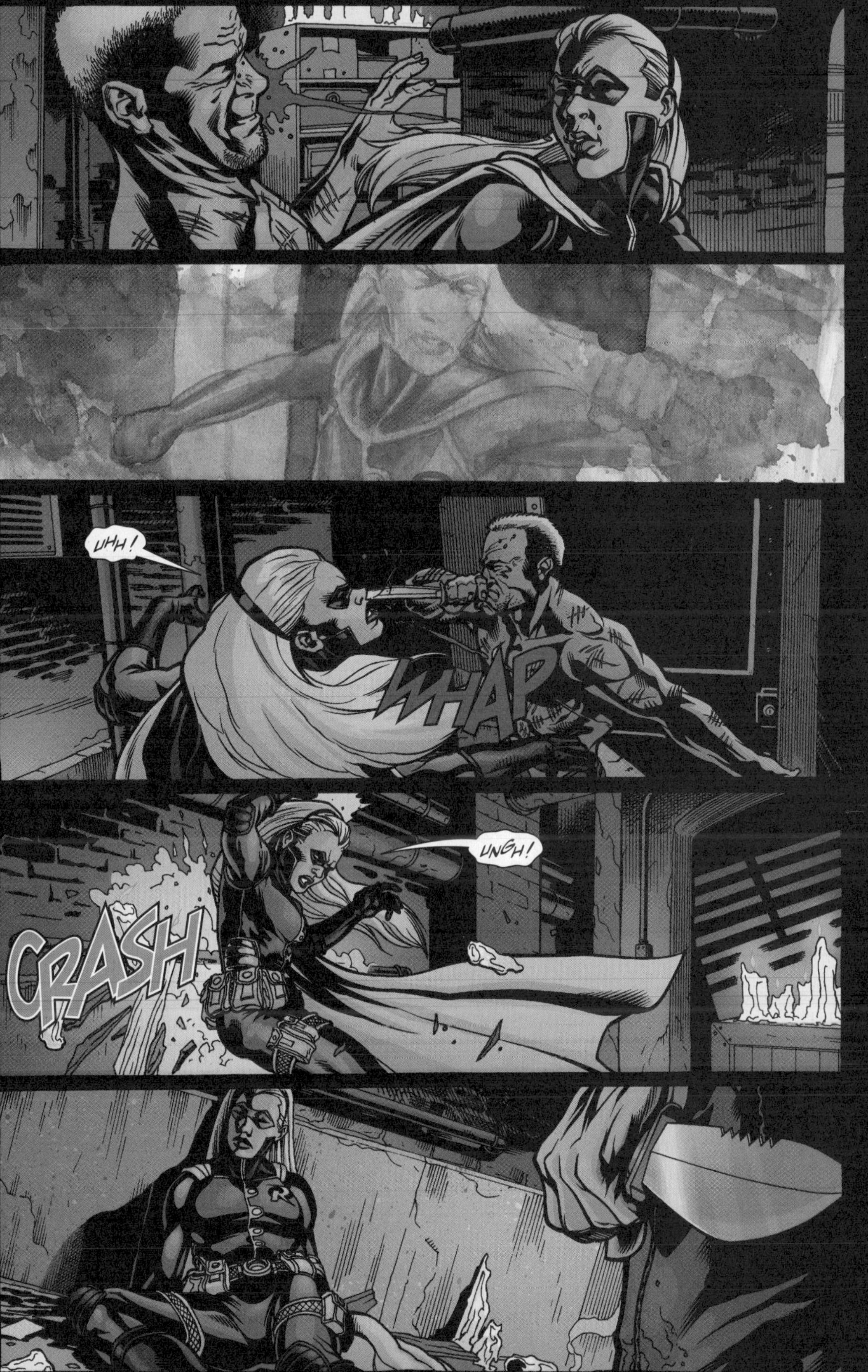
UHH!
WHAP
UNGH!
CRASH

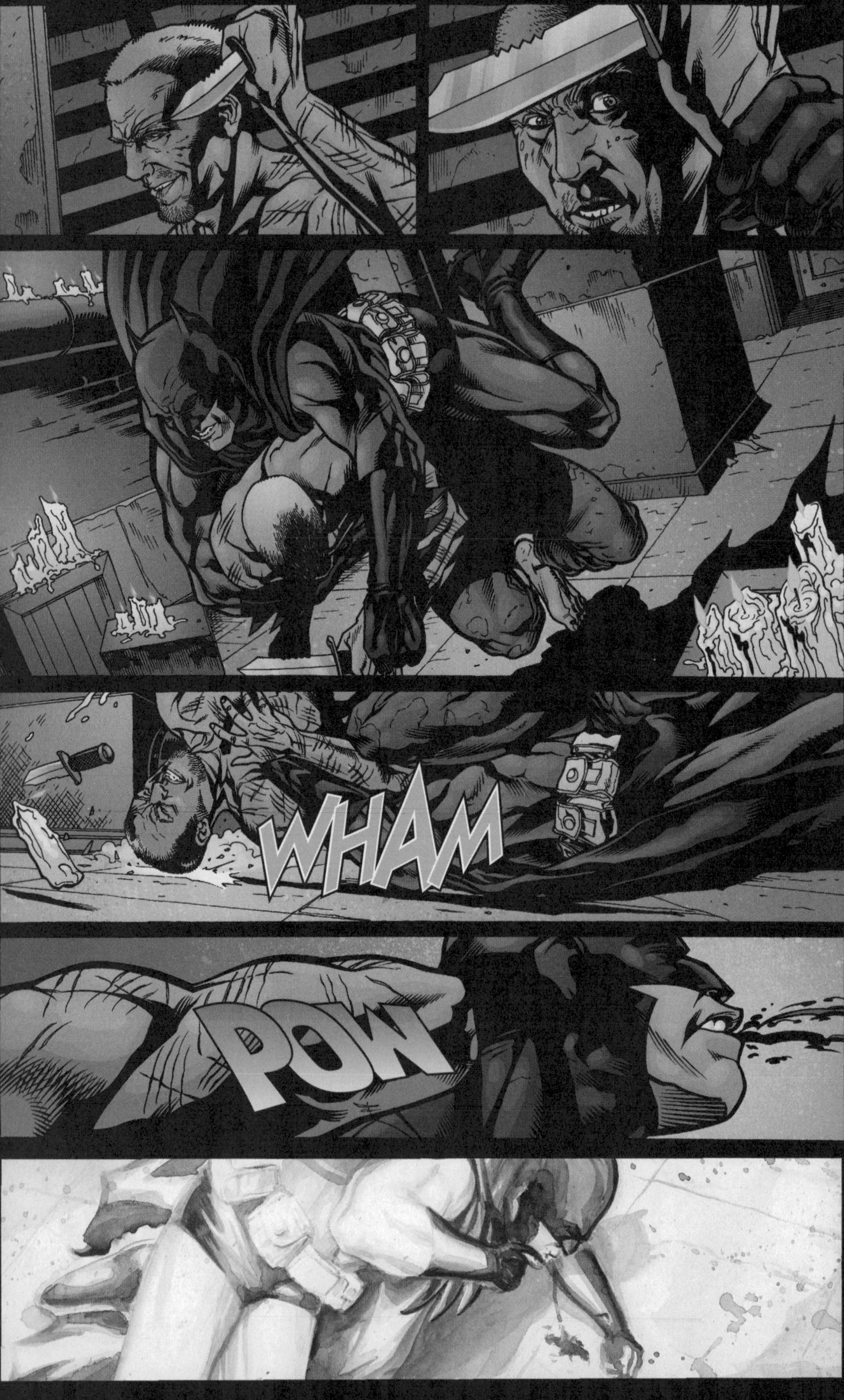
WHAM
POW

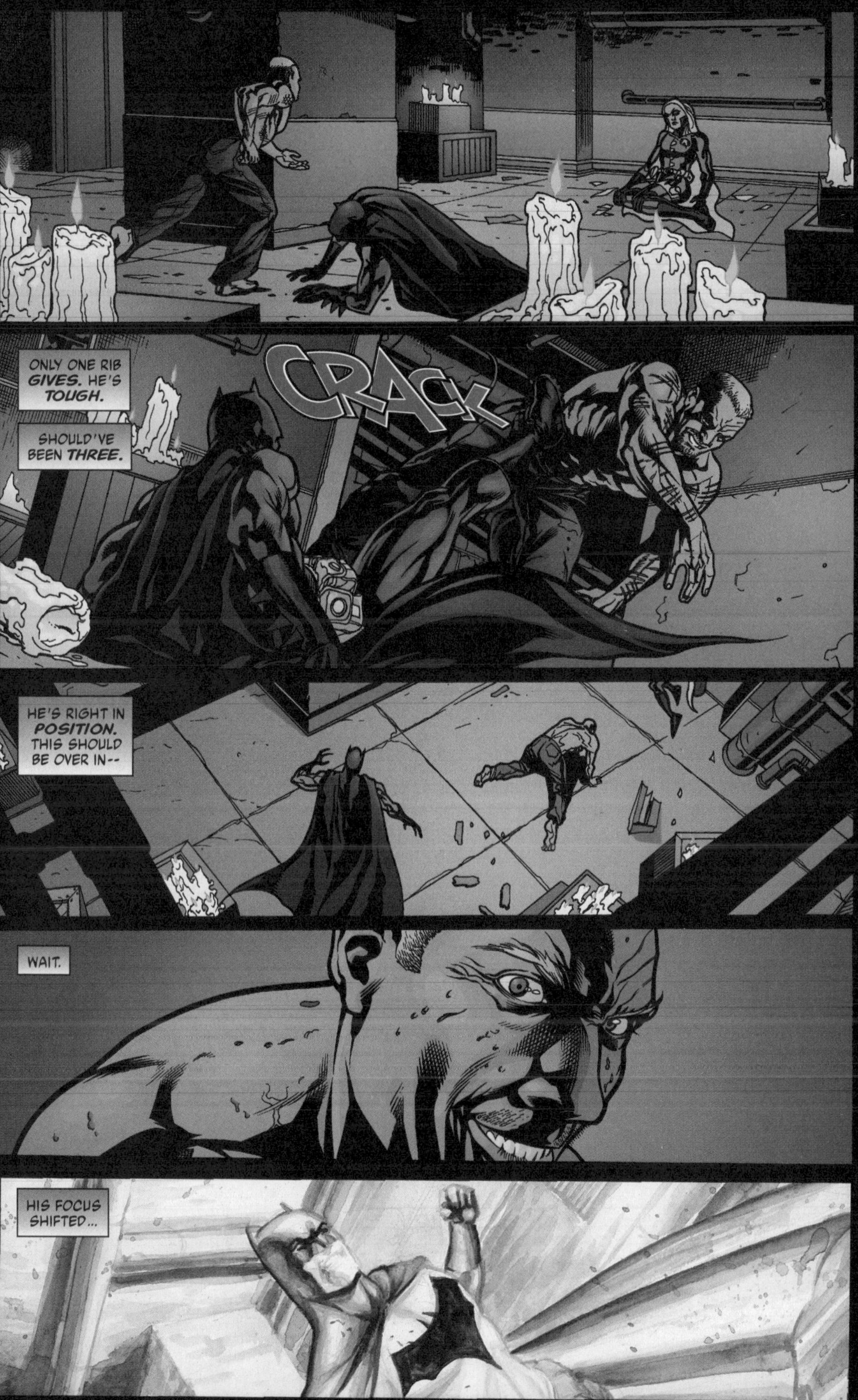
ONLY ONE RIB GIVES. HE'S TOUGH.
CRACK
SHOULD'VE BEEN THREE.
HE'S RIGHT IN POSITION. THIS SHOULD BE OVER IN--
WAIT.
HIS FOCUS SHIFTED...

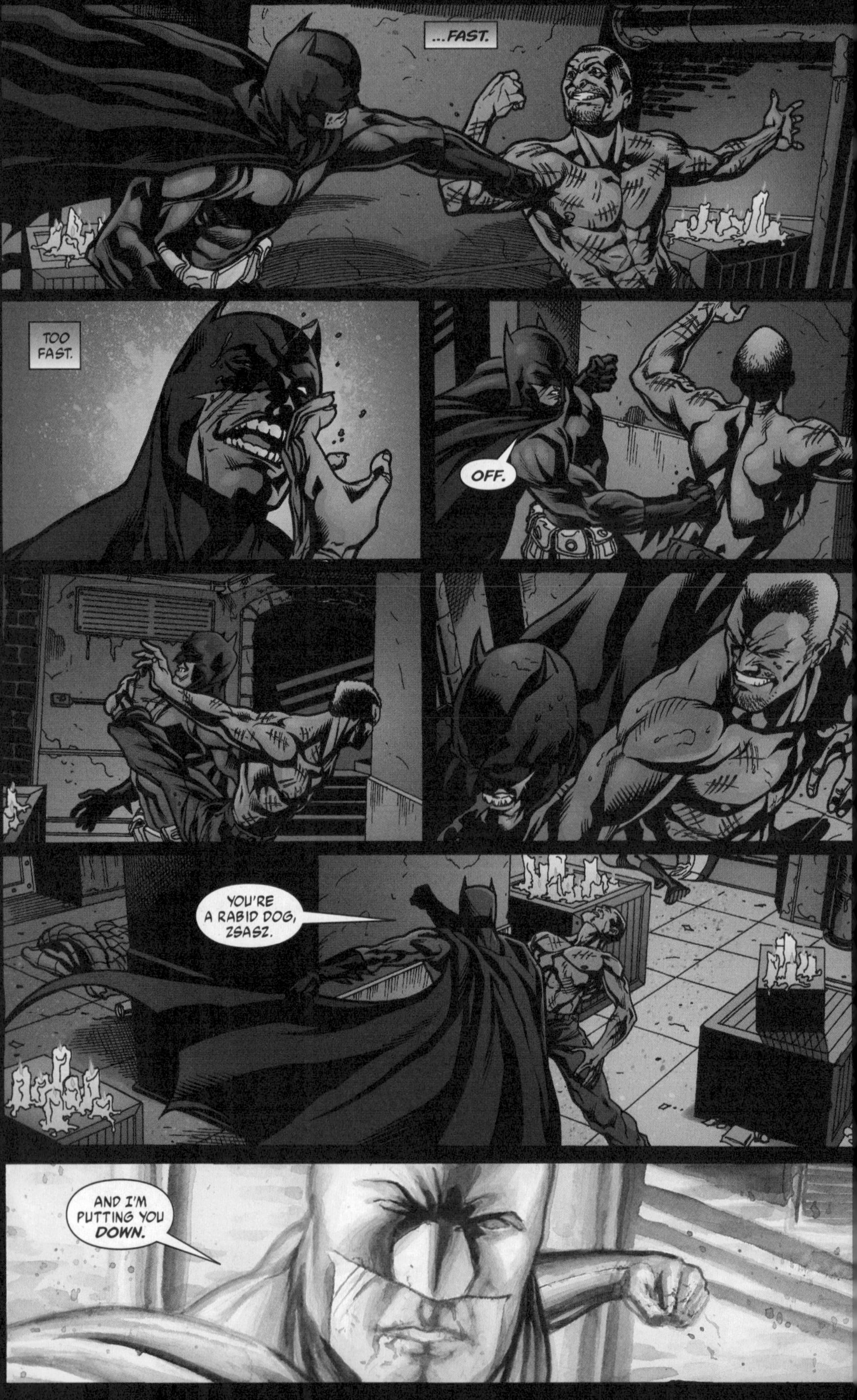
...FAST.
TOO FAST.
OFF.
YOU'RE A RABID DOG, ZSASZ.
AND I'M PUTTING YOU DOWN.

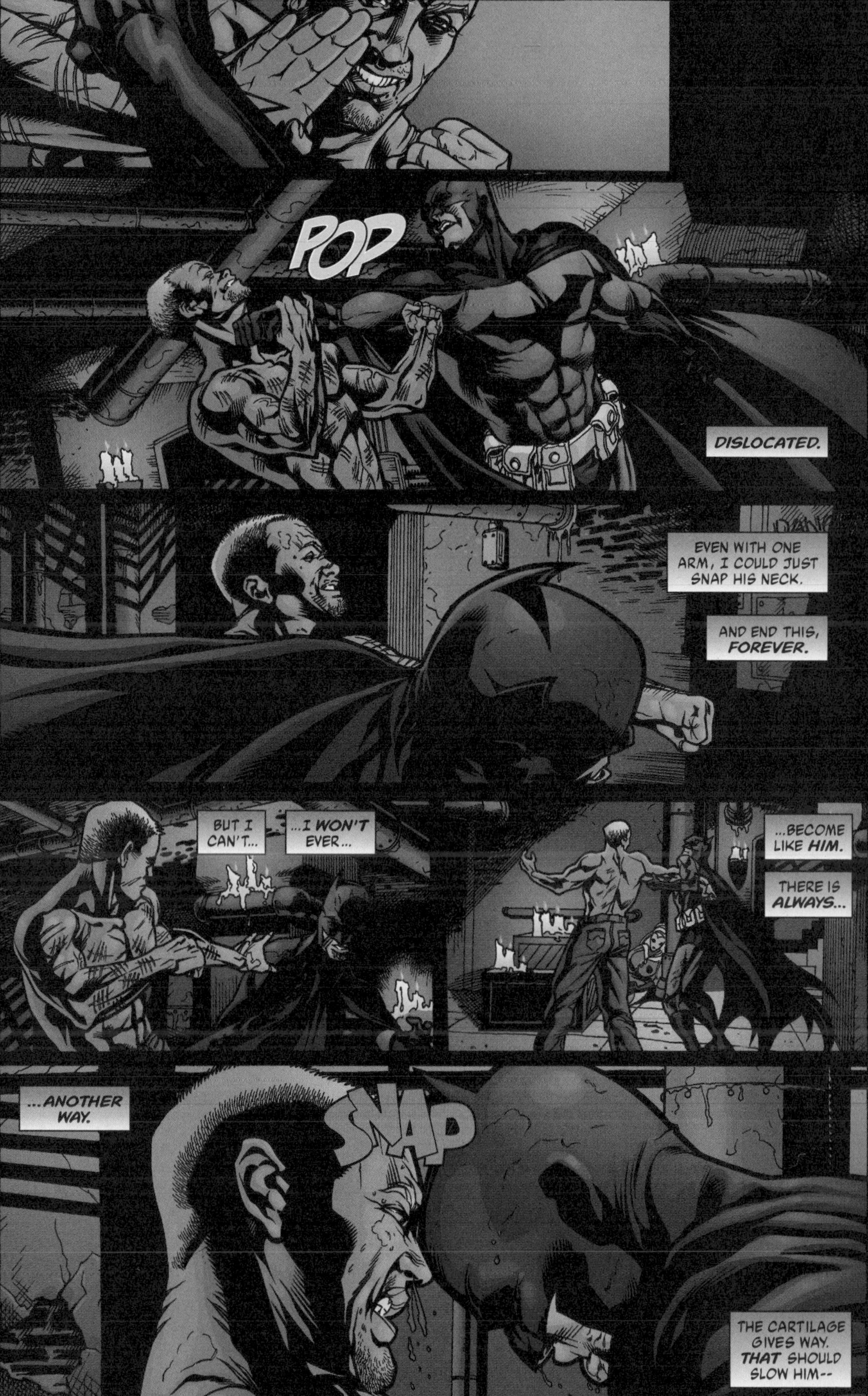
POP
DISLOCATED.
EVEN WITH ONE ARM, I COULD JUST SNAP HIS NECK.
AND END THIS, FOREVER.
BUT I CAN'T...
...I WON'T EVER...
...BECOME LIKE HIM.
THERE IS ALWAYS...
...ANOTHER WAY.
SNAP
THE CARTILAGE GIVES WAY. THAT SHOULD SLOW HIM--

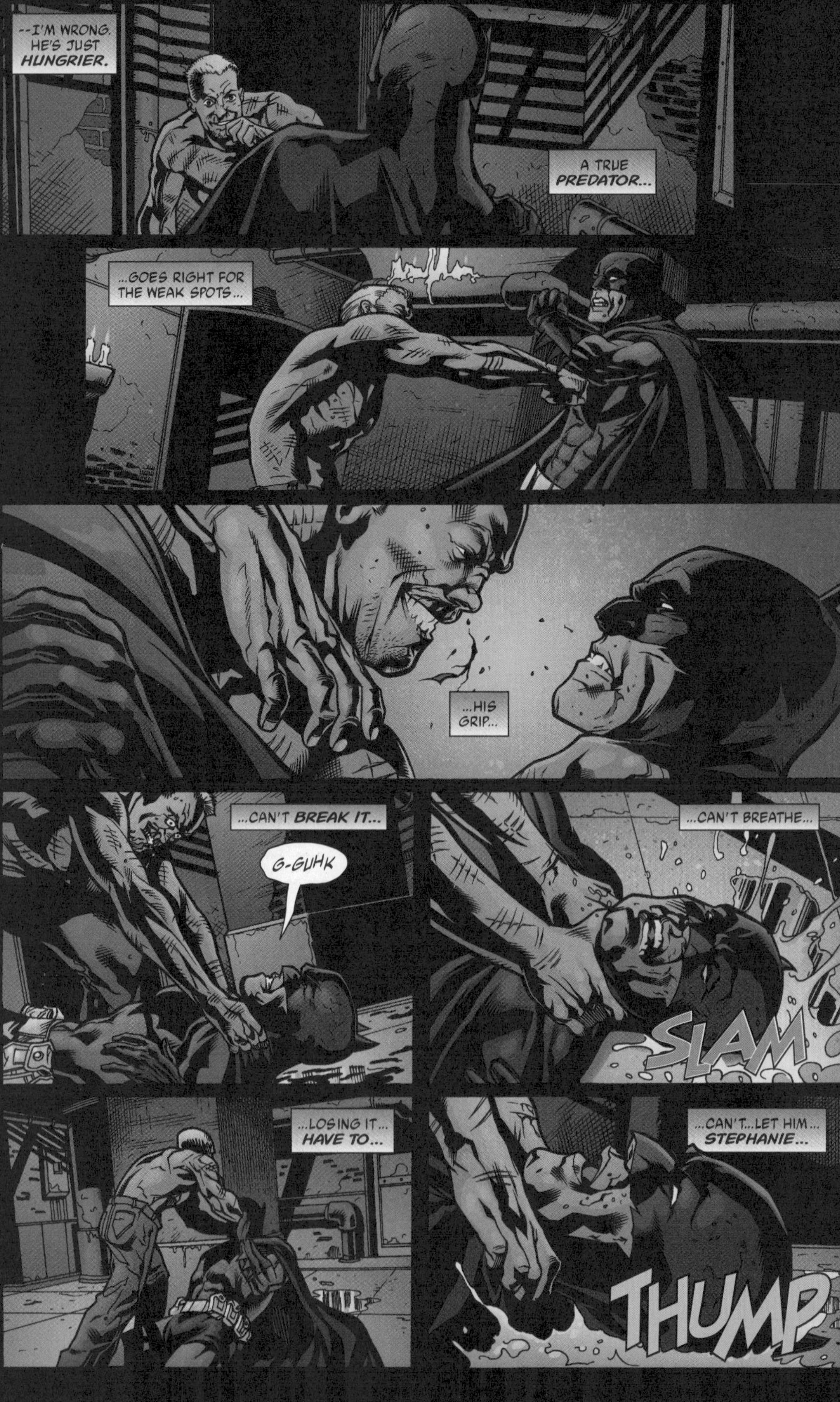
--I'M WRONG. HE'S JUST HUNGRIER.
A TRUE PREDATOR...
...GOES RIGHT FOR THE WEAK SPOTS...
...HIS GRIP...
...CAN'T BREAK IT...
G-GUHK
...CAN'T BREATHE...
SLAM
...LOSING IT... HAVE TO...
...CAN'T...LET HIM... STEPHANIE...
THUMP

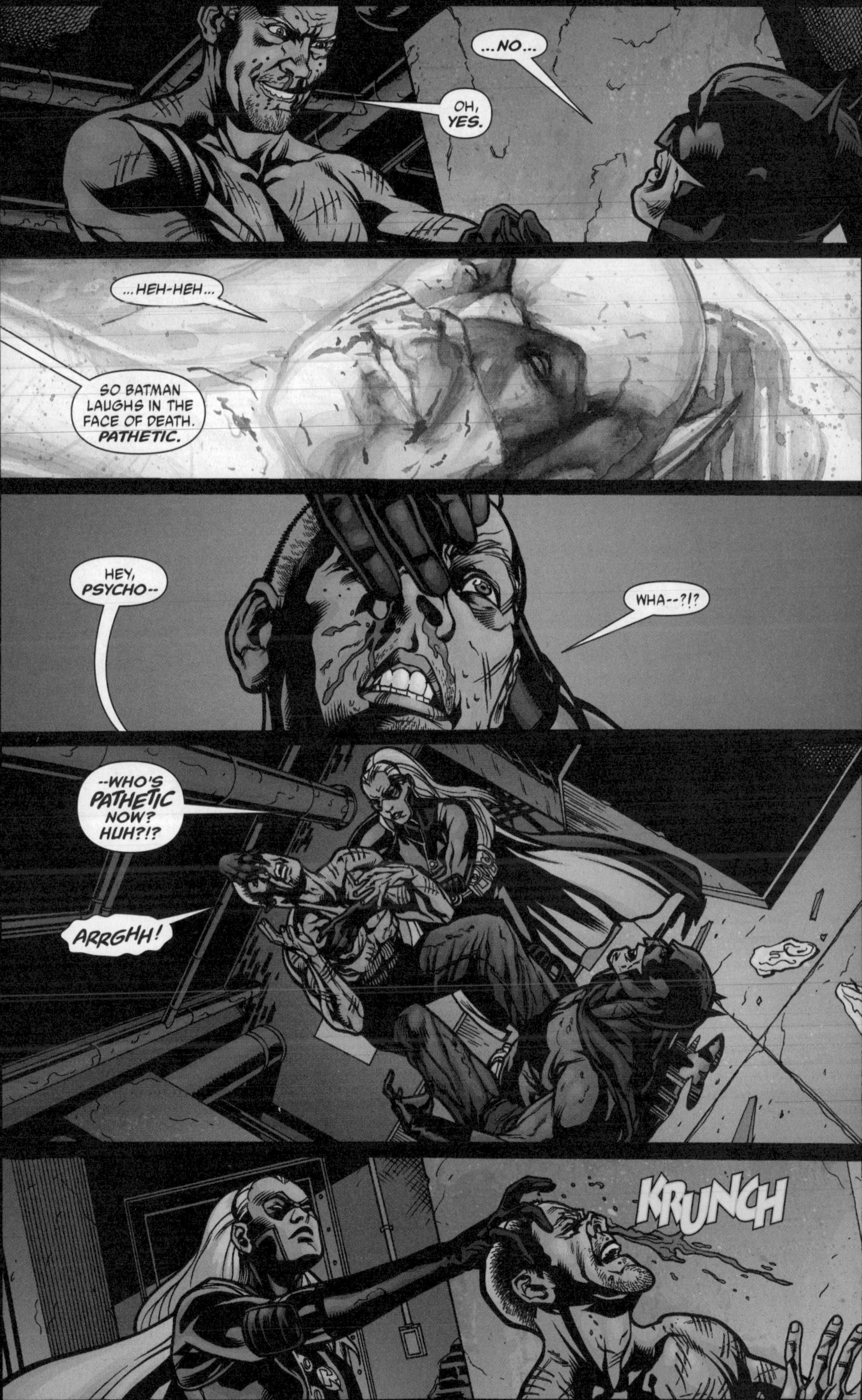
...NO...
OH, YES.
...HEH-HEH...
SO BATMAN LAUGHS IN THE FACE OF DEATH. PATHETIC.
HEY, PSYCHO--
WHA--?!?
--WHO'S PATHETIC NOW? HUH?!?
ARRGHH!
KRUNCH

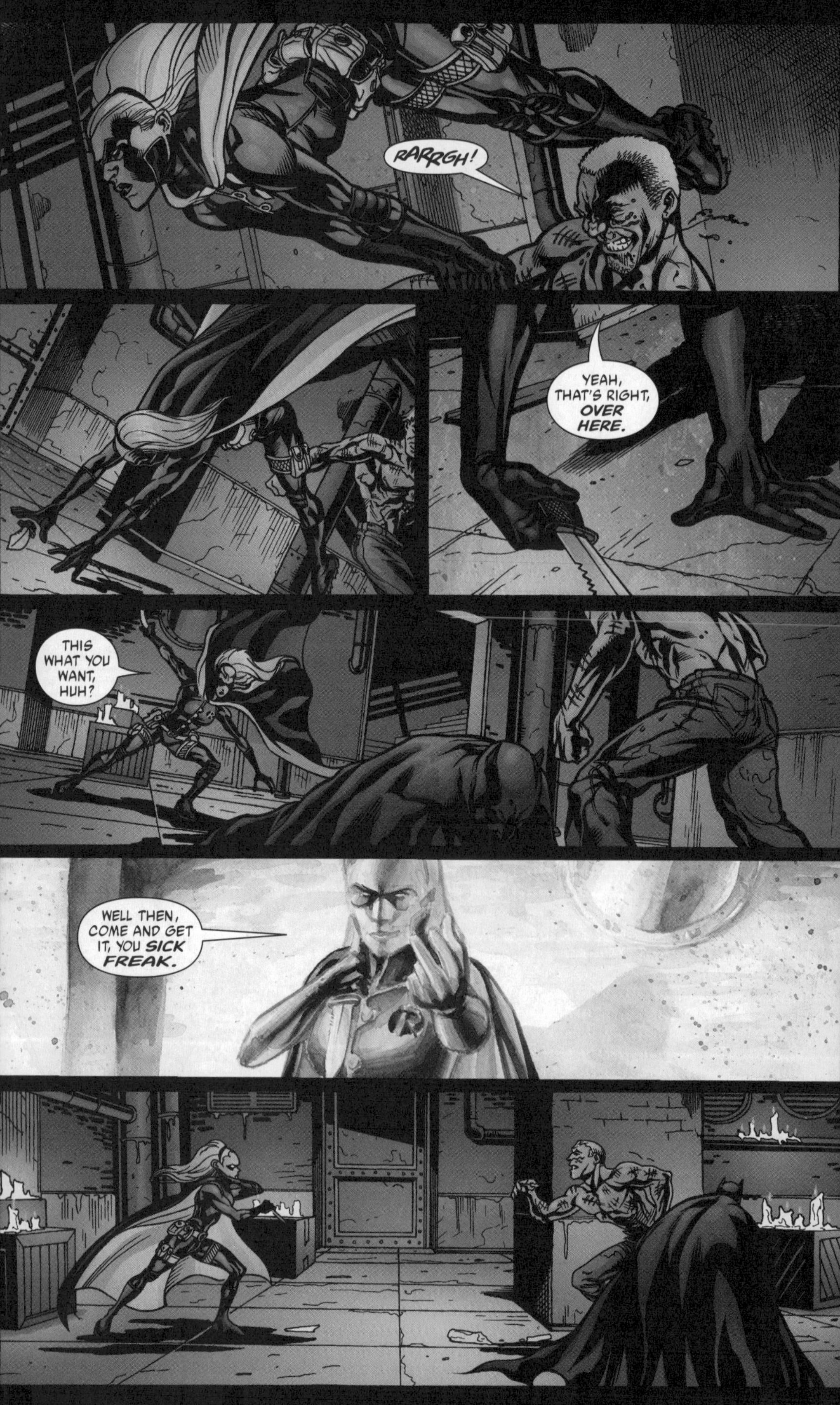
RARRGH!
YEAH, THAT'S RIGHT, OVER HERE.
THIS WHAT YOU WANT, HUH?
WELL THEN, COME AND GET IT, YOU SICK FREAK.

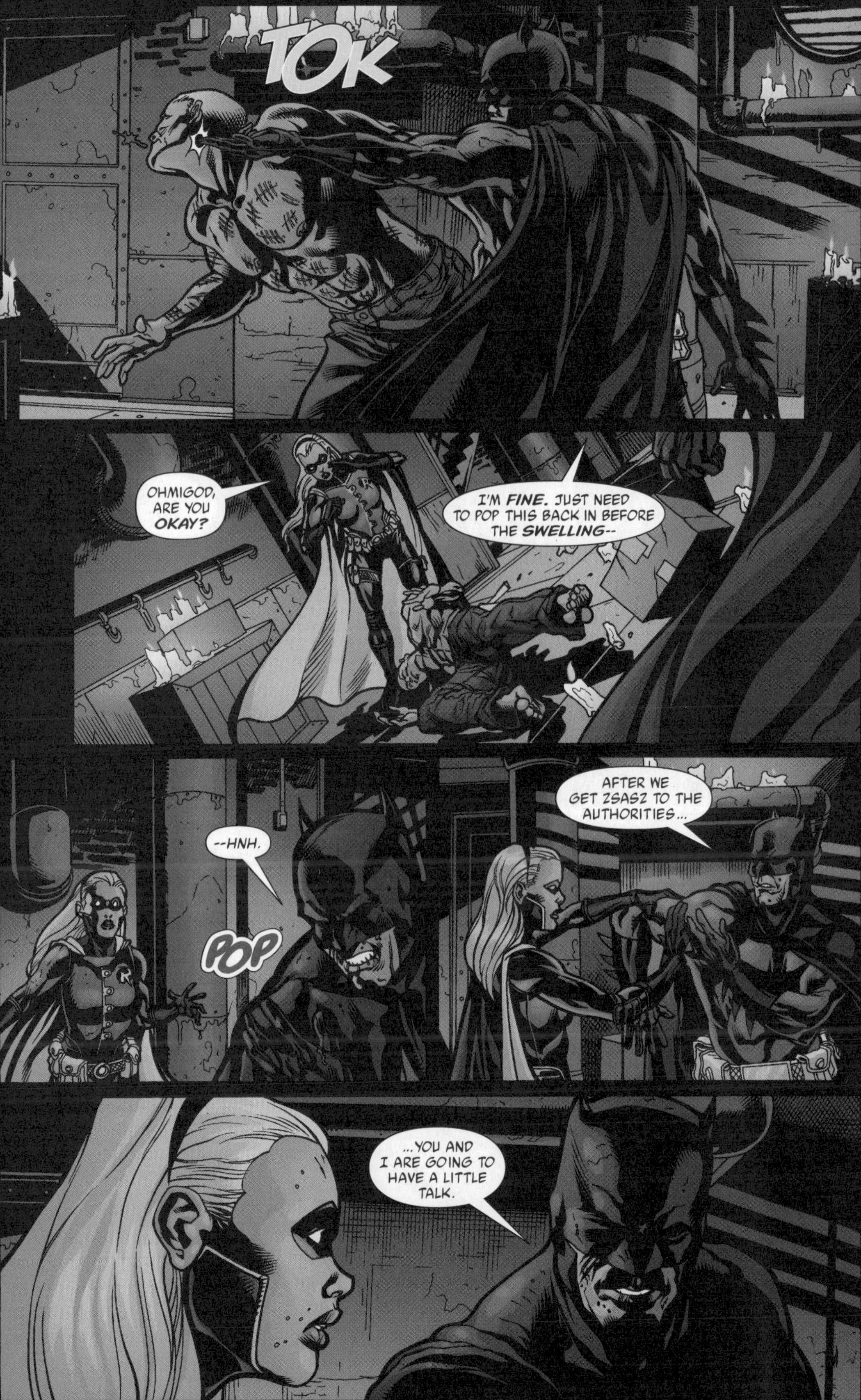
TOK
OHMIGOD, ARE YOU OKAY?
I'M FINE. JUST NEED TO POP THIS BACK IN BEFORE THE SWELLING--
--HNH.
POP
AFTER WE GET ZSASZ TO THE AUTHORITIES...
...YOU AND I ARE GOING TO HAVE A LITTLE TALK.

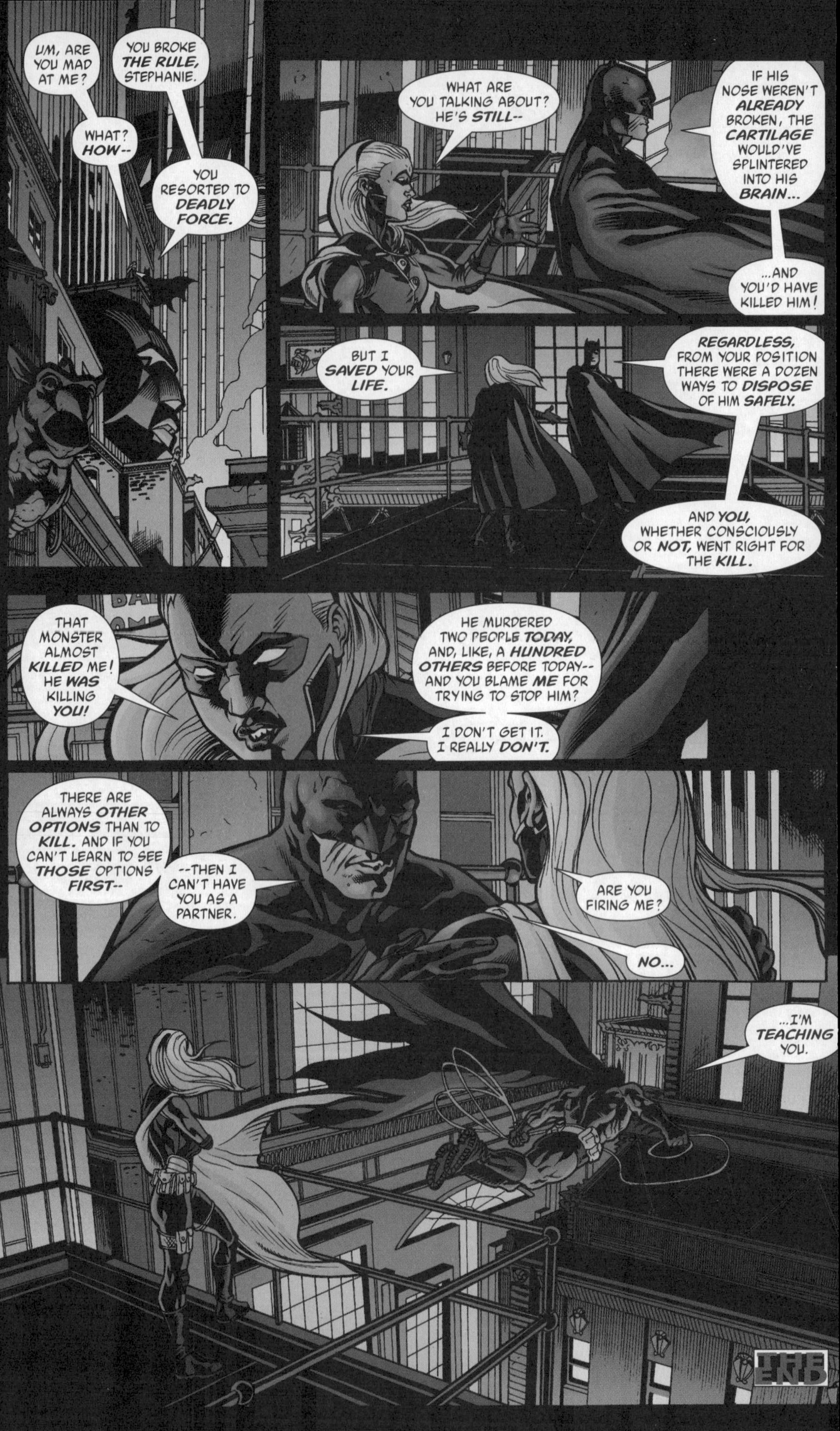

UM, ARE YOU MAD AT ME?
YOU BROKE THE RULE, STEPHANIE.
WHAT? HOW--
YOU RESORTED TO DEADLY FORCE.
WHAT ARE YOU TALKING ABOUT? HE'S STILL--
IF HIS NOSE WEREN'T ALREADY BROKEN, THE CARTILAGE WOULD'VE SPLINTERED INTO HIS BRAIN...
...AND YOU'D HAVE KILLED HIM!
BUT I SAVED YOUR LIFE.
REGARDLESS, FROM YOUR POSITION THERE WERE A DOZEN WAYS TO DISPOSE OF HIM SAFELY.
AND YOU, WHETHER CONSCIOUSLY OR NOT, WENT RIGHT FOR THE KILL.
THAT MONSTER ALMOST KILLED ME! HE WAS KILLING YOU!
HE MURDERED TWO PEOPLE TODAY, AND, LIKE, A HUNDRED OTHERS BEFORE TODAY-- AND YOU BLAME ME FOR TRYING TO STOP HIM?
I DON'T GET IT. I REALLY DON'T.
THERE ARE ALWAYS OTHER OPTIONS THAN TO KILL. AND IF YOU CAN'T LEARN TO SEE THOSE OPTIONS FIRST--
--THEN I CAN'T HAVE YOU AS A PARTNER.
ARE YOU FIRING ME?
NO...
...I'M TEACHING YOU.
THE END

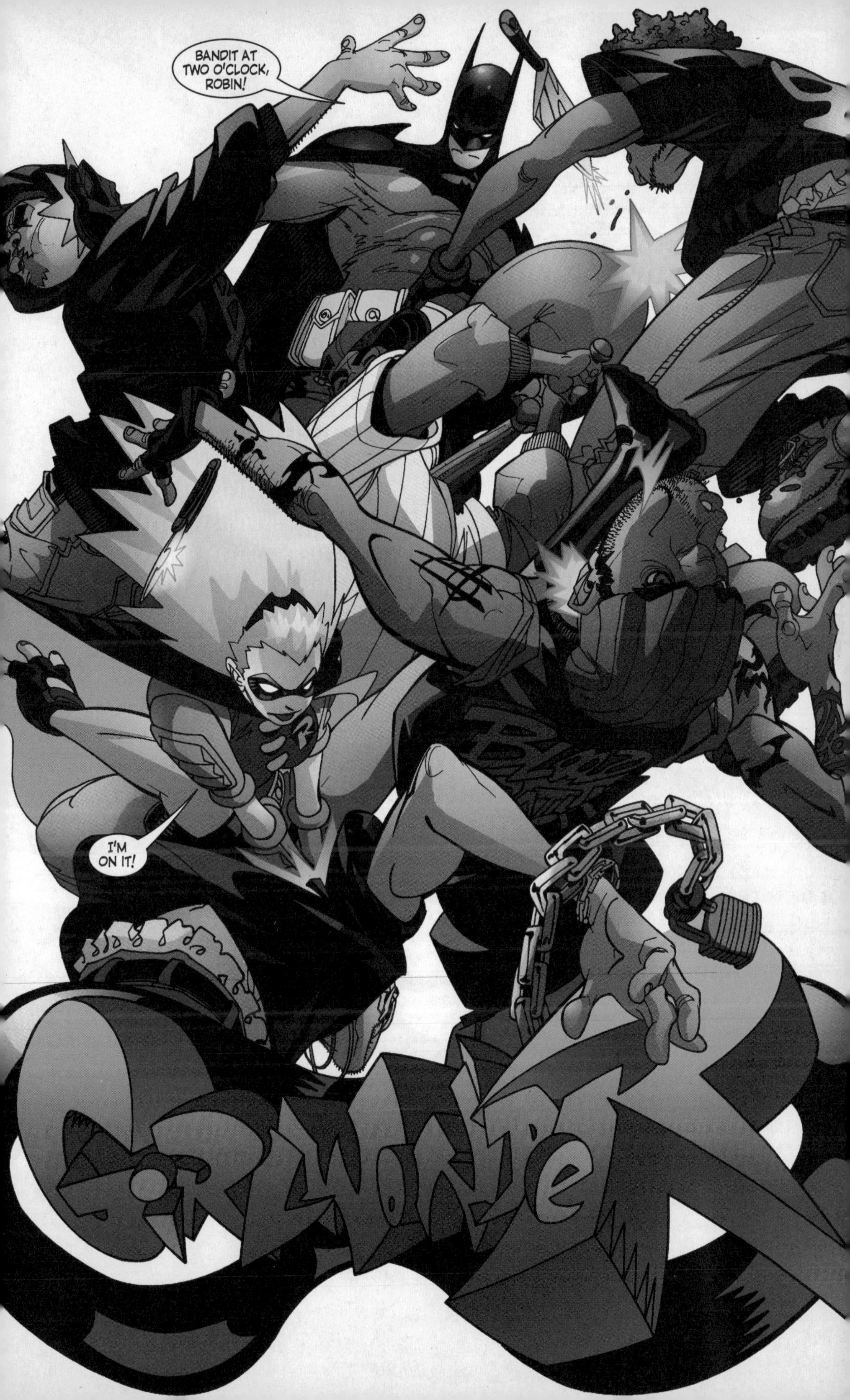
BANDIT AT TWO O'CLOCK, ROBIN!
I'M ON IT!

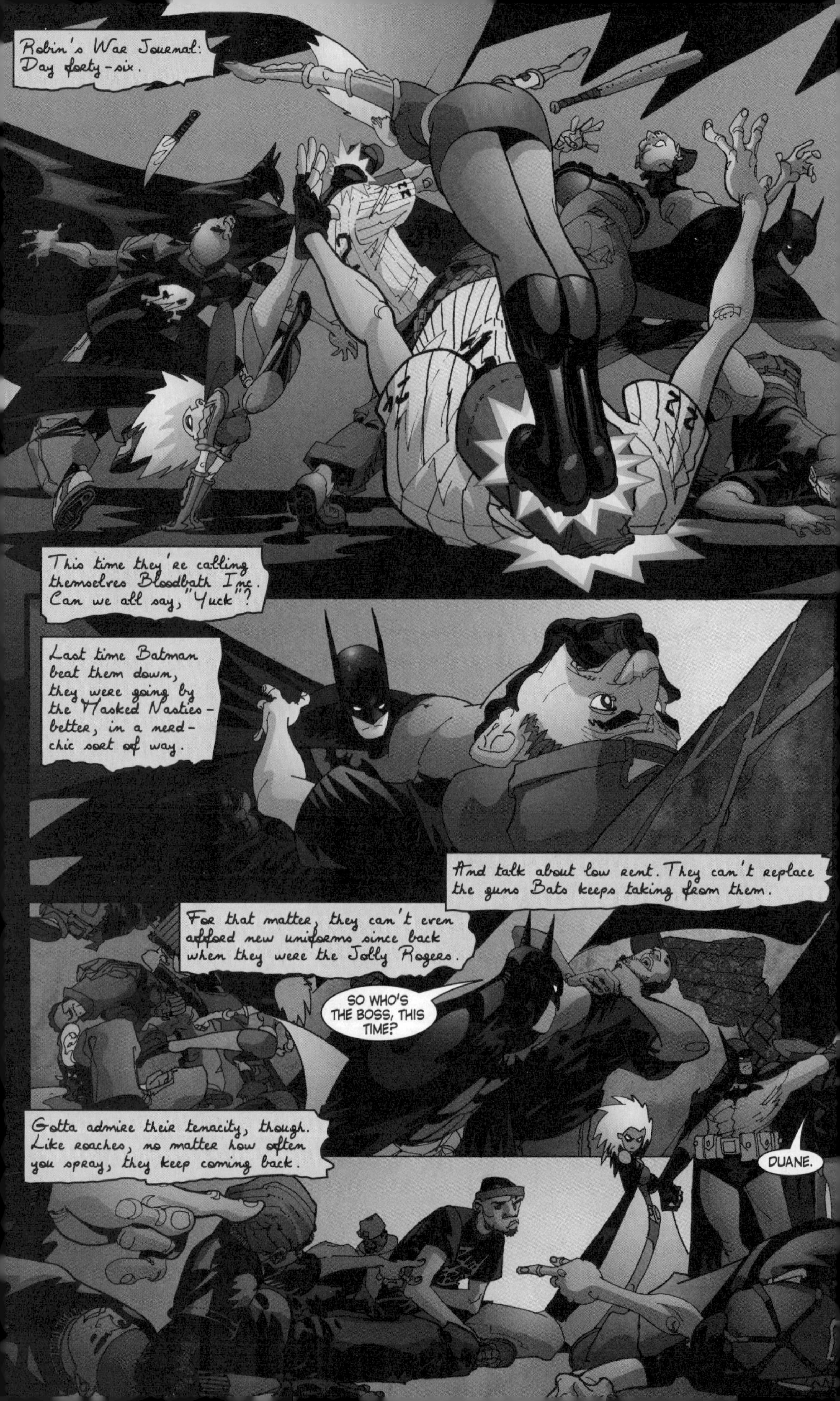
Robin's War Journal: Day forty-six.
This time they're calling themselves Bloodbath Inc. Can we all say, "Yuck"?
Last time Batman beat them down, they were going by the Masked Nasties - better, in a nerd-chic sort of way.
And talk about low rent. They can't replace the guns Bats keeps taking from them.
For that matter, they can't even afford new uniforms since back when they were the Jolly Rogers.
SO WHO'S THE BOSS, THIS TIME?
Gotta admire their tenacity, though. Like roaches, no matter how often you spray, they keep coming back.
DUANE.

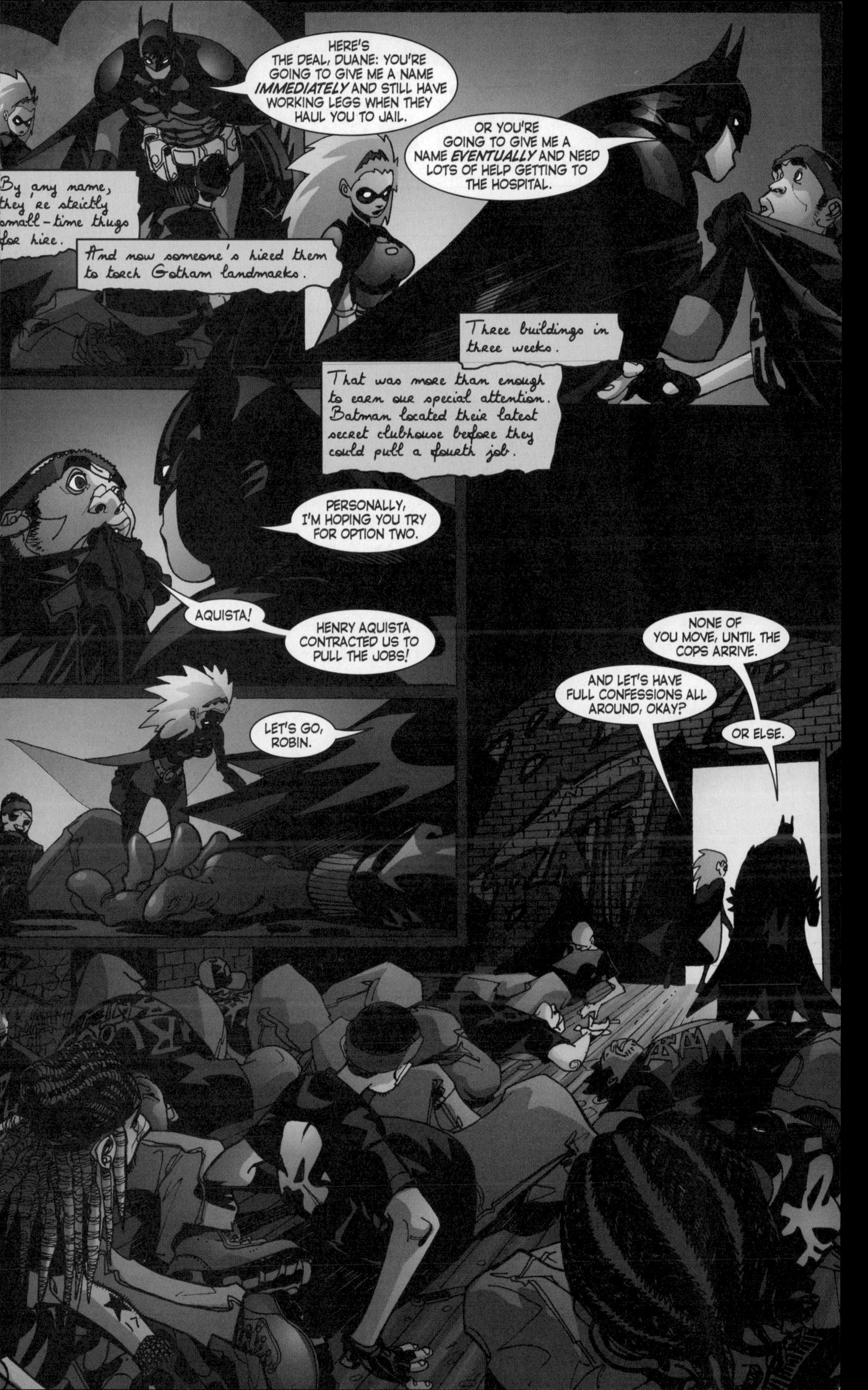

HERE'S THE DEAL, DUANE: YOU'RE GOING TO GIVE ME A NAME IMMEDIATELY AND STILL HAVE WORKING LEGS WHEN THEY HAUL YOU TO JAIL.
OR YOU'RE GOING TO GIVE ME A NAME EVENTUALLY AND NEED LOTS OF HELP GETTING TO THE HOSPITAL.
By any name, they're strictly small-time thugs for hire.
And now someone's hired them to torch Gotham landmarks.
Three buildings in three weeks.
That was more than enough to earn our special attention. Batman located their latest secret clubhouse before they could pull a fourth job.
PERSONALLY, I'M HOPING YOU TRY FOR OPTION TWO.
AQUISTA!
HENRY AQUISTA CONTRACTED US TO PULL THE JOBS!
LET'S GO, ROBIN.
NONE OF YOU MOVE, UNTIL THE COPS ARRIVE.
AND LET'S HAVE FULL CONFESSIONS ALL AROUND, OKAY?
OR ELSE.

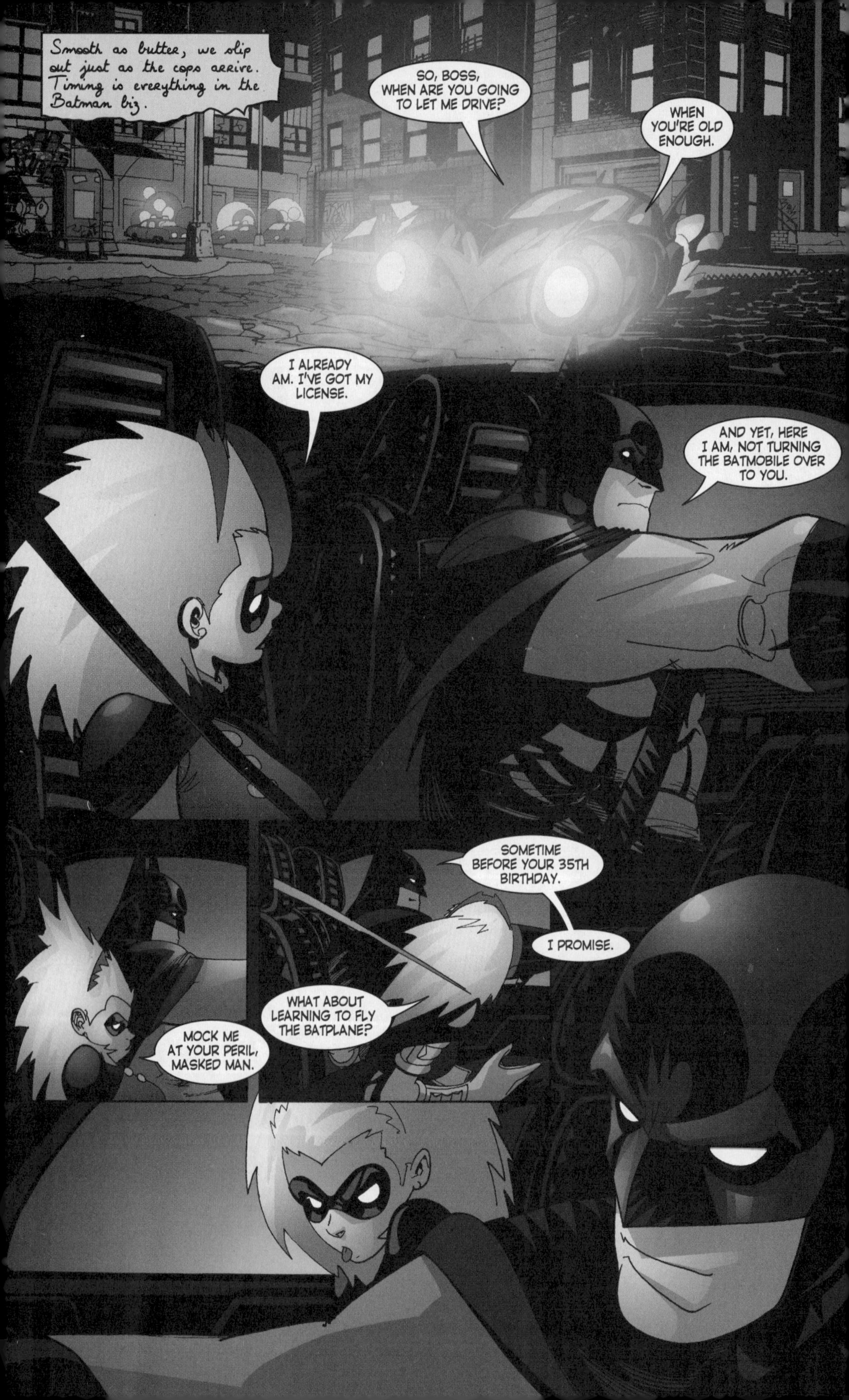
Smooth as butter, we slip out just as the cops arrive. Timing is everything in the Batman biz.
SO, BOSS, WHEN ARE YOU GOING TO LET ME DRIVE?
WHEN YOU'RE OLD ENOUGH.
I ALREADY AM. I'VE GOT MY LICENSE.
AND YET, HERE I AM, NOT TURNING THE BATMOBILE OVER TO YOU.
MOCK ME AT YOUR PERIL, MASKED MAN.
SOMETIME BEFORE YOUR 35TH BIRTHDAY.
I PROMISE.
WHAT ABOUT LEARNING TO FLY THE BATPLANE?

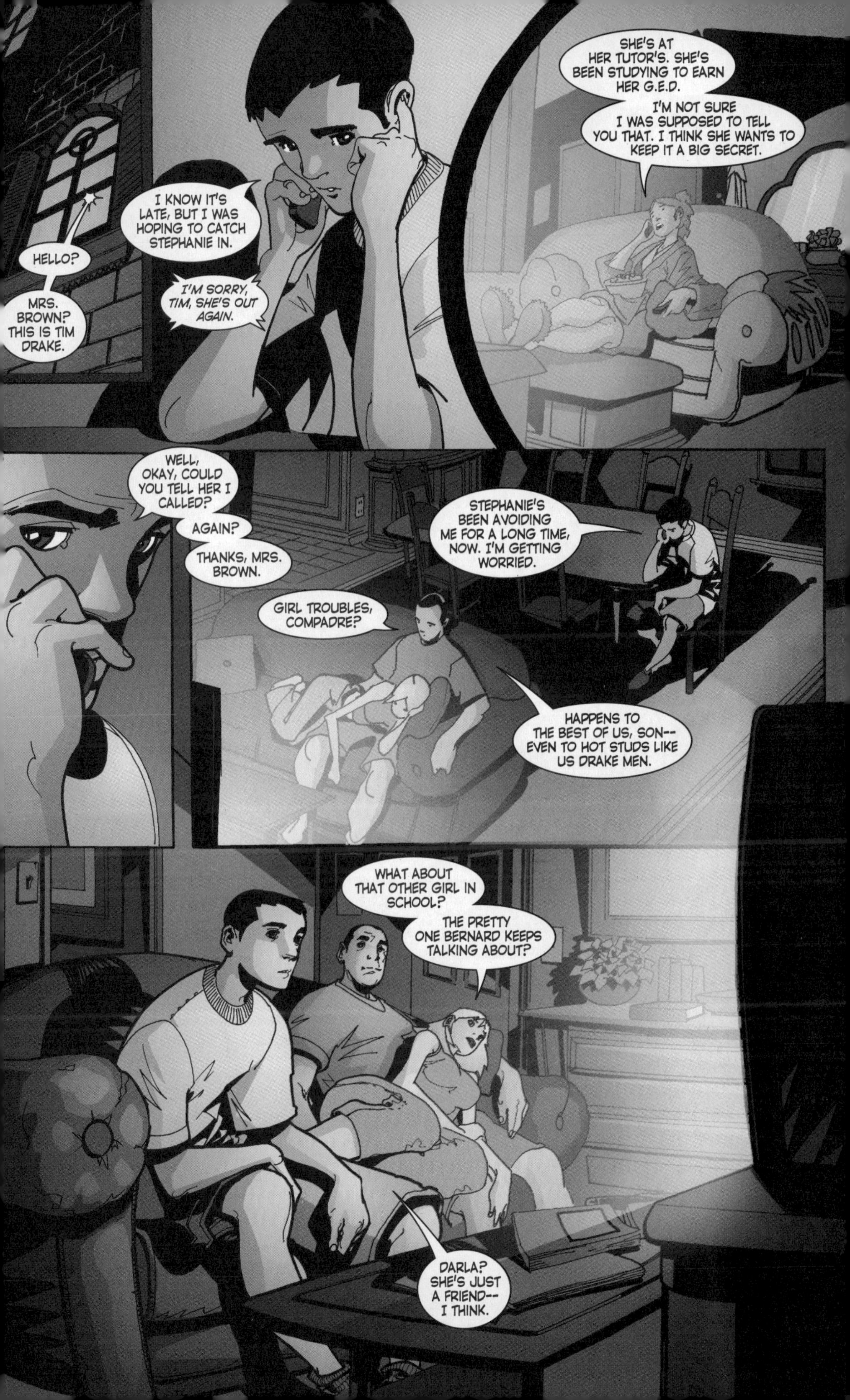
HELLO?
MRS. BROWN? THIS IS TIM DRAKE.
I KNOW IT'S LATE, BUT I WAS HOPING TO CATCH STEPHANIE IN.
I'M SORRY, TIM, SHE'S OUT AGAIN.
SHE'S AT HER TUTOR'S. SHE'S BEEN STUDYING TO EARN HER G.E.D.
I'M NOT SURE I WAS SUPPOSED TO TELL YOU THAT. I THINK SHE WANTS TO KEEP IT A BIG SECRET.
WELL, OKAY, COULD YOU TELL HER I CALLED?
AGAIN?
THANKS, MRS. BROWN.
STEPHANIE'S BEEN AVOIDING ME FOR A LONG TIME, NOW. I'M GETTING WORRIED.
GIRL TROUBLES, COMPADRE?
HAPPENS TO THE BEST OF US, SON-- EVEN TO HOT STUDS LIKE US DRAKE MEN.
WHAT ABOUT THAT OTHER GIRL IN SCHOOL?
THE PRETTY ONE BERNARD KEEPS TALKING ABOUT?
DARLA? SHE'S JUST A FRIEND-- I THINK.

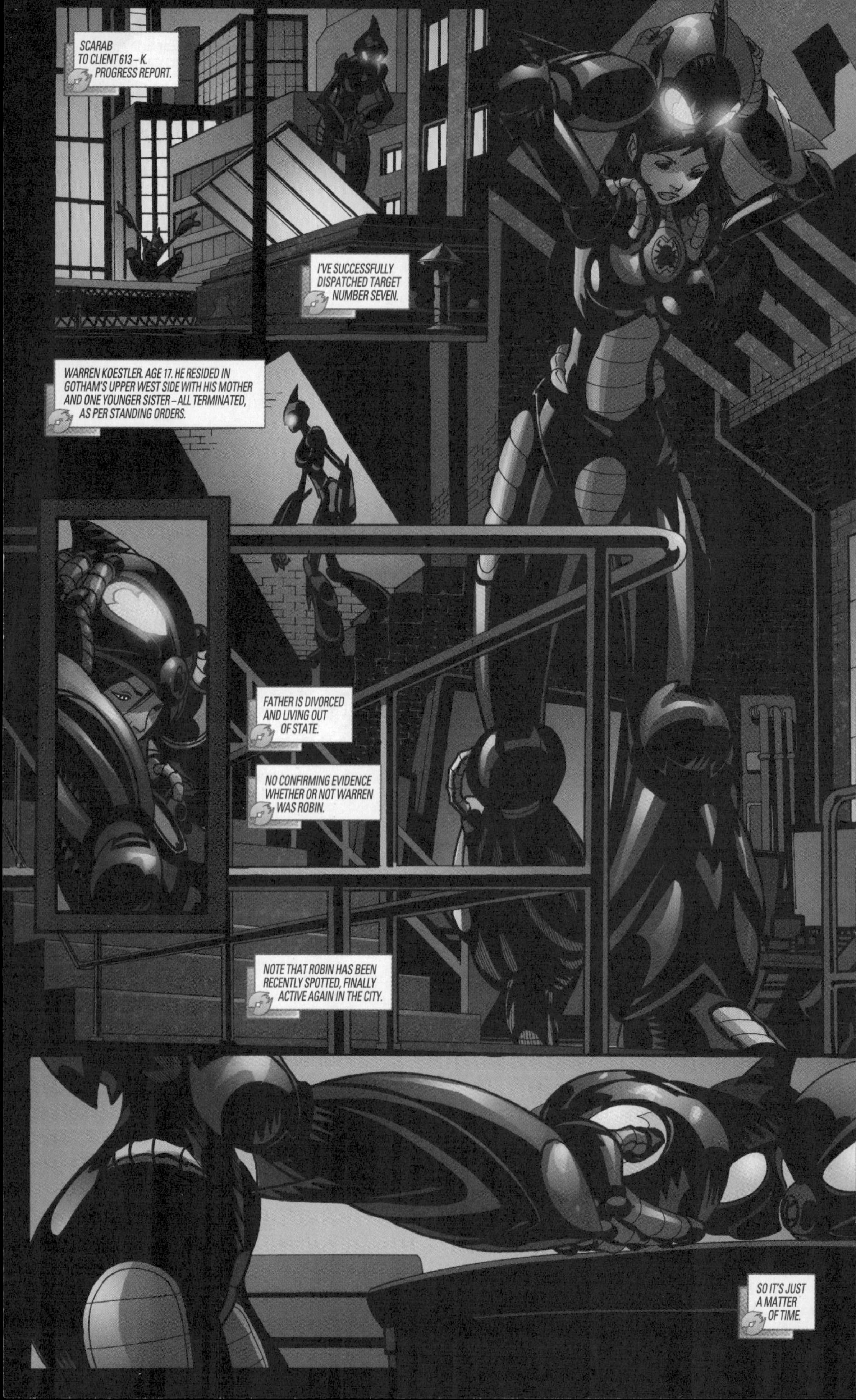
SCARAB TO CLIENT 613 – K. PROGRESS REPORT.
I'VE SUCCESSFULLY DISPATCHED TARGET NUMBER SEVEN.
WARREN KOESTLER. AGE 17. HE RESIDED IN GOTHAM'S UPPER WEST SIDE WITH HIS MOTHER AND ONE YOUNGER SISTER – ALL TERMINATED, AS PER STANDING ORDERS.
FATHER IS DIVORCED AND LIVING OUT OF STATE.
NO CONFIRMING EVIDENCE WHETHER OR NOT WARREN WAS ROBIN.
NOTE THAT ROBIN HAS BEEN RECENTLY SPOTTED, FINALLY ACTIVE AGAIN IN THE CITY.
SO IT'S JUST A MATTER OF TIME.

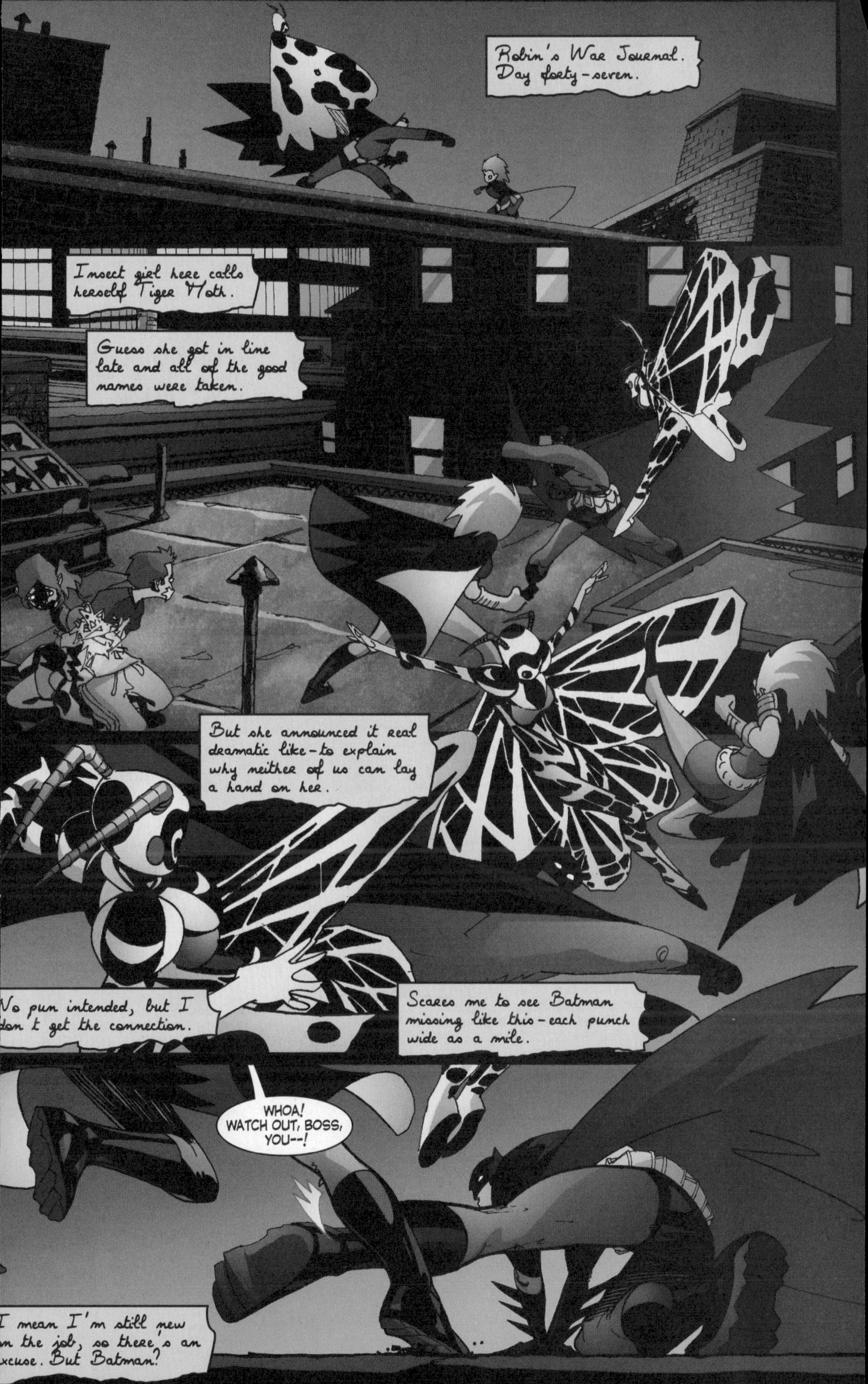
Robin's War Journal. Day forty-seven.
Insect girl here calls herself Tiger Moth.
Guess she got in line late and all of the good names were taken.
But she announced it real dramatic like—to explain why neither of us can lay a hand on her.
No pun intended, but I don't get the connection.
Scares me to see Batman missing like this—each punch wide as a mile.
WHOA! WATCH OUT, BOSS, YOU--!
I mean I'm still new on the job, so there's an excuse. But Batman?

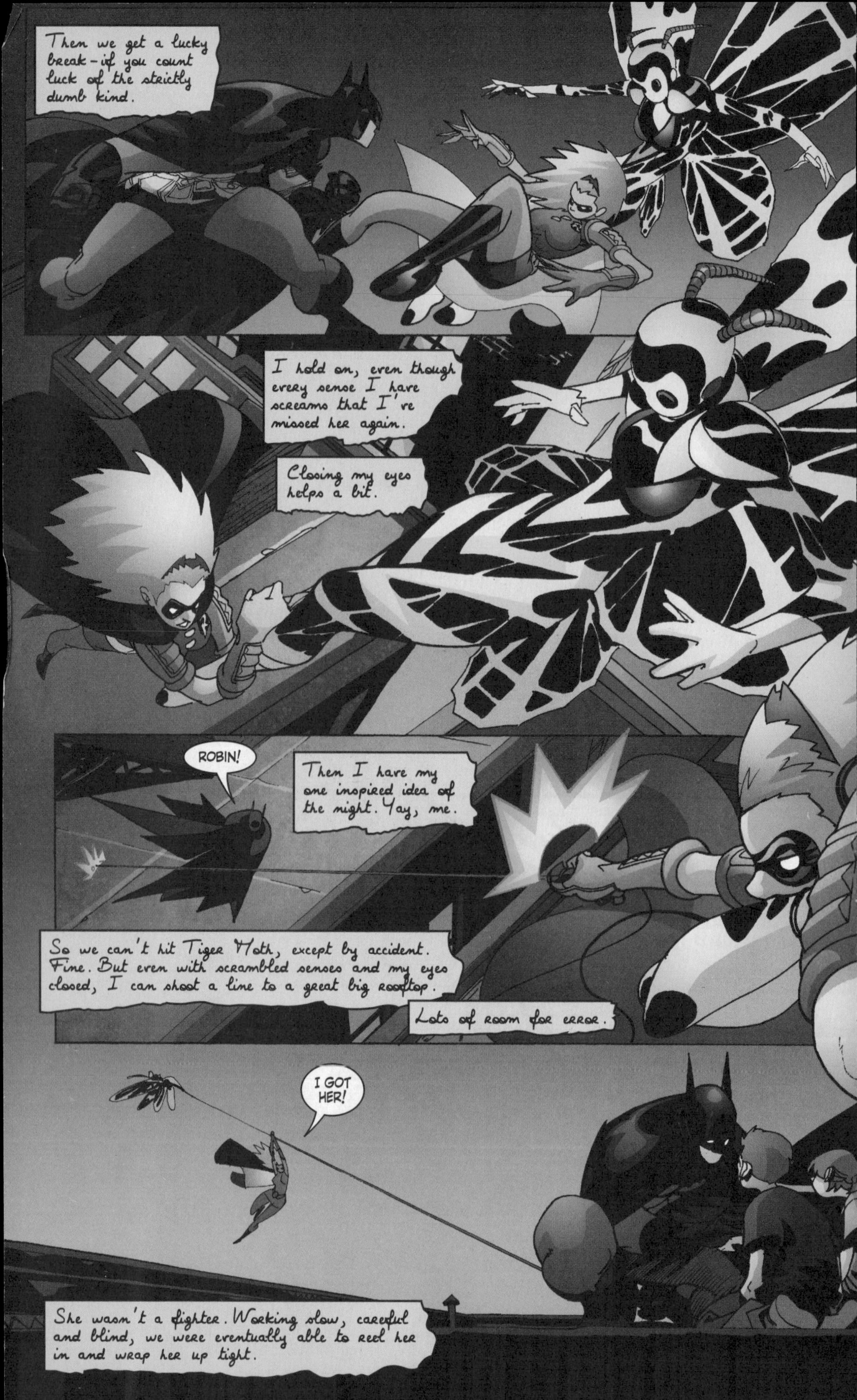
Then we get a lucky break—if you count luck of the strictly dumb kind.
I hold on, even though every sense I have screams that I've missed her again.
Closing my eyes helps a bit.
ROBIN!
Then I have my one inspired idea of the night. Yay, me.
So we can't hit Tiger Moth, except by accident. Fine. But even with scrambled senses and my eyes closed, I can shoot a line to a great big rooftop.
Lots of room for error.
I GOT HER!
She wasn't a fighter. Working slow, careful and blind, we were eventually able to reel her in and wrap her up tight.

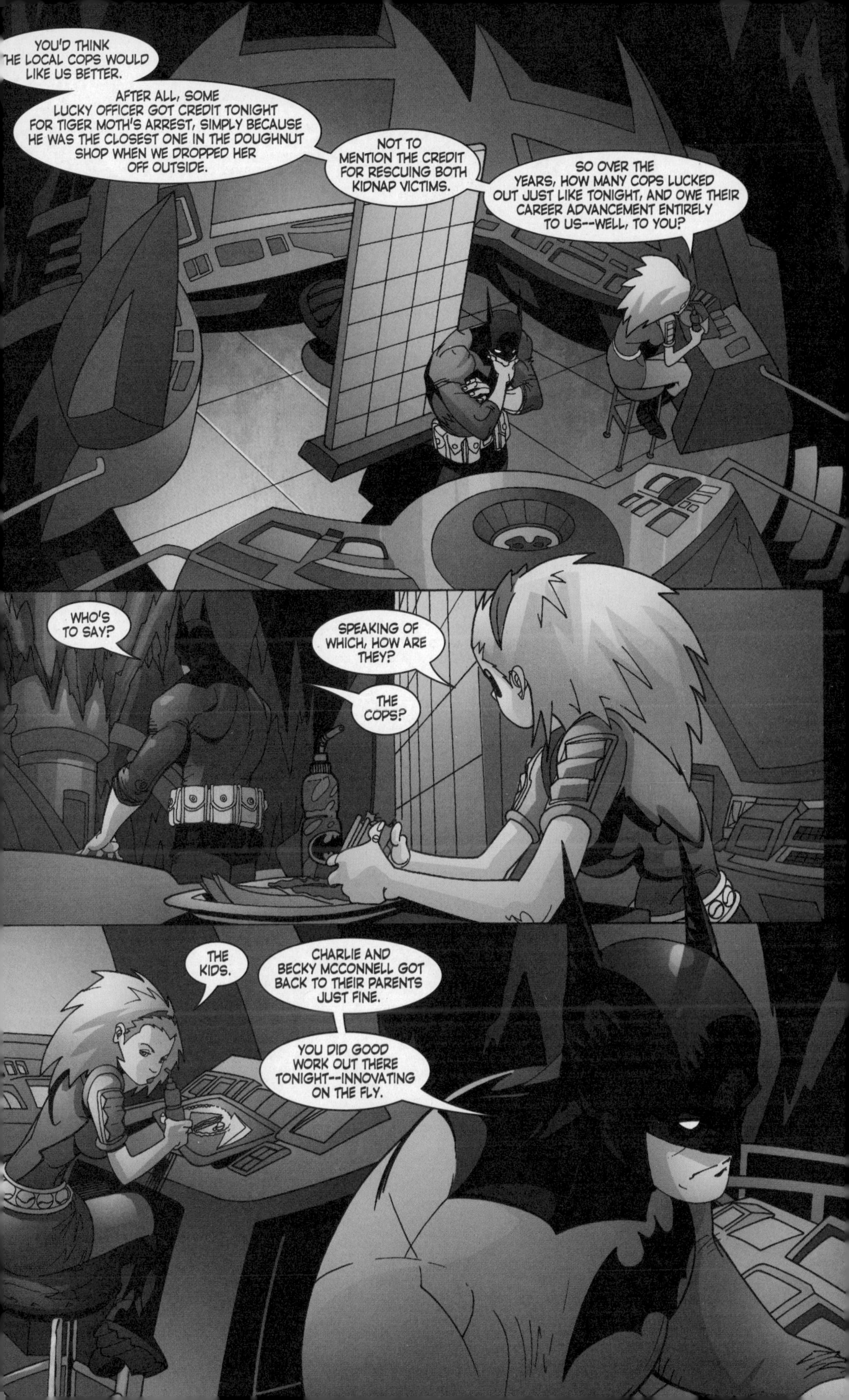
YOU'D THINK THE LOCAL COPS WOULD LIKE US BETTER.
AFTER ALL, SOME LUCKY OFFICER GOT CREDIT TONIGHT FOR TIGER MOTH'S ARREST, SIMPLY BECAUSE HE WAS THE CLOSEST ONE IN THE DOUGHNUT SHOP WHEN WE DROPPED HER OFF OUTSIDE.
NOT TO MENTION THE CREDIT FOR RESCUING BOTH KIDNAP VICTIMS.
SO OVER THE YEARS, HOW MANY COPS LUCKED OUT JUST LIKE TONIGHT, AND OWE THEIR CAREER ADVANCEMENT ENTIRELY TO US--WELL, TO YOU?
WHO'S TO SAY?
SPEAKING OF WHICH, HOW ARE THEY?
THE COPS?
THE KIDS.
CHARLIE AND BECKY McCONNELL GOT BACK TO THEIR PARENTS JUST FINE.
YOU DID GOOD WORK OUT THERE TONIGHT--INNOVATING ON THE FLY.

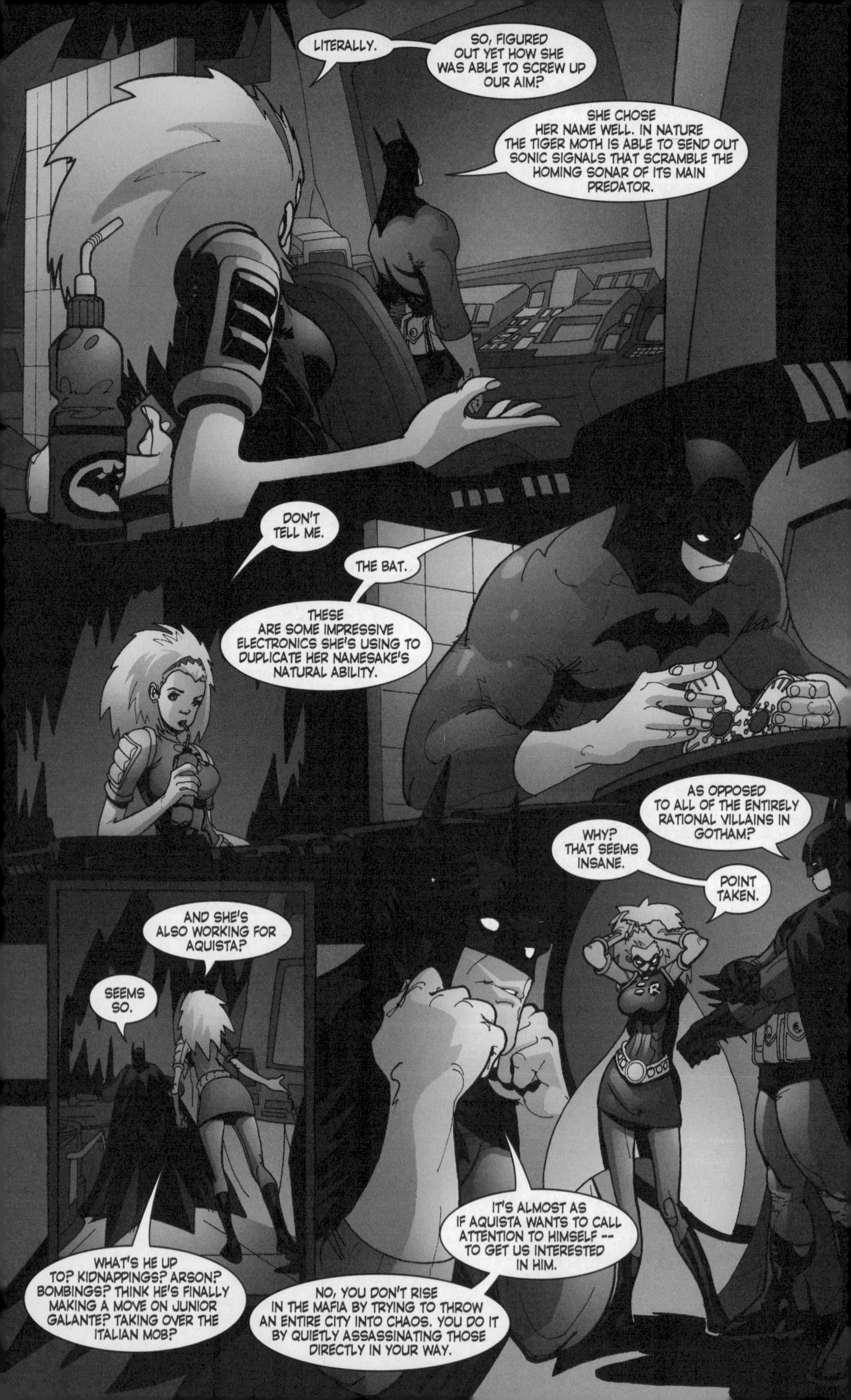
LITERALLY.
SO, FIGURED OUT YET HOW SHE WAS ABLE TO SCREW UP OUR AIM?
SHE CHOSE HER NAME WELL. IN NATURE THE TIGER MOTH IS ABLE TO SEND OUT SONIC SIGNALS THAT SCRAMBLE THE HOMING SONAR OF ITS MAIN PREDATOR.
DON'T TELL ME.
THE BAT.
THESE ARE SOME IMPRESSIVE ELECTRONICS SHE'S USING TO DUPLICATE HER NAMESAKE'S NATURAL ABILITY.
AND SHE'S ALSO WORKING FOR AQUISTA?
SEEMS SO.
WHAT'S HE UP TO? KIDNAPPINGS? ARSON? BOMBINGS? THINK HE'S FINALLY MAKING A MOVE ON JUNIOR GALANTE? TAKING OVER THE ITALIAN MOB?
NO, YOU DON'T RISE IN THE MAFIA BY TRYING TO THROW AN ENTIRE CITY INTO CHAOS. YOU DO IT BY QUIETLY ASSASSINATING THOSE DIRECTLY IN YOUR WAY.
IT'S ALMOST AS IF AQUISTA WANTS TO CALL ATTENTION TO HIMSELF -- TO GET US INTERESTED IN HIM.
WHY? THAT SEEMS INSANE.
AS OPPOSED TO ALL OF THE ENTIRELY RATIONAL VILLAINS IN GOTHAM?
POINT TAKEN.

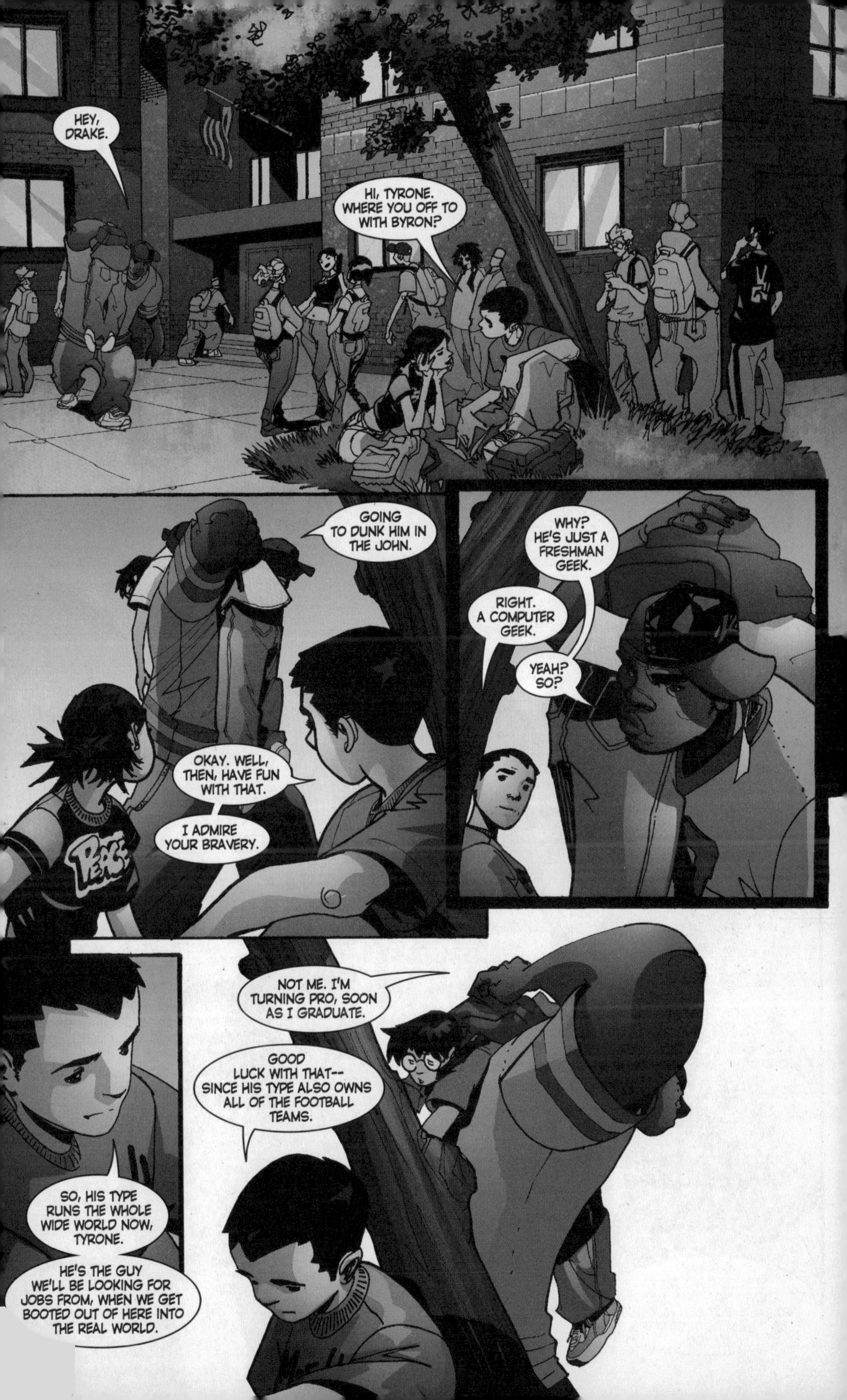
HEY, DRAKE.
HI, TYRONE. WHERE YOU OFF TO WITH BYRON?
GOING TO DUNK HIM IN THE JOHN.
WHY? HE'S JUST A FRESHMAN GEEK.
RIGHT. A COMPUTER GEEK.
YEAH? SO?
OKAY. WELL, THEN, HAVE FUN WITH THAT.
I ADMIRE YOUR BRAVERY.
NOT ME. I'M TURNING PRO, SOON AS I GRADUATE.
GOOD LUCK WITH THAT-- SINCE HIS TYPE ALSO OWNS ALL OF THE FOOTBALL TEAMS.
SO, HIS TYPE RUNS THE WHOLE WIDE WORLD NOW, TYRONE.
HE'S THE GUY WE'LL BE LOOKING FOR JOBS FROM, WHEN WE GET BOOTED OUT OF HERE INTO THE REAL WORLD.

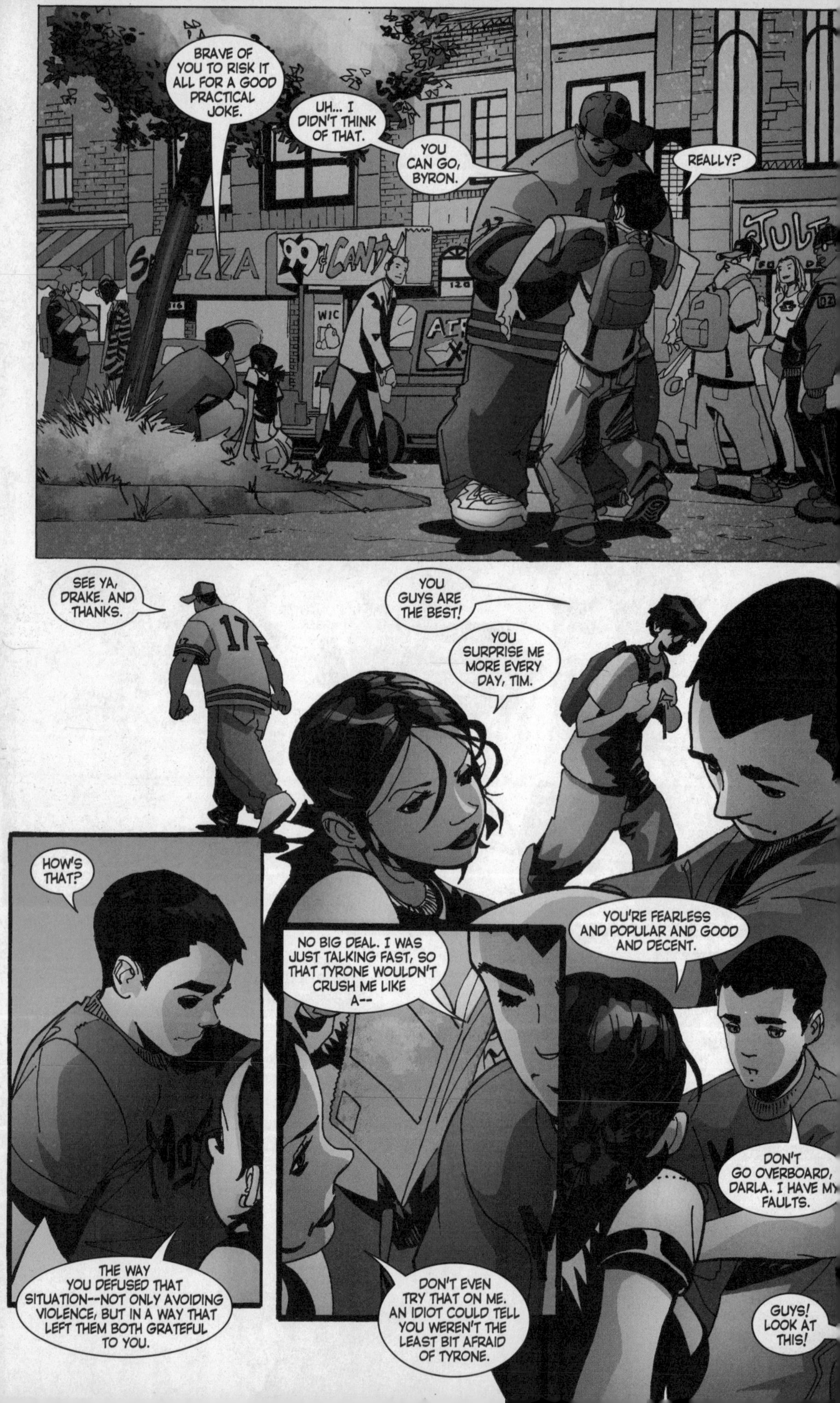
BRAVE OF YOU TO RISK IT ALL FOR A GOOD PRACTICAL JOKE.
UH... I DIDN'T THINK OF THAT.
YOU CAN GO, BYRON.
REALLY?
99¢ CANDY
PIZZA
SEE YA, DRAKE. AND THANKS.
YOU GUYS ARE THE BEST!
YOU SURPRISE ME MORE EVERY DAY, TIM.
HOW'S THAT?
THE WAY YOU DEFUSED THAT SITUATION--NOT ONLY AVOIDING VIOLENCE, BUT IN A WAY THAT LEFT THEM BOTH GRATEFUL TO YOU.
NO BIG DEAL. I WAS JUST TALKING FAST, SO THAT TYRONE WOULDN'T CRUSH ME LIKE A--
DON'T EVEN TRY THAT ON ME. AN IDIOT COULD TELL YOU WEREN'T THE LEAST BIT AFRAID OF TYRONE.
YOU'RE FEARLESS AND POPULAR AND GOOD AND DECENT.
DON'T GO OVERBOARD, DARLA. I HAVE MY FAULTS.
GUYS! LOOK AT THIS!

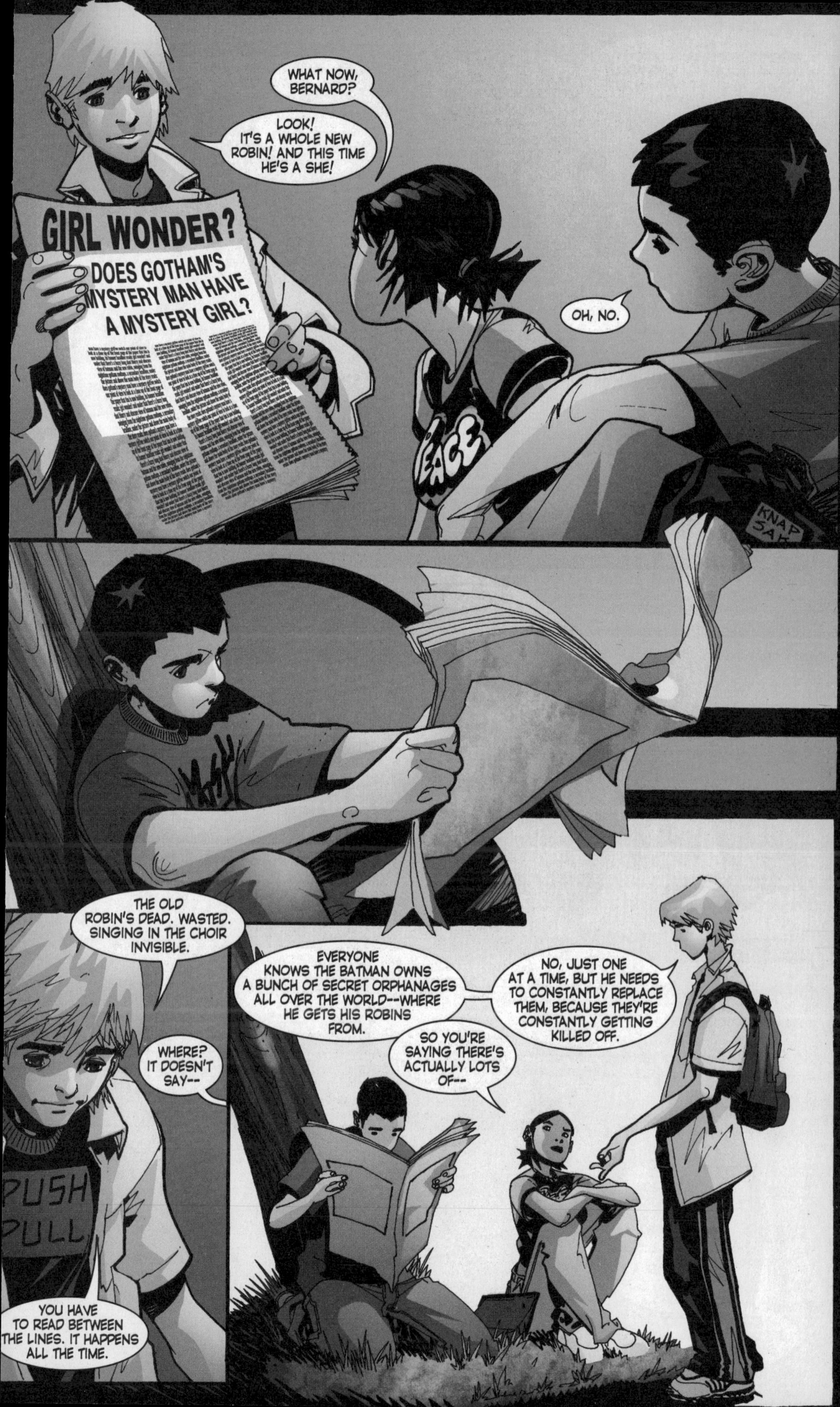
WHAT NOW, BERNARD?
LOOK! IT'S A WHOLE NEW ROBIN! AND THIS TIME HE'S A SHE!
GIRL WONDER?
DOES GOTHAM'S MYSTERY MAN HAVE A MYSTERY GIRL?
OH, NO.
PEACE
KNAP SAK
THE OLD ROBIN'S DEAD. WASTED. SINGING IN THE CHOIR INVISIBLE.
WHERE? IT DOESN'T SAY--
YOU HAVE TO READ BETWEEN THE LINES. IT HAPPENS ALL THE TIME.
PUSH PULL
EVERYONE KNOWS THE BATMAN OWNS A BUNCH OF SECRET ORPHANAGES ALL OVER THE WORLD--WHERE HE GETS HIS ROBINS FROM.
SO YOU'RE SAYING THERE'S ACTUALLY LOTS OF--
NO, JUST ONE AT A TIME, BUT HE NEEDS TO CONSTANTLY REPLACE THEM, BECAUSE THEY'RE CONSTANTLY GETTING KILLED OFF.

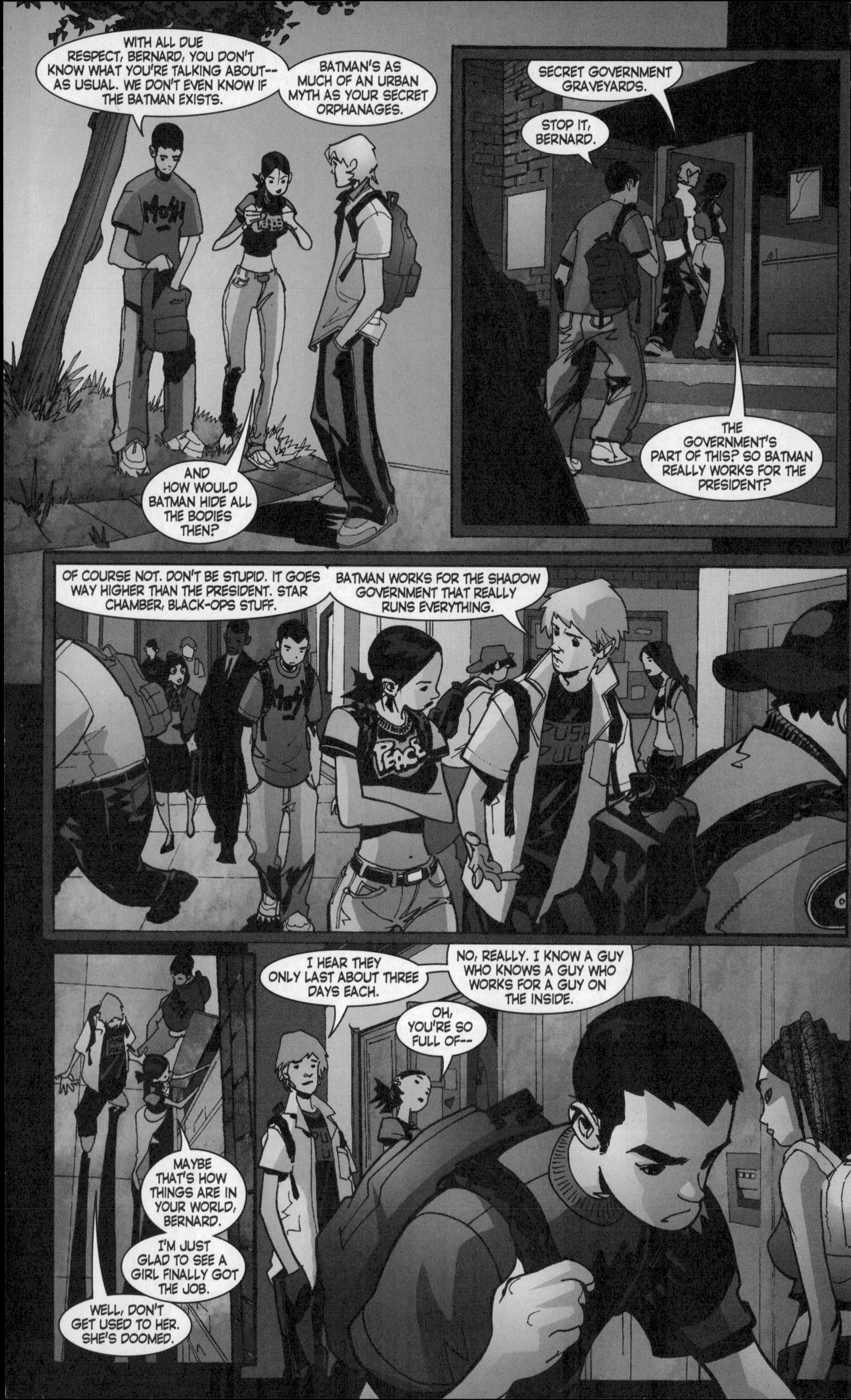
WITH ALL DUE RESPECT, BERNARD, YOU DON'T KNOW WHAT YOU'RE TALKING ABOUT-- AS USUAL. WE DON'T EVEN KNOW IF THE BATMAN EXISTS.
BATMAN'S AS MUCH OF AN URBAN MYTH AS YOUR SECRET ORPHANAGES.
AND HOW WOULD BATMAN HIDE ALL THE BODIES THEN?
SECRET GOVERNMENT GRAVEYARDS.
STOP IT, BERNARD.
THE GOVERNMENT'S PART OF THIS? SO BATMAN REALLY WORKS FOR THE PRESIDENT?
OF COURSE NOT. DON'T BE STUPID. IT GOES WAY HIGHER THAN THE PRESIDENT. STAR CHAMBER, BLACK-OPS STUFF.
BATMAN WORKS FOR THE SHADOW GOVERNMENT THAT REALLY RUNS EVERYTHING.
I HEAR THEY ONLY LAST ABOUT THREE DAYS EACH.
NO, REALLY. I KNOW A GUY WHO KNOWS A GUY WHO WORKS FOR A GUY ON THE INSIDE.
OH, YOU'RE SO FULL OF--
MAYBE THAT'S HOW THINGS ARE IN YOUR WORLD, BERNARD.
I'M JUST GLAD TO SEE A GIRL FINALLY GOT THE JOB.
WELL, DON'T GET USED TO HER. SHE'S DOOMED.

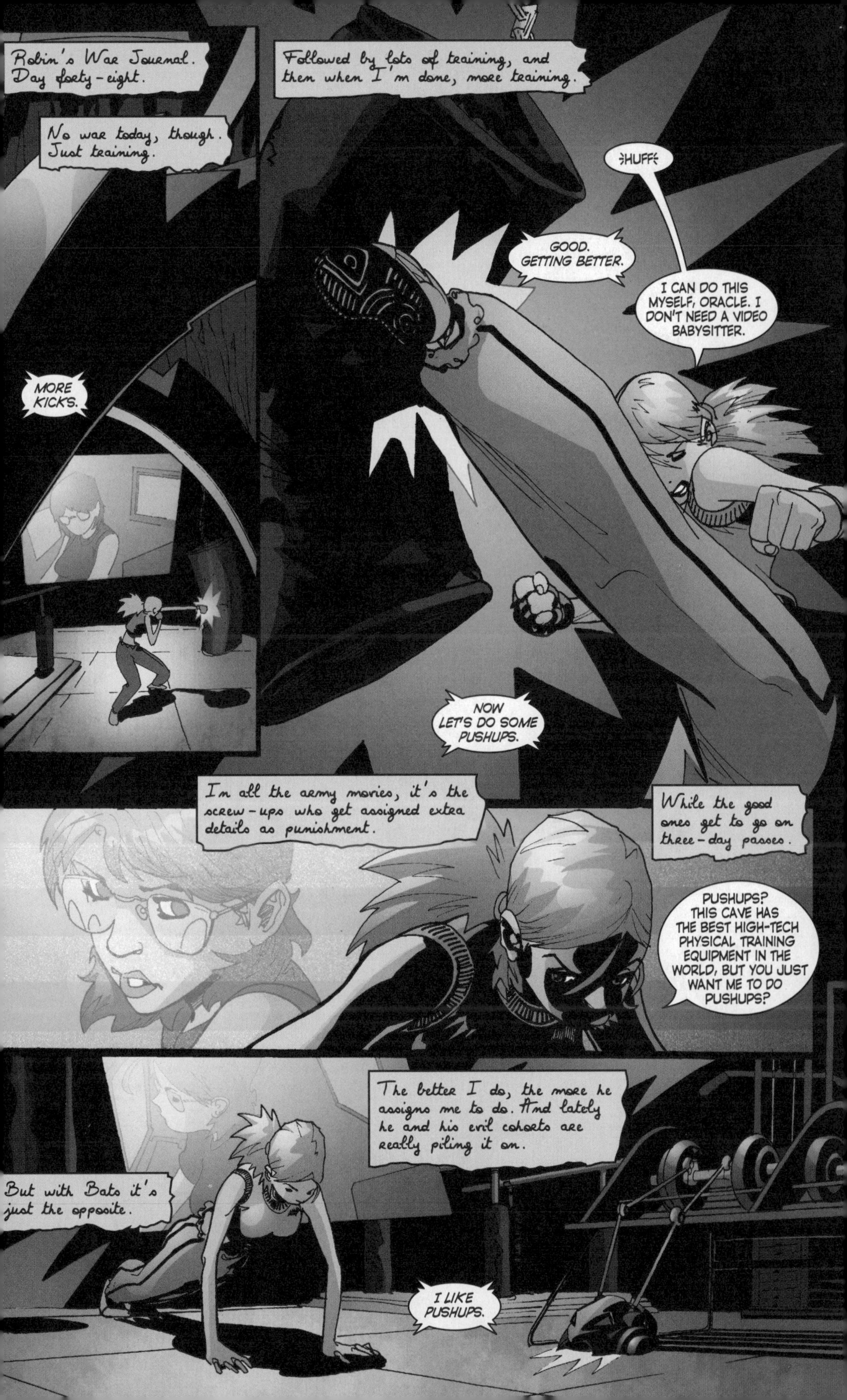
Robin's War Journal. Day forty-eight.
No war today, though. Just training.
MORE KICKS.
Followed by lots of training, and then when I'm done, more training.
GOOD. GETTING BETTER.
HUFF
I CAN DO THIS MYSELF, ORACLE. I DON'T NEED A VIDEO BABYSITTER.
NOW LET'S DO SOME PUSHUPS.
In all the army movies, it's the screw-ups who get assigned extra details as punishment.
While the good ones get to go on three-day passes.
PUSHUPS? THIS CAVE HAS THE BEST HIGH-TECH PHYSICAL TRAINING EQUIPMENT IN THE WORLD, BUT YOU JUST WANT ME TO DO PUSHUPS?
But with Bats it's just the opposite.
The better I do, the more he assigns me to do. And lately he and his evil cohorts are really piling it on.
I LIKE PUSHUPS.

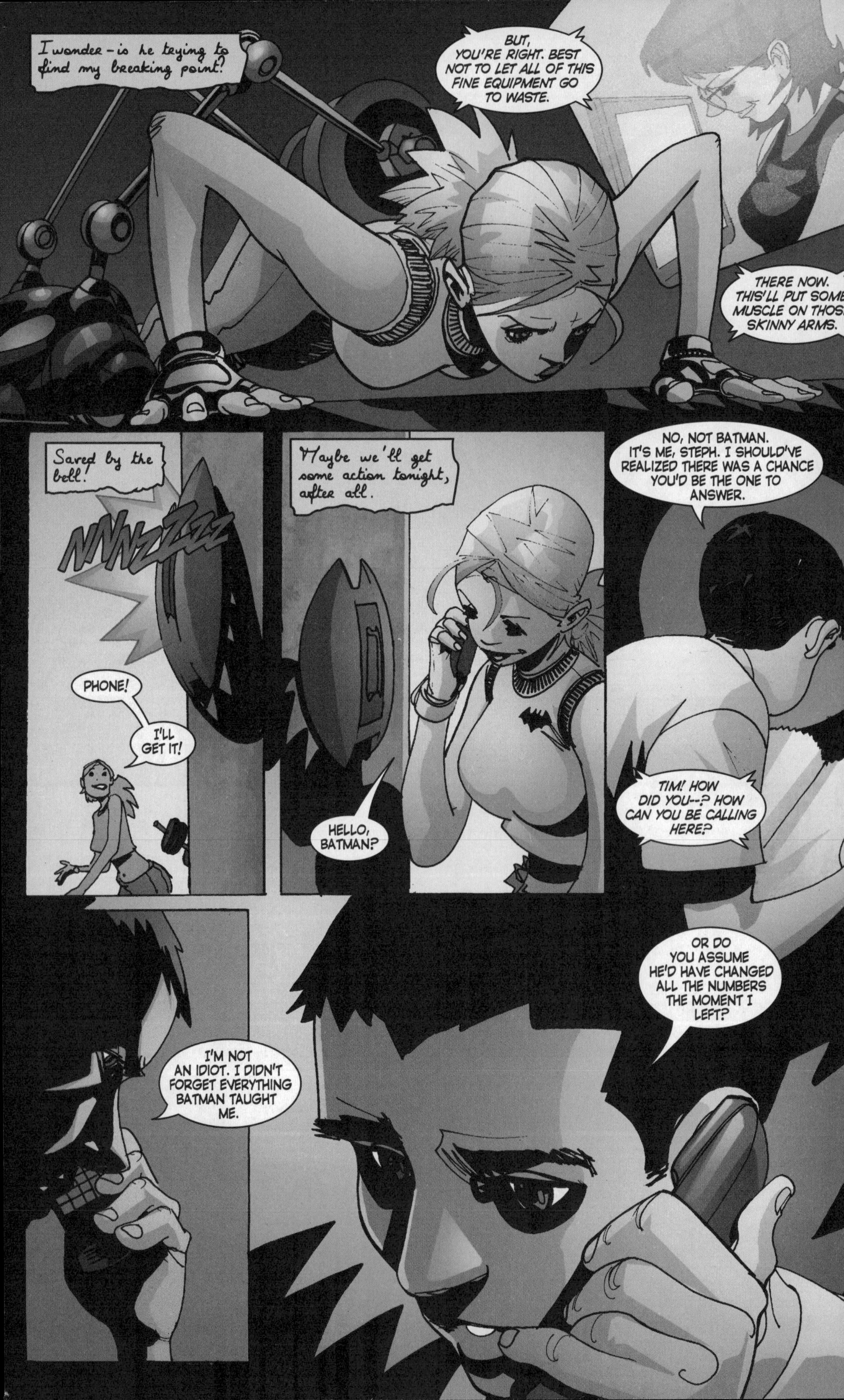
I wonder—is he trying to find my breaking point?
BUT, YOU'RE RIGHT. BEST NOT TO LET ALL OF THIS FINE EQUIPMENT GO TO WASTE.
THERE NOW. THIS'LL PUT SOME MUSCLE ON THOS SKINNY ARMS.
Saved by the bell!
NNNZZZZ
PHONE!
I'LL GET IT!
Maybe we'll get some action tonight, after all.
HELLO, BATMAN?
NO, NOT BATMAN. IT'S ME, STEPH. I SHOULD'VE REALIZED THERE WAS A CHANCE YOU'D BE THE ONE TO ANSWER.
TIM! HOW DID YOU--? HOW CAN YOU BE CALLING HERE?
OR DO YOU ASSUME HE'D HAVE CHANGED ALL THE NUMBERS THE MOMENT I LEFT?
I'M NOT AN IDIOT. I DIDN'T FORGET EVERYTHING BATMAN TAUGHT ME.

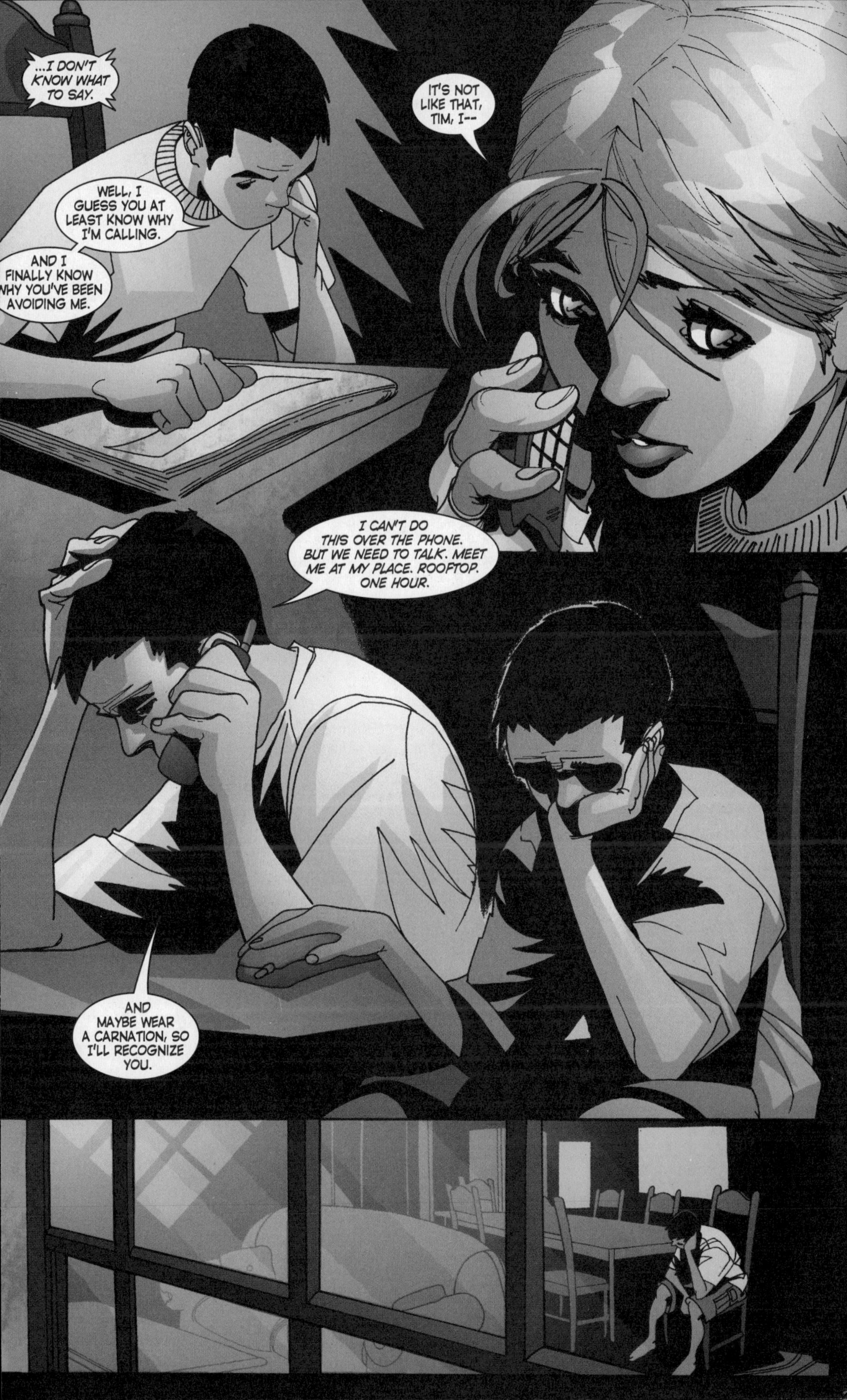
...I DON'T KNOW WHAT TO SAY.
IT'S NOT LIKE THAT, TIM, I--
WELL, I GUESS YOU AT LEAST KNOW WHY I'M CALLING.
AND I FINALLY KNOW WHY YOU'VE BEEN AVOIDING ME.
I CAN'T DO THIS OVER THE PHONE. BUT WE NEED TO TALK. MEET ME AT MY PLACE. ROOFTOP. ONE HOUR.
AND MAYBE WEAR A CARNATION, SO I'LL RECOGNIZE YOU.

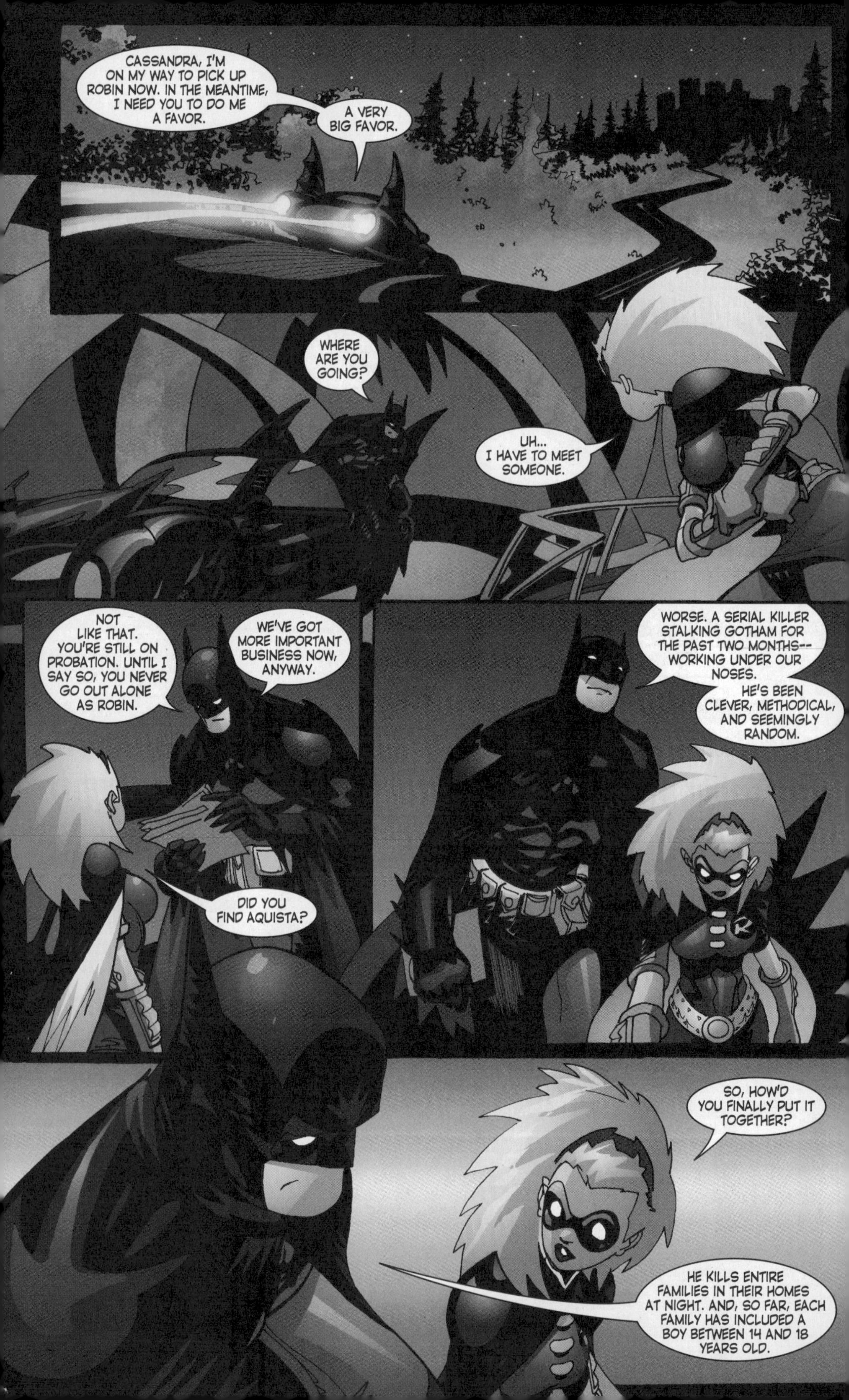
CASSANDRA, I'M ON MY WAY TO PICK UP ROBIN NOW. IN THE MEANTIME, I NEED YOU TO DO ME A FAVOR.
A VERY BIG FAVOR.
WHERE ARE YOU GOING?
UH... I HAVE TO MEET SOMEONE.
NOT LIKE THAT. YOU'RE STILL ON PROBATION. UNTIL I SAY SO, YOU NEVER GO OUT ALONE AS ROBIN.
WE'VE GOT MORE IMPORTANT BUSINESS NOW, ANYWAY.
DID YOU FIND AQUISTA?
WORSE. A SERIAL KILLER STALKING GOTHAM FOR THE PAST TWO MONTHS-- WORKING UNDER OUR NOSES.
HE'S BEEN CLEVER, METHODICAL, AND SEEMINGLY RANDOM.
SO, HOW'D YOU FINALLY PUT IT TOGETHER?
HE KILLS ENTIRE FAMILIES IN THEIR HOMES AT NIGHT. AND, SO FAR, EACH FAMILY HAS INCLUDED A BOY BETWEEN 14 AND 18 YEARS OLD.

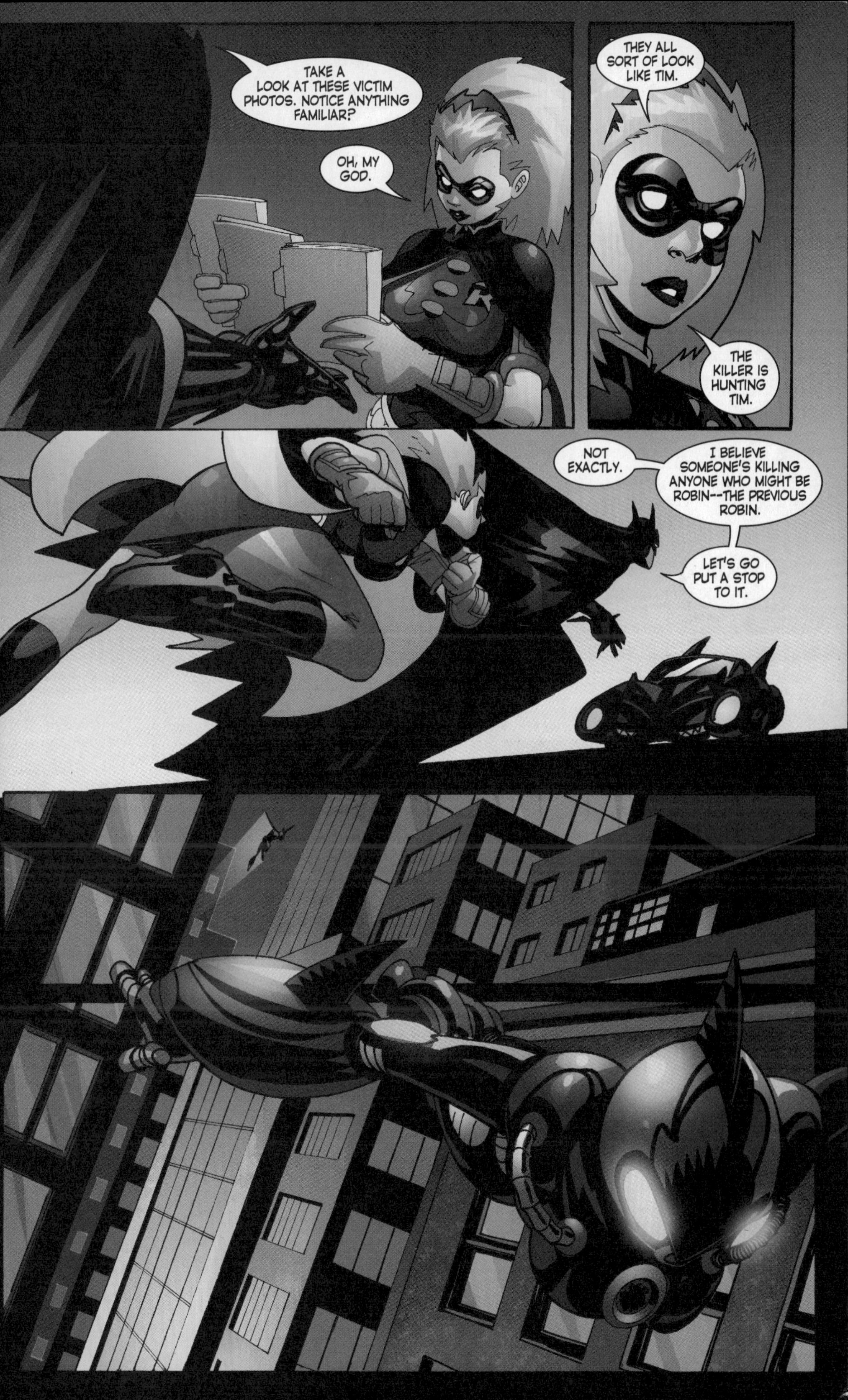

TAKE A LOOK AT THESE VICTIM PHOTOS. NOTICE ANYTHING FAMILIAR?
OH, MY GOD.
THEY ALL SORT OF LOOK LIKE TIM.
THE KILLER IS HUNTING TIM.
NOT EXACTLY.
I BELIEVE SOMEONE'S KILLING ANYONE WHO MIGHT BE ROBIN--THE PREVIOUS ROBIN.
LET'S GO PUT A STOP TO IT.

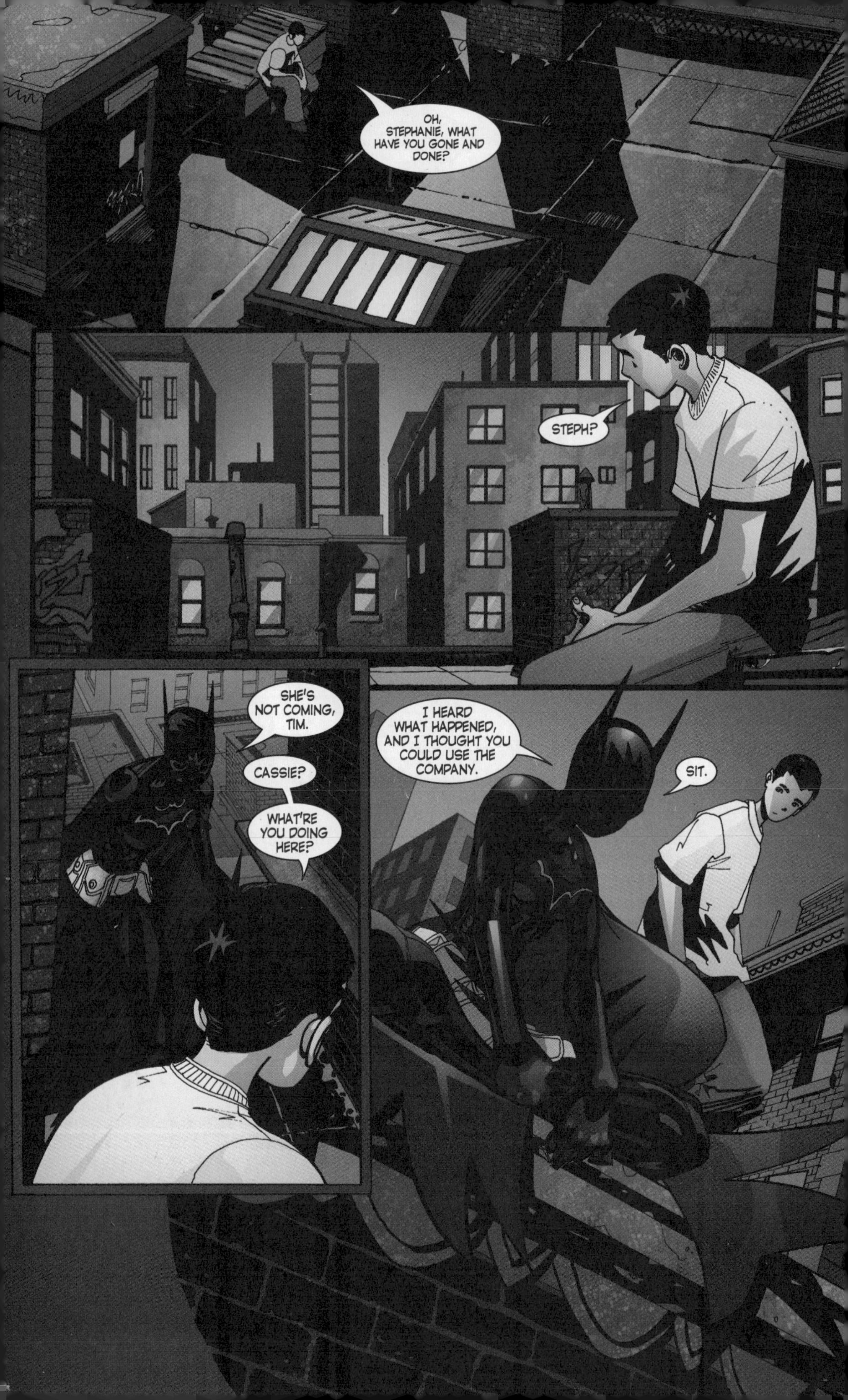
OH, STEPHANIE, WHAT HAVE YOU GONE AND DONE?
STEPH?
SHE'S NOT COMING, TIM.
CASSIE?
WHAT'RE YOU DOING HERE?
I HEARD WHAT HAPPENED, AND I THOUGHT YOU COULD USE THE COMPANY.
SIT.

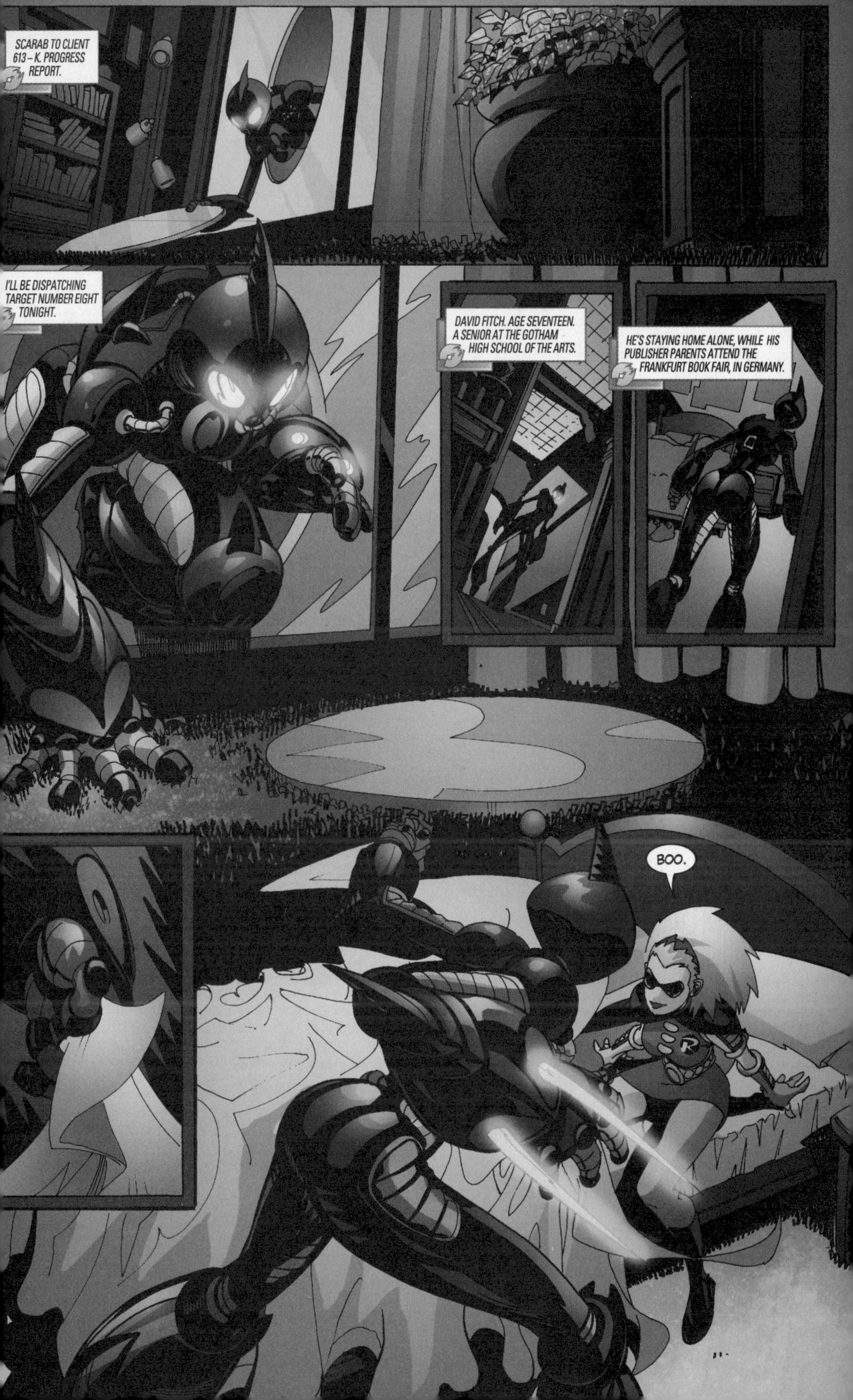
SCARAB TO CLIENT 613–K. PROGRESS REPORT.
I'LL BE DISPATCHING TARGET NUMBER EIGHT TONIGHT.
DAVID FITCH. AGE SEVENTEEN. A SENIOR AT THE GOTHAM HIGH SCHOOL OF THE ARTS.
HE'S STAYING HOME ALONE, WHILE HIS PUBLISHER PARENTS ATTEND THE FRANKFURT BOOK FAIR, IN GERMANY.
BOO.

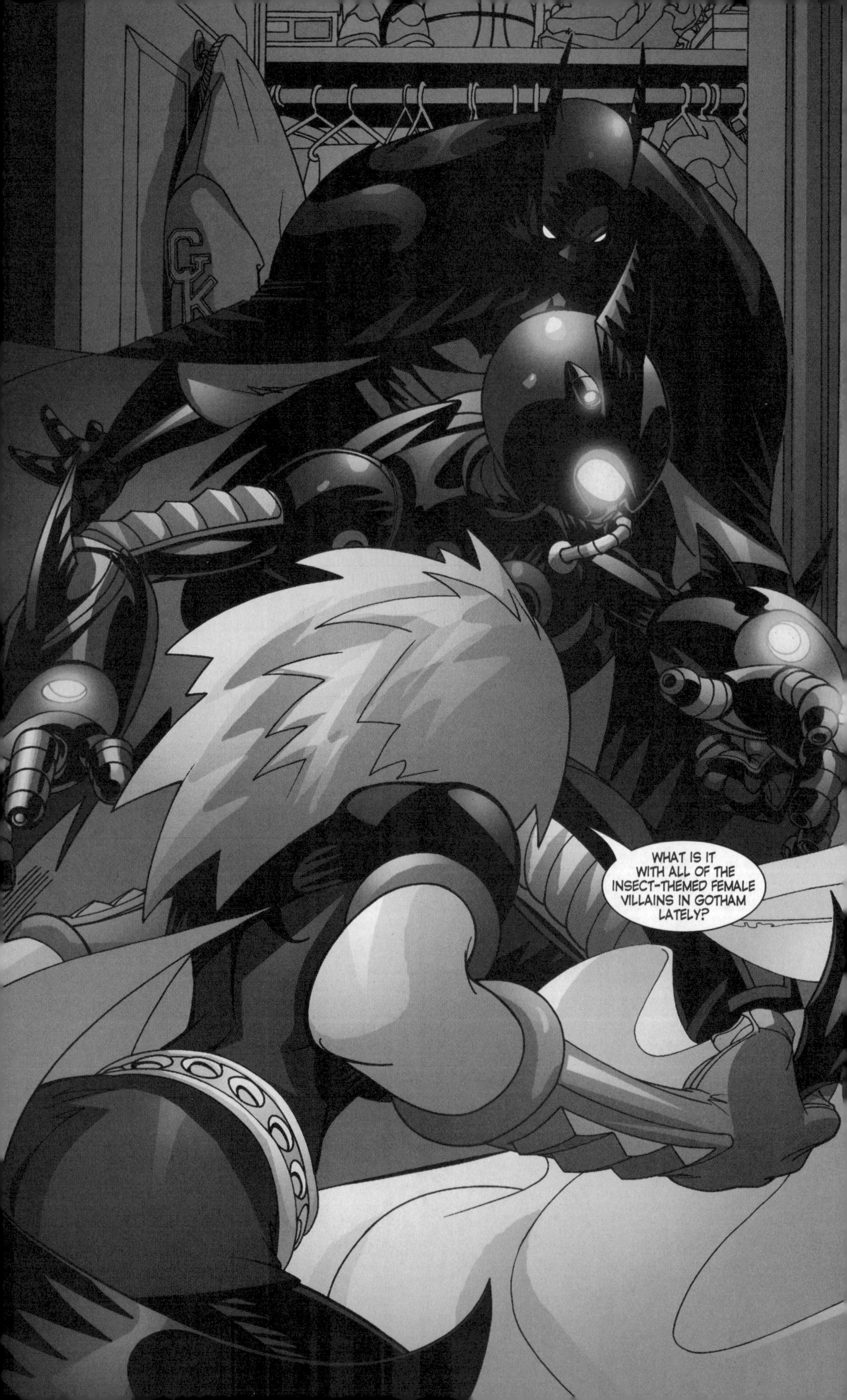
WHAT IS IT WITH ALL OF THE INSECT-THEMED FEMALE VILLAINS IN GOTHAM LATELY?

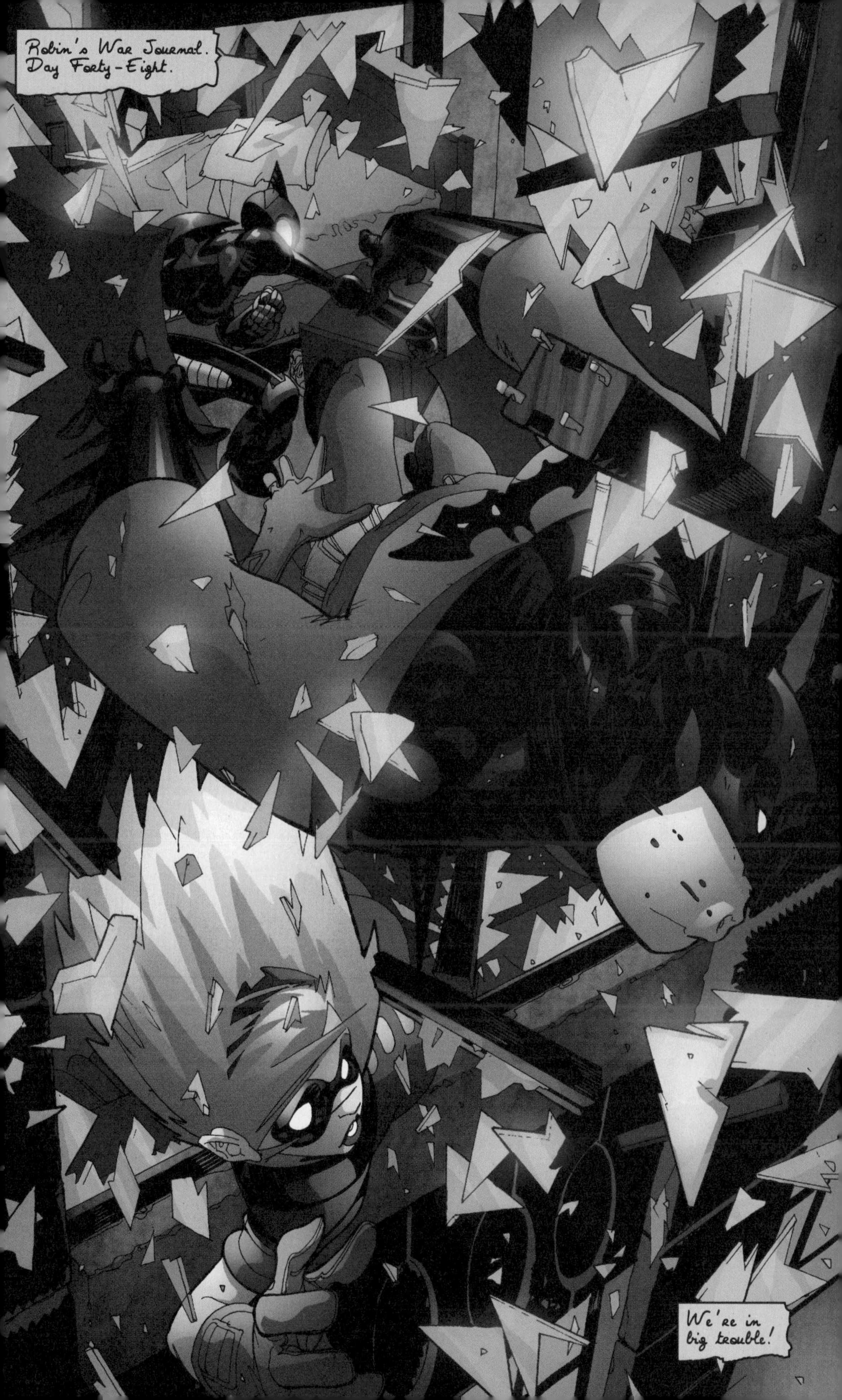
Robin's War Journal. Day Forty-Eight.
We're in big trouble!

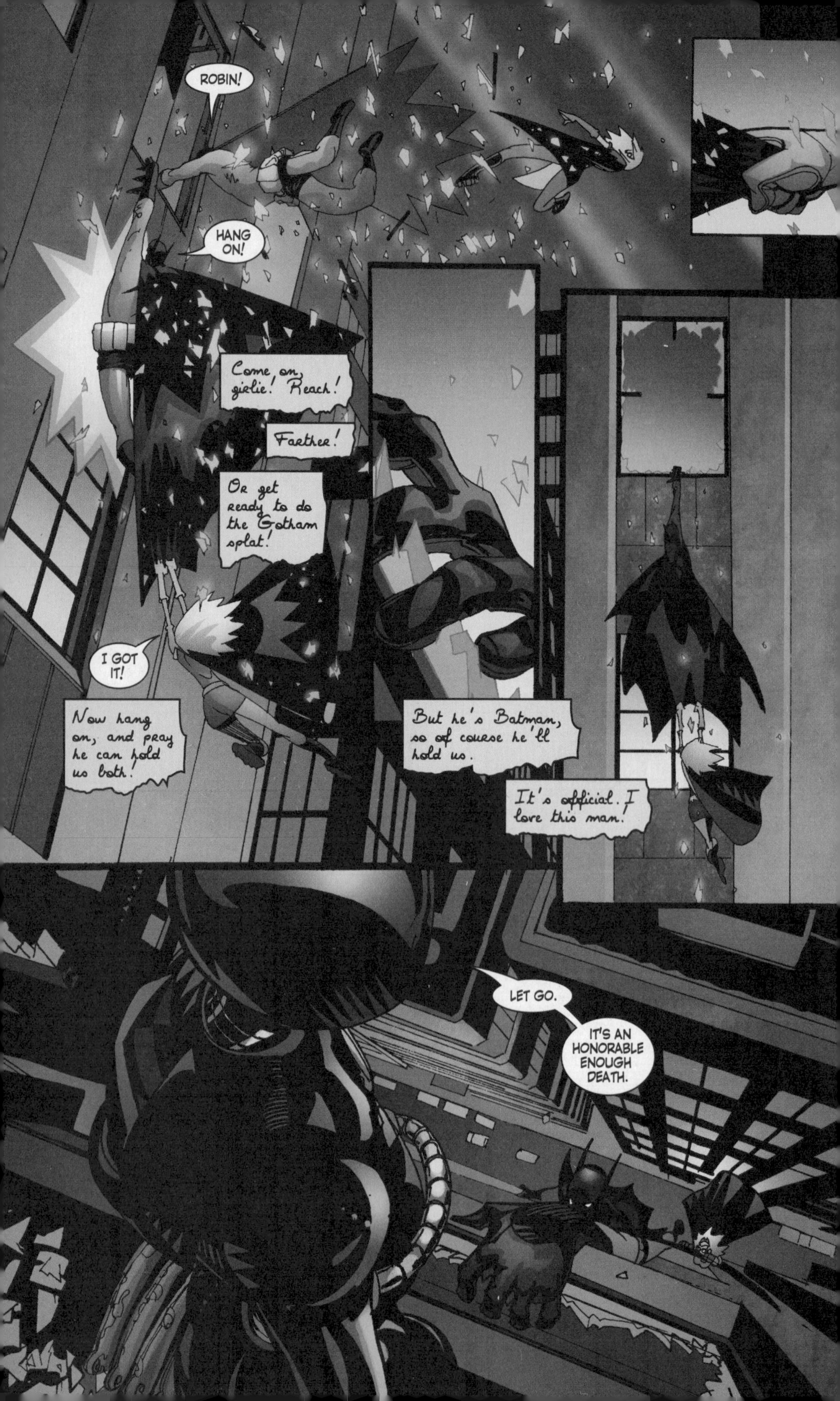

ROBIN!
HANG ON!
Come on, girlie! Reach!
Farther!
Or get ready to do the Gotham splat!
I GOT IT!
Now hang on, and pray he can hold us both!
But he's Batman, so of course he'll hold us.
It's official. I love this man!
LET GO.
IT'S AN HONORABLE ENOUGH DEATH.

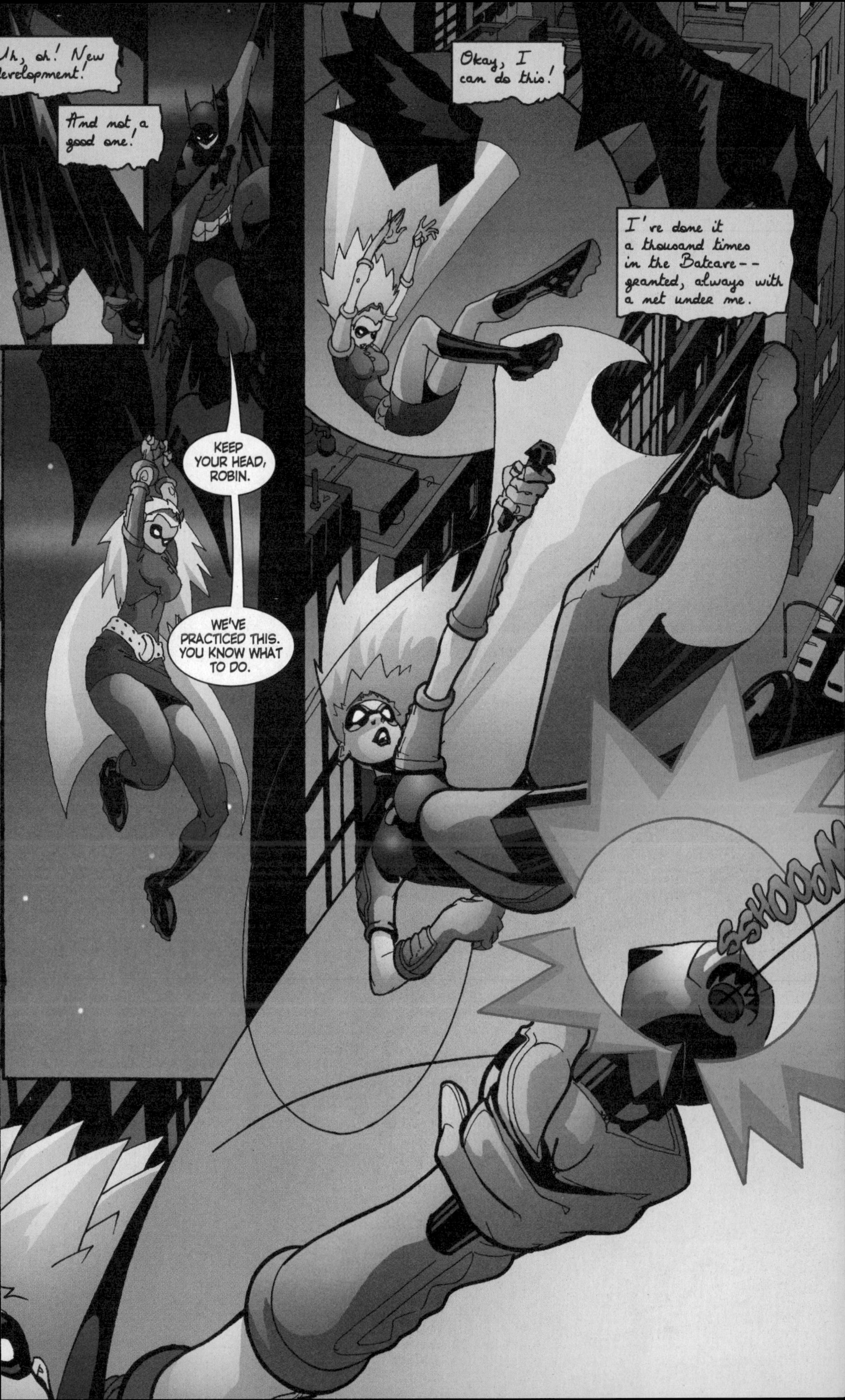
h, oh! New evelopment!
And not a good one!
KEEP YOUR HEAD, ROBIN.
WE'VE PRACTICED THIS. YOU KNOW WHAT TO DO.
Okay, I can do this!
I've done it a thousand times in the Batcave-- granted, always with a net under me.
SSHOOO

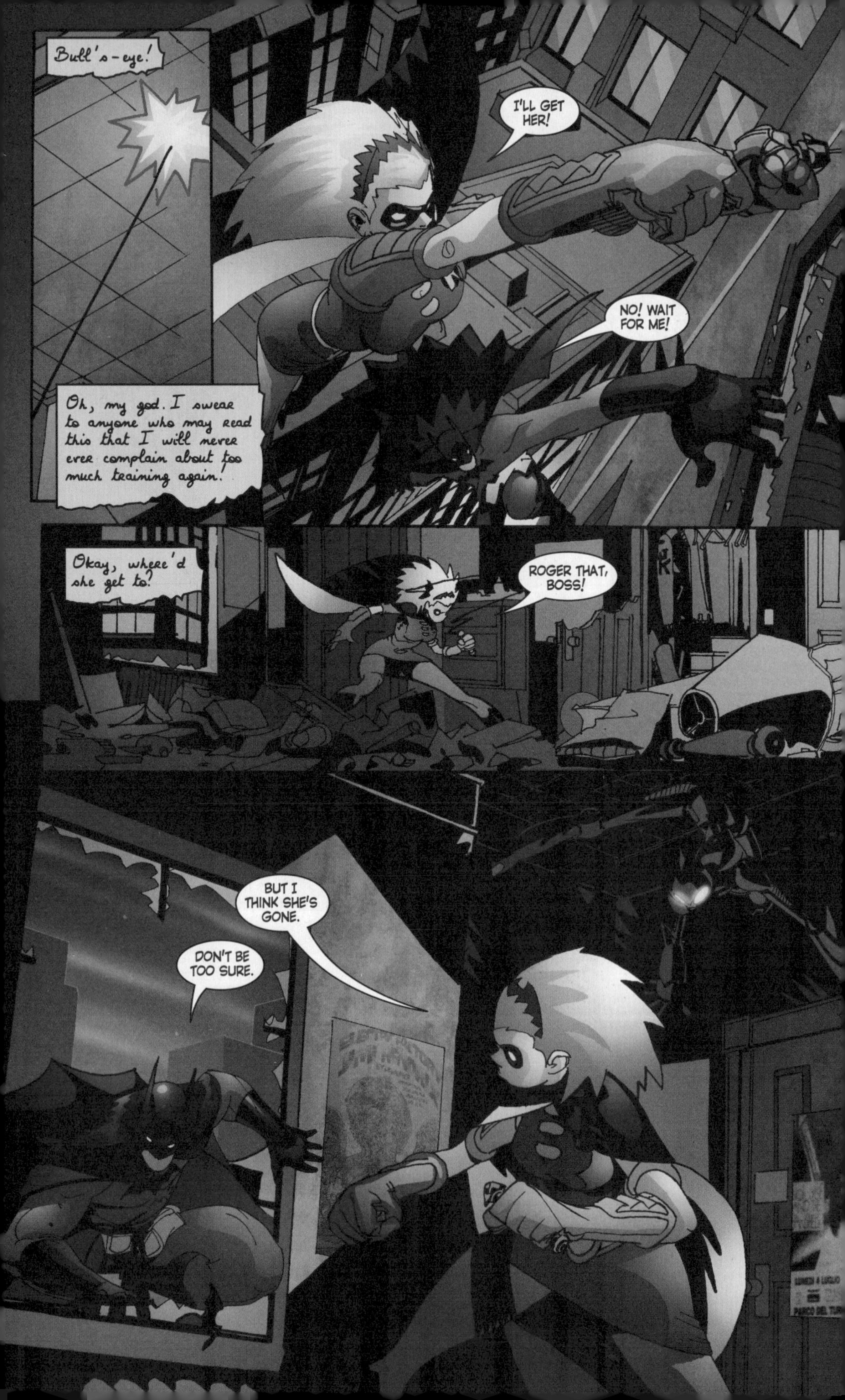
Bull's-eye!
I'LL GET HER!
NO! WAIT FOR ME!
Oh, my god. I swear to anyone who may read this that I will never ever complain about too much training again.
Okay, where'd she get to?
ROGER THAT, BOSS!
BUT I THINK SHE'S GONE.
DON'T BE TOO SURE.

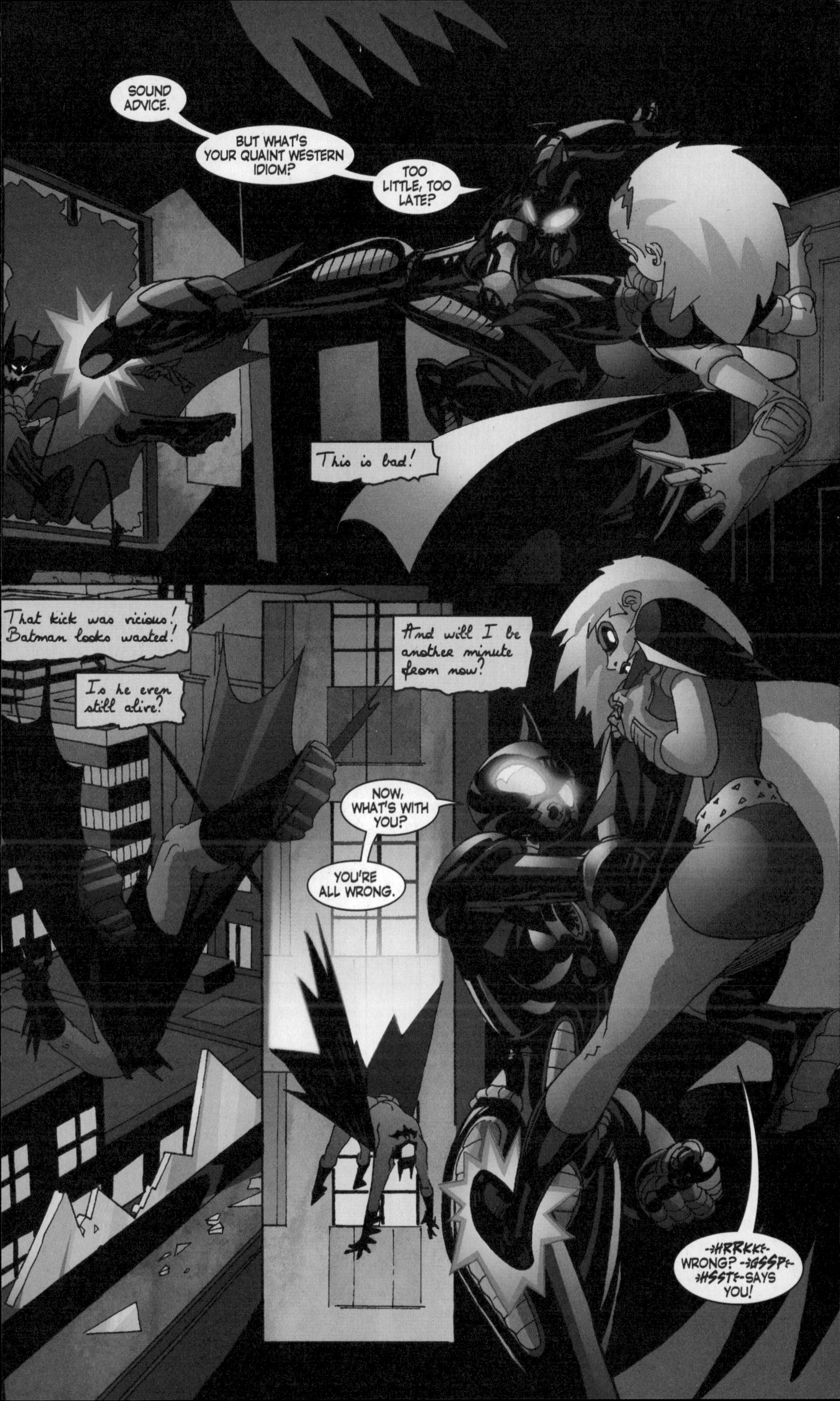
SOUND ADVICE.
BUT WHAT'S YOUR QUAINT WESTERN IDIOM?
TOO LITTLE, TOO LATE?
This is bad!
That kick was vicious! Batman looks wasted!
Is he even still alive?
And will I be another minute from now?
NOW, WHAT'S WITH YOU?
YOU'RE ALL WRONG.
-HRRKK- WRONG? -GSSP- -HSST- SAYS YOU!

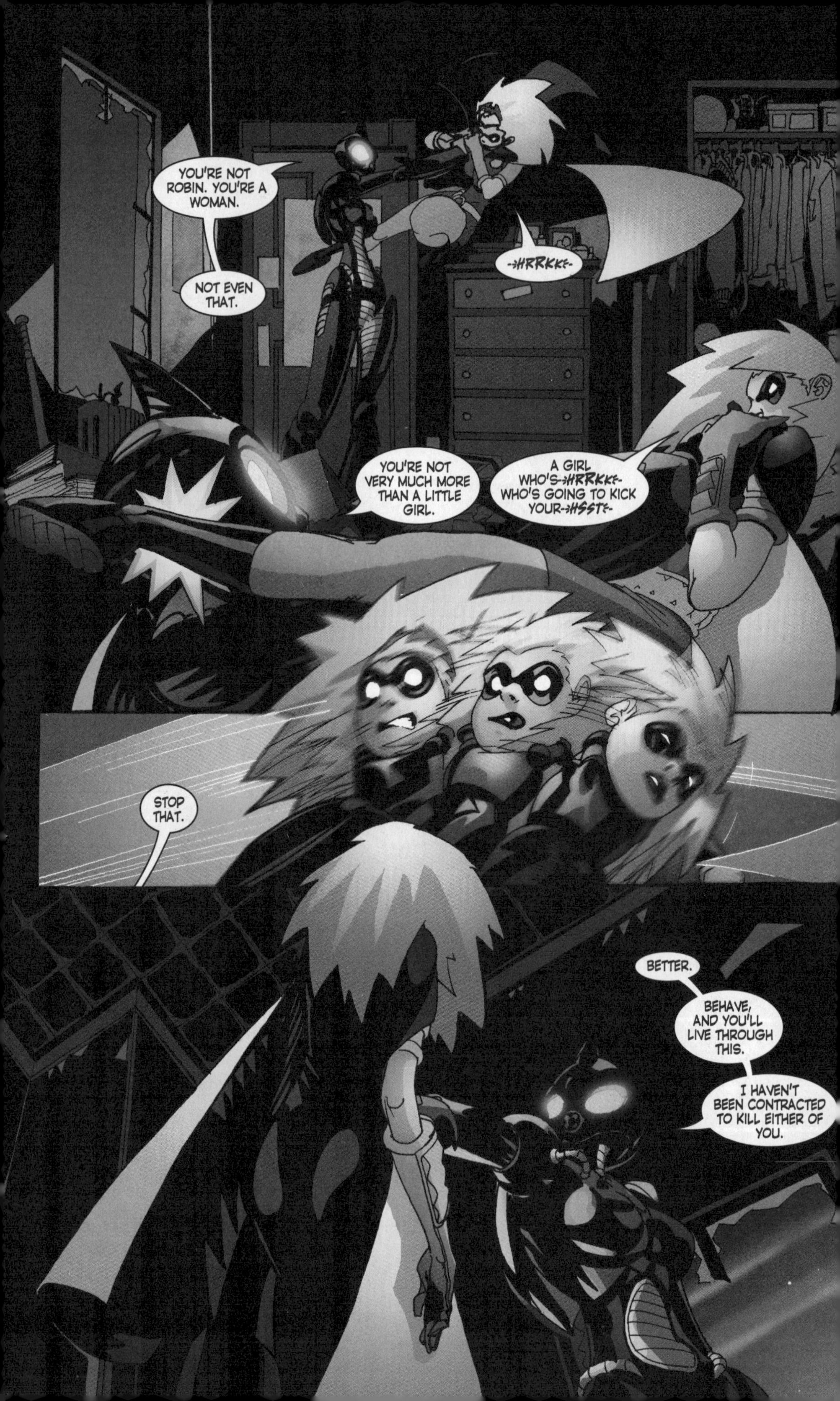
YOU'RE NOT ROBIN. YOU'RE A WOMAN.
NOT EVEN THAT.
-HRRKK-
YOU'RE NOT VERY MUCH MORE THAN A LITTLE GIRL.
A GIRL WHO'S-HRRKK- WHO'S GOING TO KICK YOUR-HSST-
STOP THAT.
BETTER.
BEHAVE, AND YOU'LL LIVE THROUGH THIS.
I HAVEN'T BEEN CONTRACTED TO KILL EITHER OF YOU.

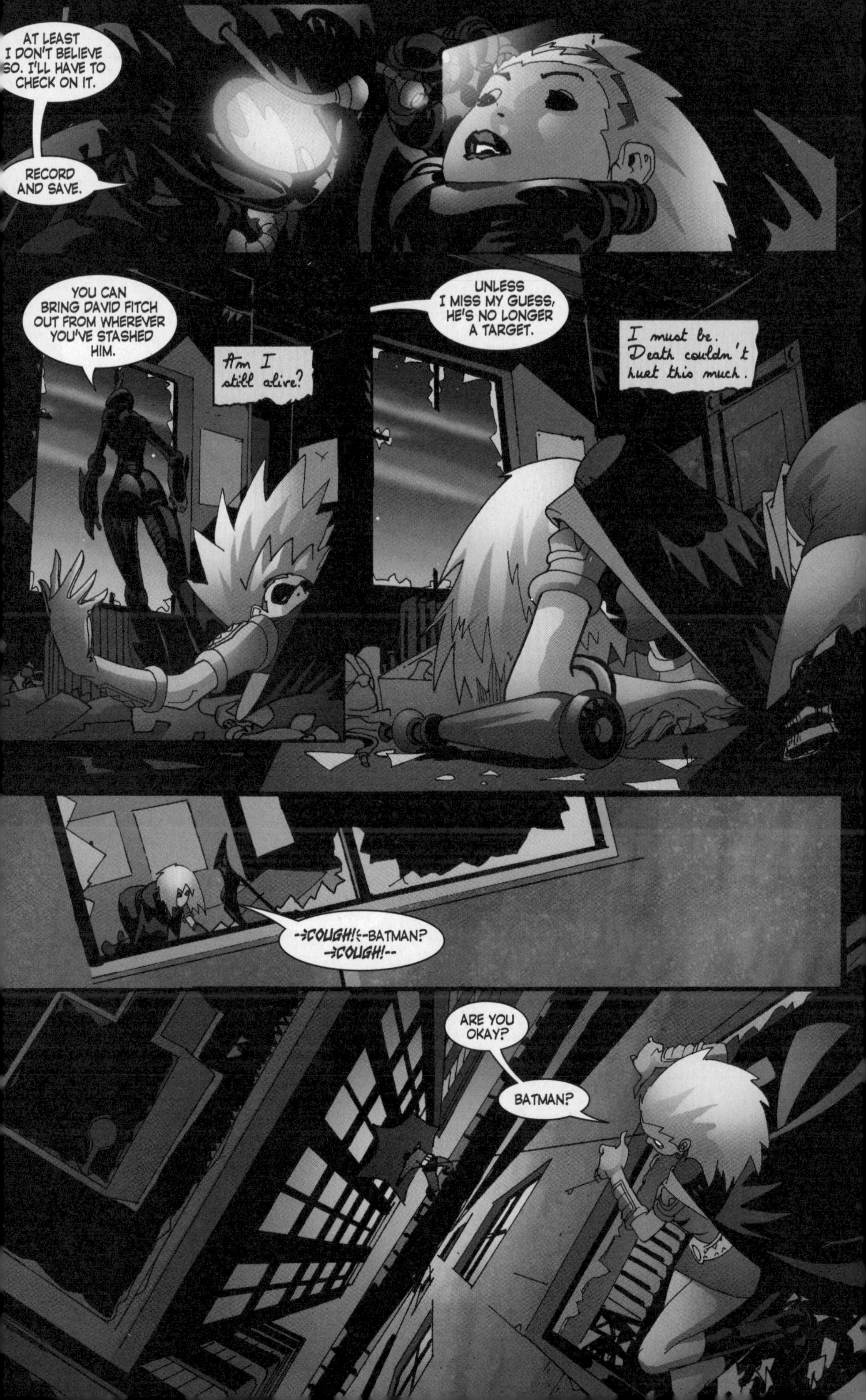
AT LEAST I DON'T BELIEVE SO. I'LL HAVE TO CHECK ON IT.
RECORD AND SAVE.
YOU CAN BRING DAVID FITCH OUT FROM WHEREVER YOU'VE STASHED HIM.
Am I still alive?
UNLESS I MISS MY GUESS, HE'S NO LONGER A TARGET.
I must be. Death couldn't hurt this much.
--COUGH!--BATMAN? --COUGH!--
ARE YOU OKAY?
BATMAN?

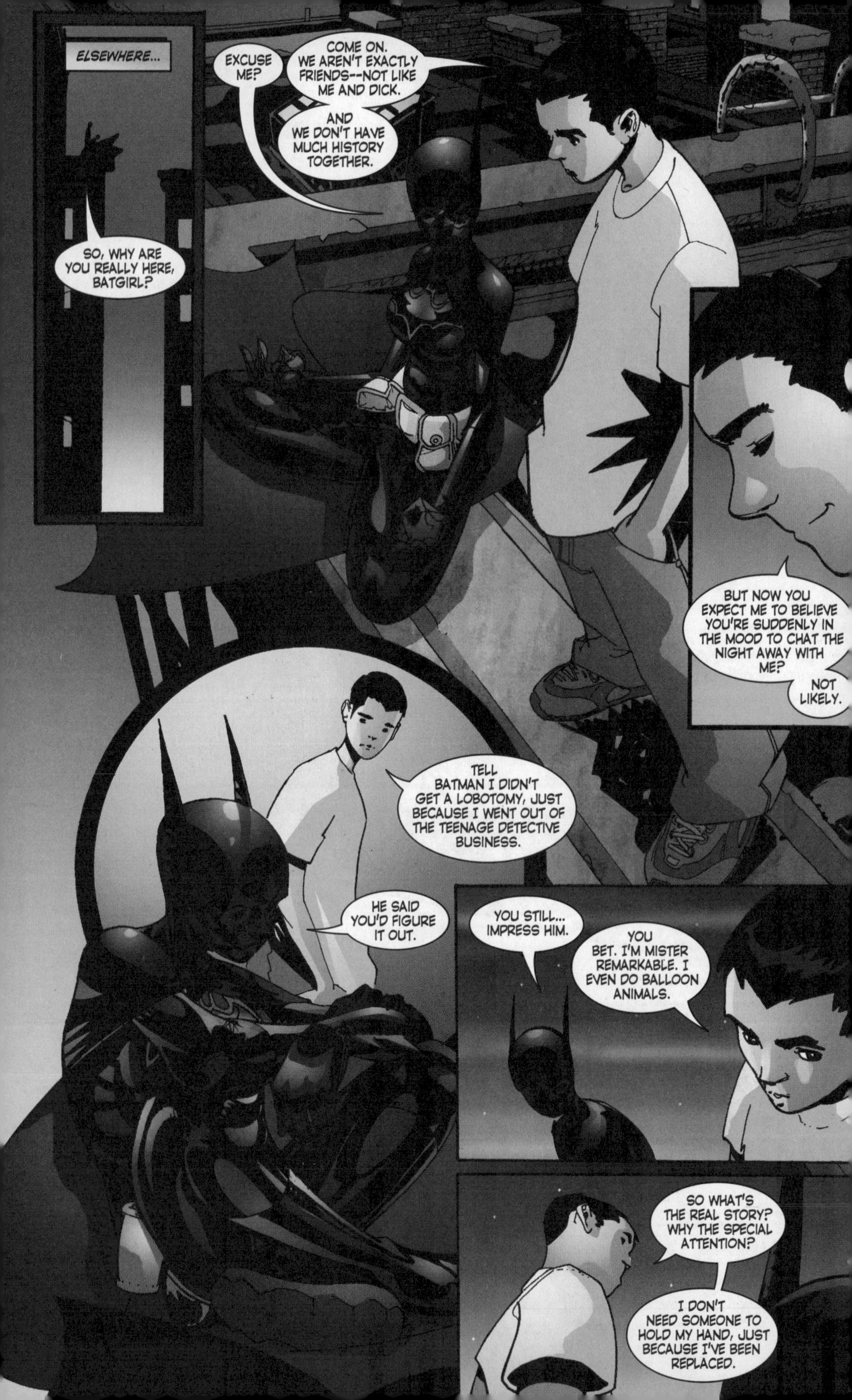
ELSEWHERE...
SO, WHY ARE YOU REALLY HERE, BATGIRL?
EXCUSE ME?
COME ON. WE AREN'T EXACTLY FRIENDS--NOT LIKE ME AND DICK.
AND WE DON'T HAVE MUCH HISTORY TOGETHER.
BUT NOW YOU EXPECT ME TO BELIEVE YOU'RE SUDDENLY IN THE MOOD TO CHAT THE NIGHT AWAY WITH ME?
NOT LIKELY.
TELL BATMAN I DIDN'T GET A LOBOTOMY, JUST BECAUSE I WENT OUT OF THE TEENAGE DETECTIVE BUSINESS.
HE SAID YOU'D FIGURE IT OUT.
YOU STILL... IMPRESS HIM.
YOU BET. I'M MISTER REMARKABLE. I EVEN DO BALLOON ANIMALS.
SO WHAT'S THE REAL STORY? WHY THE SPECIAL ATTENTION?
I DON'T NEED SOMEONE TO HOLD MY HAND, JUST BECAUSE I'VE BEEN REPLACED.

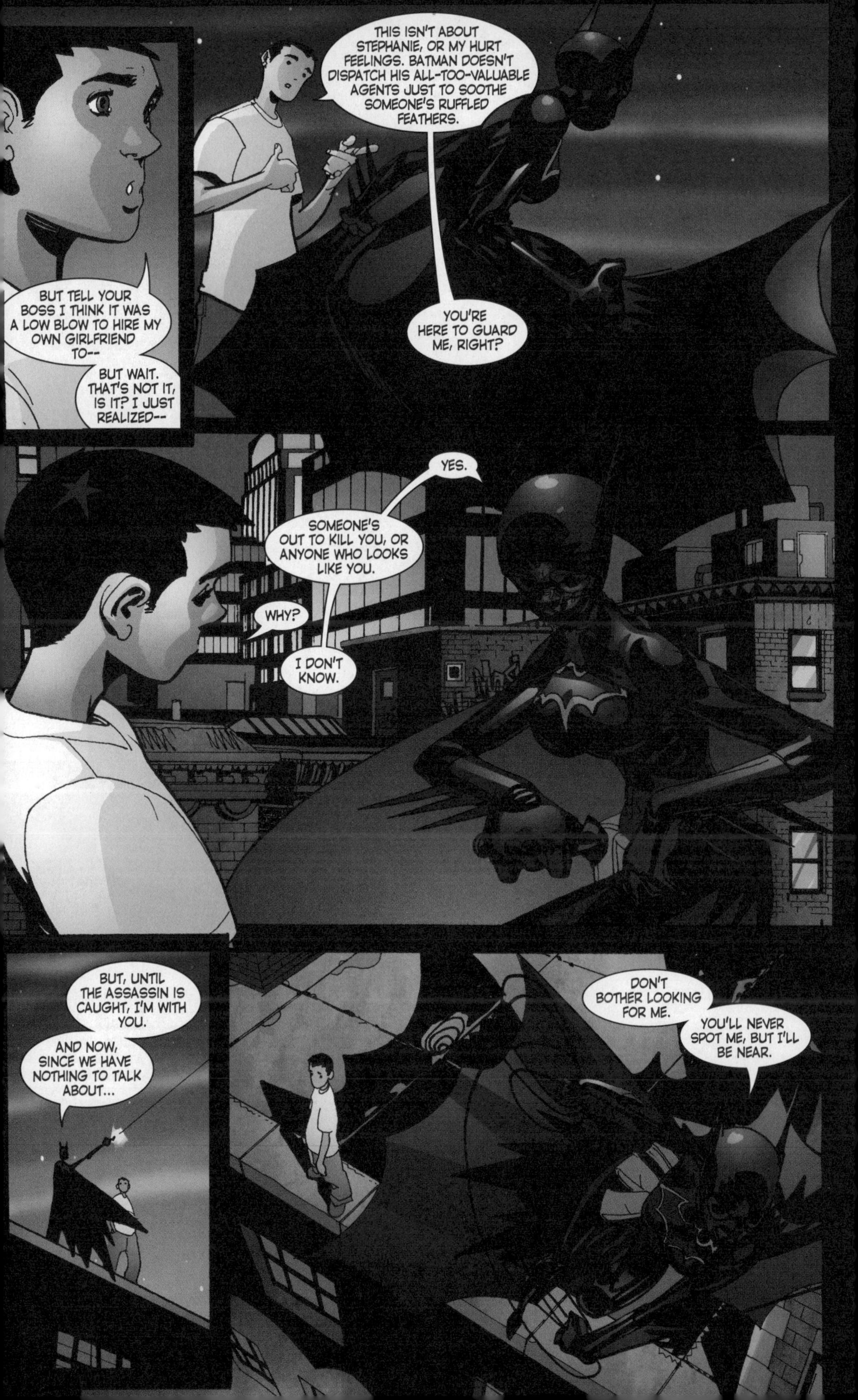
BUT TELL YOUR BOSS I THINK IT WAS A LOW BLOW TO HIRE MY OWN GIRLFRIEND TO--
BUT WAIT. THAT'S NOT IT, IS IT? I JUST REALIZED--
THIS ISN'T ABOUT STEPHANIE, OR MY HURT FEELINGS. BATMAN DOESN'T DISPATCH HIS ALL-TOO-VALUABLE AGENTS JUST TO SOOTHE SOMEONE'S RUFFLED FEATHERS.
YOU'RE HERE TO GUARD ME, RIGHT?
YES.
SOMEONE'S OUT TO KILL YOU, OR ANYONE WHO LOOKS LIKE YOU.
WHY?
I DON'T KNOW.
BUT, UNTIL THE ASSASSIN IS CAUGHT, I'M WITH YOU.
AND NOW, SINCE WE HAVE NOTHING TO TALK ABOUT...
DON'T BOTHER LOOKING FOR ME.
YOU'LL NEVER SPOT ME, BUT I'LL BE NEAR.

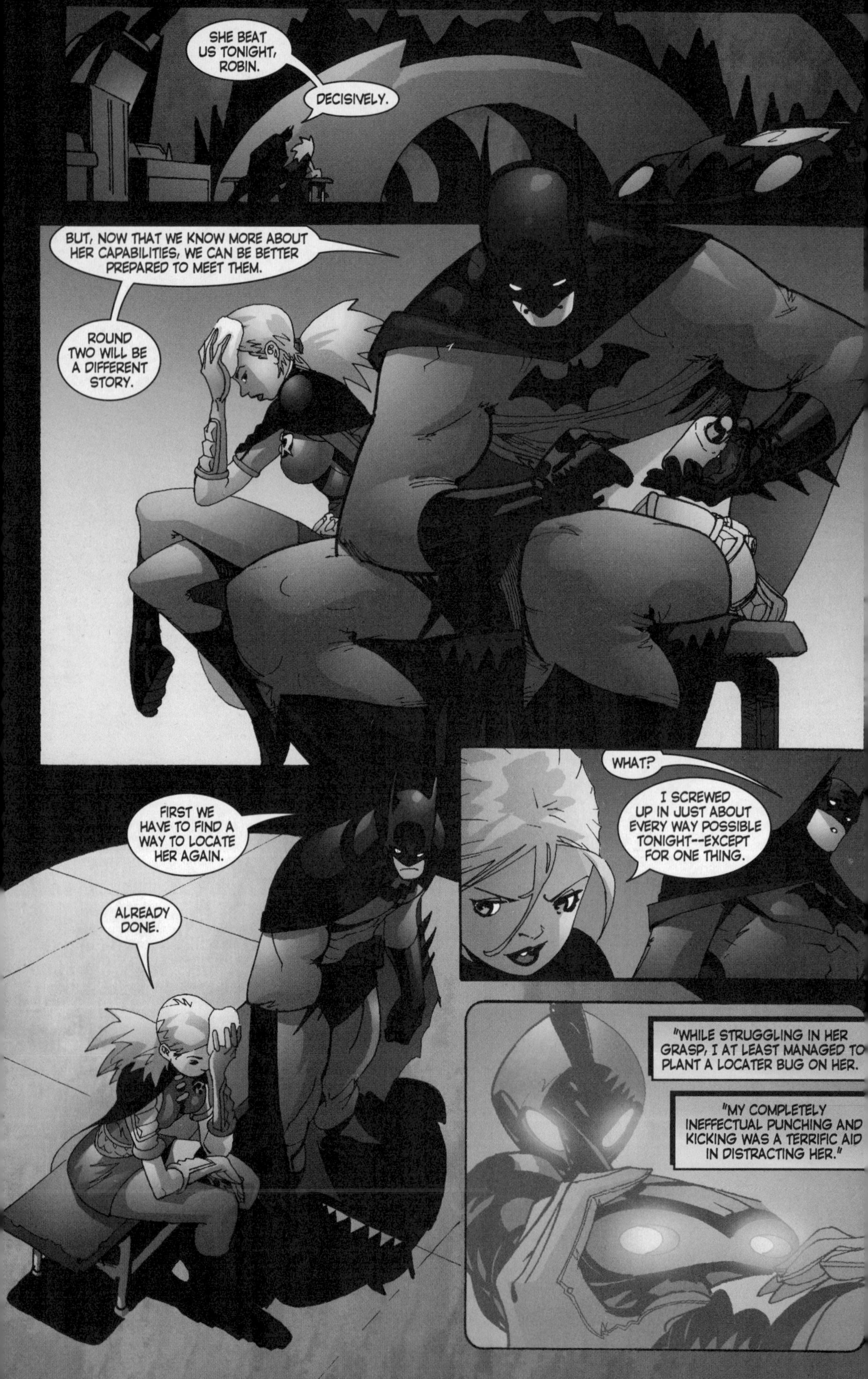
SHE BEAT US TONIGHT, ROBIN.
DECISIVELY.
BUT, NOW THAT WE KNOW MORE ABOUT HER CAPABILITIES, WE CAN BE BETTER PREPARED TO MEET THEM.
ROUND TWO WILL BE A DIFFERENT STORY.
FIRST WE HAVE TO FIND A WAY TO LOCATE HER AGAIN.
ALREADY DONE.
WHAT?
I SCREWED UP IN JUST ABOUT EVERY WAY POSSIBLE TONIGHT--EXCEPT FOR ONE THING.
"WHILE STRUGGLING IN HER GRASP, I AT LEAST MANAGED TO PLANT A LOCATER BUG ON HER.
"MY COMPLETELY INEFFECTUAL PUNCHING AND KICKING WAS A TERRIFIC AID IN DISTRACTING HER."

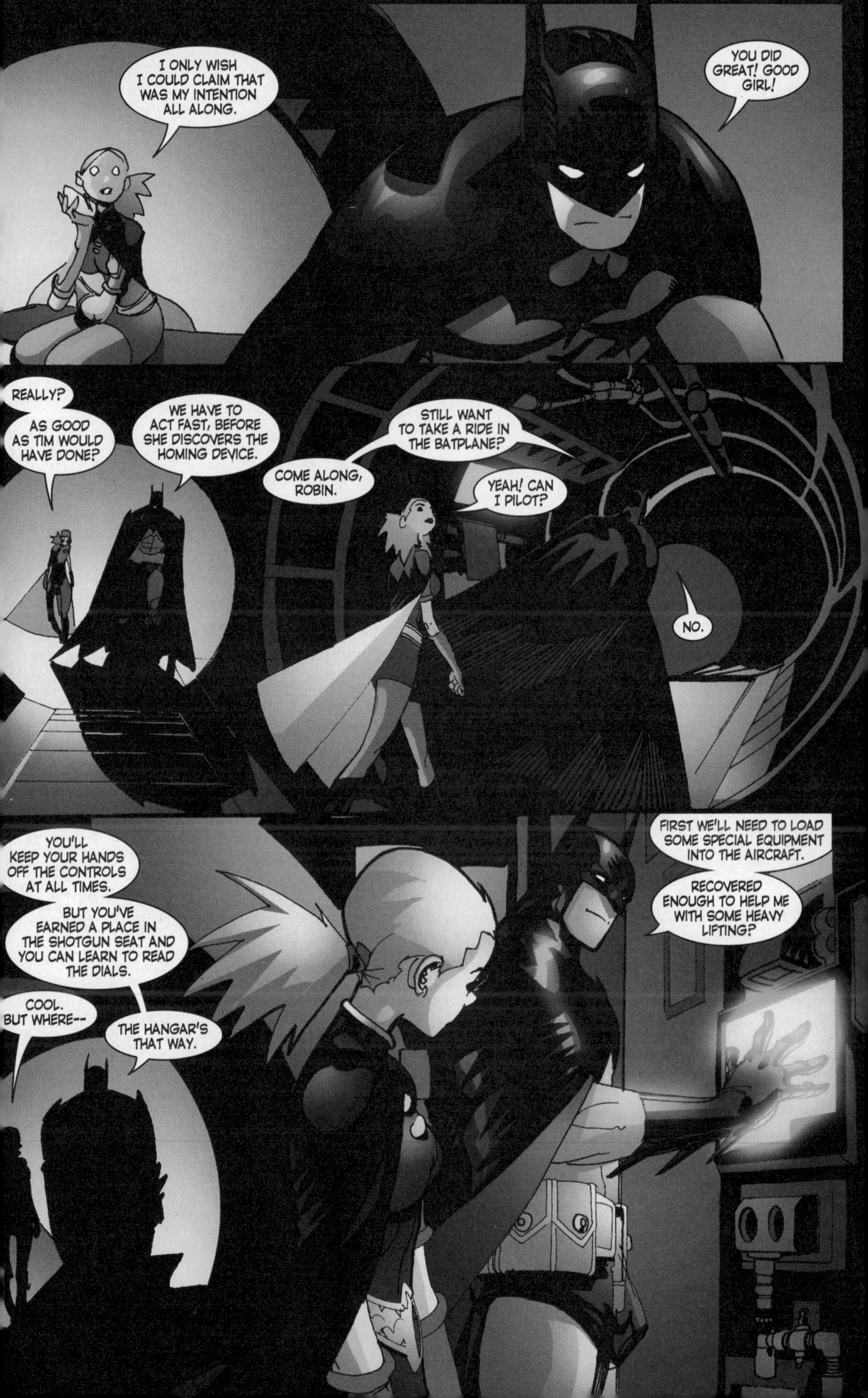
I ONLY WISH I COULD CLAIM THAT WAS MY INTENTION ALL ALONG.
YOU DID GREAT! GOOD GIRL!
REALLY?
AS GOOD AS TIM WOULD HAVE DONE?
WE HAVE TO ACT FAST, BEFORE SHE DISCOVERS THE HOMING DEVICE.
STILL WANT TO TAKE A RIDE IN THE BATPLANE?
COME ALONG, ROBIN.
YEAH! CAN I PILOT?
NO.
YOU'LL KEEP YOUR HANDS OFF THE CONTROLS AT ALL TIMES.
BUT YOU'VE EARNED A PLACE IN THE SHOTGUN SEAT AND YOU CAN LEARN TO READ THE DIALS.
COOL. BUT WHERE--
THE HANGAR'S THAT WAY.
FIRST WE'LL NEED TO LOAD SOME SPECIAL EQUIPMENT INTO THE AIRCRAFT.
RECOVERED ENOUGH TO HELP ME WITH SOME HEAVY LIFTING?

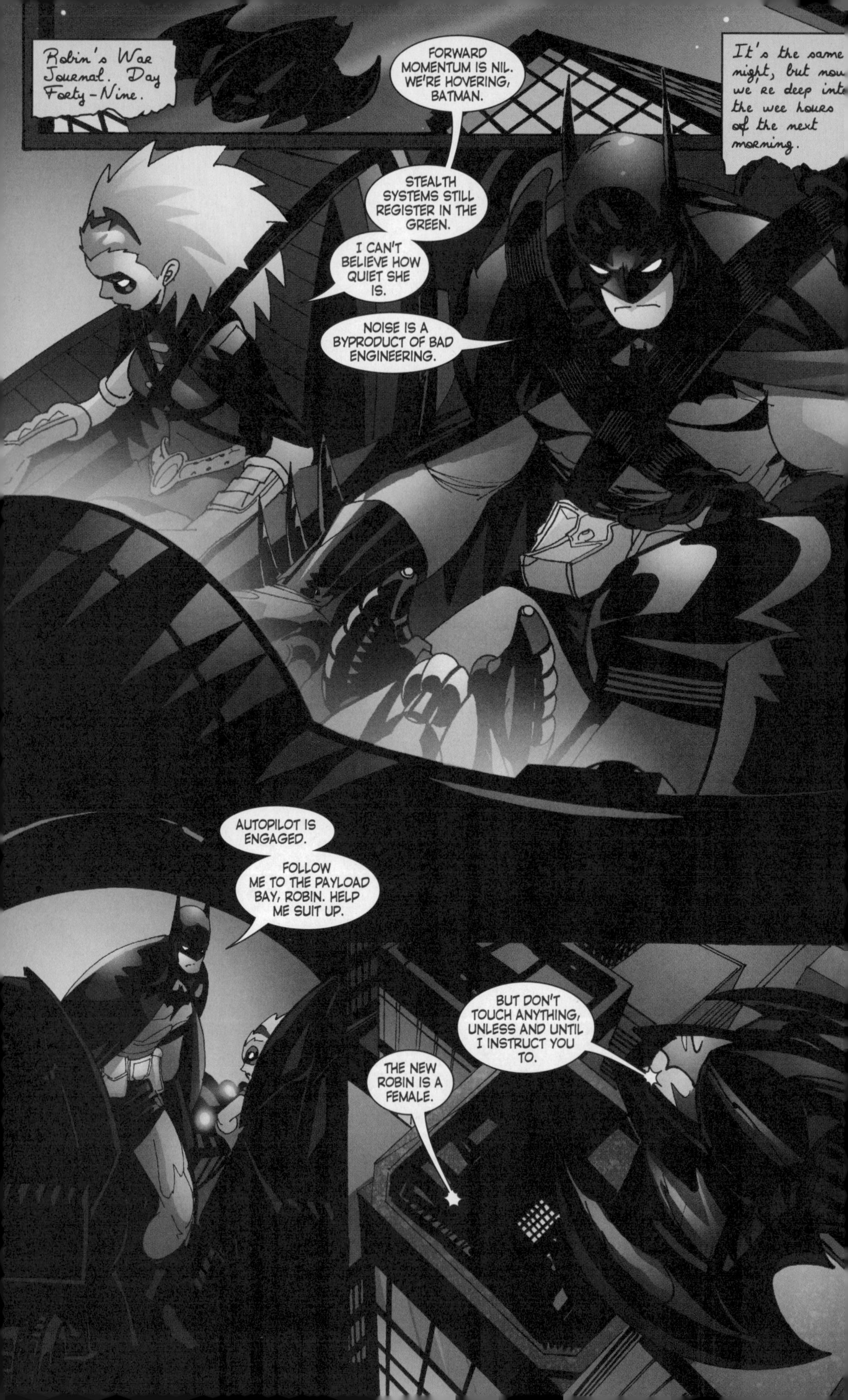
Robin's War Journal. Day Forty-Nine.
It's the same night, but now we're deep into the wee hours of the next morning.
FORWARD MOMENTUM IS NIL. WE'RE HOVERING, BATMAN.
STEALTH SYSTEMS STILL REGISTER IN THE GREEN.
I CAN'T BELIEVE HOW QUIET SHE IS.
NOISE IS A BYPRODUCT OF BAD ENGINEERING.
AUTOPILOT IS ENGAGED.
FOLLOW ME TO THE PAYLOAD BAY, ROBIN. HELP ME SUIT UP.
BUT DON'T TOUCH ANYTHING, UNLESS AND UNTIL I INSTRUCT YOU TO.
THE NEW ROBIN IS A FEMALE.

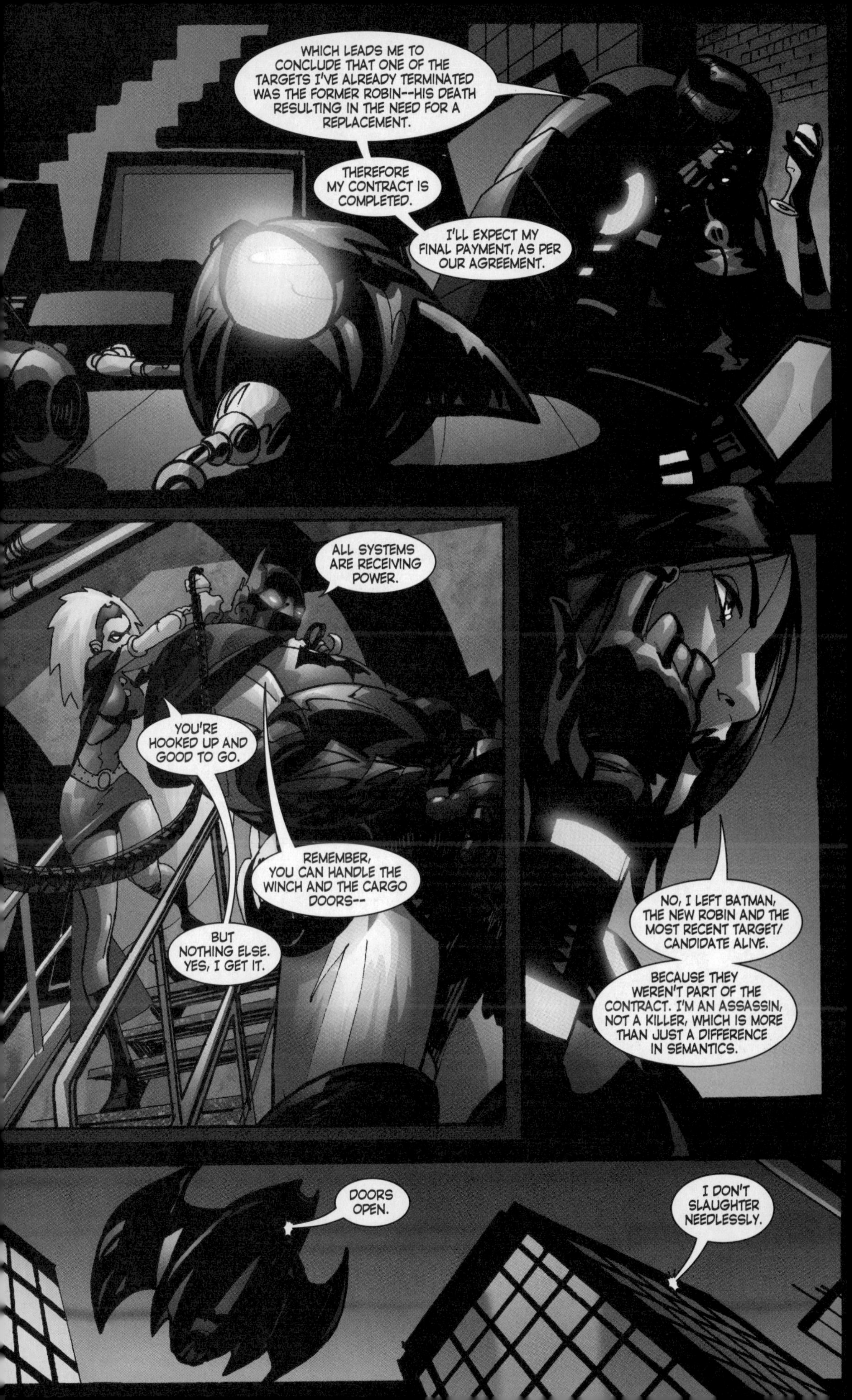
WHICH LEADS ME TO CONCLUDE THAT ONE OF THE TARGETS I'VE ALREADY TERMINATED WAS THE FORMER ROBIN--HIS DEATH RESULTING IN THE NEED FOR A REPLACEMENT.
THEREFORE MY CONTRACT IS COMPLETED.
I'LL EXPECT MY FINAL PAYMENT, AS PER OUR AGREEMENT.
ALL SYSTEMS ARE RECEIVING POWER.
YOU'RE HOOKED UP AND GOOD TO GO.
REMEMBER, YOU CAN HANDLE THE WINCH AND THE CARGO DOORS--
BUT NOTHING ELSE. YES, I GET IT.
NO, I LEFT BATMAN, THE NEW ROBIN AND THE MOST RECENT TARGET/ CANDIDATE ALIVE.
BECAUSE THEY WEREN'T PART OF THE CONTRACT. I'M AN ASSASSIN, NOT A KILLER, WHICH IS MORE THAN JUST A DIFFERENCE IN SEMANTICS.
DOORS OPEN.
I DON'T SLAUGHTER NEEDLESSLY.

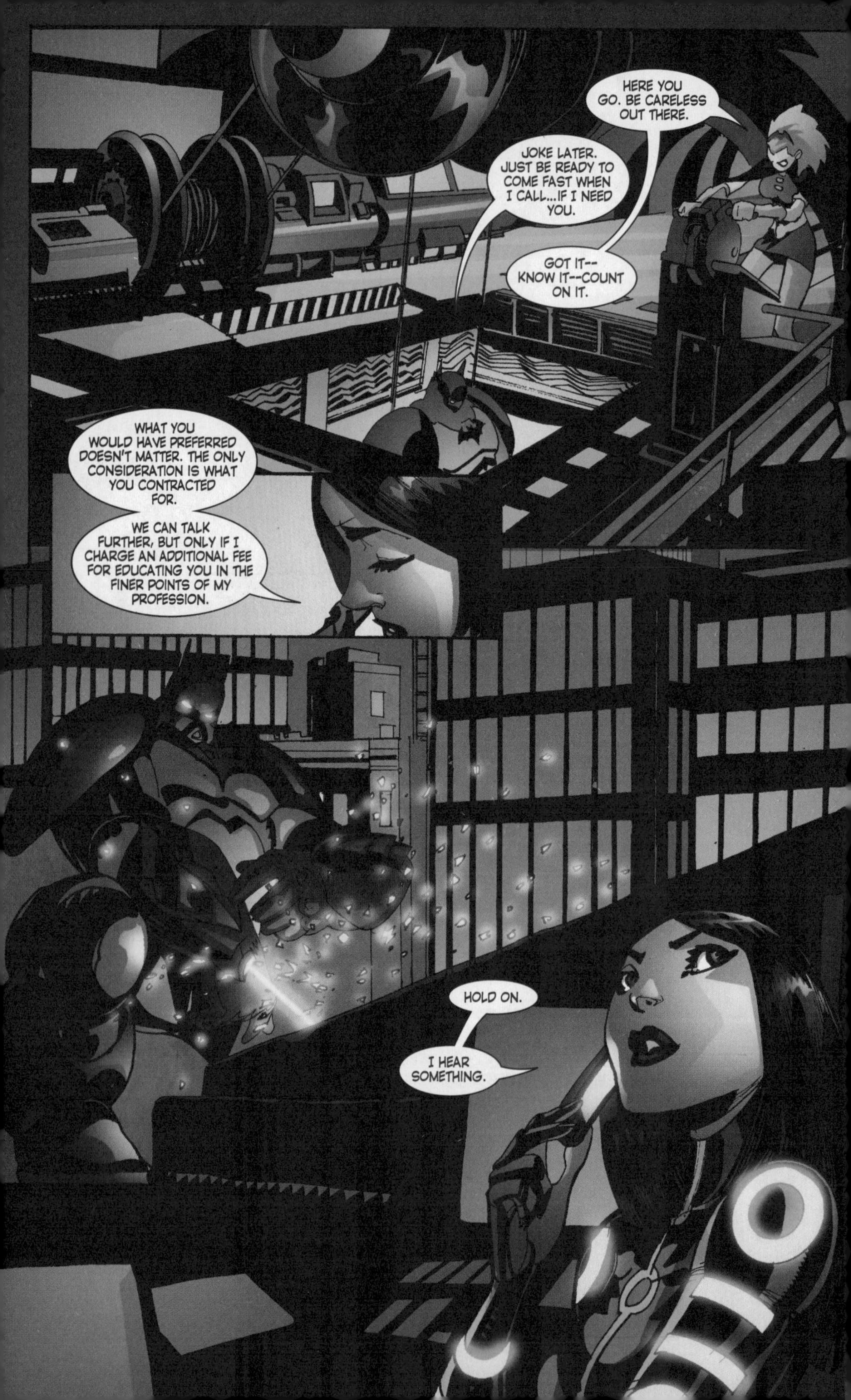
HERE YOU GO. BE CARELESS OUT THERE.
JOKE LATER. JUST BE READY TO COME FAST WHEN I CALL...IF I NEED YOU.
GOT IT--KNOW IT--COUNT ON IT.
WHAT YOU WOULD HAVE PREFERRED DOESN'T MATTER. THE ONLY CONSIDERATION IS WHAT YOU CONTRACTED FOR.
WE CAN TALK FURTHER, BUT ONLY IF I CHARGE AN ADDITIONAL FEE FOR EDUCATING YOU IN THE FINER POINTS OF MY PROFESSION.
HOLD ON.
I HEAR SOMETHING.

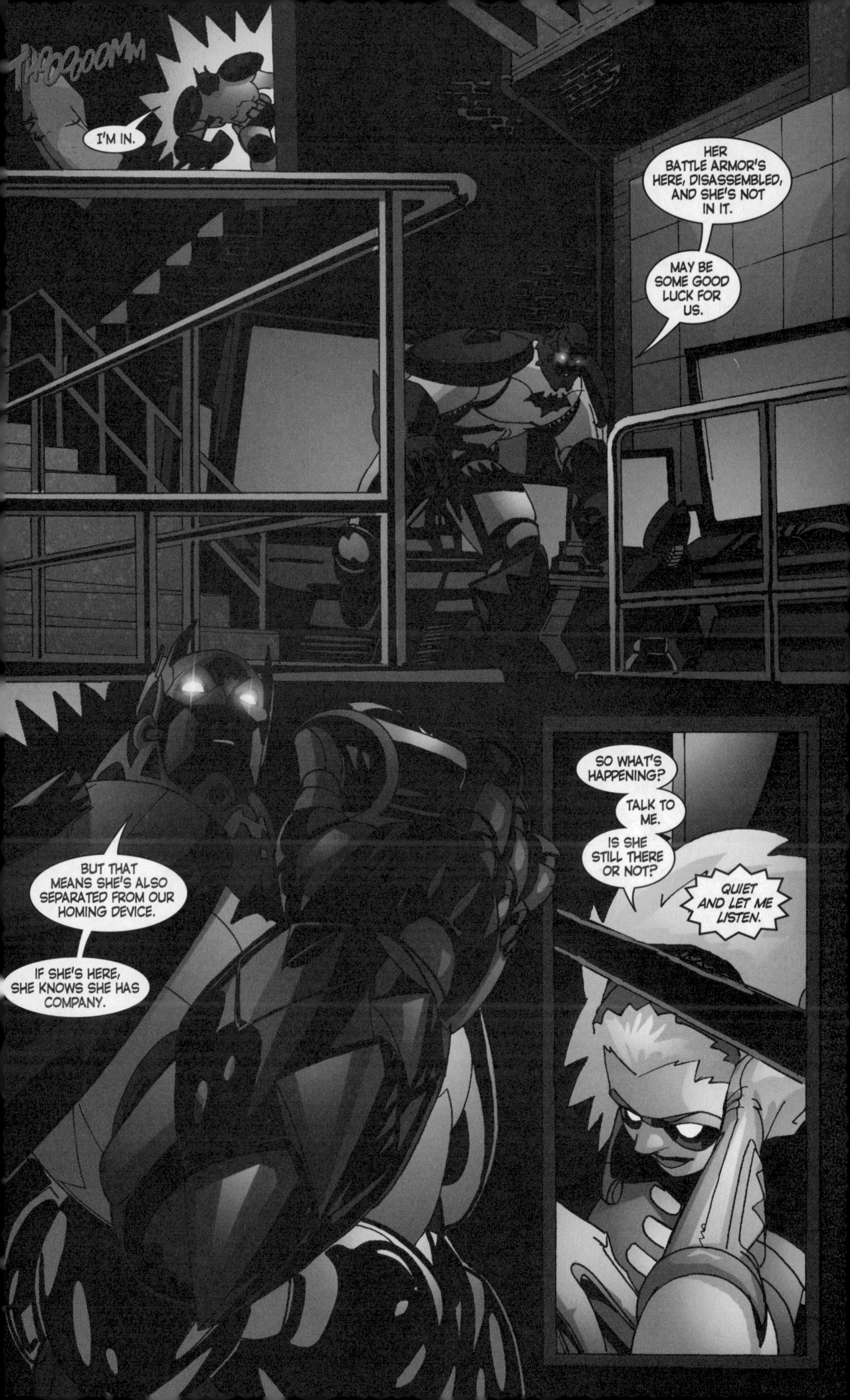
THROOOOMM
I'M IN.
HER BATTLE ARMOR'S HERE, DISASSEMBLED, AND SHE'S NOT IN IT.
MAY BE SOME GOOD LUCK FOR US.
BUT THAT MEANS SHE'S ALSO SEPARATED FROM OUR HOMING DEVICE.
IF SHE'S HERE, SHE KNOWS SHE HAS COMPANY.
SO WHAT'S HAPPENING?
TALK TO ME.
IS SHE STILL THERE OR NOT?
QUIET AND LET ME LISTEN.

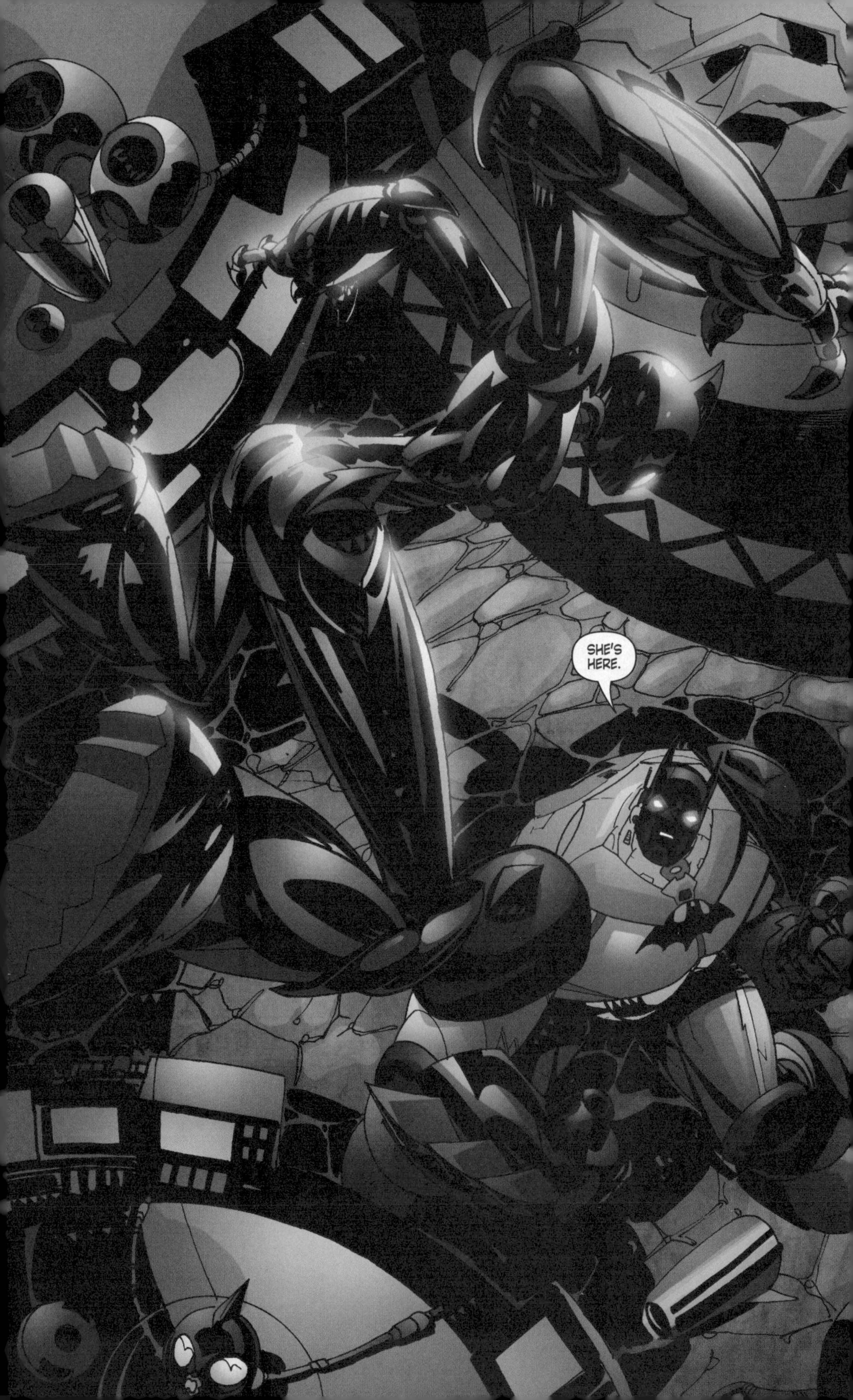
SHE'S HERE.

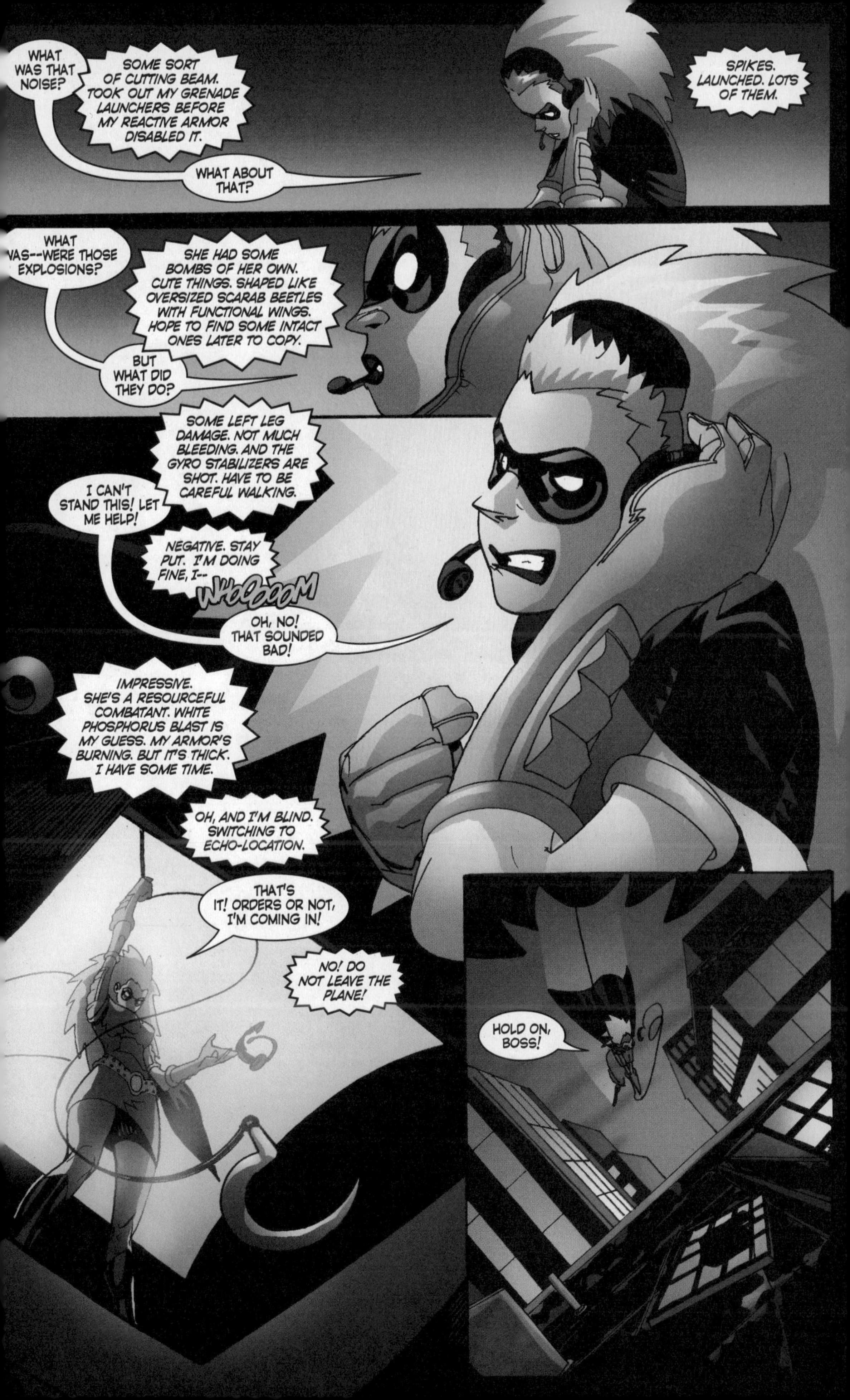
WHAT WAS THAT NOISE?
SOME SORT OF CUTTING BEAM. TOOK OUT MY GRENADE LAUNCHERS BEFORE MY REACTIVE ARMOR DISABLED IT.
WHAT ABOUT THAT?
SPIKES. LAUNCHED. LOTS OF THEM.
WHAT WAS--WERE THOSE EXPLOSIONS?
SHE HAD SOME BOMBS OF HER OWN. CUTE THINGS. SHAPED LIKE OVERSIZED SCARAB BEETLES WITH FUNCTIONAL WINGS. HOPE TO FIND SOME INTACT ONES LATER TO COPY.
BUT WHAT DID THEY DO?
SOME LEFT LEG DAMAGE. NOT MUCH BLEEDING. AND THE GYRO STABILIZERS ARE SHOT. HAVE TO BE CAREFUL WALKING.
I CAN'T STAND THIS! LET ME HELP!
NEGATIVE. STAY PUT. I'M DOING FINE, I--
WHOOOOOM
OH, NO! THAT SOUNDED BAD!
IMPRESSIVE. SHE'S A RESOURCEFUL COMBATANT. WHITE PHOSPHORUS BLAST IS MY GUESS. MY ARMOR'S BURNING. BUT IT'S THICK. I HAVE SOME TIME.
OH, AND I'M BLIND. SWITCHING TO ECHO-LOCATION.
THAT'S IT! ORDERS OR NOT, I'M COMING IN!
NO! DO NOT LEAVE THE PLANE!
HOLD ON, BOSS!

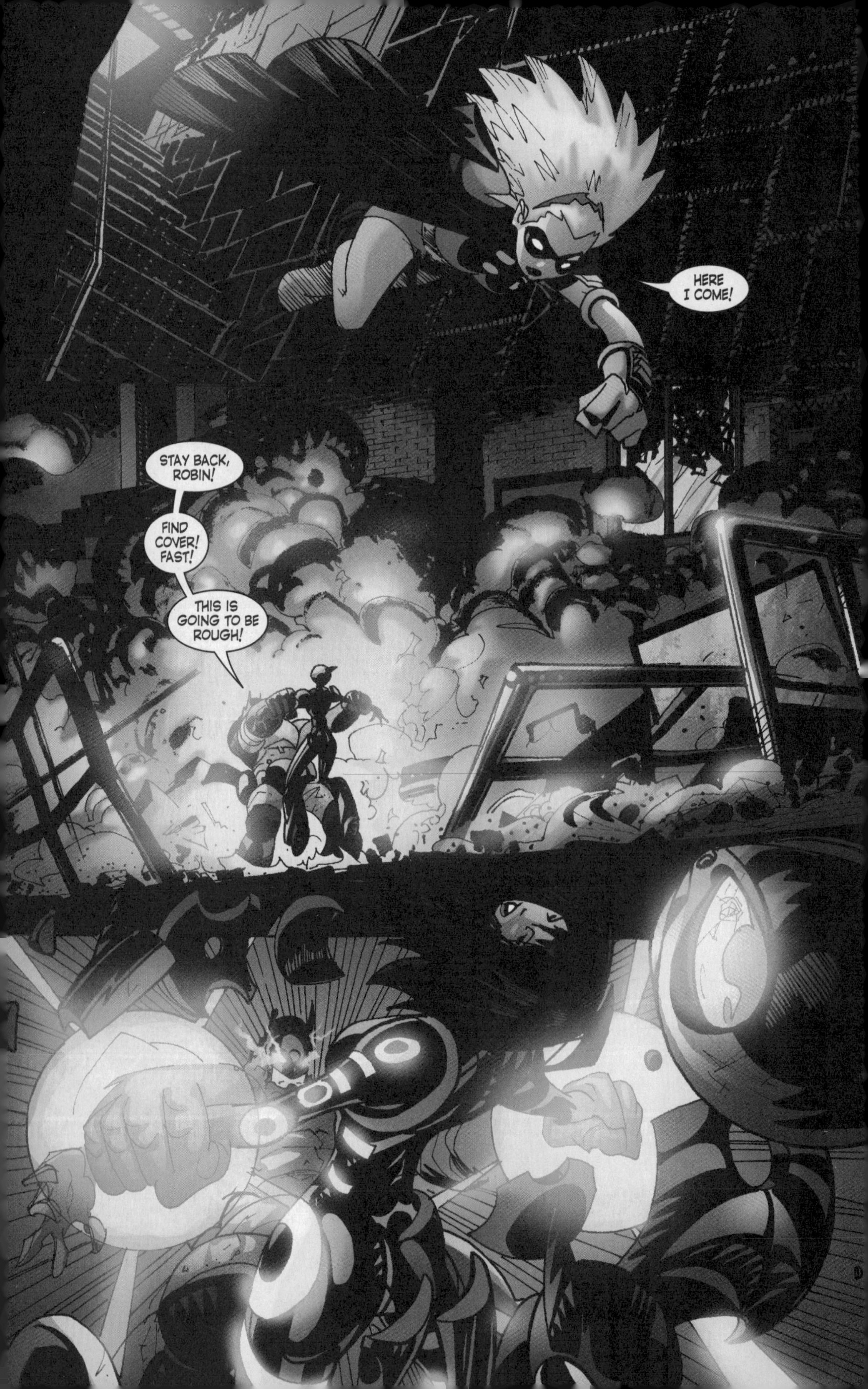
HERE I COME!
STAY BACK, ROBIN!
FIND COVER! FAST!
THIS IS GOING TO BE ROUGH!

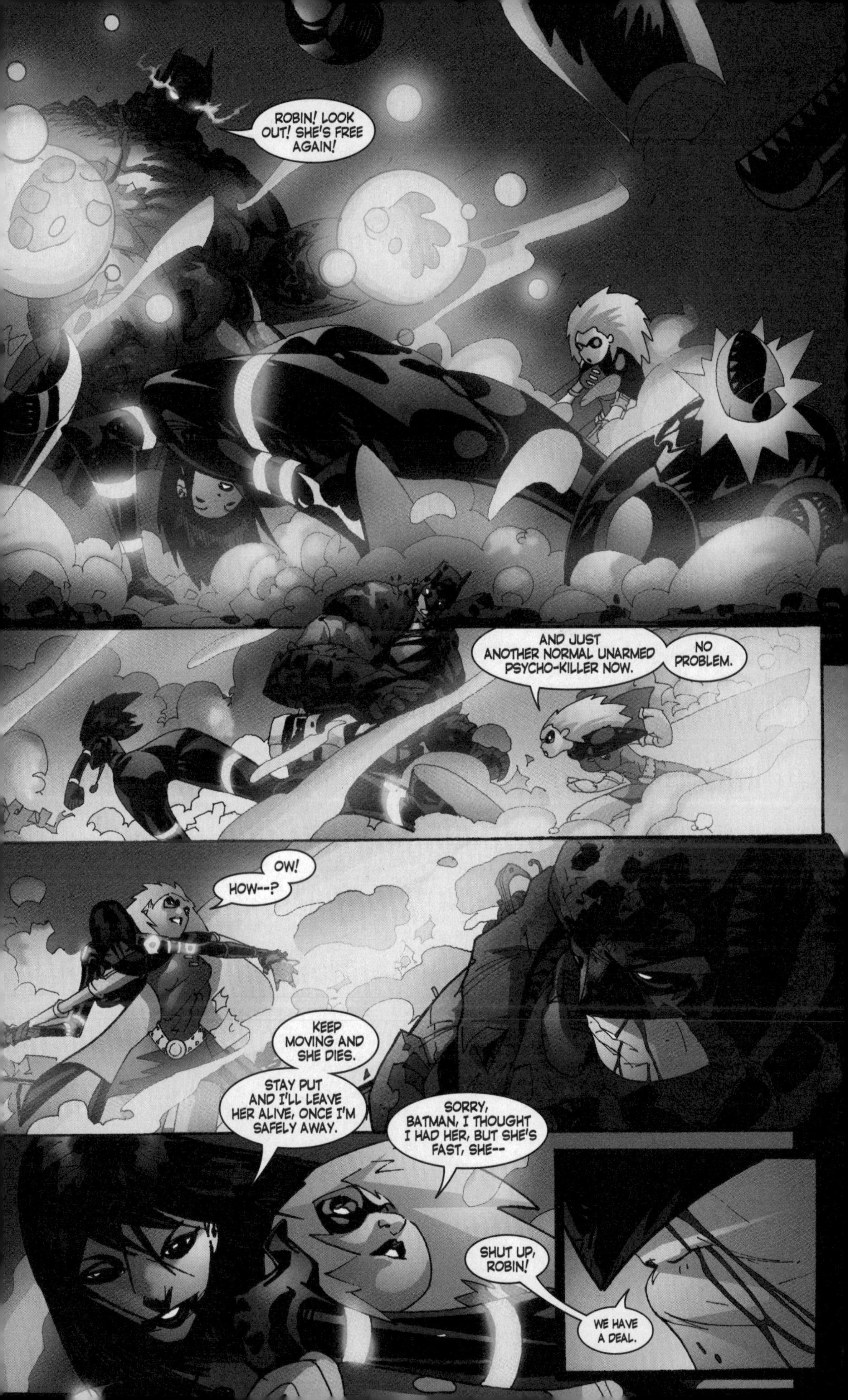
ROBIN! LOOK OUT! SHE'S FREE AGAIN!
AND JUST ANOTHER NORMAL UNARMED PSYCHO-KILLER NOW.
NO PROBLEM.
OW!
HOW--?
KEEP MOVING AND SHE DIES.
STAY PUT AND I'LL LEAVE HER ALIVE, ONCE I'M SAFELY AWAY.
SORRY, BATMAN, I THOUGHT I HAD HER, BUT SHE'S FAST, SHE--
SHUT UP, ROBIN!
WE HAVE A DEAL.

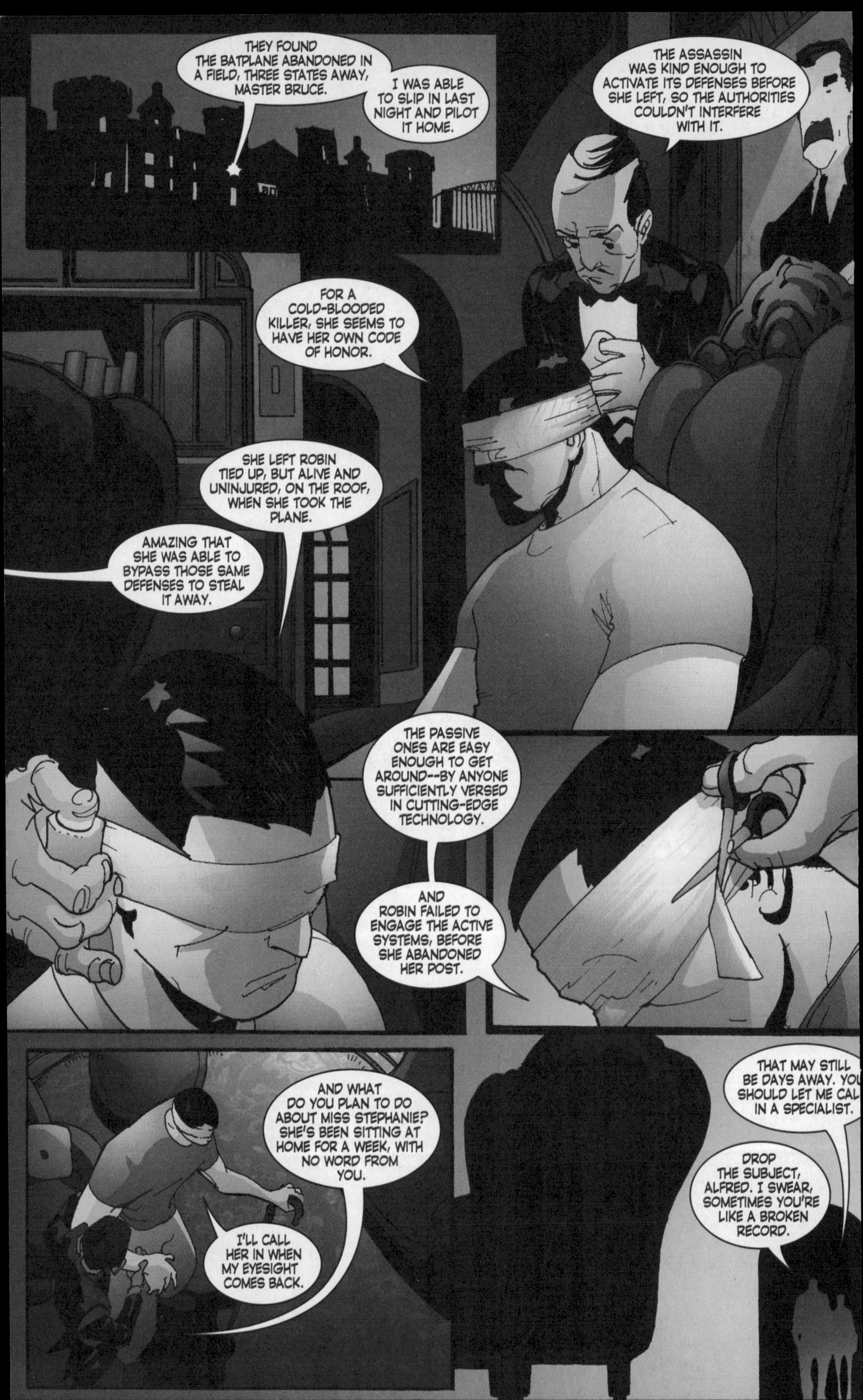
THEY FOUND THE BATPLANE ABANDONED IN A FIELD, THREE STATES AWAY, MASTER BRUCE.
I WAS ABLE TO SLIP IN LAST NIGHT AND PILOT IT HOME.
THE ASSASSIN WAS KIND ENOUGH TO ACTIVATE ITS DEFENSES BEFORE SHE LEFT, SO THE AUTHORITIES COULDN'T INTERFERE WITH IT.
FOR A COLD-BLOODED KILLER, SHE SEEMS TO HAVE HER OWN CODE OF HONOR.
SHE LEFT ROBIN TIED UP, BUT ALIVE AND UNINJURED, ON THE ROOF, WHEN SHE TOOK THE PLANE.
AMAZING THAT SHE WAS ABLE TO BYPASS THOSE SAME DEFENSES TO STEAL IT AWAY.
THE PASSIVE ONES ARE EASY ENOUGH TO GET AROUND--BY ANYONE SUFFICIENTLY VERSED IN CUTTING-EDGE TECHNOLOGY.
AND ROBIN FAILED TO ENGAGE THE ACTIVE SYSTEMS, BEFORE SHE ABANDONED HER POST.
AND WHAT DO YOU PLAN TO DO ABOUT MISS STEPHANIE? SHE'S BEEN SITTING AT HOME FOR A WEEK, WITH NO WORD FROM YOU.
I'LL CALL HER IN WHEN MY EYESIGHT COMES BACK.
THAT MAY STILL BE DAYS AWAY. YOU SHOULD LET ME CAL IN A SPECIALIST.
DROP THE SUBJECT, ALFRED. I SWEAR, SOMETIMES YOU'RE LIKE A BROKEN RECORD.

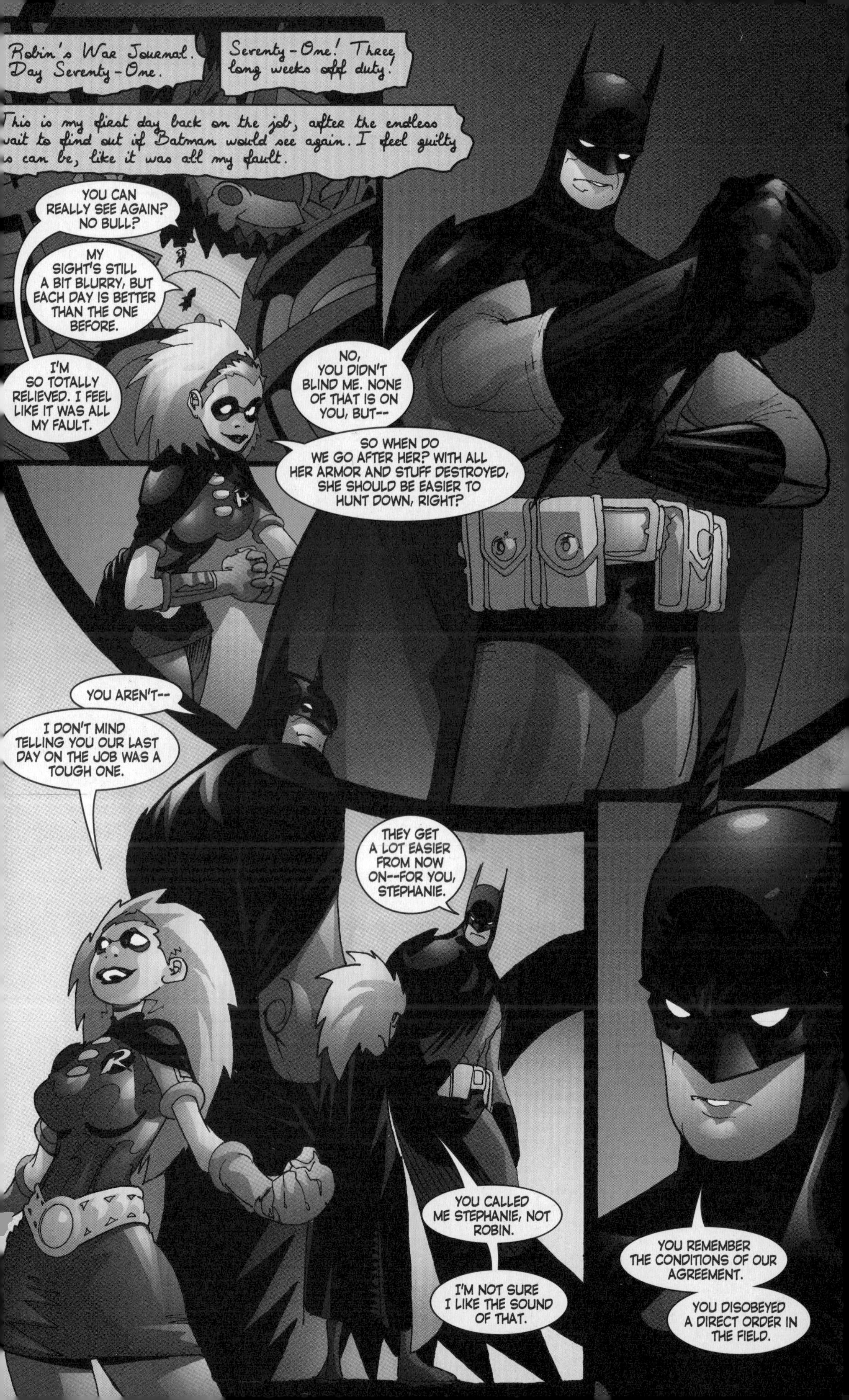
Robin's War Journal. Day Seventy-One.
Seventy-One! Three long weeks off duty!
This is my first day back on the job, after the endless wait to find out if Batman would see again. I feel guilty as can be, like it was all my fault.
YOU CAN REALLY SEE AGAIN? NO BULL?
MY SIGHT'S STILL A BIT BLURRY, BUT EACH DAY IS BETTER THAN THE ONE BEFORE.
I'M SO TOTALLY RELIEVED. I FEEL LIKE IT WAS ALL MY FAULT.
NO, YOU DIDN'T BLIND ME. NONE OF THAT IS ON YOU, BUT--
SO WHEN DO WE GO AFTER HER? WITH ALL HER ARMOR AND STUFF DESTROYED, SHE SHOULD BE EASIER TO HUNT DOWN, RIGHT?
YOU AREN'T--
I DON'T MIND TELLING YOU OUR LAST DAY ON THE JOB WAS A TOUGH ONE.
THEY GET A LOT EASIER FROM NOW ON--FOR YOU, STEPHANIE.
YOU CALLED ME STEPHANIE, NOT ROBIN.
I'M NOT SURE I LIKE THE SOUND OF THAT.
YOU REMEMBER THE CONDITIONS OF OUR AGREEMENT.
YOU DISOBEYED A DIRECT ORDER IN THE FIELD.

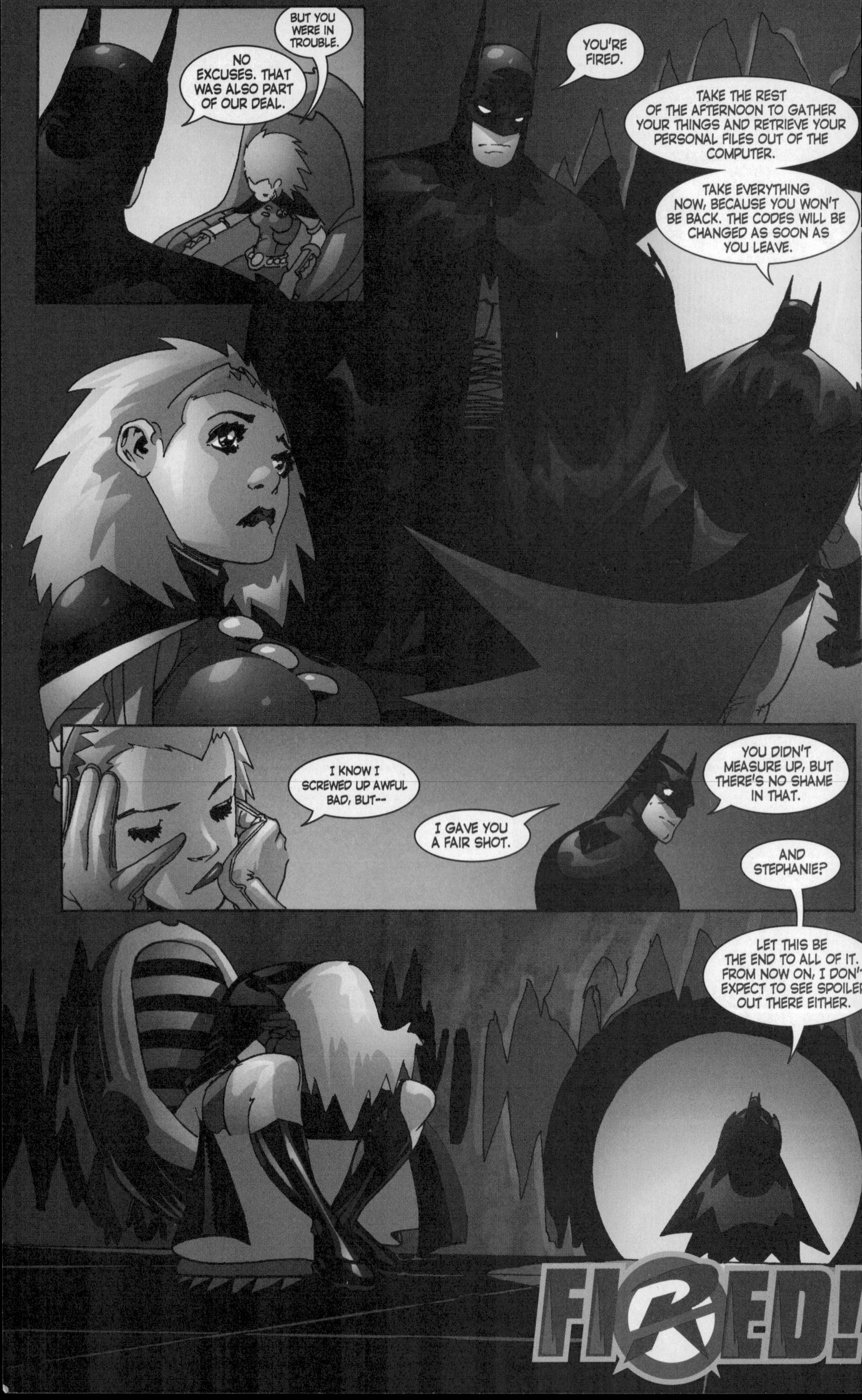

BUT YOU WERE IN TROUBLE.
NO EXCUSES. THAT WAS ALSO PART OF OUR DEAL.
YOU'RE FIRED.
TAKE THE REST OF THE AFTERNOON TO GATHER YOUR THINGS AND RETRIEVE YOUR PERSONAL FILES OUT OF THE COMPUTER.
TAKE EVERYTHING NOW, BECAUSE YOU WON'T BE BACK. THE CODES WILL BE CHANGED AS SOON AS YOU LEAVE.
I KNOW I SCREWED UP AWFUL BAD, BUT--
I GAVE YOU A FAIR SHOT.
YOU DIDN'T MEASURE UP, BUT THERE'S NO SHAME IN THAT.
AND STEPHANIE?
LET THIS BE THE END TO ALL OF IT.
FIRED!

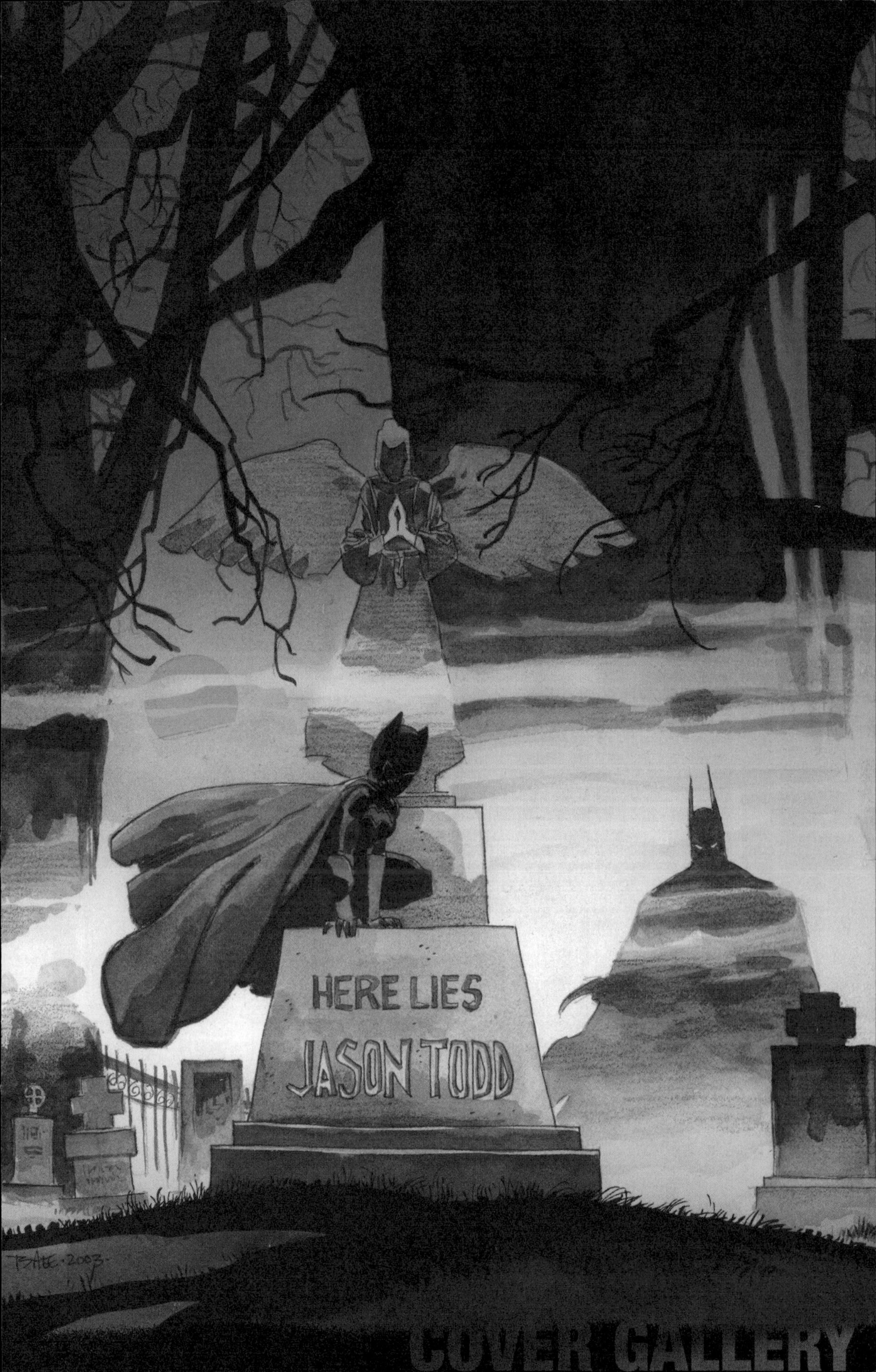
HERE LIES
JASON TODD
BALE · 2003

COVER GALLERY

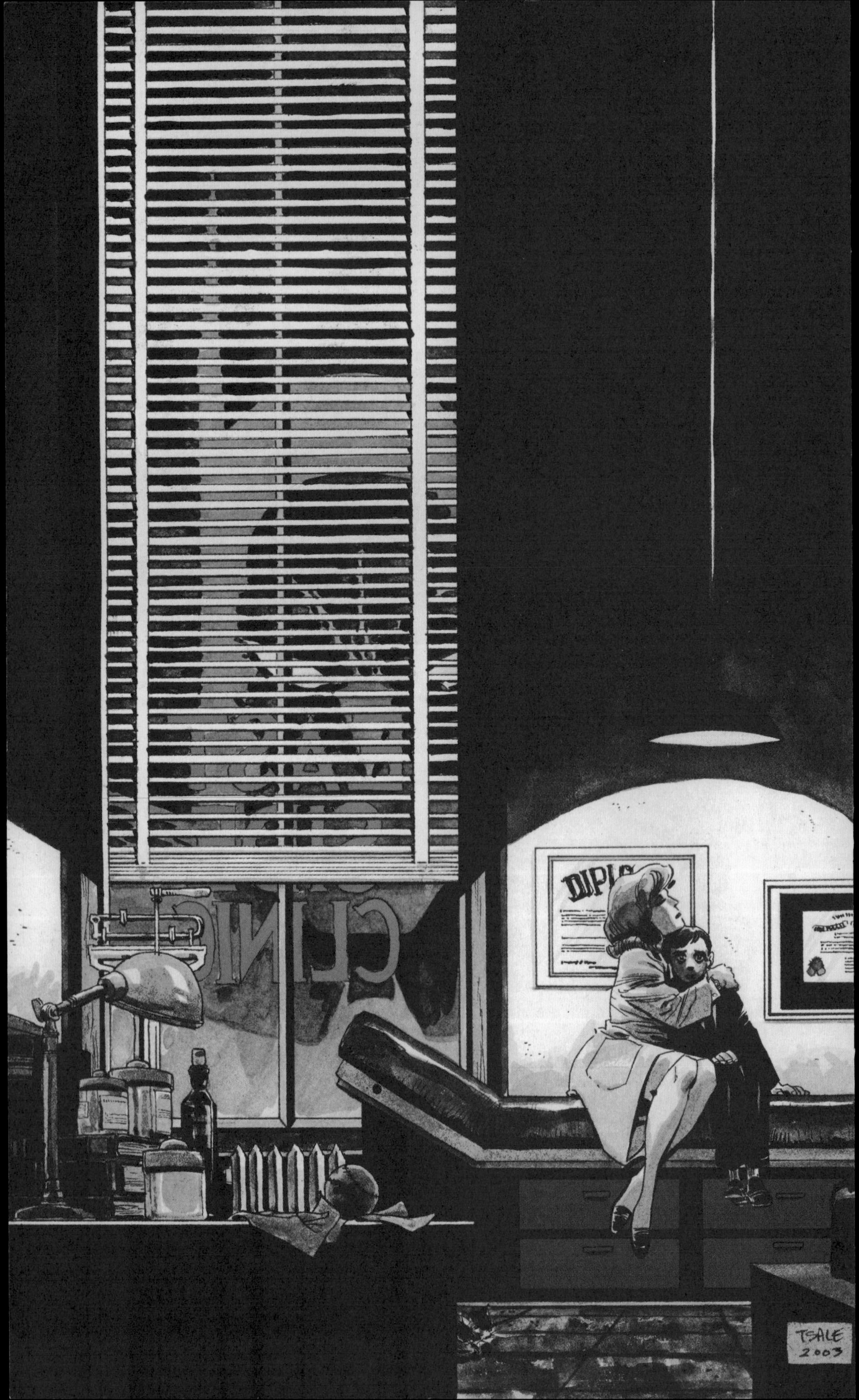
TSALE
2003

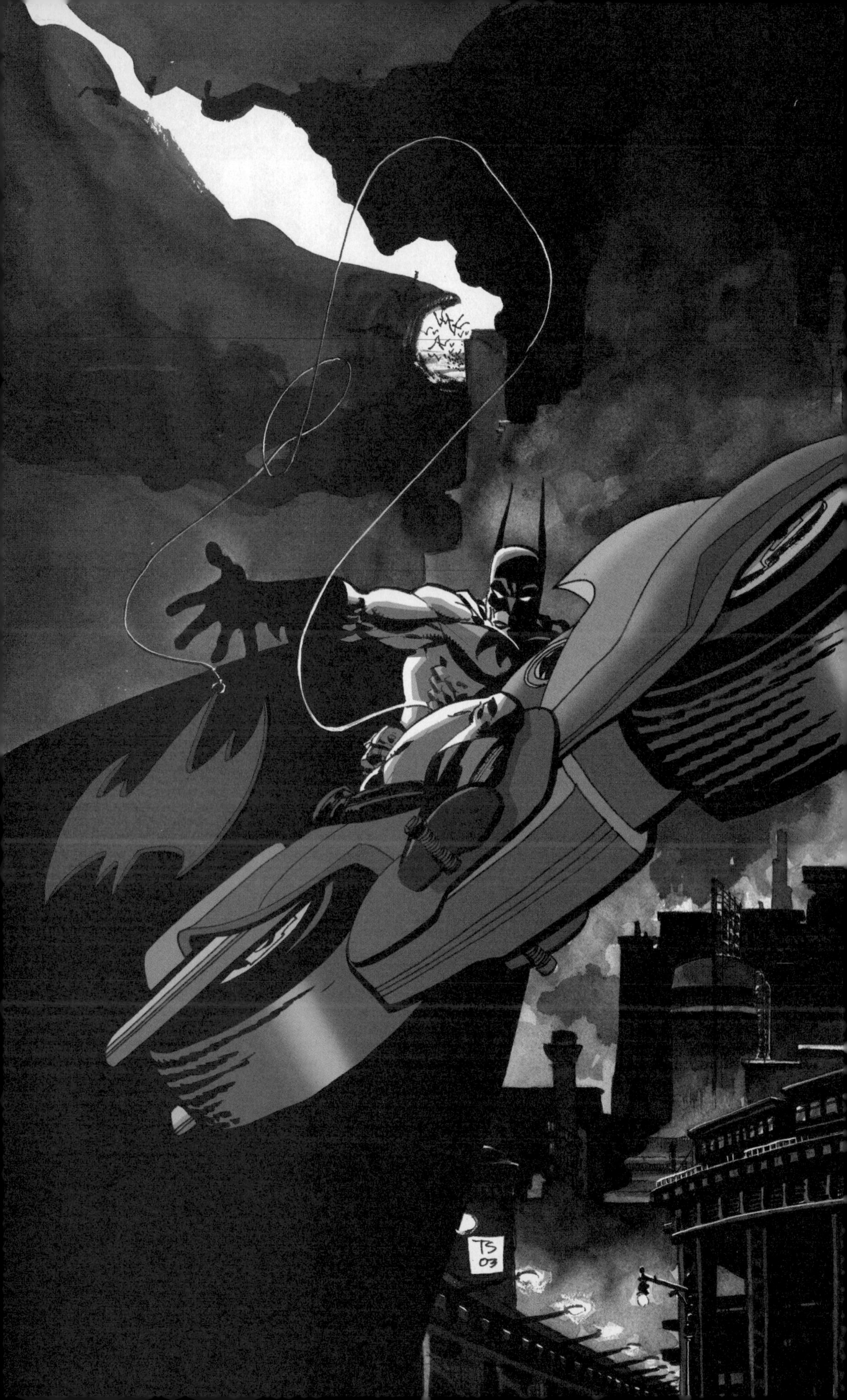

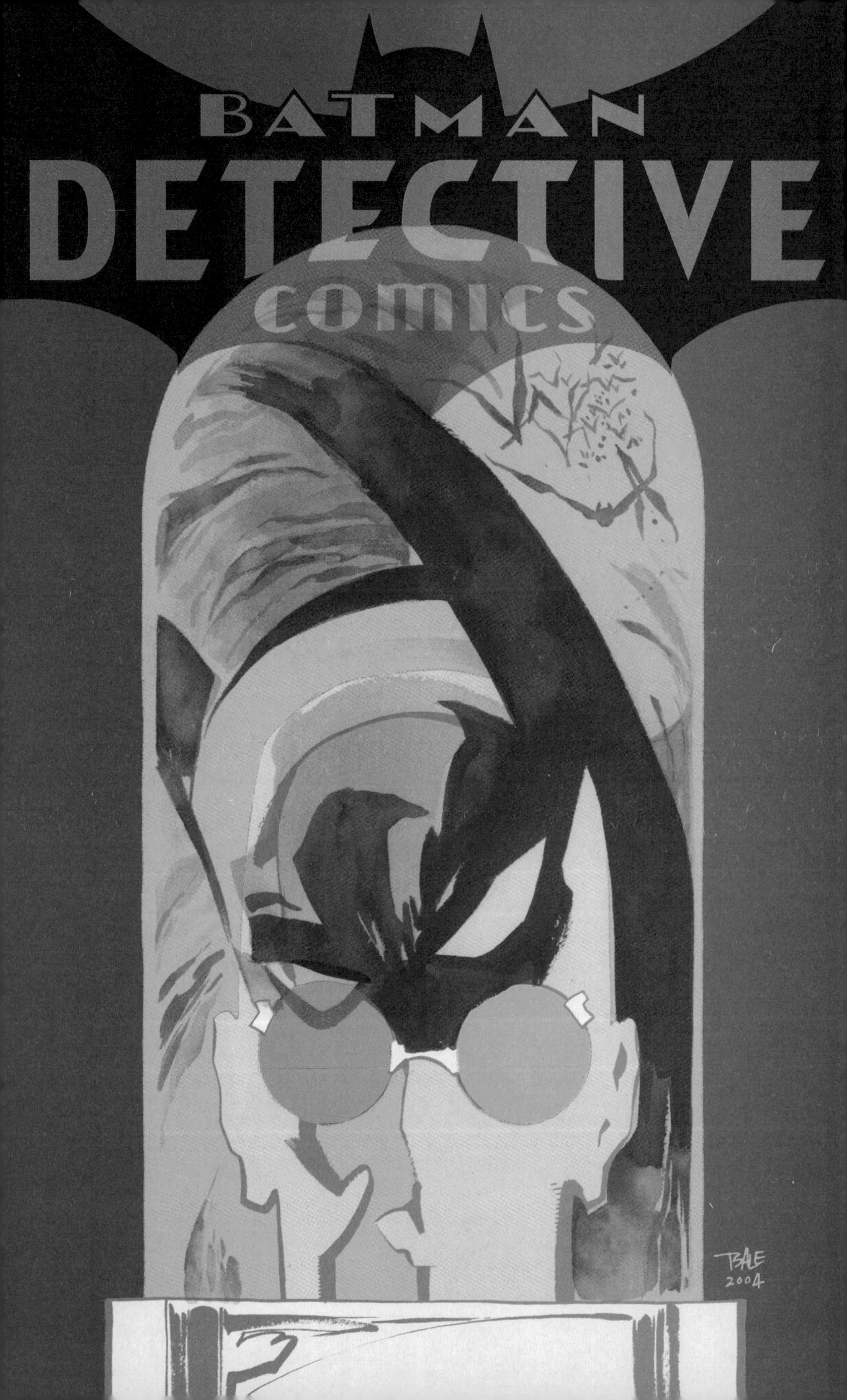
BATMAN
DETECTIVE
COMICS
TBALE
2004

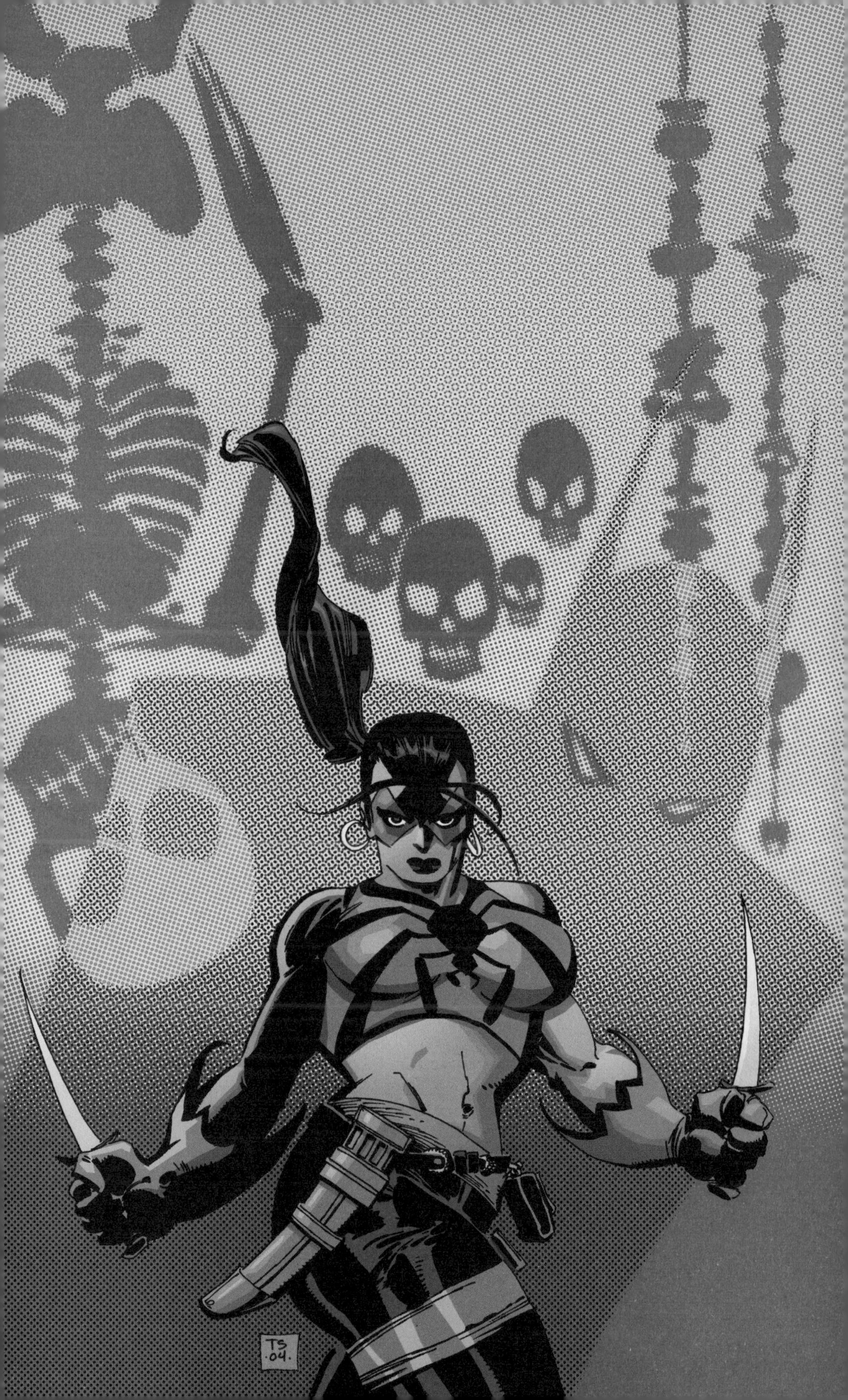
TS
.04.

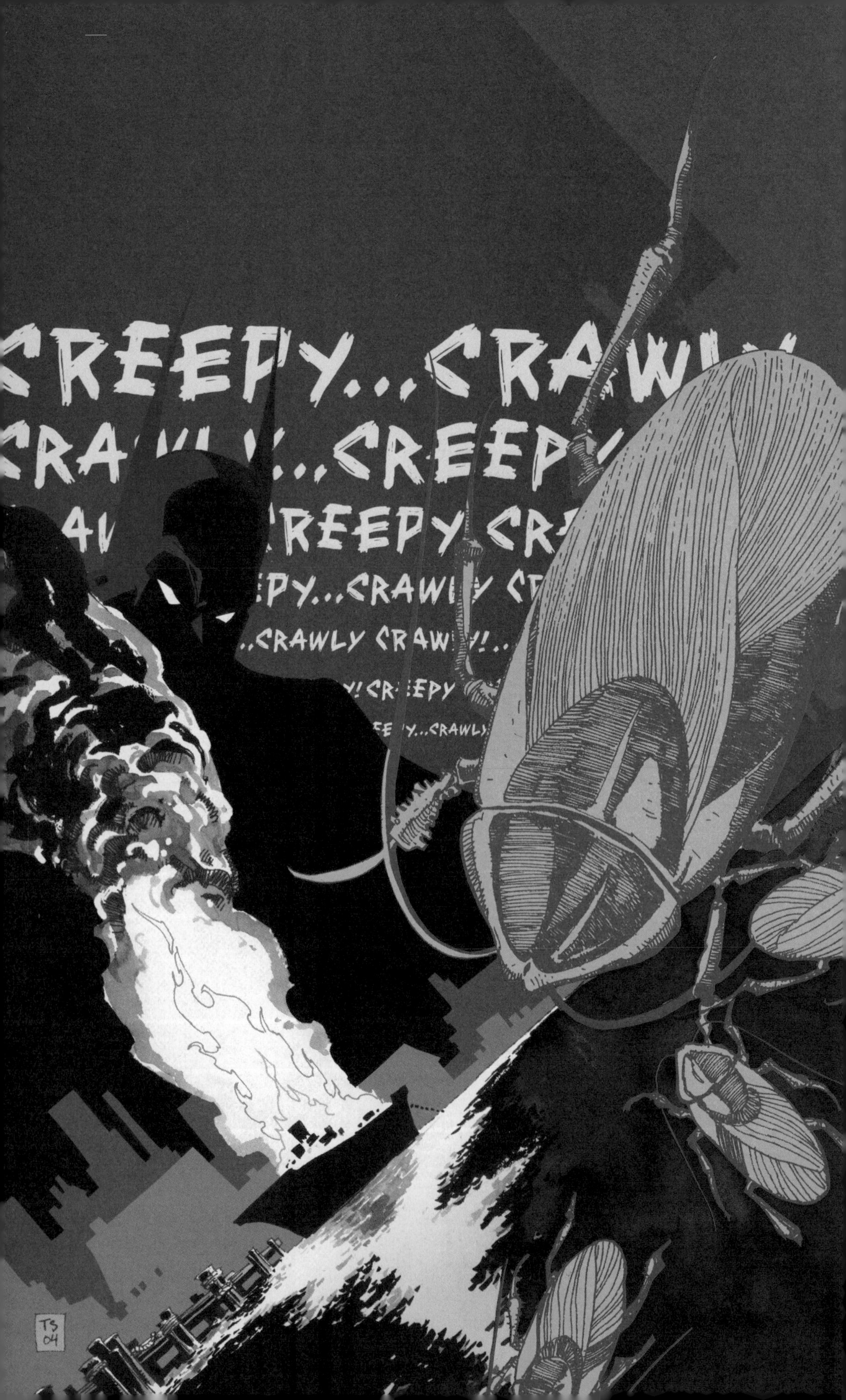

CREEPY...
...CREEP
CREEPY
PY...CRAW
...CRAWLY CRAW
CREEPY
...CRAWLY
TS 04

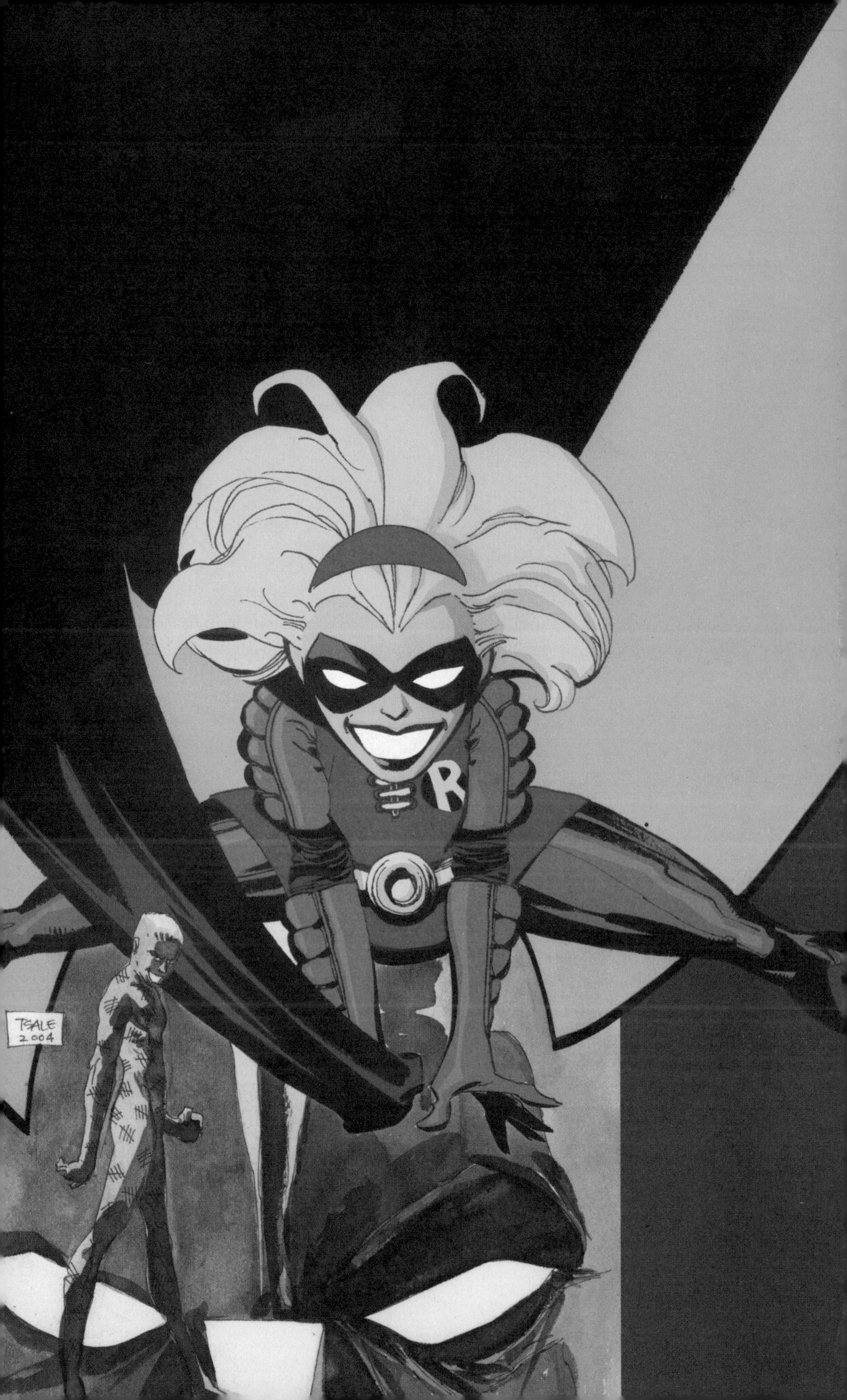
TSALE
2004

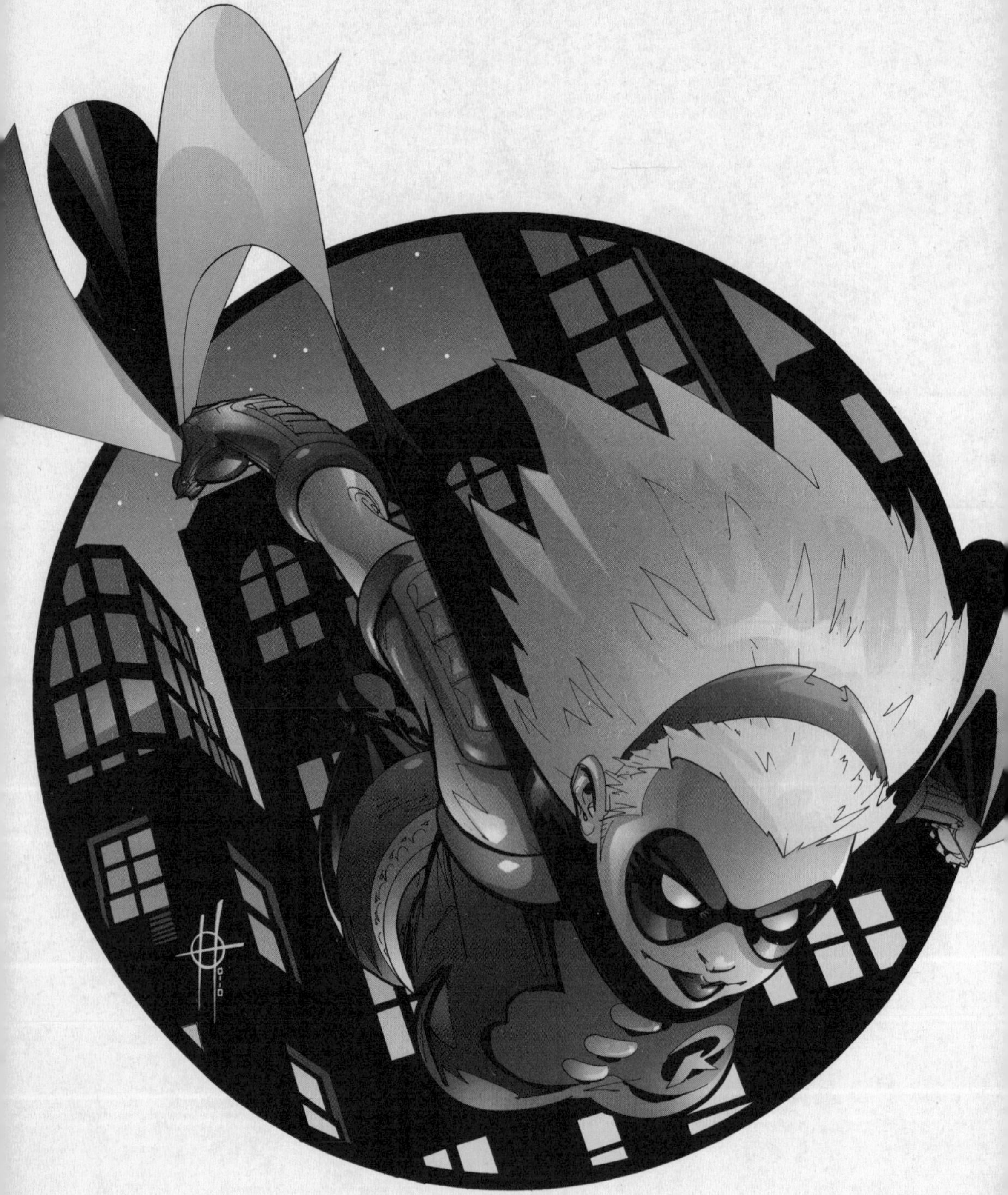

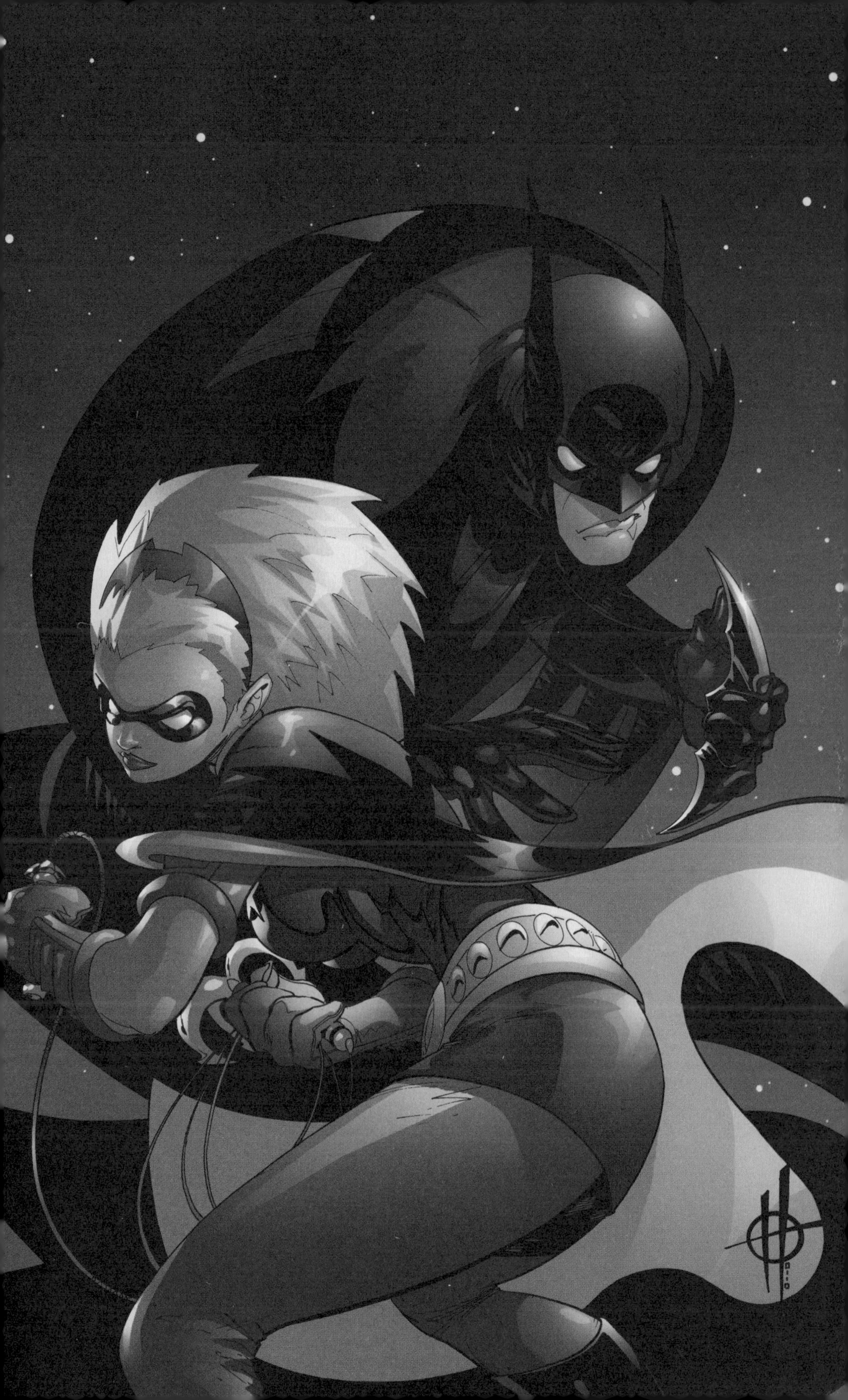

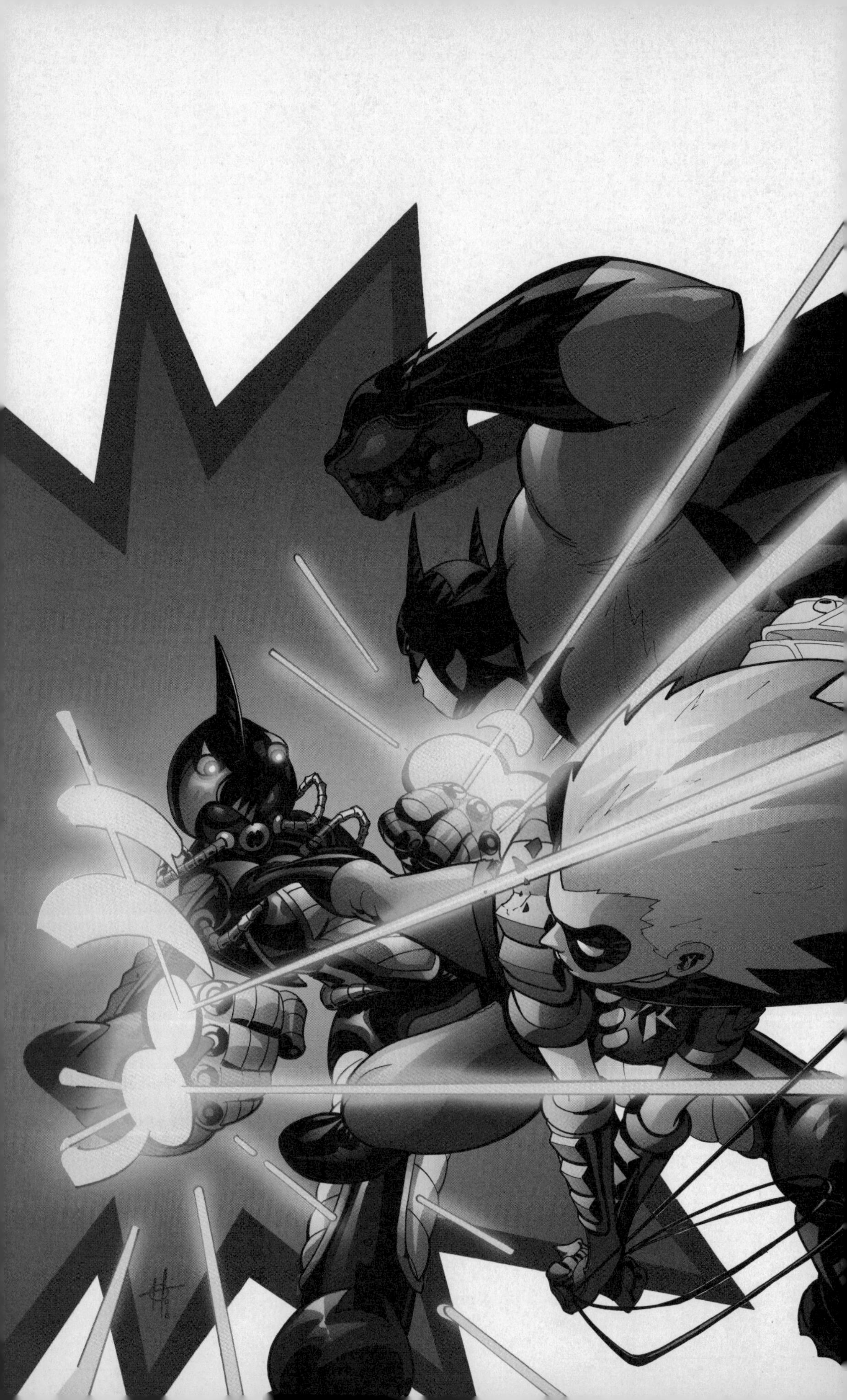

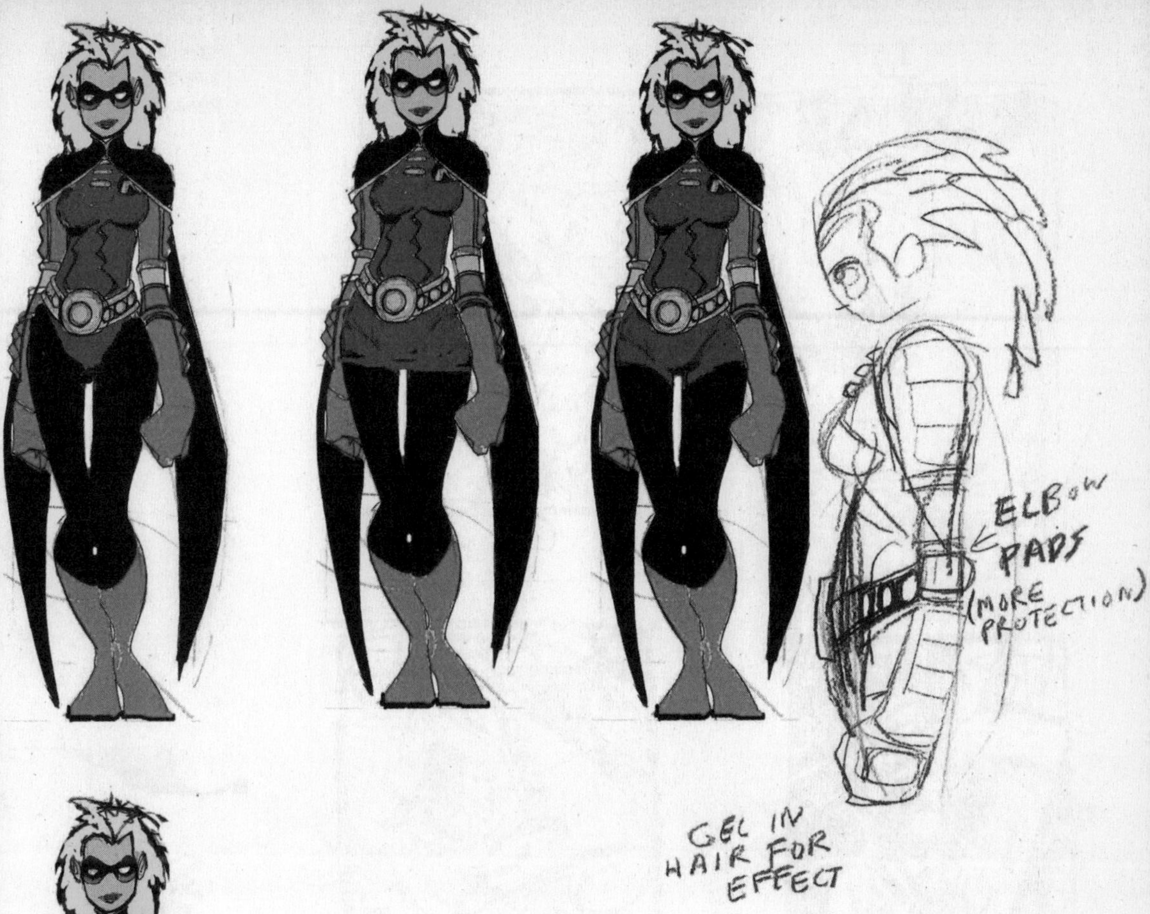
ELBOW PADS
(MORE PROTECTION)
GEL IN HAIR FOR EFFECT

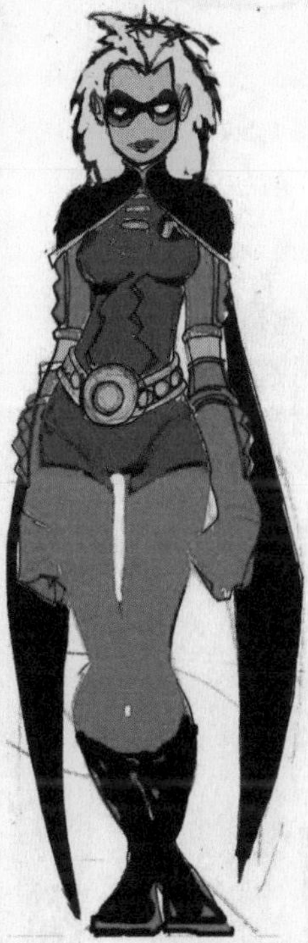

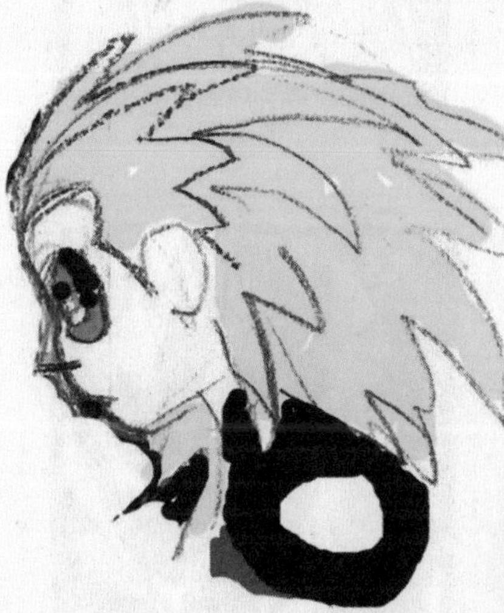

Stephanie Brown didn't have access to the best materials when designing her own Robin outfit. Creating a new costume proved a challenge to artist Damion Scott as well. He presented the editors with numerous sketches to try to imagine what a teenaged single mother could do to impress the World's Greatest Detective. Here's a look at Damion's creative process.

DESIGNING A NEW ROBIN

Sketches for various ROBIN covers, also by Damion Scott.

1
ROBIN
MASHUM
2
3
MASHUM
4
ROBIN
5
6

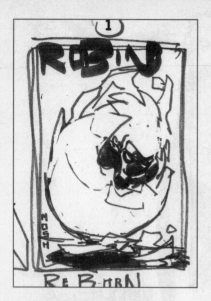

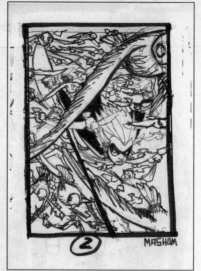

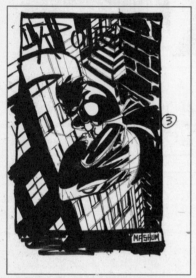

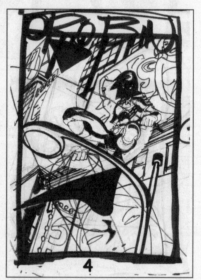

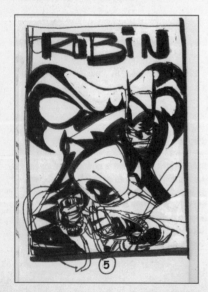

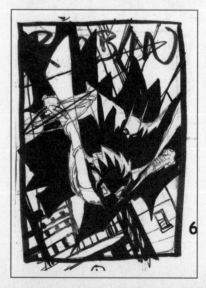

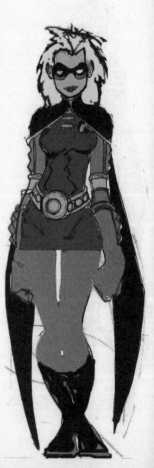

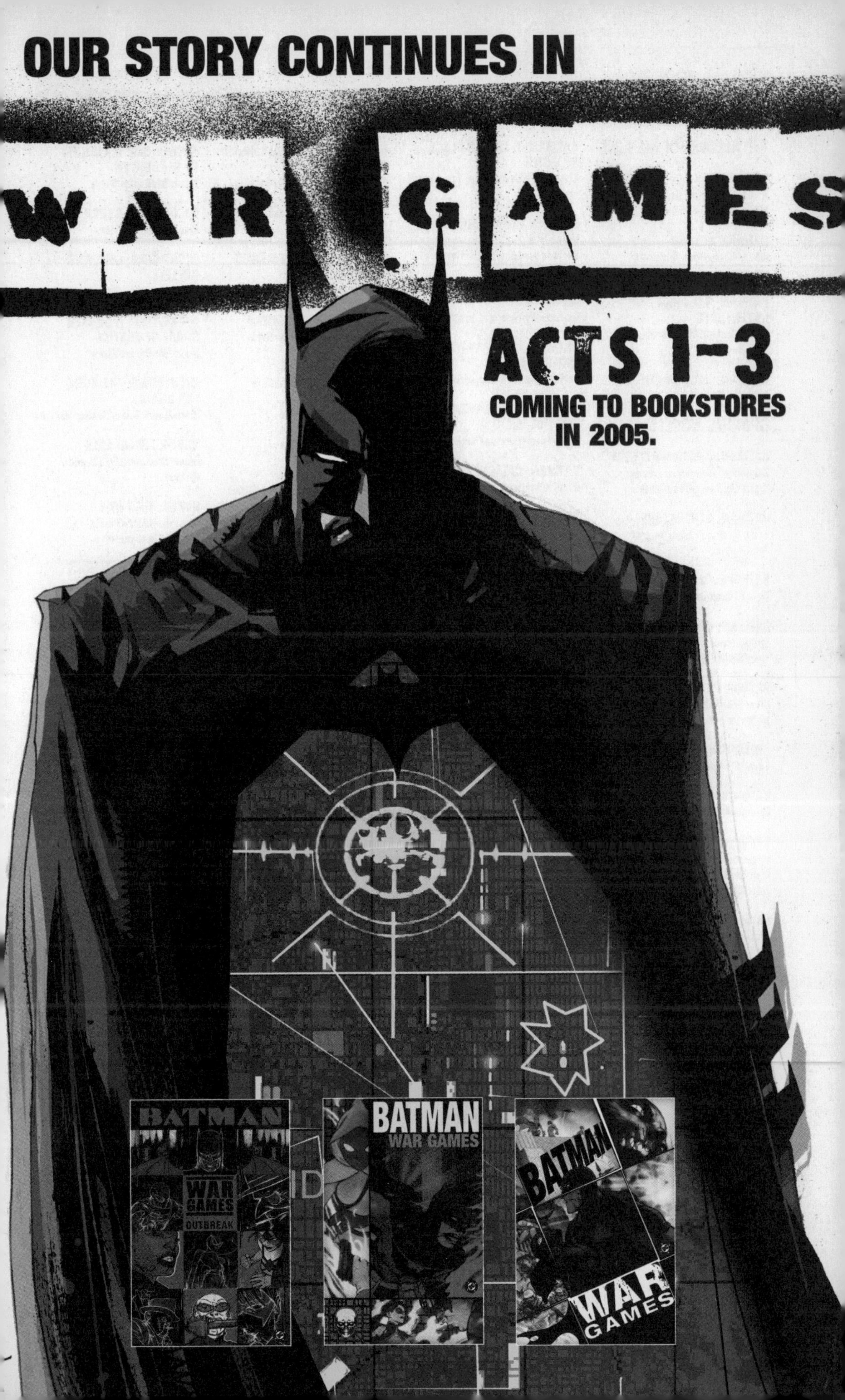
OUR STORY CONTINUES IN
WAR GAMES
ACTS 1-3
COMING TO BOOKSTORES
IN 2005.
BATMAN
WAR GAMES
OUTBREAK
BATMAN
WAR GAMES
BATMAN
WAR GAMES

B A T M A N
THE QUEST FOR JUSTICE CONTINUES IN THESE BOOKS FROM DC: